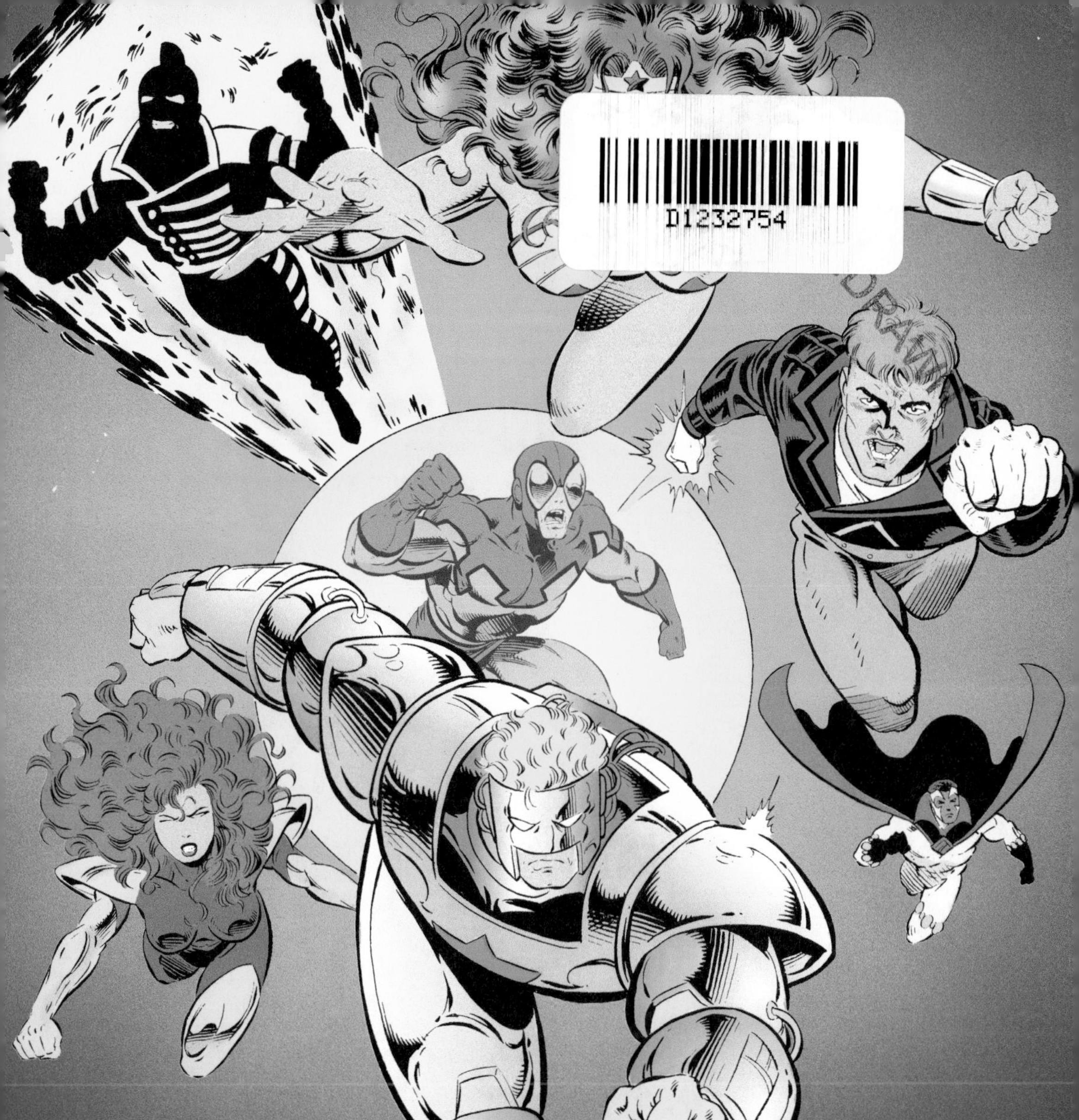

WONDER WOMAN AND JUSTICE LEAGUE AMERICA

VOLUME 1

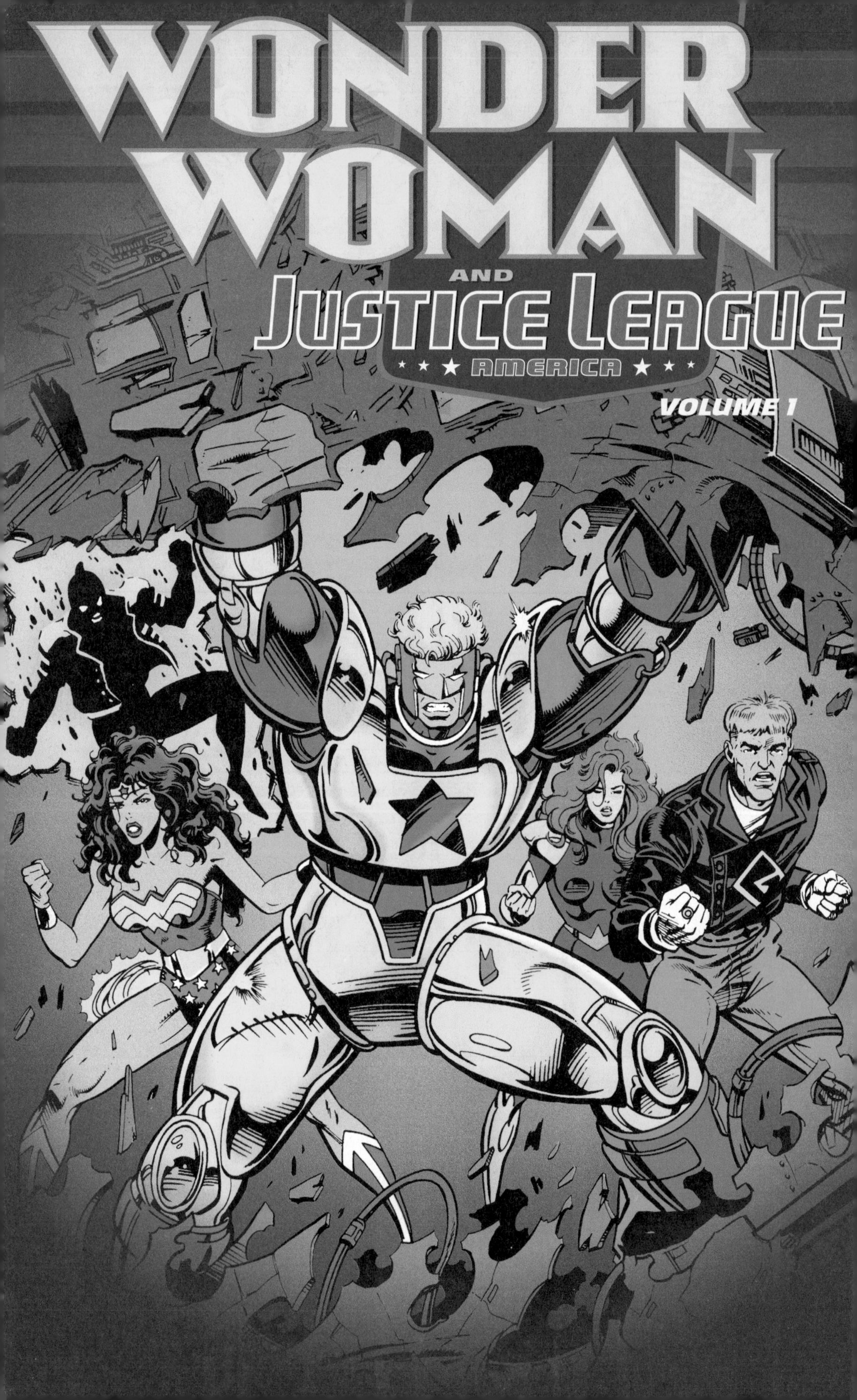
WONDER WOMAN
AND
JUSTICE LEAGUE
AMERICA
VOLUME 1

DAN VADO
CHUCK DIXON
BILL LOEBS
WRITERS

KEVIN WEST
GREG LAROCQUE
MIKE COLLINS
CHRIS HUNTER
PENCILLERS

RICK BURCHETT
KEN BRANCH
ROMEO TANGHAL
TERRY BEATTY
CARLOS GARZON
ROBERT JONES
MARK STEGBAUER
BOB DOWNS
INKERS

GENE D'ANGELO
ANTHONY TOLLIN
GINA GOING
COLORISTS

TIM HARKINS
WILLIE SCHUBERT
ALBERT DeGUZMAN
KEN BRUZENAK
LETTERERS

TOM GRUMMETT
COLLECTION COVER ART

WONDER WOMAN CREATED BY *WILLIAM MOULTON MARSTON*

BRIAN AUGUSTYN *Editor – Original Series*
RUBEN DIAZ *Assistant Editor – Original Series*
JEB WOODARD *Group Editor – Collected Editions*
PAUL SANTOS *Editor – Collected Edition*
STEVE COOK *Design Director – Books*
CURTIS KING JR. *Publication Design*
BOB HARRAS *Senior VP – Editor-in-Chief, DC Comics*

DIANE NELSON *President*
DAN DiDIO *Publisher*
JIM LEE *Publisher*
GEOFF JOHNS *President & Chief Creative Officer*
AMIT DESAI *Executive VP – Business & Marketing Strategy,
    Direct to Consumer & Global Franchise Management*
SAM ADES *Senior VP – Direct to Consumer*
BOBBIE CHASE *VP – Talent Development*
MARK CHIARELLO *Senior VP – Art, Design & Collected Editions*
JOHN CUNNINGHAM *Senior VP – Sales & Trade Marketing*
ANNE DePIES *Senior VP – Business Strategy, Finance & Administration*
DON FALLETTI *VP – Manufacturing Operations*
LAWRENCE GANEM *VP – Editorial Administration & Talent Relations*
ALISON GILL *Senior VP – Manufacturing & Operations*
HANK KANALZ *Senior VP – Editorial Strategy & Administration*
JAY KOGAN *VP – Legal Affairs*
THOMAS LOFTUS *VP – Business Affairs*
JACK MAHAN *VP – Business Affairs*
NICK J. NAPOLITANO *VP – Manufacturing Administration*
EDDIE SCANNELL *VP – Consumer Marketing*
COURTNEY SIMMONS *Senior VP – Publicity & Communications*
JIM (SKI) SOKOLOWSKI *VP – Comic Book Specialty Sales & Trade Marketing*
NANCY SPEARS *VP – Mass, Book, Digital Sales & Trade Marketing*

**WONDER WOMAN AND
JUSTICE LEAGUE AMERICA VOL. 1**

Published by DC Comics. Compilation and all new
material Copyright © 2017 DC Comics. All Rights
Reserved. Originally published in single magazine
form in JUSTICE LEAGUE AMERICA 78-85, JUSTICE
LEAGUE AMERICA ANNUAL 7, and GUY GARDNER
15. Copyright © 1993, 1994 DC Comics. All Rights
Reserved. All characters, their distinctive likenesses
and related elements featured in this publication are
trademarks of DC Comics. The stories, characters
and incidents featured in this publication are
entirely fictional. DC Comics does not read or accept
unsolicited submissions of ideas, stories or artwork.

DC Comics,
2900 West Alameda Avenue,
Burbank, CA 91505

Printed by LSC Communications, Salem, VA, USA.
2/10/17. First Printing. ISBN: 978-1-4012-6834-3

Library of Congress
Cataloging-in-Publication Data is available.

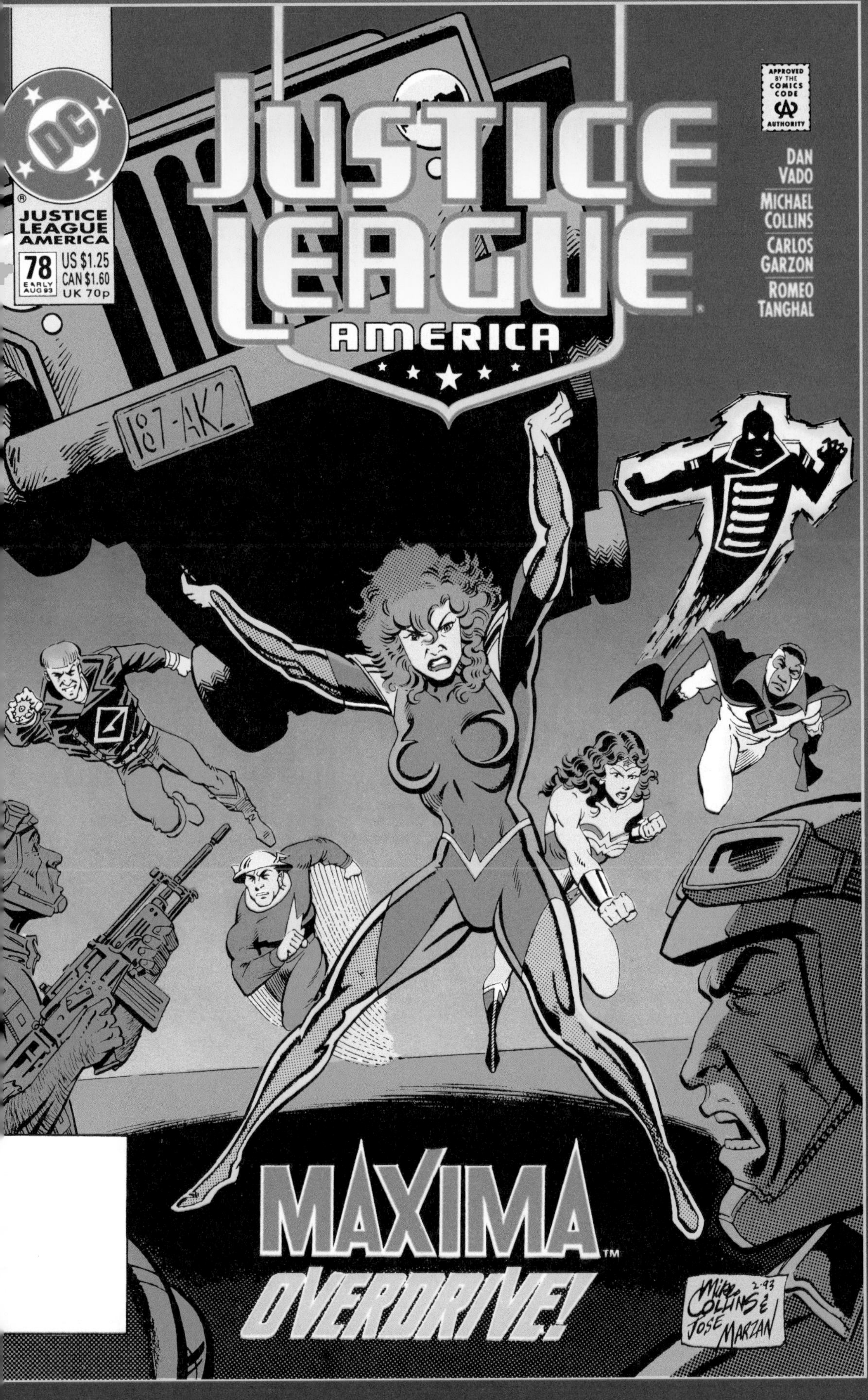
DC
JUSTICE LEAGUE AMERICA
78
EARLY AUG 93
US $1.25
CAN $1.60
UK 70p
APPROVED BY THE COMICS CODE AUTHORITY
JUSTICE LEAGUE AMERICA
DAN VADO
MICHAEL COLLINS
CARLOS GARZON
ROMEO TANGHAL
187-AK2
MAXIMA™
OVERDRIVE!
Mike Collins 2-93 & Jose Marzan

Cover art by **MIKE COLLINS**
and **JOSÉ MARZAN, JR.**

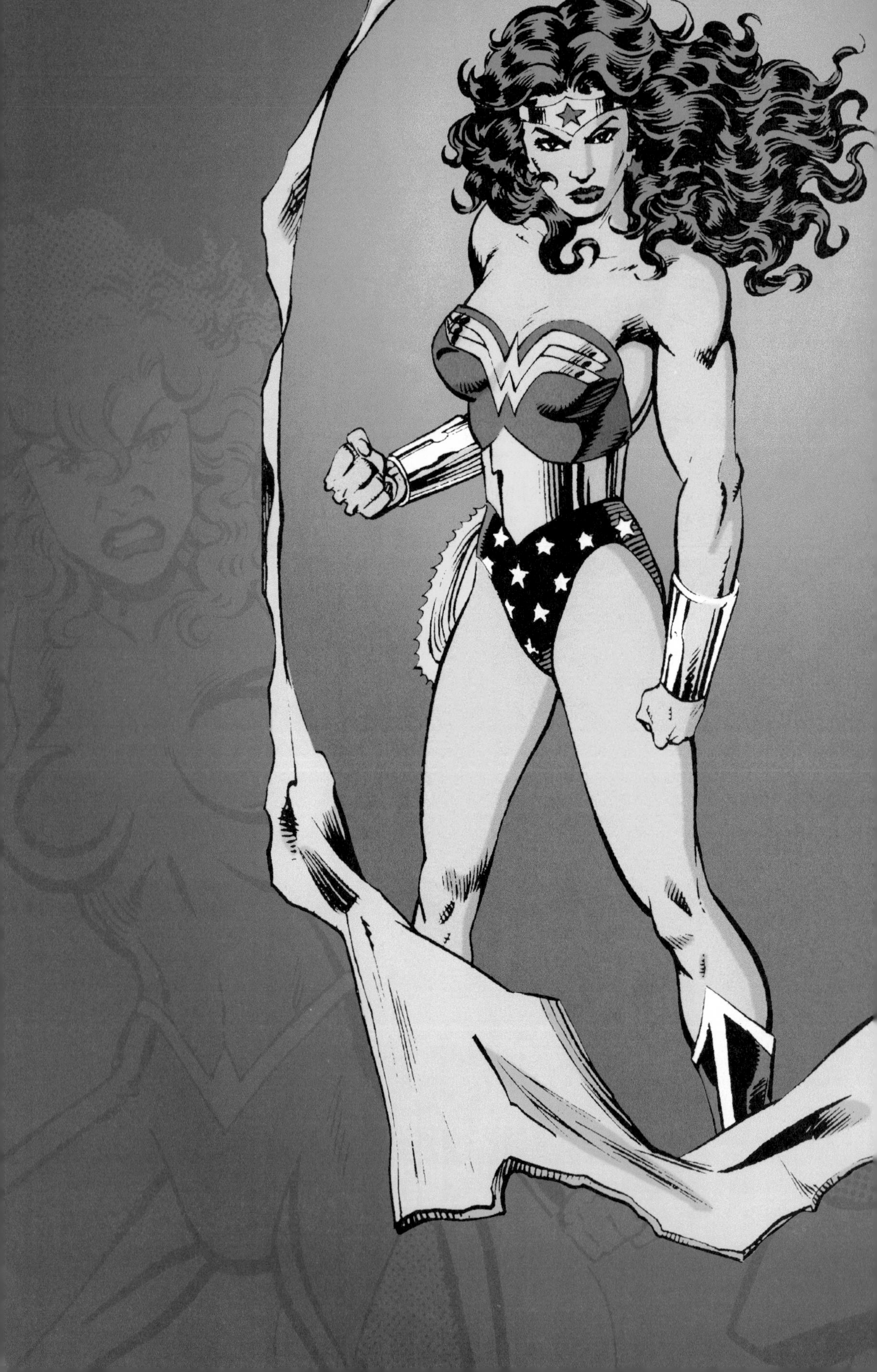

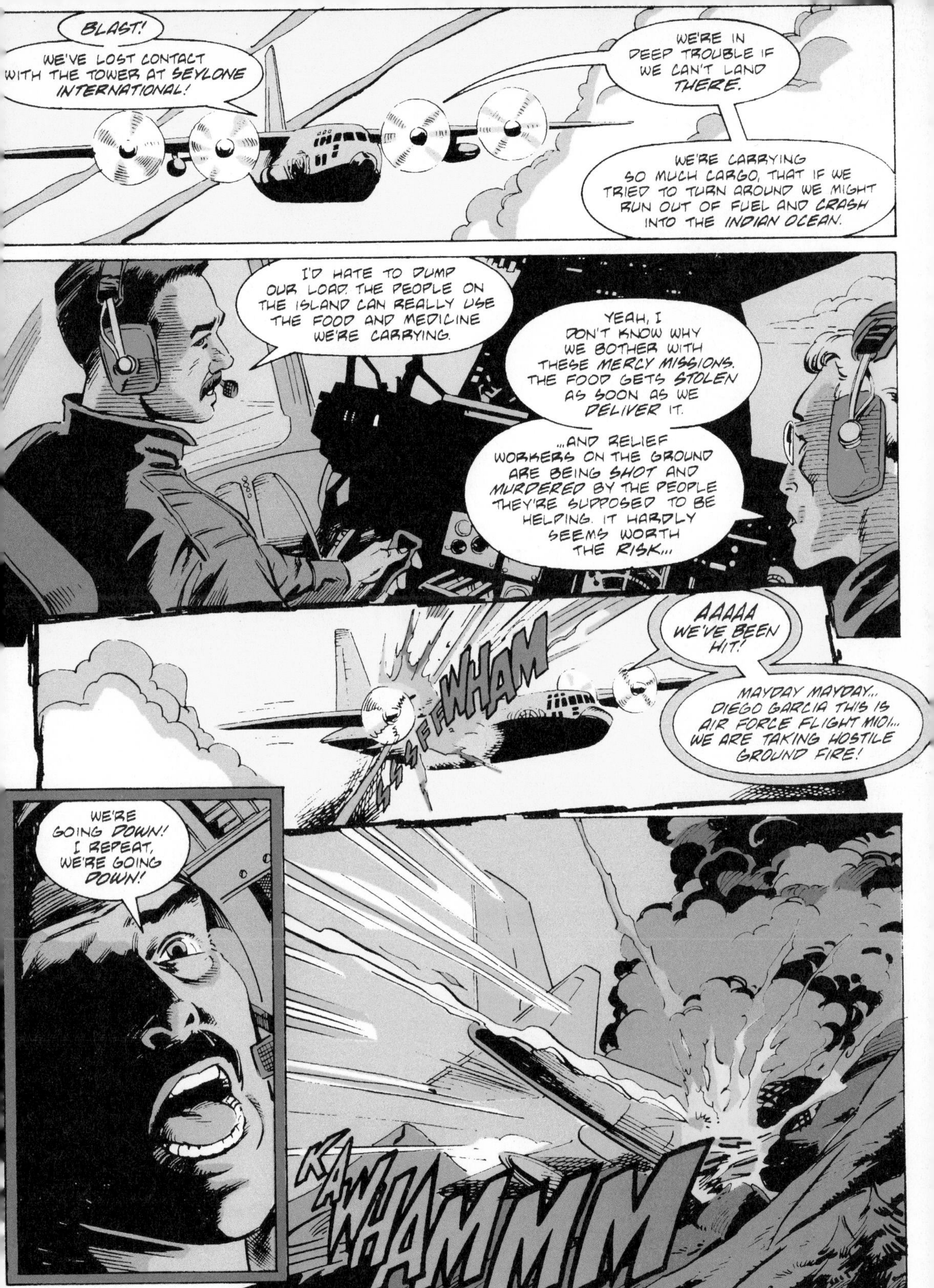
BLAST!
WE'VE LOST CONTACT WITH THE TOWER AT SEYLONE INTERNATIONAL!
WE'RE IN DEEP TROUBLE IF WE CAN'T LAND THERE.
WE'RE CARRYING SO MUCH CARGO, THAT IF WE TRIED TO TURN AROUND WE MIGHT RUN OUT OF FUEL AND CRASH INTO THE INDIAN OCEAN.
I'D HATE TO DUMP OUR LOAD. THE PEOPLE ON THE ISLAND CAN REALLY USE THE FOOD AND MEDICINE WE'RE CARRYING.
YEAH, I DON'T KNOW WHY WE BOTHER WITH THESE MERCY MISSIONS. THE FOOD GETS STOLEN AS SOON AS WE DELIVER IT.
...AND RELIEF WORKERS ON THE GROUND ARE BEING SHOT AND MURDERED BY THE PEOPLE THEY'RE SUPPOSED TO BE HELPING. IT HARDLY SEEMS WORTH THE RISK...
WHAM
AAAAA WE'VE BEEN HIT!
MAYDAY MAYDAY... DIEGO GARCIA THIS IS AIR FORCE FLIGHT M101... WE ARE TAKING HOSTILE GROUND FIRE!
WE'RE GOING DOWN! I REPEAT, WE'RE GOING DOWN!
KA-WHAMMMM

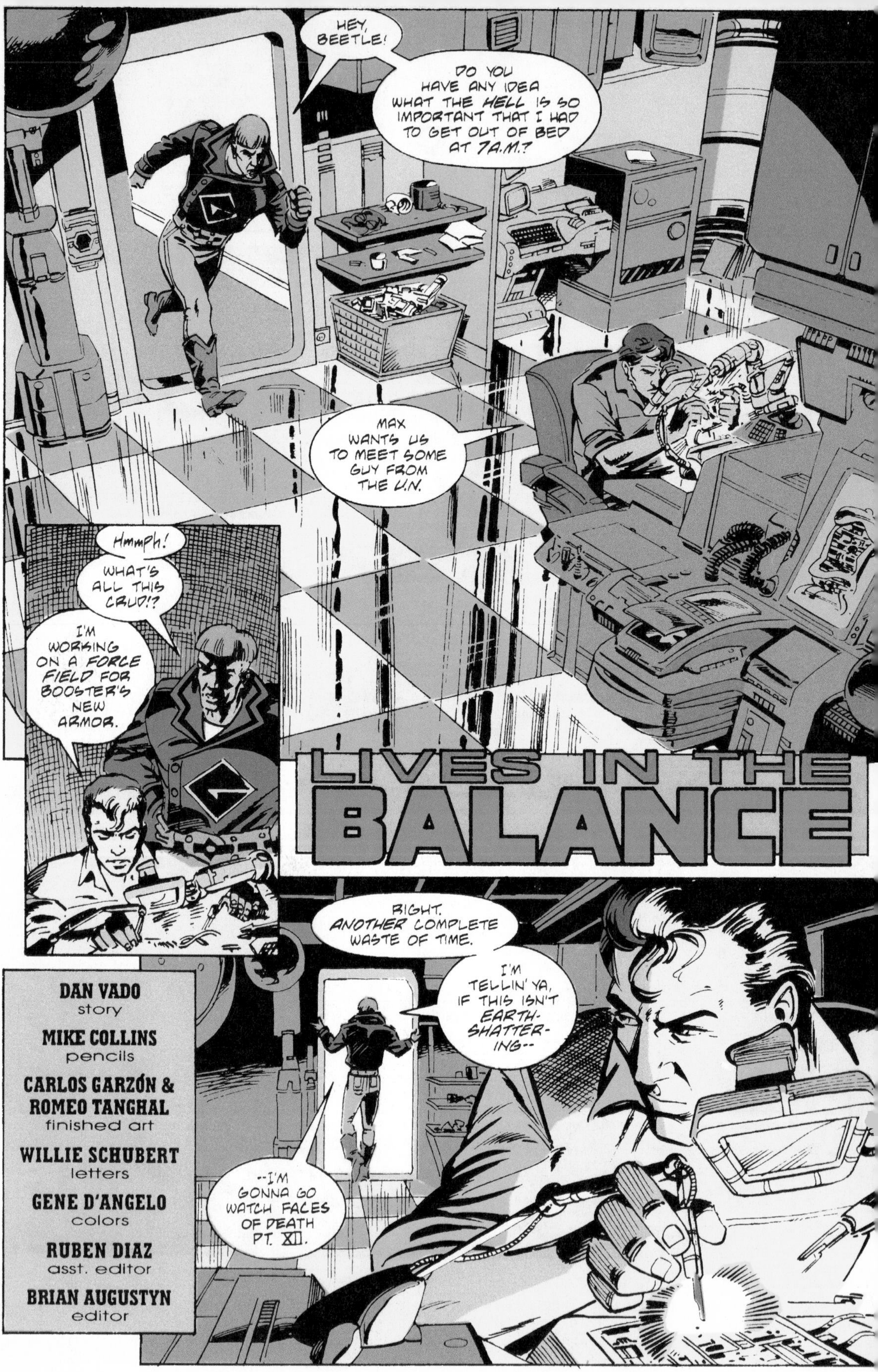
HEY, BEETLE!
DO YOU HAVE ANY IDEA WHAT THE HELL IS SO IMPORTANT THAT I HAD TO GET OUT OF BED AT 7A.M.?
MAX WANTS US TO MEET SOME GUY FROM THE U.N.
Hmmph!
WHAT'S ALL THIS CRUD!?
I'M WORKING ON A FORCE FIELD FOR BOOSTER'S NEW ARMOR.
LIVES IN THE BALANCE
RIGHT. ANOTHER COMPLETE WASTE OF TIME.
I'M TELLIN' YA, IF THIS ISN'T EARTH-SHATTER-ING--
--I'M GONNA GO WATCH FACES OF DEATH PT. XII.
DAN VADO story
MIKE COLLINS pencils
CARLOS GARZÓN & ROMEO TANGHAL finished art
WILLIE SCHUBERT letters
GENE D'ANGELO colors
RUBEN DIAZ asst. editor
BRIAN AUGUSTYN editor

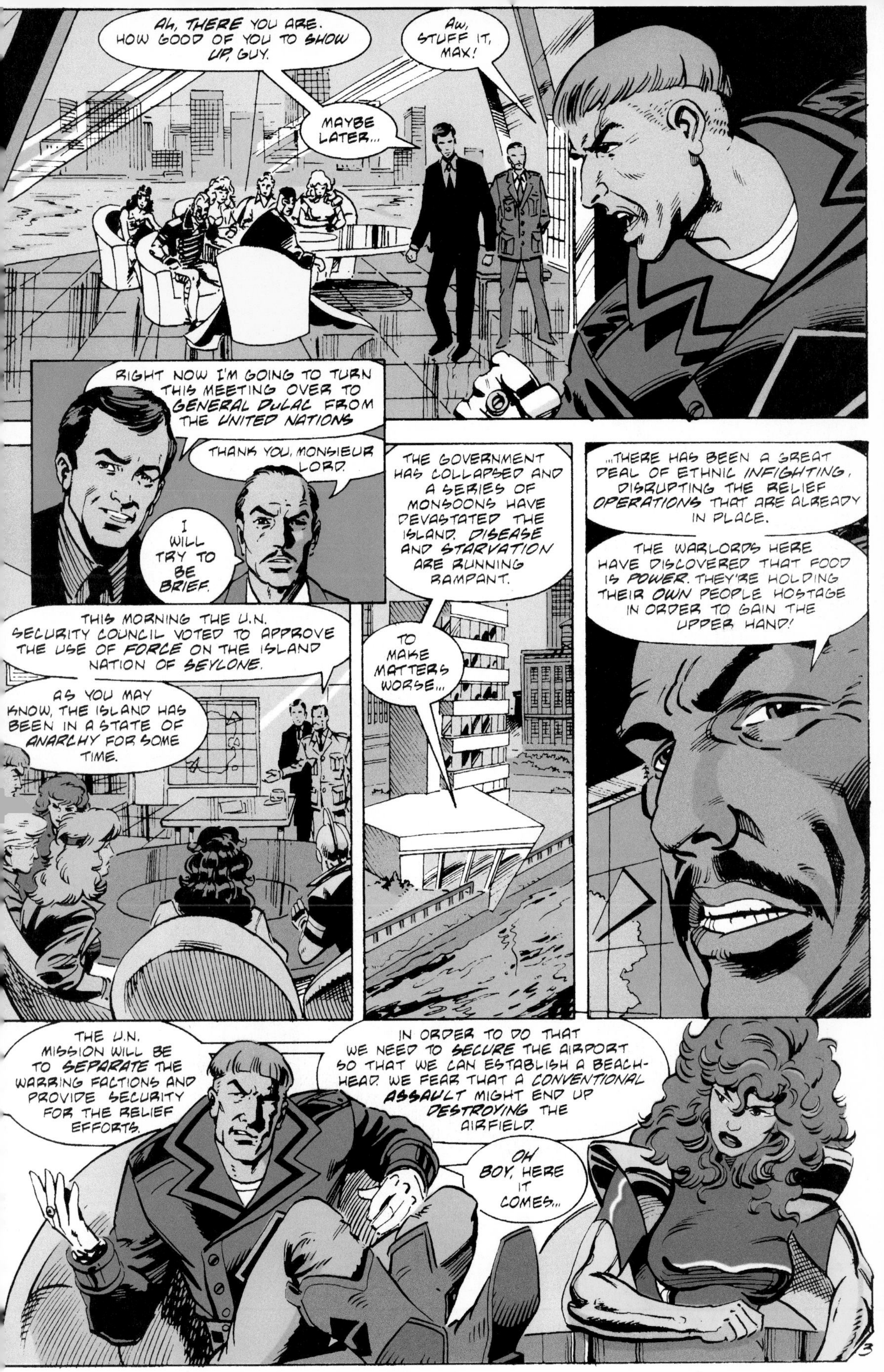
AH, THERE YOU ARE. HOW GOOD OF YOU TO SHOW UP, GUY.
AW, STUFF IT, MAX!
MAYBE LATER...
RIGHT NOW I'M GOING TO TURN THIS MEETING OVER TO GENERAL DULAC FROM THE UNITED NATIONS
THANK YOU, MONSIEUR LORD.
I WILL TRY TO BE BRIEF.
THIS MORNING THE U.N. SECURITY COUNCIL VOTED TO APPROVE THE USE OF FORCE ON THE ISLAND NATION OF SEYLONE.
AS YOU MAY KNOW, THE ISLAND HAS BEEN IN A STATE OF ANARCHY FOR SOME TIME.
THE GOVERNMENT HAS COLLAPSED AND A SERIES OF MONSOONS HAVE DEVASTATED THE ISLAND. DISEASE AND STARVATION ARE RUNNING RAMPANT.
TO MAKE MATTERS WORSE...
...THERE HAS BEEN A GREAT DEAL OF ETHNIC INFIGHTING, DISRUPTING THE RELIEF OPERATIONS THAT ARE ALREADY IN PLACE.
THE WARLORDS HERE HAVE DISCOVERED THAT FOOD IS POWER. THEY'RE HOLDING THEIR OWN PEOPLE HOSTAGE IN ORDER TO GAIN THE UPPER HAND!
THE U.N. MISSION WILL BE TO SEPARATE THE WARRING FACTIONS AND PROVIDE SECURITY FOR THE RELIEF EFFORTS.
IN ORDER TO DO THAT WE NEED TO SECURE THE AIRPORT SO THAT WE CAN ESTABLISH A BEACH-HEAD. WE FEAR THAT A CONVENTIONAL ASSAULT MIGHT END UP DESTROYING THE AIRFIELD.
OH BOY, HERE IT COMES...

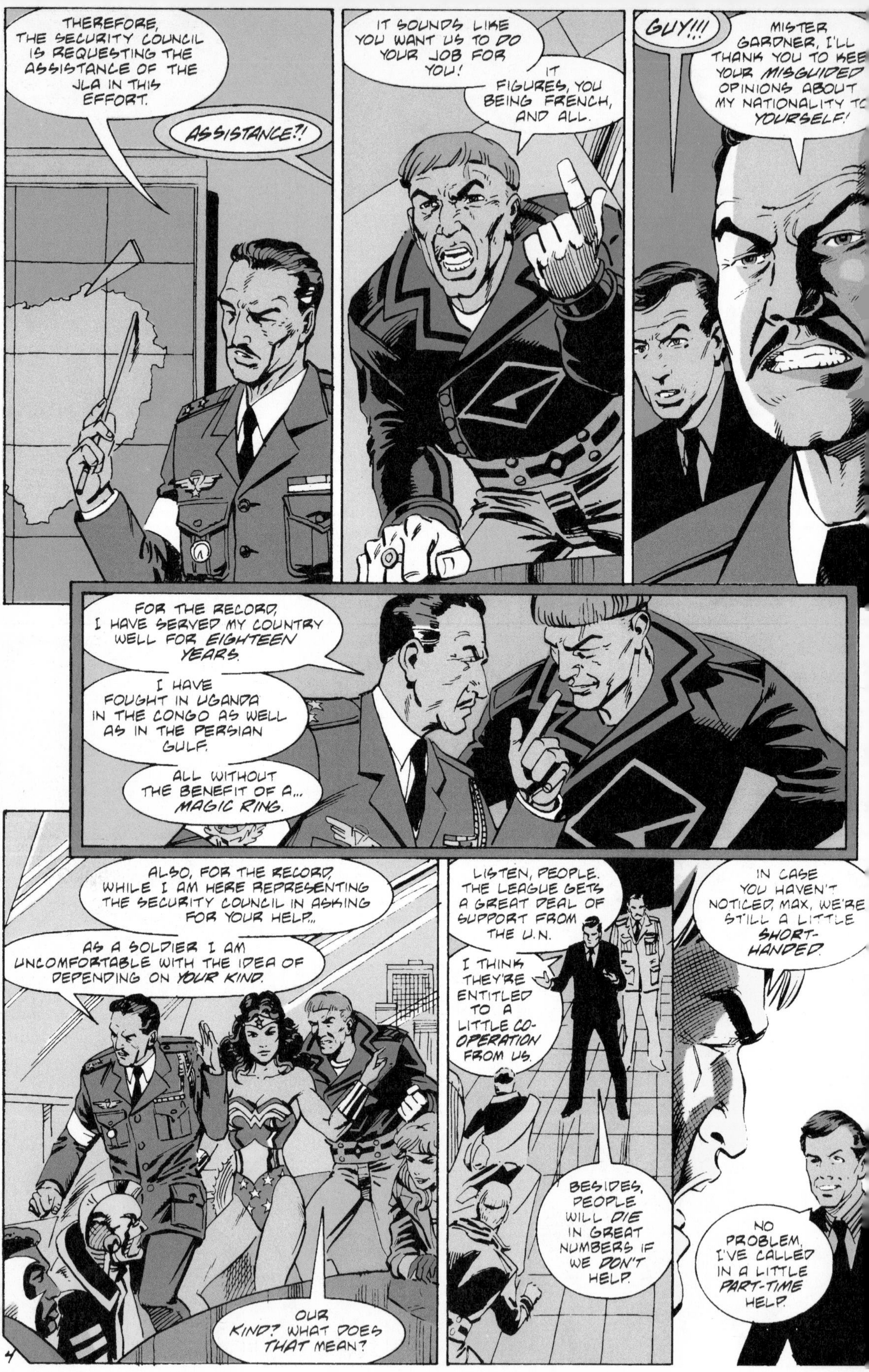
THEREFORE, THE SECURITY COUNCIL IS REQUESTING THE ASSISTANCE OF THE JLA IN THIS EFFORT.
ASSISTANCE?!
IT SOUNDS LIKE YOU WANT US TO DO YOUR JOB FOR YOU!
IT FIGURES, YOU BEING FRENCH, AND ALL.
GUY!!!
MISTER GARDNER, I'LL THANK YOU TO KEEP YOUR MISGUIDED OPINIONS ABOUT MY NATIONALITY TO YOURSELF!
FOR THE RECORD, I HAVE SERVED MY COUNTRY WELL FOR EIGHTEEN YEARS.
I HAVE FOUGHT IN UGANDA IN THE CONGO AS WELL AS IN THE PERSIAN GULF.
ALL WITHOUT THE BENEFIT OF A... MAGIC RING.
ALSO, FOR THE RECORD, WHILE I AM HERE REPRESENTING THE SECURITY COUNCIL IN ASKING FOR YOUR HELP...
AS A SOLDIER I AM UNCOMFORTABLE WITH THE IDEA OF DEPENDING ON YOUR KIND.
OUR KIND? WHAT DOES THAT MEAN?
LISTEN, PEOPLE. THE LEAGUE GETS A GREAT DEAL OF SUPPORT FROM THE U.N.
I THINK THEY'RE ENTITLED TO A LITTLE CO-OPERATION FROM US.
BESIDES, PEOPLE WILL DIE IN GREAT NUMBERS IF WE DON'T HELP.
IN CASE YOU HAVEN'T NOTICED, MAX, WE'RE STILL A LITTLE SHORT-HANDED.
NO PROBLEM, I'VE CALLED IN A LITTLE PART-TIME HELP.

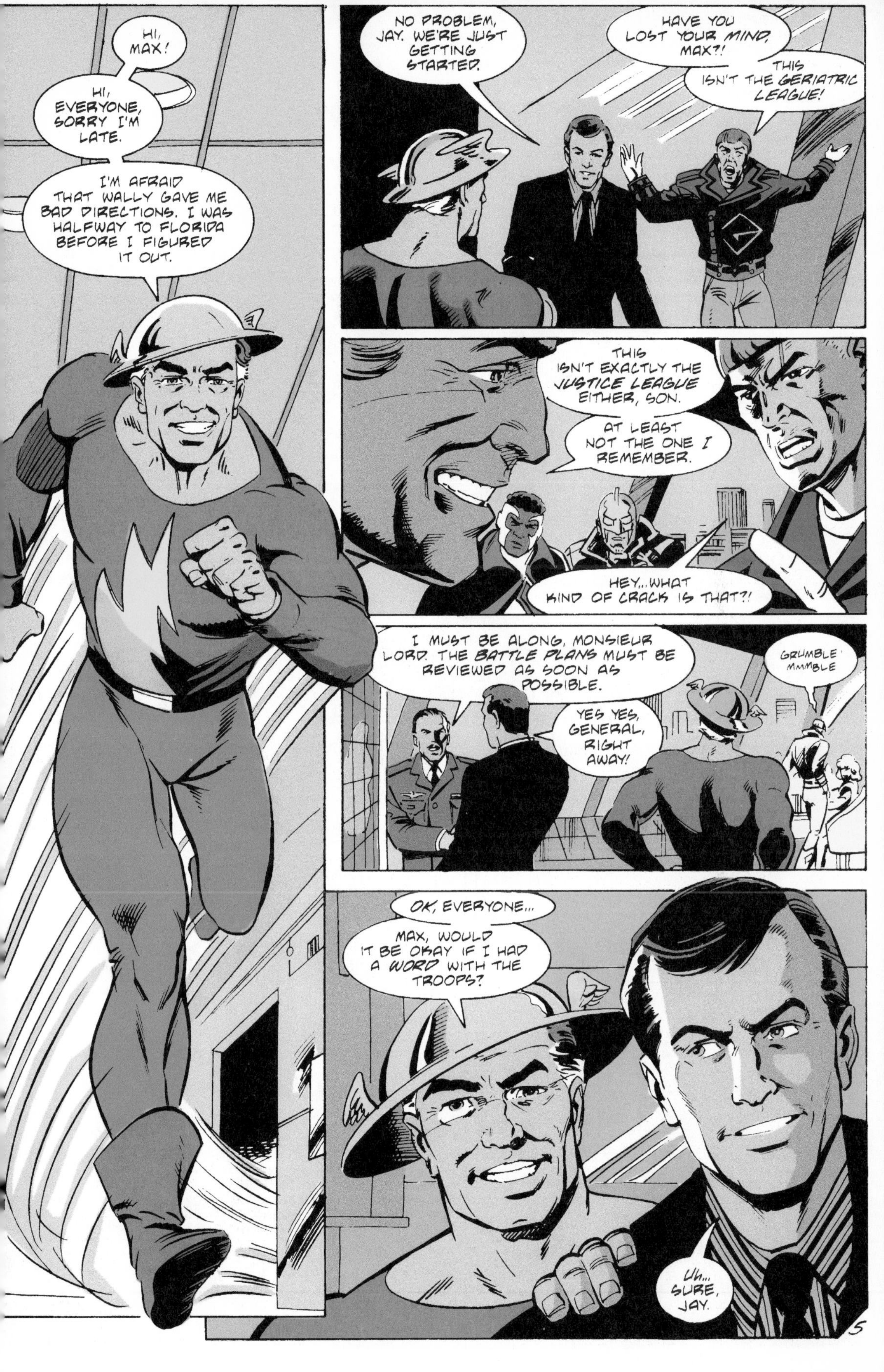
HI, MAX!
HI, EVERYONE, SORRY I'M LATE.
I'M AFRAID THAT WALLY GAVE ME BAD DIRECTIONS. I WAS HALFWAY TO FLORIDA BEFORE I FIGURED IT OUT.
NO PROBLEM, JAY. WE'RE JUST GETTING STARTED.
HAVE YOU LOST YOUR *MIND*, MAX?!
THIS ISN'T THE *GERIATRIC LEAGUE!*
THIS ISN'T EXACTLY THE *JUSTICE LEAGUE* EITHER, SON.
AT LEAST NOT THE ONE *I* REMEMBER.
HEY... WHAT KIND OF CRACK IS THAT?!
I MUST BE ALONG, MONSIEUR LORD. THE *BATTLE PLANS* MUST BE REVIEWED AS SOON AS POSSIBLE.
YES YES, GENERAL, RIGHT AWAY!
GRUMBLE MMMBLE
OK, EVERYONE...
MAX, WOULD IT BE OKAY IF I HAD A *WORD* WITH THE TROOPS?
Uh... SURE, JAY.

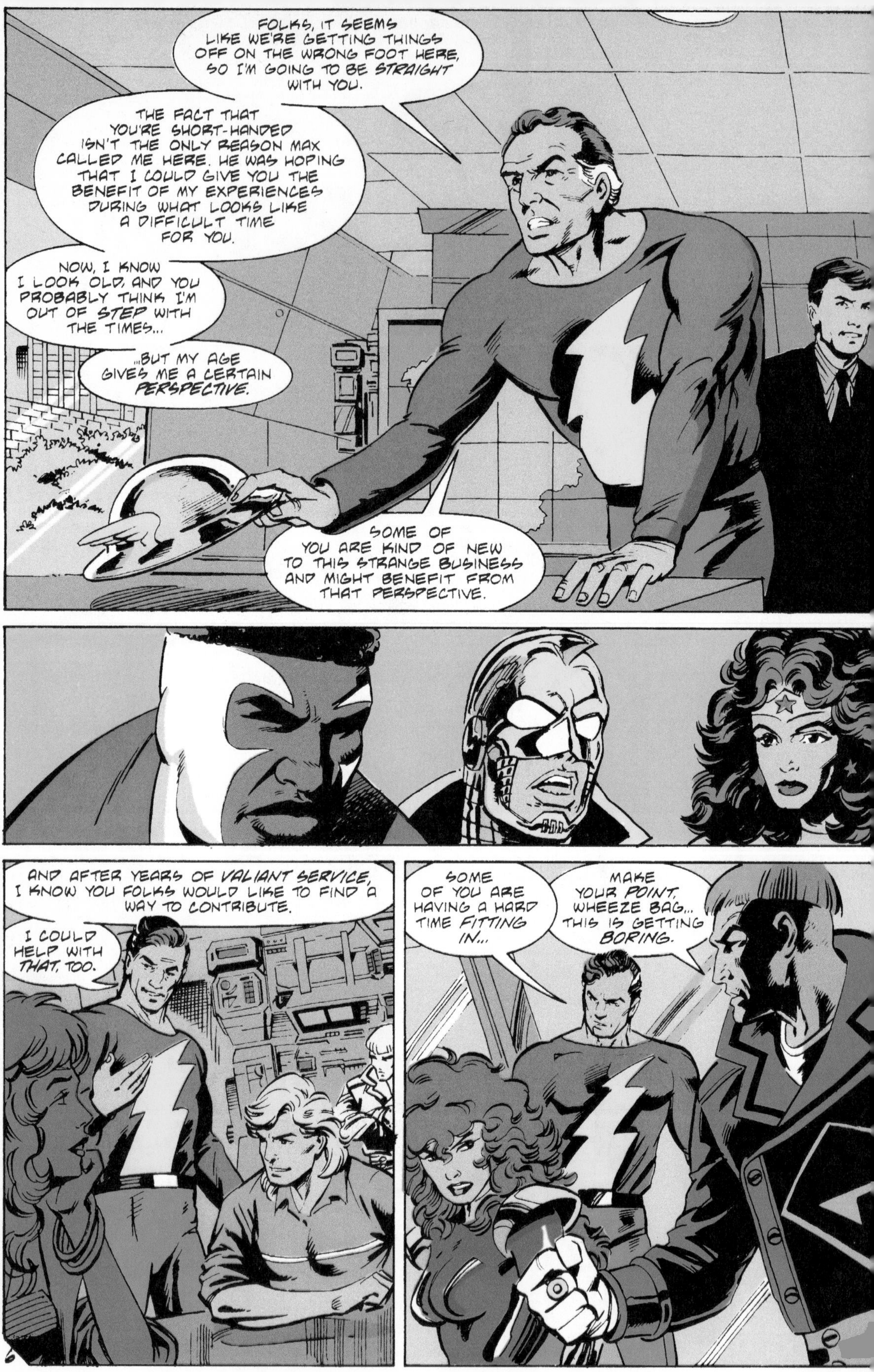
FOLKS, IT SEEMS LIKE WE'RE GETTING THINGS OFF ON THE WRONG FOOT HERE, SO I'M GOING TO BE STRAIGHT WITH YOU.
THE FACT THAT YOU'RE SHORT-HANDED ISN'T THE ONLY REASON MAX CALLED ME HERE. HE WAS HOPING THAT I COULD GIVE YOU THE BENEFIT OF MY EXPERIENCES DURING WHAT LOOKS LIKE A DIFFICULT TIME FOR YOU.
NOW, I KNOW I LOOK OLD, AND YOU PROBABLY THINK I'M OUT OF STEP WITH THE TIMES...
...BUT MY AGE GIVES ME A CERTAIN PERSPECTIVE.
SOME OF YOU ARE KIND OF NEW TO THIS STRANGE BUSINESS AND MIGHT BENEFIT FROM THAT PERSPECTIVE.
AND AFTER YEARS OF VALIANT SERVICE, I KNOW YOU FOLKS WOULD LIKE TO FIND A WAY TO CONTRIBUTE.
I COULD HELP WITH THAT, TOO.
SOME OF YOU ARE HAVING A HARD TIME FITTING IN...
MAKE YOUR POINT, WHEEZE BAG... THIS IS GETTING BORING.

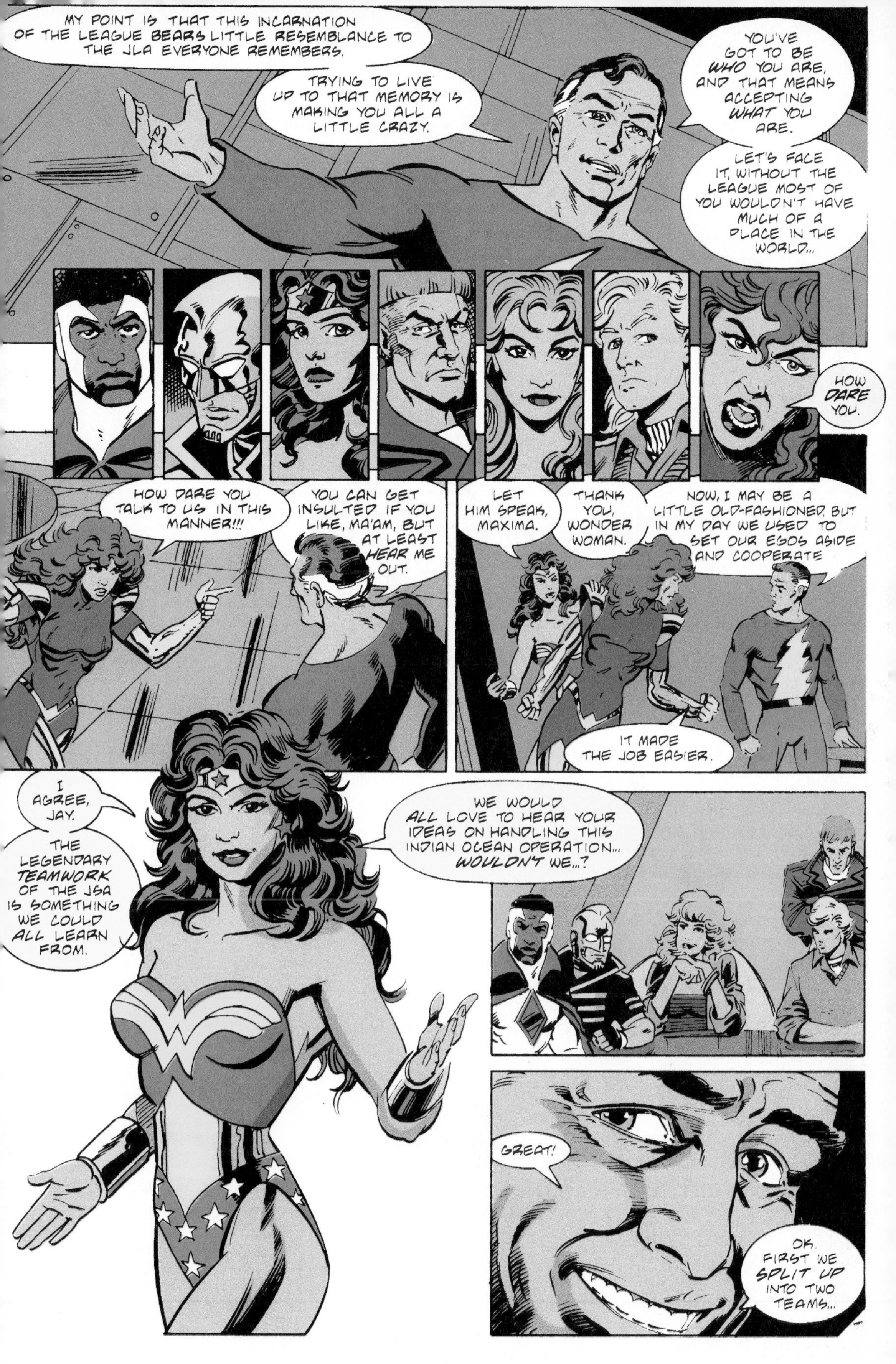

MY POINT IS THAT THIS INCARNATION OF THE LEAGUE BEARS LITTLE RESEMBLANCE TO THE JLA EVERYONE REMEMBERS.
TRYING TO LIVE UP TO THAT MEMORY IS MAKING YOU ALL A LITTLE CRAZY.
YOU'VE GOT TO BE WHO YOU ARE, AND THAT MEANS ACCEPTING WHAT YOU ARE.
LET'S FACE IT, WITHOUT THE LEAGUE MOST OF YOU WOULDN'T HAVE MUCH OF A PLACE IN THE WORLD...
HOW DARE YOU.
HOW DARE YOU TALK TO US IN THIS MANNER!!!
YOU CAN GET INSULTED IF YOU LIKE, MA'AM, BUT AT LEAST HEAR ME OUT.
LET HIM SPEAK, MAXIMA.
THANK YOU, WONDER WOMAN.
NOW, I MAY BE A LITTLE OLD-FASHIONED, BUT IN MY DAY WE USED TO SET OUR EGOS ASIDE AND COOPERATE
IT MADE THE JOB EASIER.
I AGREE, JAY.
THE LEGENDARY TEAMWORK OF THE JSA IS SOMETHING WE COULD ALL LEARN FROM.
WE WOULD ALL LOVE TO HEAR YOUR IDEAS ON HANDLING THIS INDIAN OCEAN OPERATION... WOULDN'T WE...?
GREAT!
OK. FIRST WE SPLIT UP INTO TWO TEAMS...

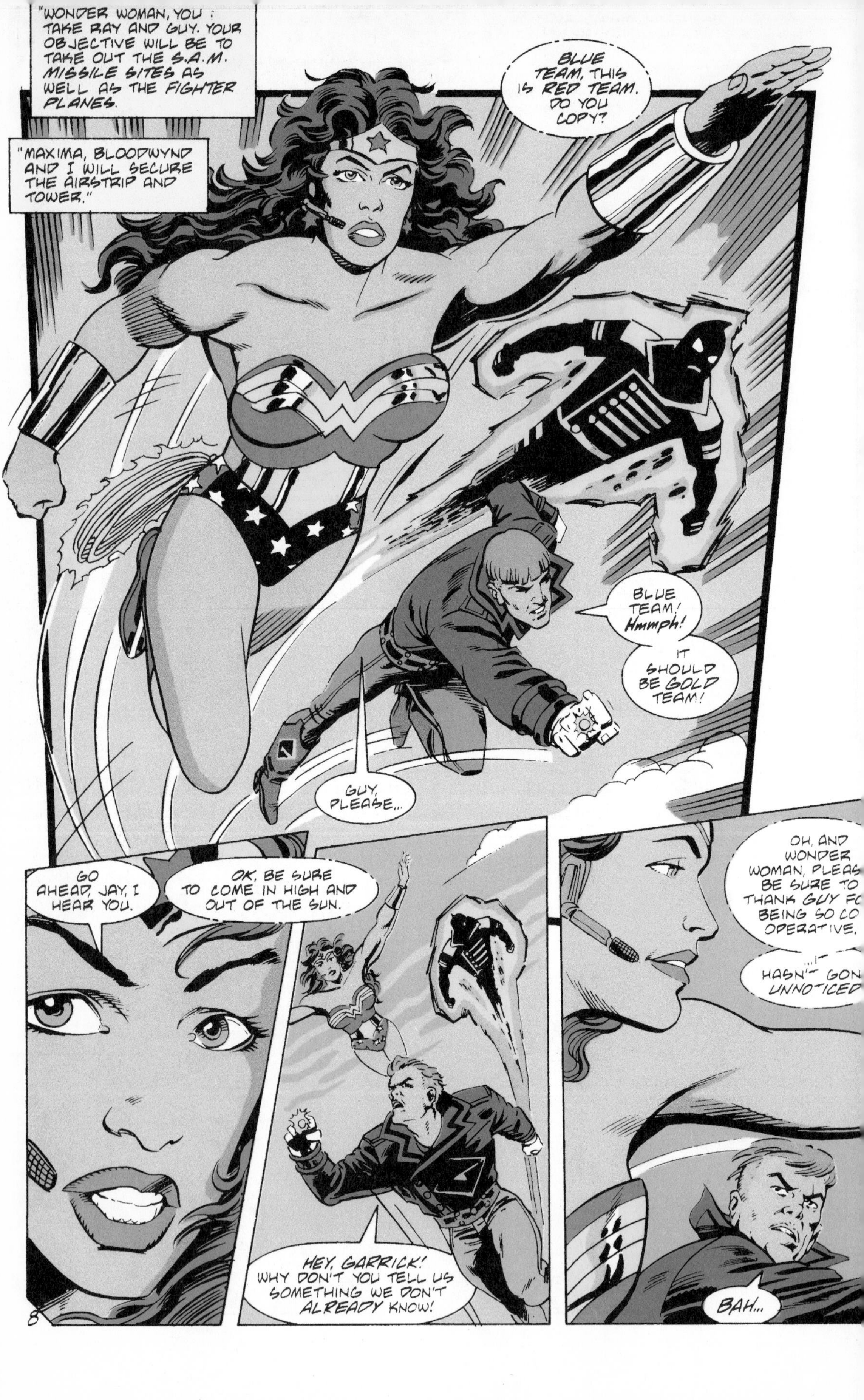
"WONDER WOMAN, YOU : TAKE RAY AND GUY. YOUR OBJECTIVE WILL BE TO TAKE OUT THE S.A.M. MISSILE SITES AS WELL AS THE FIGHTER PLANES.
"MAXIMA, BLOODWYND AND I WILL SECURE THE AIRSTRIP AND TOWER."
BLUE TEAM, THIS IS RED TEAM. DO YOU COPY?
BLUE TEAM! Hmmph!
IT SHOULD BE GOLD TEAM!
GUY, PLEASE...
GO AHEAD, JAY, I HEAR YOU.
OK, BE SURE TO COME IN HIGH AND OUT OF THE SUN.
HEY, GARRICK! WHY DON'T YOU TELL US SOMETHING WE DON'T ALREADY KNOW!
OH, AND WONDER WOMAN, PLEAS BE SURE TO THANK GUY FO BEING SO CO OPERATIVE.
...IT HASN'T GON UNNOTICED
BAH...

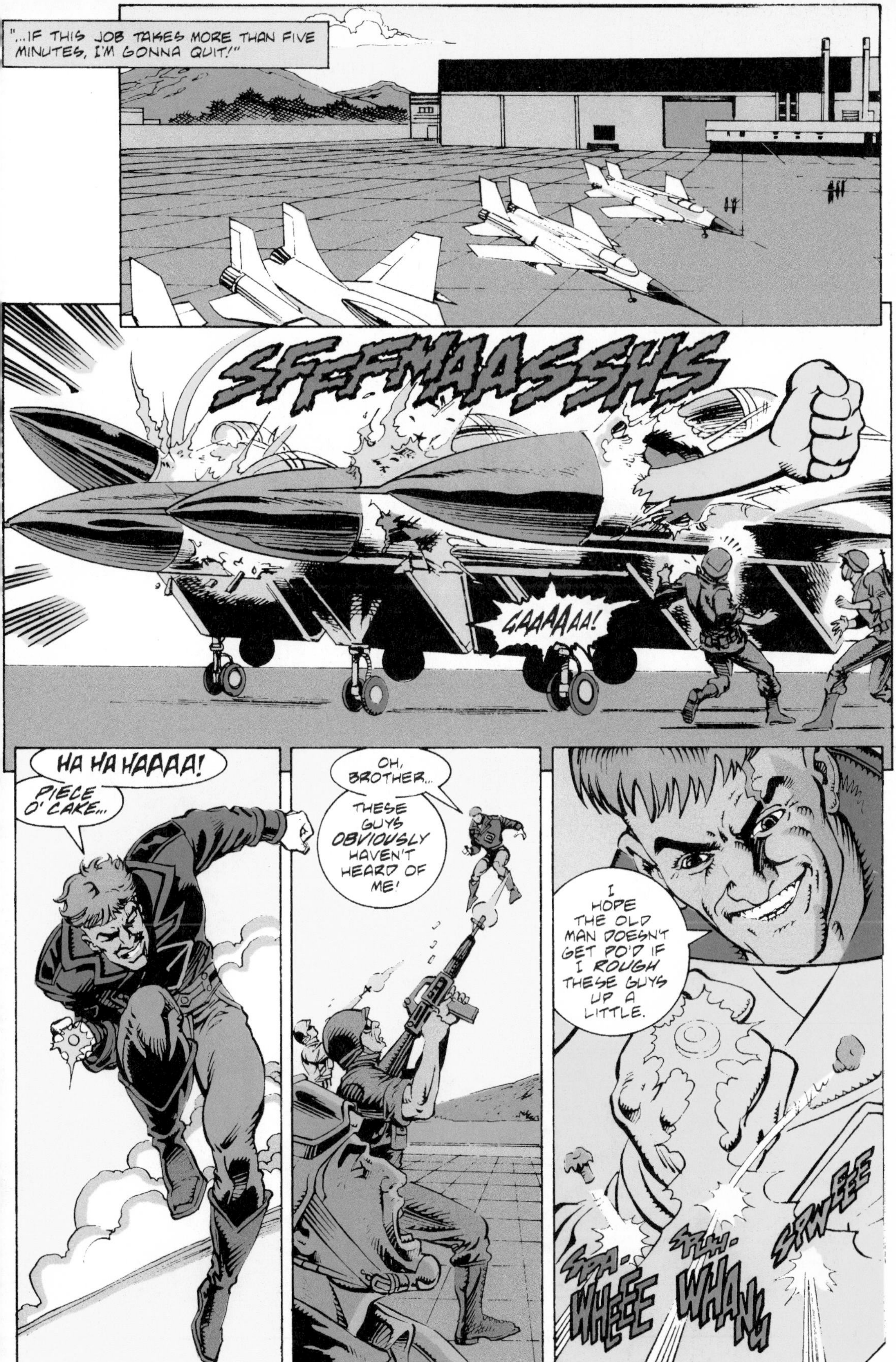
"...IF THIS JOB TAKES MORE THAN FIVE MINUTES, I'M GONNA QUIT!"
SFFFMAASSHS
GAAAAAA!
HA HA HAAAA!
PIECE O' CAKE...
OH, BROTHER...
THESE GUYS OBVIOUSLY HAVEN'T HEARD OF ME!
I HOPE THE OLD MAN DOESN'T GET PO'D IF I ROUGH THESE GUYS UP A LITTLE.
SPA-WHEEE
SPUH-WHANG
SPWEEE

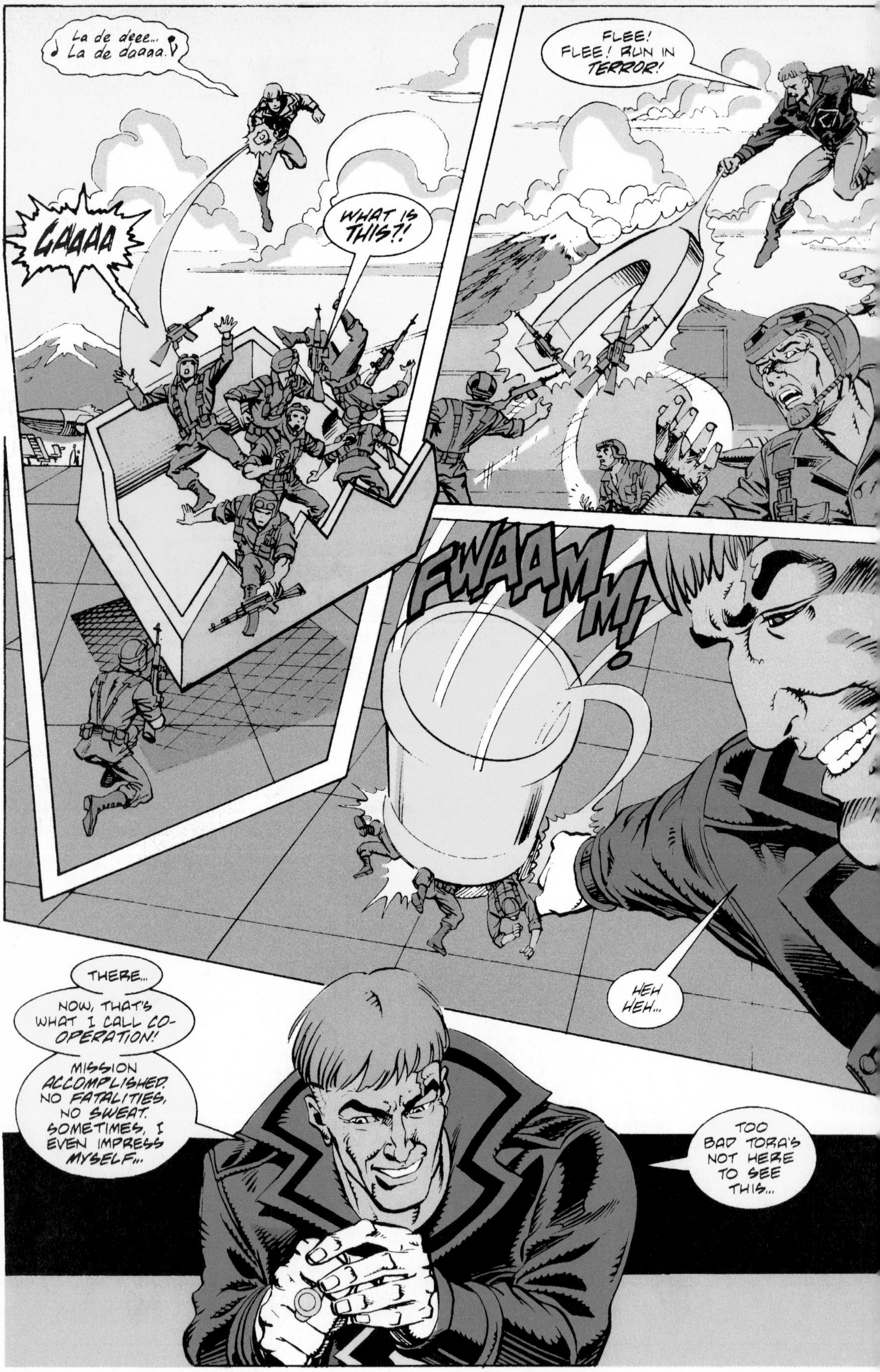
La de deee... La de daaaa.
GAAAA
WHAT IS THIS?!
FLEE! FLEE! RUN IN TERROR!
FWAAMM!
HEH HEH...
THERE...
NOW, THAT'S WHAT I CALL CO-OPERATION!
MISSION ACCOMPLISHED. NO FATALITIES, NO SWEAT. SOMETIMES, I EVEN IMPRESS MYSELF...
TOO BAD TORA'S NOT HERE TO SEE THIS...

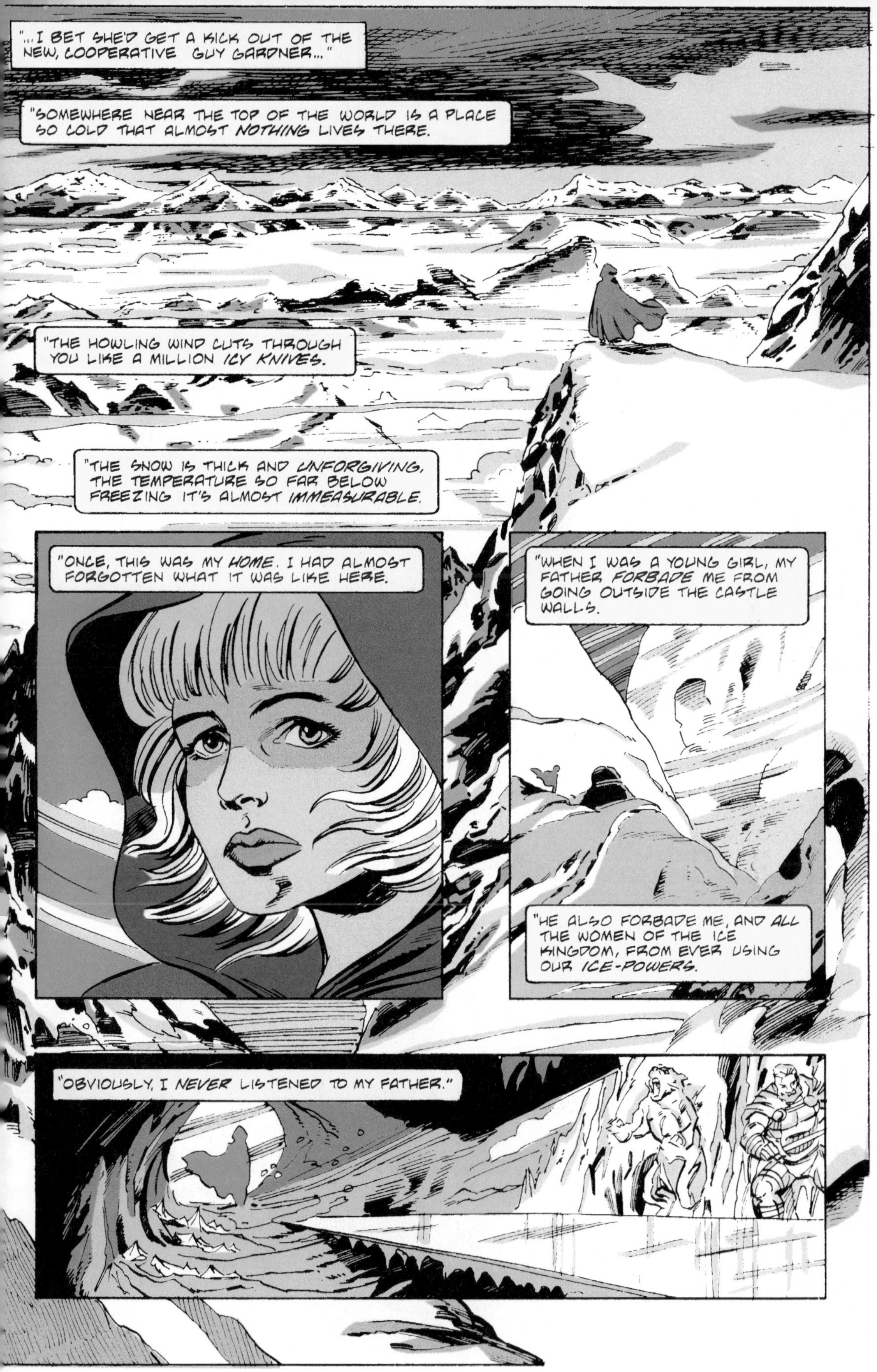
"...I BET SHE'D GET A KICK OUT OF THE NEW, COOPERATIVE GUY GARDNER..."
"SOMEWHERE NEAR THE TOP OF THE WORLD IS A PLACE SO COLD THAT ALMOST NOTHING LIVES THERE.
"THE HOWLING WIND CUTS THROUGH YOU LIKE A MILLION ICY KNIVES.
"THE SNOW IS THICK AND UNFORGIVING, THE TEMPERATURE SO FAR BELOW FREEZING IT'S ALMOST IMMEASURABLE.
"ONCE, THIS WAS MY HOME. I HAD ALMOST FORGOTTEN WHAT IT WAS LIKE HERE.
"WHEN I WAS A YOUNG GIRL, MY FATHER FORBADE ME FROM GOING OUTSIDE THE CASTLE WALLS.
"HE ALSO FORBADE ME, AND ALL THE WOMEN OF THE ICE KINGDOM, FROM EVER USING OUR ICE-POWERS.
"OBVIOUSLY, I NEVER LISTENED TO MY FATHER."

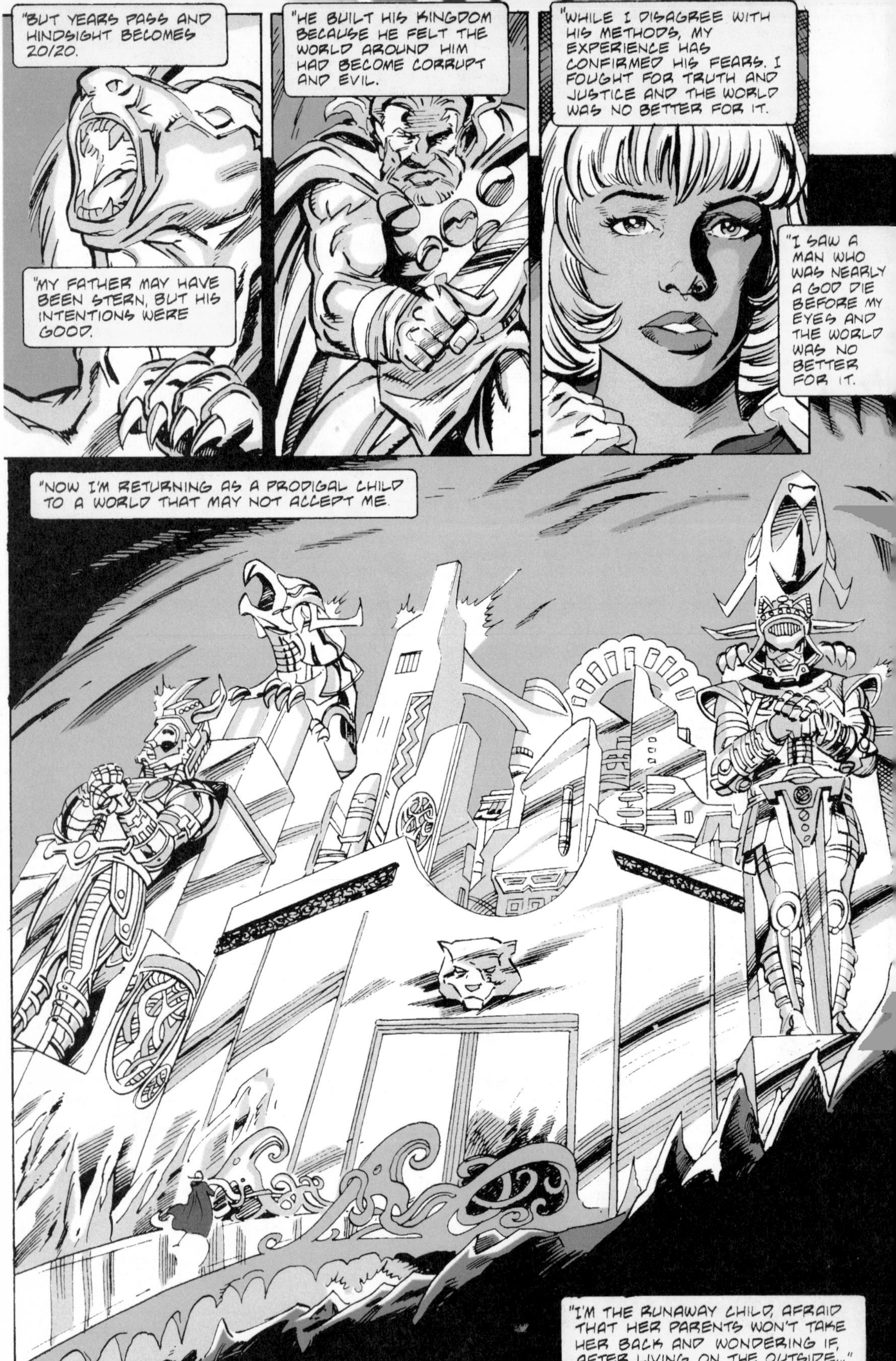
"BUT YEARS PASS AND HINDSIGHT BECOMES 20/20.
"MY FATHER MAY HAVE BEEN STERN, BUT HIS INTENTIONS WERE GOOD.
"HE BUILT HIS KINGDOM BECAUSE HE FELT THE WORLD AROUND HIM HAD BECOME CORRUPT AND EVIL.
"WHILE I DISAGREE WITH HIS METHODS, MY EXPERIENCE HAS CONFIRMED HIS FEARS. I FOUGHT FOR TRUTH AND JUSTICE AND THE WORLD WAS NO BETTER FOR IT.
"I SAW A MAN WHO WAS NEARLY A GOD DIE BEFORE MY EYES AND THE WORLD WAS NO BETTER FOR IT.
"NOW I'M RETURNING AS A PRODIGAL CHILD TO A WORLD THAT MAY NOT ACCEPT ME.
"I'M THE RUNAWAY CHILD, AFRAID THAT HER PARENTS WON'T TAKE HER BACK AND WONDERING IF, AFTER LIVING ON THE OUTSIDE..."

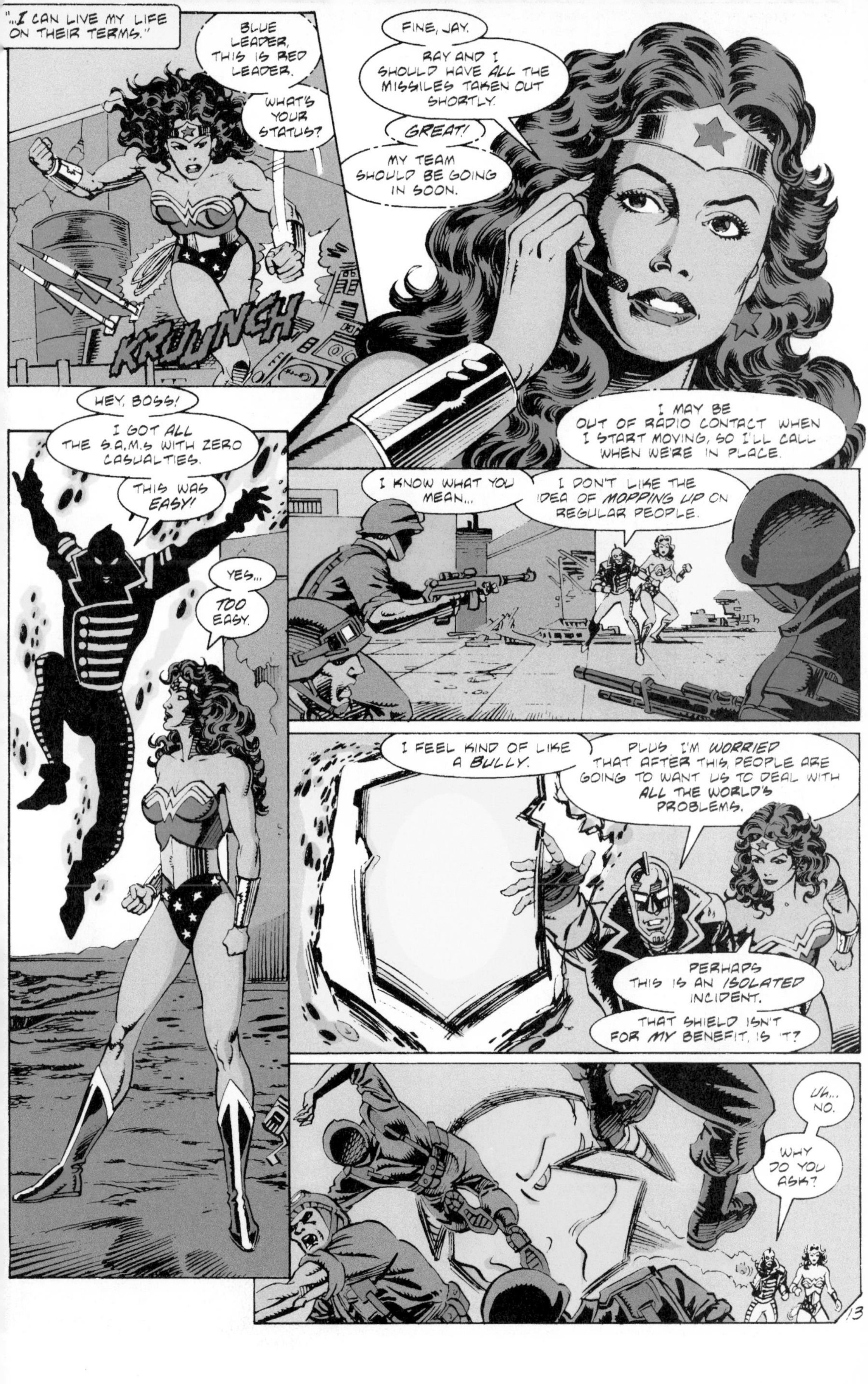
"...I CAN LIVE MY LIFE ON THEIR TERMS."
BLUE LEADER, THIS IS RED LEADER.
WHAT'S YOUR STATUS?
KRUUNCH
FINE, JAY.
RAY AND I SHOULD HAVE ALL THE MISSILES TAKEN OUT SHORTLY.
GREAT!
MY TEAM SHOULD BE GOING IN SOON.
I MAY BE OUT OF RADIO CONTACT WHEN I START MOVING, SO I'LL CALL WHEN WE'RE IN PLACE.
HEY, BOSS!
I GOT ALL THE S.A.M.s WITH ZERO CASUALTIES.
THIS WAS EASY!
YES...
TOO EASY.
I KNOW WHAT YOU MEAN...
I DON'T LIKE THE IDEA OF MOPPING UP ON REGULAR PEOPLE.
I FEEL KIND OF LIKE A BULLY.
PLUS I'M WORRIED THAT AFTER THIS, PEOPLE ARE GOING TO WANT US TO DEAL WITH ALL THE WORLD'S PROBLEMS.
PERHAPS THIS IS AN ISOLATED INCIDENT.
THAT SHIELD ISN'T FOR MY BENEFIT, IS IT?
UH... NO.
WHY DO YOU ASK?

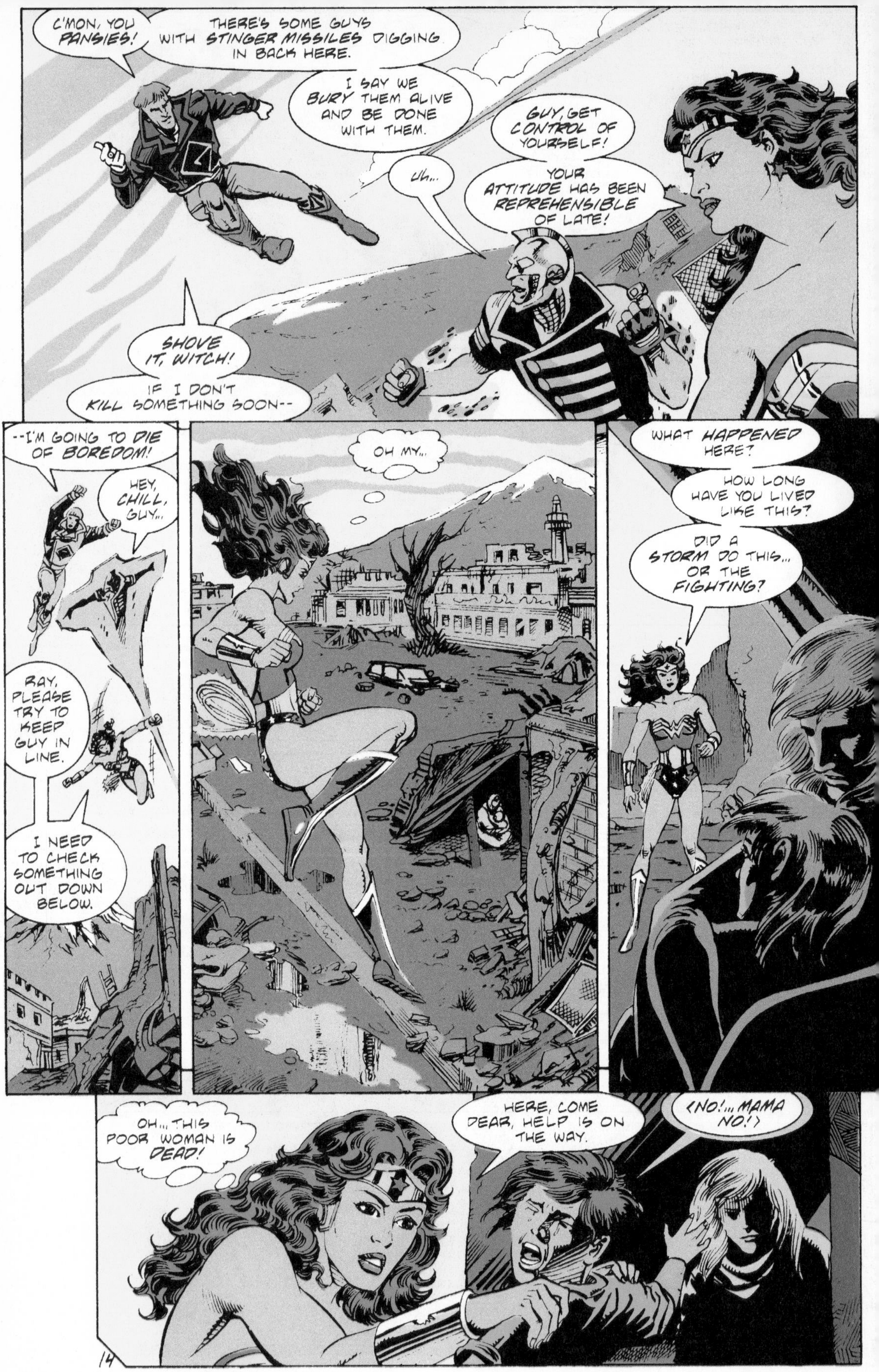
C'MON, YOU PANSIES!
THERE'S SOME GUYS WITH STINGER MISSILES DIGGING IN BACK HERE.
I SAY WE BURY THEM ALIVE AND BE DONE WITH THEM.
GUY, GET CONTROL OF YOURSELF!
YOUR ATTITUDE HAS BEEN REPREHENSIBLE OF LATE!
Uh...
SHOVE IT, WITCH!
IF I DON'T KILL SOMETHING SOON--
--I'M GOING TO DIE OF BOREDOM!
HEY, CHILL, GUY...
RAY, PLEASE TRY TO KEEP GUY IN LINE.
I NEED TO CHECK SOMETHING OUT DOWN BELOW.
OH MY...
WHAT HAPPENED HERE?
HOW LONG HAVE YOU LIVED LIKE THIS?
DID A STORM DO THIS... OR THE FIGHTING?
OH... THIS POOR WOMAN IS DEAD!
HERE, COME DEAR, HELP IS ON THE WAY.
<NO!... MAMA NO!>
14

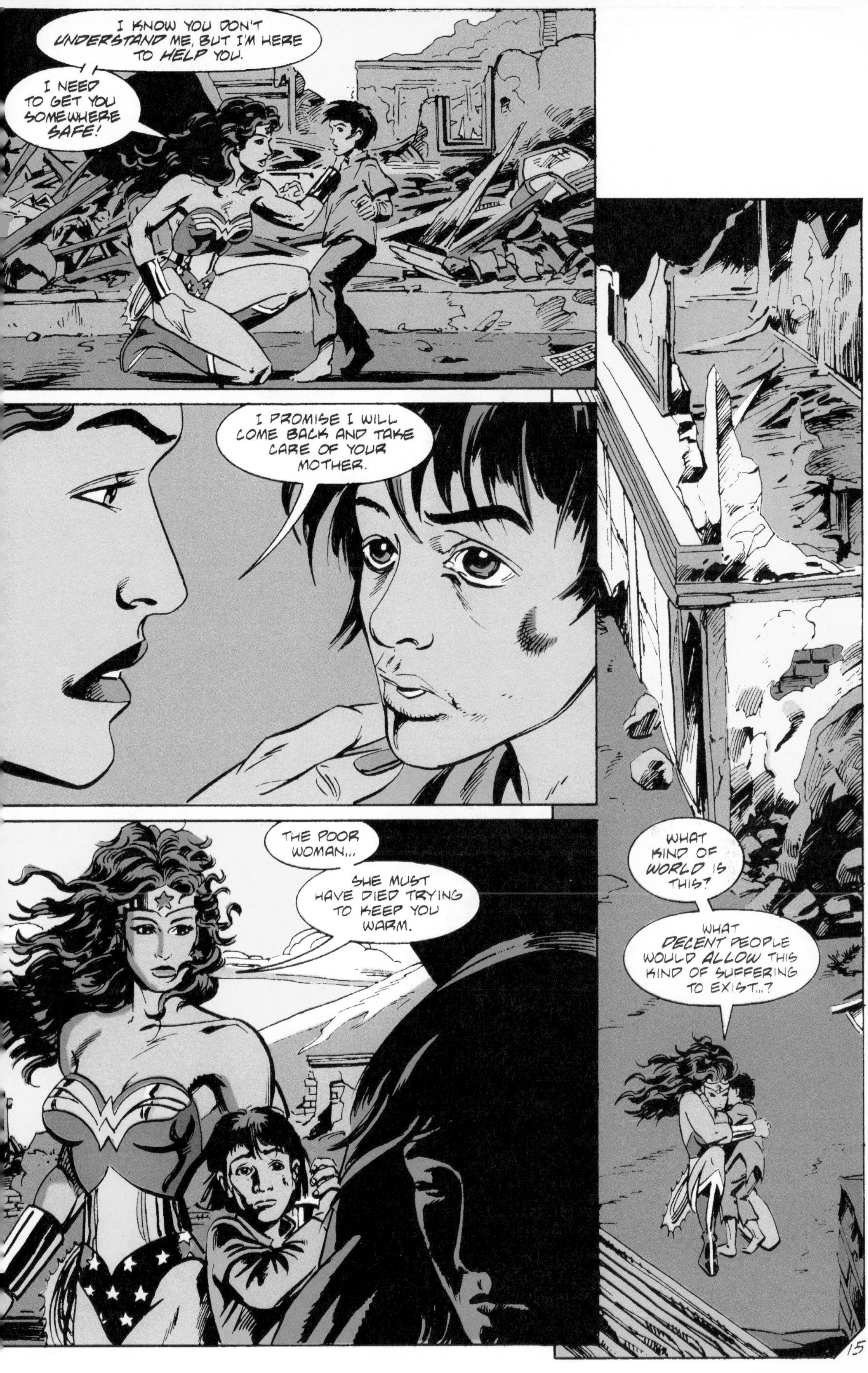
I KNOW YOU DON'T UNDERSTAND ME, BUT I'M HERE TO HELP YOU.
I NEED TO GET YOU SOMEWHERE SAFE!
I PROMISE I WILL COME BACK AND TAKE CARE OF YOUR MOTHER.
THE POOR WOMAN...
SHE MUST HAVE DIED TRYING TO KEEP YOU WARM.
WHAT KIND OF WORLD IS THIS?
WHAT DECENT PEOPLE WOULD ALLOW THIS KIND OF SUFFERING TO EXIST...?

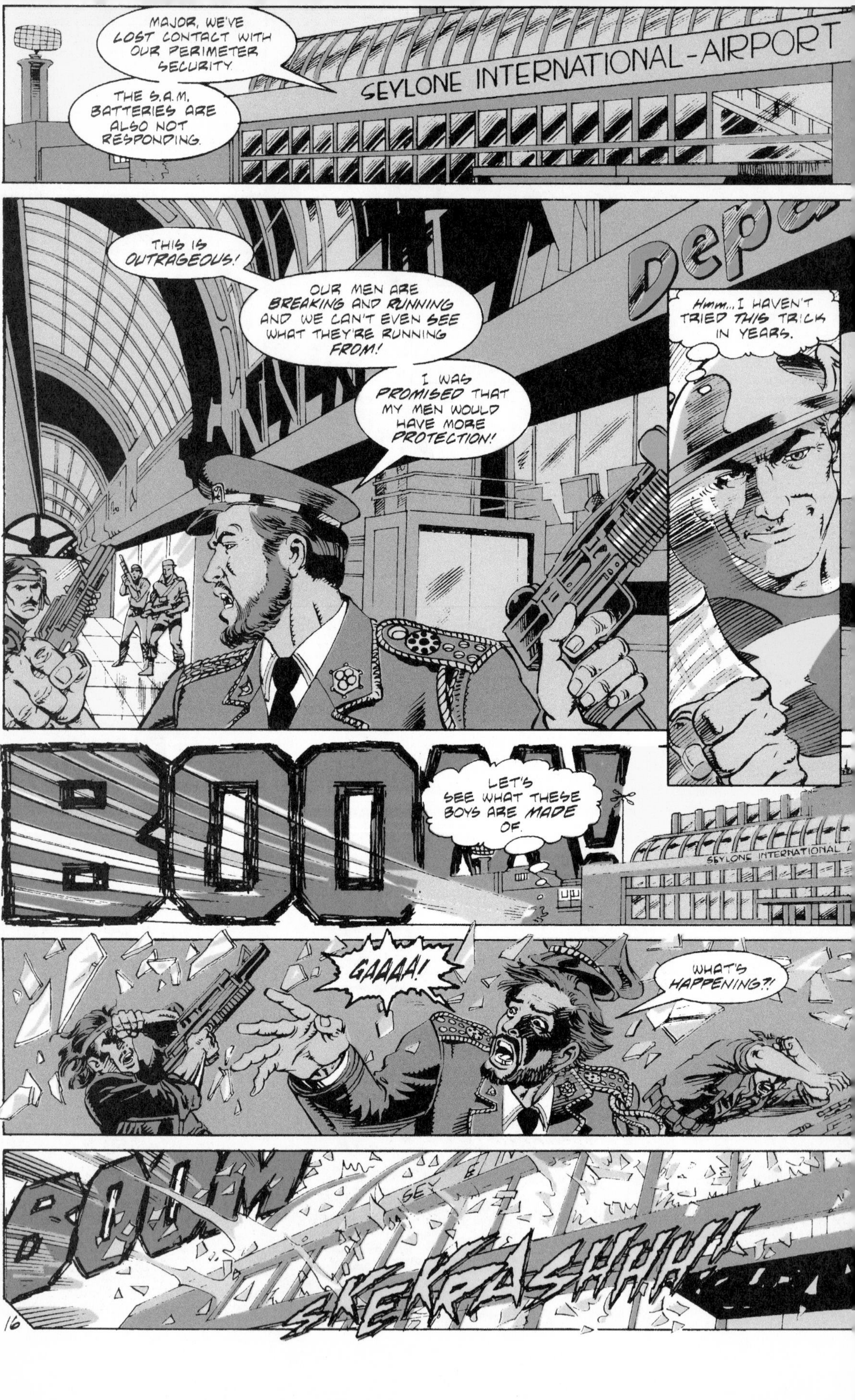
SEYLONE INTERNATIONAL-AIRPORT
MAJOR, WE'VE LOST CONTACT WITH OUR PERIMETER SECURITY.
THE S.A.M. BATTERIES ARE ALSO NOT RESPONDING.
THIS IS OUTRAGEOUS!
OUR MEN ARE BREAKING AND RUNNING AND WE CAN'T EVEN SEE WHAT THEY'RE RUNNING FROM!
I WAS PROMISED THAT MY MEN WOULD HAVE MORE PROTECTION!
Hmm... I HAVEN'T TRIED THIS TRICK IN YEARS.
BOOM!
LET'S SEE WHAT THESE BOYS ARE MADE OF.
SEYLONE INTERNATIONAL
GAAAA!
WHAT'S HAPPENING?!
BOOM!
SKEKRASHHH!

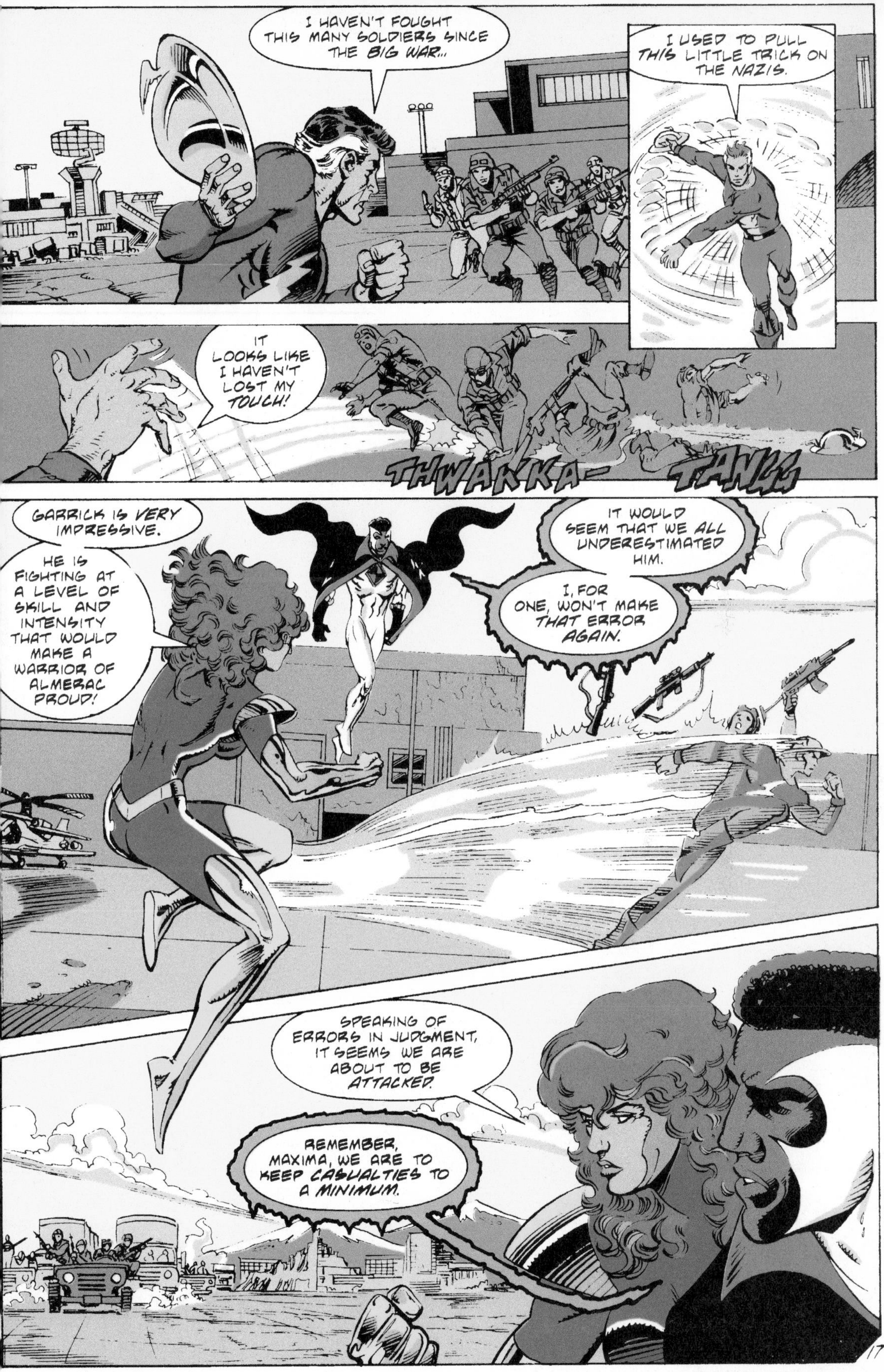
I HAVEN'T FOUGHT THIS MANY SOLDIERS SINCE THE BIG WAR...
I USED TO PULL THIS LITTLE TRICK ON THE NAZIS.
IT LOOKS LIKE I HAVEN'T LOST MY TOUCH!
THWAKKA-
TANG
GARRICK IS VERY IMPRESSIVE.
HE IS FIGHTING AT A LEVEL OF SKILL AND INTENSITY THAT WOULD MAKE A WARRIOR OF ALMERAC PROUD!
IT WOULD SEEM THAT WE ALL UNDERESTIMATED HIM.
I, FOR ONE, WON'T MAKE THAT ERROR AGAIN.
SPEAKING OF ERRORS IN JUDGMENT, IT SEEMS WE ARE ABOUT TO BE ATTACKED.
REMEMBER, MAXIMA, WE ARE TO KEEP CASUALTIES TO A MINIMUM.

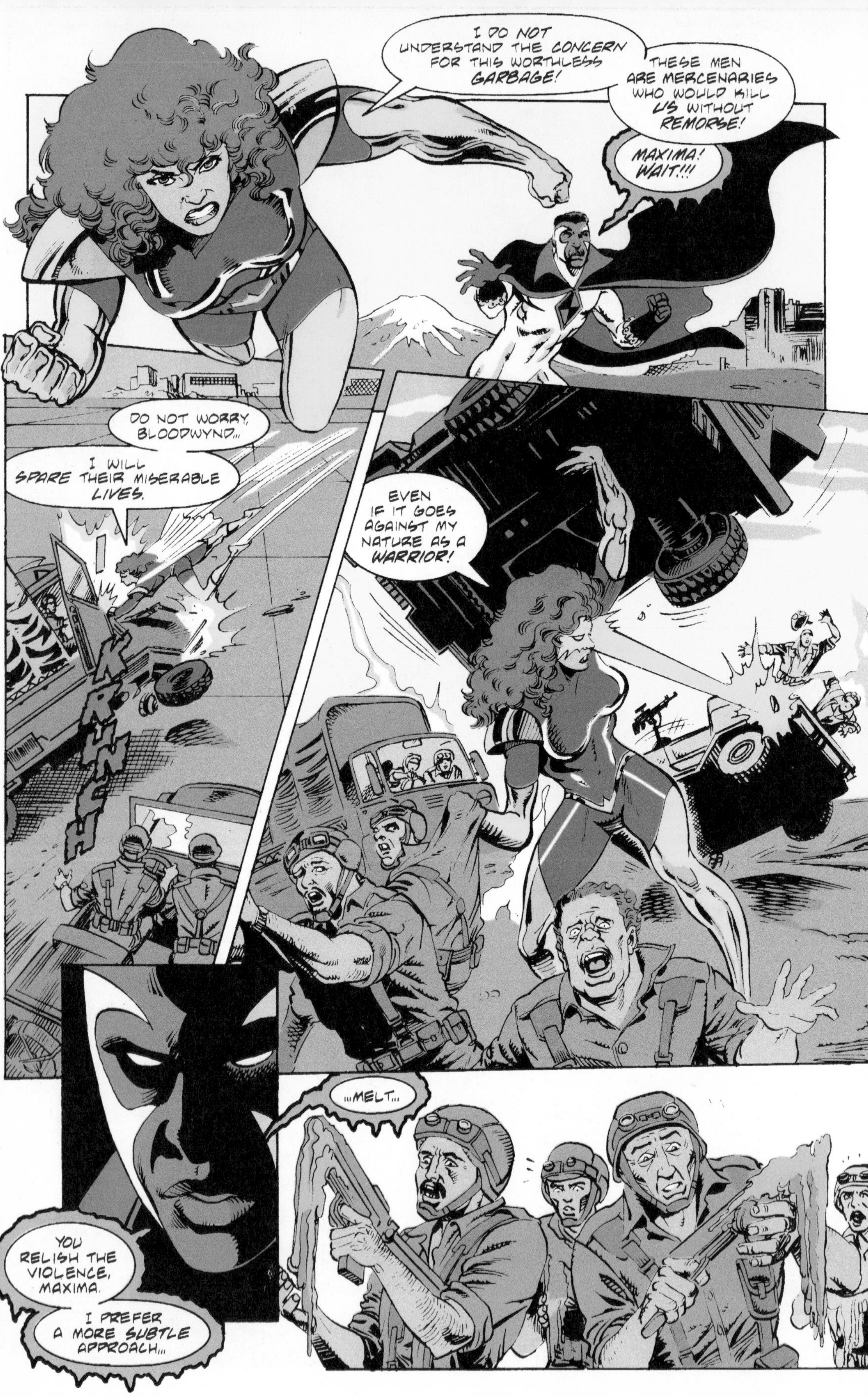
I DO NOT UNDERSTAND THE CONCERN FOR THIS WORTHLESS GARBAGE!
THESE MEN ARE MERCENARIES WHO WOULD KILL US WITHOUT REMORSE!
MAXIMA! WAIT!!!
DO NOT WORRY, BLOODWYND...
I WILL SPARE THEIR MISERABLE LIVES.
KRUNCH
EVEN IF IT GOES AGAINST MY NATURE AS A WARRIOR!
...MELT...
YOU RELISH THE VIOLENCE, MAXIMA.
I PREFER A MORE SUBTLE APPROACH...

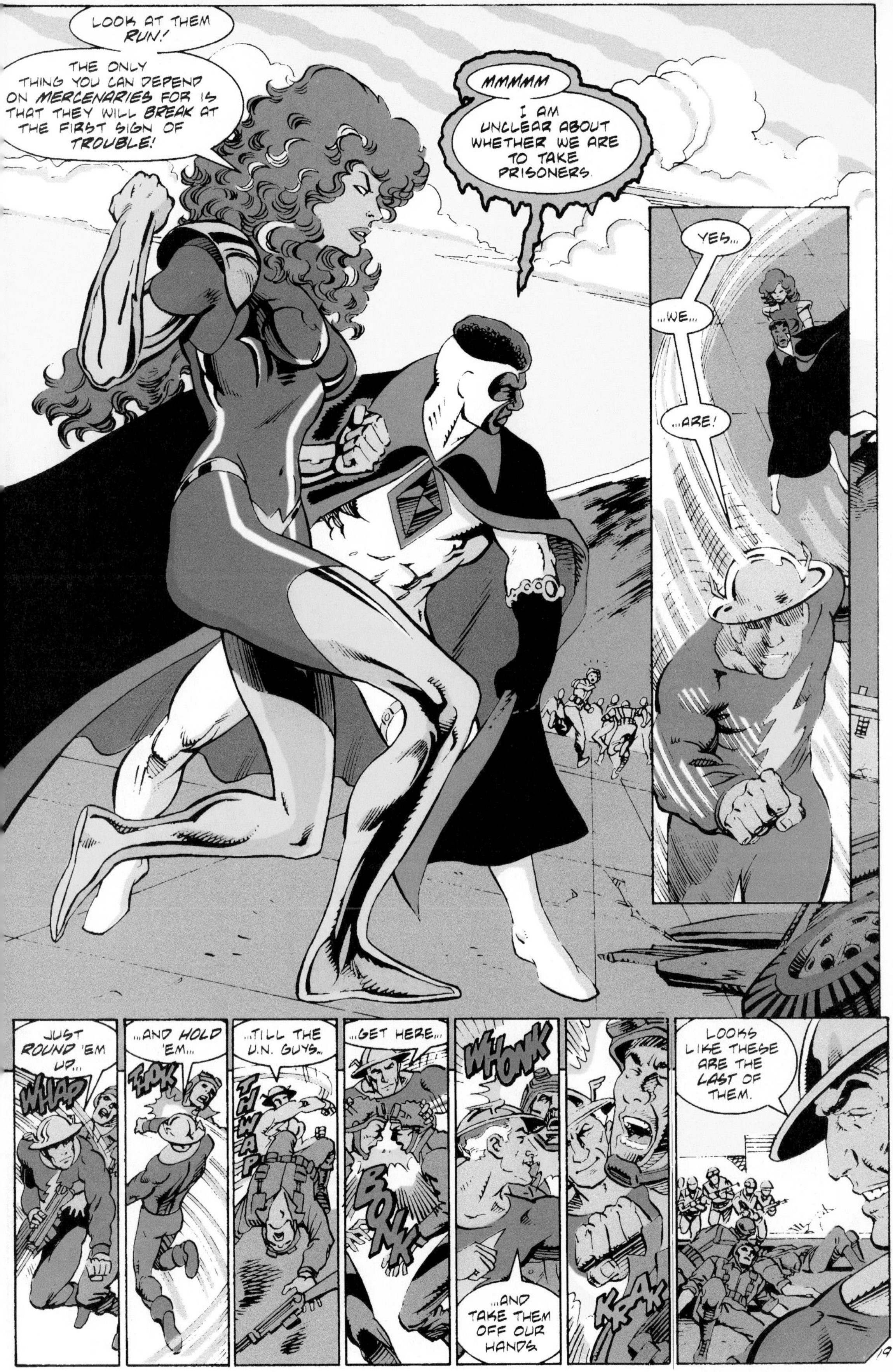

LOOK AT THEM RUN!
THE ONLY THING YOU CAN DEPEND ON MERCENARIES FOR IS THAT THEY WILL BREAK AT THE FIRST SIGN OF TROUBLE!
MMMMM
I AM UNCLEAR ABOUT WHETHER WE ARE TO TAKE PRISONERS.
YES...
...WE...
...ARE!
JUST ROUND 'EM UP...
WHAP
...AND HOLD 'EM...
...TILL THE U.N. GUYS...
THWAP
...GET HERE...
BONK
WHONK
...AND TAKE THEM OFF OUR HANDS.
KRAK
LOOKS LIKE THESE ARE THE LAST OF THEM.

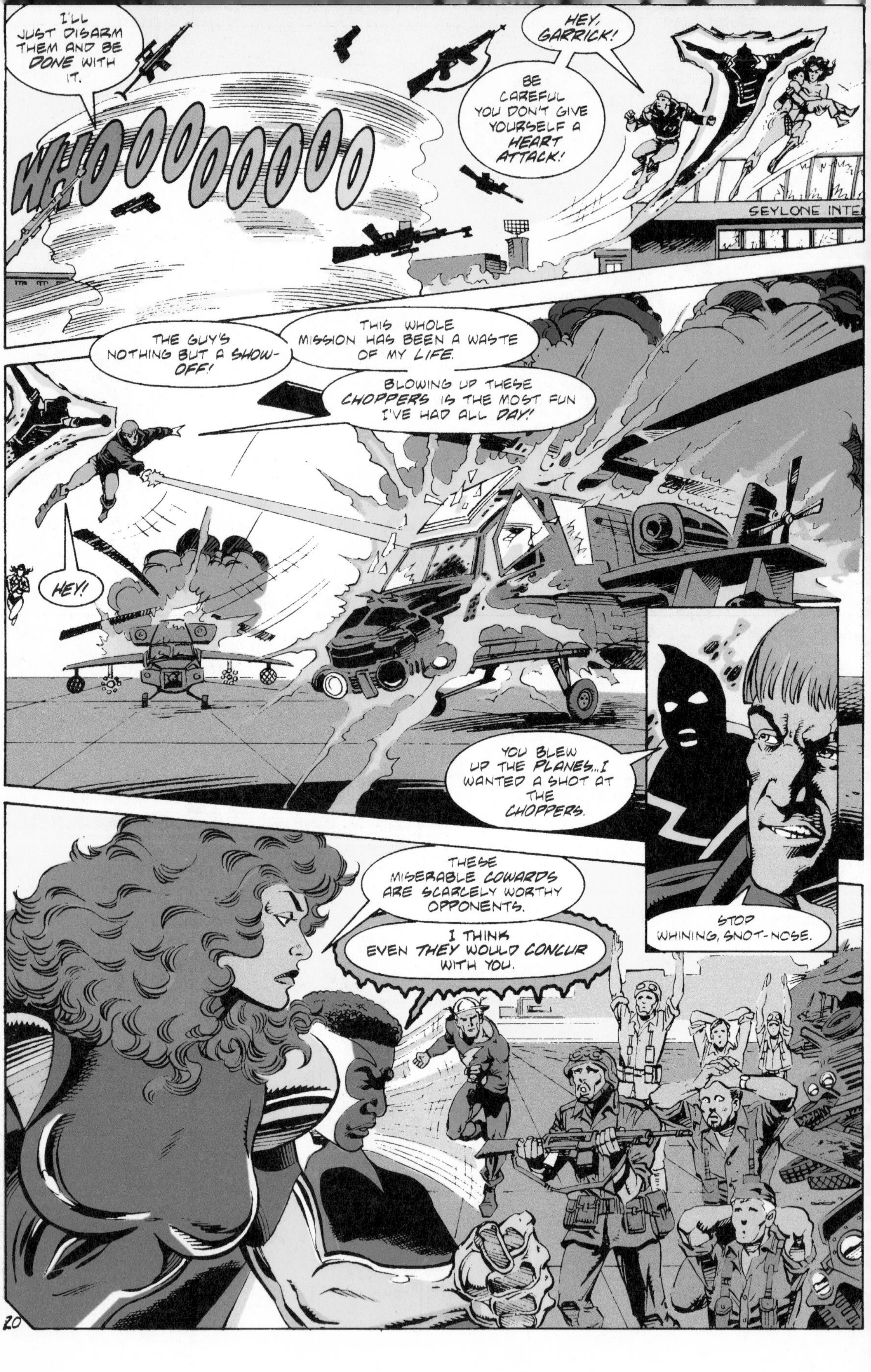
I'LL JUST DISARM THEM AND BE DONE WITH IT.
WHOOOOOOOO
HEY, GARRICK!
BE CAREFUL YOU DON'T GIVE YOURSELF A HEART ATTACK!
SEYLONE INTE
THE GUY'S NOTHING BUT A SHOW-OFF!
THIS WHOLE MISSION HAS BEEN A WASTE OF MY LIFE.
BLOWING UP THESE CHOPPERS IS THE MOST FUN I'VE HAD ALL DAY!
HEY!
YOU BLEW UP THE PLANES...I WANTED A SHOT AT THE CHOPPERS.
STOP WHINING, SNOT-NOSE.
THESE MISERABLE COWARDS ARE SCARCELY WORTHY OPPONENTS.
I THINK EVEN THEY WOULD CONCUR WITH YOU.

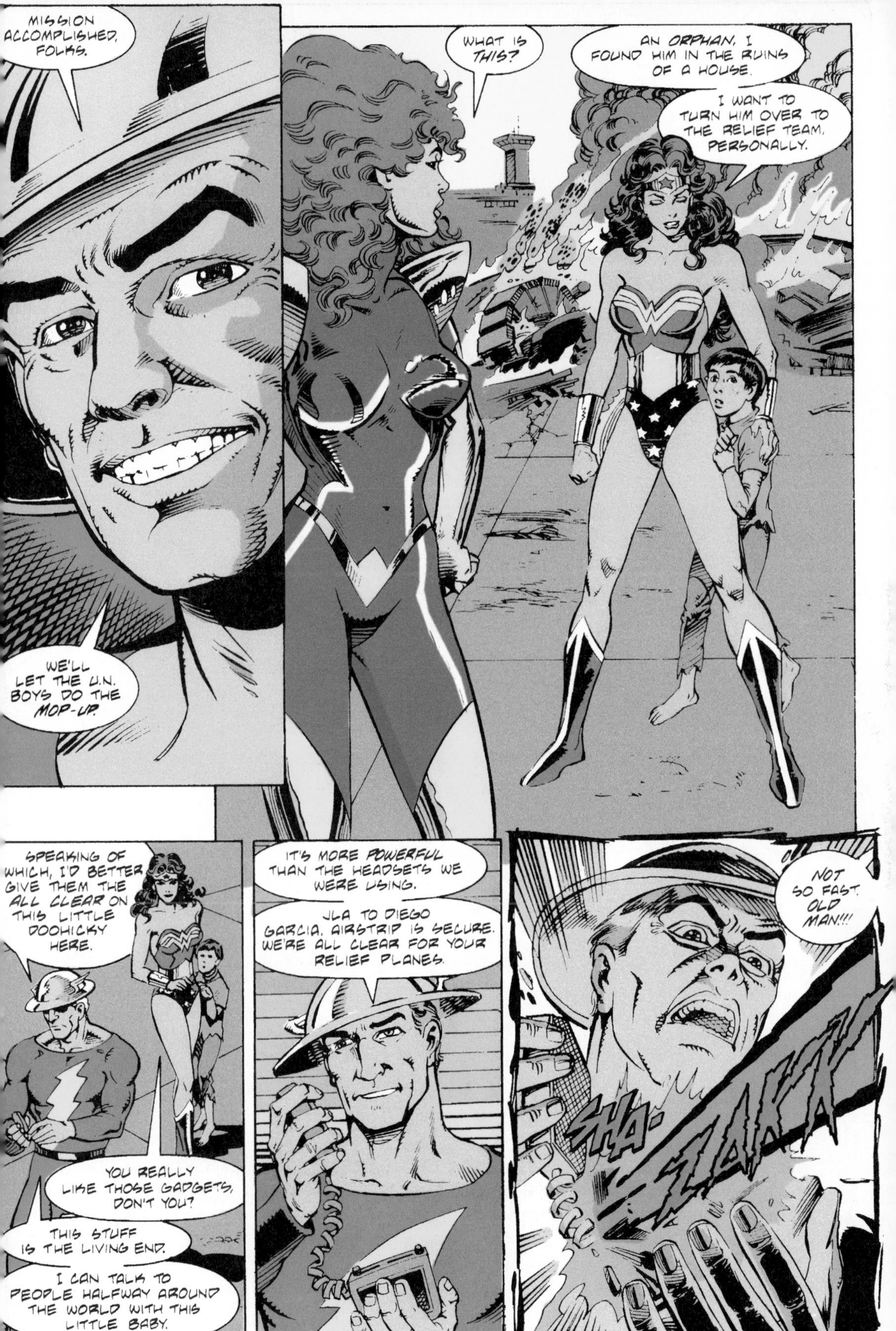

MISSION ACCOMPLISHED, FOLKS.
WE'LL LET THE U.N. BOYS DO THE MOP-UP.
WHAT IS THIS?
AN ORPHAN. I FOUND HIM IN THE RUINS OF A HOUSE.
I WANT TO TURN HIM OVER TO THE RELIEF TEAM, PERSONALLY.
SPEAKING OF WHICH, I'D BETTER GIVE THEM THE ALL CLEAR ON THIS LITTLE DOOHICKY HERE.
YOU REALLY LIKE THOSE GADGETS, DON'T YOU?
THIS STUFF IS THE LIVING END.
I CAN TALK TO PEOPLE HALFWAY AROUND THE WORLD WITH THIS LITTLE BABY.
IT'S MORE POWERFUL THAN THE HEADSETS WE WERE USING.
JLA TO DIEGO GARCIA. AIRSTRIP IS SECURE. WE'RE ALL CLEAR FOR YOUR RELIEF PLANES.
NOT SO FAST, OLD MAN!!!
SHA-ZAKK!

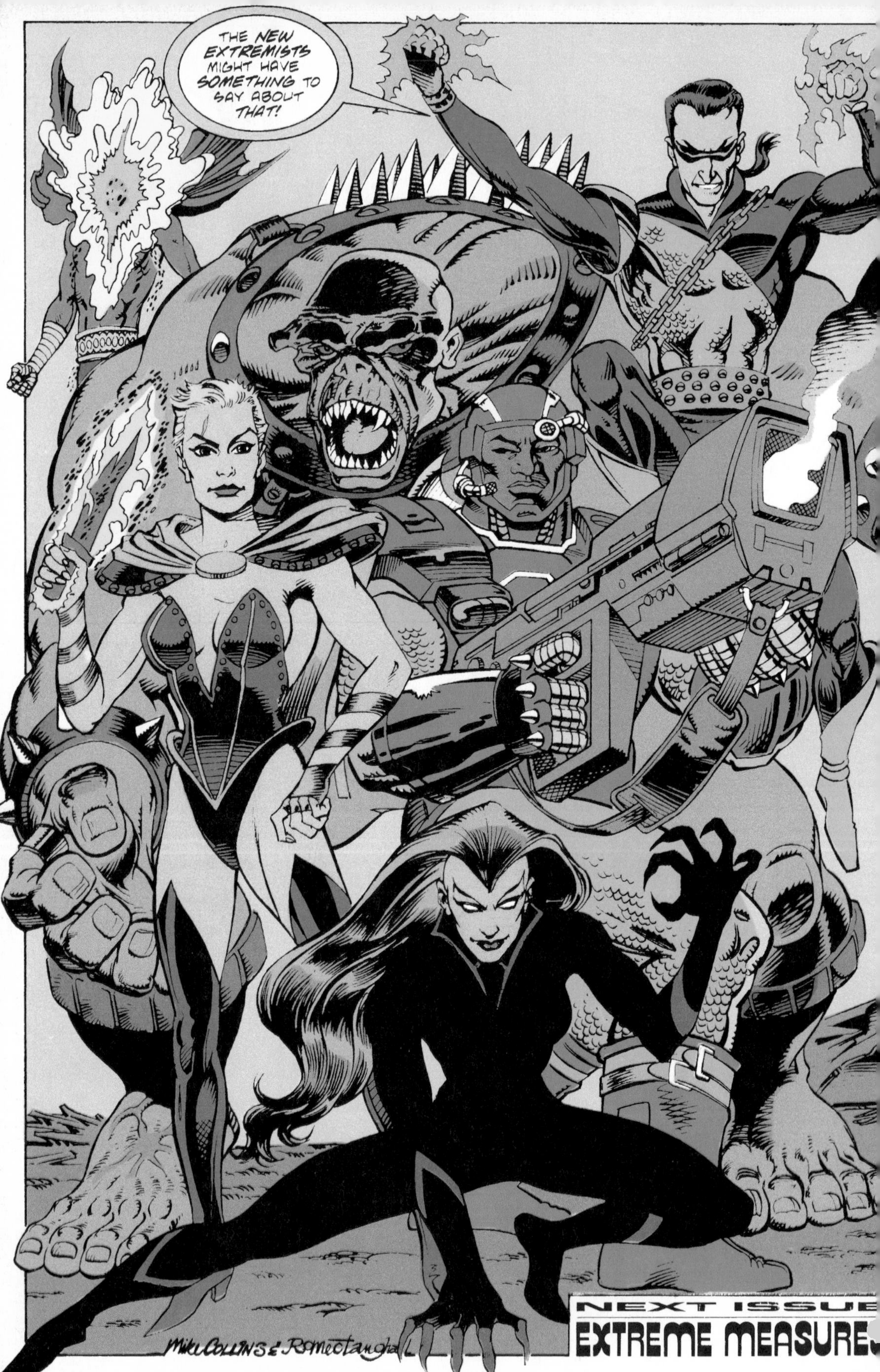
THE NEW EXTREMISTS MIGHT HAVE SOMETHING TO SAY ABOUT THAT!
MIKE COLLINS & ROMEO TANGHAL
NEXT ISSUE
EXTREME MEASURES

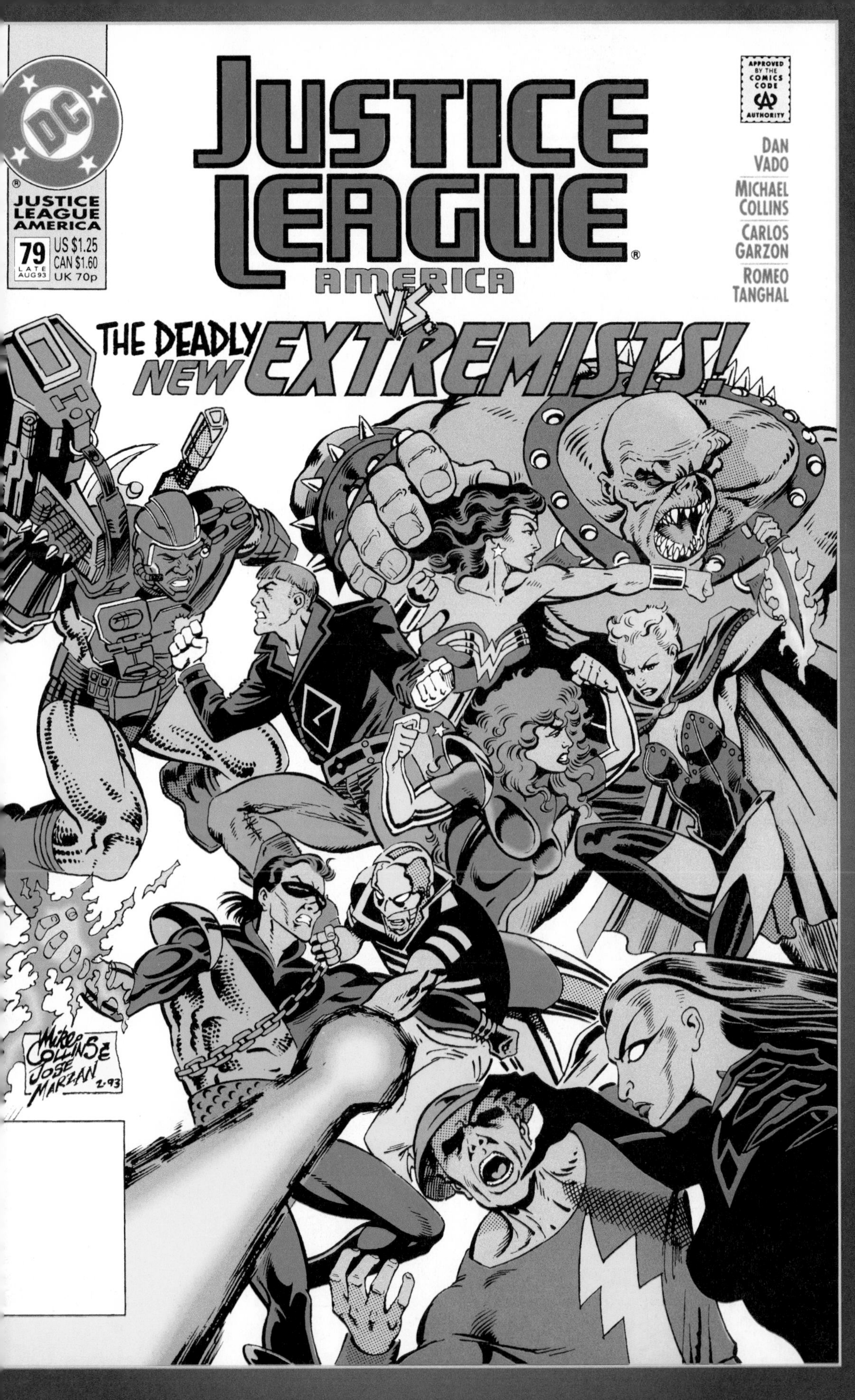
DC
JUSTICE LEAGUE AMERICA
79
LATE AUG 93
US $1.25
CAN $1.60
UK 70p
JUSTICE LEAGUE AMERICA
APPROVED BY THE COMICS CODE AUTHORITY
DAN VADO
MICHAEL COLLINS
CARLOS GARZON
ROMEO TANGHAL
VS.
THE DEADLY NEW EXTREMISTS!
MIKE COLLINS & JOSE MARZAN 2-93

Cover art by **MIKE COLLINS**
and **JOSÉ MARZAN, JR.**

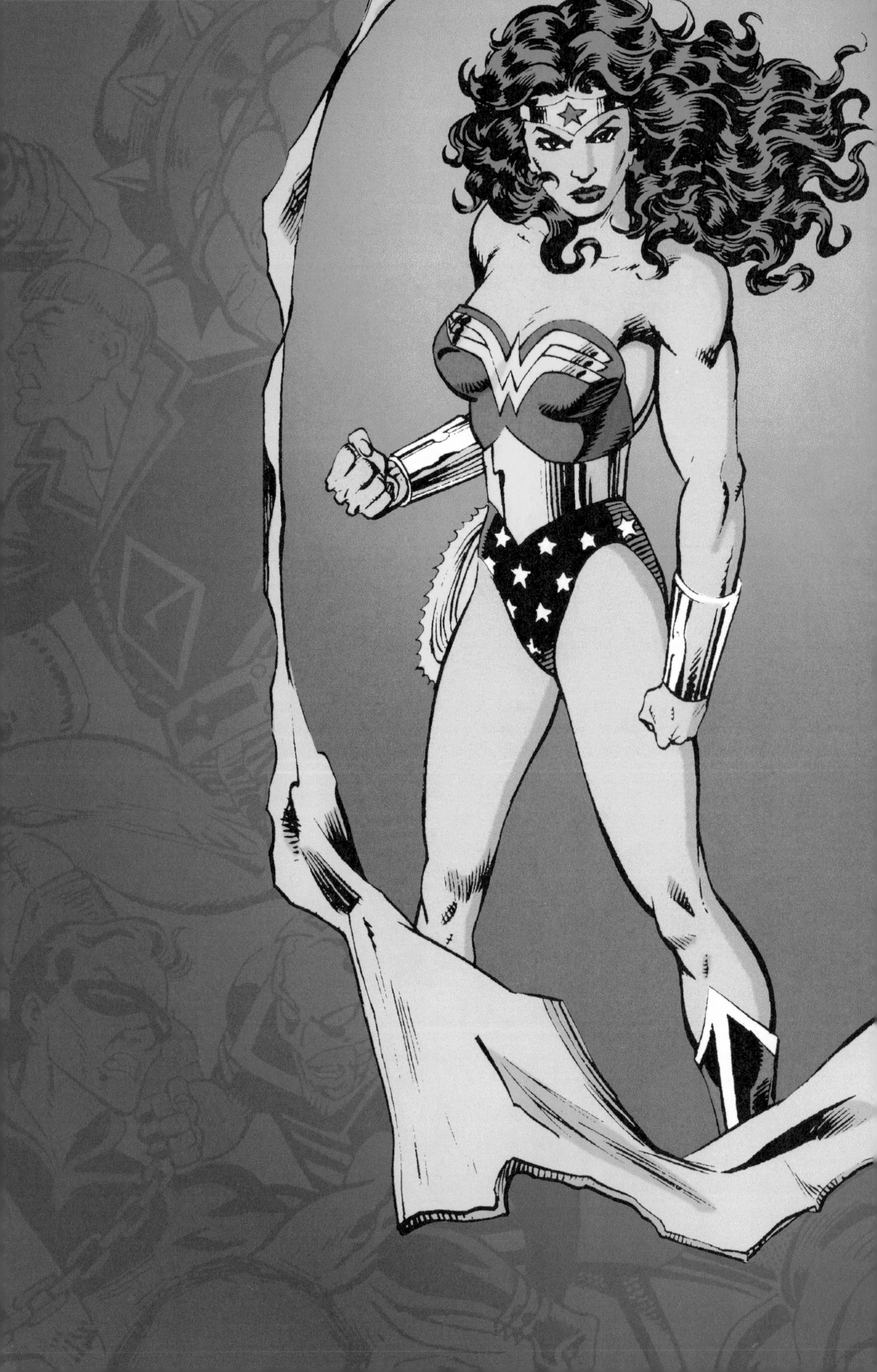

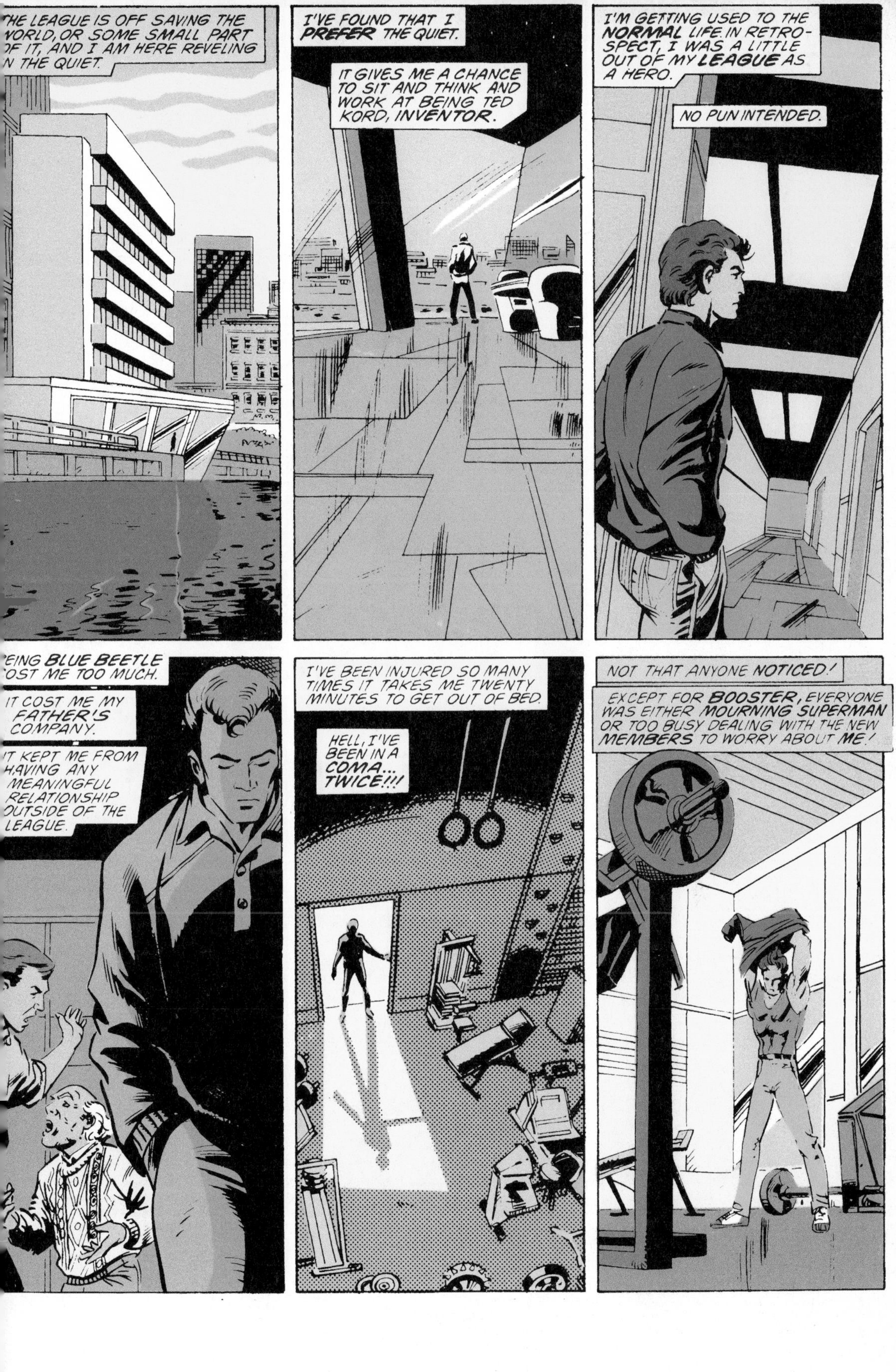
THE LEAGUE IS OFF SAVING THE WORLD, OR SOME SMALL PART OF IT, AND I AM HERE REVELING IN THE QUIET.
I'VE FOUND THAT I PREFER THE QUIET.
IT GIVES ME A CHANCE TO SIT AND THINK AND WORK AT BEING TED KORD, INVENTOR.
I'M GETTING USED TO THE NORMAL LIFE. IN RETROSPECT, I WAS A LITTLE OUT OF MY LEAGUE AS A HERO.
NO PUN INTENDED.
BEING BLUE BEETLE COST ME TOO MUCH.
IT COST ME MY FATHER'S COMPANY.
IT KEPT ME FROM HAVING ANY MEANINGFUL RELATIONSHIP OUTSIDE OF THE LEAGUE.
I'VE BEEN INJURED SO MANY TIMES IT TAKES ME TWENTY MINUTES TO GET OUT OF BED.
HELL, I'VE BEEN IN A COMA... TWICE!!!
NOT THAT ANYONE NOTICED!
EXCEPT FOR BOOSTER, EVERYONE WAS EITHER MOURNING SUPERMAN OR TOO BUSY DEALING WITH THE NEW MEMBERS TO WORRY ABOUT ME!

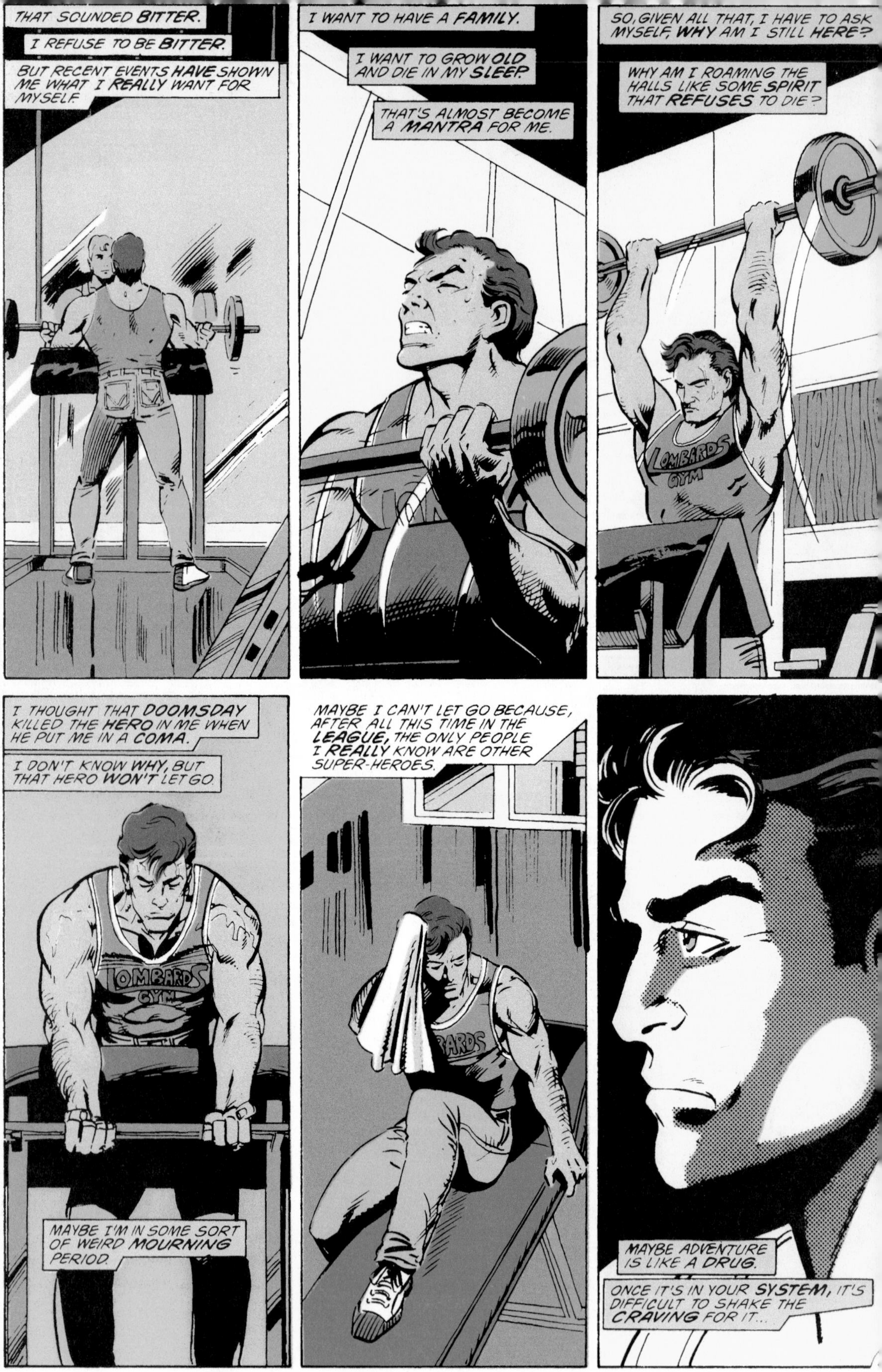
THAT SOUNDED BITTER.
I REFUSE TO BE BITTER.
BUT RECENT EVENTS HAVE SHOWN ME WHAT I REALLY WANT FOR MYSELF.
I WANT TO HAVE A FAMILY.
I WANT TO GROW OLD AND DIE IN MY SLEEP.
THAT'S ALMOST BECOME A MANTRA FOR ME.
SO, GIVEN ALL THAT, I HAVE TO ASK MYSELF, WHY AM I STILL HERE?
WHY AM I ROAMING THE HALLS LIKE SOME SPIRIT THAT REFUSES TO DIE?
LOMBARDS GYM
I THOUGHT THAT DOOMSDAY KILLED THE HERO IN ME WHEN HE PUT ME IN A COMA.
I DON'T KNOW WHY, BUT THAT HERO WON'T LET GO.
LOMBARDS GYM
MAYBE I'M IN SOME SORT OF WEIRD MOURNING PERIOD.
MAYBE I CAN'T LET GO BECAUSE, AFTER ALL THIS TIME IN THE LEAGUE, THE ONLY PEOPLE I REALLY KNOW ARE OTHER SUPER-HEROES.
MAYBE ADVENTURE IS LIKE A DRUG.
ONCE IT'S IN YOUR SYSTEM, IT'S DIFFICULT TO SHAKE THE CRAVING FOR IT...

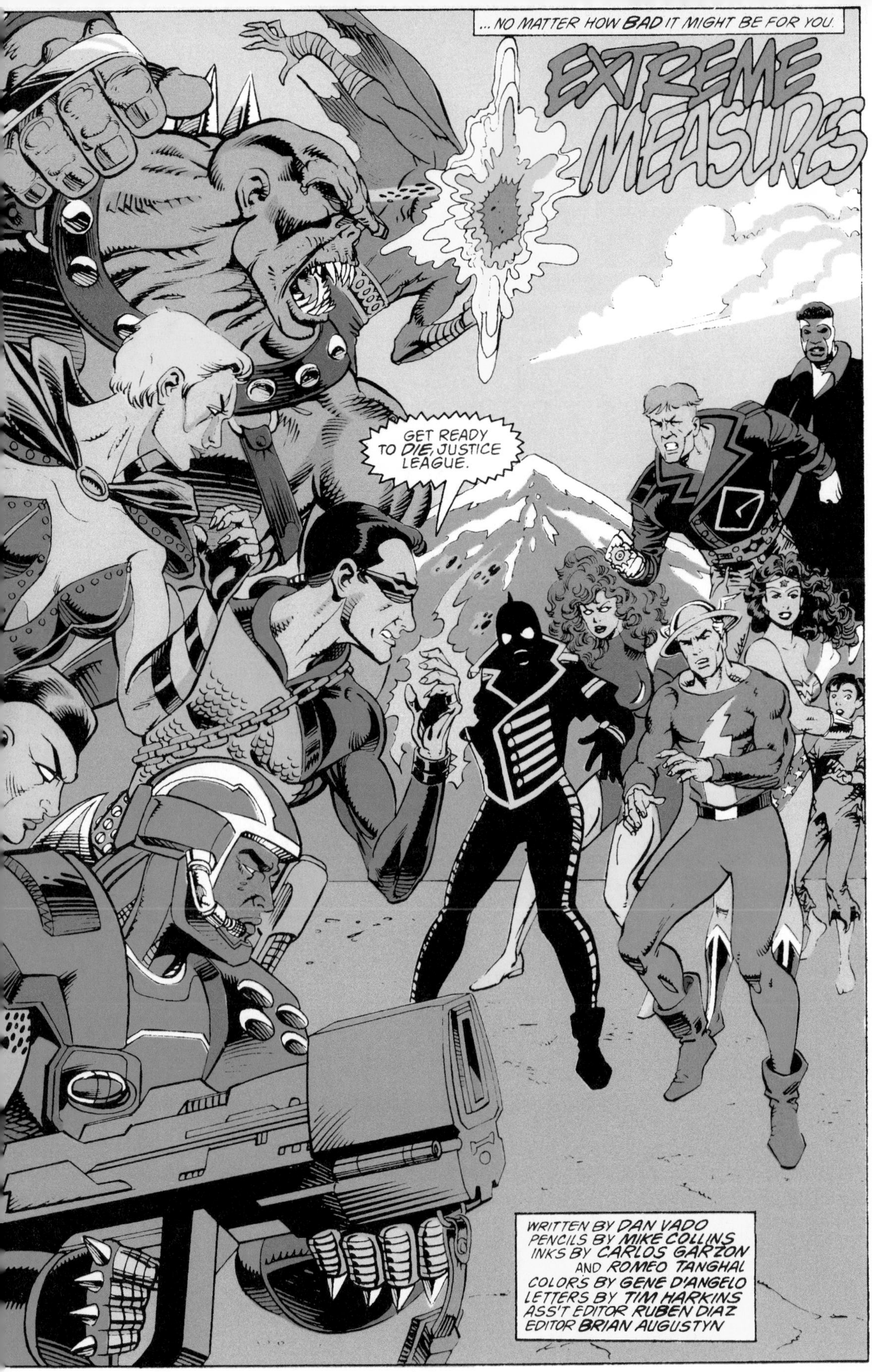
...NO MATTER HOW BAD IT MIGHT BE FOR YOU.
EXTREME MEASURES
GET READY TO DIE, JUSTICE LEAGUE.
WRITTEN BY DAN VADO
PENCILS BY MIKE COLLINS
INKS BY CARLOS GARZON AND ROMEO TANGHAL
COLORS BY GENE D'ANGELO
LETTERS BY TIM HARKINS
ASS'T EDITOR RUBEN DIAZ
EDITOR BRIAN AUGUSTYN

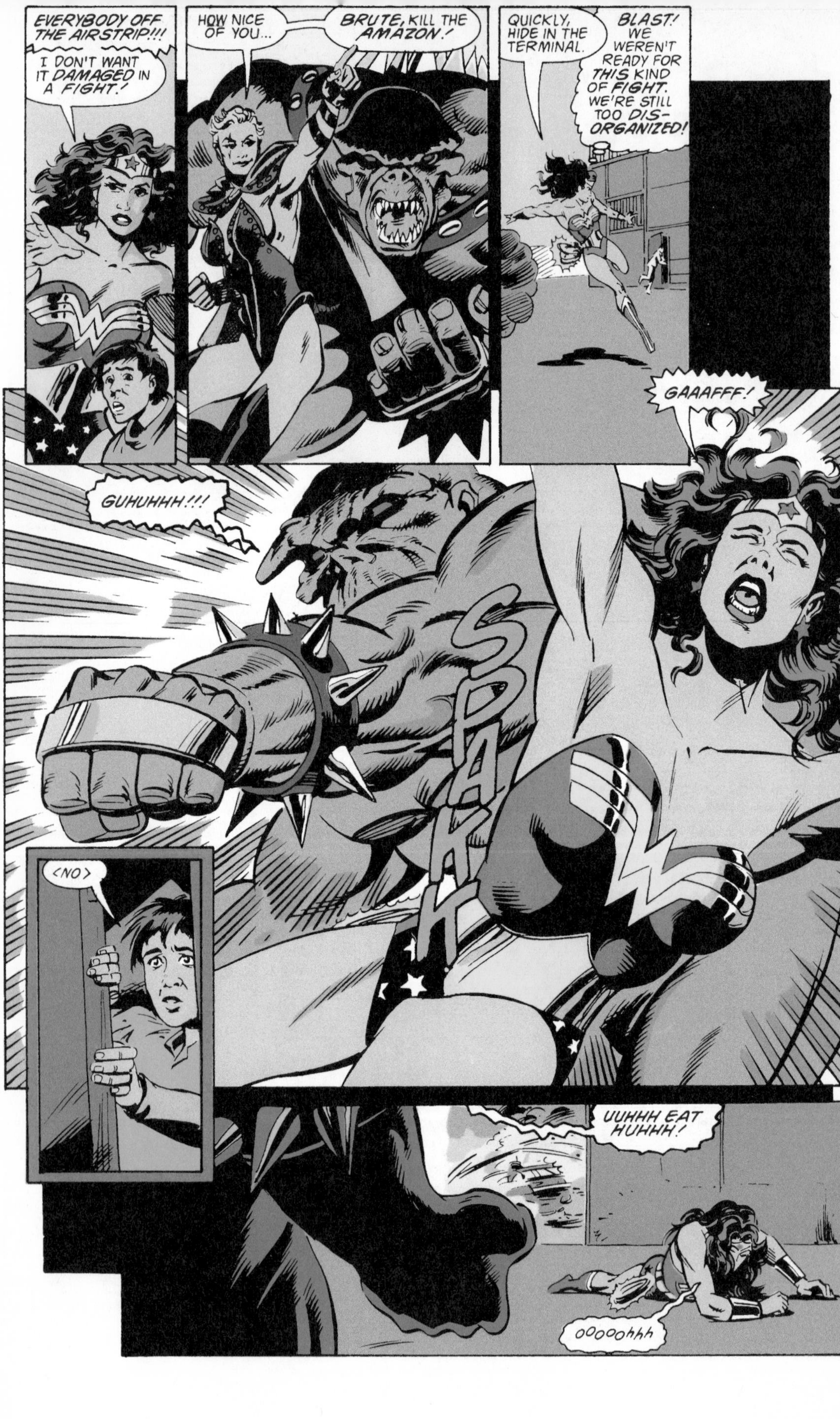
EVERYBODY OFF THE AIRSTRIP!!!
I DON'T WANT IT DAMAGED IN A FIGHT.!
HOW NICE OF YOU...
BRUTE, KILL THE AMAZON.!
QUICKLY, HIDE IN THE TERMINAL.
BLAST.! WE WEREN'T READY FOR THIS KIND OF FIGHT. WE'RE STILL TOO DIS-ORGANIZED!
GAAAFFF!
GUHUHHH!!!
SPAKK
<NO>
UUHHH EAT HUHHH!
OOOOOhhh

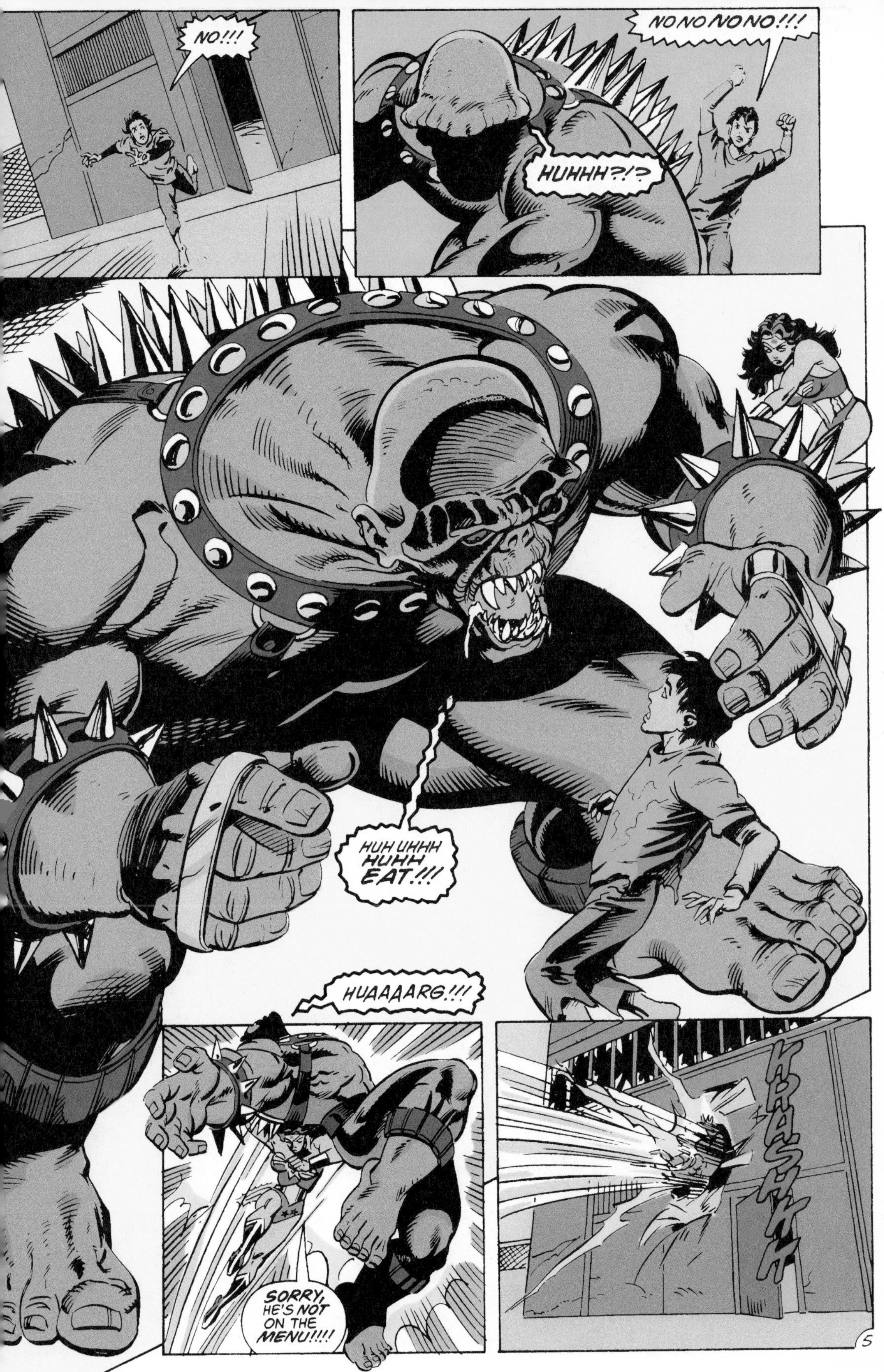
NO!!!
NONONONONO!!!
HUHHH?!?
HUH UHHH HUHH EAT!!!
HUAAAARG!!!
SORRY, HE'S NOT ON THE MENU!!!!
KRASHHH

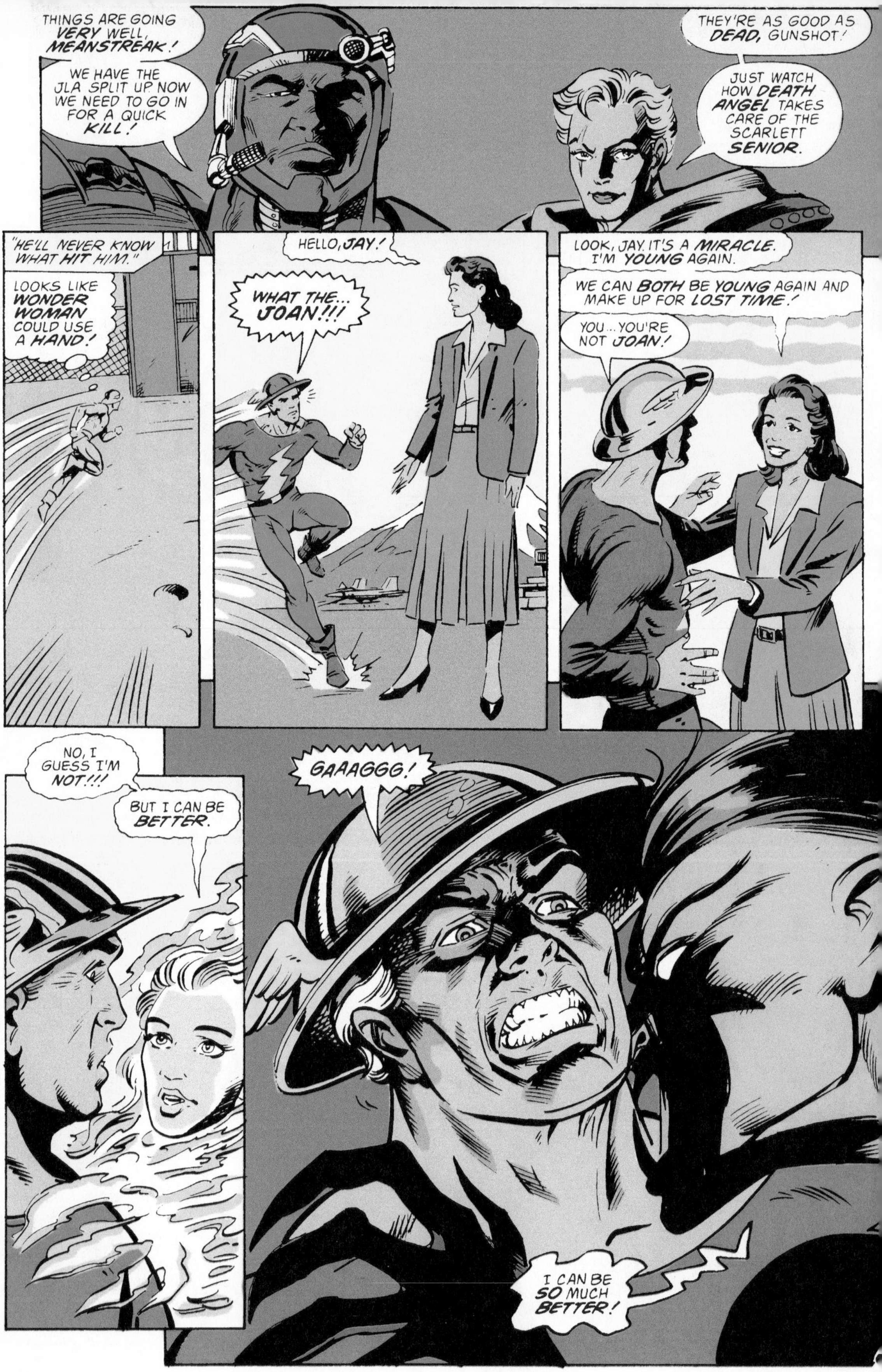

THINGS ARE GOING VERY WELL, MEANSTREAK!
WE HAVE THE JLA SPLIT UP NOW WE NEED TO GO IN FOR A QUICK KILL!
THEY'RE AS GOOD AS DEAD, GUNSHOT!
JUST WATCH HOW DEATH ANGEL TAKES CARE OF THE SCARLETT SENIOR.
"HE'LL NEVER KNOW WHAT HIT HIM."
LOOKS LIKE WONDER WOMAN COULD USE A HAND!
HELLO, JAY!
WHAT THE... JOAN!!!
LOOK, JAY. IT'S A MIRACLE. I'M YOUNG AGAIN.
WE CAN BOTH BE YOUNG AGAIN AND MAKE UP FOR LOST TIME!
YOU... YOU'RE NOT JOAN!
NO, I GUESS I'M NOT!!!
BUT I CAN BE BETTER.
GAAAGGG!
I CAN BE SO MUCH BETTER!

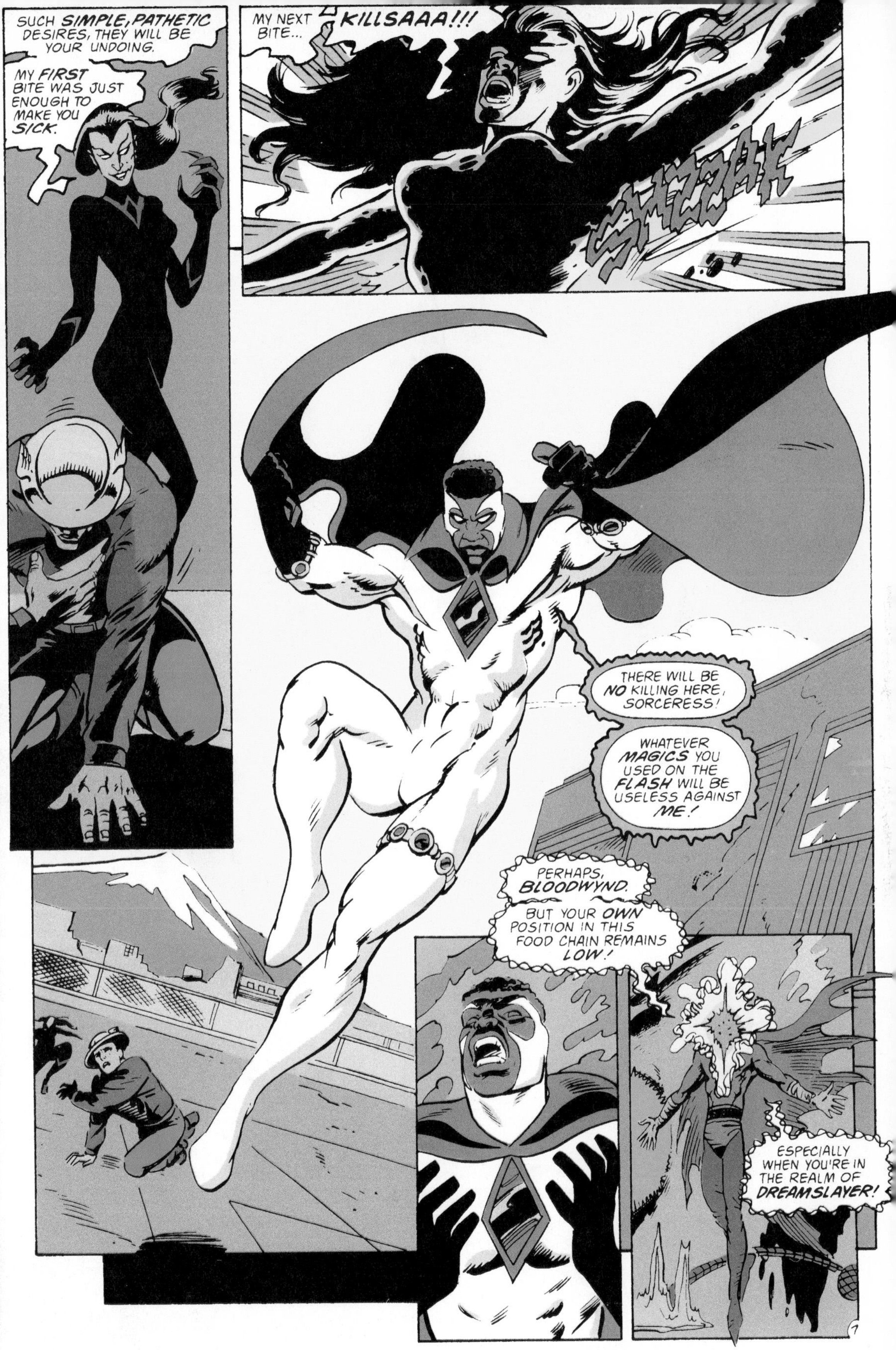
SUCH SIMPLE, PATHETIC DESIRES, THEY WILL BE YOUR UNDOING.
MY FIRST BITE WAS JUST ENOUGH TO MAKE YOU SICK.
MY NEXT BITE...
KILLSAAA!!!
SHZZAK
THERE WILL BE NO KILLING HERE, SORCERESS!
WHATEVER MAGICS YOU USED ON THE FLASH WILL BE USELESS AGAINST ME!
PERHAPS, BLOODWYND.
BUT YOUR OWN POSITION IN THIS FOOD CHAIN REMAINS LOW!
ESPECIALLY WHEN YOU'RE IN THE REALM OF DREAMSLAYER!
7

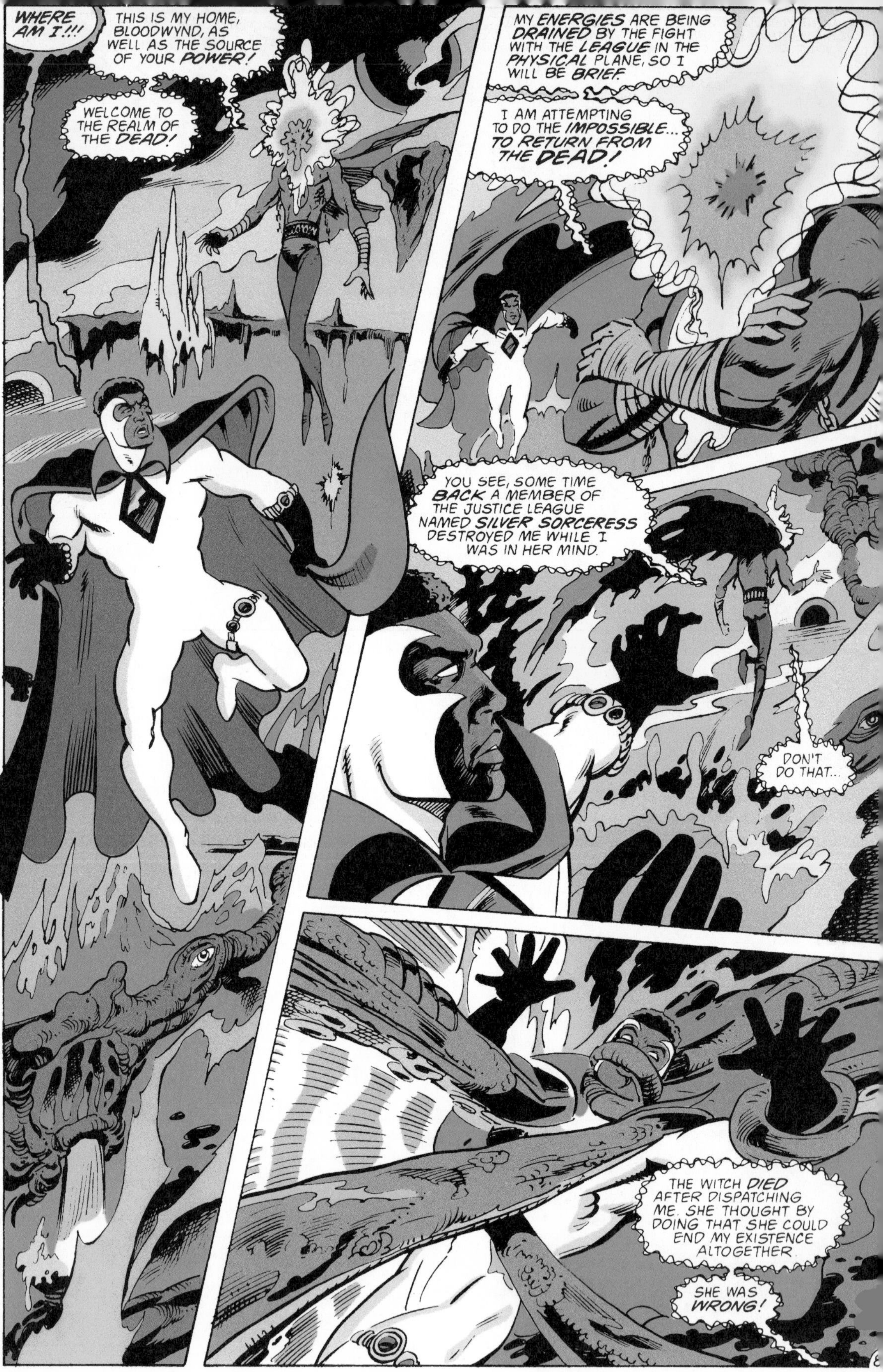

WHERE AM I!!!
THIS IS MY HOME, BLOODWYND, AS WELL AS THE SOURCE OF YOUR POWER!
WELCOME TO THE REALM OF THE DEAD!
MY ENERGIES ARE BEING DRAINED BY THE FIGHT WITH THE LEAGUE IN THE PHYSICAL PLANE, SO I WILL BE BRIEF.
I AM ATTEMPTING TO DO THE IMPOSSIBLE... TO RETURN FROM THE DEAD!
YOU SEE, SOME TIME BACK A MEMBER OF THE JUSTICE LEAGUE NAMED SILVER SORCERESS DESTROYED ME WHILE I WAS IN HER MIND.
DON'T DO THAT...
THE WITCH DIED AFTER DISPATCHING ME. SHE THOUGHT BY DOING THAT SHE COULD END MY EXISTENCE ALTOGETHER.
SHE WAS WRONG!

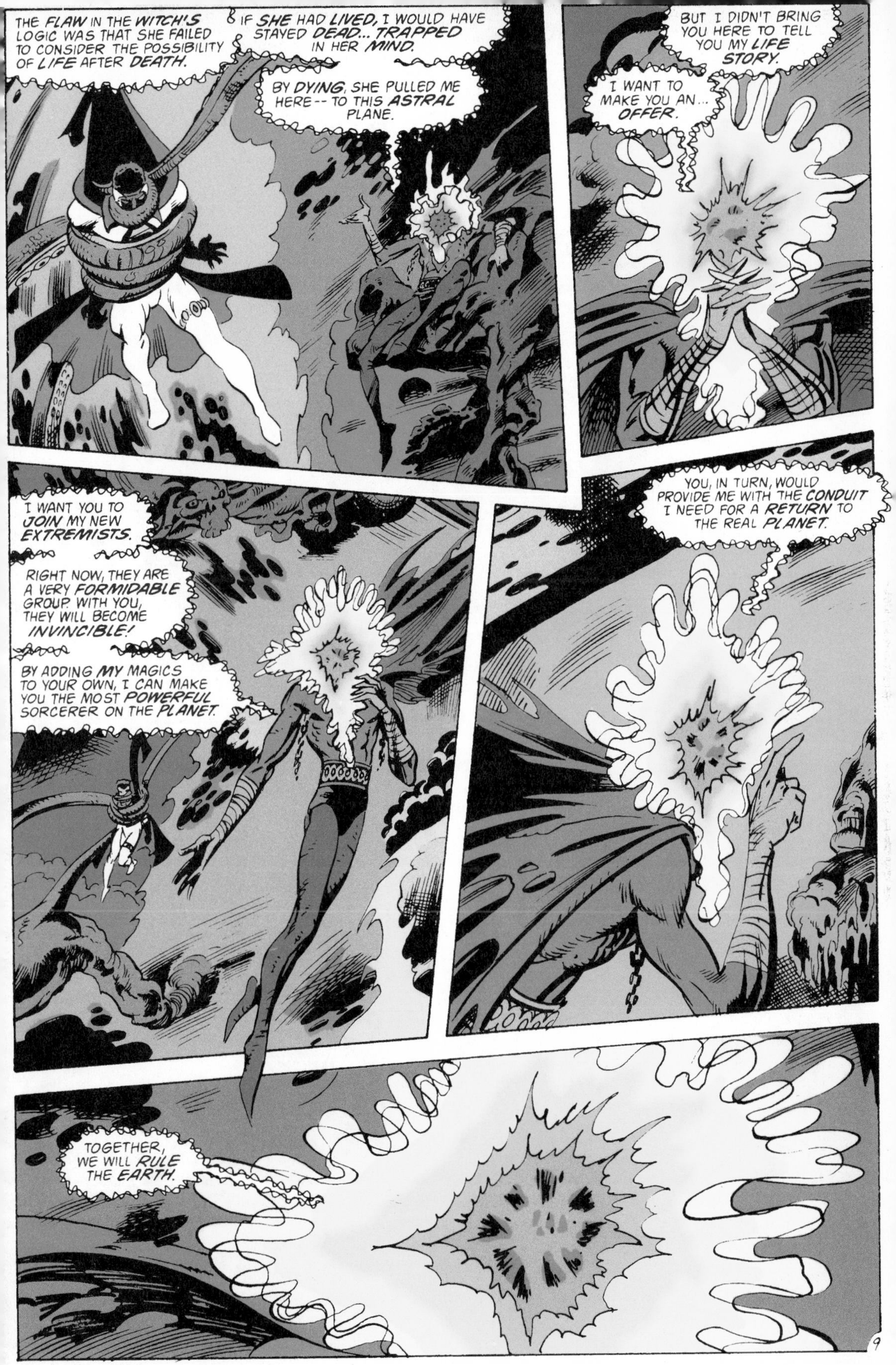

THE FLAW IN THE WITCH'S LOGIC WAS THAT SHE FAILED TO CONSIDER THE POSSIBILITY OF LIFE AFTER DEATH.
IF SHE HAD LIVED, I WOULD HAVE STAYED DEAD... TRAPPED IN HER MIND.
BY DYING, SHE PULLED ME HERE-- TO THIS ASTRAL PLANE.
BUT I DIDN'T BRING YOU HERE TO TELL YOU MY LIFE STORY.
I WANT TO MAKE YOU AN... OFFER.
I WANT YOU TO JOIN MY NEW EXTREMISTS.
RIGHT NOW, THEY ARE A VERY FORMIDABLE GROUP. WITH YOU, THEY WILL BECOME INVINCIBLE!
BY ADDING MY MAGICS TO YOUR OWN, I CAN MAKE YOU THE MOST POWERFUL SORCERER ON THE PLANET.
YOU, IN TURN, WOULD PROVIDE ME WITH THE CONDUIT I NEED FOR A RETURN TO THE REAL PLANET.
TOGETHER, WE WILL RULE THE EARTH.

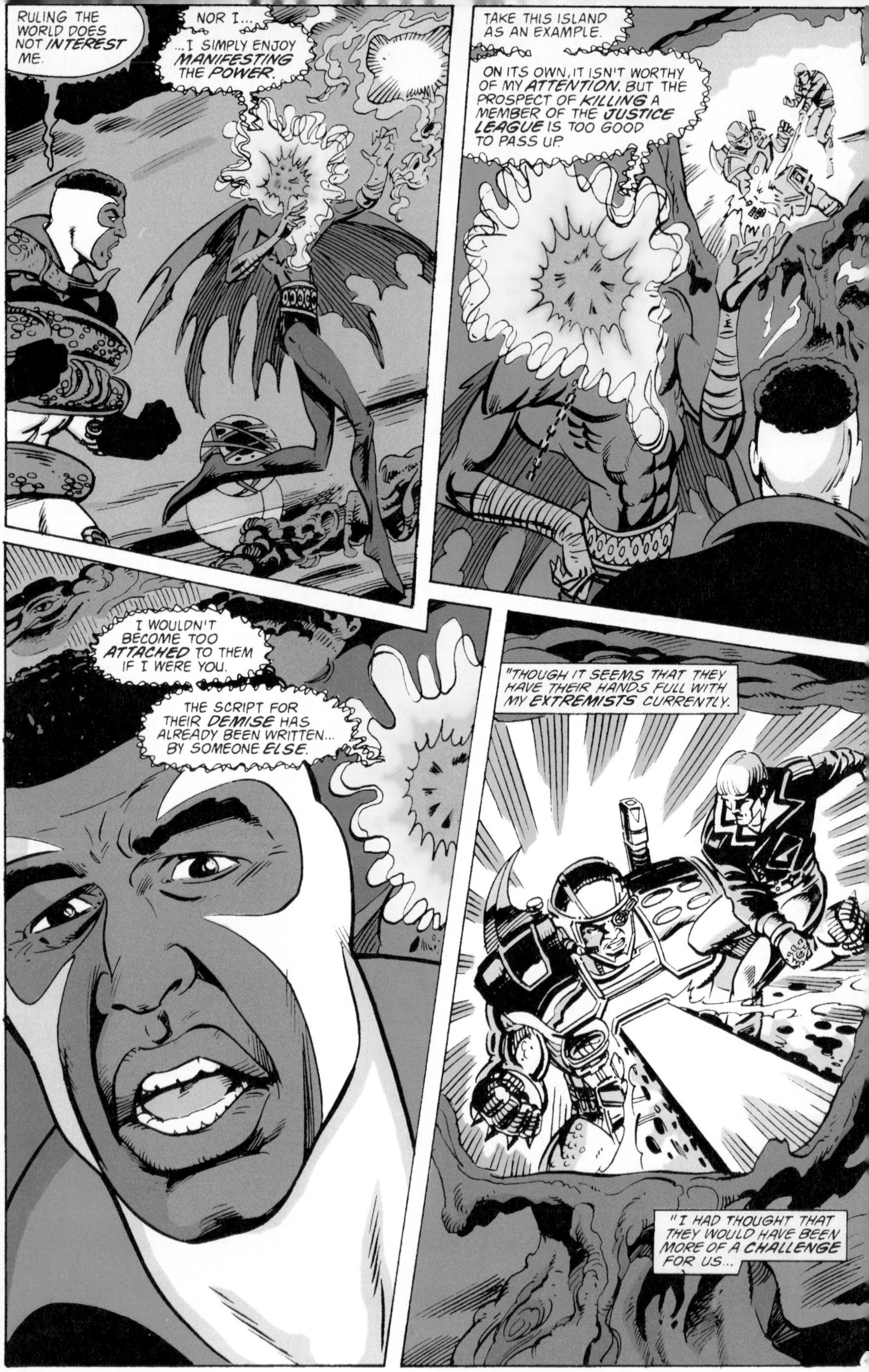
RULING THE WORLD DOES NOT INTEREST ME.
NOR I...
...I SIMPLY ENJOY MANIFESTING THE POWER.
TAKE THIS ISLAND AS AN EXAMPLE.
ON ITS OWN, IT ISN'T WORTHY OF MY ATTENTION. BUT THE PROSPECT OF KILLING A MEMBER OF THE JUSTICE LEAGUE IS TOO GOOD TO PASS UP.
I WOULDN'T BECOME TOO ATTACHED TO THEM IF I WERE YOU.
THE SCRIPT FOR THEIR DEMISE HAS ALREADY BEEN WRITTEN... BY SOMEONE ELSE.
"THOUGH IT SEEMS THAT THEY HAVE THEIR HANDS FULL WITH MY EXTREMISTS CURRENTLY.
"I HAD THOUGHT THAT THEY WOULD HAVE BEEN MORE OF A CHALLENGE FOR US...

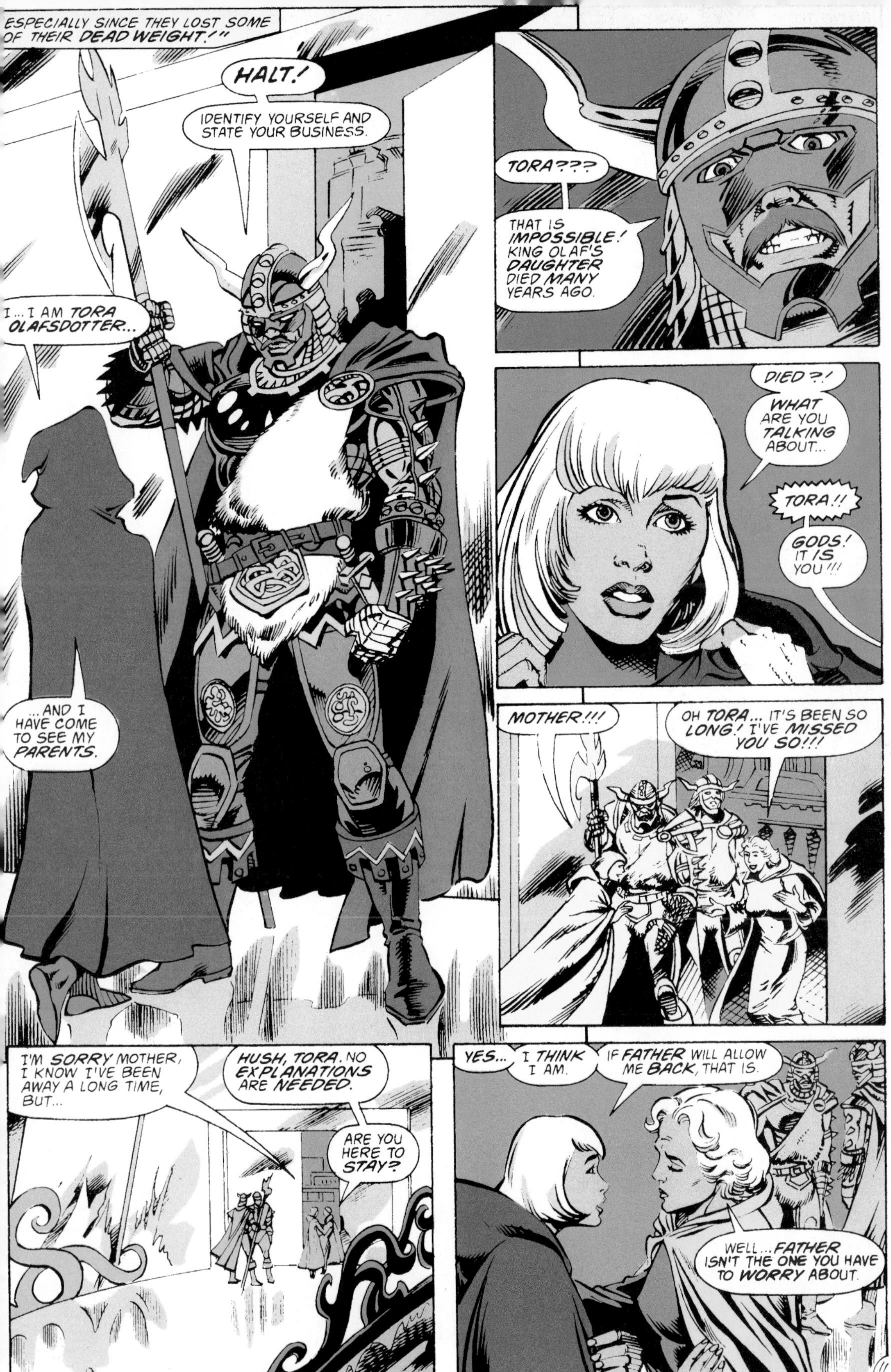
ESPECIALLY SINCE THEY LOST SOME OF THEIR DEAD WEIGHT!"
HALT!
IDENTIFY YOURSELF AND STATE YOUR BUSINESS.
I... I AM TORA OLAFSDOTTER...
...AND I HAVE COME TO SEE MY PARENTS.
TORA???
THAT IS IMPOSSIBLE! KING OLAF'S DAUGHTER DIED MANY YEARS AGO.
DIED?!
WHAT ARE YOU TALKING ABOUT...
TORA!!
GODS! IT IS YOU!!!
MOTHER!!!
OH TORA... IT'S BEEN SO LONG! I'VE MISSED YOU SO!!!
I'M SORRY MOTHER, I KNOW I'VE BEEN AWAY A LONG TIME, BUT...
HUSH, TORA. NO EXPLANATIONS ARE NEEDED.
ARE YOU HERE TO STAY?
YES...
I THINK I AM.
IF FATHER WILL ALLOW ME BACK, THAT IS.
WELL... FATHER ISN'T THE ONE YOU HAVE TO WORRY ABOUT.
11

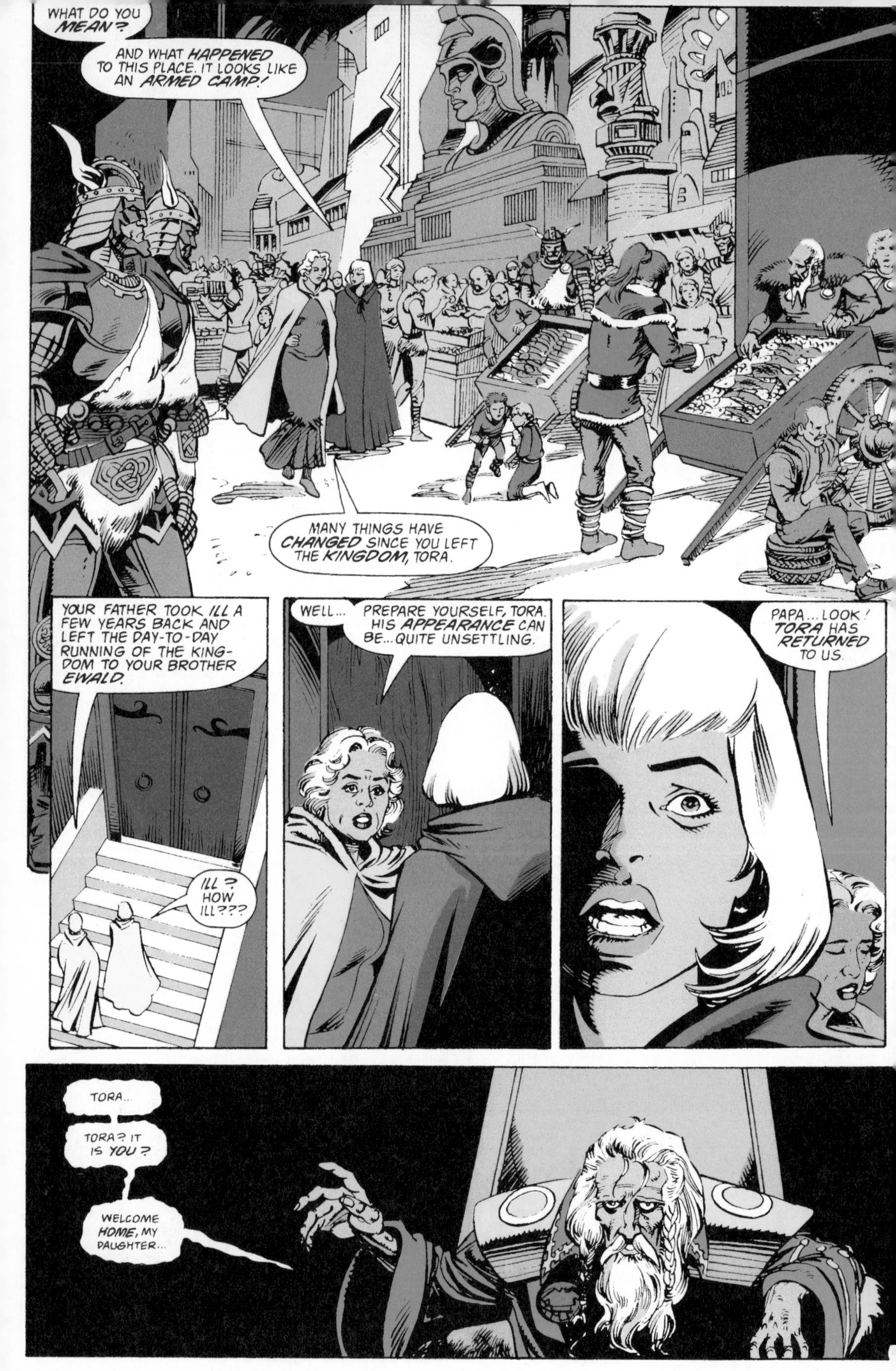
WHAT DO YOU MEAN?
AND WHAT HAPPENED TO THIS PLACE. IT LOOKS LIKE AN ARMED CAMP!
MANY THINGS HAVE CHANGED SINCE YOU LEFT THE KINGDOM, TORA.
YOUR FATHER TOOK ILL A FEW YEARS BACK AND LEFT THE DAY-TO-DAY RUNNING OF THE KINGDOM TO YOUR BROTHER EWALD.
ILL? HOW ILL???
WELL...
PREPARE YOURSELF, TORA. HIS APPEARANCE CAN BE...QUITE UNSETTLING.
PAPA...LOOK! TORA HAS RETURNED TO US.
TORA...
TORA? IT IS YOU?
WELCOME HOME, MY DAUGHTER...

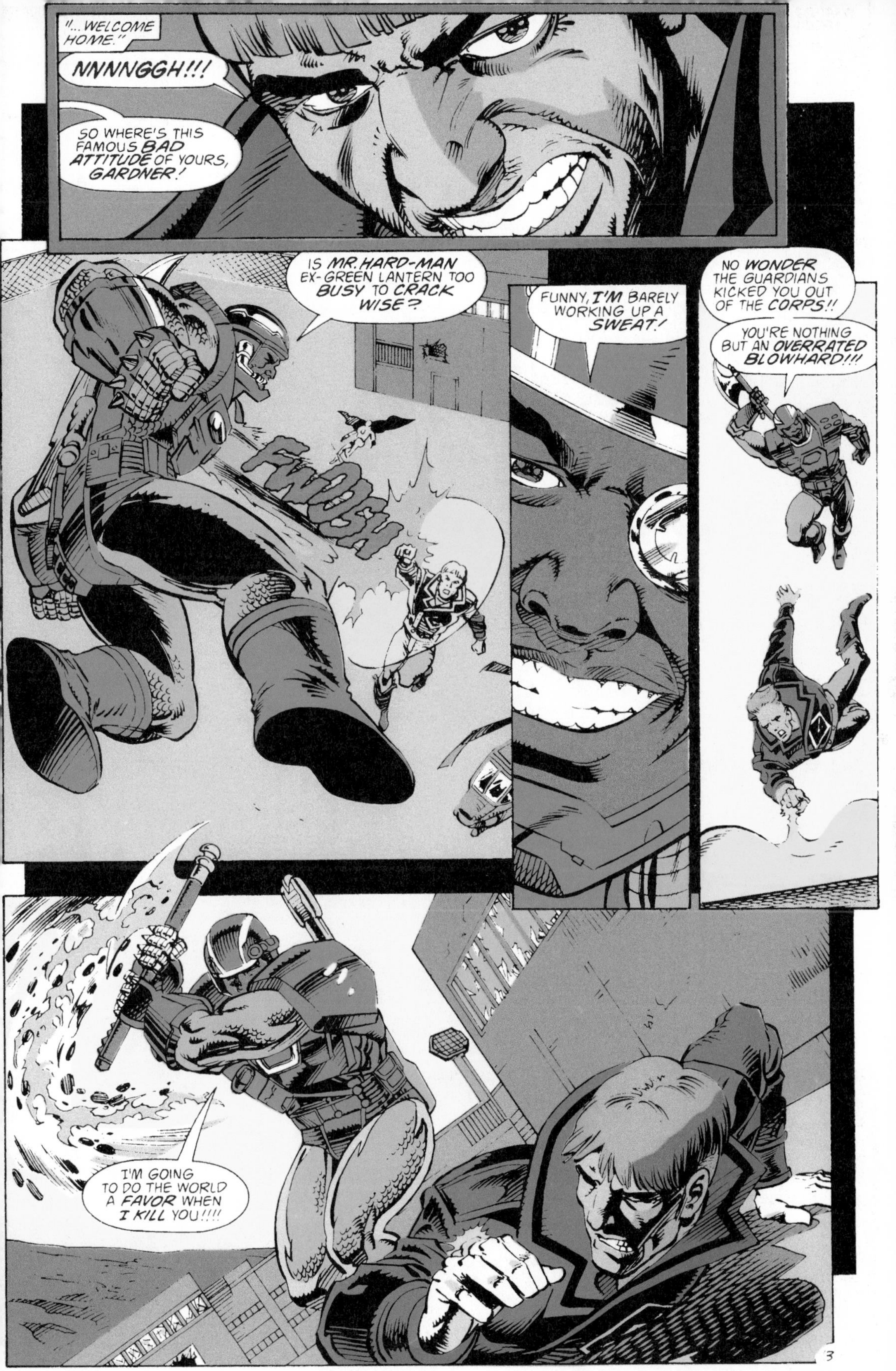
"...WELCOME HOME."
NNNNGGH!!!
SO WHERE'S THIS FAMOUS BAD ATTITUDE OF YOURS, GARDNER!
IS MR. HARD-MAN EX-GREEN LANTERN TOO BUSY TO CRACK WISE?
FWOSH
FUNNY, I'M BARELY WORKING UP A SWEAT!
NO WONDER THE GUARDIANS KICKED YOU OUT OF THE CORPS!!
YOU'RE NOTHING BUT AN OVERRATED BLOWHARD!!!
I'M GOING TO DO THE WORLD A FAVOR WHEN I KILL YOU!!!!

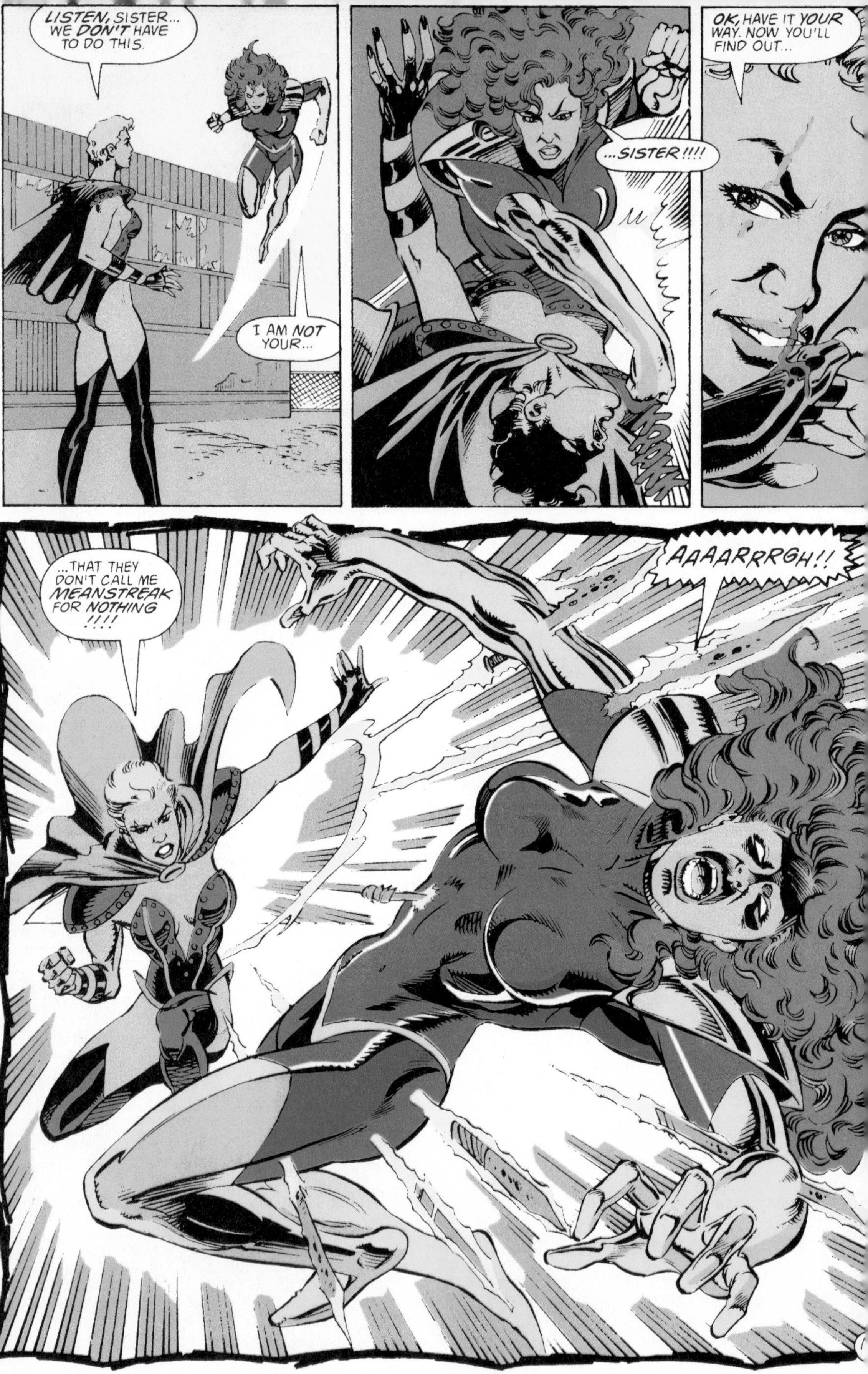
LISTEN, SISTER... WE DON'T HAVE TO DO THIS.
I AM NOT YOUR...
...SISTER!!!!
OK, HAVE IT YOUR WAY. NOW YOU'LL FIND OUT...
...THAT THEY DON'T CALL ME MEANSTREAK FOR NOTHING!!!!
AAAARRRGH!!

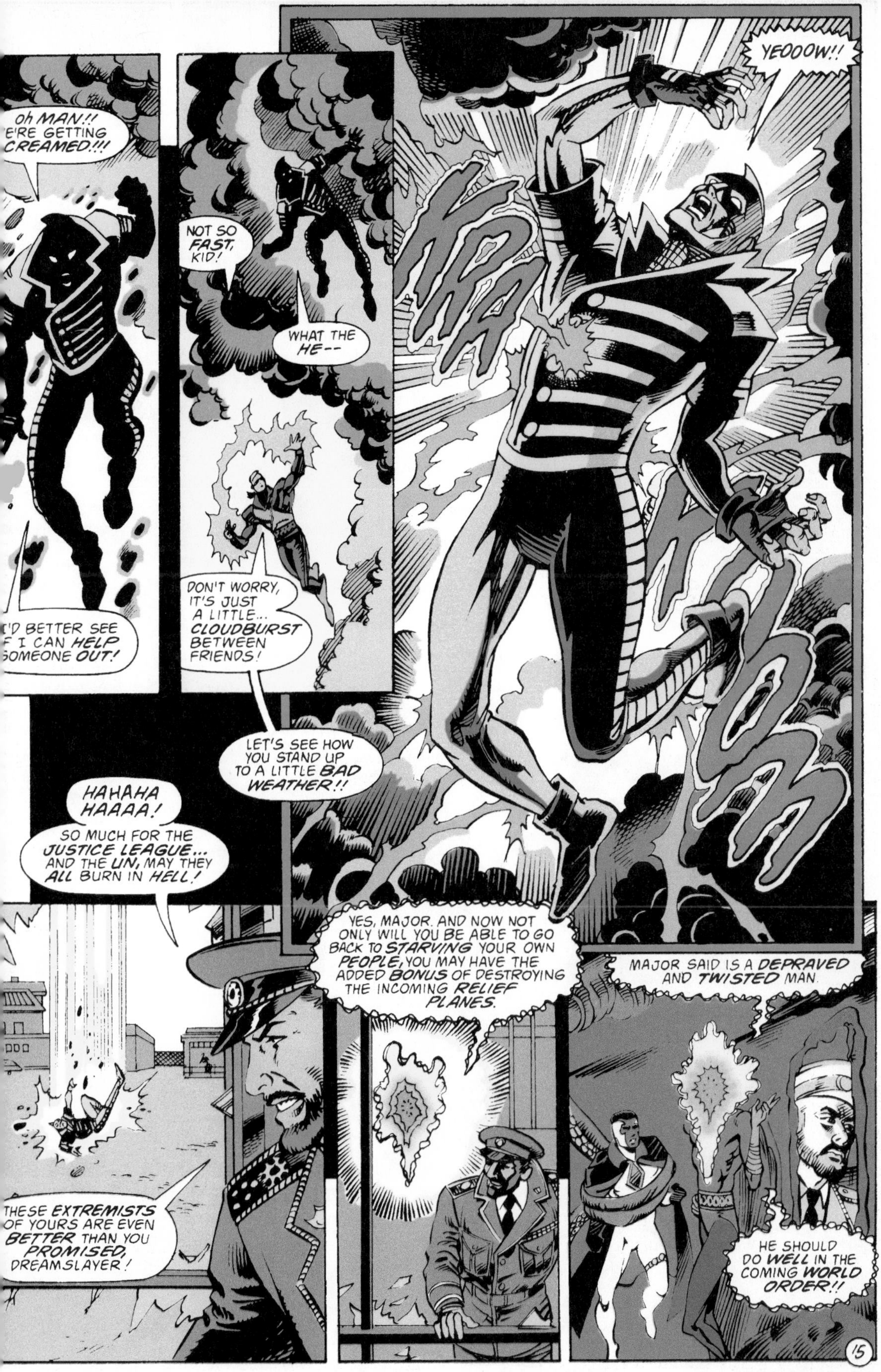
oh MAN!! E'RE GETTING CREAMED!!!
'D BETTER SEE F I CAN HELP SOMEONE OUT!
NOT SO FAST, KID!
WHAT THE HE--
DON'T WORRY, IT'S JUST A LITTLE... CLOUDBURST BETWEEN FRIENDS!
LET'S SEE HOW YOU STAND UP TO A LITTLE BAD WEATHER!!
YEOOOW!!
KRA
HAHAHA HAAAA!
SO MUCH FOR THE JUSTICE LEAGUE... AND THE UN, MAY THEY ALL BURN IN HELL!
THESE EXTREMISTS OF YOURS ARE EVEN BETTER THAN YOU PROMISED, DREAMSLAYER!
YES, MAJOR. AND NOW NOT ONLY WILL YOU BE ABLE TO GO BACK TO STARVING YOUR OWN PEOPLE, YOU MAY HAVE THE ADDED BONUS OF DESTROYING THE INCOMING RELIEF PLANES.
MAJOR SAID IS A DEPRAVED AND TWISTED MAN.
HE SHOULD DO WELL IN THE COMING WORLD ORDER!!

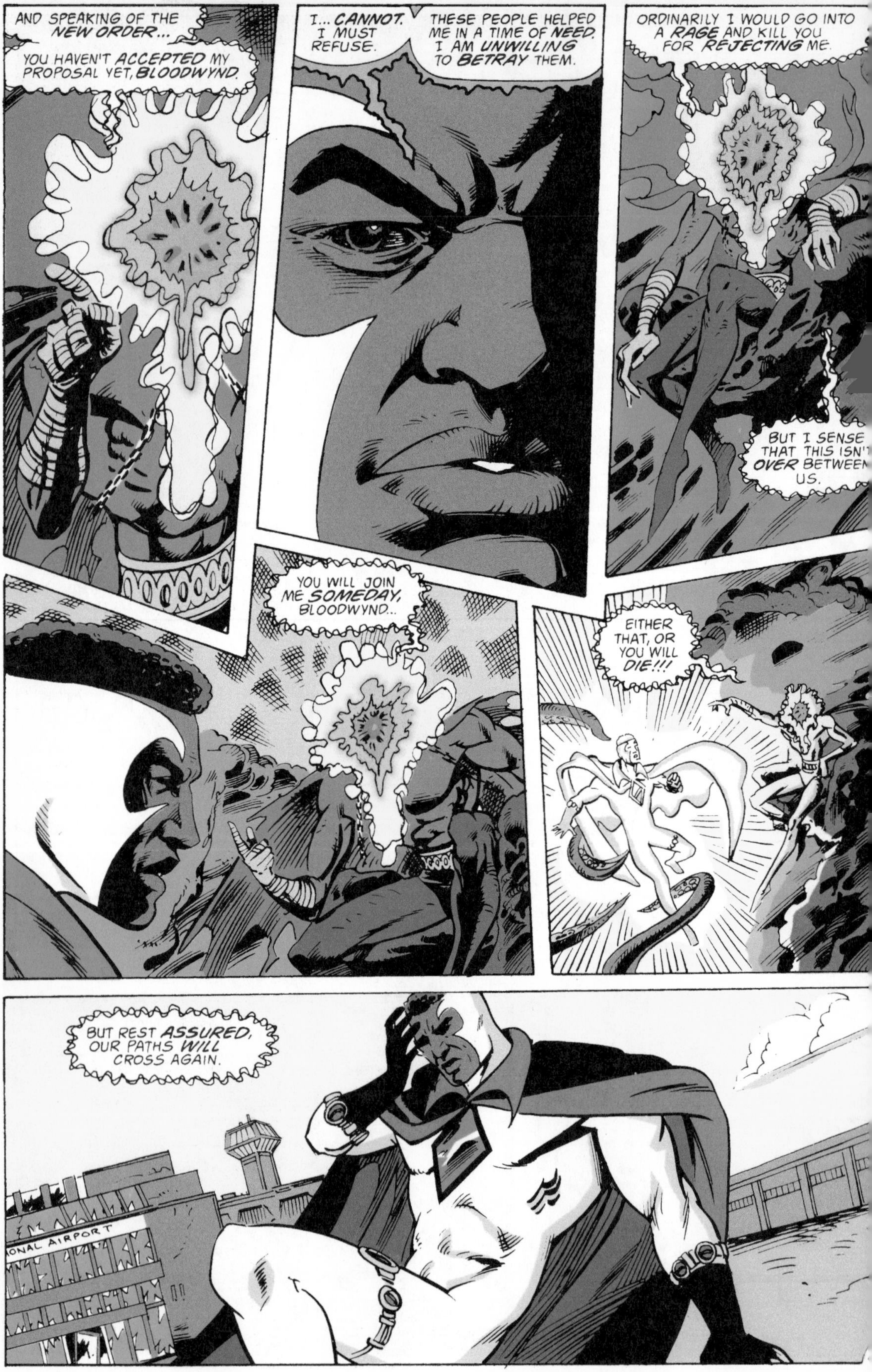
AND SPEAKING OF THE NEW ORDER...
YOU HAVEN'T ACCEPTED MY PROPOSAL YET, BLOODWYND.
I... CANNOT. I MUST REFUSE.
THESE PEOPLE HELPED ME IN A TIME OF NEED. I AM UNWILLING TO BETRAY THEM.
ORDINARILY I WOULD GO INTO A RAGE AND KILL YOU FOR REJECTING ME.
BUT I SENSE THAT THIS ISN'T OVER BETWEEN US.
YOU WILL JOIN ME SOMEDAY, BLOODWYND...
EITHER THAT, OR YOU WILL DIE!!!
BUT REST ASSURED, OUR PATHS WILL CROSS AGAIN.
ONAL AIRPORT

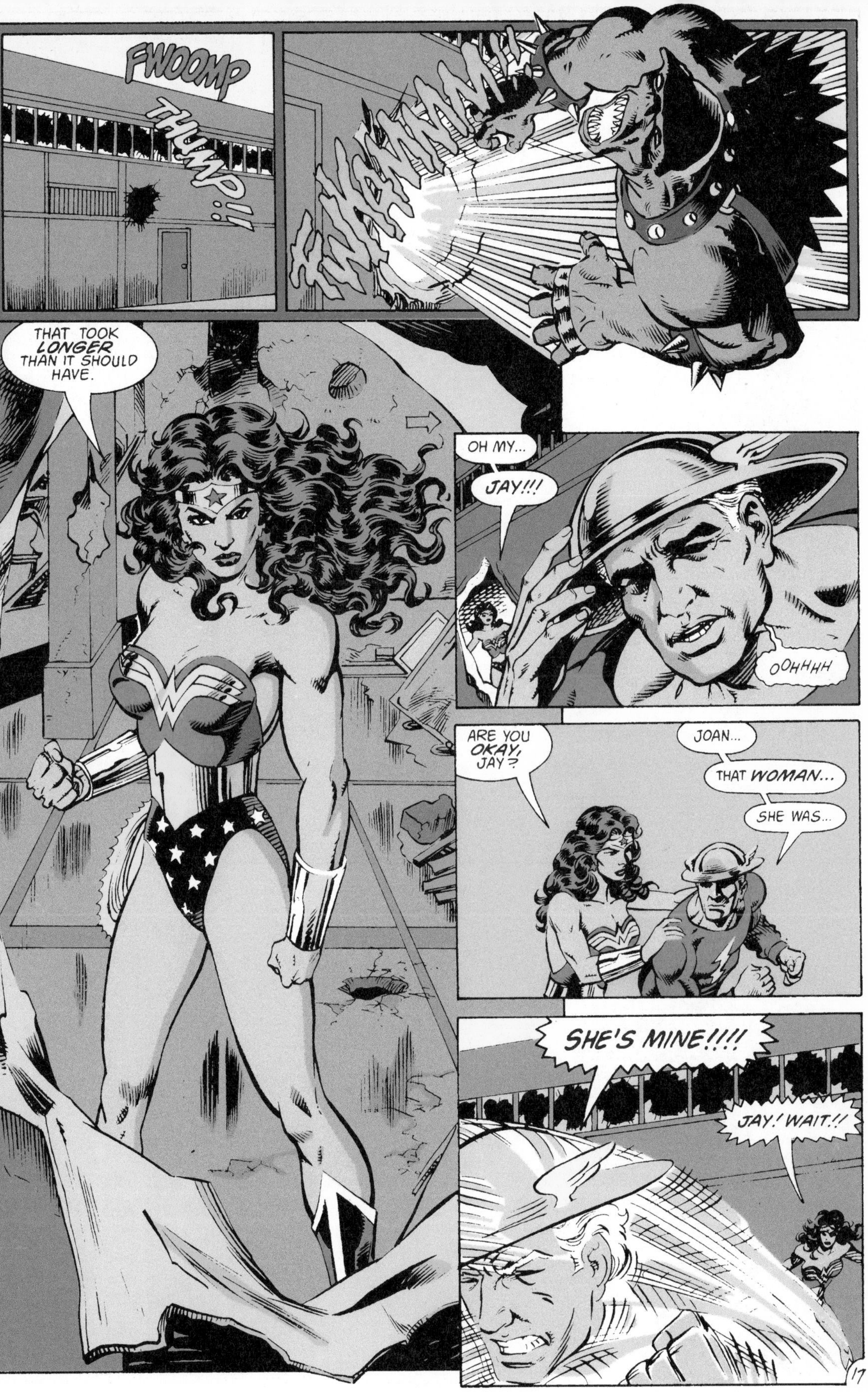

FWOOMP
THUMP!!
THWAMM!!
THAT TOOK LONGER THAN IT SHOULD HAVE.
OH MY...
JAY!!!
OOHHHH
ARE YOU OKAY, JAY?
JOAN...
THAT WOMAN...
SHE WAS...
SHE'S MINE!!!!
JAY! WAIT!!

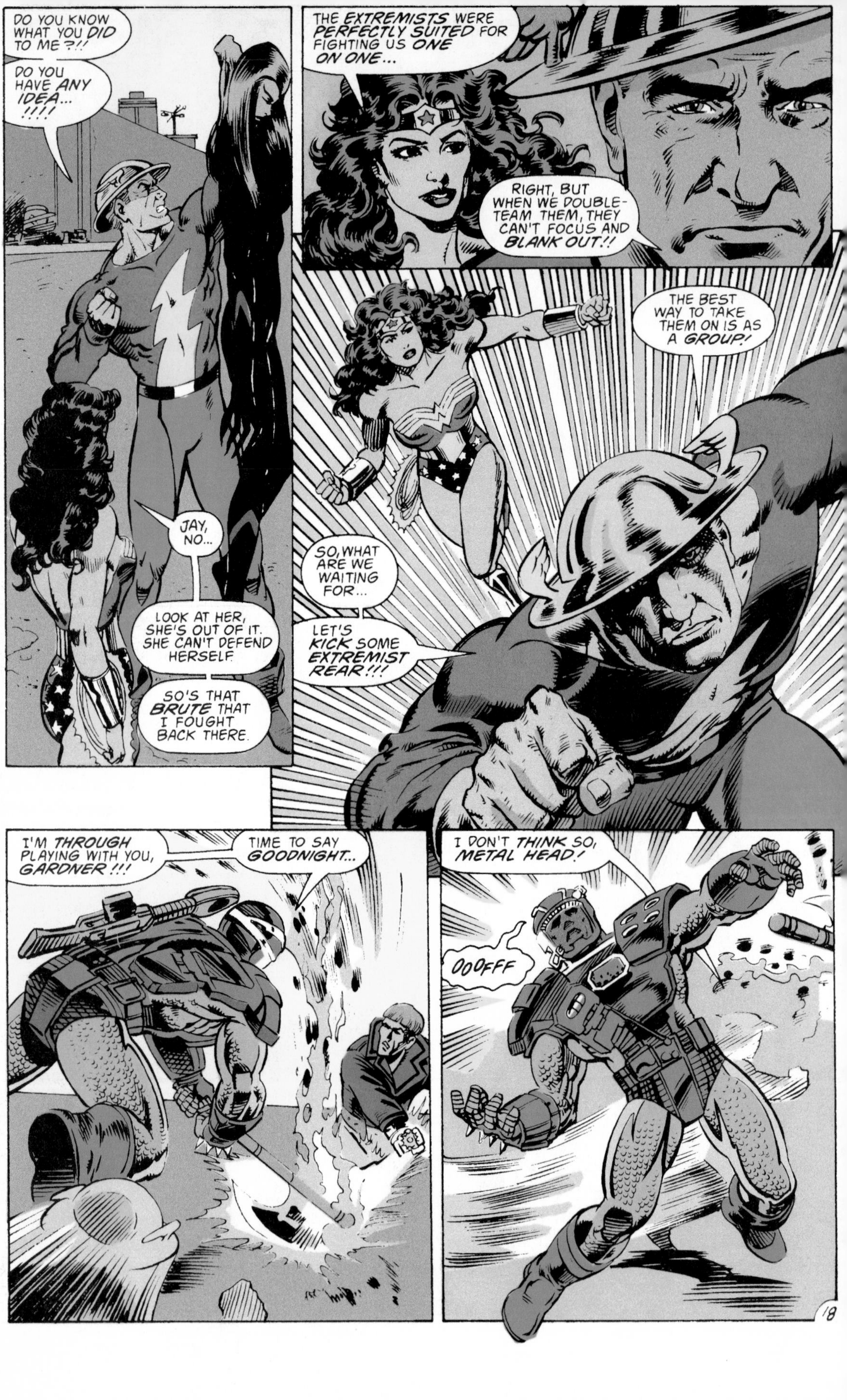
DO YOU KNOW WHAT YOU DID TO ME?!!
DO YOU HAVE ANY IDEA... !!!!
JAY, NO...
LOOK AT HER, SHE'S OUT OF IT. SHE CAN'T DEFEND HERSELF.
SO'S THAT BRUTE THAT I FOUGHT BACK THERE.
THE EXTREMISTS WERE PERFECTLY SUITED FOR FIGHTING US ONE ON ONE...
RIGHT, BUT WHEN WE DOUBLE-TEAM THEM, THEY CAN'T FOCUS AND BLANK OUT!!
THE BEST WAY TO TAKE THEM ON IS AS A GROUP!
SO, WHAT ARE WE WAITING FOR...
LET'S KICK SOME EXTREMIST REAR!!!
I'M THROUGH PLAYING WITH YOU, GARDNER!!!
TIME TO SAY GOODNIGHT...
I DON'T THINK SO, METAL HEAD!
OOOFFF
18

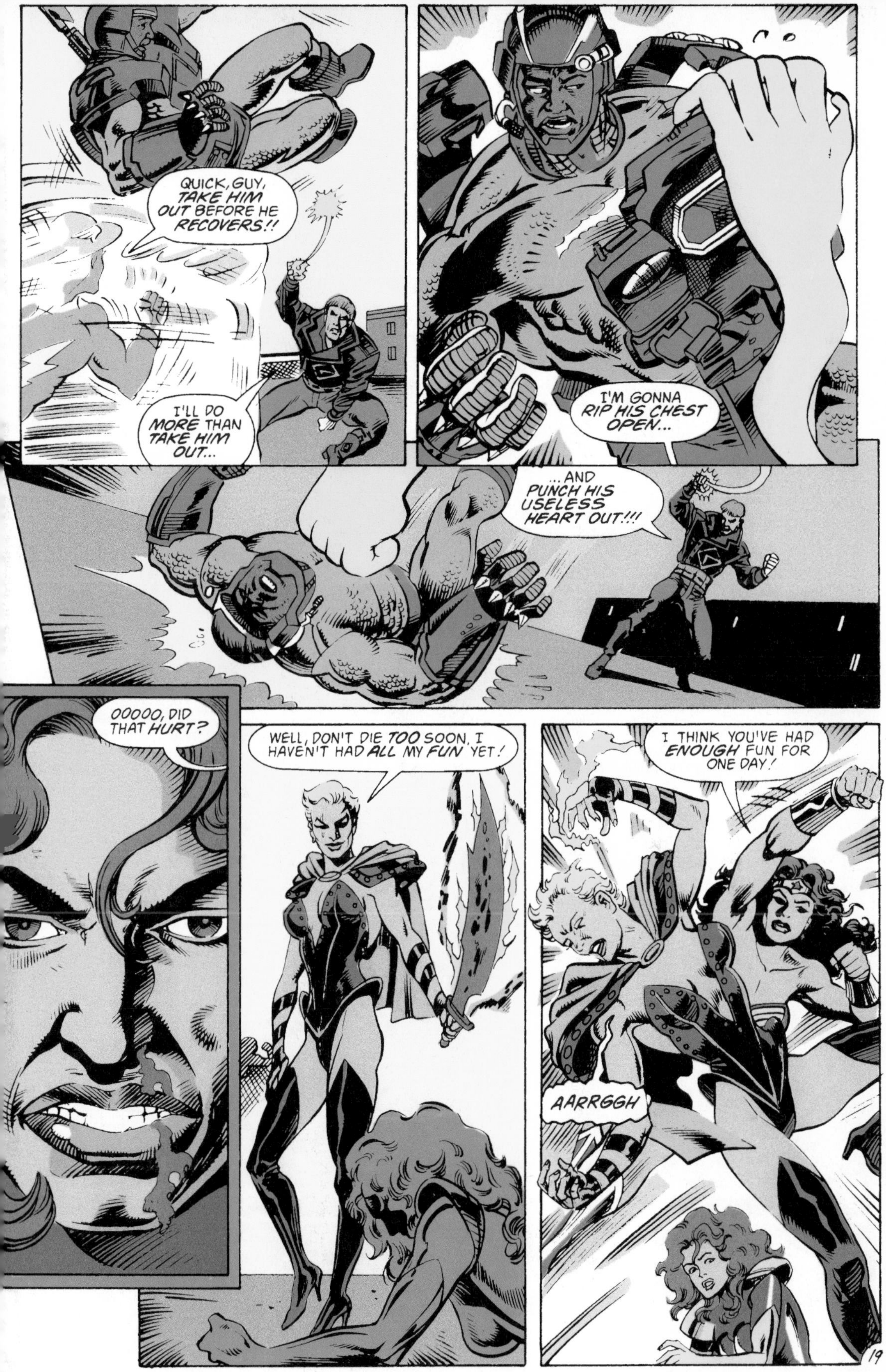
QUICK, GUY, TAKE HIM OUT BEFORE HE RECOVERS!!
I'LL DO MORE THAN TAKE HIM OUT...
I'M GONNA RIP HIS CHEST OPEN...
...AND PUNCH HIS USELESS HEART OUT!!!
OOOOO, DID THAT HURT?
WELL, DON'T DIE TOO SOON, I HAVEN'T HAD ALL MY FUN YET!
I THINK YOU'VE HAD ENOUGH FUN FOR ONE DAY!
AARRGGH

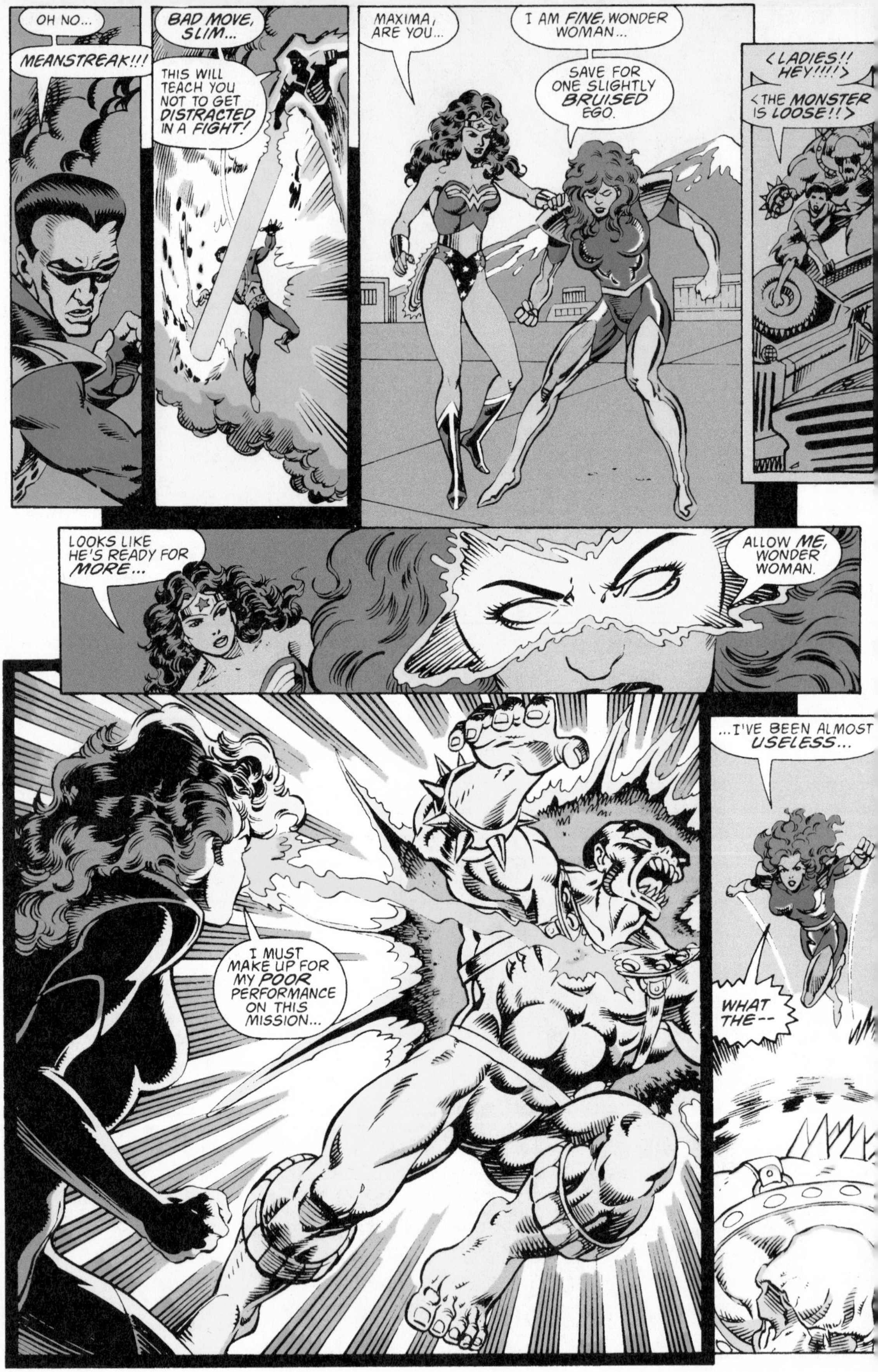
OH NO...
MEANSTREAK!!!
BAD MOVE, SLIM...
THIS WILL TEACH YOU NOT TO GET DISTRACTED IN A FIGHT!
MAXIMA, ARE YOU...
I AM FINE, WONDER WOMAN...
SAVE FOR ONE SLIGHTLY BRUISED EGO.
<LADIES!! HEY!!!!>
<THE MONSTER IS LOOSE!!>
LOOKS LIKE HE'S READY FOR MORE...
ALLOW ME, WONDER WOMAN.
I MUST MAKE UP FOR MY POOR PERFORMANCE ON THIS MISSION...
...I'VE BEEN ALMOST USELESS...
WHAT THE--

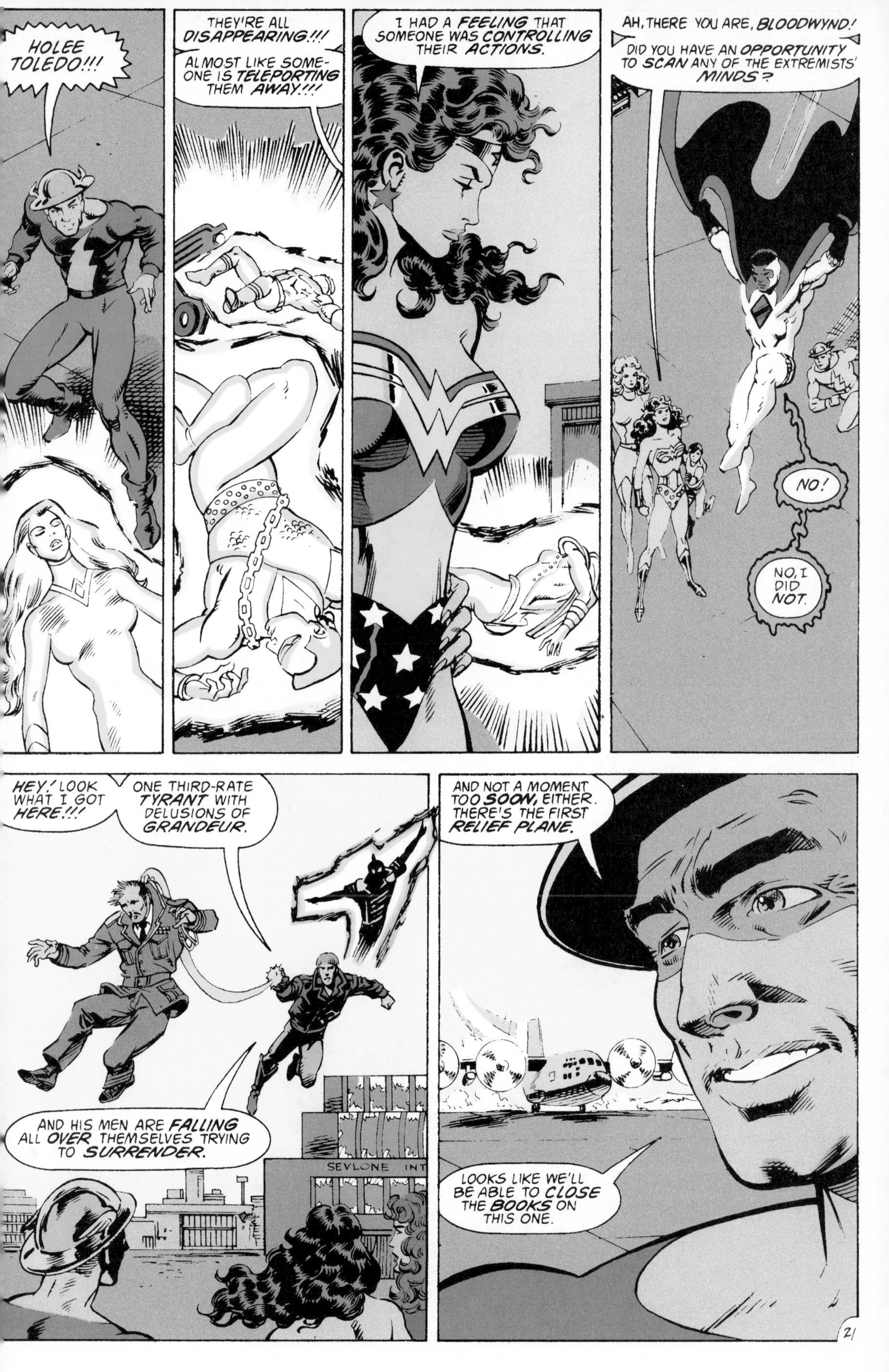

HOLEE TOLEDO!!!
THEY'RE ALL DISAPPEARING!!!
ALMOST LIKE SOME-ONE IS TELEPORTING THEM AWAY!!!
I HAD A FEELING THAT SOMEONE WAS CONTROLLING THEIR ACTIONS.
AH, THERE YOU ARE, BLOODWYND!
DID YOU HAVE AN OPPORTUNITY TO SCAN ANY OF THE EXTREMISTS' MINDS?
NO!
NO, I DID NOT.
HEY! LOOK WHAT I GOT HERE!!!
ONE THIRD-RATE TYRANT WITH DELUSIONS OF GRANDEUR.
AND HIS MEN ARE FALLING ALL OVER THEMSELVES TRYING TO SURRENDER.
SEVLONE INT
AND NOT A MOMENT TOO SOON, EITHER. THERE'S THE FIRST RELIEF PLANE.
LOOKS LIKE WE'LL BE ABLE TO CLOSE THE BOOKS ON THIS ONE.

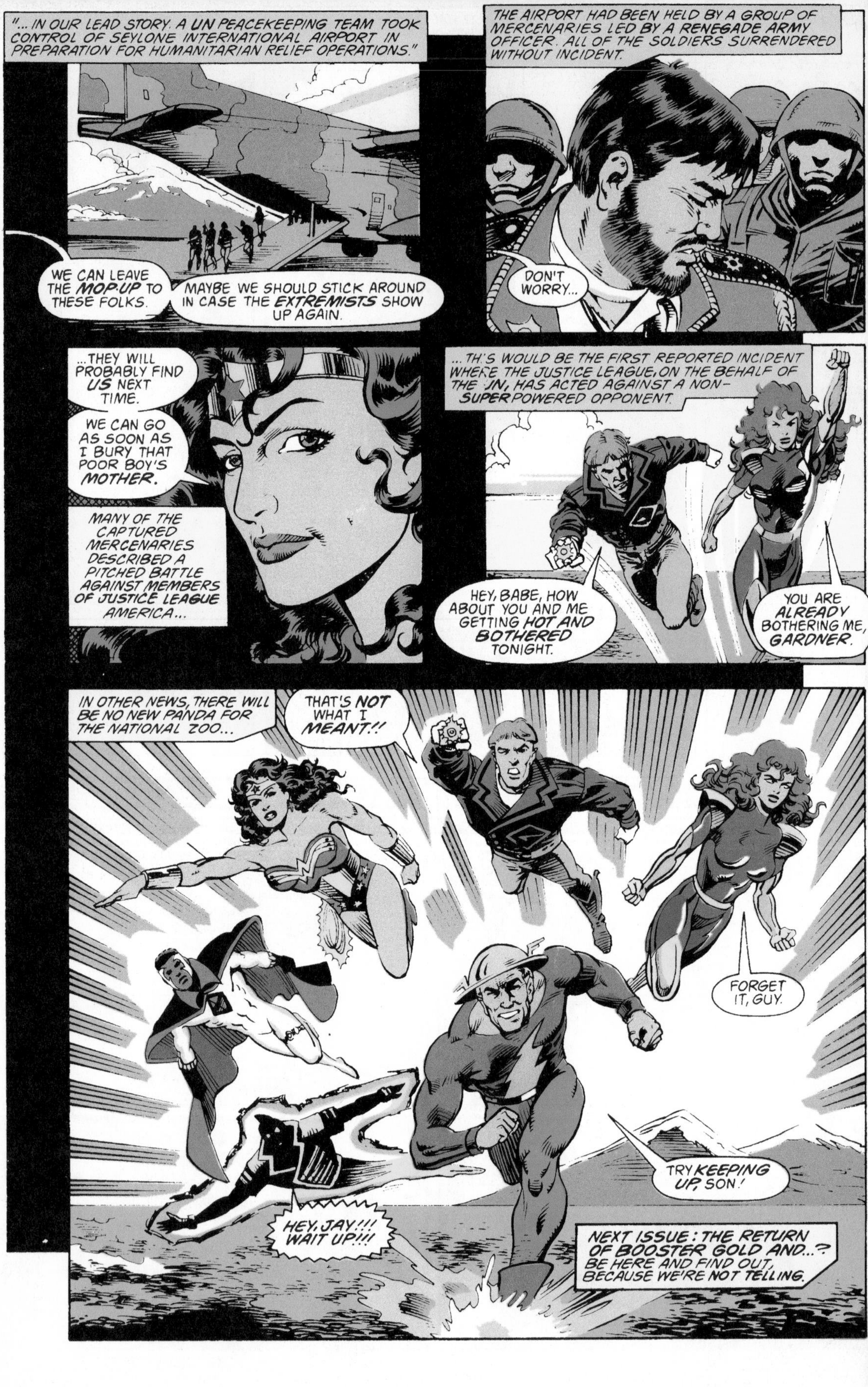
"...IN OUR LEAD STORY. A UN PEACEKEEPING TEAM TOOK CONTROL OF SEYLONE INTERNATIONAL AIRPORT IN PREPARATION FOR HUMANITARIAN RELIEF OPERATIONS."
WE CAN LEAVE THE MOP-UP TO THESE FOLKS.
MAYBE WE SHOULD STICK AROUND IN CASE THE EXTREMISTS SHOW UP AGAIN.
THE AIRPORT HAD BEEN HELD BY A GROUP OF MERCENARIES LED BY A RENEGADE ARMY OFFICER. ALL OF THE SOLDIERS SURRENDERED WITHOUT INCIDENT.
DON'T WORRY...
...THEY WILL PROBABLY FIND US NEXT TIME.
WE CAN GO AS SOON AS I BURY THAT POOR BOY'S MOTHER.
MANY OF THE CAPTURED MERCENARIES DESCRIBED A PITCHED BATTLE AGAINST MEMBERS OF JUSTICE LEAGUE AMERICA...
...THIS WOULD BE THE FIRST REPORTED INCIDENT WHERE THE JUSTICE LEAGUE, ON THE BEHALF OF THE UN, HAS ACTED AGAINST A NON-SUPERPOWERED OPPONENT.
HEY, BABE, HOW ABOUT YOU AND ME GETTING HOT AND BOTHERED TONIGHT.
YOU ARE ALREADY BOTHERING ME, GARDNER.
IN OTHER NEWS, THERE WILL BE NO NEW PANDA FOR THE NATIONAL ZOO...
THAT'S NOT WHAT I MEANT!!
FORGET IT, GUY.
TRY KEEPING UP, SON!
HEY, JAY!!! WAIT UP!!!
NEXT ISSUE: THE RETURN OF BOOSTER GOLD AND...? BE HERE AND FIND OUT, BECAUSE WE'RE NOT TELLING.

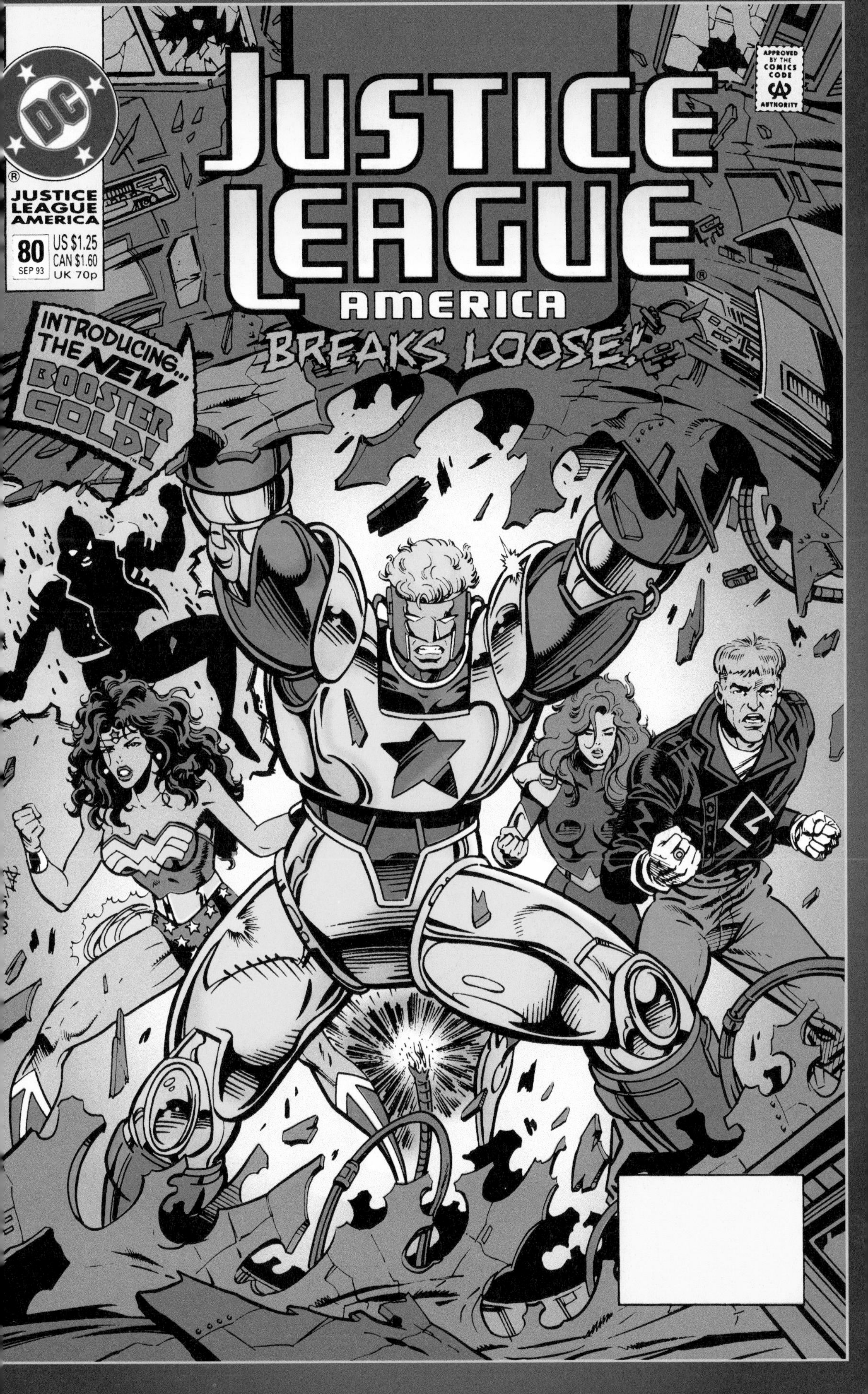
DC
JUSTICE LEAGUE AMERICA
80
SEP 93
US $1.25
CAN $1.60
UK 70p
APPROVED BY THE COMICS CODE AUTHORITY
JUSTICE LEAGUE AMERICA
BREAKS LOOSE!
INTRODUCING... THE NEW BOOSTER GOLD!

Cover art by **KEVIN WEST**
and **RICK BURCHETT**

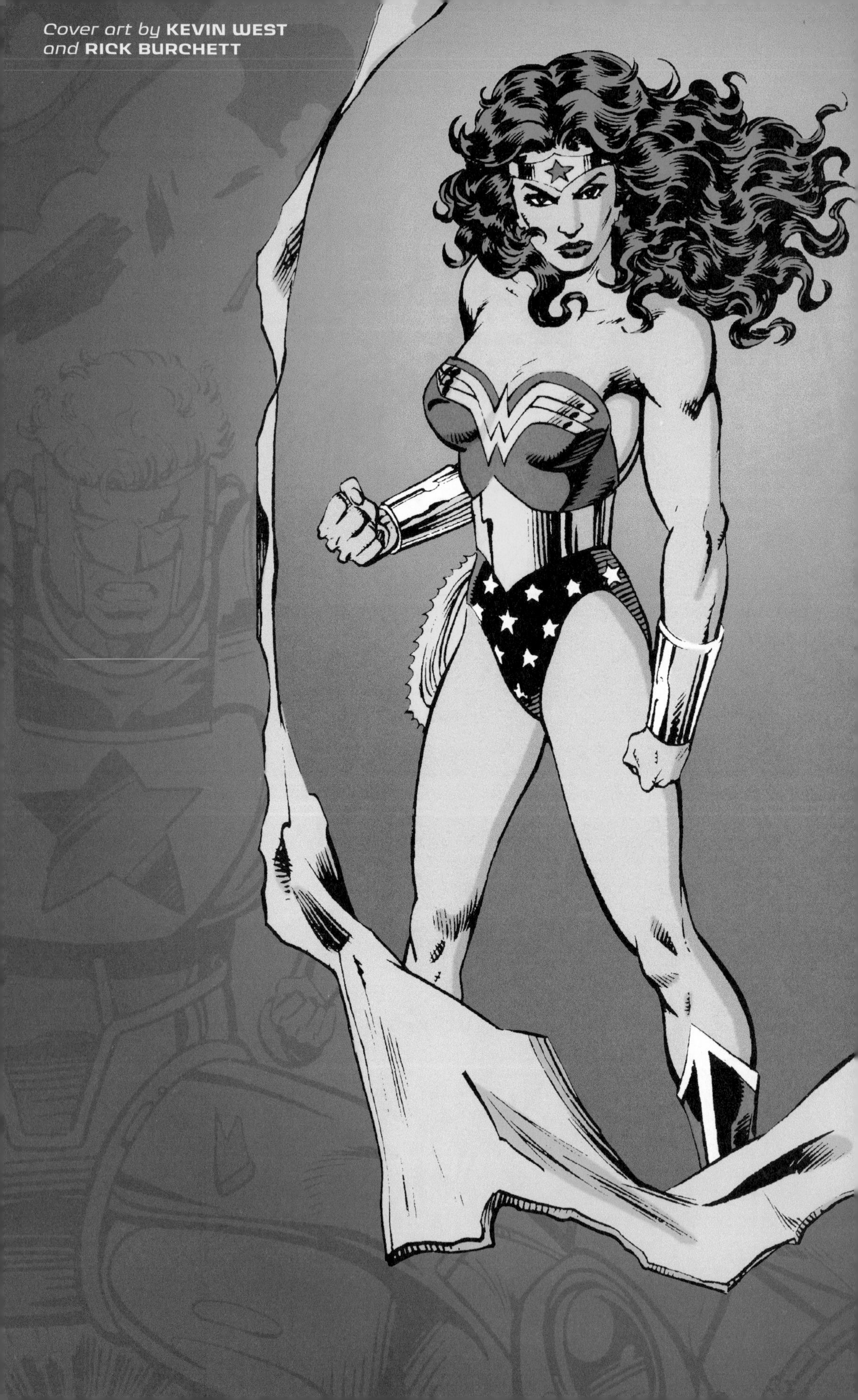

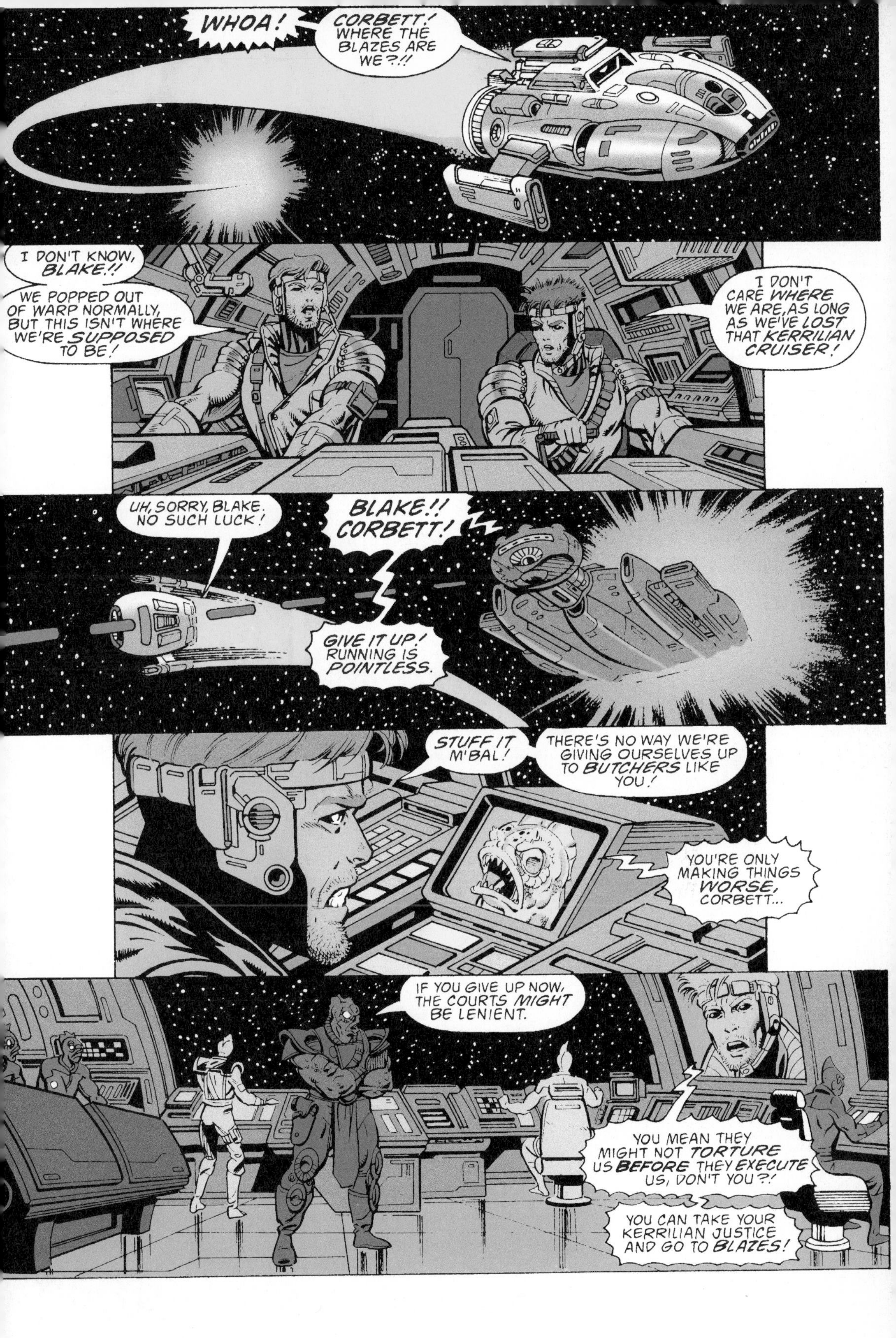
WHOA!
CORBETT! WHERE THE BLAZES ARE WE?!!
I DON'T KNOW, BLAKE!!
WE POPPED OUT OF WARP NORMALLY, BUT THIS ISN'T WHERE WE'RE SUPPOSED TO BE!
I DON'T CARE WHERE WE ARE, AS LONG AS WE'VE LOST THAT KERRILIAN CRUISER!
UH, SORRY, BLAKE. NO SUCH LUCK!
BLAKE!! CORBETT!
GIVE IT UP! RUNNING IS POINTLESS.
STUFF IT M'BAL!
THERE'S NO WAY WE'RE GIVING OURSELVES UP TO BUTCHERS LIKE YOU!
YOU'RE ONLY MAKING THINGS WORSE, CORBETT...
IF YOU GIVE UP NOW, THE COURTS MIGHT BE LENIENT.
YOU MEAN THEY MIGHT NOT TORTURE US BEFORE THEY EXECUTE US, DON'T YOU?!
YOU CAN TAKE YOUR KERRILIAN JUSTICE AND GO TO BLAZES!

HEH. I GUESS I TOLD *HIM*.

YEAH, NICE GOING, *SMART GUY!*

NOW WHERE ARE WE *GOING!*

THAT SMALL BLUE PLANET *MIGHT* HAVE AN ATMOSPHERE WE CAN BREATHE...

ASSUMING WE SURVIVE THE TRIP THERE.

DAMN THEM!

IF THE COUNCIL DIDN'T WANT THEM *ALIVE*, I'D *BLOW* THEM AWAY AND SAVE US THE TROUBLE OF THE CHASE!

D'BARRI! WHAT SYSTEM IS THIS?

IT'S AN *UNCHARTED* SYSTEM, SIR. I'M NOT EVEN SURE HOW WE GOT HERE.

THE PLANET THEY'RE HEADED FOR IS RELATIVELY SMALL AND DENSELY POPULATED IN ITS COASTAL REGIONS.

ATMOSPHERIC SAMPLES SUGGEST A GREAT DEAL OF INDUSTRIAL ACTIVITY. NOTHING WE CAN'T HANDLE, THOUGH.

LET'S TRY TO GET THEM *BEFORE* THEY GET THERE. GET A TRACTOR BEAM READY...

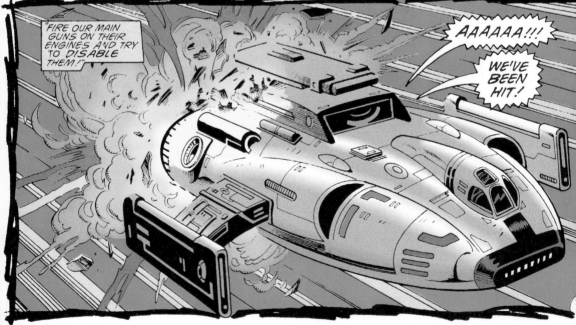

"FIRE OUR MAIN GUNS ON THEIR ENGINES AND TRY TO *DISABLE* THEM!"

AAAAAA!!!

WE'VE BEEN HIT!

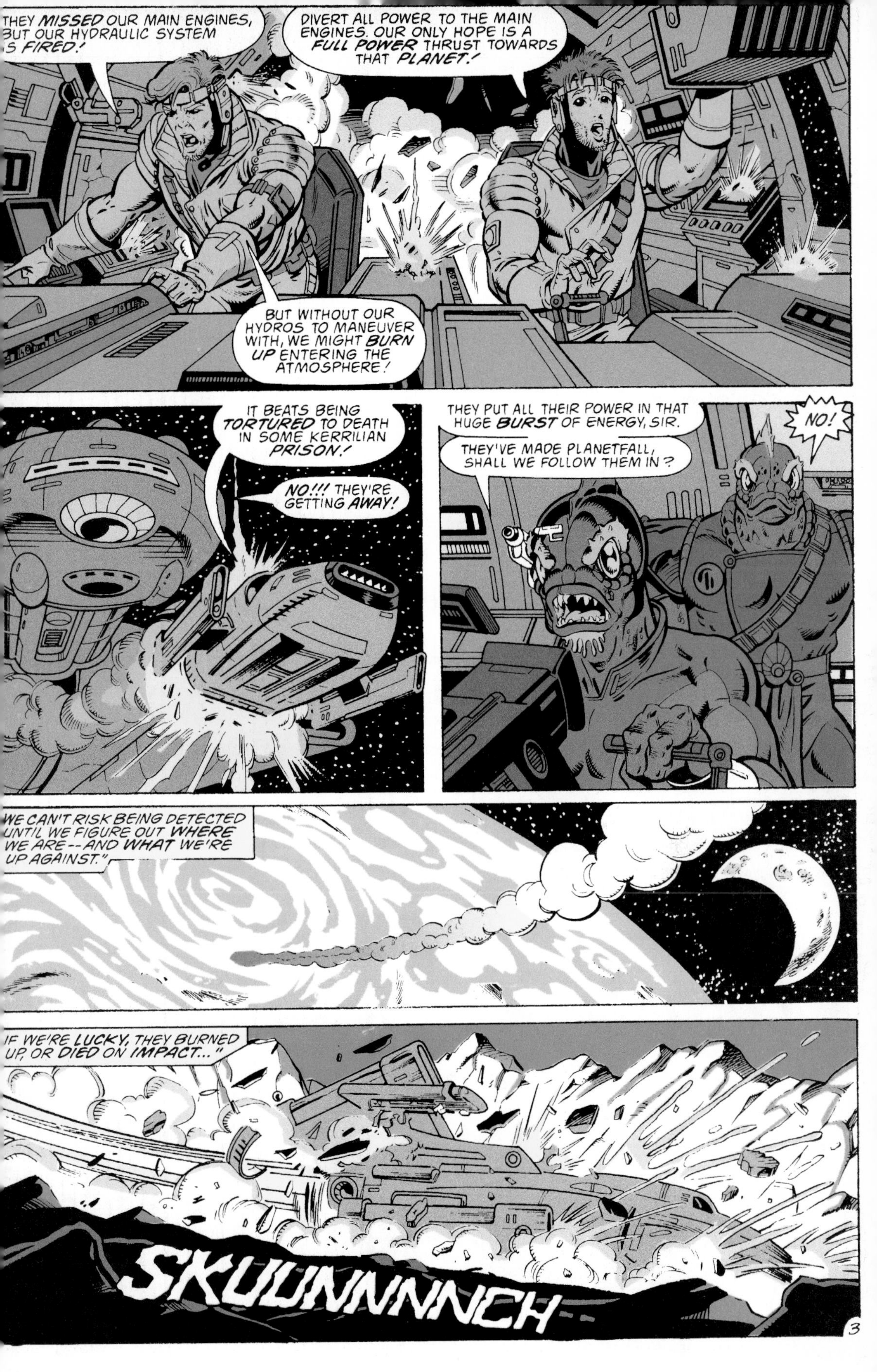
THEY MISSED OUR MAIN ENGINES, BUT OUR HYDRAULIC SYSTEM IS FIRED!
DIVERT ALL POWER TO THE MAIN ENGINES. OUR ONLY HOPE IS A FULL POWER THRUST TOWARDS THAT PLANET!
BUT WITHOUT OUR HYDROS TO MANEUVER WITH, WE MIGHT BURN UP ENTERING THE ATMOSPHERE!
IT BEATS BEING TORTURED TO DEATH IN SOME KERRILIAN PRISON!
NO!!! THEY'RE GETTING AWAY!
THEY PUT ALL THEIR POWER IN THAT HUGE BURST OF ENERGY, SIR.
THEY'VE MADE PLANETFALL, SHALL WE FOLLOW THEM IN?
NO!
WE CAN'T RISK BEING DETECTED UNTIL WE FIGURE OUT WHERE WE ARE -- AND WHAT WE'RE UP AGAINST."
IF WE'RE LUCKY, THEY BURNED UP, OR DIED ON IMPACT..."
SKUUNNNNCH

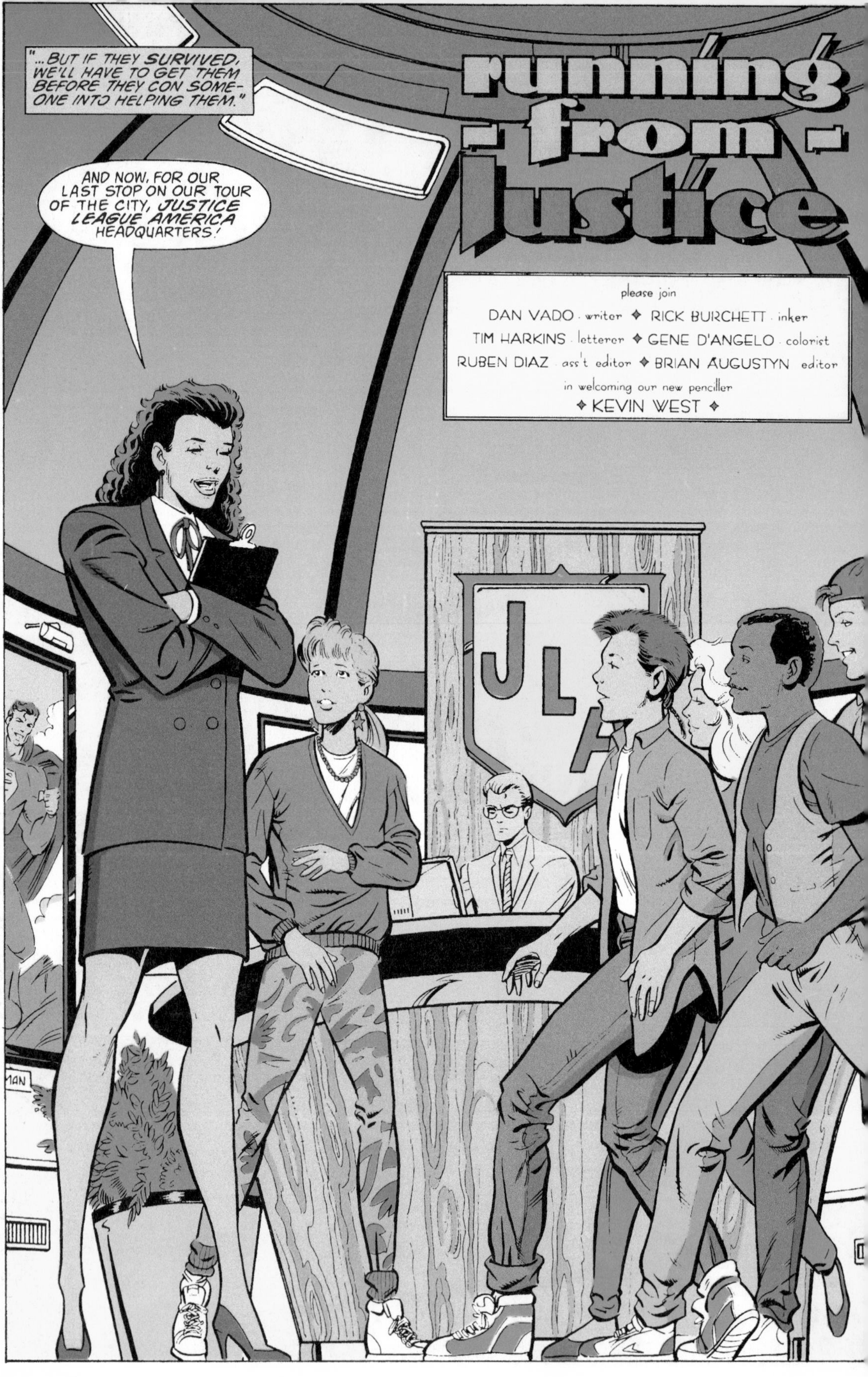

"...BUT IF THEY SURVIVED, WE'LL HAVE TO GET THEM BEFORE THEY CON SOMEONE INTO HELPING THEM."
running from justice
please join
DAN VADO · writer ✦ RICK BURCHETT · inker
TIM HARKINS · letterer ✦ GENE D'ANGELO · colorist
RUBEN DIAZ · ass't editor ✦ BRIAN AUGUSTYN editor
in welcoming our new penciller
✦ KEVIN WEST ✦
AND NOW, FOR OUR LAST STOP ON OUR TOUR OF THE CITY, JUSTICE LEAGUE AMERICA HEADQUARTERS!
JLA

HIS NEW LOBBY AREA DOUBLES AS AN INFORMATION CENTER AND A *HALL OF FAME* HONORING SOME OF THE JUSTICE LEAGUE'S MOST NOTABLE MEMBERS AND ACHIEVEMENTS.

WOW, *BAD!*

I WONDER IF WE'LL SEE ANY *REAL* SUPER-HEROES TODAY?

SORRY, KID. ALL THE *REAL* SUPER-HEROES ARE BUSY...

I GUESS YOU'LL HAVE TO SETTLE FOR *US.*

FIRE!!!

BAD DOG SIT

WHOA...

...*YOU'RE* THAT FIRE CHICK! I SAW YOU ON TV FIGHTING THAT *DOOMSDUDE* THAT OFFED SUPERMAN.

BAD DOG SIT

YEAH, WELL, SUPERMAN WASN'T THE *ONLY* PERSON THAT LOST SOMETHING IN THAT FIGHT.

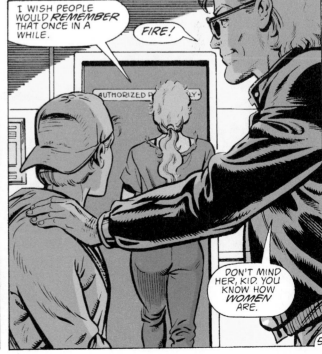

I WISH PEOPLE WOULD *REMEMBER* THAT ONCE IN A WHILE.

FIRE!

AUTHORIZED P   ONLY

DON'T MIND HER, KID. YOU KNOW HOW *WOMEN* ARE.

5

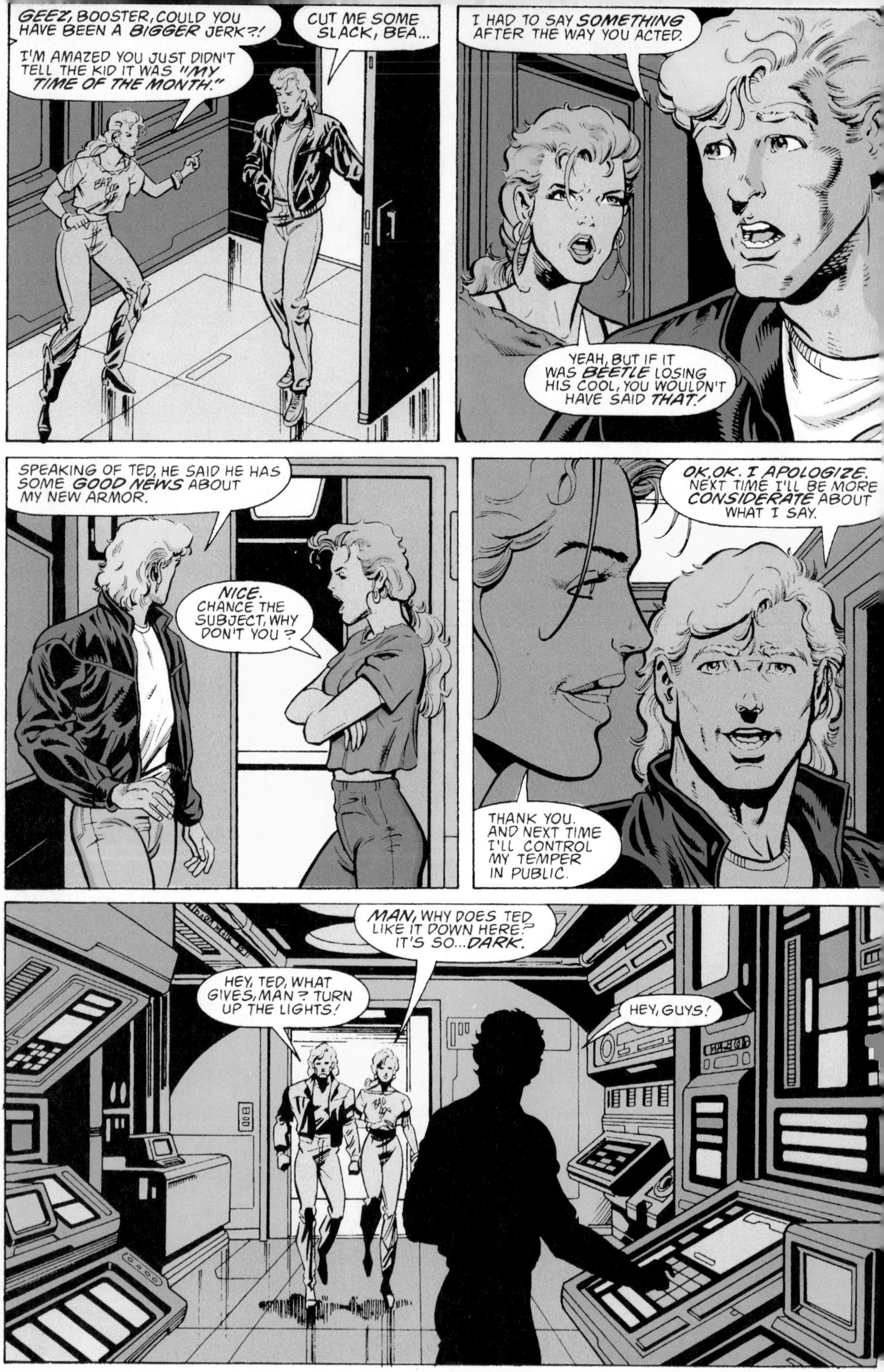
GEEZ, BOOSTER, COULD YOU HAVE BEEN A BIGGER JERK?!
I'M AMAZED YOU JUST DIDN'T TELL THE KID IT WAS "MY TIME OF THE MONTH."
CUT ME SOME SLACK, BEA...
I HAD TO SAY SOMETHING AFTER THE WAY YOU ACTED.
YEAH, BUT IF IT WAS BEETLE LOSING HIS COOL, YOU WOULDN'T HAVE SAID THAT!
SPEAKING OF TED, HE SAID HE HAS SOME GOOD NEWS ABOUT MY NEW ARMOR.
NICE. CHANGE THE SUBJECT, WHY DON'T YOU?
OK, OK. I APOLOGIZE. NEXT TIME I'LL BE MORE CONSIDERATE ABOUT WHAT I SAY.
THANK YOU. AND NEXT TIME I'LL CONTROL MY TEMPER IN PUBLIC.
HEY, TED, WHAT GIVES, MAN? TURN UP THE LIGHTS!
MAN, WHY DOES TED LIKE IT DOWN HERE? IT'S SO...DARK.
HEY, GUYS!

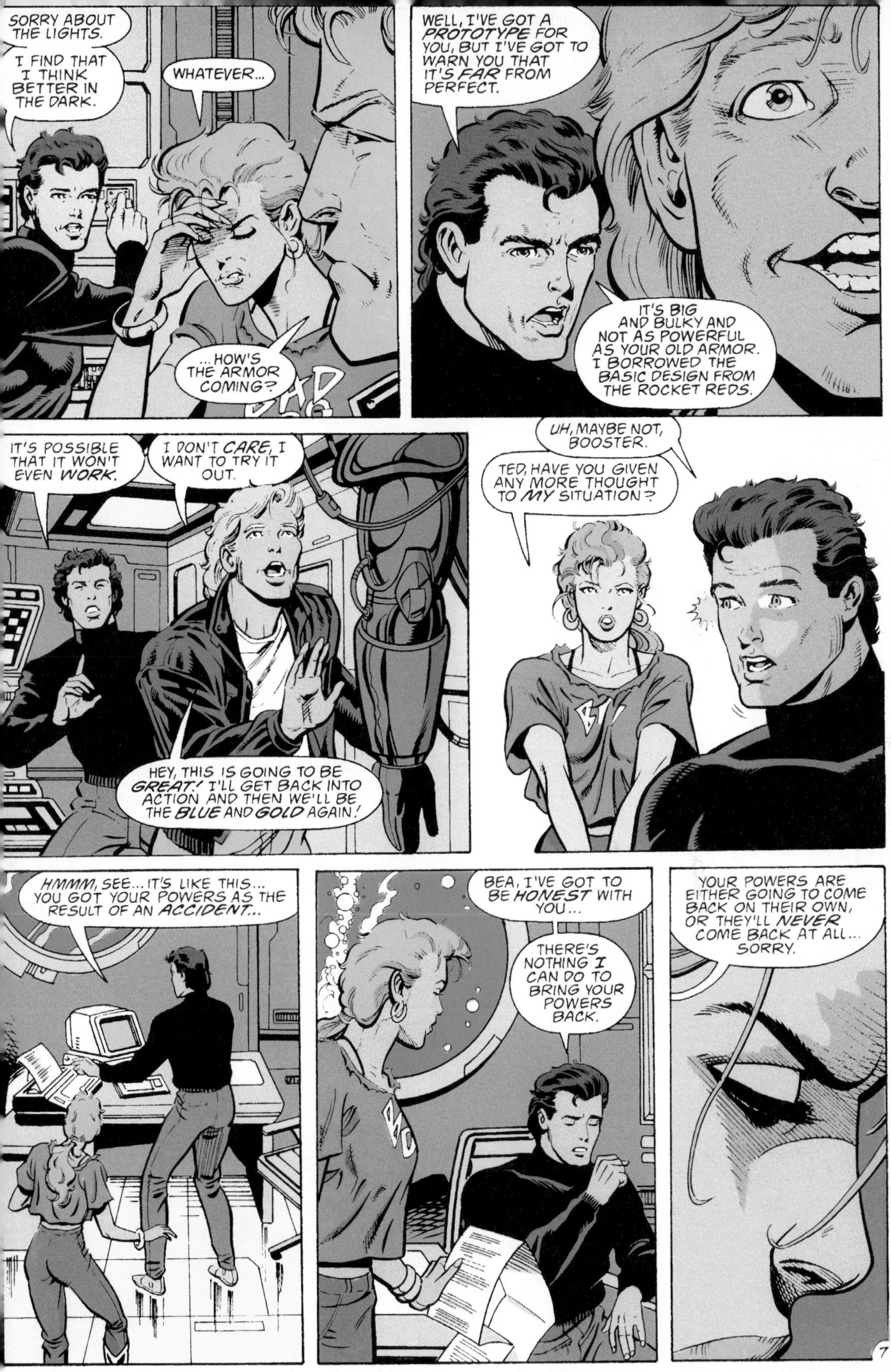
SORRY ABOUT THE LIGHTS.
I FIND THAT I THINK BETTER IN THE DARK.
WHATEVER...
...HOW'S THE ARMOR COMING?
WELL, I'VE GOT A PROTOTYPE FOR YOU, BUT I'VE GOT TO WARN YOU THAT IT'S FAR FROM PERFECT.
IT'S BIG AND BULKY AND NOT AS POWERFUL AS YOUR OLD ARMOR. I BORROWED THE BASIC DESIGN FROM THE ROCKET REDS.
IT'S POSSIBLE THAT IT WON'T EVEN WORK.
I DON'T CARE, I WANT TO TRY IT OUT.
HEY, THIS IS GOING TO BE GREAT! I'LL GET BACK INTO ACTION AND THEN WE'LL BE THE BLUE AND GOLD AGAIN!
UH, MAYBE NOT, BOOSTER.
TED, HAVE YOU GIVEN ANY MORE THOUGHT TO MY SITUATION?
HMMM, SEE... IT'S LIKE THIS... YOU GOT YOUR POWERS AS THE RESULT OF AN ACCIDENT...
BEA, I'VE GOT TO BE HONEST WITH YOU...
THERE'S NOTHING I CAN DO TO BRING YOUR POWERS BACK.
YOUR POWERS ARE EITHER GOING TO COME BACK ON THEIR OWN, OR THEY'LL NEVER COME BACK AT ALL... SORRY.

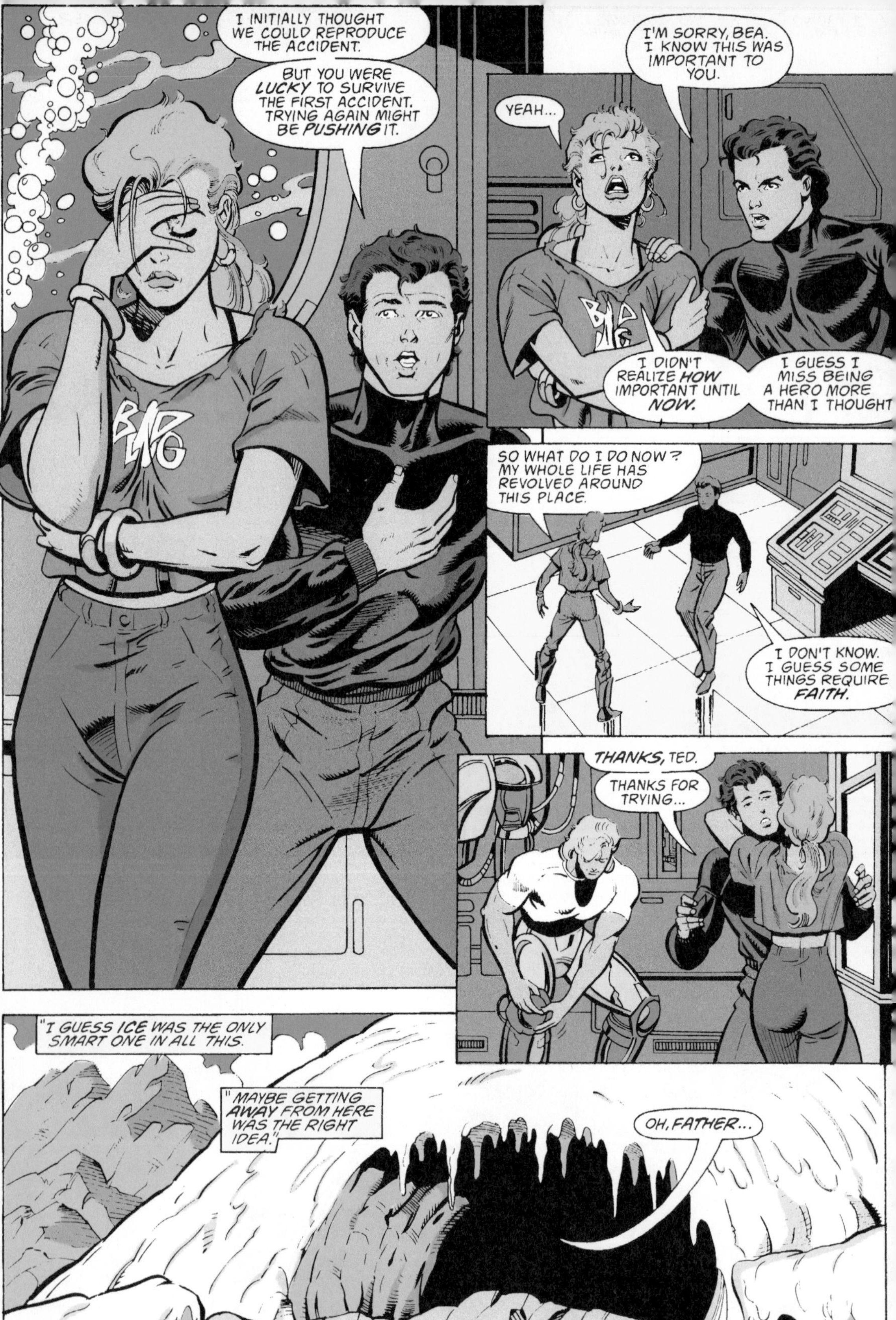

I INITIALLY THOUGHT WE COULD REPRODUCE THE ACCIDENT.
BUT YOU WERE LUCKY TO SURVIVE THE FIRST ACCIDENT. TRYING AGAIN MIGHT BE PUSHING IT.
YEAH...
I'M SORRY, BEA. I KNOW THIS WAS IMPORTANT TO YOU.
I DIDN'T REALIZE HOW IMPORTANT UNTIL NOW.
I GUESS I MISS BEING A HERO MORE THAN I THOUGHT.
SO WHAT DO I DO NOW? MY WHOLE LIFE HAS REVOLVED AROUND THIS PLACE.
I DON'T KNOW. I GUESS SOME THINGS REQUIRE FAITH.
THANKS, TED.
THANKS FOR TRYING...
"I GUESS ICE WAS THE ONLY SMART ONE IN ALL THIS.
"MAYBE GETTING AWAY FROM HERE WAS THE RIGHT IDEA."
OH, FATHER...
8

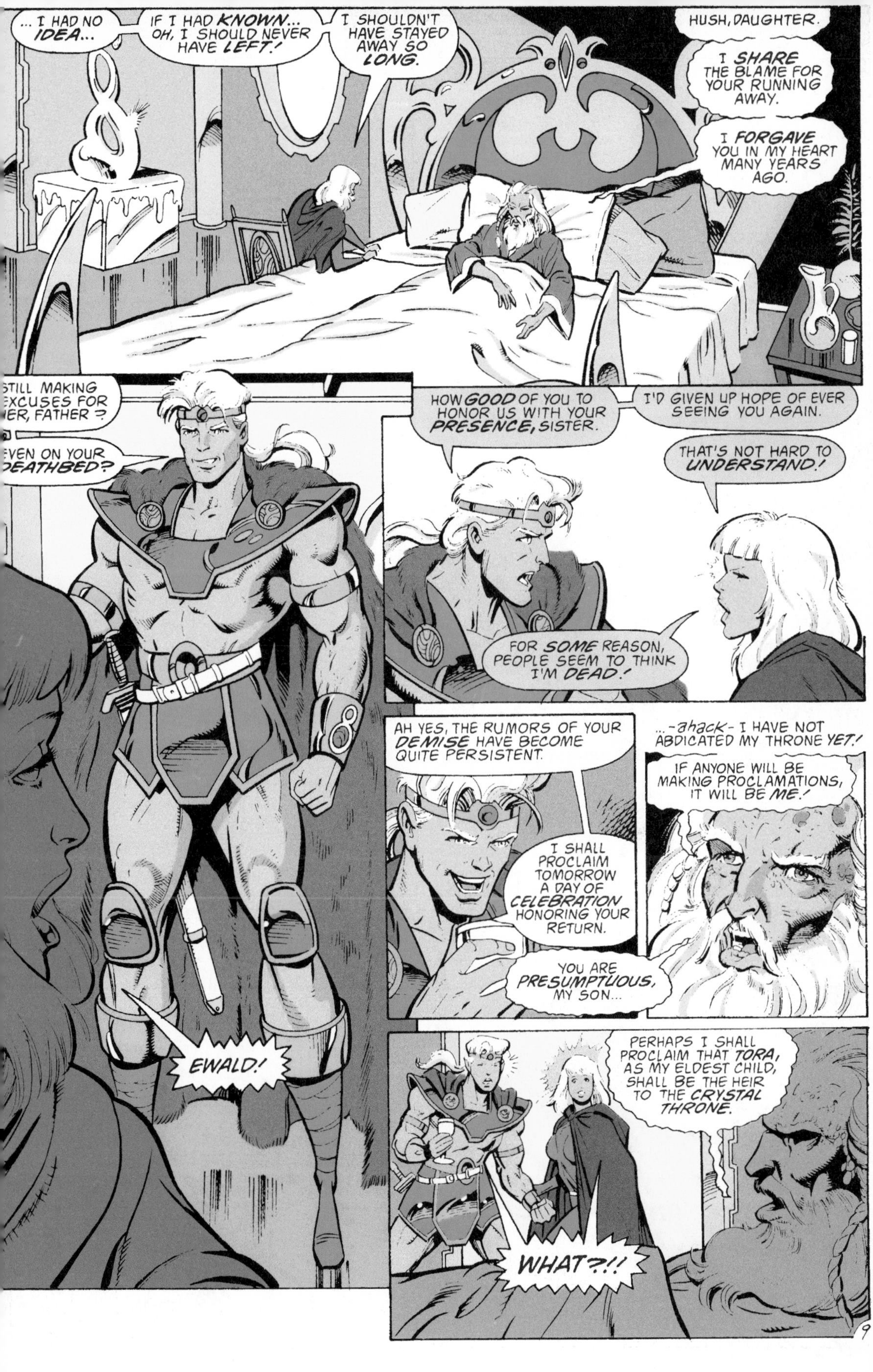

... I HAD NO IDEA...
IF I HAD KNOWN... OH, I SHOULD NEVER HAVE LEFT!
I SHOULDN'T HAVE STAYED AWAY SO LONG.
HUSH, DAUGHTER.
I SHARE THE BLAME FOR YOUR RUNNING AWAY.
I FORGAVE YOU IN MY HEART MANY YEARS AGO.
STILL MAKING EXCUSES FOR HER, FATHER?
EVEN ON YOUR DEATHBED?
EWALD!
HOW GOOD OF YOU TO HONOR US WITH YOUR PRESENCE, SISTER.
I'D GIVEN UP HOPE OF EVER SEEING YOU AGAIN.
THAT'S NOT HARD TO UNDERSTAND!
FOR SOME REASON, PEOPLE SEEM TO THINK I'M DEAD!
AH YES, THE RUMORS OF YOUR DEMISE HAVE BECOME QUITE PERSISTENT.
I SHALL PROCLAIM TOMORROW A DAY OF CELEBRATION HONORING YOUR RETURN.
YOU ARE PRESUMPTUOUS, MY SON...
...-ahack- I HAVE NOT ABDICATED MY THRONE YET!
IF ANYONE WILL BE MAKING PROCLAMATIONS, IT WILL BE ME!
PERHAPS I SHALL PROCLAIM THAT TORA, AS MY ELDEST CHILD, SHALL BE THE HEIR TO THE CRYSTAL THRONE.
WHAT?!!

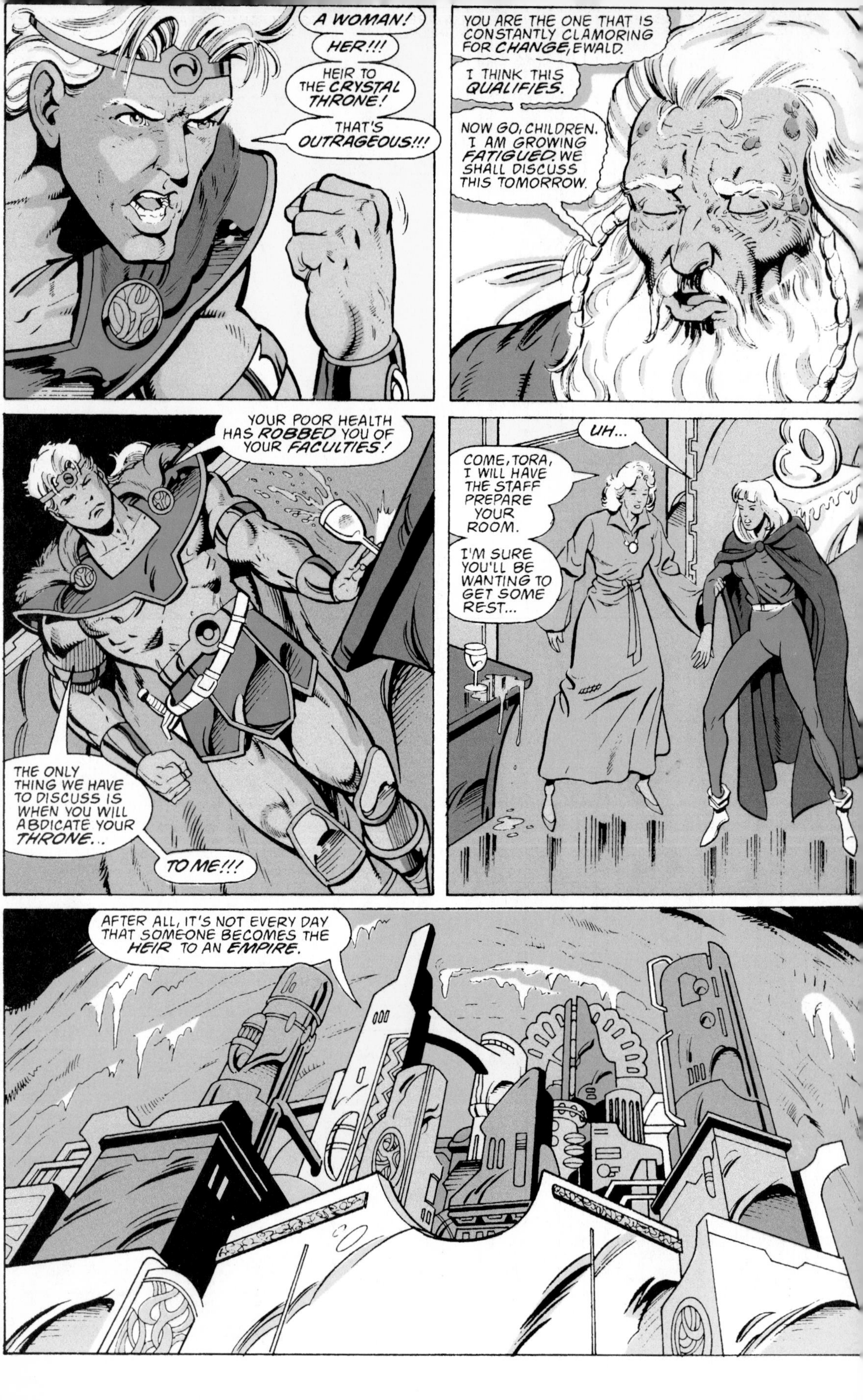
A WOMAN!
HER!!!
HEIR TO THE CRYSTAL THRONE!
THAT'S OUTRAGEOUS!!!
YOU ARE THE ONE THAT IS CONSTANTLY CLAMORING FOR CHANGE, EWALD.
I THINK THIS QUALIFIES.
NOW GO, CHILDREN. I AM GROWING FATIGUED. WE SHALL DISCUSS THIS TOMORROW.
YOUR POOR HEALTH HAS ROBBED YOU OF YOUR FACULTIES!
THE ONLY THING WE HAVE TO DISCUSS IS WHEN YOU WILL ABDICATE YOUR THRONE...
TO ME!!!
UH...
COME, TORA, I WILL HAVE THE STAFF PREPARE YOUR ROOM.
I'M SURE YOU'LL BE WANTING TO GET SOME REST...
AFTER ALL, IT'S NOT EVERY DAY THAT SOMEONE BECOMES THE HEIR TO AN EMPIRE.

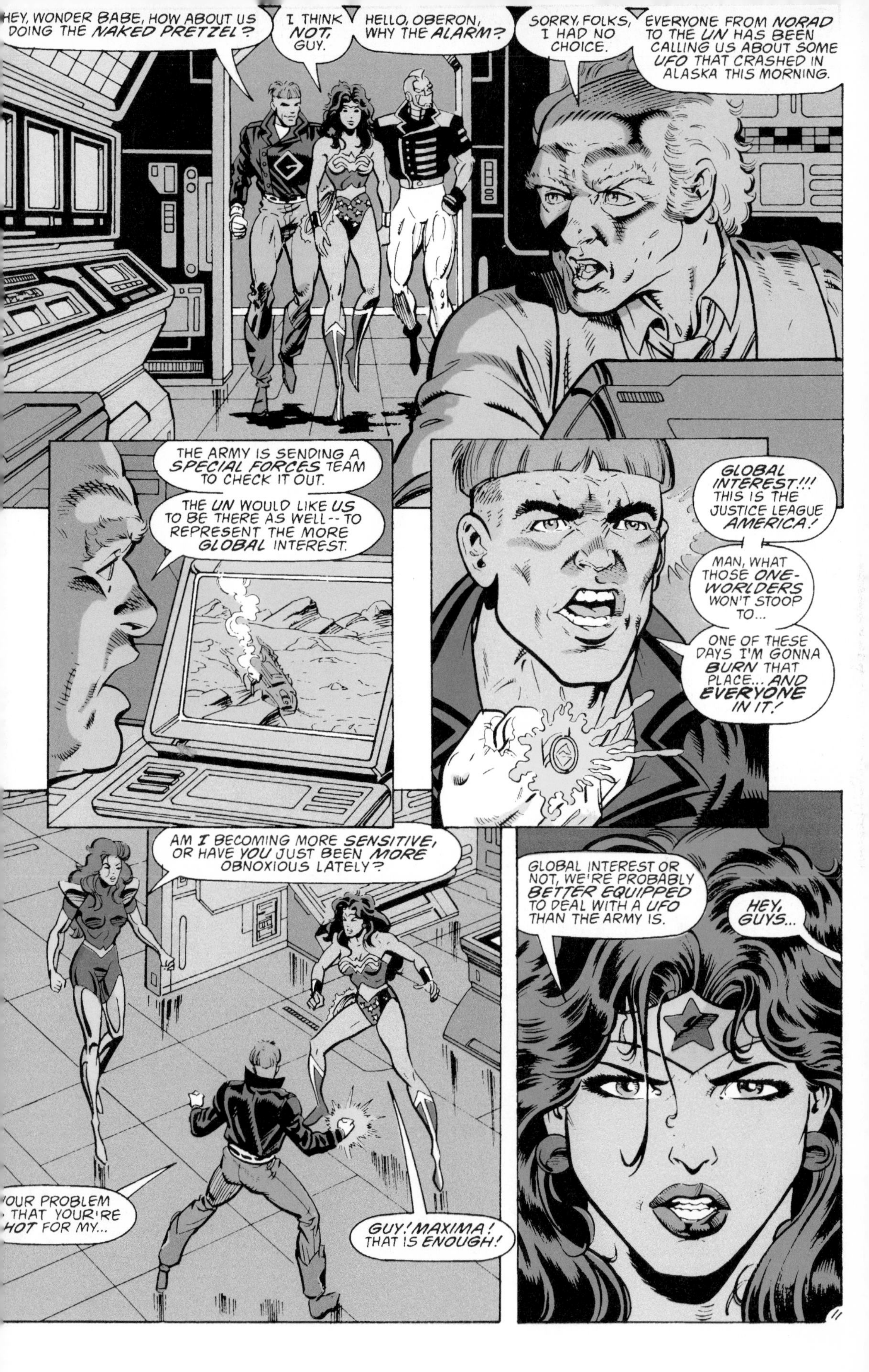
HEY, WONDER BABE, HOW ABOUT US DOING THE NAKED PRETZEL?
I THINK NOT, GUY.
HELLO, OBERON, WHY THE ALARM?
SORRY, FOLKS, I HAD NO CHOICE.
EVERYONE FROM NORAD TO THE UN HAS BEEN CALLING US ABOUT SOME UFO THAT CRASHED IN ALASKA THIS MORNING.
THE ARMY IS SENDING A SPECIAL FORCES TEAM TO CHECK IT OUT.
THE UN WOULD LIKE US TO BE THERE AS WELL-- TO REPRESENT THE MORE GLOBAL INTEREST.
GLOBAL INTEREST!!! THIS IS THE JUSTICE LEAGUE AMERICA!
MAN, WHAT THOSE ONE-WORLDERS WON'T STOOP TO...
ONE OF THESE DAYS I'M GONNA BURN THAT PLACE... AND EVERYONE IN IT!
AM I BECOMING MORE SENSITIVE, OR HAVE YOU JUST BEEN MORE OBNOXIOUS LATELY?
YOUR PROBLEM IS THAT YOU'RE HOT FOR MY...
GUY! MAXIMA! THAT IS ENOUGH!
GLOBAL INTEREST OR NOT, WE'RE PROBABLY BETTER EQUIPPED TO DEAL WITH A UFO THAN THE ARMY IS.
HEY, GUYS...

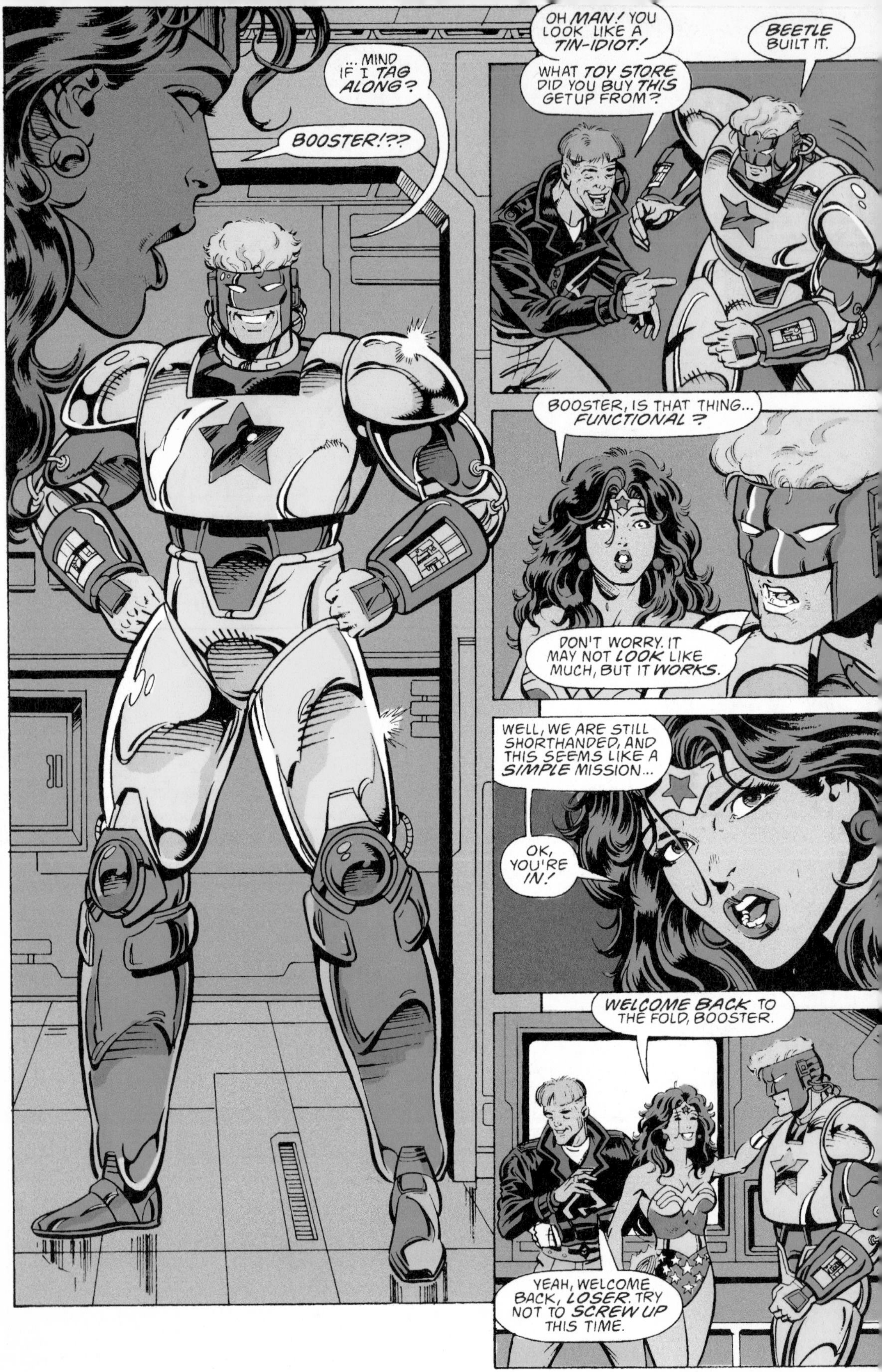

... MIND IF I TAG ALONG?
BOOSTER!??
OH MAN! YOU LOOK LIKE A TIN-IDIOT!
WHAT TOY STORE DID YOU BUY THIS GETUP FROM?
BEETLE BUILT IT.
BOOSTER, IS THAT THING... FUNCTIONAL?
DON'T WORRY. IT MAY NOT LOOK LIKE MUCH, BUT IT WORKS.
WELL, WE ARE STILL SHORTHANDED, AND THIS SEEMS LIKE A SIMPLE MISSION...
OK, YOU'RE IN!
WELCOME BACK TO THE FOLD, BOOSTER.
YEAH, WELCOME BACK, LOSER. TRY NOT TO SCREW UP THIS TIME.

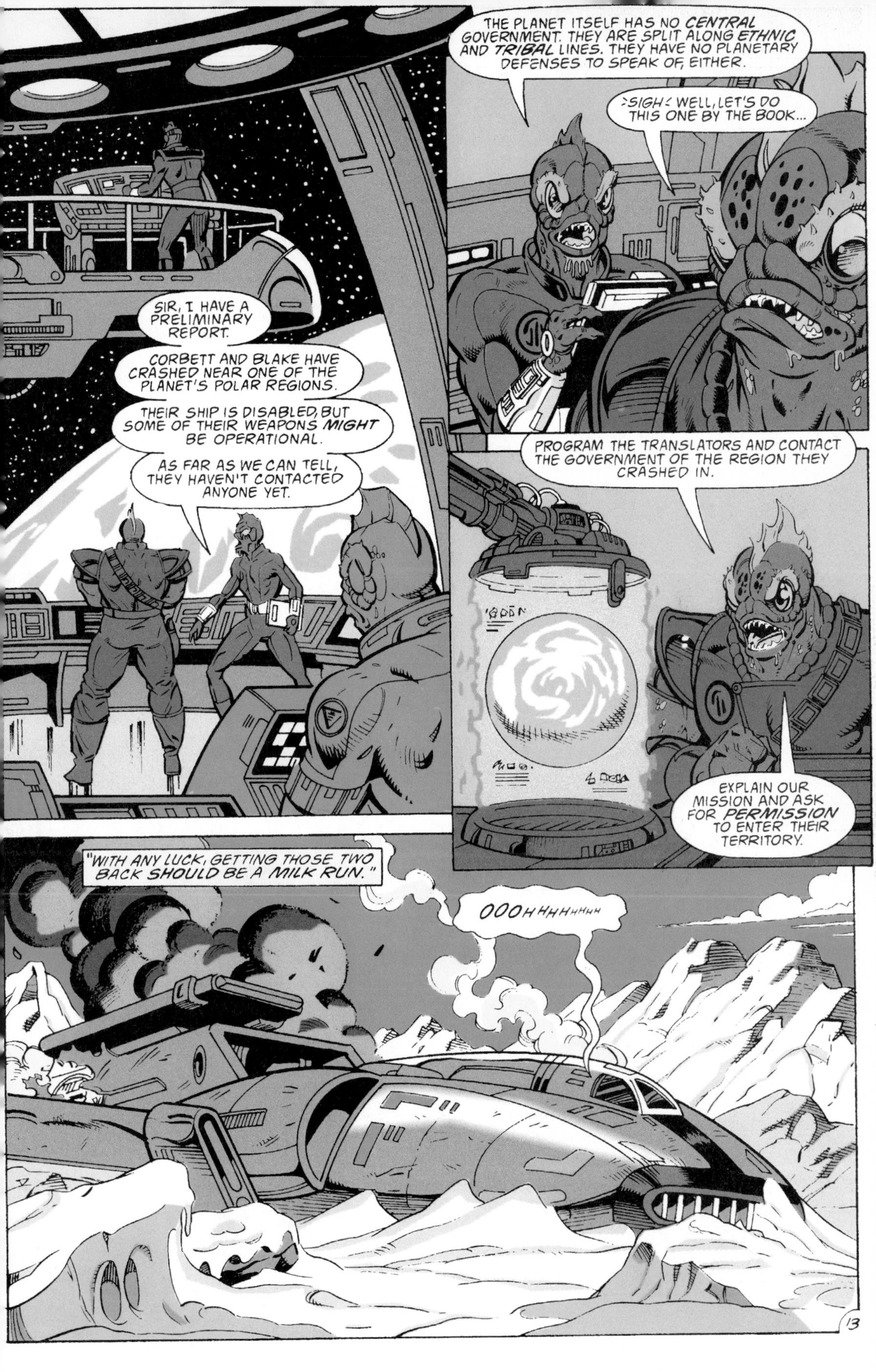
SIR, I HAVE A PRELIMINARY REPORT.
CORBETT AND BLAKE HAVE CRASHED NEAR ONE OF THE PLANET'S POLAR REGIONS.
THEIR SHIP IS DISABLED, BUT SOME OF THEIR WEAPONS MIGHT BE OPERATIONAL.
AS FAR AS WE CAN TELL, THEY HAVEN'T CONTACTED ANYONE YET.
THE PLANET ITSELF HAS NO CENTRAL GOVERNMENT. THEY ARE SPLIT ALONG ETHNIC AND TRIBAL LINES. THEY HAVE NO PLANETARY DEFENSES TO SPEAK OF, EITHER.
>SIGH< WELL, LET'S DO THIS ONE BY THE BOOK...
PROGRAM THE TRANSLATORS AND CONTACT THE GOVERNMENT OF THE REGION THEY CRASHED IN.
EXPLAIN OUR MISSION AND ASK FOR PERMISSION TO ENTER THEIR TERRITORY.
"WITH ANY LUCK, GETTING THOSE TWO BACK SHOULD BE A MILK RUN."
OOOHHHHHHHH

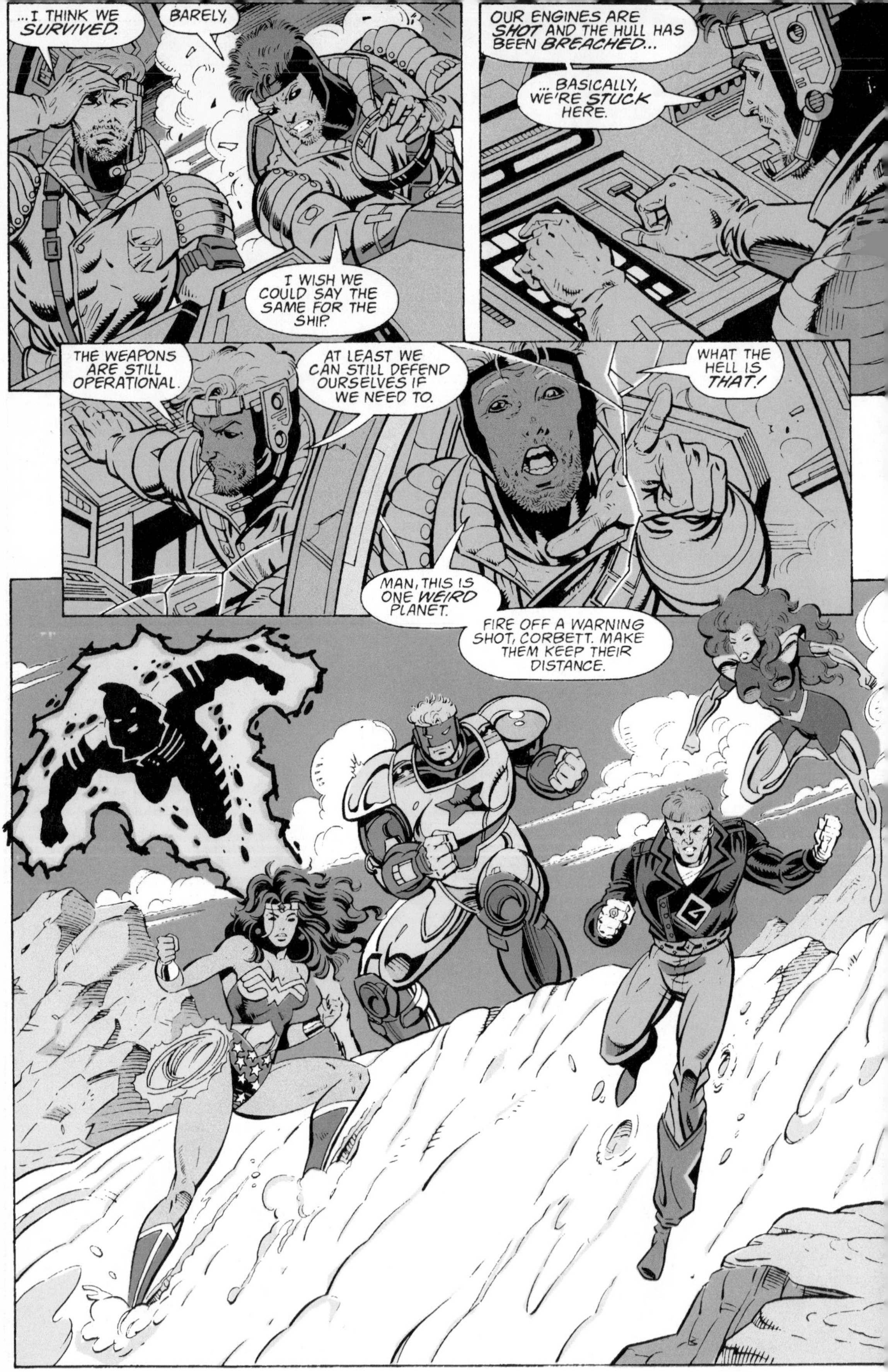
...I THINK WE SURVIVED.
BARELY,
I WISH WE COULD SAY THE SAME FOR THE SHIP.
OUR ENGINES ARE SHOT AND THE HULL HAS BEEN BREACHED...
... BASICALLY, WE'RE STUCK HERE.
THE WEAPONS ARE STILL OPERATIONAL.
AT LEAST WE CAN STILL DEFEND OURSELVES IF WE NEED TO.
WHAT THE HELL IS THAT!
MAN, THIS IS ONE WEIRD PLANET.
FIRE OFF A WARNING SHOT, CORBETT. MAKE THEM KEEP THEIR DISTANCE.

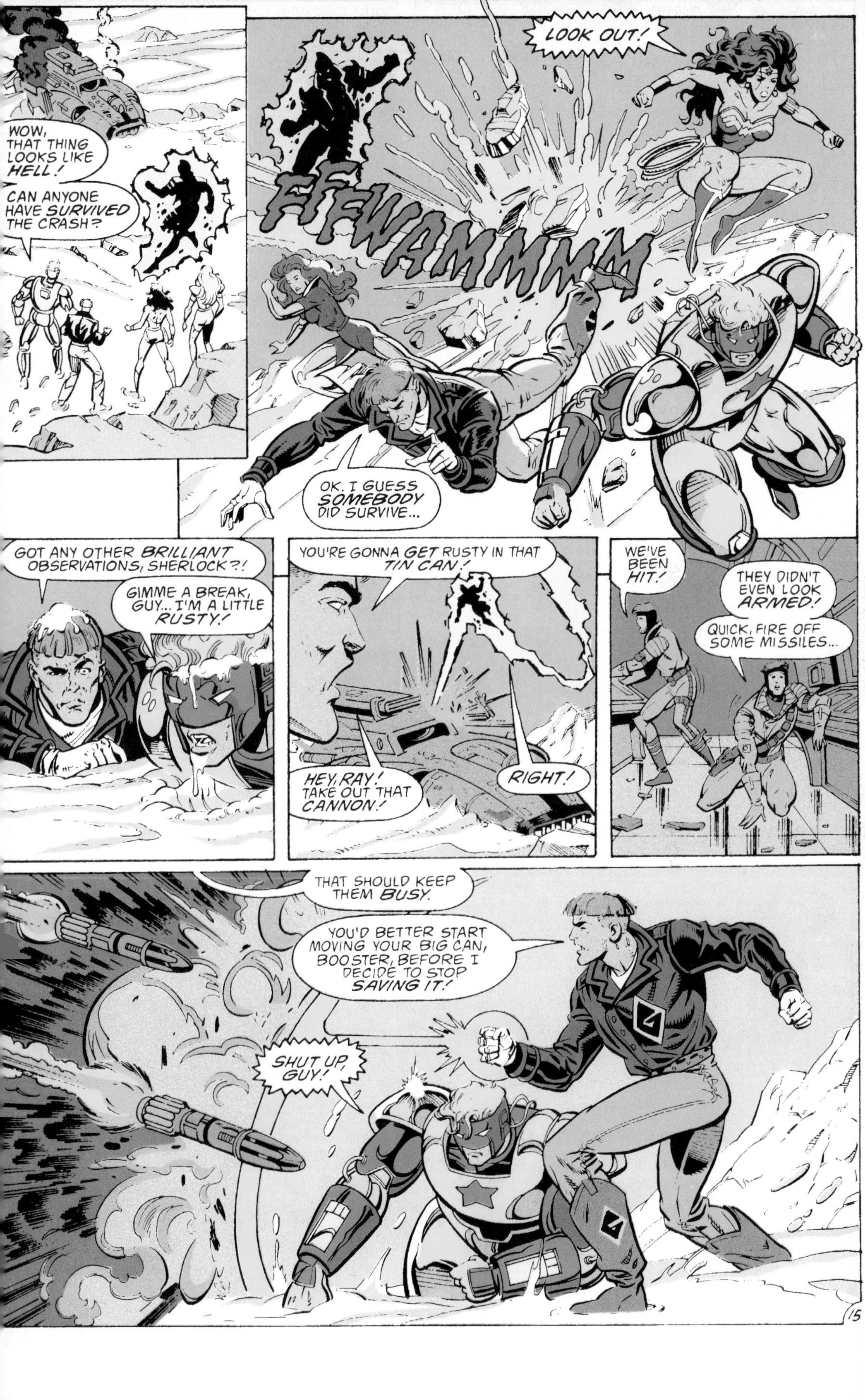
WOW, THAT THING LOOKS LIKE HELL!
CAN ANYONE HAVE SURVIVED THE CRASH?
LOOK OUT!
FFFWAMMMMM
OK. I GUESS SOMEBODY DID SURVIVE...
GOT ANY OTHER BRILLIANT OBSERVATIONS, SHERLOCK?!
GIMME A BREAK, GUY... I'M A LITTLE RUSTY!
YOU'RE GONNA GET RUSTY IN THAT TIN CAN!
HEY, RAY! TAKE OUT THAT CANNON!
RIGHT!
WE'VE BEEN HIT!
THEY DIDN'T EVEN LOOK ARMED!
QUICK, FIRE OFF SOME MISSILES...
THAT SHOULD KEEP THEM BUSY.
YOU'D BETTER START MOVING YOUR BIG CAN, BOOSTER, BEFORE I DECIDE TO STOP SAVING IT!
SHUT UP, GUY!

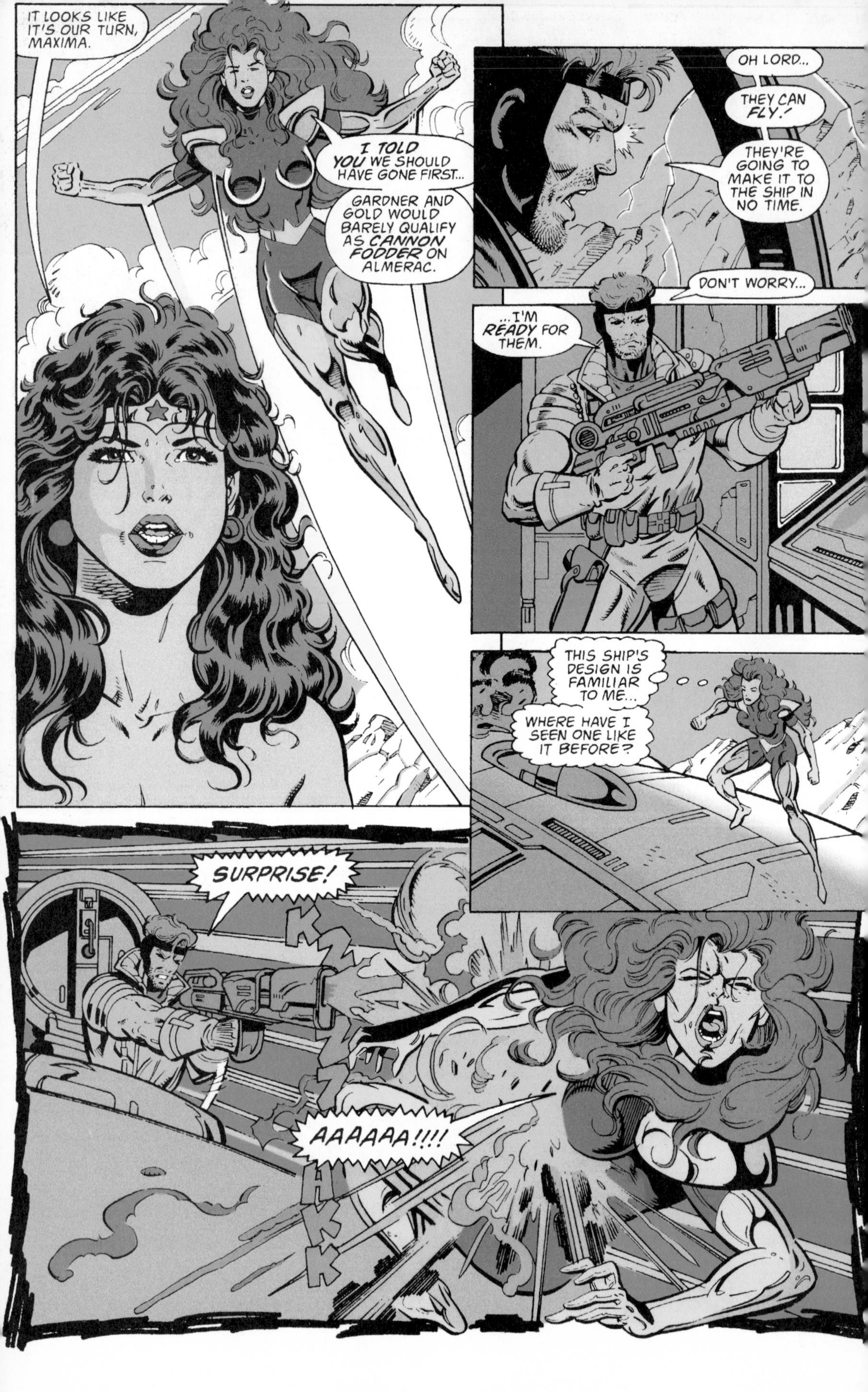
IT LOOKS LIKE IT'S OUR TURN, MAXIMA.
I TOLD YOU WE SHOULD HAVE GONE FIRST...
GARDNER AND GOLD WOULD BARELY QUALIFY AS CANNON FODDER ON ALMERAC.
OH LORD...
THEY CAN FLY!
THEY'RE GOING TO MAKE IT TO THE SHIP IN NO TIME.
DON'T WORRY...
...I'M READY FOR THEM.
THIS SHIP'S DESIGN IS FAMILIAR TO ME...
WHERE HAVE I SEEN ONE LIKE IT BEFORE?
SURPRISE!
AAAAAA!!!!

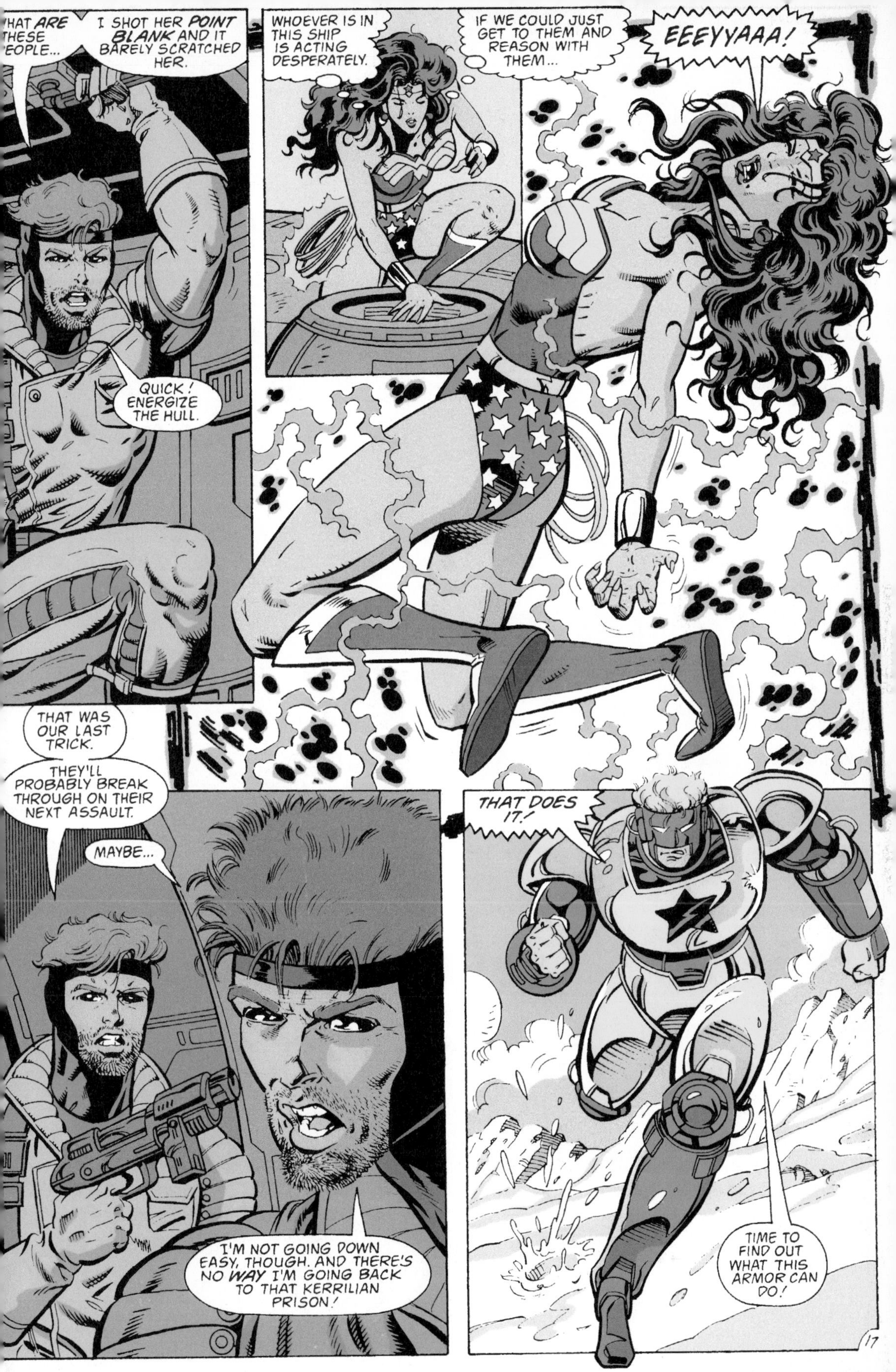
WHAT ARE THESE PEOPLE...
I SHOT HER POINT BLANK AND IT BARELY SCRATCHED HER.
QUICK! ENERGIZE THE HULL.
WHOEVER IS IN THIS SHIP IS ACTING DESPERATELY.
IF WE COULD JUST GET TO THEM AND REASON WITH THEM...
EEEYYAAA!
THAT WAS OUR LAST TRICK.
THEY'LL PROBABLY BREAK THROUGH ON THEIR NEXT ASSAULT.
MAYBE...
I'M NOT GOING DOWN EASY, THOUGH. AND THERE'S NO WAY I'M GOING BACK TO THAT KERRILIAN PRISON!
THAT DOES IT!
TIME TO FIND OUT WHAT THIS ARMOR CAN DO!

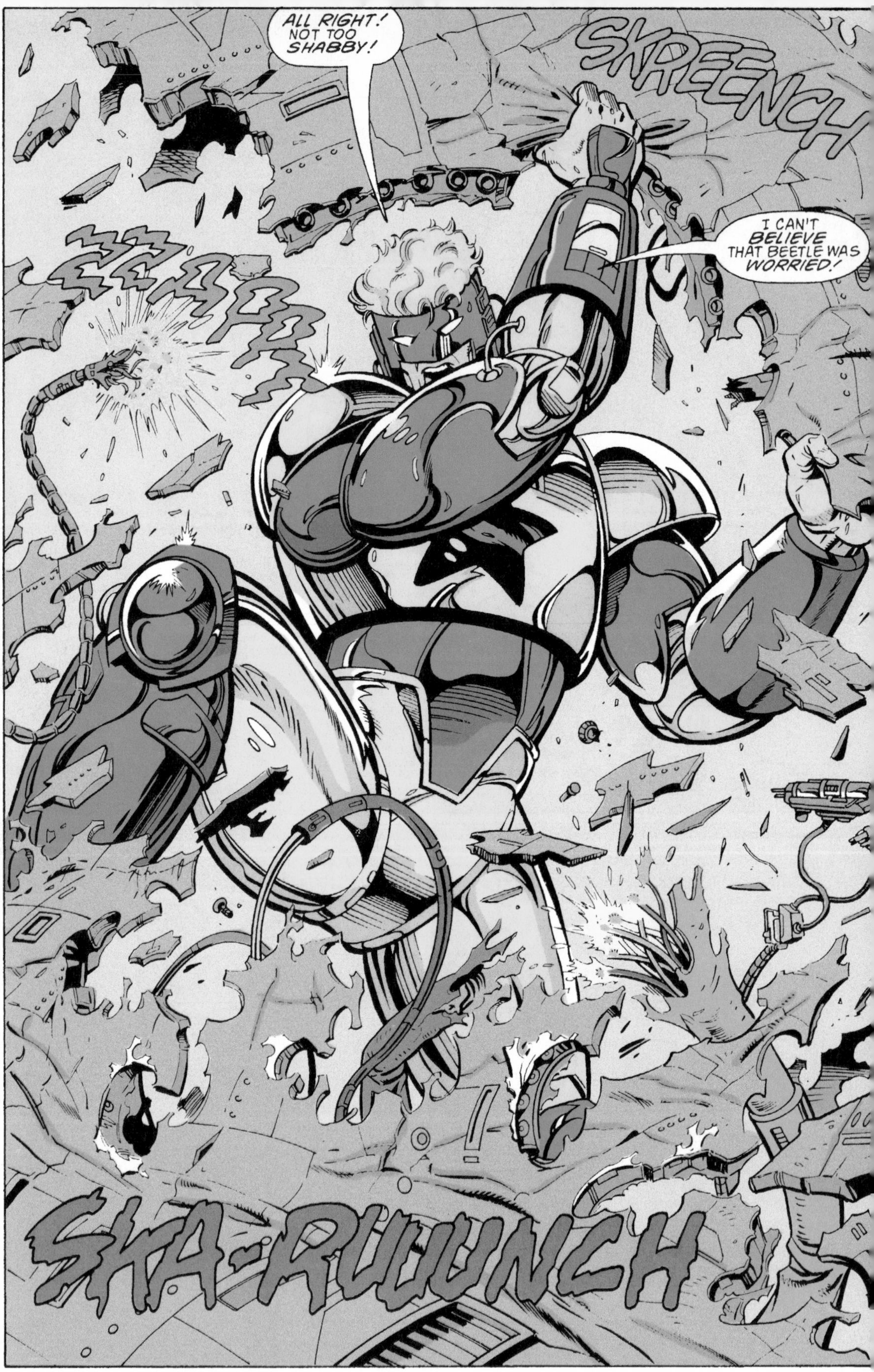
ALL RIGHT! NOT TOO SHABBY!
SKREEENCH
ZZZAPP
I CAN'T BELIEVE THAT BEETLE WAS WORRIED!
SKA-RUUUNCH

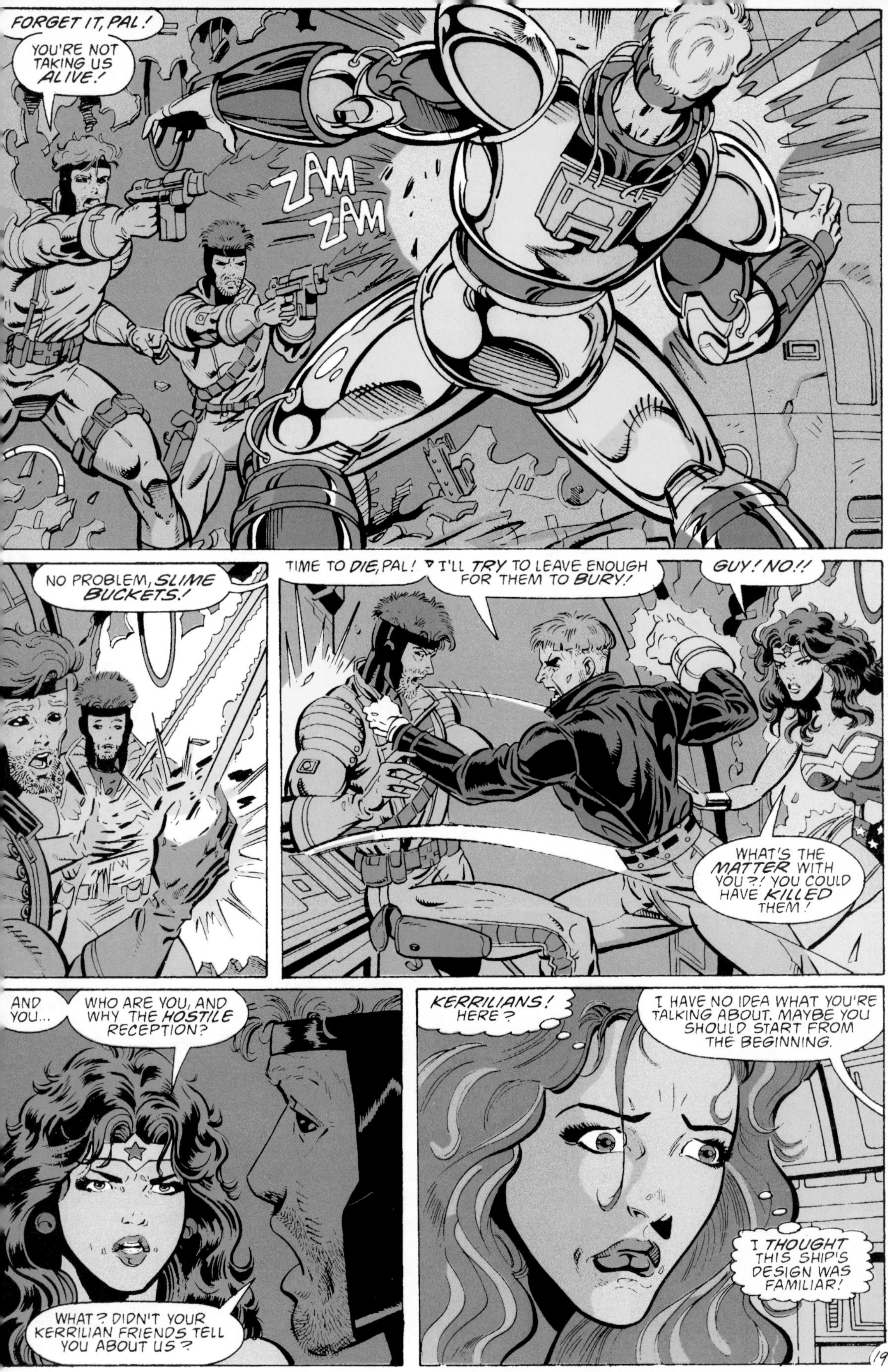

FORGET IT, PAL!
YOU'RE NOT TAKING US ALIVE!
ZAM ZAM
NO PROBLEM, SLIME BUCKETS!
TIME TO DIE, PAL!
I'LL TRY TO LEAVE ENOUGH FOR THEM TO BURY!
GUY! NO!!
WHAT'S THE MATTER WITH YOU?! YOU COULD HAVE KILLED THEM!
AND YOU...
WHO ARE YOU, AND WHY THE HOSTILE RECEPTION?
WHAT? DIDN'T YOUR KERRILIAN FRIENDS TELL YOU ABOUT US?
KERRILIANS! HERE?
I HAVE NO IDEA WHAT YOU'RE TALKING ABOUT. MAYBE YOU SHOULD START FROM THE BEGINNING.
I THOUGHT THIS SHIP'S DESIGN WAS FAMILIAR!

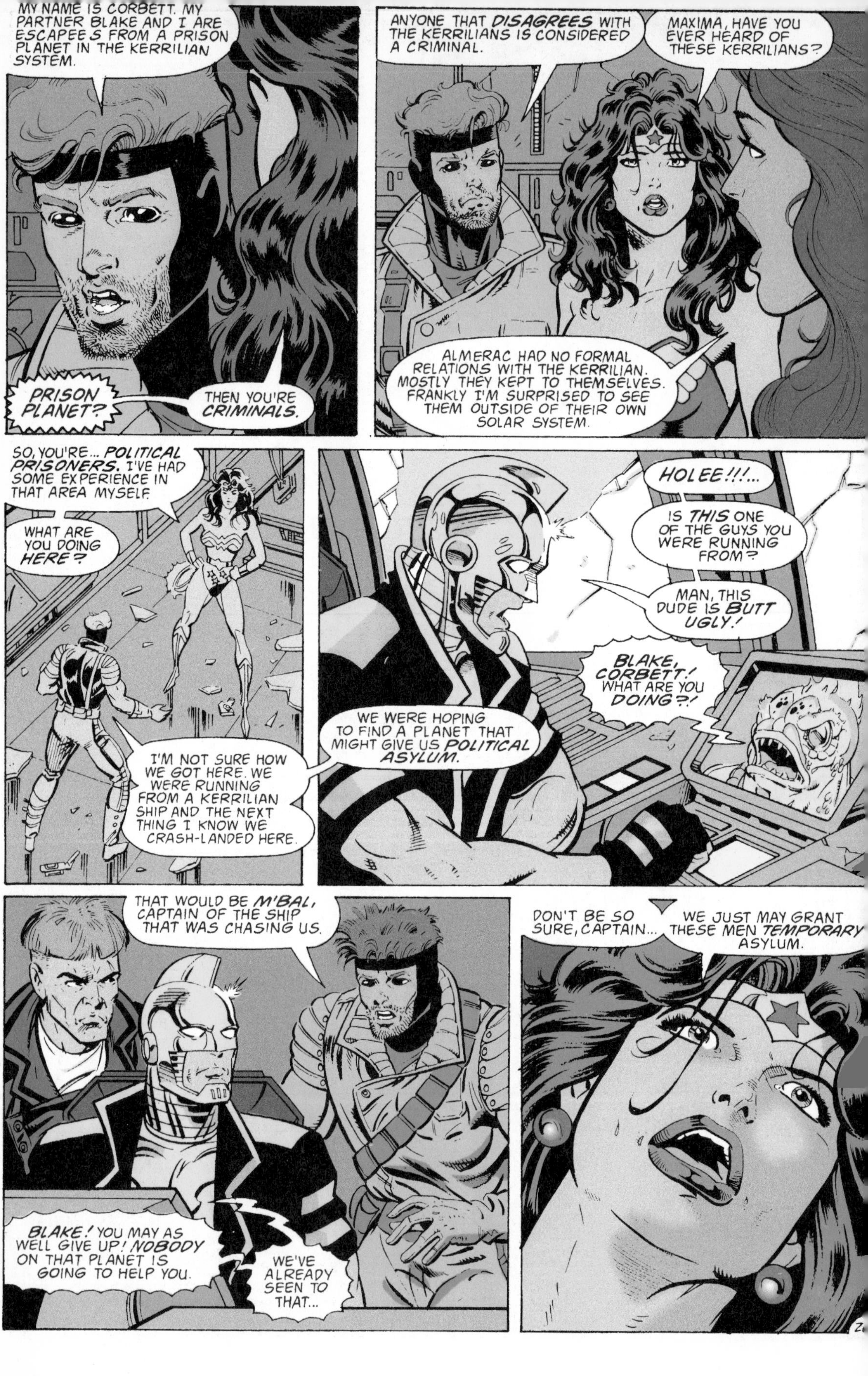
MY NAME IS CORBETT. MY PARTNER BLAKE AND I ARE ESCAPEES FROM A PRISON PLANET IN THE KERRILIAN SYSTEM.
PRISON PLANET?
THEN YOU'RE CRIMINALS.
ANYONE THAT DISAGREES WITH THE KERRILIANS IS CONSIDERED A CRIMINAL.
MAXIMA, HAVE YOU EVER HEARD OF THESE KERRILIANS?
ALMERAC HAD NO FORMAL RELATIONS WITH THE KERRILIAN. MOSTLY THEY KEPT TO THEMSELVES. FRANKLY I'M SURPRISED TO SEE THEM OUTSIDE OF THEIR OWN SOLAR SYSTEM.
SO, YOU'RE... POLITICAL PRISONERS. I'VE HAD SOME EXPERIENCE IN THAT AREA MYSELF.
WHAT ARE YOU DOING HERE?
I'M NOT SURE HOW WE GOT HERE. WE WERE RUNNING FROM A KERRILIAN SHIP AND THE NEXT THING I KNOW WE CRASH-LANDED HERE.
WE WERE HOPING TO FIND A PLANET THAT MIGHT GIVE US POLITICAL ASYLUM.
HOLEE!!!...
IS THIS ONE OF THE GUYS YOU WERE RUNNING FROM?
MAN, THIS DUDE IS BUTT UGLY!
BLAKE, CORBETT! WHAT ARE YOU DOING?!
THAT WOULD BE M'BAL, CAPTAIN OF THE SHIP THAT WAS CHASING US.
BLAKE! YOU MAY AS WELL GIVE UP! NOBODY ON THAT PLANET IS GOING TO HELP YOU.
WE'VE ALREADY SEEN TO THAT...
DON'T BE SO SURE, CAPTAIN...
WE JUST MAY GRANT THESE MEN TEMPORARY ASYLUM.

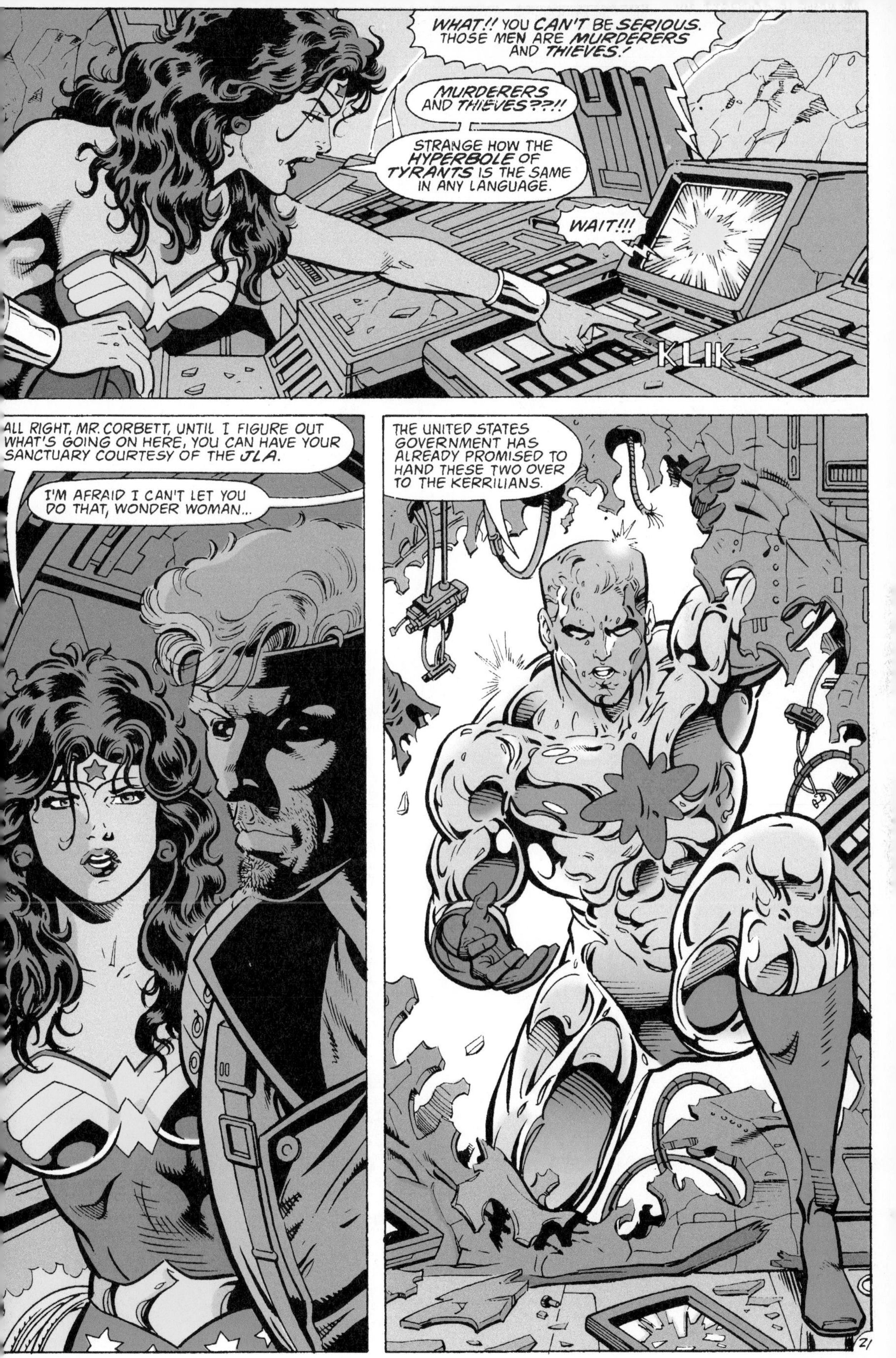
WHAT!! YOU CAN'T BE SERIOUS. THOSE MEN ARE MURDERERS AND THIEVES!
MURDERERS AND THIEVES??!!
STRANGE HOW THE HYPERBOLE OF TYRANTS IS THE SAME IN ANY LANGUAGE.
WAIT!!!
KLIK
ALL RIGHT, MR. CORBETT, UNTIL I FIGURE OUT WHAT'S GOING ON HERE, YOU CAN HAVE YOUR SANCTUARY COURTESY OF THE JLA.
I'M AFRAID I CAN'T LET YOU DO THAT, WONDER WOMAN...
THE UNITED STATES GOVERNMENT HAS ALREADY PROMISED TO HAND THESE TWO OVER TO THE KERRILIANS.
21

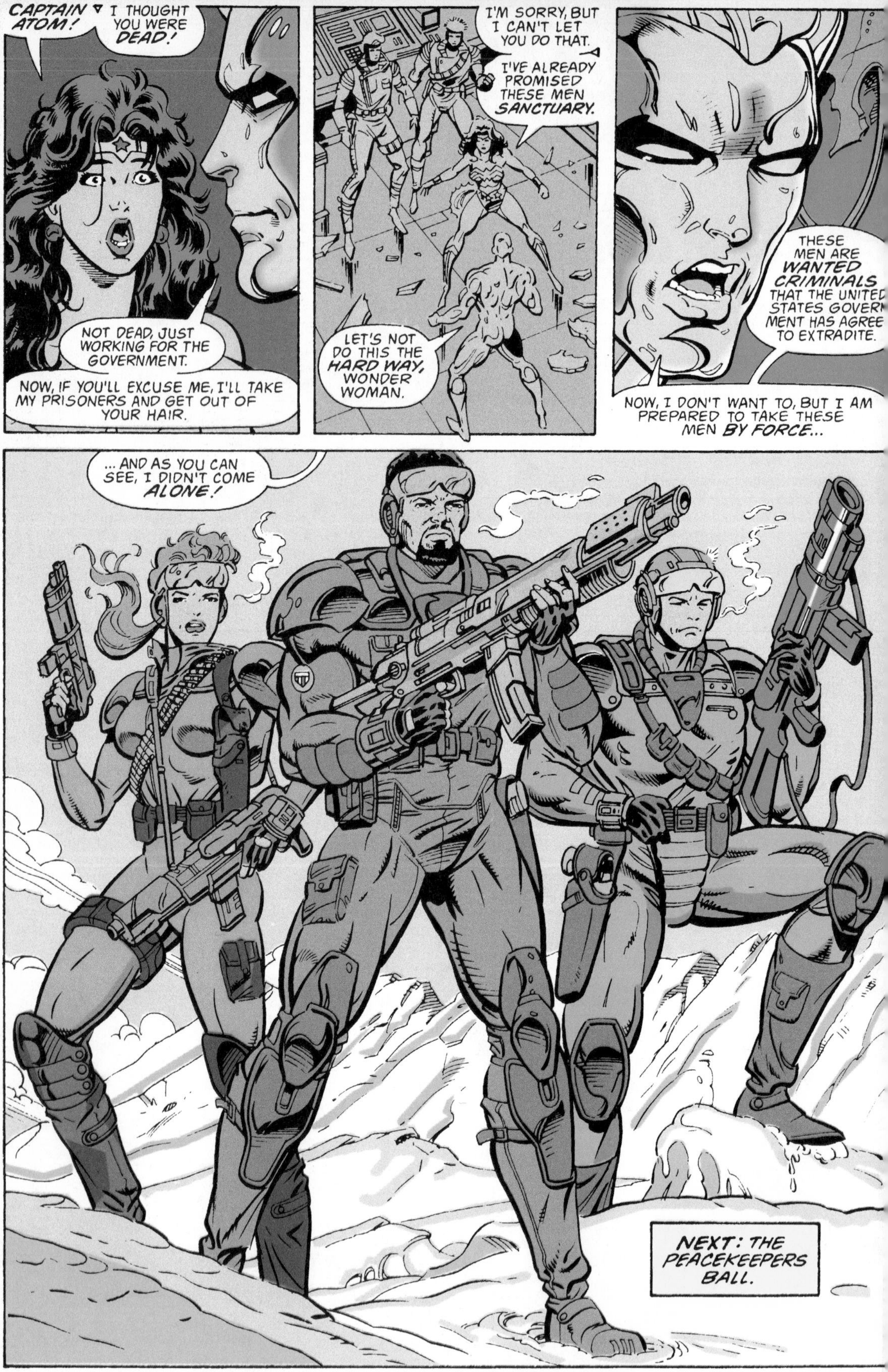

CAPTAIN ATOM!
I THOUGHT YOU WERE DEAD!
NOT DEAD, JUST WORKING FOR THE GOVERNMENT.
NOW, IF YOU'LL EXCUSE ME, I'LL TAKE MY PRISONERS AND GET OUT OF YOUR HAIR.
I'M SORRY, BUT I CAN'T LET YOU DO THAT.
I'VE ALREADY PROMISED THESE MEN SANCTUARY.
LET'S NOT DO THIS THE HARD WAY, WONDER WOMAN.
THESE MEN ARE WANTED CRIMINALS THAT THE UNITED STATES GOVERNMENT HAS AGREED TO EXTRADITE.
NOW, I DON'T WANT TO, BUT I AM PREPARED TO TAKE THESE MEN BY FORCE...
...AND AS YOU CAN SEE, I DIDN'T COME ALONE!
NEXT: THE PEACEKEEPERS BALL.

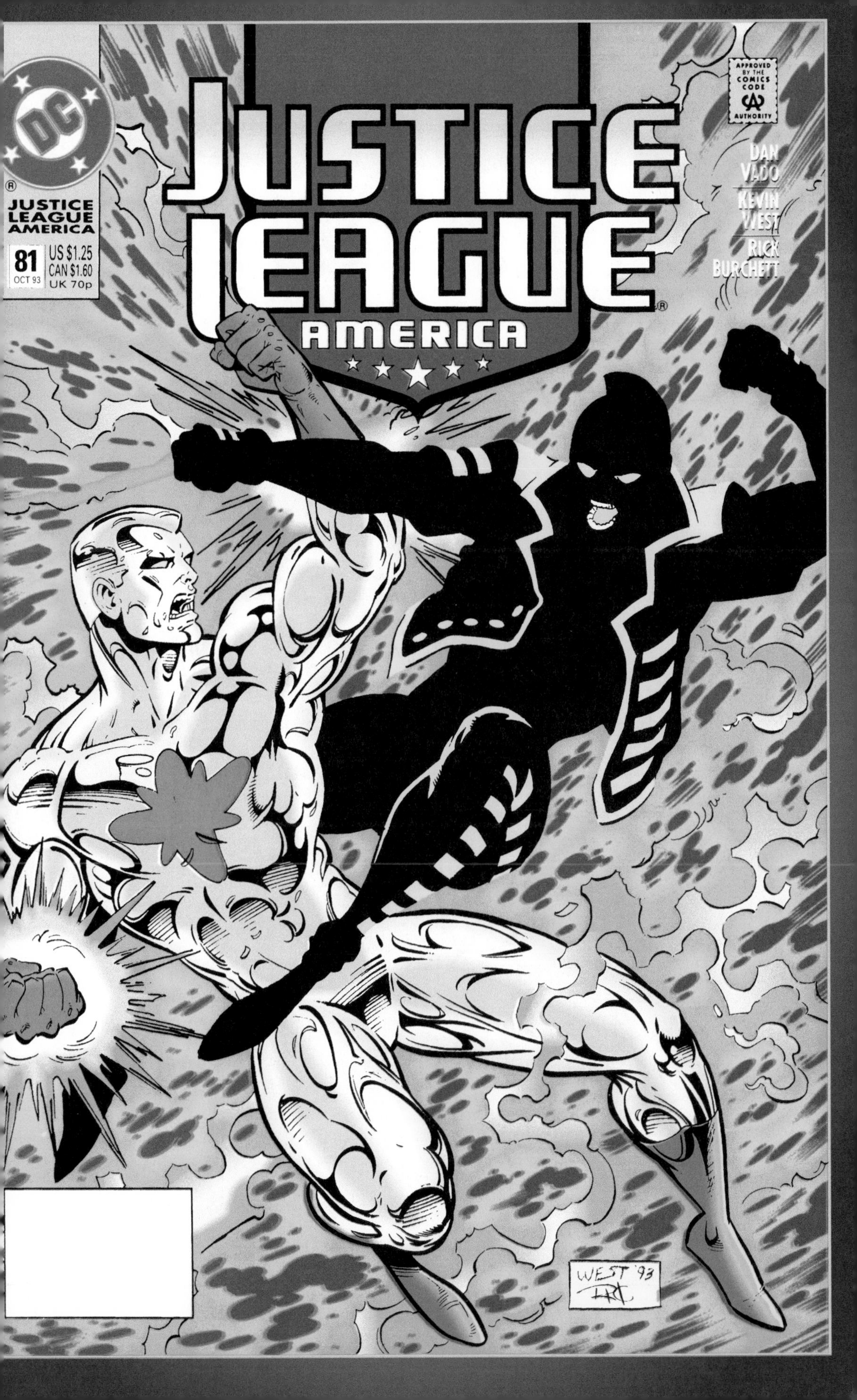

JUSTICE LEAGUE AMERICA
81
OCT 93
US $1.25
CAN $1.60
UK 70p
APPROVED BY THE COMICS CODE AUTHORITY
JUSTICE LEAGUE AMERICA
DAN VADO
KEVIN WEST
RICK BURCHETT
WEST '93

Cover art by **KEVIN WEST**
and **RICK BURCHETT**

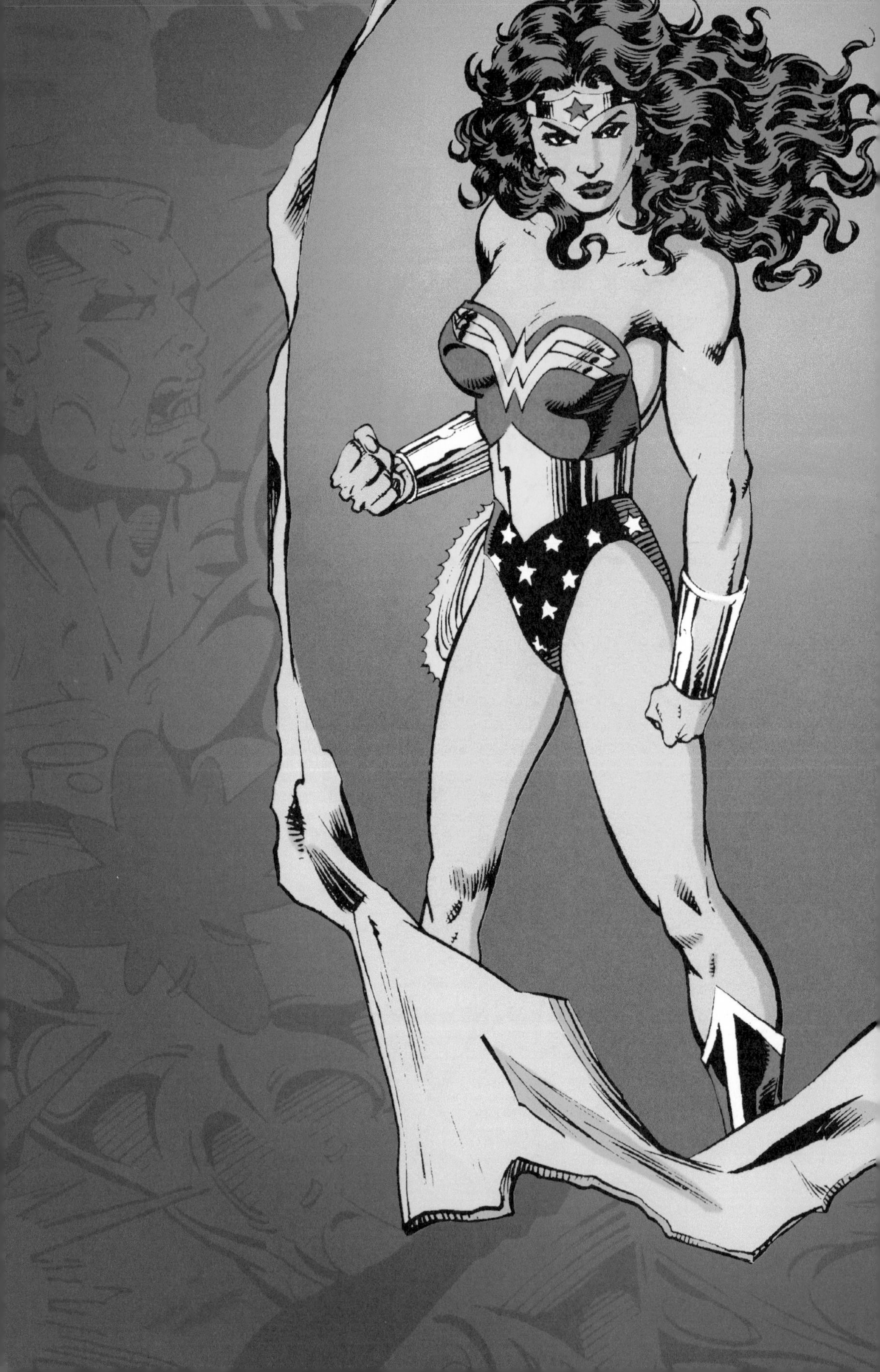

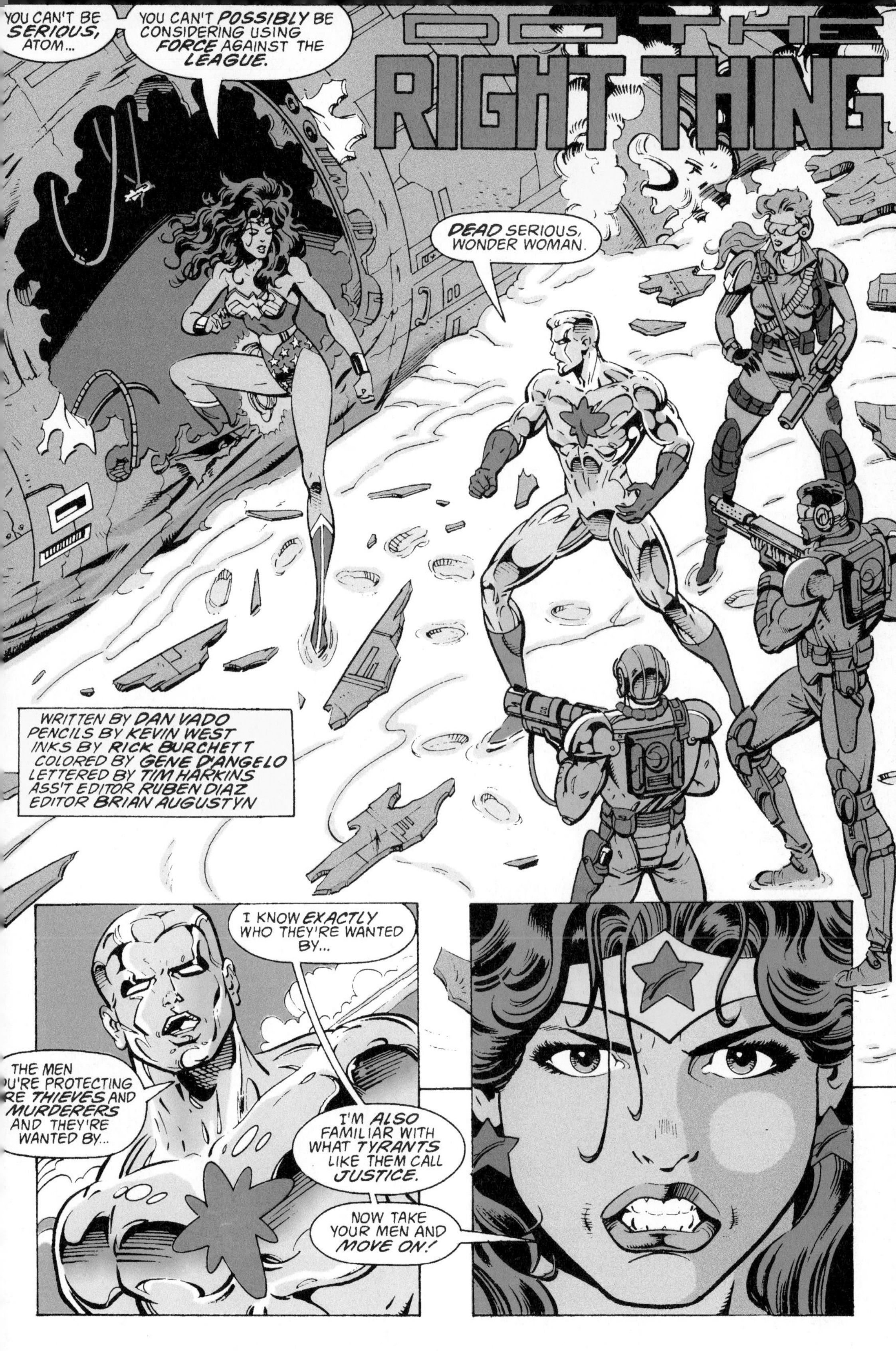

DO THE RIGHT THING
YOU CAN'T BE SERIOUS, ATOM...
YOU CAN'T POSSIBLY BE CONSIDERING USING FORCE AGAINST THE LEAGUE.
DEAD SERIOUS, WONDER WOMAN.
WRITTEN BY DAN VADO
PENCILS BY KEVIN WEST
INKS BY RICK BURCHETT
COLORED BY GENE D'ANGELO
LETTERED BY TIM HARKINS
ASS'T EDITOR RUBEN DIAZ
EDITOR BRIAN AUGUSTYN
THE MEN
U'RE PROTECTING
RE THIEVES AND MURDERERS AND THEY'RE WANTED BY...
I KNOW EXACTLY WHO THEY'RE WANTED BY...
I'M ALSO FAMILIAR WITH WHAT TYRANTS LIKE THEM CALL JUSTICE.
NOW TAKE YOUR MEN AND MOVE ON!

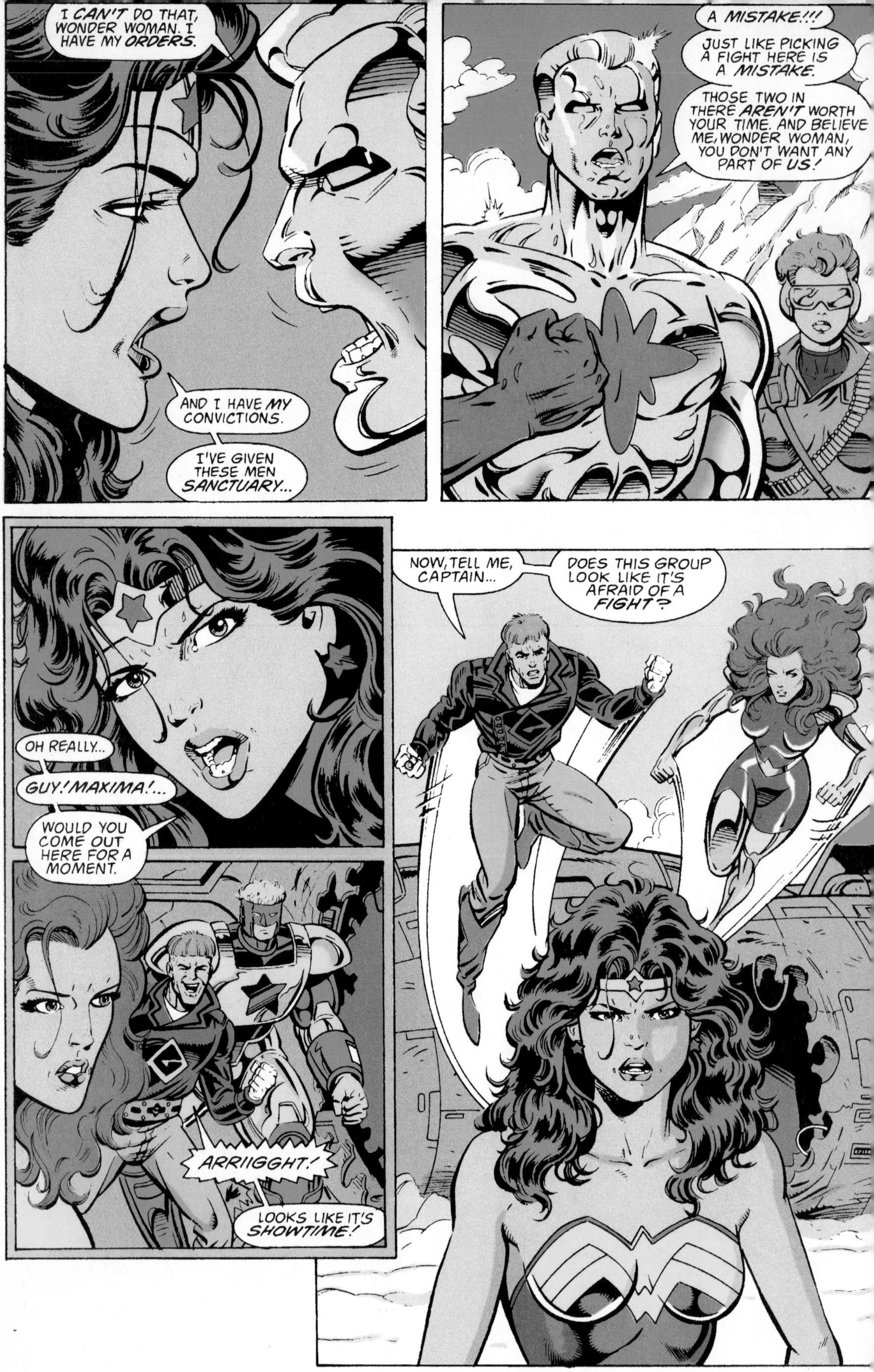

I CAN'T DO THAT, WONDER WOMAN. I HAVE MY ORDERS.
AND I HAVE MY CONVICTIONS.
I'VE GIVEN THESE MEN SANCTUARY...
A MISTAKE!!!
JUST LIKE PICKING A FIGHT HERE IS A MISTAKE.
THOSE TWO IN THERE AREN'T WORTH YOUR TIME. AND BELIEVE ME, WONDER WOMAN, YOU DON'T WANT ANY PART OF US!
OH REALLY...
GUY! MAXIMA!...
WOULD YOU COME OUT HERE FOR A MOMENT.
ARRIIGGHT!
LOOKS LIKE IT'S SHOWTIME!
NOW, TELL ME, CAPTAIN...
DOES THIS GROUP LOOK LIKE IT'S AFRAID OF A FIGHT?

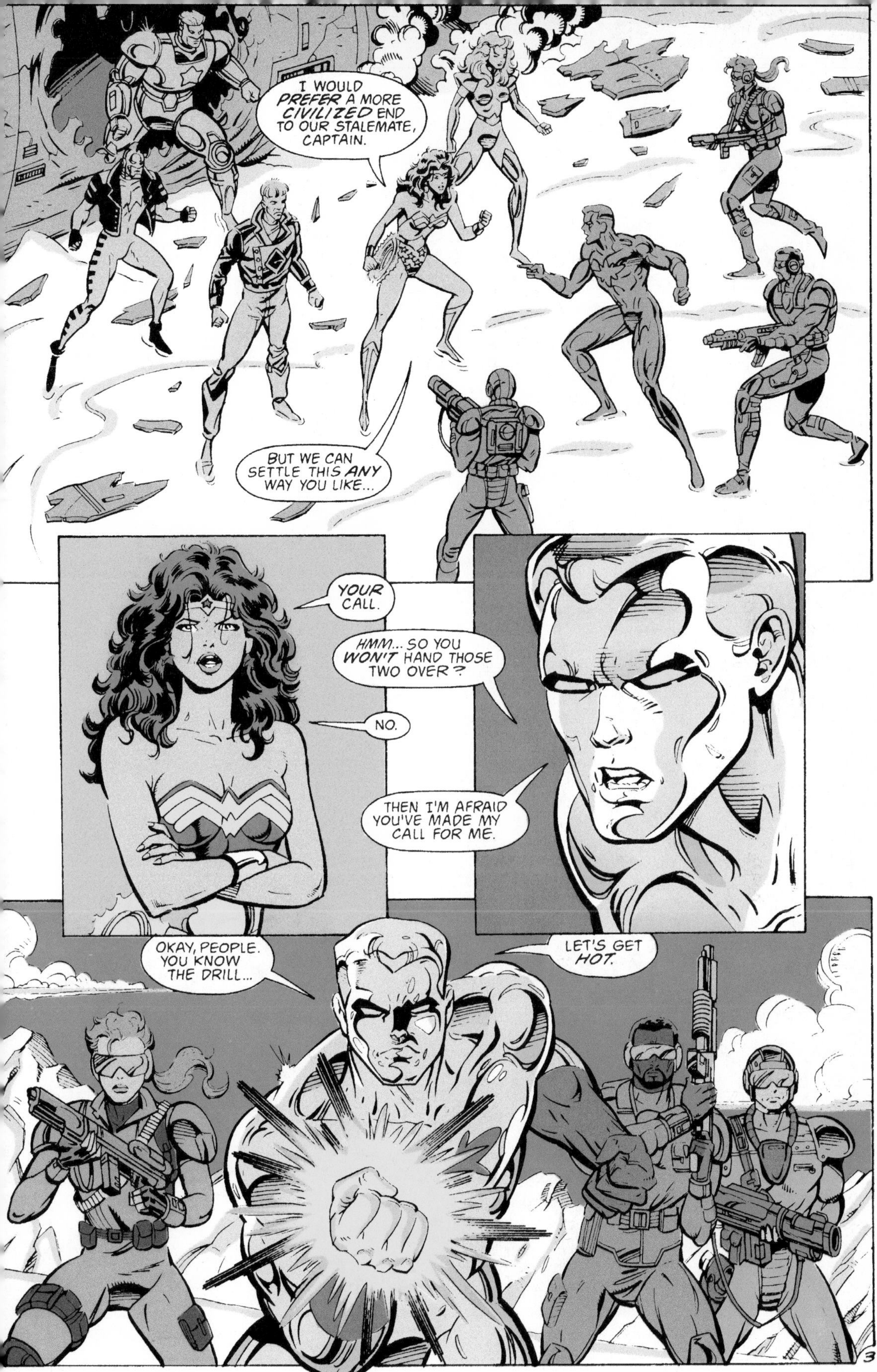
I WOULD PREFER A MORE CIVILIZED END TO OUR STALEMATE, CAPTAIN.
BUT WE CAN SETTLE THIS ANY WAY YOU LIKE...
YOUR CALL.
HMM... SO YOU WON'T HAND THOSE TWO OVER?
NO.
THEN I'M AFRAID YOU'VE MADE MY CALL FOR ME.
OKAY, PEOPLE. YOU KNOW THE DRILL...
LET'S GET HOT.

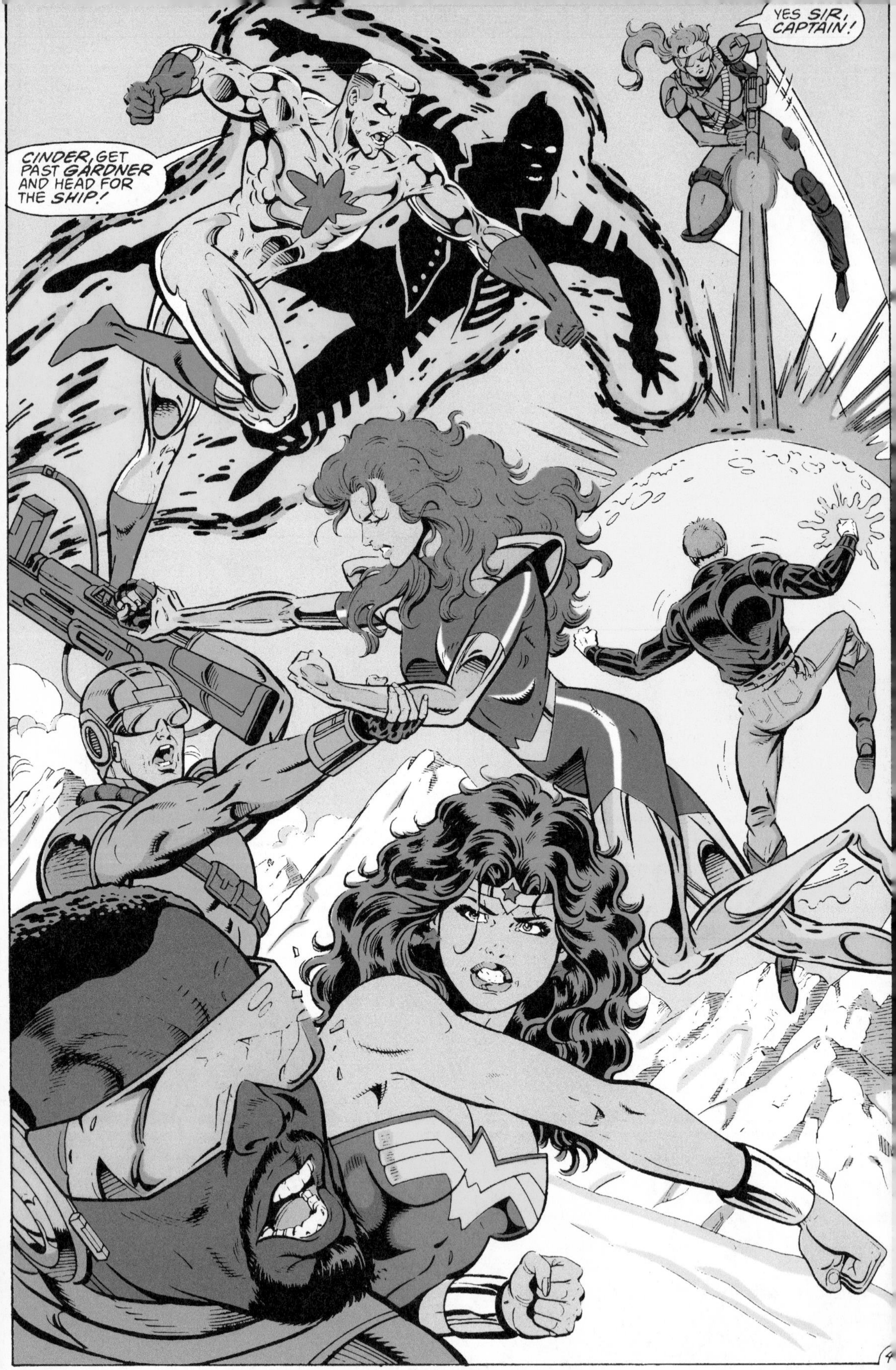
YES SIR, CAPTAIN!
CINDER, GET PAST GARDNER AND HEAD FOR THE SHIP!

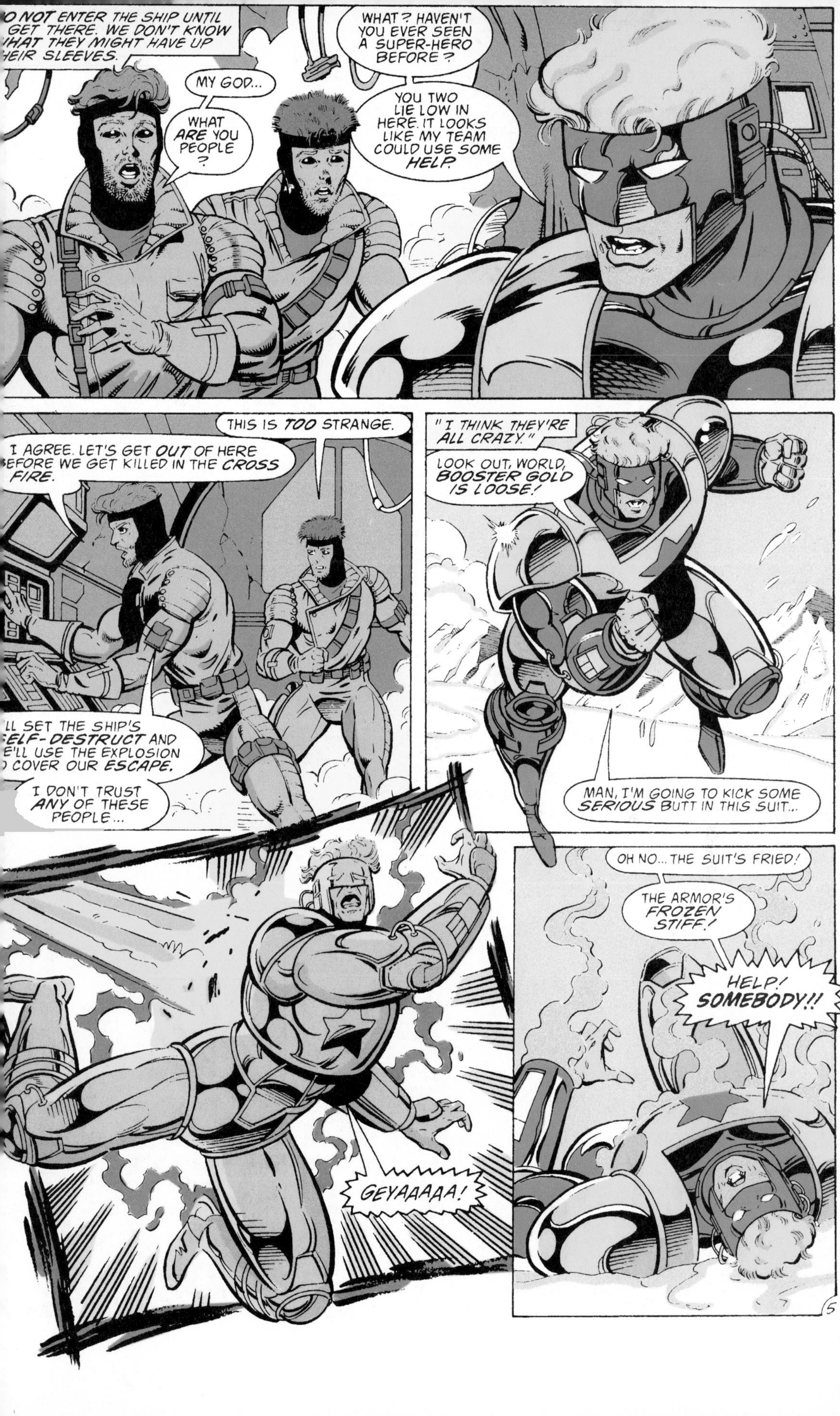

O NOT ENTER THE SHIP UNTIL GET THERE. WE DON'T KNOW HAT THEY MIGHT HAVE UP HEIR SLEEVES.
MY GOD...
WHAT ARE YOU PEOPLE ?
WHAT? HAVEN'T YOU EVER SEEN A SUPER-HERO BEFORE?
YOU TWO LIE LOW IN HERE. IT LOOKS LIKE MY TEAM COULD USE SOME HELP.
THIS IS TOO STRANGE.
I AGREE. LET'S GET OUT OF HERE EFORE WE GET KILLED IN THE CROSS FIRE.
LL SET THE SHIP'S ELF-DESTRUCT AND E'LL USE THE EXPLOSION O COVER OUR ESCAPE.
I DON'T TRUST ANY OF THESE PEOPLE...
"I THINK THEY'RE ALL CRAZY."
LOOK OUT, WORLD, BOOSTER GOLD IS LOOSE!
MAN, I'M GOING TO KICK SOME SERIOUS BUTT IN THIS SUIT...
GEYAAAAA!
OH NO... THE SUIT'S FRIED!
THE ARMOR'S FROZEN STIFF!
HELP! SOMEBODY!!

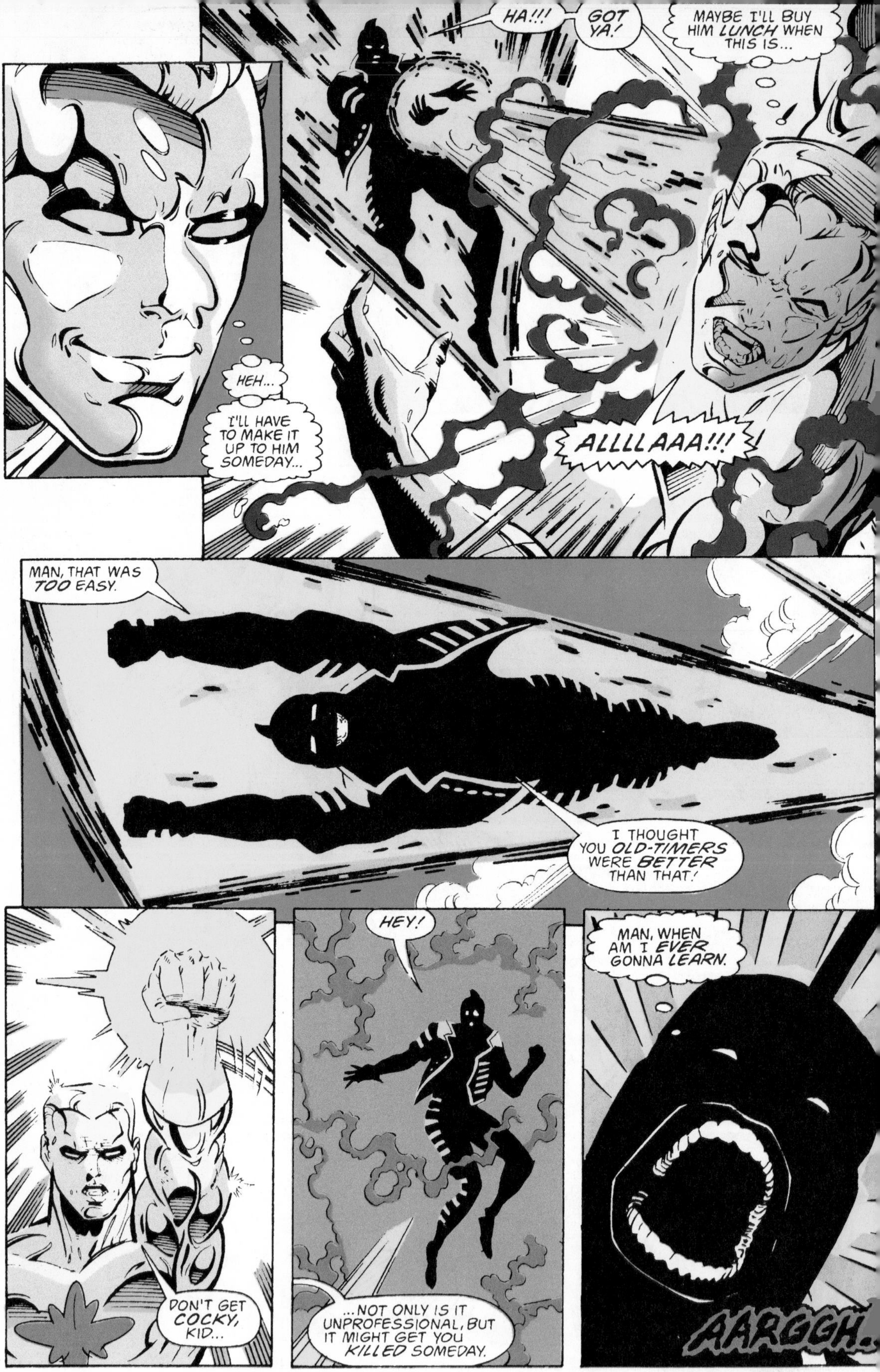
HA!!!
GOT YA!
MAYBE I'LL BUY HIM LUNCH WHEN THIS IS...
HEH...
I'LL HAVE TO MAKE IT UP TO HIM SOMEDAY...
ALLLLAAA!!!
MAN, THAT WAS TOO EASY.
I THOUGHT YOU OLD-TIMERS WERE BETTER THAN THAT!
DON'T GET COCKY, KID...
HEY!
...NOT ONLY IS IT UNPROFESSIONAL, BUT IT MIGHT GET YOU KILLED SOMEDAY.
MAN, WHEN AM I EVER GONNA LEARN.
AARGGH...

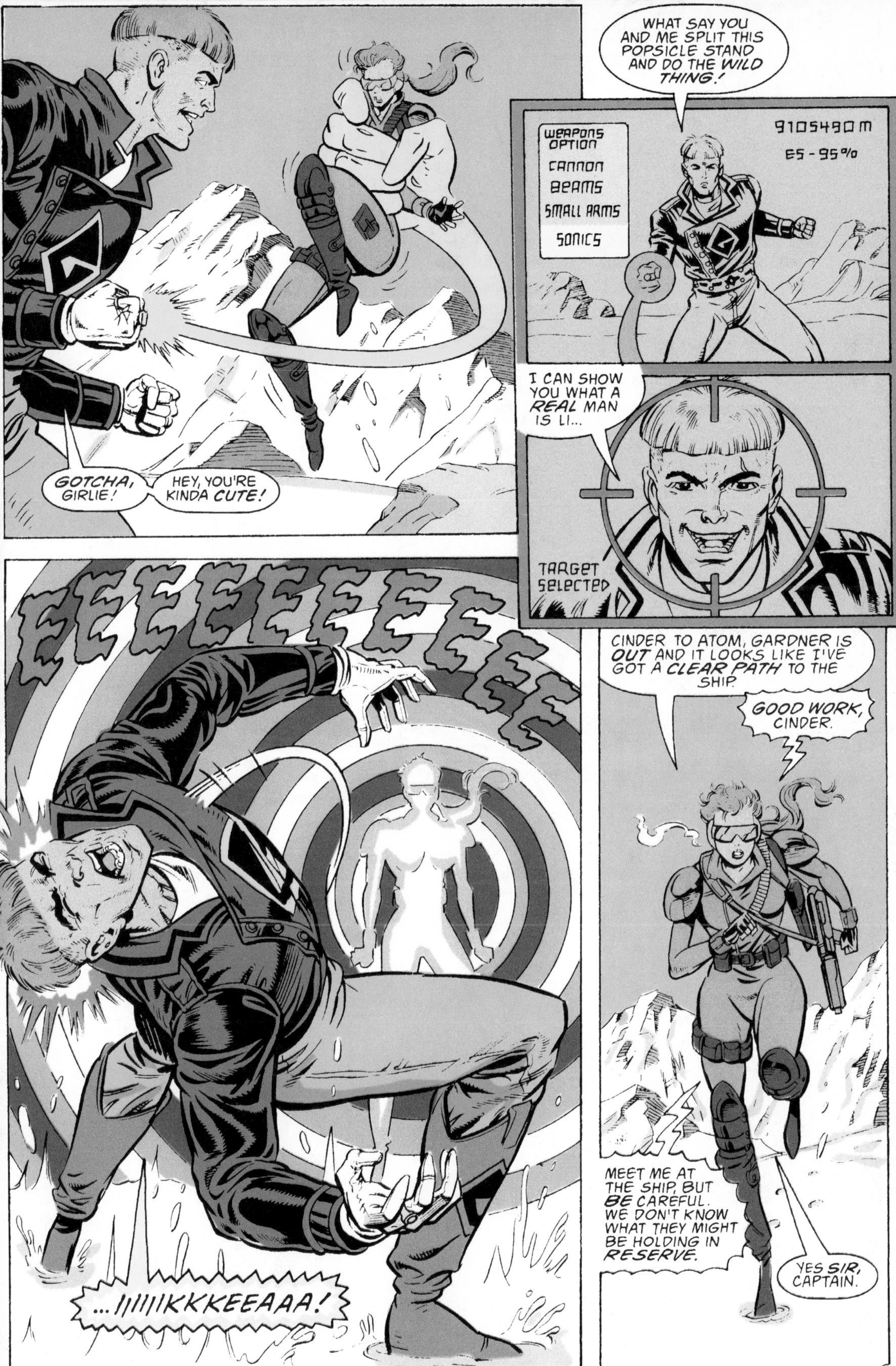
GOTCHA, GIRLIE!
HEY, YOU'RE KINDA CUTE!
WHAT SAY YOU AND ME SPLIT THIS POPSICLE STAND AND DO THE WILD THING!
WEAPONS OPTION
CANNON
BEAMS
SMALL ARMS
SONICS
9105490 M
ES - 95%
I CAN SHOW YOU WHAT A REAL MAN IS LI...
TARGET SELECTED
EEEEEEEEEEEE
...IIIIIIKKKEEAAA!
CINDER TO ATOM, GARDNER IS OUT AND IT LOOKS LIKE I'VE GOT A CLEAR PATH TO THE SHIP.
GOOD WORK, CINDER.
MEET ME AT THE SHIP, BUT BE CAREFUL. WE DON'T KNOW WHAT THEY MIGHT BE HOLDING IN RESERVE.
YES SIR, CAPTAIN.

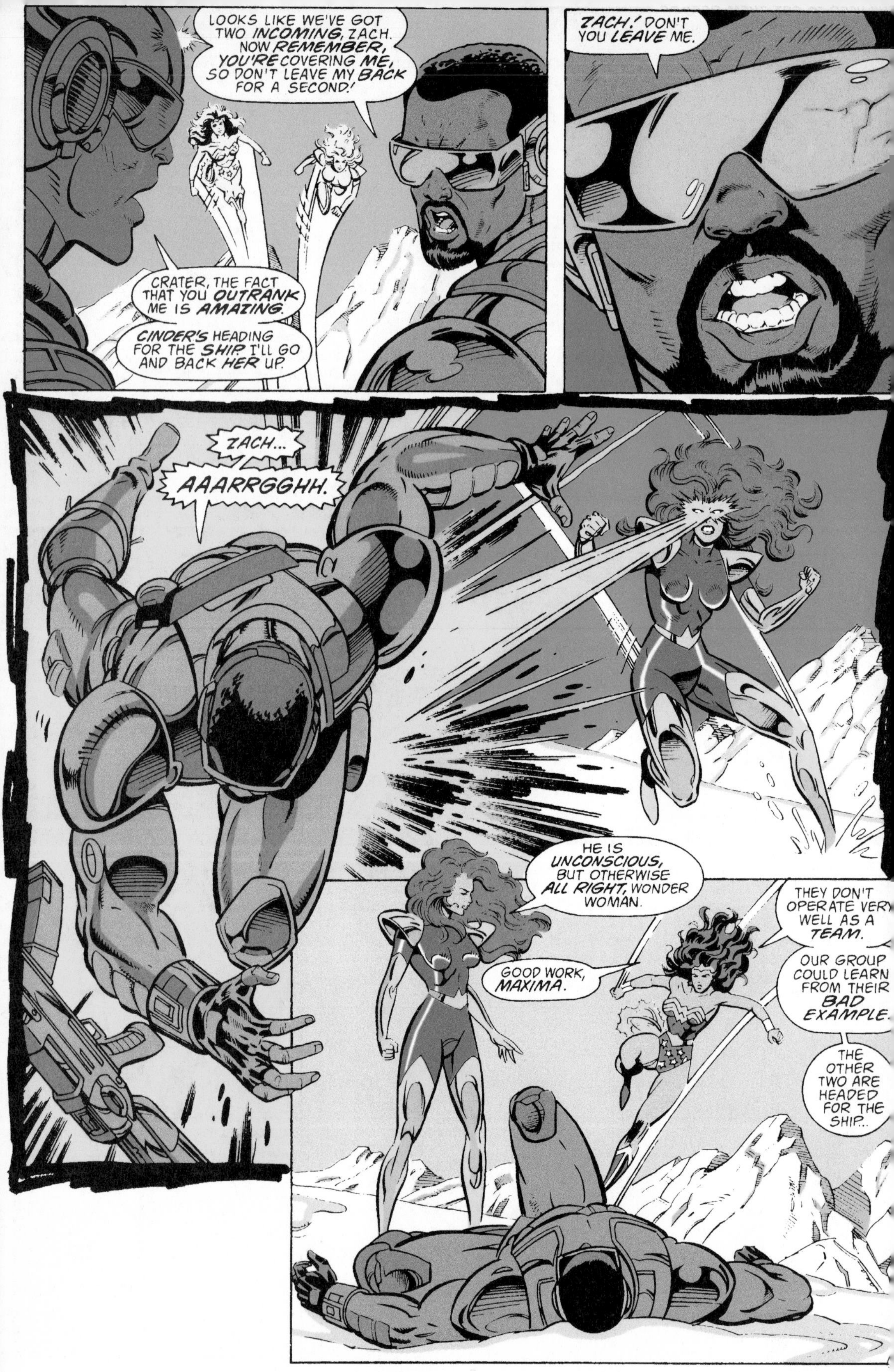

LOOKS LIKE WE'VE GOT TWO INCOMING, ZACH. NOW REMEMBER, YOU'RE COVERING ME, SO DON'T LEAVE MY BACK FOR A SECOND!
CRATER, THE FACT THAT YOU OUTRANK ME IS AMAZING.
CINDER'S HEADING FOR THE SHIP. I'LL GO AND BACK HER UP.
ZACH! DON'T YOU LEAVE ME.
ZACH...
AAARRGGHH.
HE IS UNCONSCIOUS, BUT OTHERWISE ALL RIGHT, WONDER WOMAN.
GOOD WORK, MAXIMA.
THEY DON'T OPERATE VERY WELL AS A TEAM.
OUR GROUP COULD LEARN FROM THEIR BAD EXAMPLE.
THE OTHER TWO ARE HEADED FOR THE SHIP...

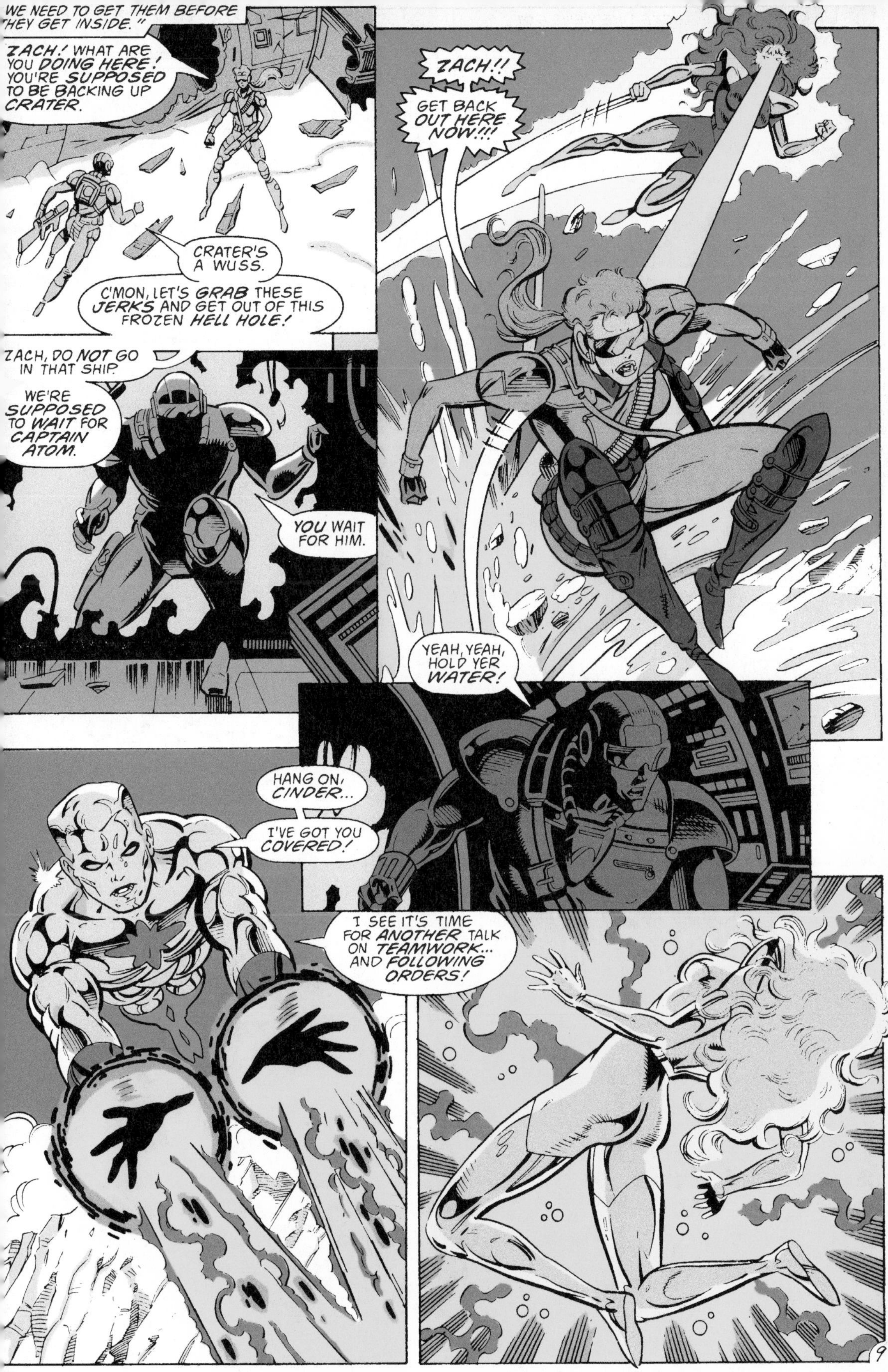

WE NEED TO GET THEM BEFORE THEY GET INSIDE."
ZACH! WHAT ARE YOU DOING HERE! YOU'RE SUPPOSED TO BE BACKING UP CRATER.
CRATER'S A WUSS.
C'MON, LET'S GRAB THESE JERKS AND GET OUT OF THIS FROZEN HELL HOLE!
ZACH!!
GET BACK OUT HERE NOW!!!
ZACH, DO NOT GO IN THAT SHIP.
WE'RE SUPPOSED TO WAIT FOR CAPTAIN ATOM.
YOU WAIT FOR HIM.
YEAH, YEAH, HOLD YER WATER!
HANG ON, CINDER...
I'VE GOT YOU COVERED!
I SEE IT'S TIME FOR ANOTHER TALK ON TEAMWORK... AND FOLLOWING ORDERS!

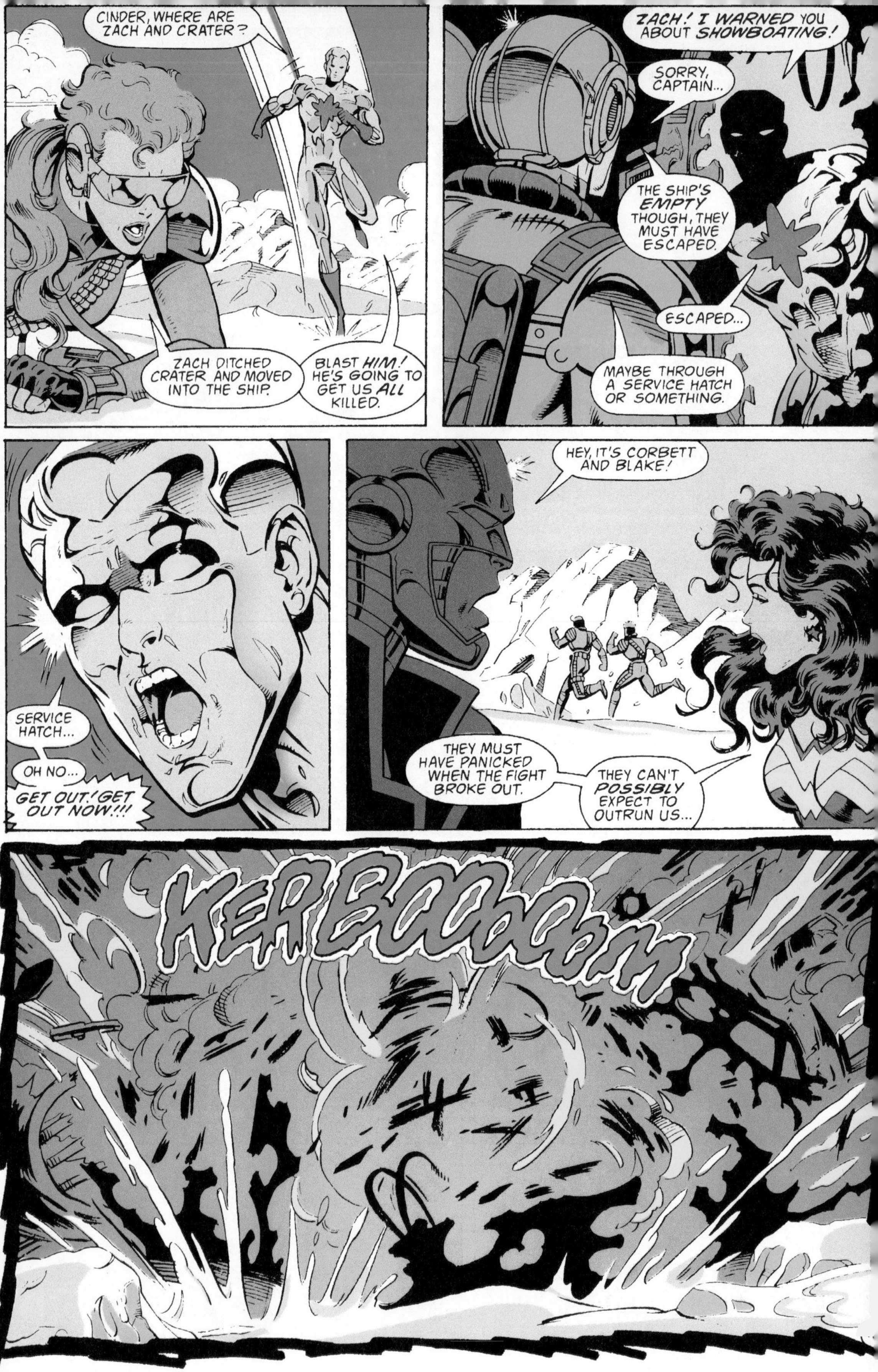
CINDER, WHERE ARE ZACH AND CRATER?
ZACH DITCHED CRATER AND MOVED INTO THE SHIP.
BLAST HIM! HE'S GOING TO GET US ALL KILLED.
ZACH! I WARNED YOU ABOUT SHOWBOATING!
SORRY, CAPTAIN...
THE SHIP'S EMPTY THOUGH, THEY MUST HAVE ESCAPED.
ESCAPED...
MAYBE THROUGH A SERVICE HATCH OR SOMETHING.
SERVICE HATCH...
OH NO...
GET OUT! GET OUT NOW!!!
HEY, IT'S CORBETT AND BLAKE!
THEY MUST HAVE PANICKED WHEN THE FIGHT BROKE OUT.
THEY CAN'T POSSIBLY EXPECT TO OUTRUN US...
KERBOOOOOM

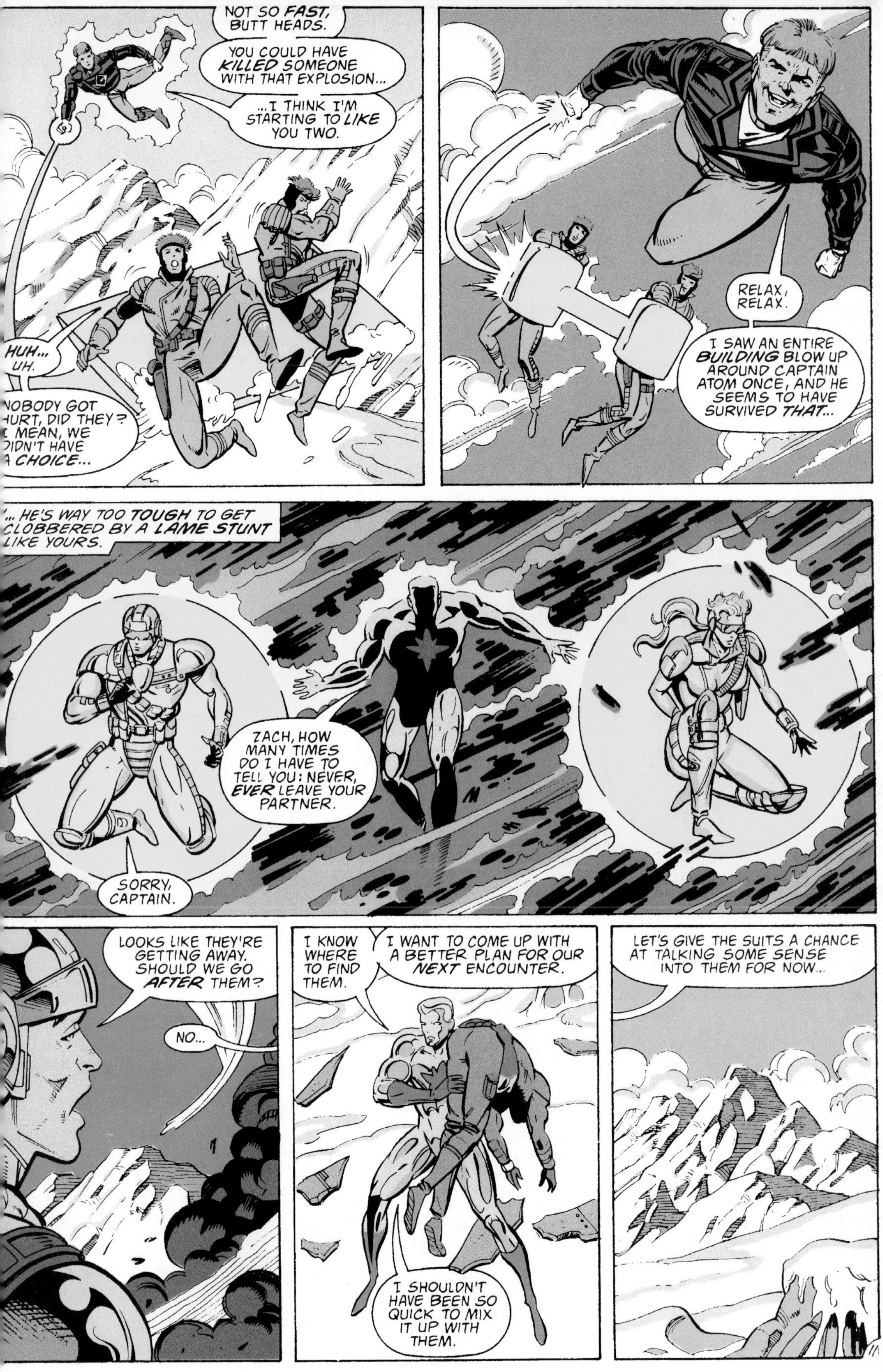
NOT SO FAST, BUTT HEADS.
YOU COULD HAVE KILLED SOMEONE WITH THAT EXPLOSION...
...I THINK I'M STARTING TO LIKE YOU TWO.
HUH... UH.
NOBODY GOT HURT, DID THEY? I MEAN, WE DIDN'T HAVE A CHOICE...
RELAX, RELAX.
I SAW AN ENTIRE BUILDING BLOW UP AROUND CAPTAIN ATOM ONCE, AND HE SEEMS TO HAVE SURVIVED THAT...
...HE'S WAY TOO TOUGH TO GET CLOBBERED BY A LAME STUNT LIKE YOURS.
ZACH, HOW MANY TIMES DO I HAVE TO TELL YOU: NEVER, EVER LEAVE YOUR PARTNER.
SORRY, CAPTAIN.
LOOKS LIKE THEY'RE GETTING AWAY. SHOULD WE GO AFTER THEM?
NO...
I KNOW WHERE TO FIND THEM.
I WANT TO COME UP WITH A BETTER PLAN FOR OUR NEXT ENCOUNTER.
I SHOULDN'T HAVE BEEN SO QUICK TO MIX IT UP WITH THEM.
LET'S GIVE THE SUITS A CHANCE AT TALKING SOME SENSE INTO THEM FOR NOW...

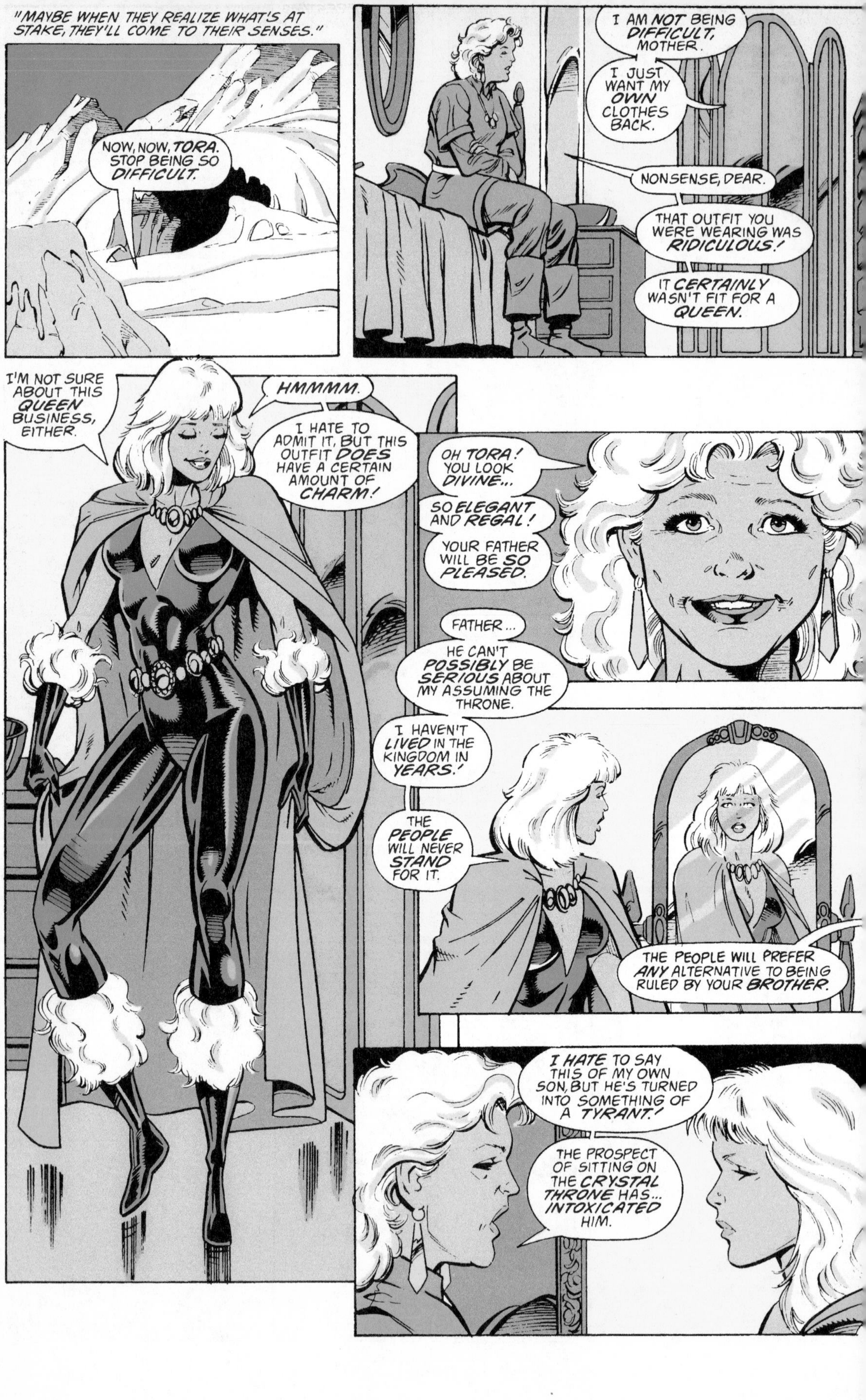
"MAYBE WHEN THEY REALIZE WHAT'S AT STAKE, THEY'LL COME TO THEIR SENSES."
NOW, NOW, TORA. STOP BEING SO DIFFICULT.
I AM NOT BEING DIFFICULT, MOTHER.
I JUST WANT MY OWN CLOTHES BACK.
NONSENSE, DEAR.
THAT OUTFIT YOU WERE WEARING WAS RIDICULOUS!
IT CERTAINLY WASN'T FIT FOR A QUEEN.
I'M NOT SURE ABOUT THIS QUEEN BUSINESS, EITHER.
HMMMM.
I HATE TO ADMIT IT, BUT THIS OUTFIT DOES HAVE A CERTAIN AMOUNT OF CHARM!
OH TORA! YOU LOOK DIVINE...
SO ELEGANT AND REGAL!
YOUR FATHER WILL BE SO PLEASED.
FATHER...
HE CAN'T POSSIBLY BE SERIOUS ABOUT MY ASSUMING THE THRONE.
I HAVEN'T LIVED IN THE KINGDOM IN YEARS!
THE PEOPLE WILL NEVER STAND FOR IT.
THE PEOPLE WILL PREFER ANY ALTERNATIVE TO BEING RULED BY YOUR BROTHER.
I HATE TO SAY THIS OF MY OWN SON, BUT HE'S TURNED INTO SOMETHING OF A TYRANT!
THE PROSPECT OF SITTING ON THE CRYSTAL THRONE HAS... INTOXICATED HIM.

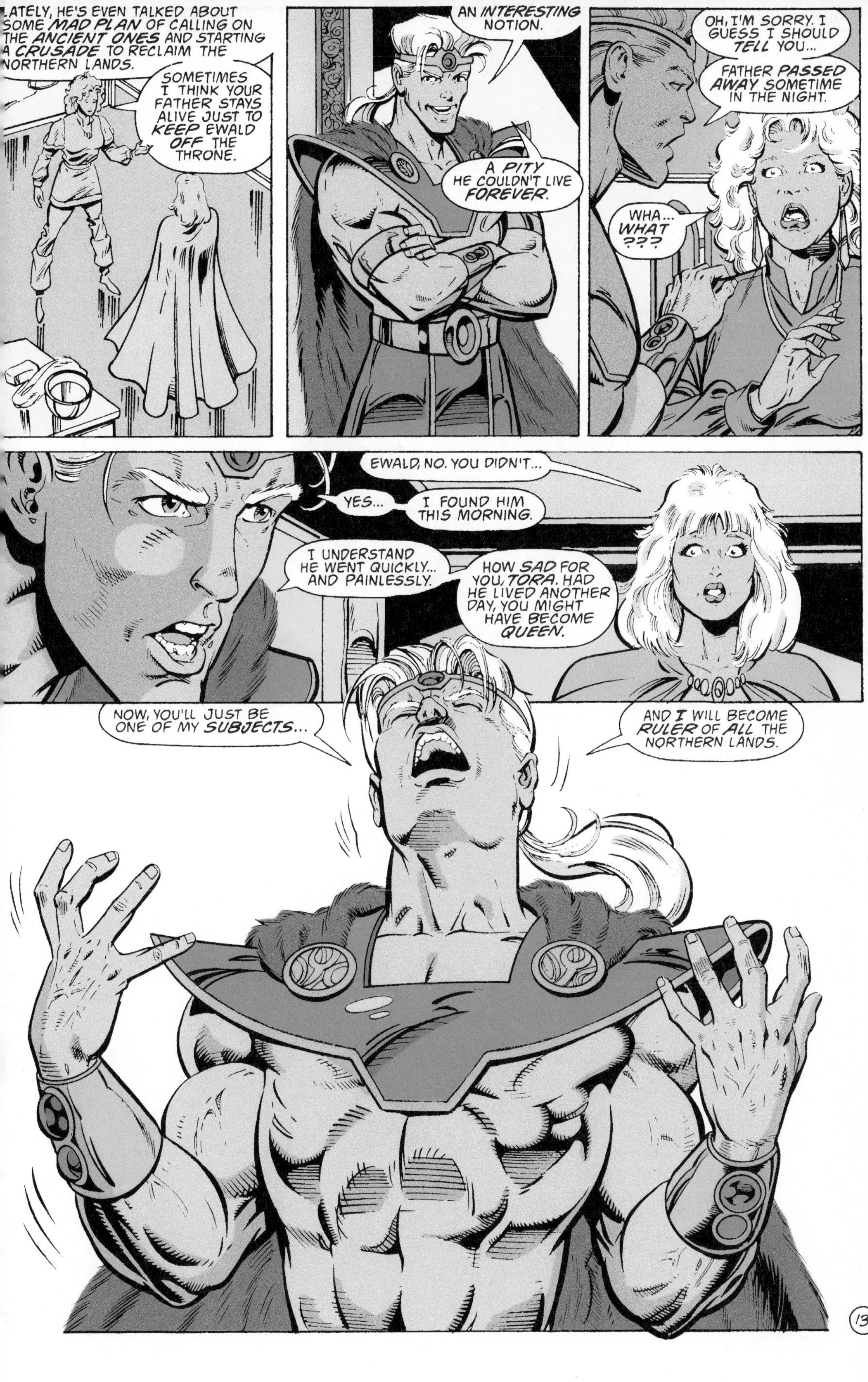
LATELY, HE'S EVEN TALKED ABOUT SOME MAD PLAN OF CALLING ON THE ANCIENT ONES AND STARTING A CRUSADE TO RECLAIM THE NORTHERN LANDS.
SOMETIMES I THINK YOUR FATHER STAYS ALIVE JUST TO KEEP EWALD OFF THE THRONE.
AN INTERESTING NOTION.
A PITY HE COULDN'T LIVE FOREVER.
OH, I'M SORRY. I GUESS I SHOULD TELL YOU...
FATHER PASSED AWAY SOMETIME IN THE NIGHT.
WHA... WHAT ???
EWALD, NO. YOU DIDN'T...
YES...
I FOUND HIM THIS MORNING.
I UNDERSTAND HE WENT QUICKLY... AND PAINLESSLY.
HOW SAD FOR YOU, TORA. HAD HE LIVED ANOTHER DAY, YOU MIGHT HAVE BECOME QUEEN.
NOW, YOU'LL JUST BE ONE OF MY SUBJECTS...
AND I WILL BECOME RULER OF ALL THE NORTHERN LANDS.

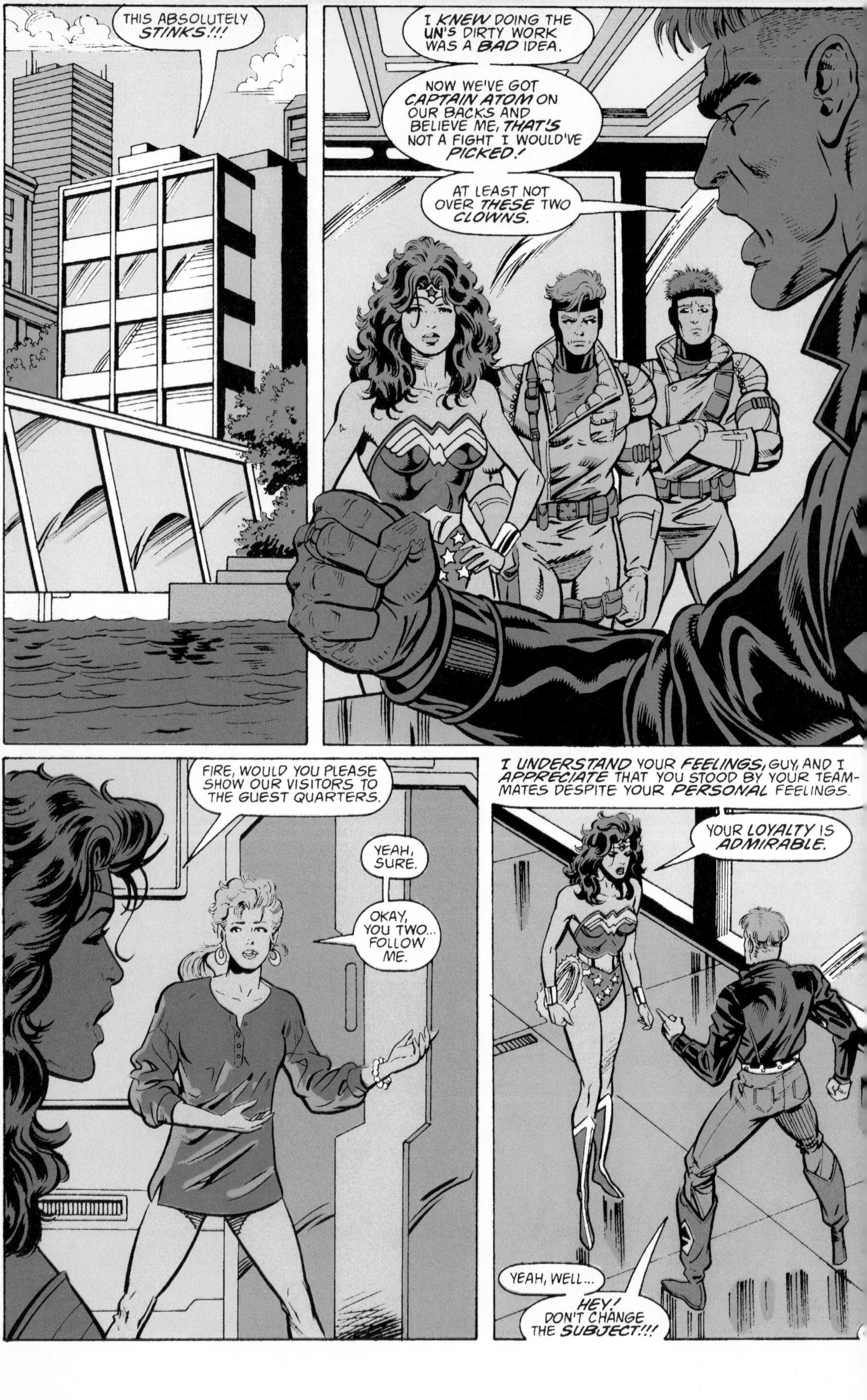

THIS ABSOLUTELY STINKS!!!
I KNEW DOING THE UN'S DIRTY WORK WAS A BAD IDEA.
NOW WE'VE GOT CAPTAIN ATOM ON OUR BACKS AND BELIEVE ME, THAT'S NOT A FIGHT I WOULD'VE PICKED!
AT LEAST NOT OVER THESE TWO CLOWNS.
FIRE, WOULD YOU PLEASE SHOW OUR VISITORS TO THE GUEST QUARTERS.
YEAH, SURE.
OKAY, YOU TWO... FOLLOW ME.
I UNDERSTAND YOUR FEELINGS, GUY, AND I APPRECIATE THAT YOU STOOD BY YOUR TEAM-MATES DESPITE YOUR PERSONAL FEELINGS.
YOUR LOYALTY IS ADMIRABLE.
YEAH, WELL...
HEY! DON'T CHANGE THE SUBJECT!!!

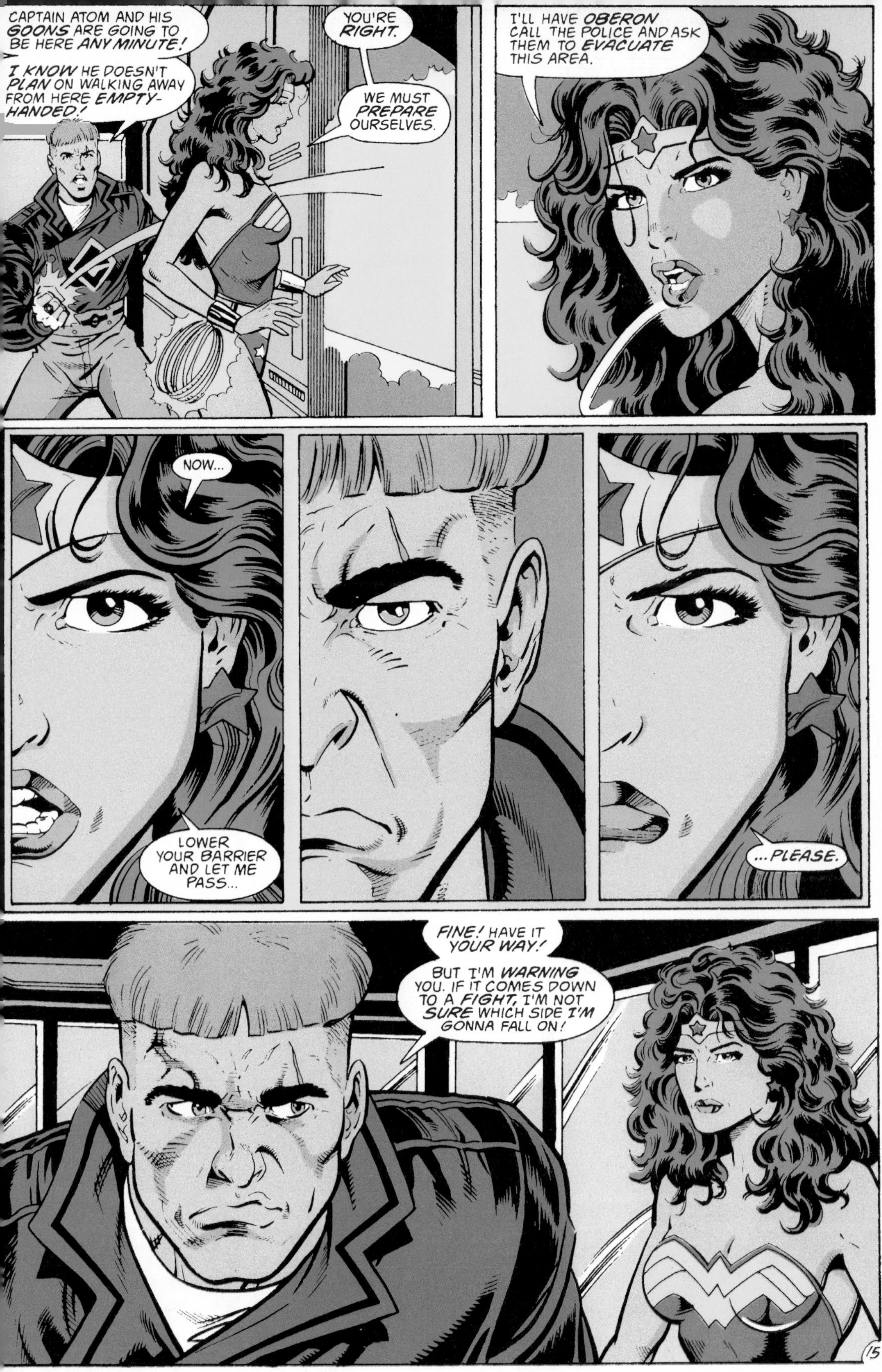
CAPTAIN ATOM AND HIS GOONS ARE GOING TO BE HERE ANY MINUTE!
I KNOW HE DOESN'T PLAN ON WALKING AWAY FROM HERE EMPTY-HANDED!
YOU'RE RIGHT.
WE MUST PREPARE OURSELVES.
I'LL HAVE OBERON CALL THE POLICE AND ASK THEM TO EVACUATE THIS AREA.
NOW...
LOWER YOUR BARRIER AND LET ME PASS...
...PLEASE.
FINE! HAVE IT YOUR WAY!
BUT I'M WARNING YOU. IF IT COMES DOWN TO A FIGHT, I'M NOT SURE WHICH SIDE I'M GONNA FALL ON!
15

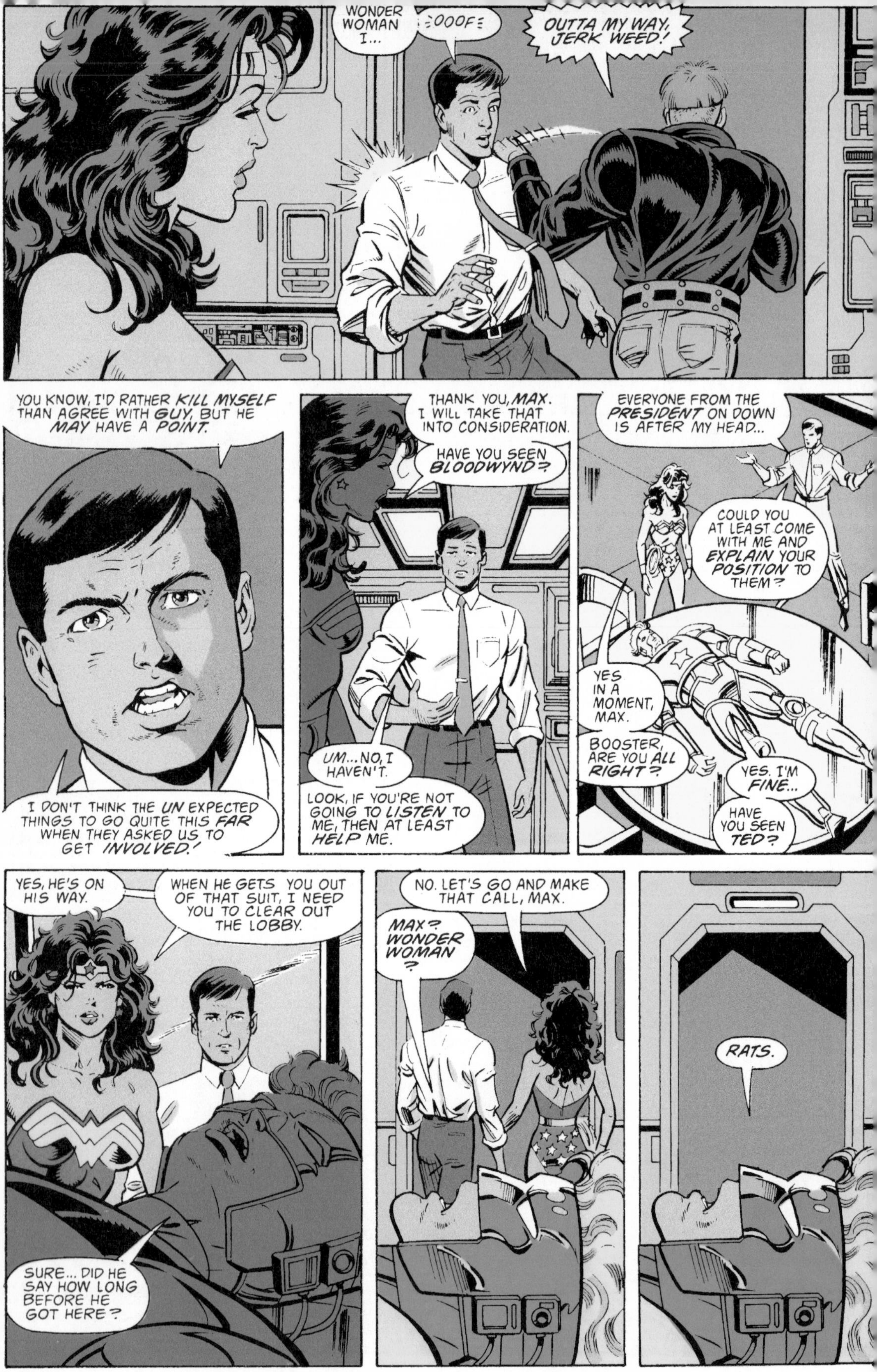
WONDER WOMAN I...
OOOF
OUTTA MY WAY, JERK WEED!
YOU KNOW, I'D RATHER KILL MYSELF THAN AGREE WITH GUY, BUT HE MAY HAVE A POINT.
I DON'T THINK THE UN EXPECTED THINGS TO GO QUITE THIS FAR WHEN THEY ASKED US TO GET INVOLVED!
THANK YOU, MAX. I WILL TAKE THAT INTO CONSIDERATION.
HAVE YOU SEEN BLOODWYND?
UM... NO, I HAVEN'T.
LOOK, IF YOU'RE NOT GOING TO LISTEN TO ME, THEN AT LEAST HELP ME.
EVERYONE FROM THE PRESIDENT ON DOWN IS AFTER MY HEAD...
COULD YOU AT LEAST COME WITH ME AND EXPLAIN YOUR POSITION TO THEM?
YES IN A MOMENT, MAX.
BOOSTER, ARE YOU ALL RIGHT?
YES. I'M FINE...
HAVE YOU SEEN TED?
YES, HE'S ON HIS WAY.
WHEN HE GETS YOU OUT OF THAT SUIT, I NEED YOU TO CLEAR OUT THE LOBBY.
SURE... DID HE SAY HOW LONG BEFORE HE GOT HERE?
NO. LET'S GO AND MAKE THAT CALL, MAX.
MAX? WONDER WOMAN ?
RATS.

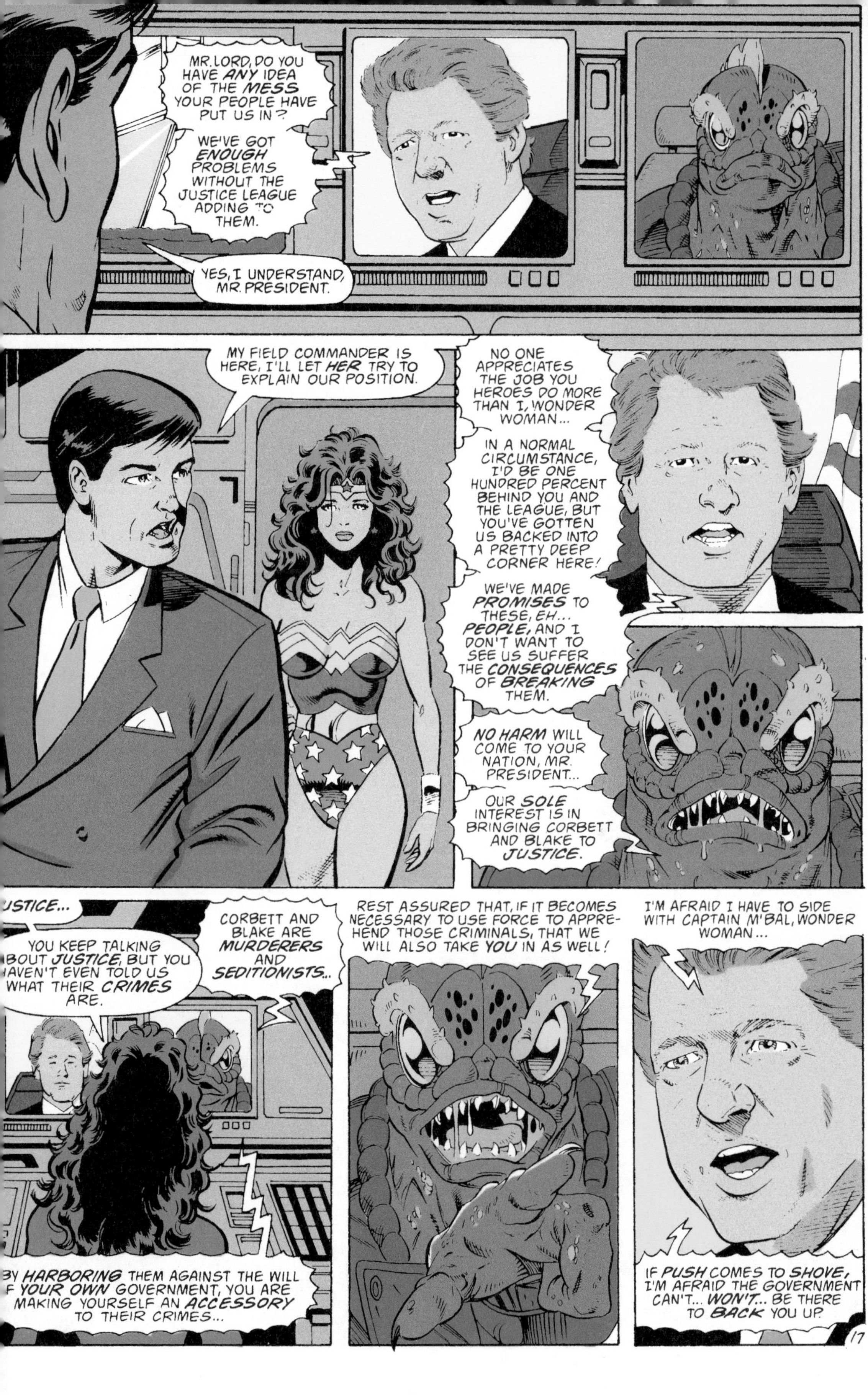
MR. LORD, DO YOU HAVE ANY IDEA OF THE MESS YOUR PEOPLE HAVE PUT US IN?
WE'VE GOT ENOUGH PROBLEMS WITHOUT THE JUSTICE LEAGUE ADDING TO THEM.
YES, I UNDERSTAND, MR. PRESIDENT.
MY FIELD COMMANDER IS HERE. I'LL LET HER TRY TO EXPLAIN OUR POSITION.
NO ONE APPRECIATES THE JOB YOU HEROES DO MORE THAN I, WONDER WOMAN...
IN A NORMAL CIRCUMSTANCE, I'D BE ONE HUNDRED PERCENT BEHIND YOU AND THE LEAGUE, BUT YOU'VE GOTTEN US BACKED INTO A PRETTY DEEP CORNER HERE!
WE'VE MADE PROMISES TO THESE, EH... PEOPLE, AND I DON'T WANT TO SEE US SUFFER THE CONSEQUENCES OF BREAKING THEM.
NO HARM WILL COME TO YOUR NATION, MR. PRESIDENT...
OUR SOLE INTEREST IS IN BRINGING CORBETT AND BLAKE TO JUSTICE.
USTICE...
YOU KEEP TALKING BOUT JUSTICE, BUT YOU HAVEN'T EVEN TOLD US WHAT THEIR CRIMES ARE.
CORBETT AND BLAKE ARE MURDERERS AND SEDITIONISTS...
BY HARBORING THEM AGAINST THE WILL F YOUR OWN GOVERNMENT, YOU ARE MAKING YOURSELF AN ACCESSORY TO THEIR CRIMES...
REST ASSURED THAT, IF IT BECOMES NECESSARY TO USE FORCE TO APPREHEND THOSE CRIMINALS, THAT WE WILL ALSO TAKE YOU IN AS WELL!
I'M AFRAID I HAVE TO SIDE WITH CAPTAIN M'BAL, WONDER WOMAN...
IF PUSH COMES TO SHOVE, I'M AFRAID THE GOVERNMENT CAN'T... WON'T... BE THERE TO BACK YOU UP.

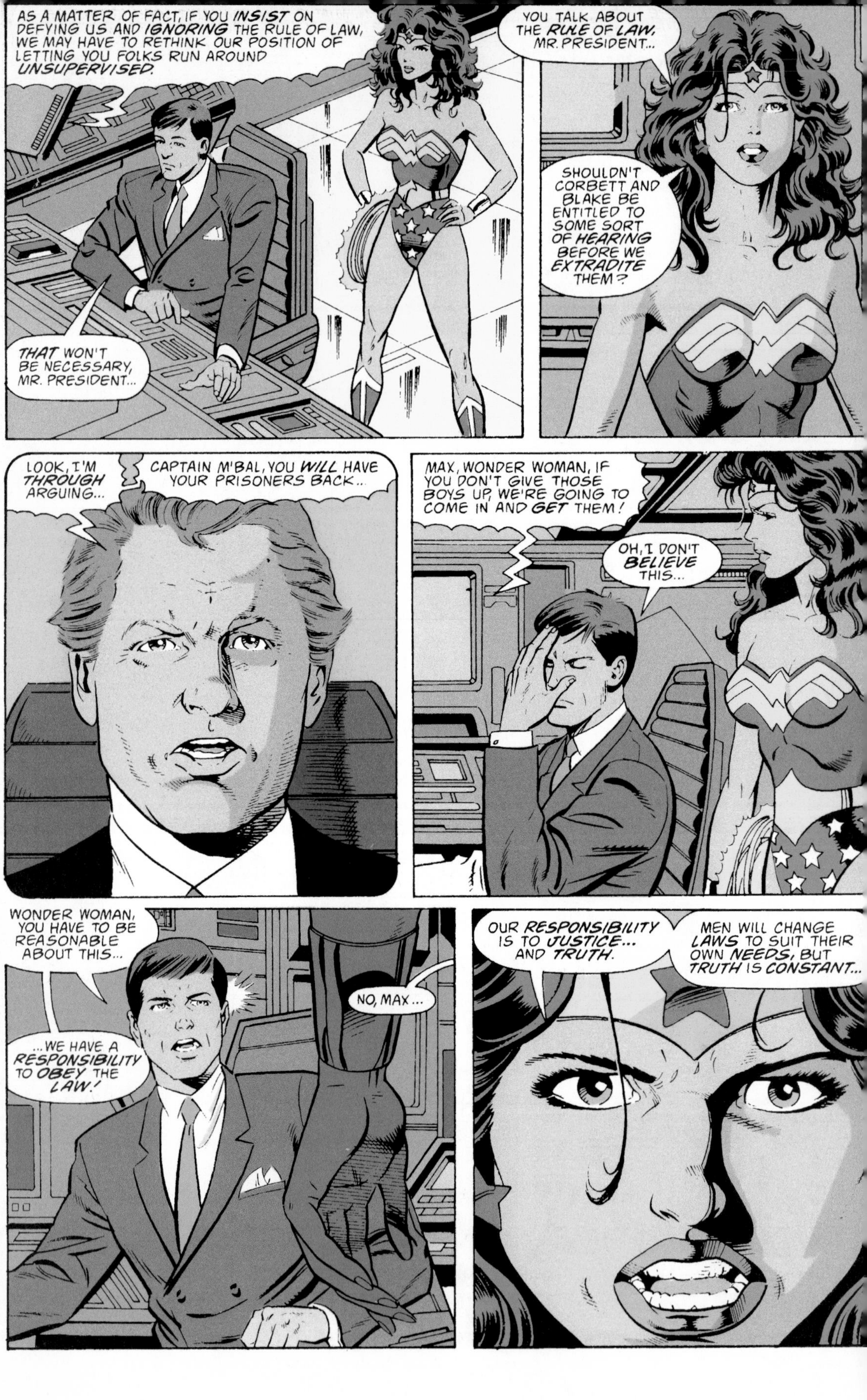
AS A MATTER OF FACT, IF YOU INSIST ON DEFYING US AND IGNORING THE RULE OF LAW, WE MAY HAVE TO RETHINK OUR POSITION OF LETTING YOU FOLKS RUN AROUND UNSUPERVISED.
THAT WON'T BE NECESSARY, MR. PRESIDENT...
YOU TALK ABOUT THE RULE OF LAW, MR. PRESIDENT...
SHOULDN'T CORBETT AND BLAKE BE ENTITLED TO SOME SORT OF HEARING BEFORE WE EXTRADITE THEM?
LOOK, I'M THROUGH ARGUING...
CAPTAIN M'BAL, YOU WILL HAVE YOUR PRISONERS BACK...
MAX, WONDER WOMAN, IF YOU DON'T GIVE THOSE BOYS UP, WE'RE GOING TO COME IN AND GET THEM!
OH, I DON'T BELIEVE THIS...
WONDER WOMAN, YOU HAVE TO BE REASONABLE ABOUT THIS...
...WE HAVE A RESPONSIBILITY TO OBEY THE LAW!
NO, MAX...
OUR RESPONSIBILITY IS TO JUSTICE... AND TRUTH.
MEN WILL CHANGE LAWS TO SUIT THEIR OWN NEEDS, BUT TRUTH IS CONSTANT...

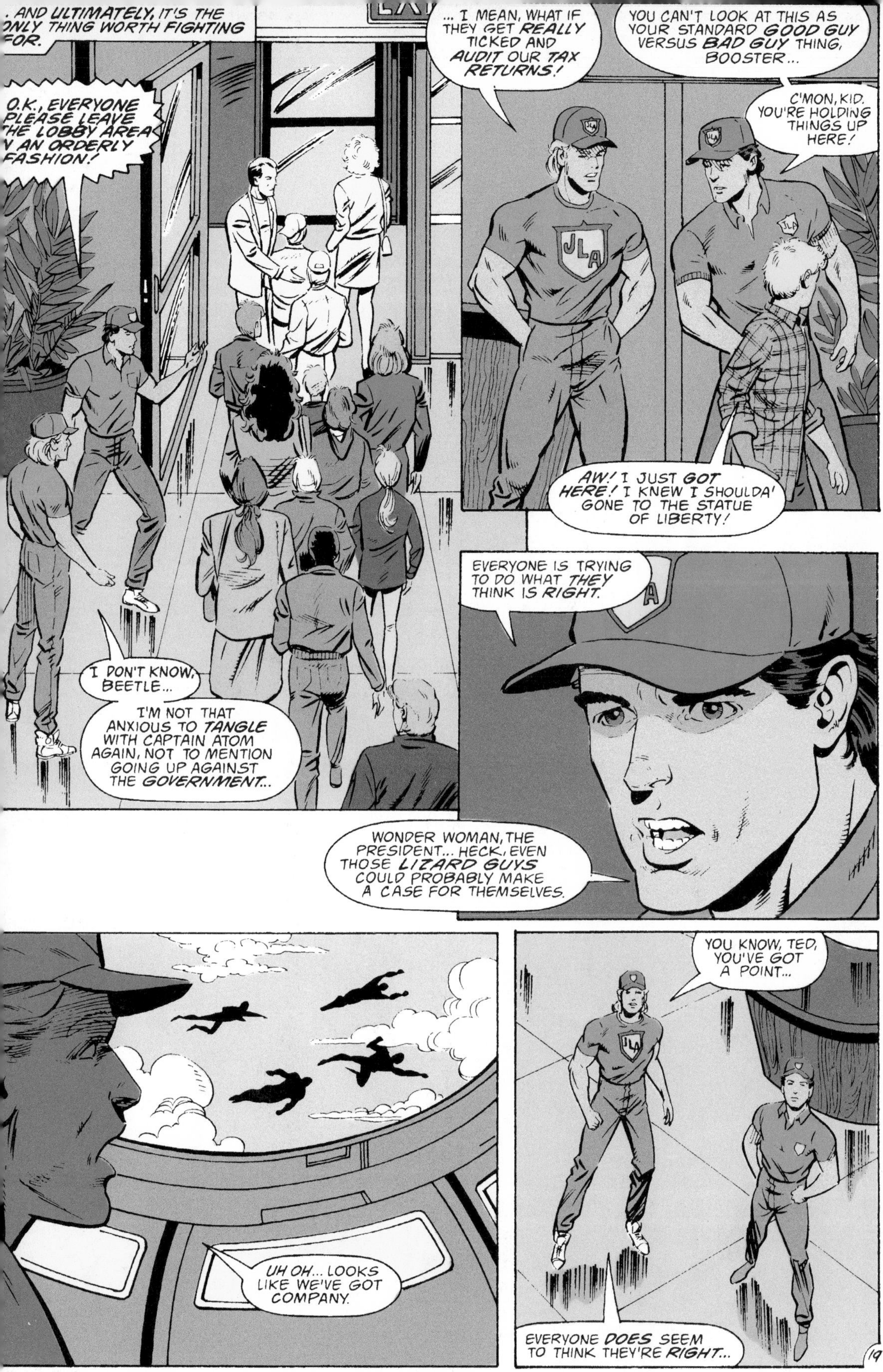

. AND ULTIMATELY, IT'S THE ONLY THING WORTH FIGHTING FOR.
O.K., EVERYONE PLEASE LEAVE THE LOBBY AREA IN AN ORDERLY FASHION!
... I MEAN, WHAT IF THEY GET REALLY TICKED AND AUDIT OUR TAX RETURNS!
YOU CAN'T LOOK AT THIS AS YOUR STANDARD GOOD GUY VERSUS BAD GUY THING, BOOSTER...
C'MON, KID. YOU'RE HOLDING THINGS UP HERE!
AW! I JUST GOT HERE! I KNEW I SHOULDA' GONE TO THE STATUE OF LIBERTY!
I DON'T KNOW, BEETLE...
I'M NOT THAT ANXIOUS TO TANGLE WITH CAPTAIN ATOM AGAIN, NOT TO MENTION GOING UP AGAINST THE GOVERNMENT...
EVERYONE IS TRYING TO DO WHAT THEY THINK IS RIGHT.
WONDER WOMAN, THE PRESIDENT... HECK, EVEN THOSE LIZARD GUYS COULD PROBABLY MAKE A CASE FOR THEMSELVES.
UH OH... LOOKS LIKE WE'VE GOT COMPANY.
YOU KNOW, TED, YOU'VE GOT A POINT...
EVERYONE DOES SEEM TO THINK THEY'RE RIGHT...

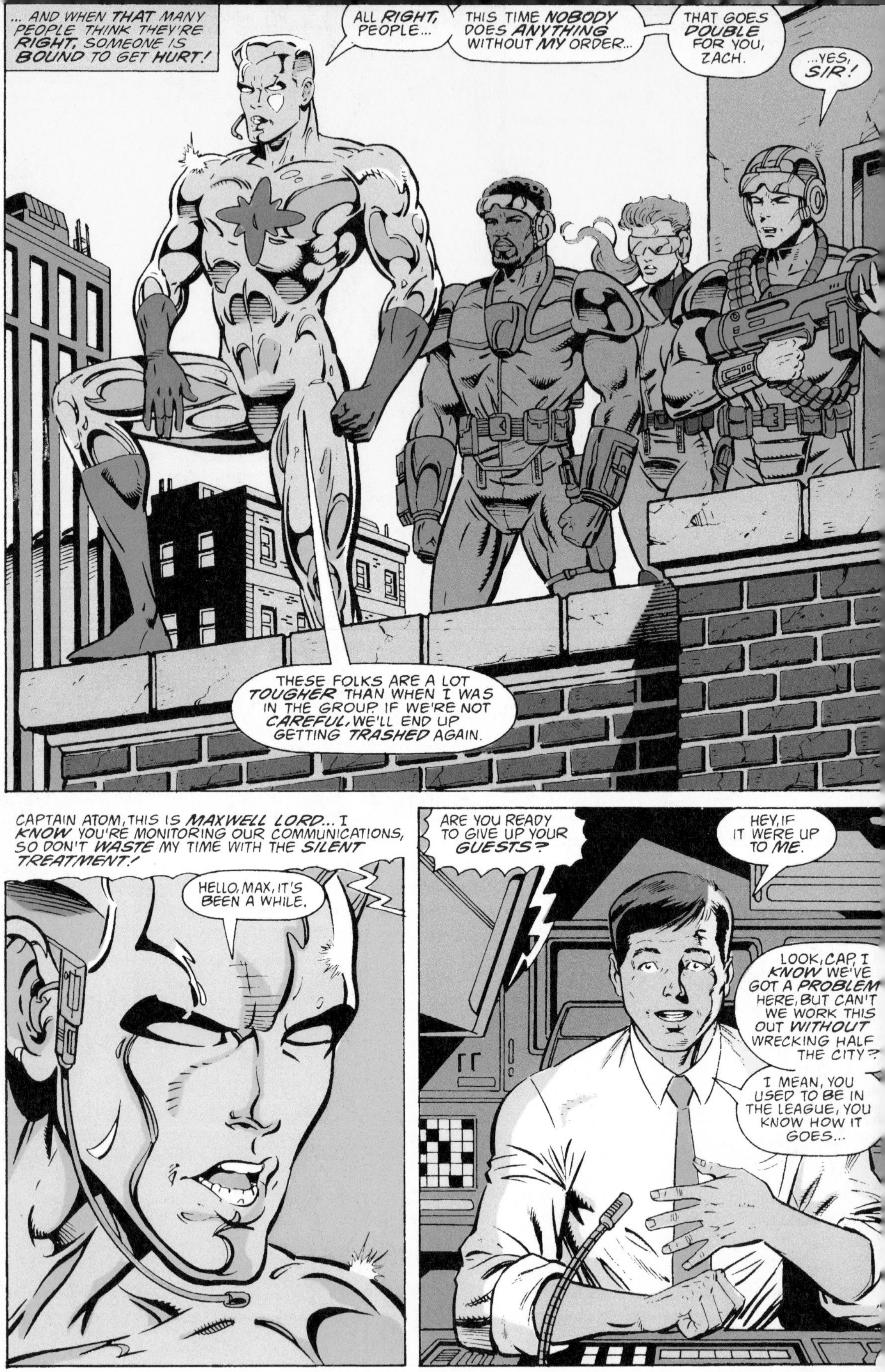
... AND WHEN THAT MANY PEOPLE THINK THEY'RE RIGHT, SOMEONE IS BOUND TO GET HURT!
ALL RIGHT, PEOPLE...
THIS TIME NOBODY DOES ANYTHING WITHOUT MY ORDER...
THAT GOES DOUBLE FOR YOU, ZACH.
...YES, SIR!
THESE FOLKS ARE A LOT TOUGHER THAN WHEN I WAS IN THE GROUP. IF WE'RE NOT CAREFUL, WE'LL END UP GETTING TRASHED AGAIN.
CAPTAIN ATOM, THIS IS MAXWELL LORD... I KNOW YOU'RE MONITORING OUR COMMUNICATIONS, SO DON'T WASTE MY TIME WITH THE SILENT TREATMENT!
HELLO, MAX, IT'S BEEN A WHILE.
ARE YOU READY TO GIVE UP YOUR GUESTS?
HEY, IF IT WERE UP TO ME.
LOOK, CAP, I KNOW WE'VE GOT A PROBLEM HERE, BUT CAN'T WE WORK THIS OUT WITHOUT WRECKING HALF THE CITY?
I MEAN, YOU USED TO BE IN THE LEAGUE, YOU KNOW HOW IT GOES...

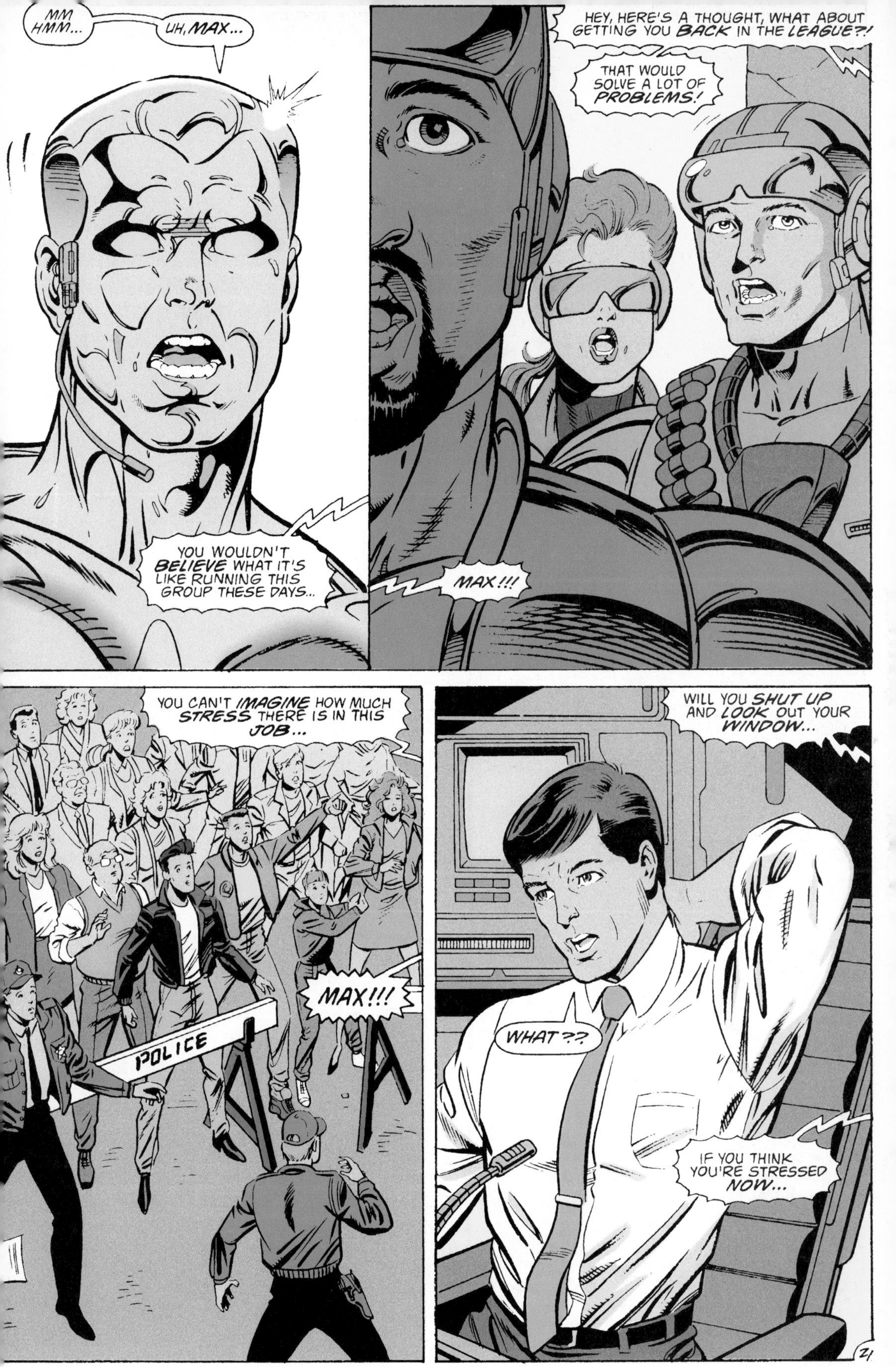
MM HMM...
UH, MAX...
HEY, HERE'S A THOUGHT, WHAT ABOUT GETTING YOU BACK IN THE LEAGUE?!
THAT WOULD SOLVE A LOT OF PROBLEMS!
YOU WOULDN'T BELIEVE WHAT IT'S LIKE RUNNING THIS GROUP THESE DAYS...
MAX!!!
YOU CAN'T IMAGINE HOW MUCH STRESS THERE IS IN THIS JOB...
MAX!!!
POLICE
WILL YOU SHUT UP AND LOOK OUT YOUR WINDOW...
WHAT??
IF YOU THINK YOU'RE STRESSED NOW...
21

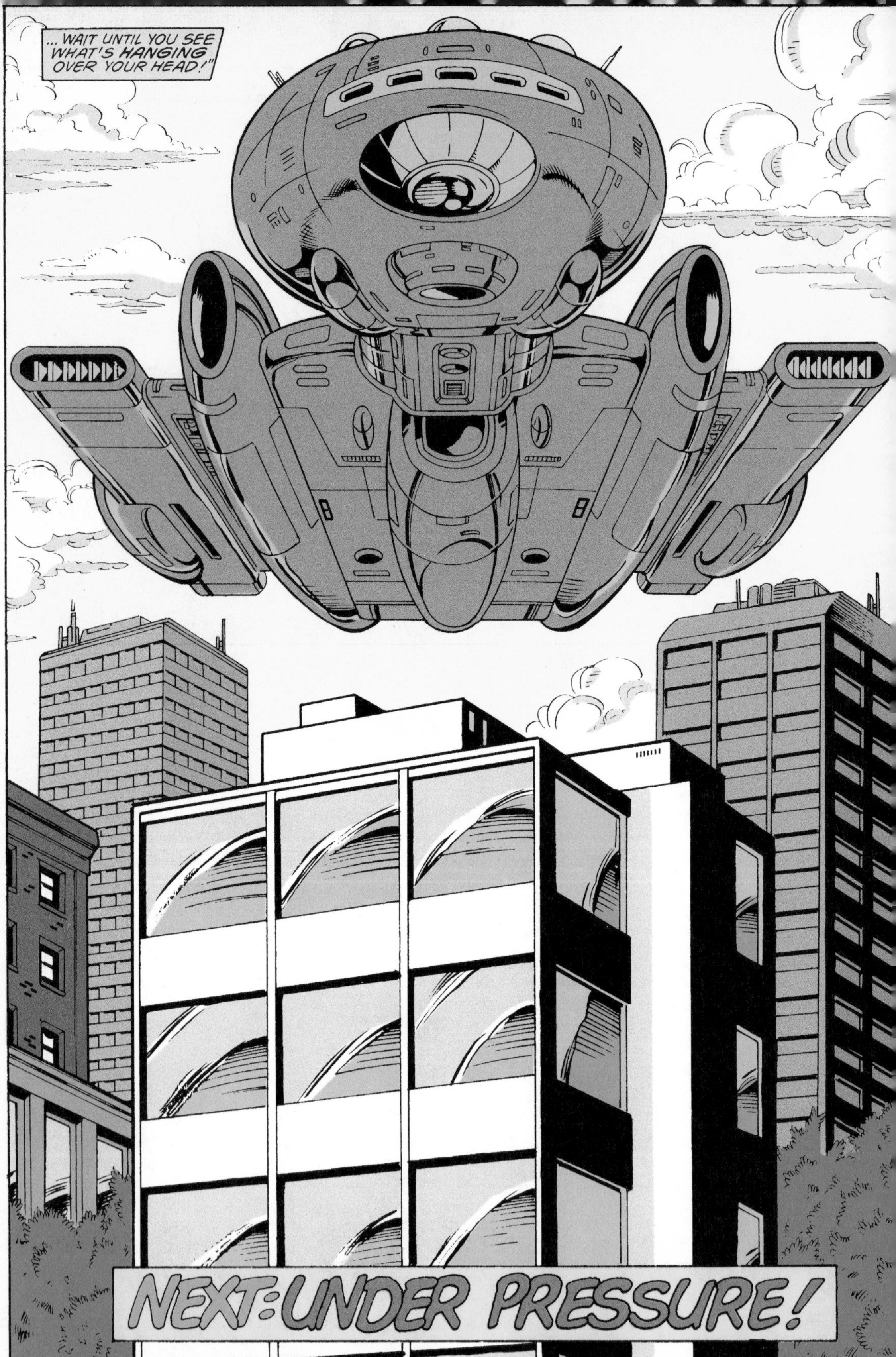
"...WAIT UNTIL YOU SEE WHAT'S HANGING OVER YOUR HEAD!"
NEXT: UNDER PRESSURE!

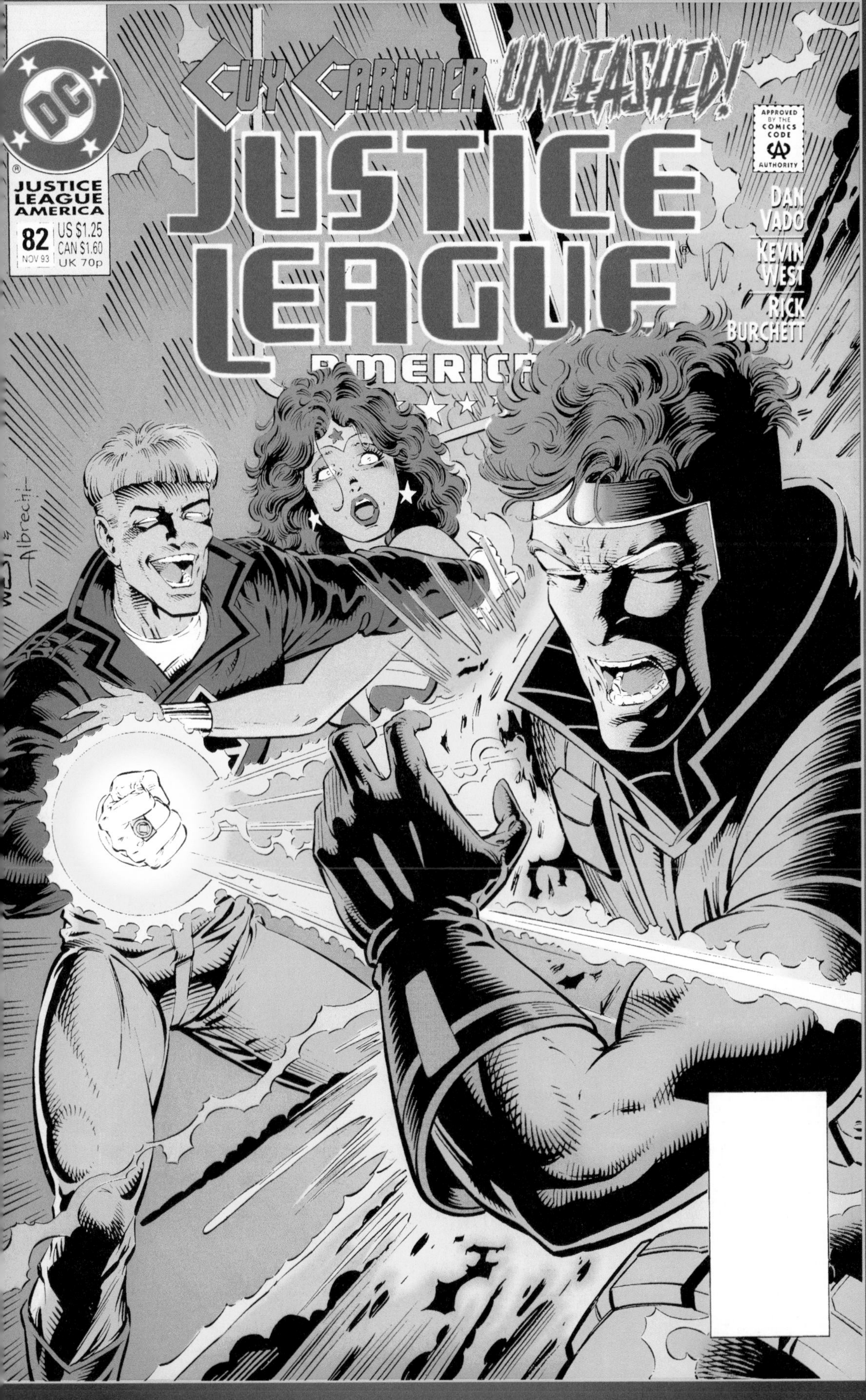

DC
JUSTICE LEAGUE AMERICA
82
NOV 93
US $1.25
CAN $1.60
UK 70p
GUY GARDNER UNLEASHED!
JUSTICE LEAGUE AMERICA
APPROVED BY THE COMICS CODE AUTHORITY
DAN VADO
KEVIN WEST
RICK BURCHETT

Cover art by **KEVIN WEST**
and **JEFF ALBRECHT**

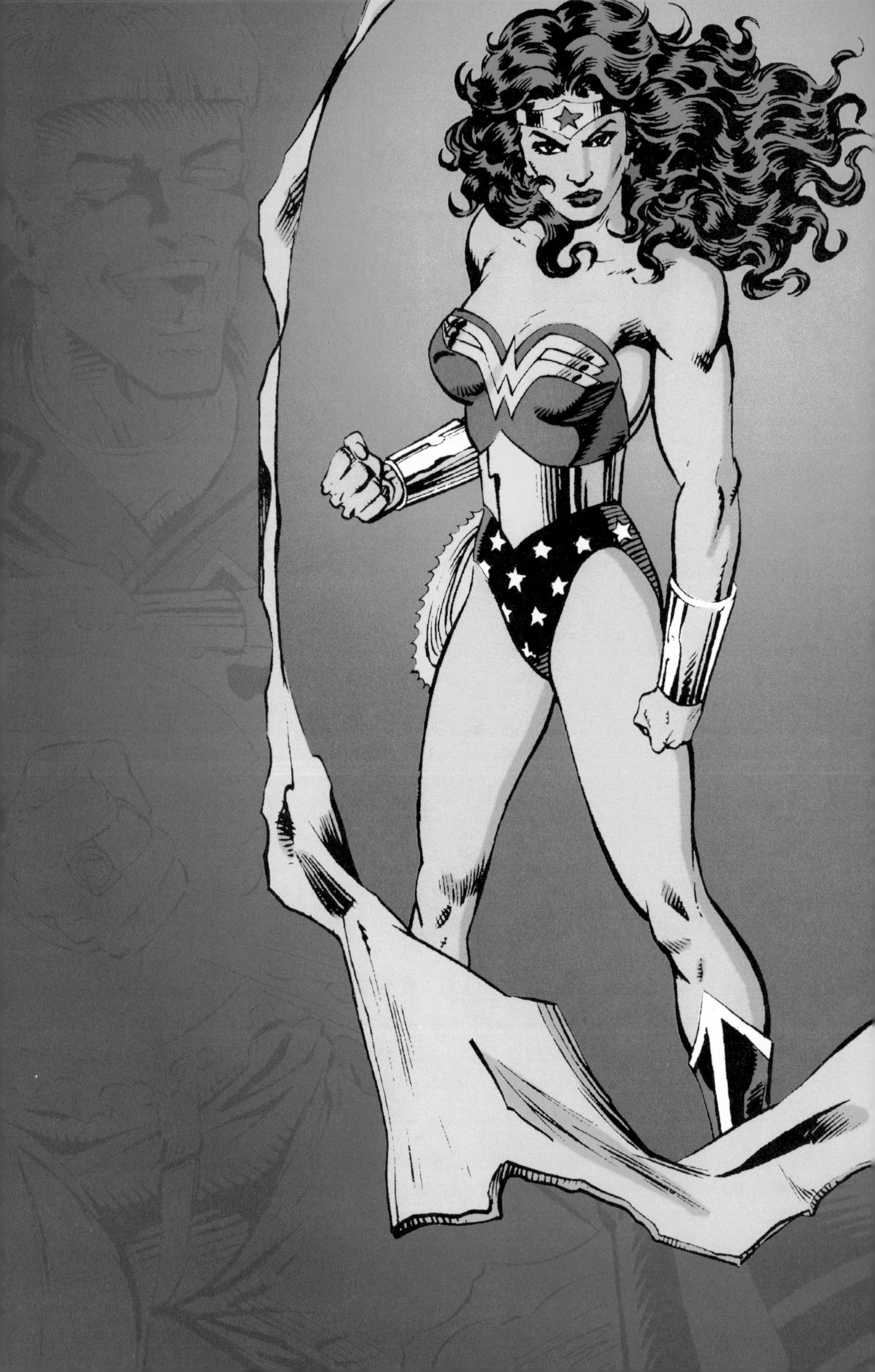

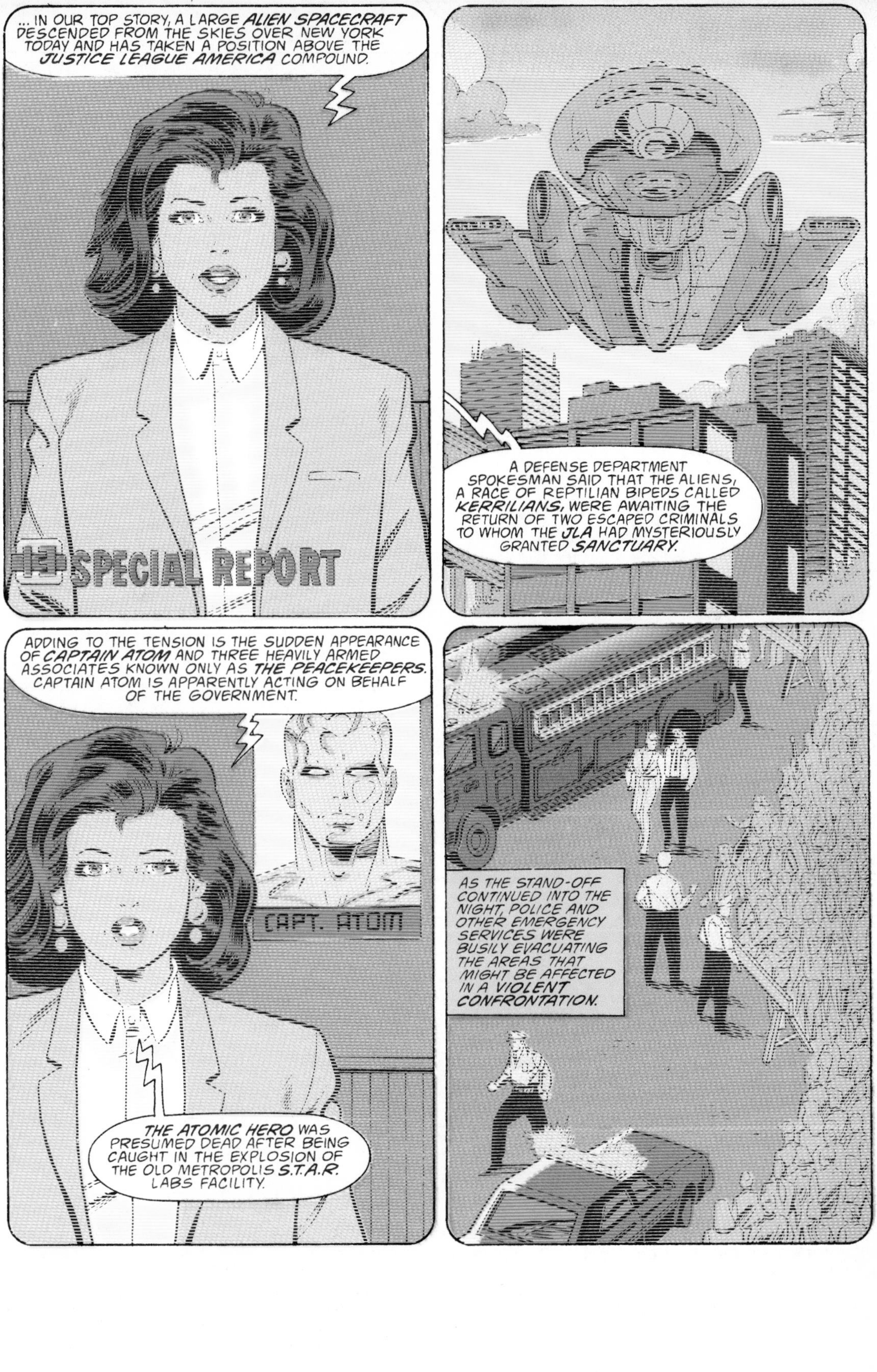
...IN OUR TOP STORY, A LARGE ALIEN SPACECRAFT DESCENDED FROM THE SKIES OVER NEW YORK TODAY AND HAS TAKEN A POSITION ABOVE THE JUSTICE LEAGUE AMERICA COMPOUND.
SPECIAL REPORT
A DEFENSE DEPARTMENT SPOKESMAN SAID THAT THE ALIENS, A RACE OF REPTILIAN BIPEDS CALLED KERRILIANS, WERE AWAITING THE RETURN OF TWO ESCAPED CRIMINALS TO WHOM THE JLA HAD MYSTERIOUSLY GRANTED SANCTUARY.
ADDING TO THE TENSION IS THE SUDDEN APPEARANCE OF CAPTAIN ATOM AND THREE HEAVILY ARMED ASSOCIATES KNOWN ONLY AS THE PEACEKEEPERS. CAPTAIN ATOM IS APPARENTLY ACTING ON BEHALF OF THE GOVERNMENT.
CAPT. ATOM
THE ATOMIC HERO WAS PRESUMED DEAD AFTER BEING CAUGHT IN THE EXPLOSION OF THE OLD METROPOLIS S.T.A.R. LABS FACILITY.
AS THE STAND-OFF CONTINUED INTO THE NIGHT, POLICE AND OTHER EMERGENCY SERVICES WERE BUSILY EVACUATING THE AREAS THAT MIGHT BE AFFECTED IN A VIOLENT CONFRONTATION.

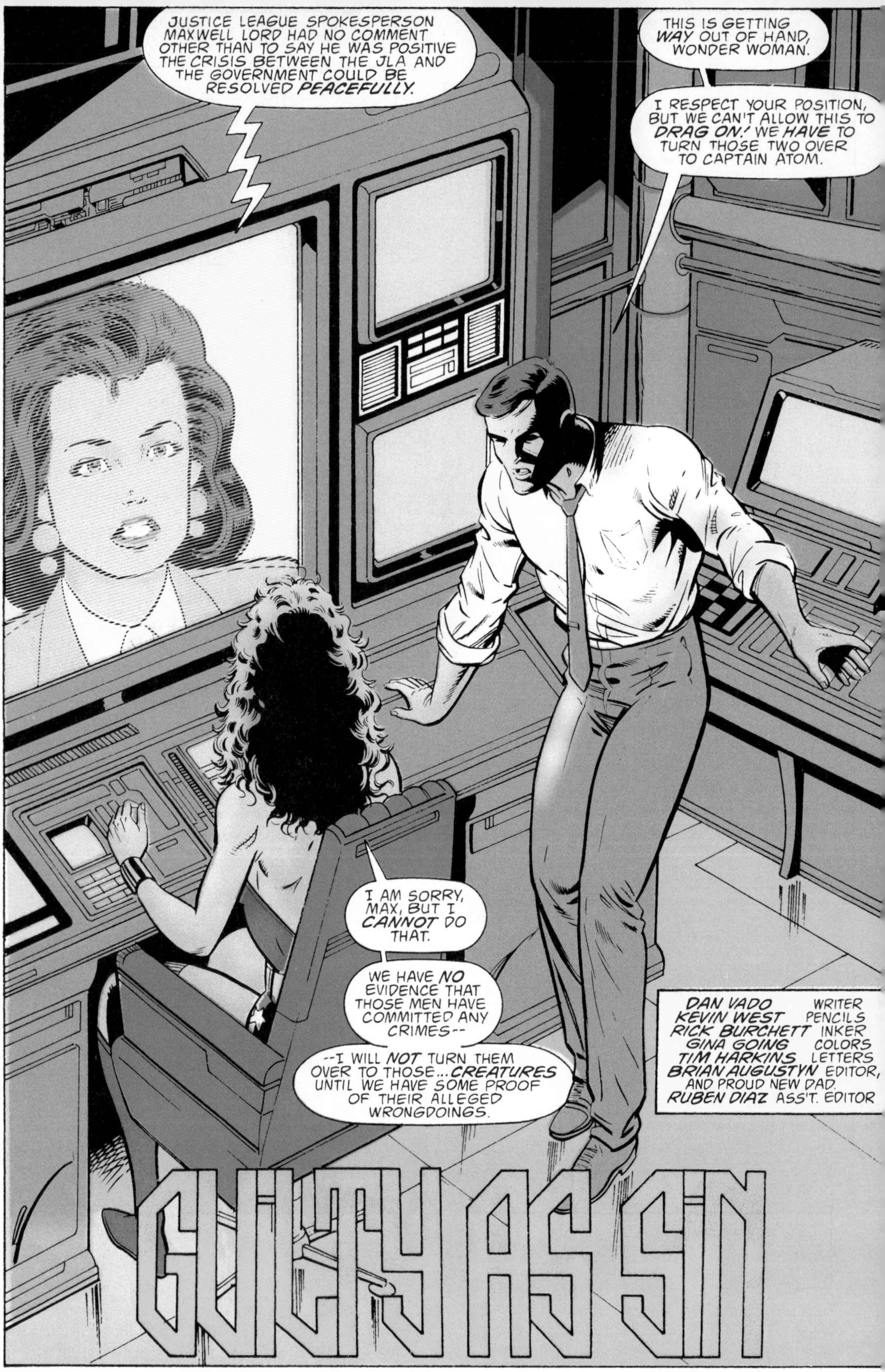

JUSTICE LEAGUE SPOKESPERSON MAXWELL LORD HAD NO COMMENT OTHER THAN TO SAY HE WAS POSITIVE THE CRISIS BETWEEN THE JLA AND THE GOVERNMENT COULD BE RESOLVED PEACEFULLY.
THIS IS GETTING WAY OUT OF HAND, WONDER WOMAN.
I RESPECT YOUR POSITION, BUT WE CAN'T ALLOW THIS TO DRAG ON! WE HAVE TO TURN THOSE TWO OVER TO CAPTAIN ATOM.
I AM SORRY, MAX, BUT I CANNOT DO THAT.
WE HAVE NO EVIDENCE THAT THOSE MEN HAVE COMMITTED ANY CRIMES--
--I WILL NOT TURN THEM OVER TO THOSE... CREATURES UNTIL WE HAVE SOME PROOF OF THEIR ALLEGED WRONGDOINGS.
DAN VADO WRITER
KEVIN WEST PENCILS
RICK BURCHETT INKER
GINA GOING COLORS
TIM HARKINS LETTERS
BRIAN AUGUSTYN EDITOR, AND PROUD NEW DAD.
RUBEN DIAZ ASS'T. EDITOR
GUILTY AS SIN

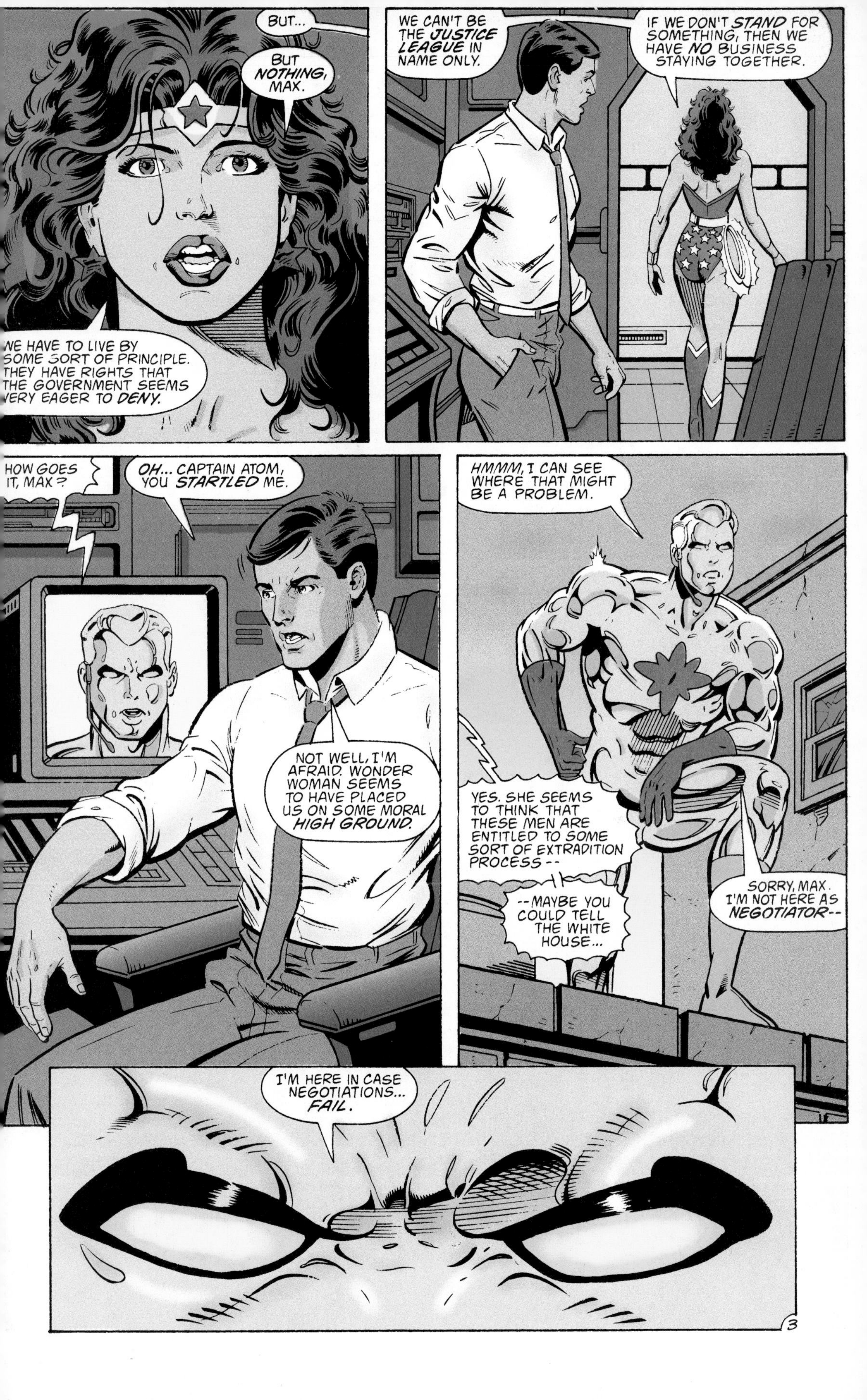
BUT...
BUT NOTHING, MAX.
WE HAVE TO LIVE BY SOME SORT OF PRINCIPLE. THEY HAVE RIGHTS THAT THE GOVERNMENT SEEMS VERY EAGER TO DENY.
WE CAN'T BE THE JUSTICE LEAGUE IN NAME ONLY.
IF WE DON'T STAND FOR SOMETHING, THEN WE HAVE NO BUSINESS STAYING TOGETHER.
HOW GOES IT, MAX?
OH... CAPTAIN ATOM, YOU STARTLED ME.
NOT WELL, I'M AFRAID. WONDER WOMAN SEEMS TO HAVE PLACED US ON SOME MORAL HIGH GROUND.
HMMM, I CAN SEE WHERE THAT MIGHT BE A PROBLEM.
YES. SHE SEEMS TO THINK THAT THESE MEN ARE ENTITLED TO SOME SORT OF EXTRADITION PROCESS --
--MAYBE YOU COULD TELL THE WHITE HOUSE...
SORRY, MAX. I'M NOT HERE AS NEGOTIATOR--
I'M HERE IN CASE NEGOTIATIONS... FAIL.

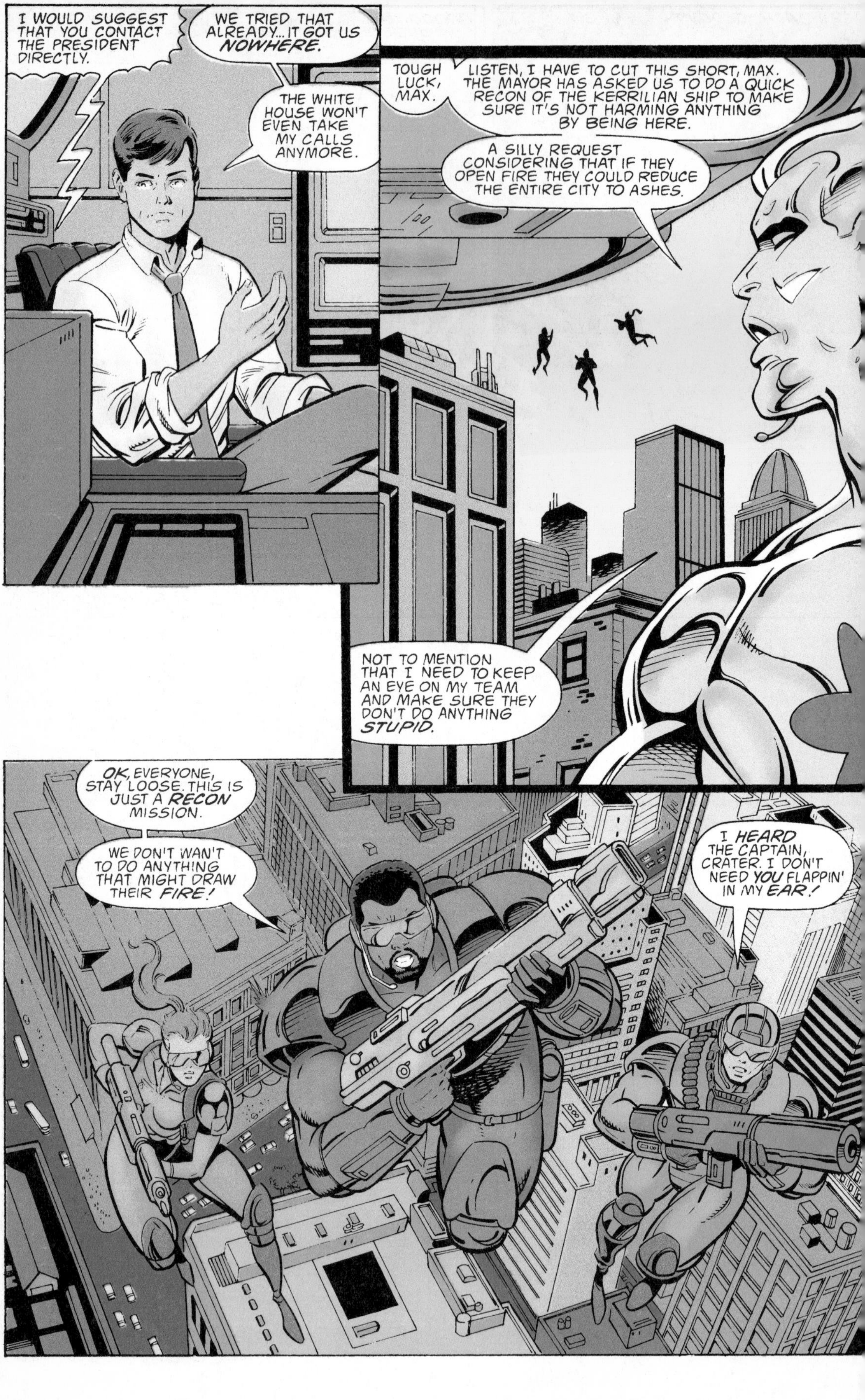

I WOULD SUGGEST THAT YOU CONTACT THE PRESIDENT DIRECTLY.
WE TRIED THAT ALREADY... IT GOT US NOWHERE.
THE WHITE HOUSE WON'T EVEN TAKE MY CALLS ANYMORE.
TOUGH LUCK, MAX.
LISTEN, I HAVE TO CUT THIS SHORT, MAX. THE MAYOR HAS ASKED US TO DO A QUICK RECON OF THE KERRILIAN SHIP TO MAKE SURE IT'S NOT HARMING ANYTHING BY BEING HERE.
A SILLY REQUEST CONSIDERING THAT IF THEY OPEN FIRE THEY COULD REDUCE THE ENTIRE CITY TO ASHES.
NOT TO MENTION THAT I NEED TO KEEP AN EYE ON MY TEAM AND MAKE SURE THEY DON'T DO ANYTHING STUPID.
OK, EVERYONE, STAY LOOSE. THIS IS JUST A RECON MISSION.
WE DON'T WAN'T TO DO ANYTHING THAT MIGHT DRAW THEIR FIRE!
I HEARD THE CAPTAIN, CRATER. I DON'T NEED YOU FLAPPIN' IN MY EAR!

LISTEN, *ZACH.* YOU DON'T HAVE TO LIKE ME, BUT AT LEAST SHOW SOME *RESPECT* FOR MY *RANK.*

OOOOO, WHAT YOU GONNA DO, CRATER. TELL *CAPTAIN ATOM* I HAVE A *BAD ATTITUDE?*

WILL YOU TWO *PIPE DOWN!* IF WE BLOW THIS MISSION WE'RE ALL GOING TO END UP REASSIGNED TO SOME *AIRBASE* IN *ALASKA.*

THESE HUMANS ARE AN *ODD LOT.* THEY SEEM TO WASTE MOST OF THEIR TIME *BICKERING* AMONGST *THEMSELVES!*

YES, CAPTAIN M'BAL. MY OBSERVATIONS ARE THAT THEY ARE A VERY DIVIDED RACE.

INDEED. THEY ARE ALSO A *HEAVILY ARMED* RACE.

FIRE A SHOT ACROSS THEIR PATH, LET'S KEEP THEM AT A DISTANCE.

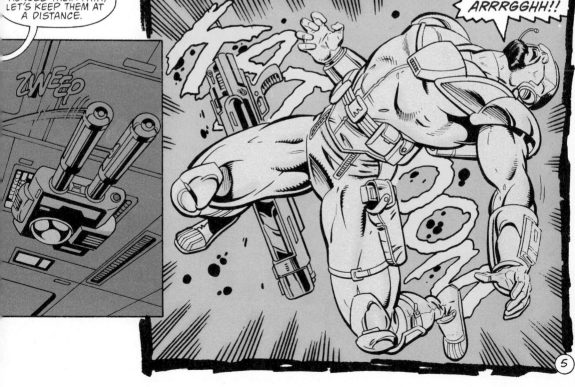

ZWEEP

ARRRGGHH!!

⑤

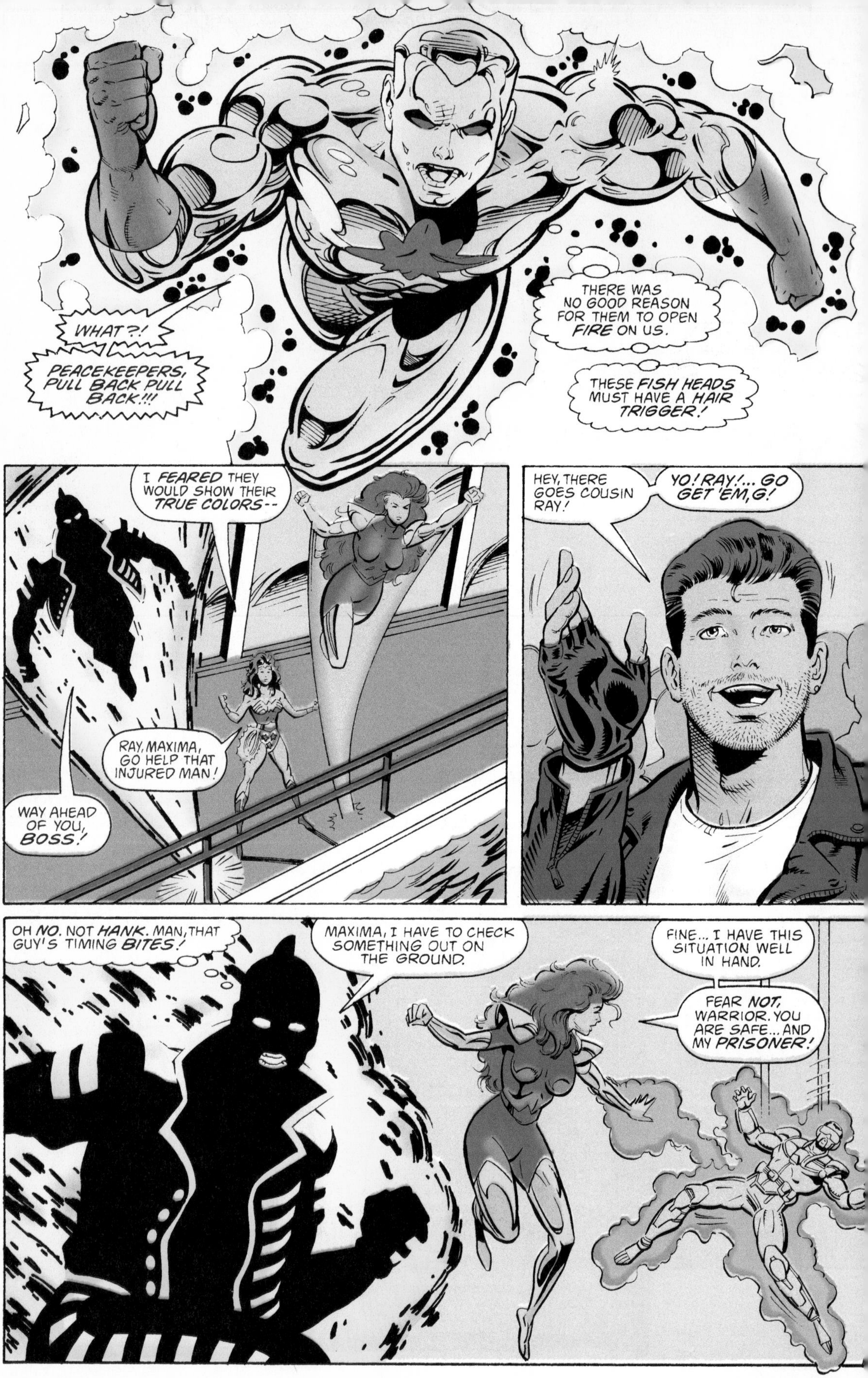
WHAT?!
PEACEKEEPERS, PULL BACK PULL BACK!!!
THERE WAS NO GOOD REASON FOR THEM TO OPEN FIRE ON US.
THESE FISH HEADS MUST HAVE A HAIR TRIGGER!
I FEARED THEY WOULD SHOW THEIR TRUE COLORS--
RAY, MAXIMA, GO HELP THAT INJURED MAN!
WAY AHEAD OF YOU, BOSS!
HEY, THERE GOES COUSIN RAY!
YO! RAY!... GO GET 'EM, G!
OH NO. NOT HANK. MAN, THAT GUY'S TIMING BITES!
MAXIMA, I HAVE TO CHECK SOMETHING OUT ON THE GROUND.
FINE... I HAVE THIS SITUATION WELL IN HAND.
FEAR NOT, WARRIOR. YOU ARE SAFE... AND MY PRISONER!

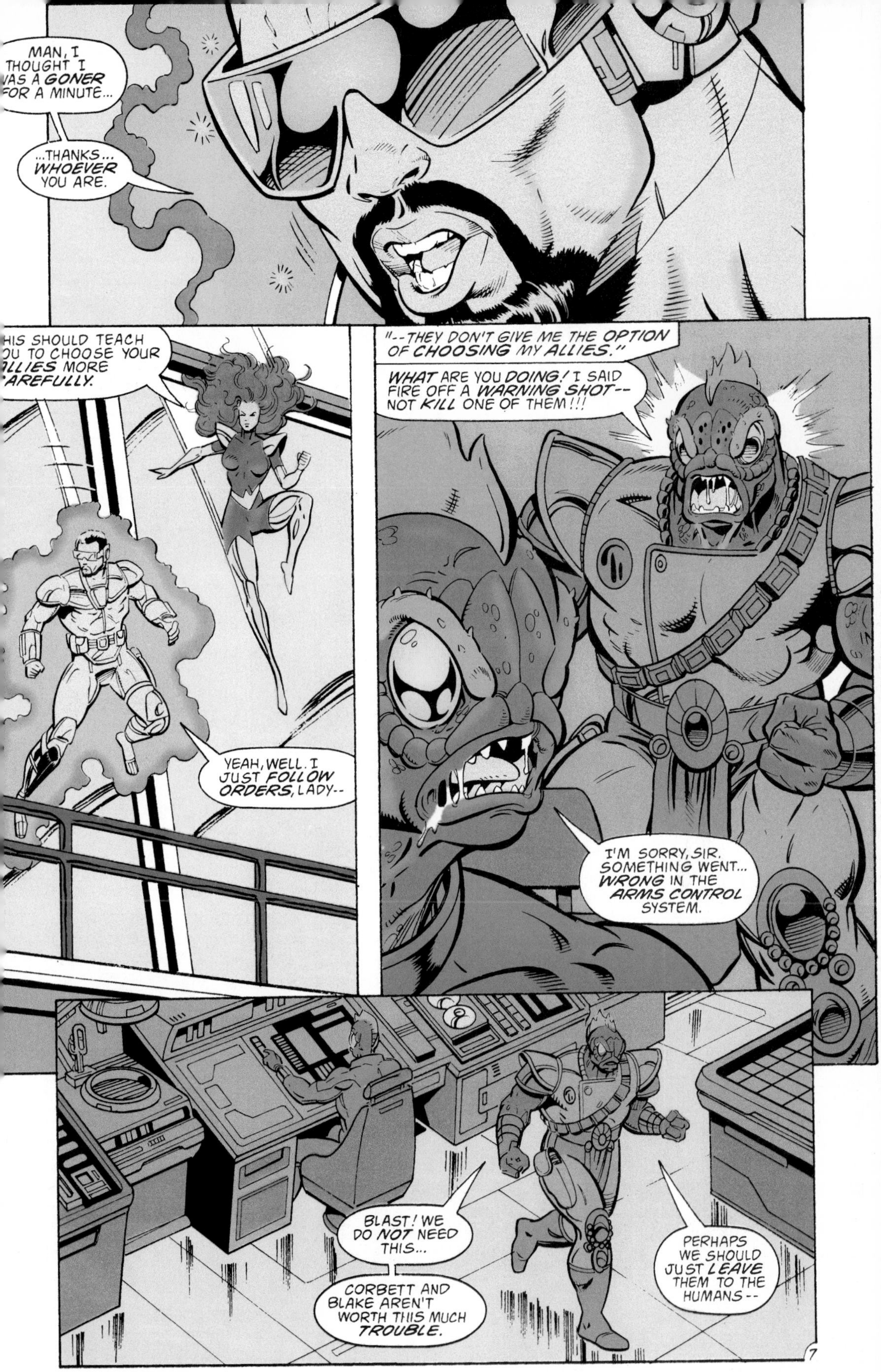

MAN, I THOUGHT I WAS A GONER FOR A MINUTE...
...THANKS... WHOEVER YOU ARE.
HIS SHOULD TEACH OU TO CHOOSE YOUR LLIES MORE AREFULLY.
YEAH, WELL. I JUST FOLLOW ORDERS, LADY--
"--THEY DON'T GIVE ME THE OPTION OF CHOOSING MY ALLIES."
WHAT ARE YOU DOING! I SAID FIRE OFF A WARNING SHOT-- NOT KILL ONE OF THEM!!!
I'M SORRY, SIR. SOMETHING WENT... WRONG IN THE ARMS CONTROL SYSTEM.
BLAST! WE DO NOT NEED THIS...
CORBETT AND BLAKE AREN'T WORTH THIS MUCH TROUBLE.
PERHAPS WE SHOULD JUST LEAVE THEM TO THE HUMANS--

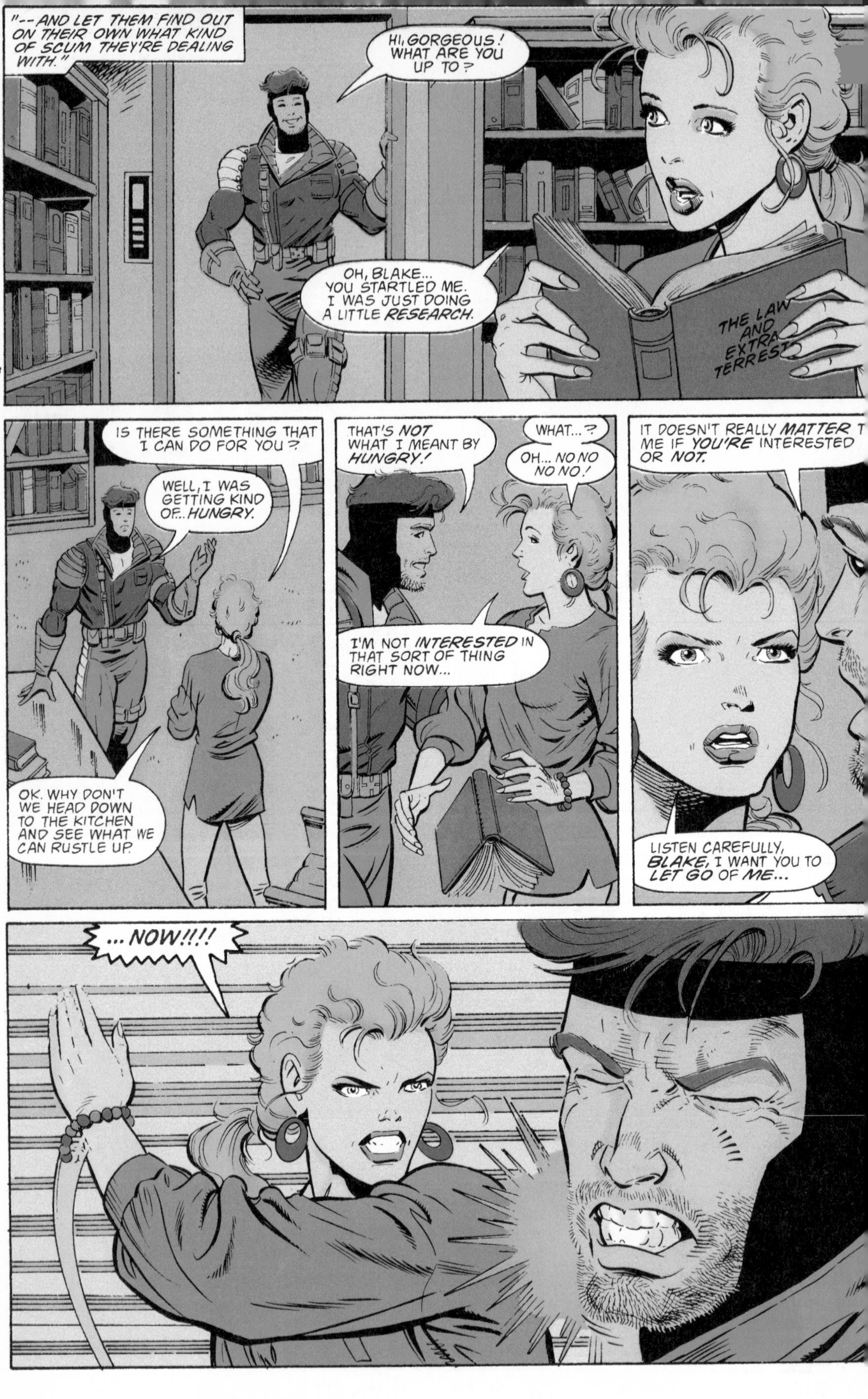
"--AND LET THEM FIND OUT ON THEIR OWN WHAT KIND OF SCUM THEY'RE DEALING WITH."
HI, GORGEOUS! WHAT ARE YOU UP TO?
OH, BLAKE... YOU STARTLED ME. I WAS JUST DOING A LITTLE RESEARCH.
THE LAW AND EXTRA TERREST
IS THERE SOMETHING THAT I CAN DO FOR YOU?
WELL, I WAS GETTING KIND OF... HUNGRY.
OK. WHY DON'T WE HEAD DOWN TO THE KITCHEN AND SEE WHAT WE CAN RUSTLE UP.
THAT'S NOT WHAT I MEANT BY HUNGRY!
WHAT...?
OH... NO NO NO NO!
I'M NOT INTERESTED IN THAT SORT OF THING RIGHT NOW...
IT DOESN'T REALLY MATTER T ME IF YOU'RE INTERESTED OR NOT.
LISTEN CAREFULLY, BLAKE, I WANT YOU TO LET GO OF ME...
...NOW!!!!

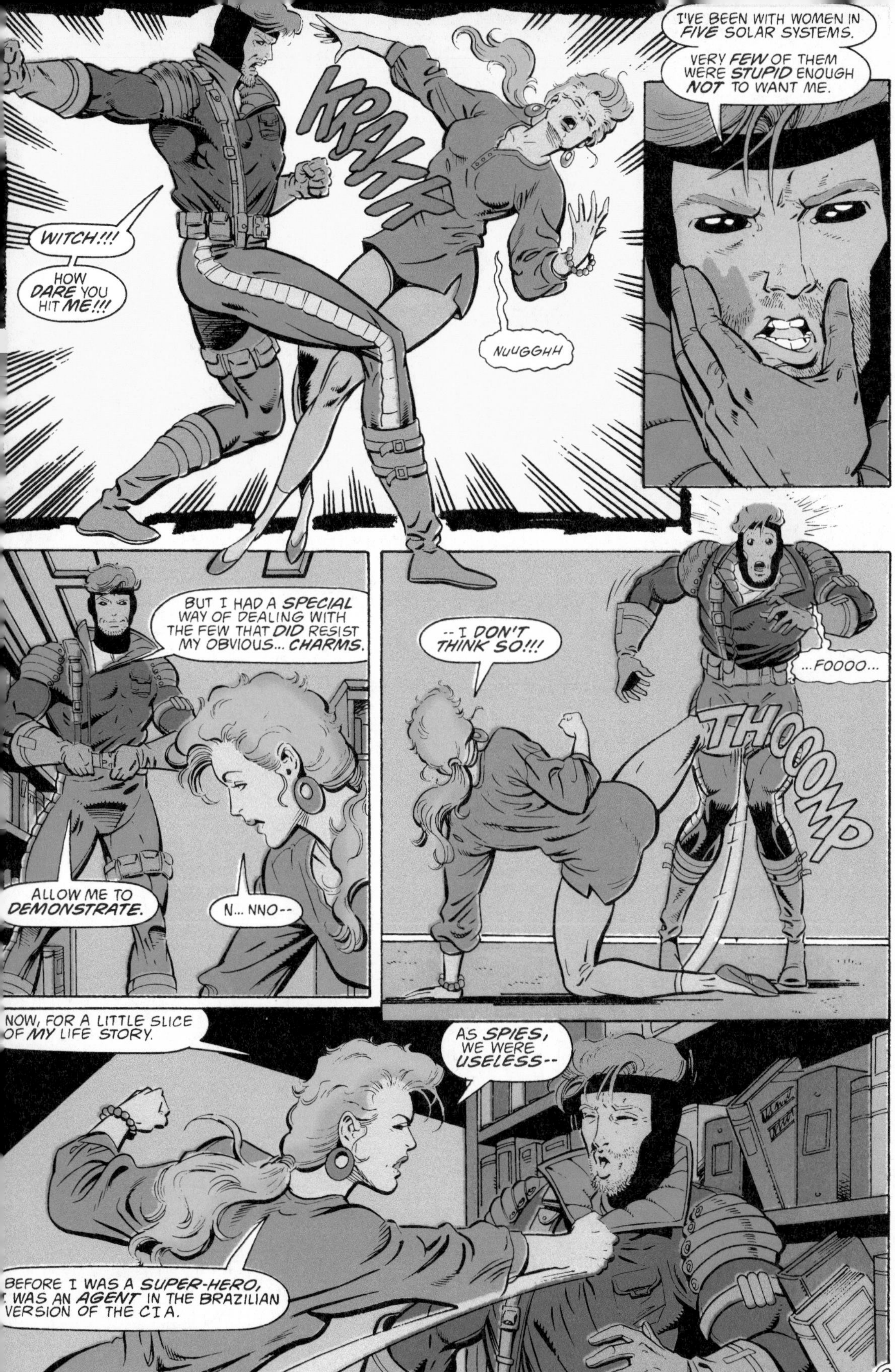
WITCH!!!
HOW DARE YOU HIT ME!!!
KRAKK
NUUGGHH
I'VE BEEN WITH WOMEN IN FIVE SOLAR SYSTEMS.
VERY FEW OF THEM WERE STUPID ENOUGH NOT TO WANT ME.
BUT I HAD A SPECIAL WAY OF DEALING WITH THE FEW THAT DID RESIST MY OBVIOUS... CHARMS.
ALLOW ME TO DEMONSTRATE.
N... NNO--
-- I DON'T THINK SO!!!
...FOOOO...
THHOOOMP
NOW, FOR A LITTLE SLICE OF MY LIFE STORY.
AS SPIES, WE WERE USELESS--
BEFORE I WAS A SUPER-HERO, I WAS AN AGENT IN THE BRAZILIAN VERSION OF THE CIA.

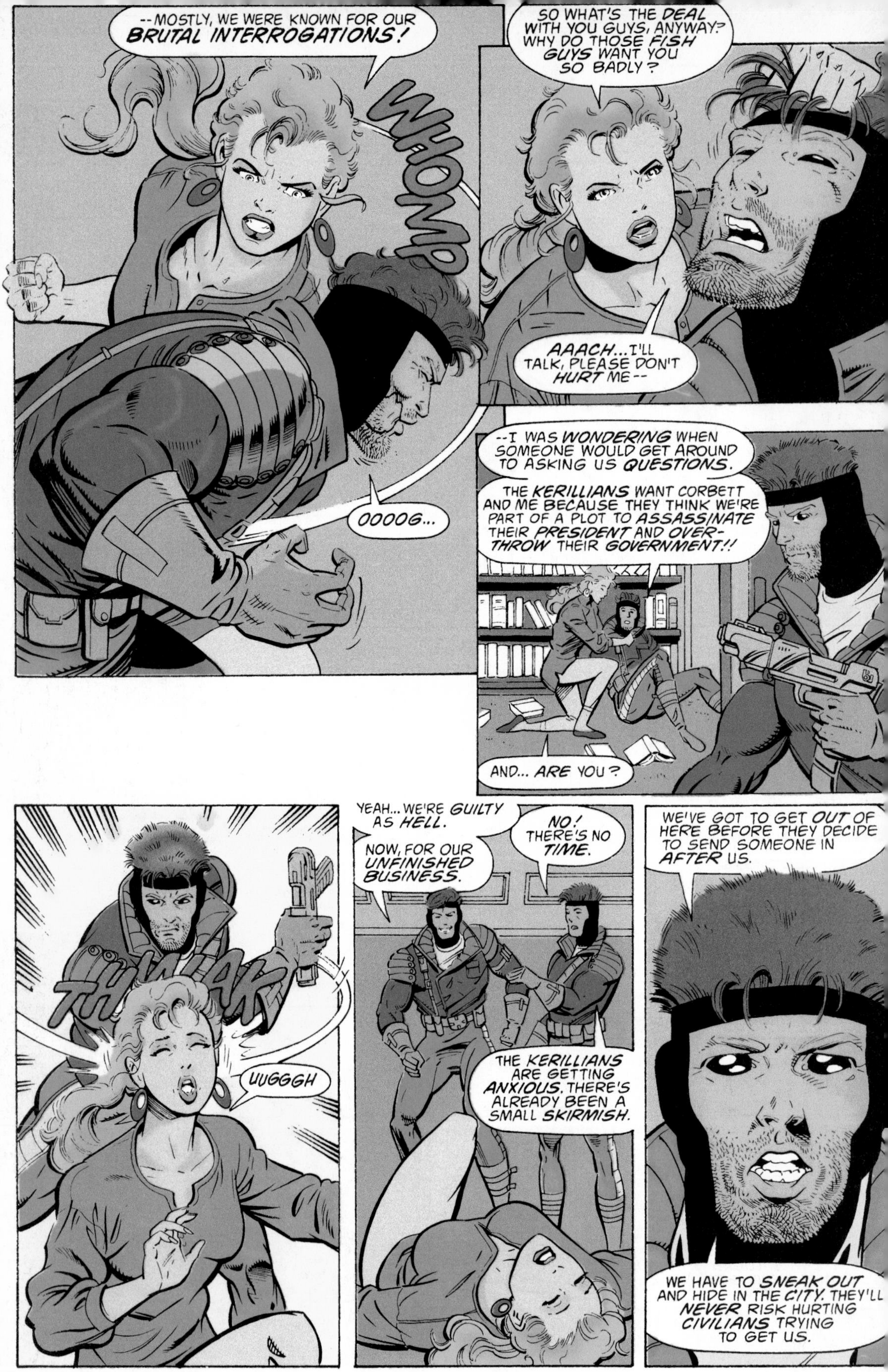
--MOSTLY, WE WERE KNOWN FOR OUR BRUTAL INTERROGATIONS!
WHOMP
OOOOG...
SO WHAT'S THE DEAL WITH YOU GUYS, ANYWAY? WHY DO THOSE FISH GUYS WANT YOU SO BADLY?
AAACH...I'LL TALK, PLEASE DON'T HURT ME--
--I WAS WONDERING WHEN SOMEONE WOULD GET AROUND TO ASKING US QUESTIONS.
THE KERILLIANS WANT CORBETT AND ME BECAUSE THEY THINK WE'RE PART OF A PLOT TO ASSASSINATE THEIR PRESIDENT AND OVERTHROW THEIR GOVERNMENT!!
AND... ARE YOU?
THWAK
UUGGGH
YEAH... WE'RE GUILTY AS HELL.
NOW, FOR OUR UNFINISHED BUSINESS.
NO! THERE'S NO TIME.
THE KERILLIANS ARE GETTING ANXIOUS. THERE'S ALREADY BEEN A SMALL SKIRMISH.
WE'VE GOT TO GET OUT OF HERE BEFORE THEY DECIDE TO SEND SOMEONE IN AFTER US.
WE HAVE TO SNEAK OUT AND HIDE IN THE CITY. THEY'LL NEVER RISK HURTING CIVILIANS TRYING TO GET US.

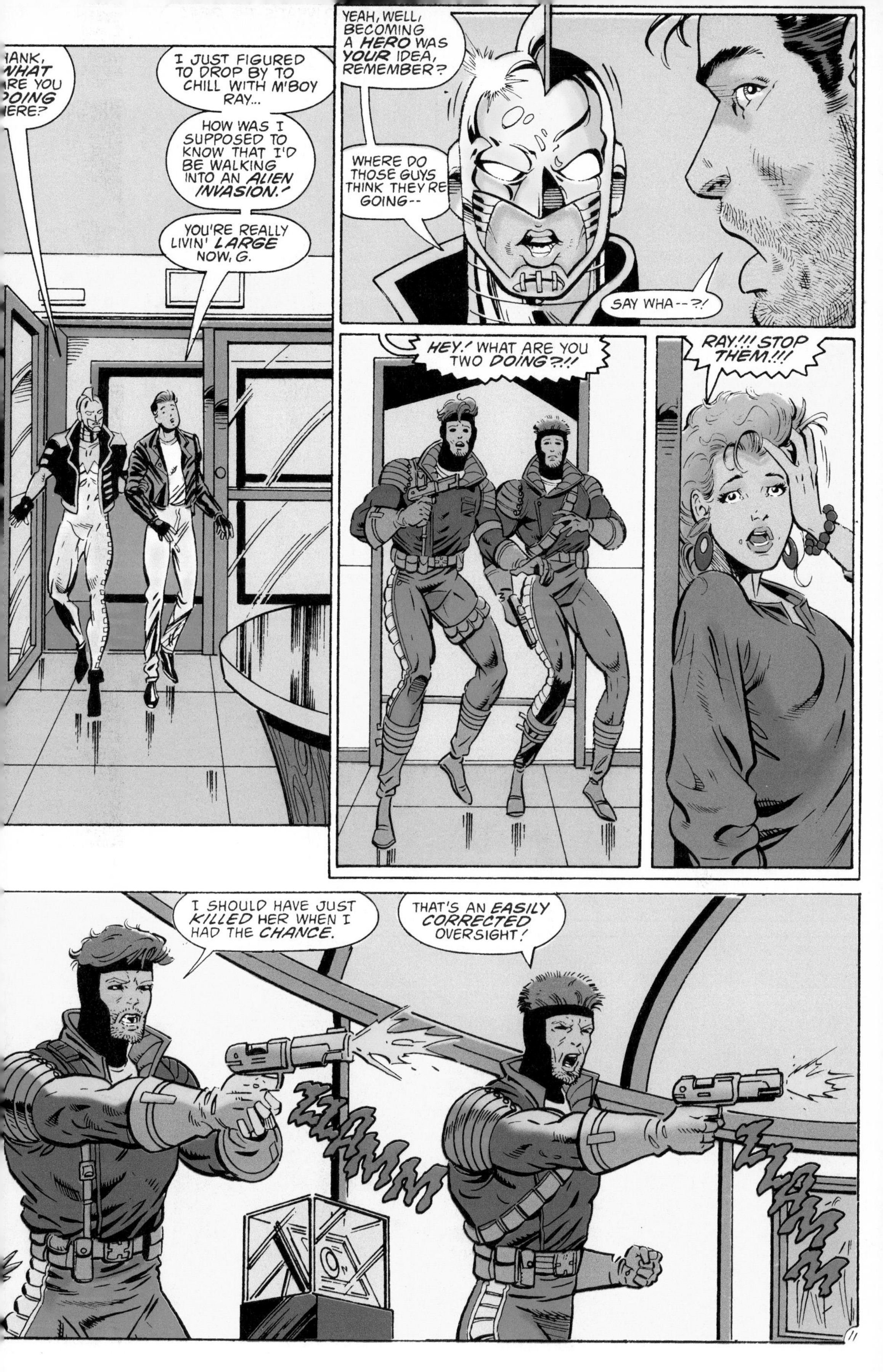

HANK, WHAT ARE YOU DOING HERE?
I JUST FIGURED TO DROP BY TO CHILL WITH M'BOY RAY...
HOW WAS I SUPPOSED TO KNOW THAT I'D BE WALKING INTO AN ALIEN INVASION!
YOU'RE REALLY LIVIN' LARGE NOW, G.
YEAH, WELL, BECOMING A HERO WAS YOUR IDEA, REMEMBER?
WHERE DO THOSE GUYS THINK THEY'RE GOING--
SAY WHA--?!
HEY! WHAT ARE YOU TWO DOING?!!
RAY!!! STOP THEM!!!
I SHOULD HAVE JUST KILLED HER WHEN I HAD THE CHANCE.
THAT'S AN EASILY CORRECTED OVERSIGHT!
ZZAMMM
ZZAMMM
11

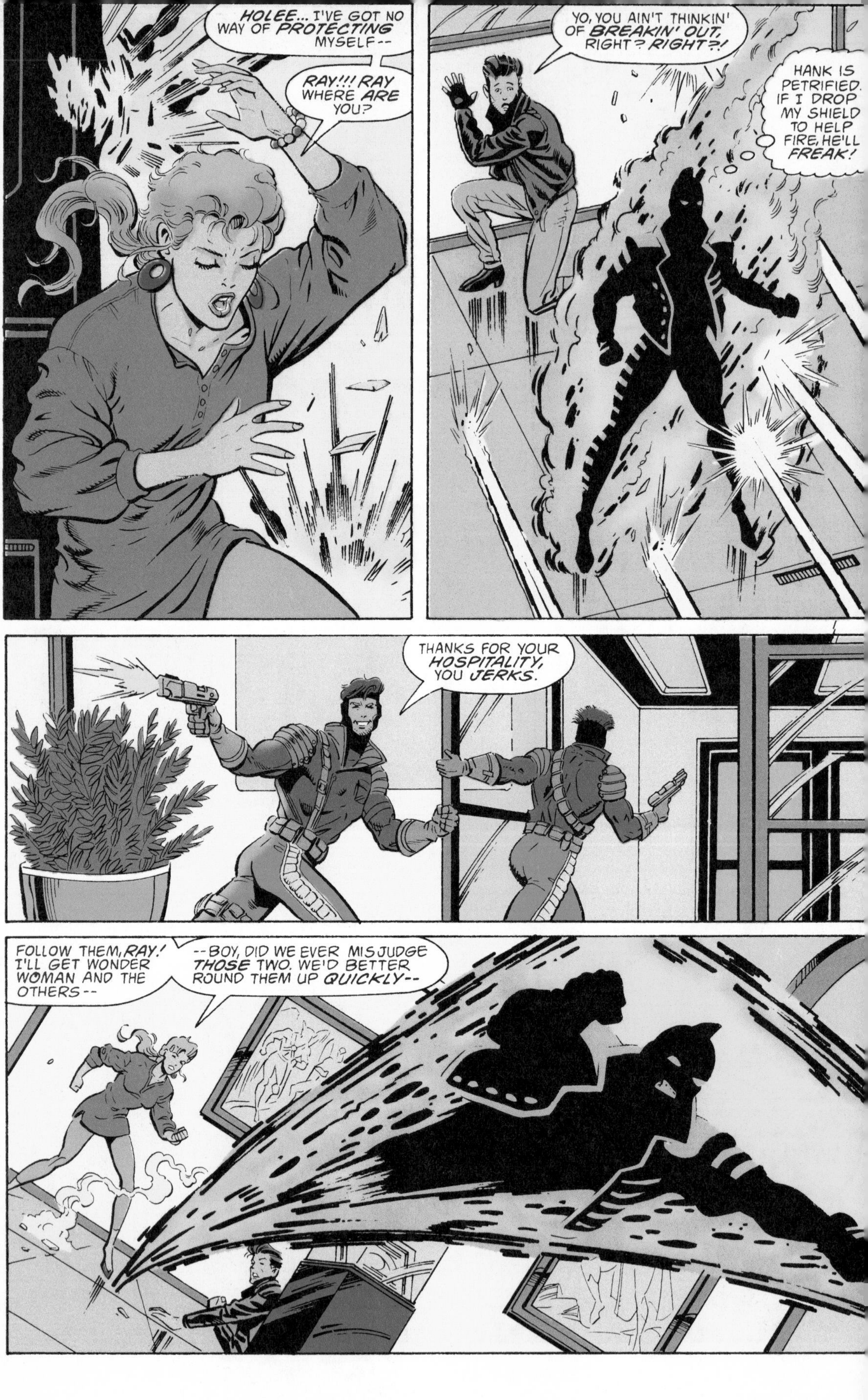
HOLEE... I'VE GOT NO WAY OF PROTECTING MYSELF--
RAY!!! RAY WHERE ARE YOU?
YO, YOU AIN'T THINKIN' OF BREAKIN' OUT, RIGHT? RIGHT?!
HANK IS PETRIFIED. IF I DROP MY SHIELD TO HELP FIRE, HE'LL FREAK!
THANKS FOR YOUR HOSPITALITY, YOU JERKS.
FOLLOW THEM, RAY! I'LL GET WONDER WOMAN AND THE OTHERS--
--BOY, DID WE EVER MISJUDGE THOSE TWO. WE'D BETTER ROUND THEM UP QUICKLY--

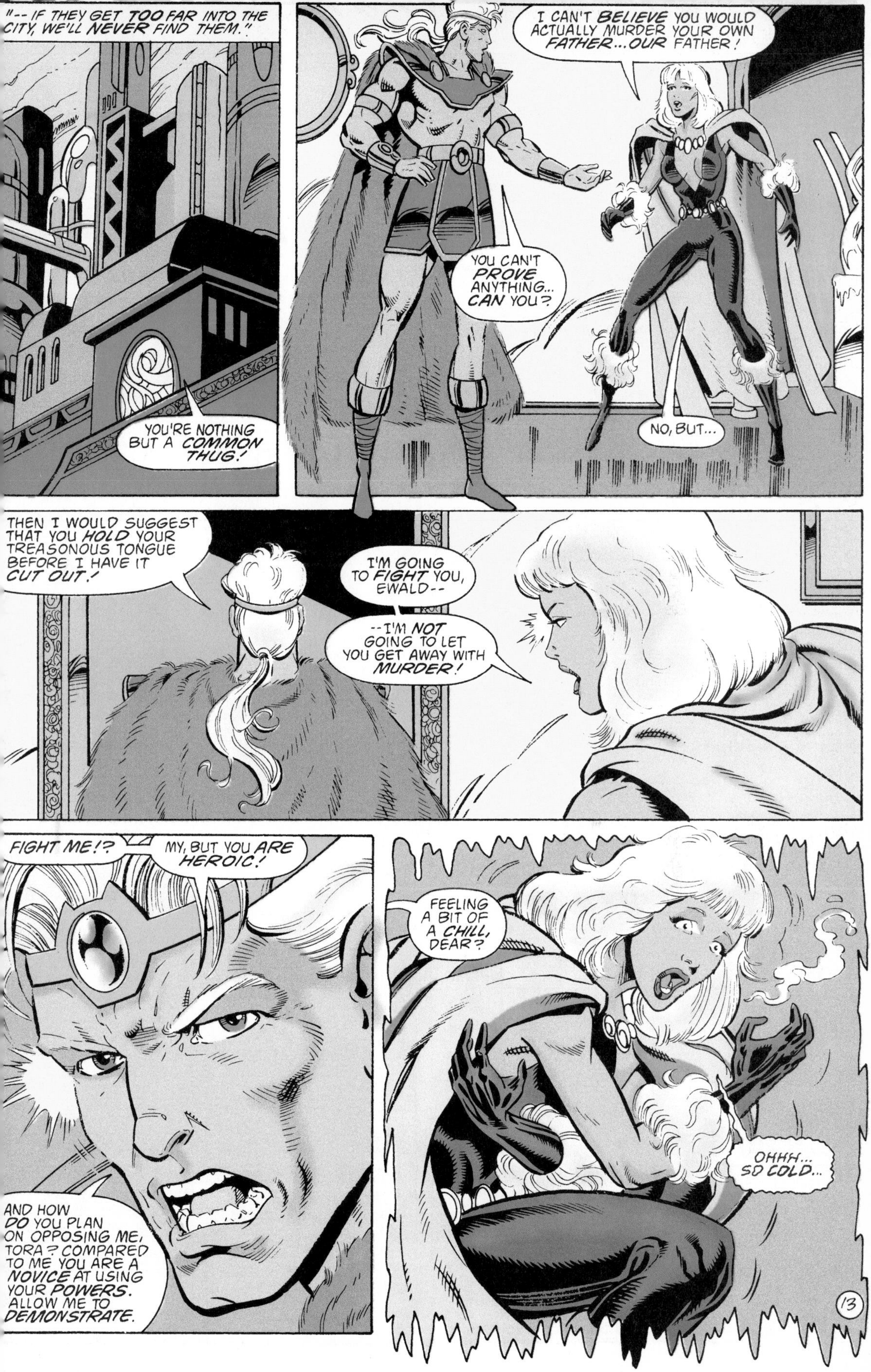
"-- IF THEY GET TOO FAR INTO THE CITY, WE'LL NEVER FIND THEM."
YOU'RE NOTHING BUT A COMMON THUG!
I CAN'T BELIEVE YOU WOULD ACTUALLY MURDER YOUR OWN FATHER...OUR FATHER!
YOU CAN'T PROVE ANYTHING... CAN YOU?
NO, BUT...
THEN I WOULD SUGGEST THAT YOU HOLD YOUR TREASONOUS TONGUE BEFORE I HAVE IT CUT OUT!
I'M GOING TO FIGHT YOU, EWALD--
--I'M NOT GOING TO LET YOU GET AWAY WITH MURDER!
FIGHT ME!?
MY, BUT YOU ARE HEROIC!
AND HOW DO YOU PLAN ON OPPOSING ME, TORA? COMPARED TO ME YOU ARE A NOVICE AT USING YOUR POWERS. ALLOW ME TO DEMONSTRATE.
FEELING A BIT OF A CHILL, DEAR?
OHHH... SO COLD...

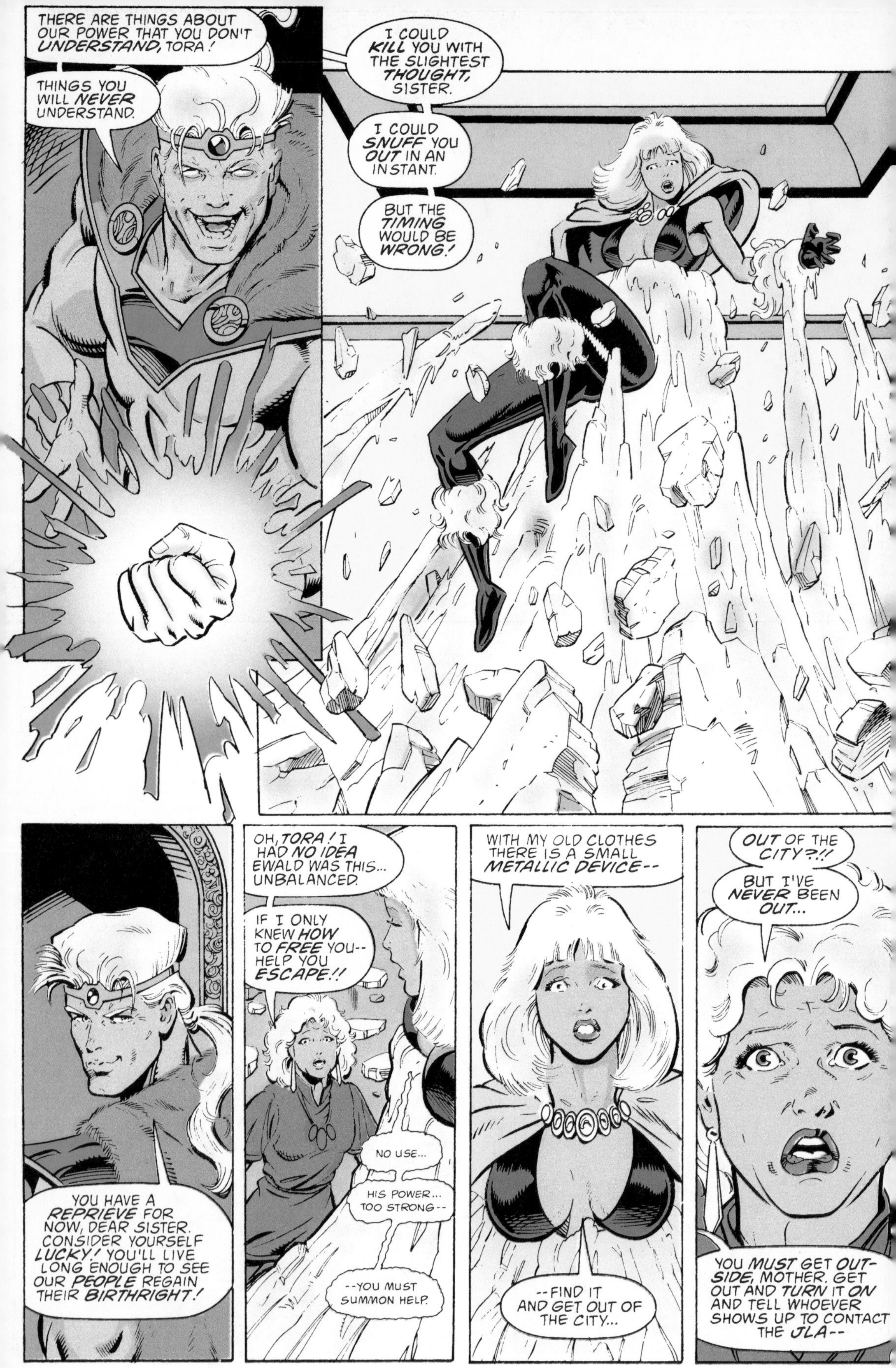

THERE ARE THINGS ABOUT OUR POWER THAT YOU DON'T UNDERSTAND, TORA!
THINGS YOU WILL NEVER UNDERSTAND.
I COULD KILL YOU WITH THE SLIGHTEST THOUGHT, SISTER.
I COULD SNUFF YOU OUT IN AN INSTANT.
BUT THE TIMING WOULD BE WRONG!
YOU HAVE A REPRIEVE FOR NOW, DEAR SISTER. CONSIDER YOURSELF LUCKY! YOU'LL LIVE LONG ENOUGH TO SEE OUR PEOPLE REGAIN THEIR BIRTHRIGHT!
OH, TORA! I HAD NO IDEA EWALD WAS THIS... UNBALANCED.
IF I ONLY KNEW HOW TO FREE YOU-- HELP YOU ESCAPE!!
NO USE...
HIS POWER... TOO STRONG--
--YOU MUST SUMMON HELP.
WITH MY OLD CLOTHES THERE IS A SMALL METALLIC DEVICE--
--FIND IT AND GET OUT OF THE CITY...
OUT OF THE CITY?!!
BUT I'VE NEVER BEEN OUT...
YOU MUST GET OUTSIDE, MOTHER. GET OUT AND TURN IT ON AND TELL WHOEVER SHOWS UP TO CONTACT THE JLA--

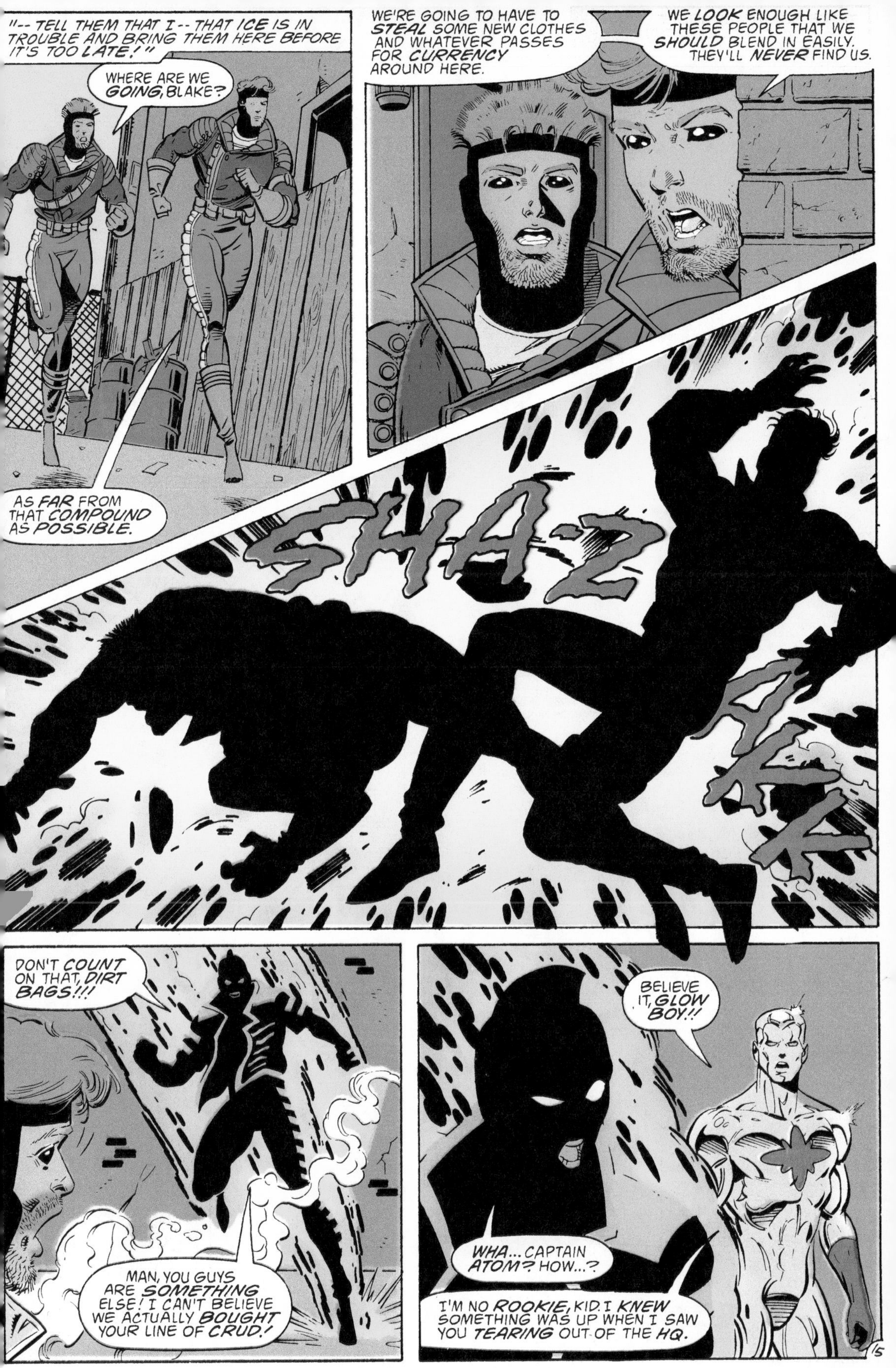

"-- TELL THEM THAT I -- THAT ICE IS IN TROUBLE AND BRING THEM HERE BEFORE IT'S TOO LATE!"
WHERE ARE WE GOING, BLAKE?
AS FAR FROM THAT COMPOUND AS POSSIBLE.
WE'RE GOING TO HAVE TO STEAL SOME NEW CLOTHES AND WHATEVER PASSES FOR CURRENCY AROUND HERE.
WE LOOK ENOUGH LIKE THESE PEOPLE THAT WE SHOULD BLEND IN EASILY. THEY'LL NEVER FIND US.
SHA-ZAKK
DON'T COUNT ON THAT, DIRT BAGS!!!
MAN, YOU GUYS ARE SOMETHING ELSE! I CAN'T BELIEVE WE ACTUALLY BOUGHT YOUR LINE OF CRUD!
BELIEVE IT, GLOW BOY!!
WHA... CAPTAIN ATOM? HOW...?
I'M NO ROOKIE, KID. I KNEW SOMETHING WAS UP WHEN I SAW YOU TEARING OUT OF THE HQ.

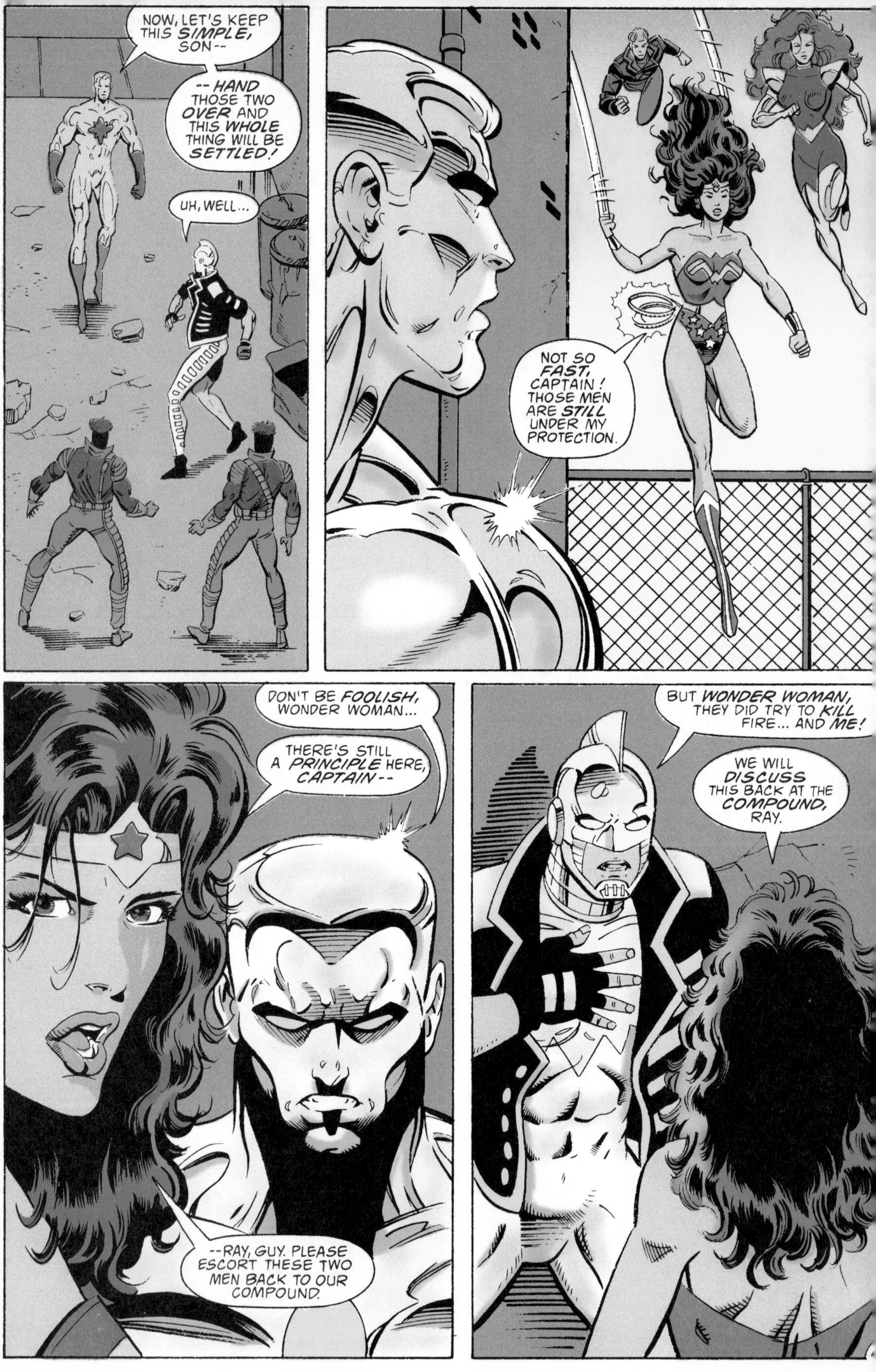
NOW, LET'S KEEP THIS SIMPLE, SON--
--HAND THOSE TWO OVER AND THIS WHOLE THING WILL BE SETTLED!
UH, WELL...
NOT SO FAST, CAPTAIN! THOSE MEN ARE STILL UNDER MY PROTECTION.
DON'T BE FOOLISH, WONDER WOMAN...
THERE'S STILL A PRINCIPLE HERE, CAPTAIN--
--RAY, GUY. PLEASE ESCORT THESE TWO MEN BACK TO OUR COMPOUND.
BUT WONDER WOMAN, THEY DID TRY TO KILL FIRE... AND ME!
WE WILL DISCUSS THIS BACK AT THE COMPOUND, RAY.

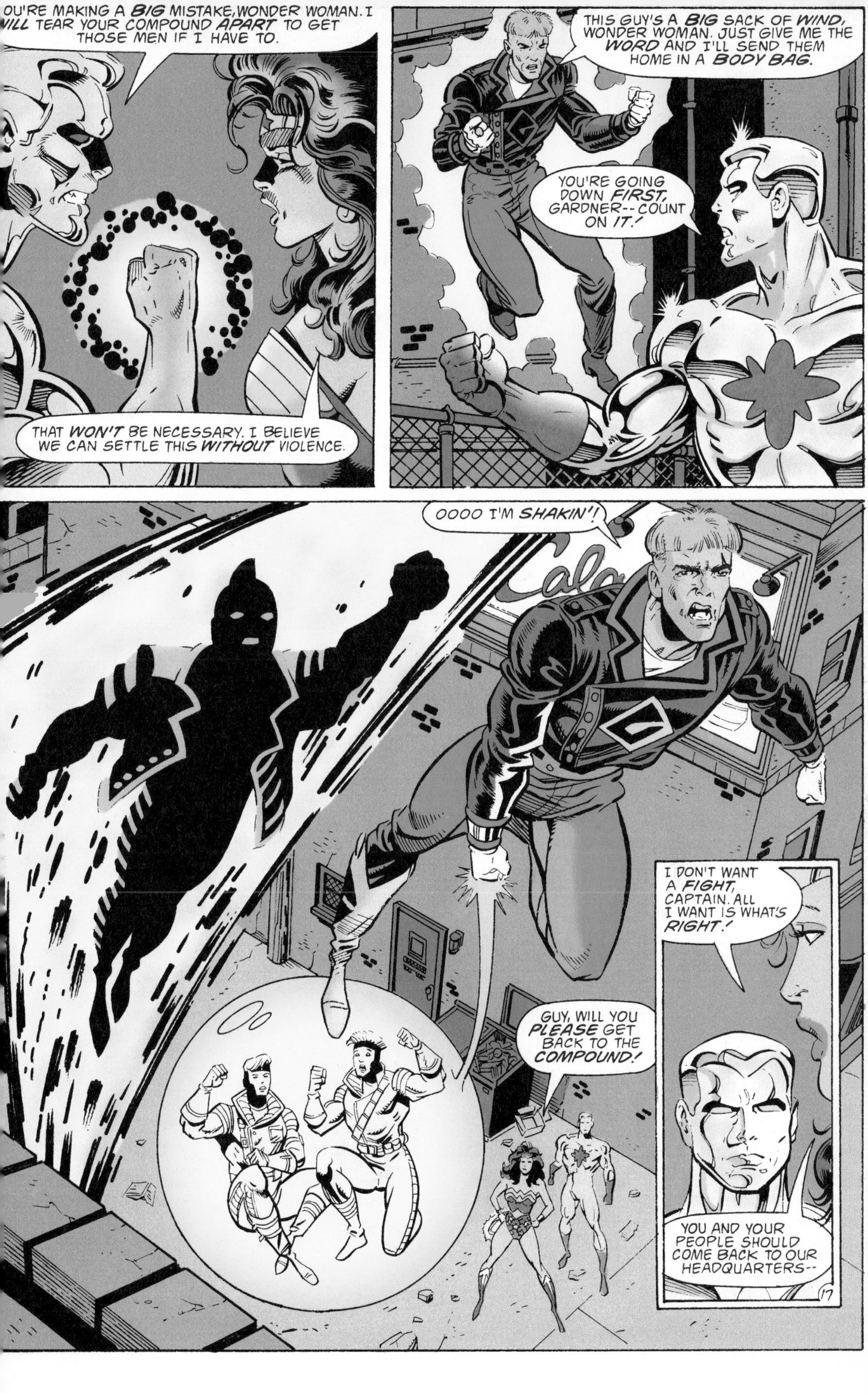
OU'RE MAKING A BIG MISTAKE, WONDER WOMAN. I WILL TEAR YOUR COMPOUND APART TO GET THOSE MEN IF I HAVE TO.
THAT WON'T BE NECESSARY. I BELIEVE WE CAN SETTLE THIS WITHOUT VIOLENCE.
THIS GUY'S A BIG SACK OF WIND, WONDER WOMAN. JUST GIVE ME THE WORD AND I'LL SEND THEM HOME IN A BODY BAG.
YOU'RE GOING DOWN FIRST, GARDNER-- COUNT ON IT!
OOOO I'M SHAKIN'!
GUY, WILL YOU PLEASE GET BACK TO THE COMPOUND!
I DON'T WANT A FIGHT, CAPTAIN. ALL I WANT IS WHAT'S RIGHT!
YOU AND YOUR PEOPLE SHOULD COME BACK TO OUR HEADQUARTERS--
17

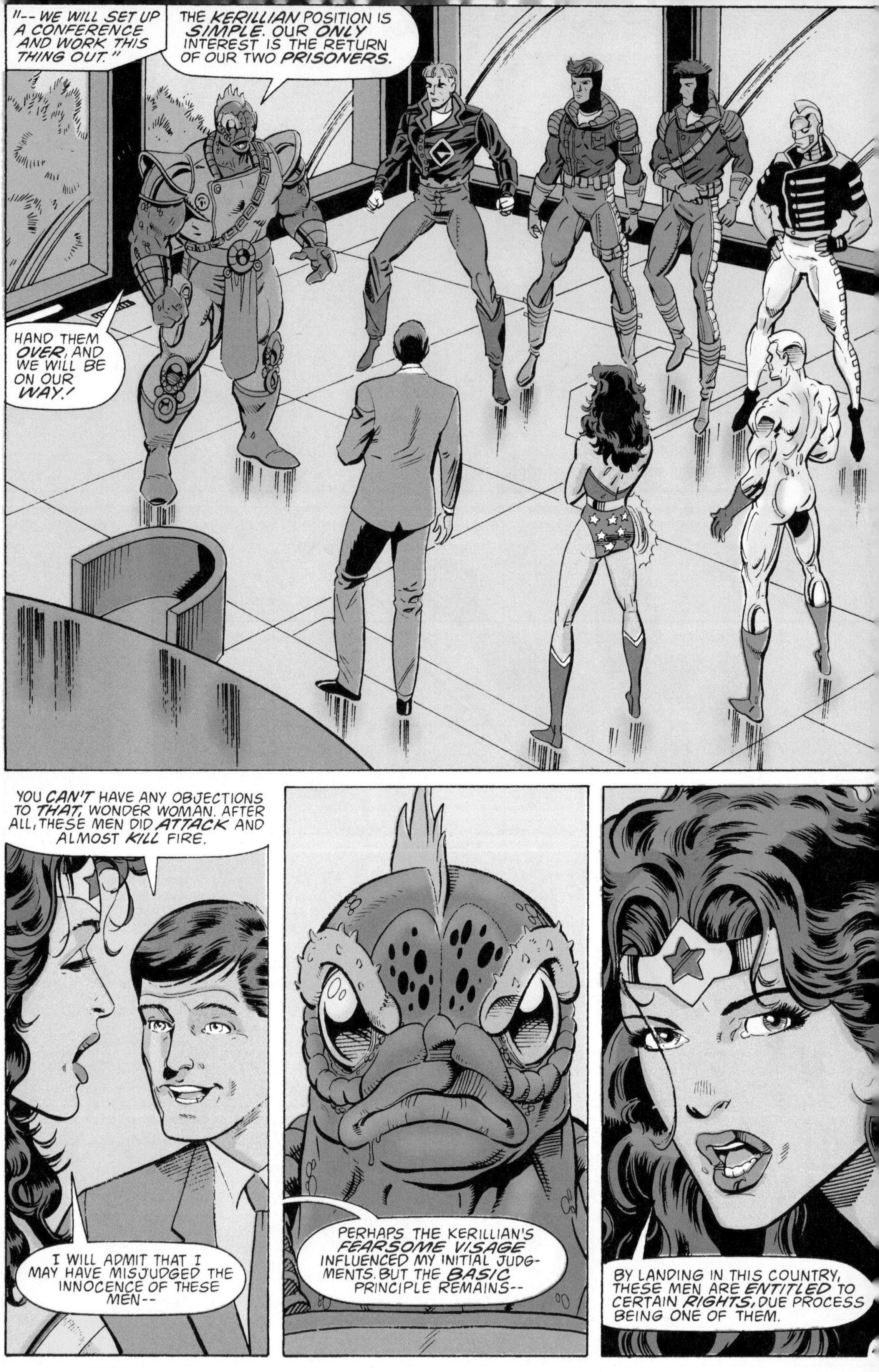
"-- WE WILL SET UP A CONFERENCE AND WORK THIS THING OUT."
THE KERILLIAN POSITION IS SIMPLE. OUR ONLY INTEREST IS THE RETURN OF OUR TWO PRISONERS.
HAND THEM OVER, AND WE WILL BE ON OUR WAY!
YOU CAN'T HAVE ANY OBJECTIONS TO THAT, WONDER WOMAN. AFTER ALL, THESE MEN DID ATTACK AND ALMOST KILL FIRE.
I WILL ADMIT THAT I MAY HAVE MISJUDGED THE INNOCENCE OF THESE MEN--
PERHAPS THE KERILLIAN'S FEARSOME VISAGE INFLUENCED MY INITIAL JUDGMENTS. BUT THE BASIC PRINCIPLE REMAINS--
BY LANDING IN THIS COUNTRY, THESE MEN ARE ENTITLED TO CERTAIN RIGHTS, DUE PROCESS BEING ONE OF THEM.

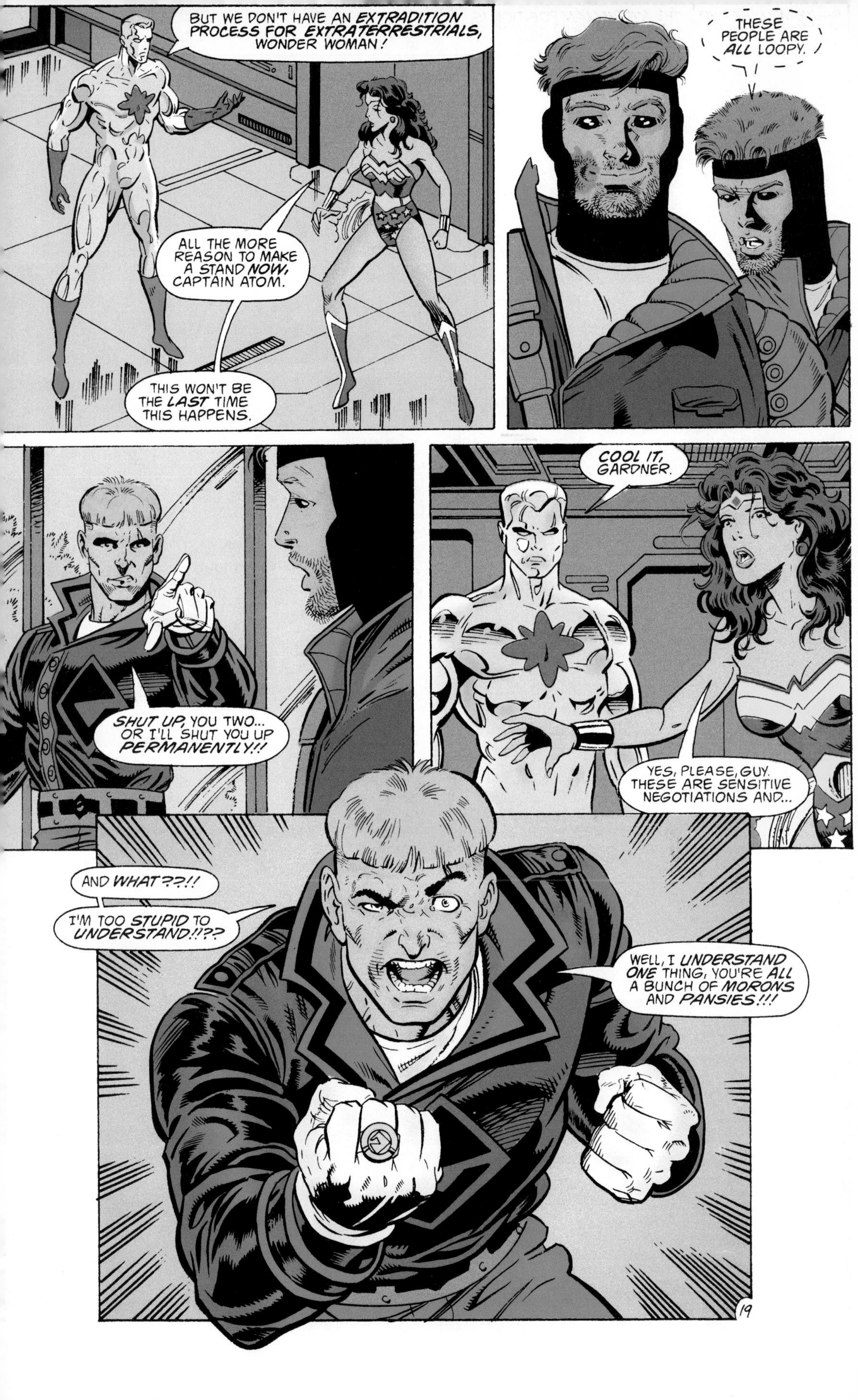

BUT WE DON'T HAVE AN *EXTRADITION PROCESS* FOR *EXTRATERRESTRIALS,* WONDER WOMAN!
ALL THE MORE REASON TO MAKE A STAND *NOW,* CAPTAIN ATOM.
THIS WON'T BE THE *LAST* TIME THIS HAPPENS.
THESE PEOPLE ARE *ALL* LOOPY.
SHUT UP, YOU TWO... OR I'LL SHUT YOU UP *PERMANENTLY!!*
COOL IT, GARDNER.
YES, PLEASE, GUY. THESE ARE SENSITIVE NEGOTIATIONS AND...
AND *WHAT??!!*
I'M TOO *STUPID* TO *UNDERSTAND!!??*
WELL, I *UNDERSTAND ONE* THING, YOU'RE *ALL* A BUNCH OF *MORONS* AND *PANSIES!!!*

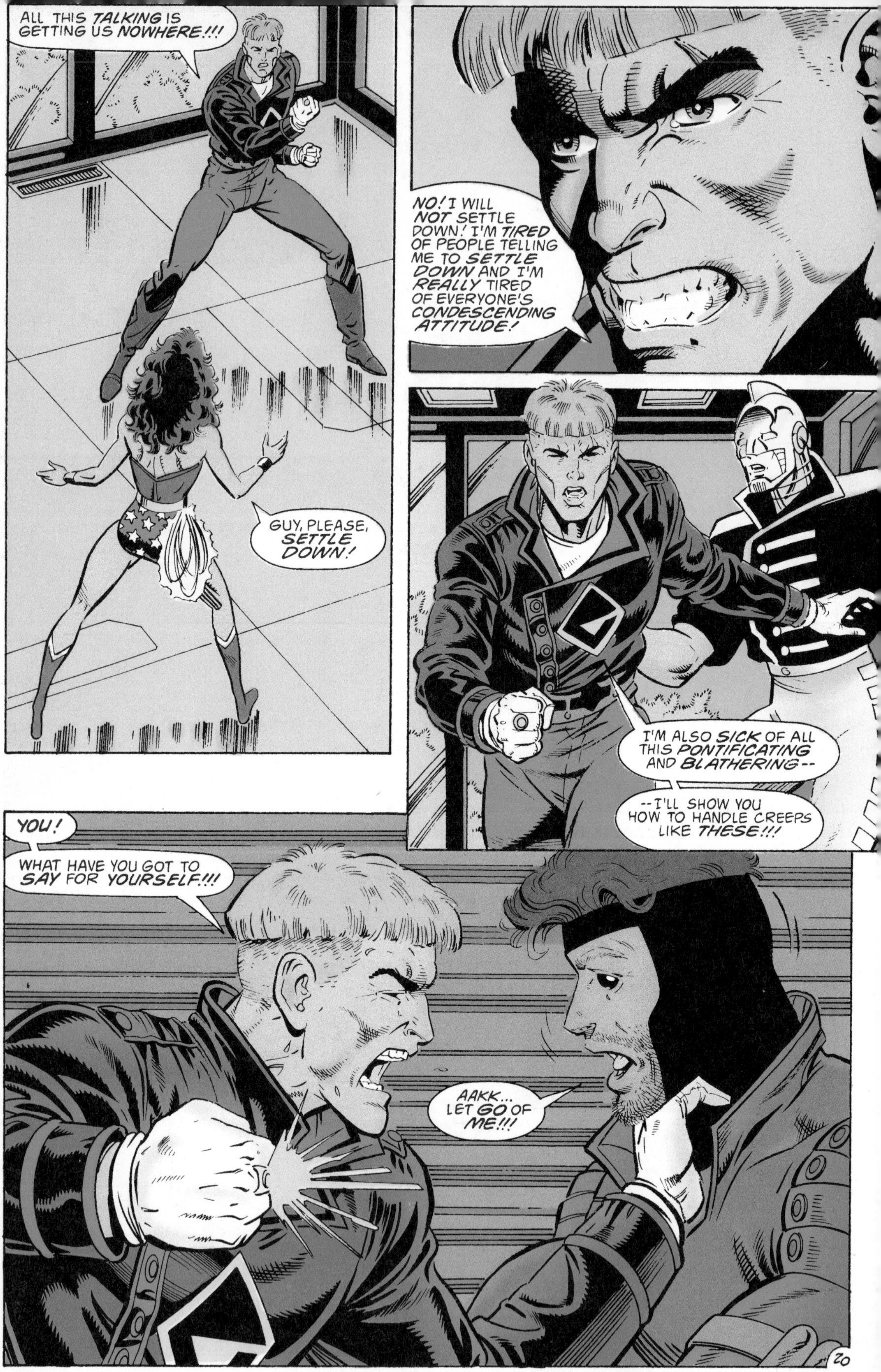
ALL THIS TALKING IS GETTING US NOWHERE!!!
GUY, PLEASE, SETTLE DOWN!
NO! I WILL NOT SETTLE DOWN! I'M TIRED OF PEOPLE TELLING ME TO SETTLE DOWN AND I'M REALLY TIRED OF EVERYONE'S CONDESCENDING ATTITUDE!
I'M ALSO SICK OF ALL THIS PONTIFICATING AND BLATHERING--
--I'LL SHOW YOU HOW TO HANDLE CREEPS LIKE THESE!!!
YOU!
WHAT HAVE YOU GOT TO SAY FOR YOURSELF!!!
AAKK... LET GO OF ME!!!
20

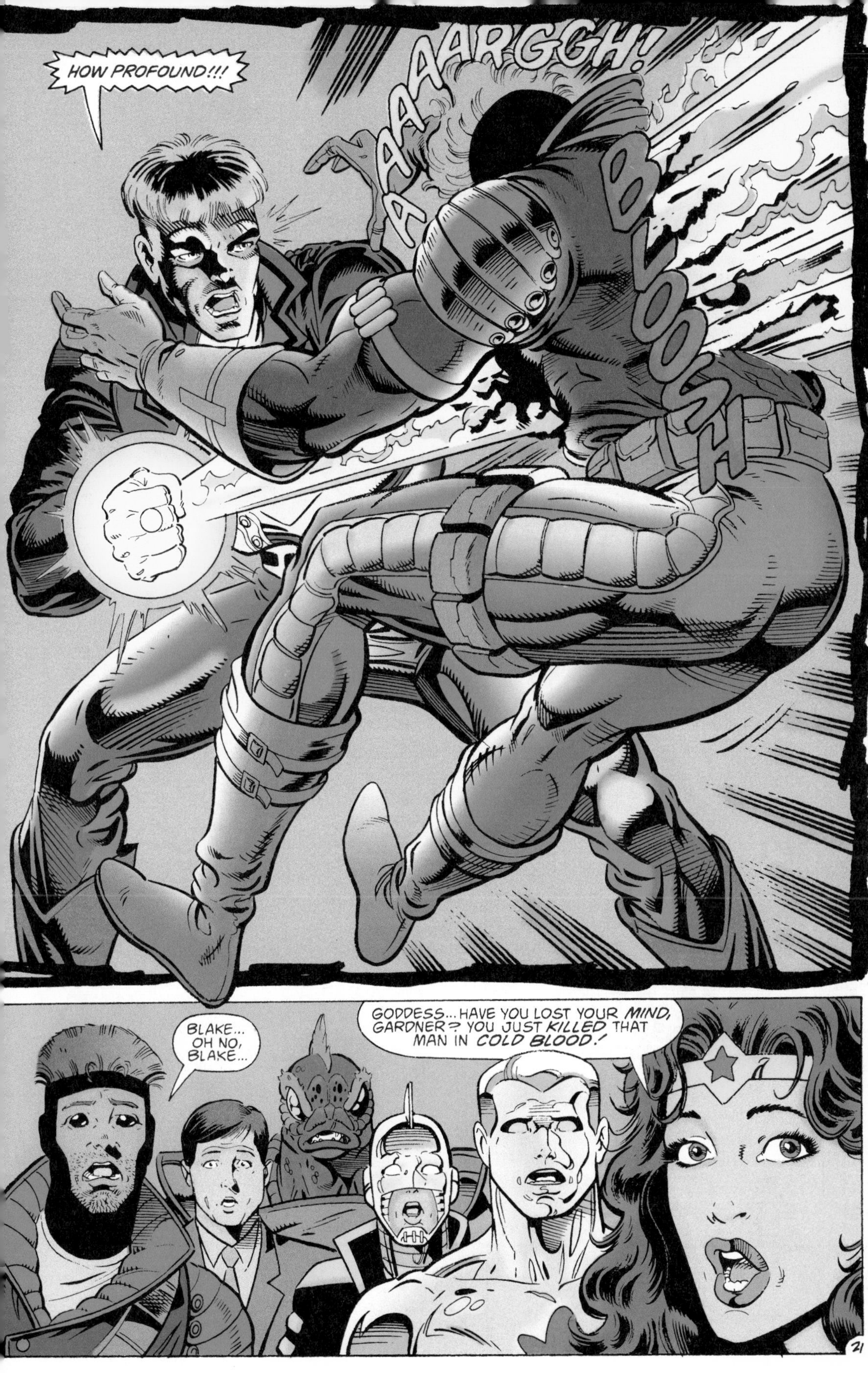
HOW PROFOUND!!!
AAAAARGGH!
BLOOOSH
BLAKE... OH NO, BLAKE...
GODDESS... HAVE YOU LOST YOUR MIND, GARDNER? YOU JUST KILLED THAT MAN IN COLD BLOOD!

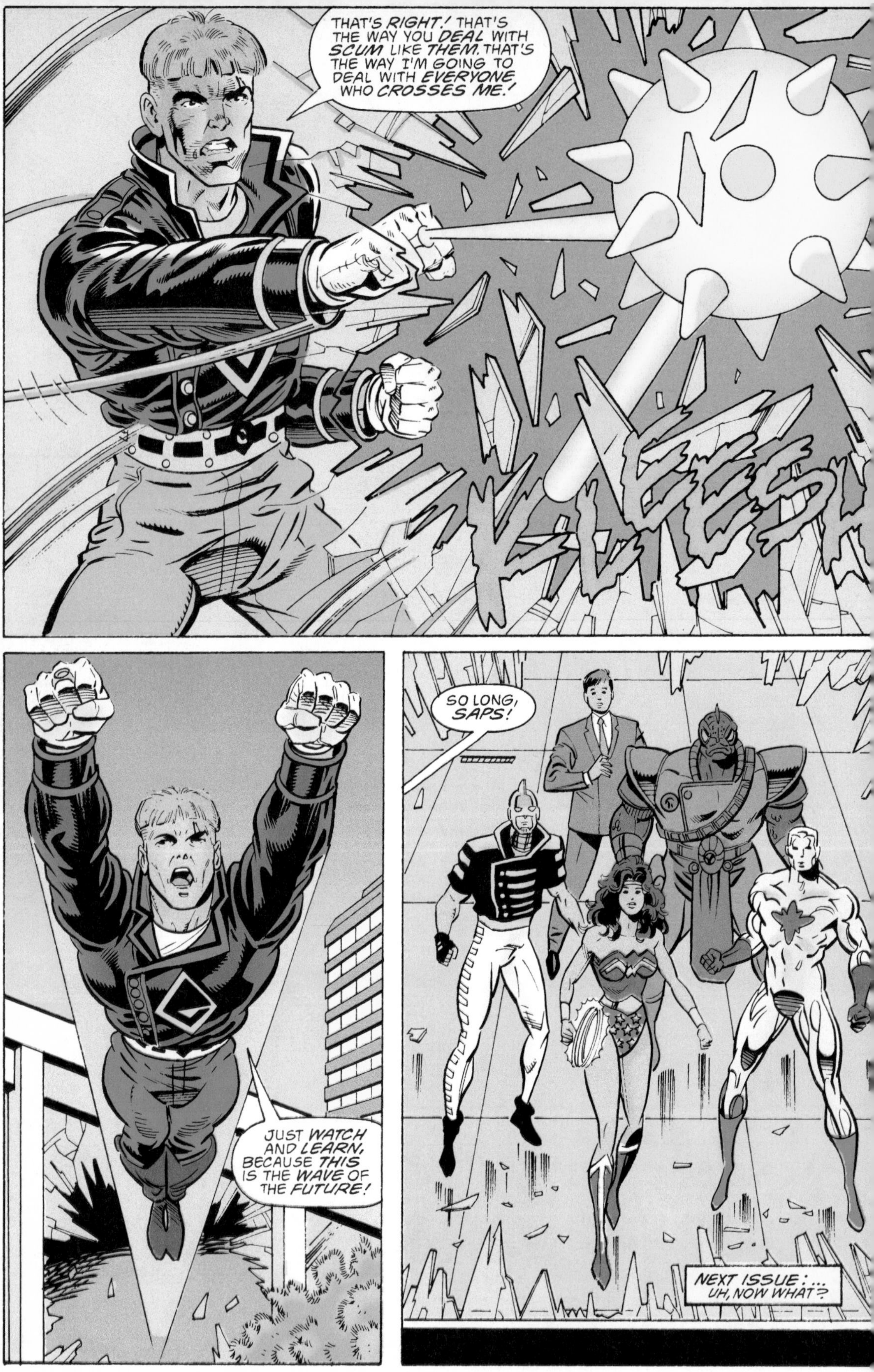
THAT'S RIGHT! THAT'S THE WAY YOU DEAL WITH SCUM LIKE THEM. THAT'S THE WAY I'M GOING TO DEAL WITH EVERYONE WHO CROSSES ME!
JUST WATCH AND LEARN, BECAUSE THIS IS THE WAVE OF THE FUTURE!
SO LONG, SAPS!
NEXT ISSUE: ... UH, NOW WHAT?

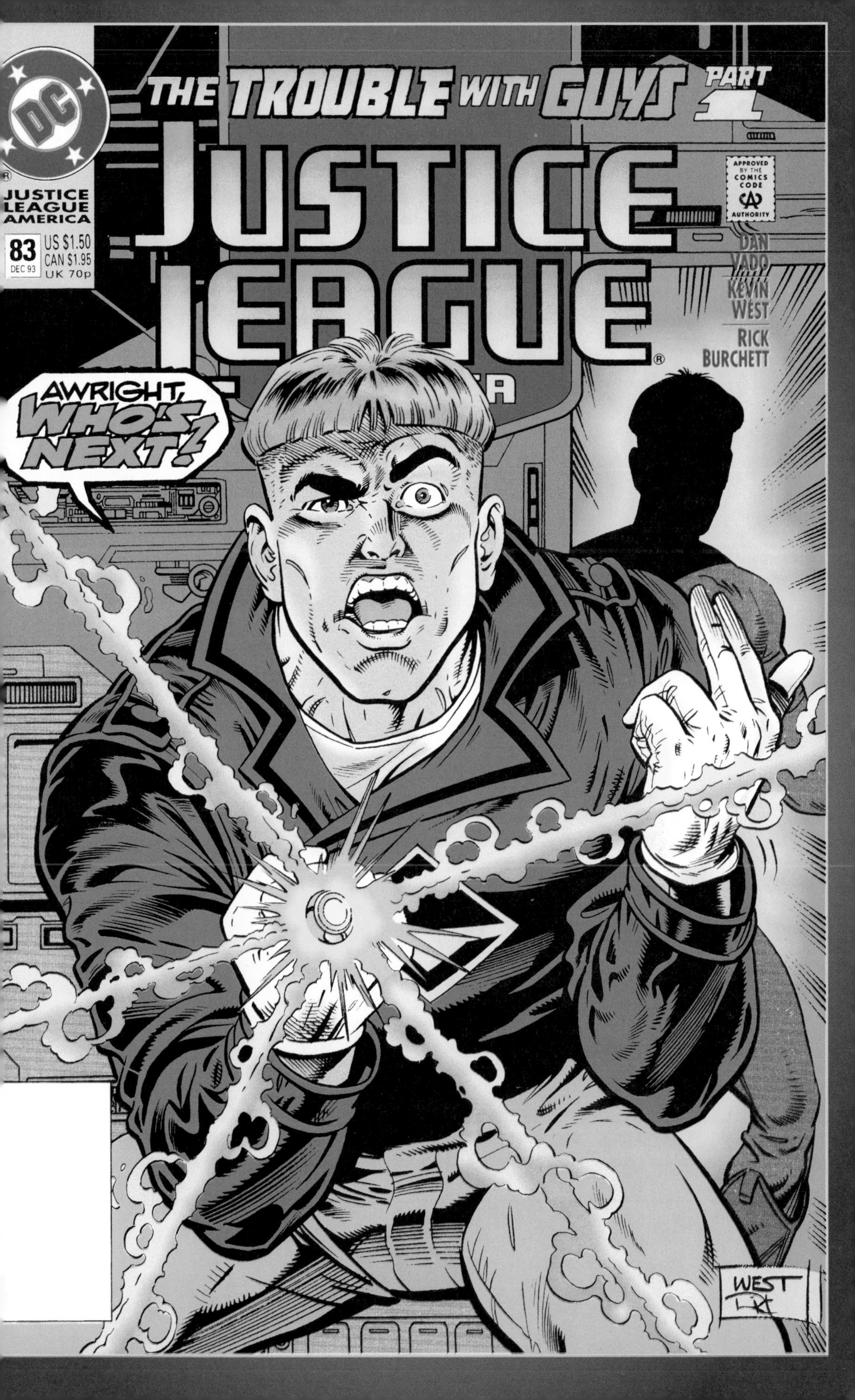
THE TROUBLE WITH GUYS PART 1
JUSTICE LEAGUE
JUSTICE LEAGUE AMERICA
83 DEC 93
US $1.50
CAN $1.95
UK 70p
APPROVED BY THE COMICS CODE AUTHORITY
DAN VADO
KEVIN WEST
RICK BURCHETT
AWRIGHT, WHO'S NEXT?!
WEST

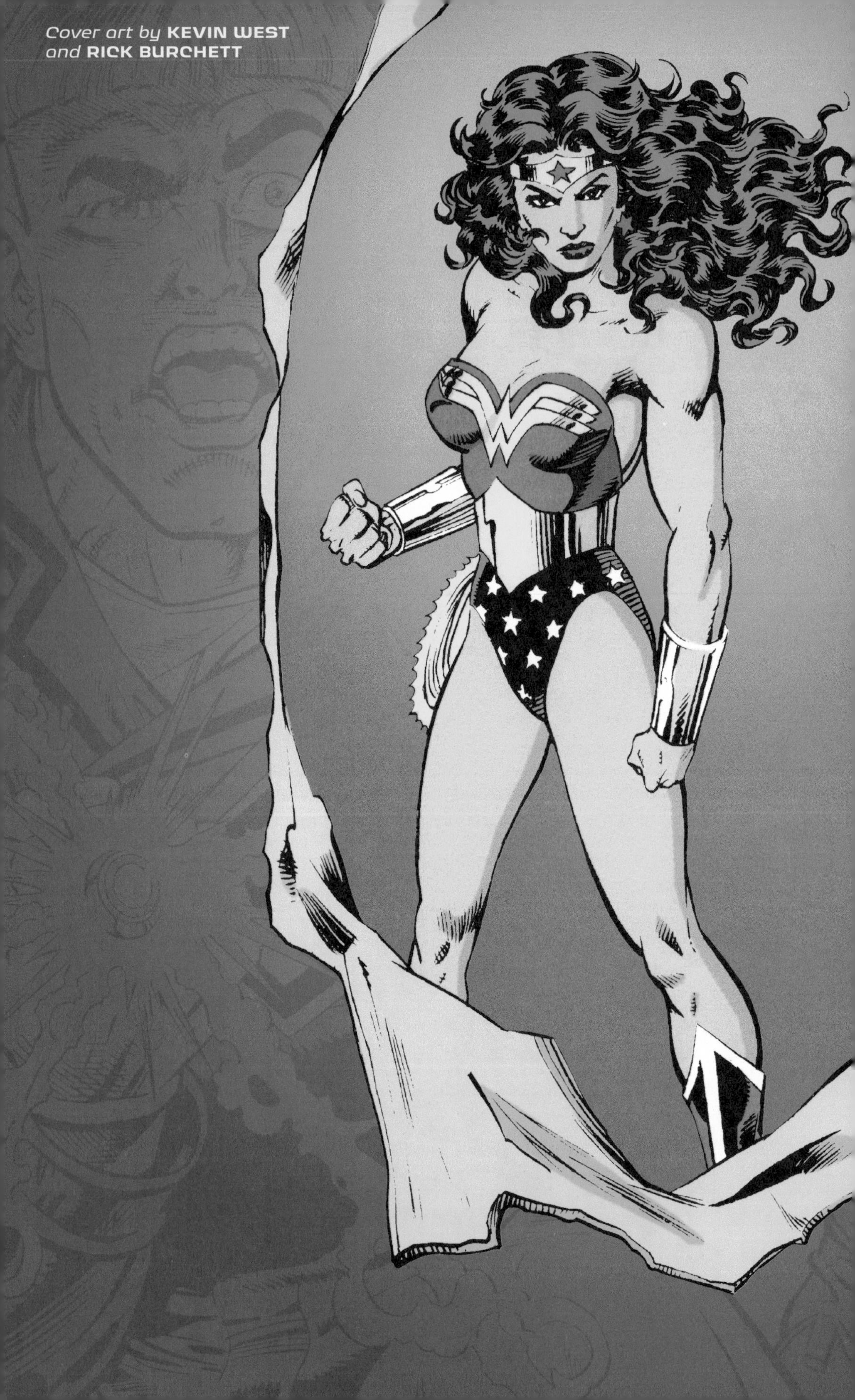

Cover art by **KEVIN WEST**
and **RICK BURCHETT**

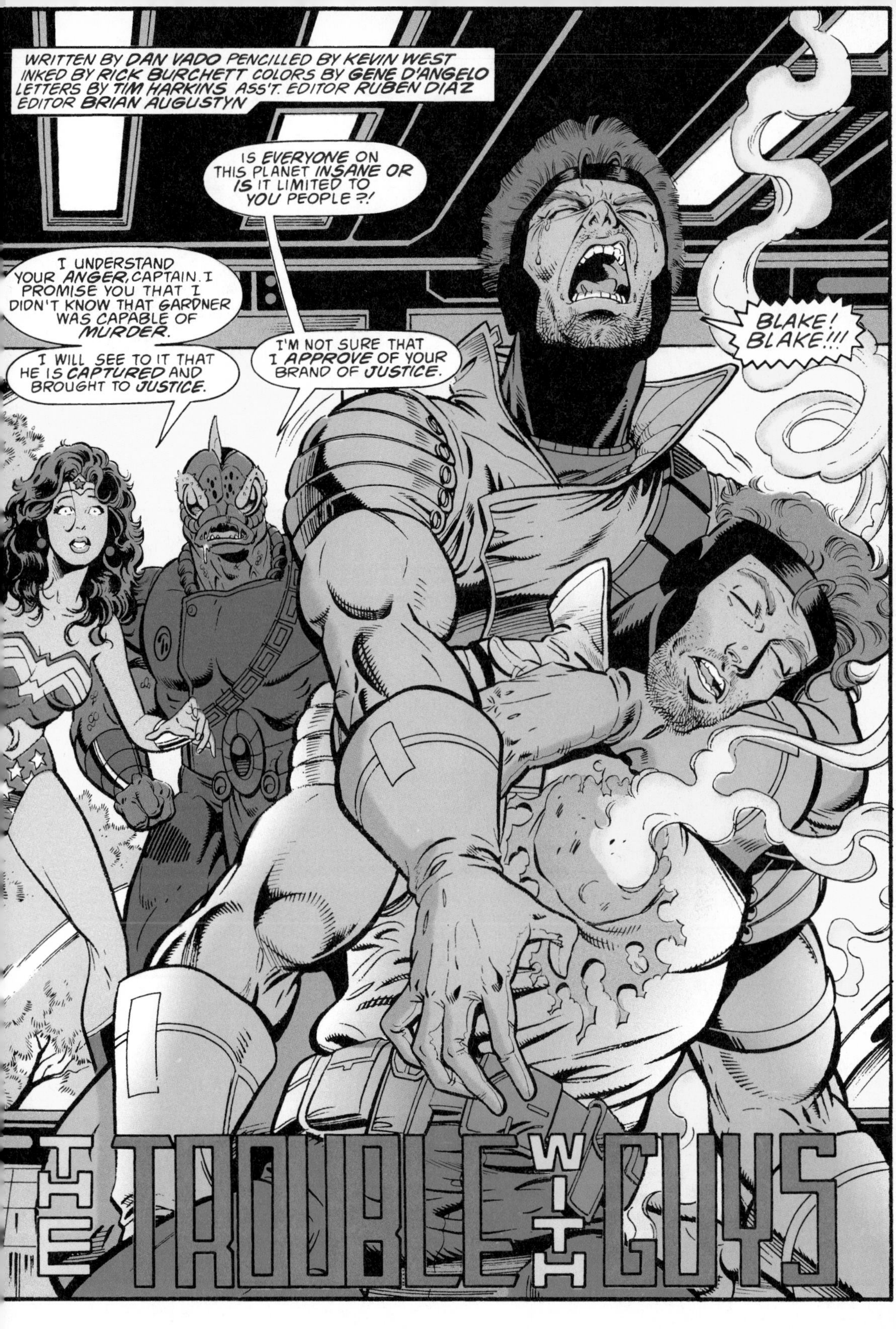
WRITTEN BY DAN VADO PENCILLED BY KEVIN WEST INKED BY RICK BURCHETT COLORS BY GENE D'ANGELO LETTERS BY TIM HARKINS ASS'T. EDITOR RUBEN DIAZ EDITOR BRIAN AUGUSTYN
IS EVERYONE ON THIS PLANET INSANE OR IS IT LIMITED TO YOU PEOPLE ?!
I UNDERSTAND YOUR ANGER, CAPTAIN. I PROMISE YOU THAT I DIDN'T KNOW THAT GARDNER WAS CAPABLE OF MURDER.
I WILL SEE TO IT THAT HE IS CAPTURED AND BROUGHT TO JUSTICE.
I'M NOT SURE THAT I APPROVE OF YOUR BRAND OF JUSTICE.
BLAKE! BLAKE!!!
THE TROUBLE WITH GUYS

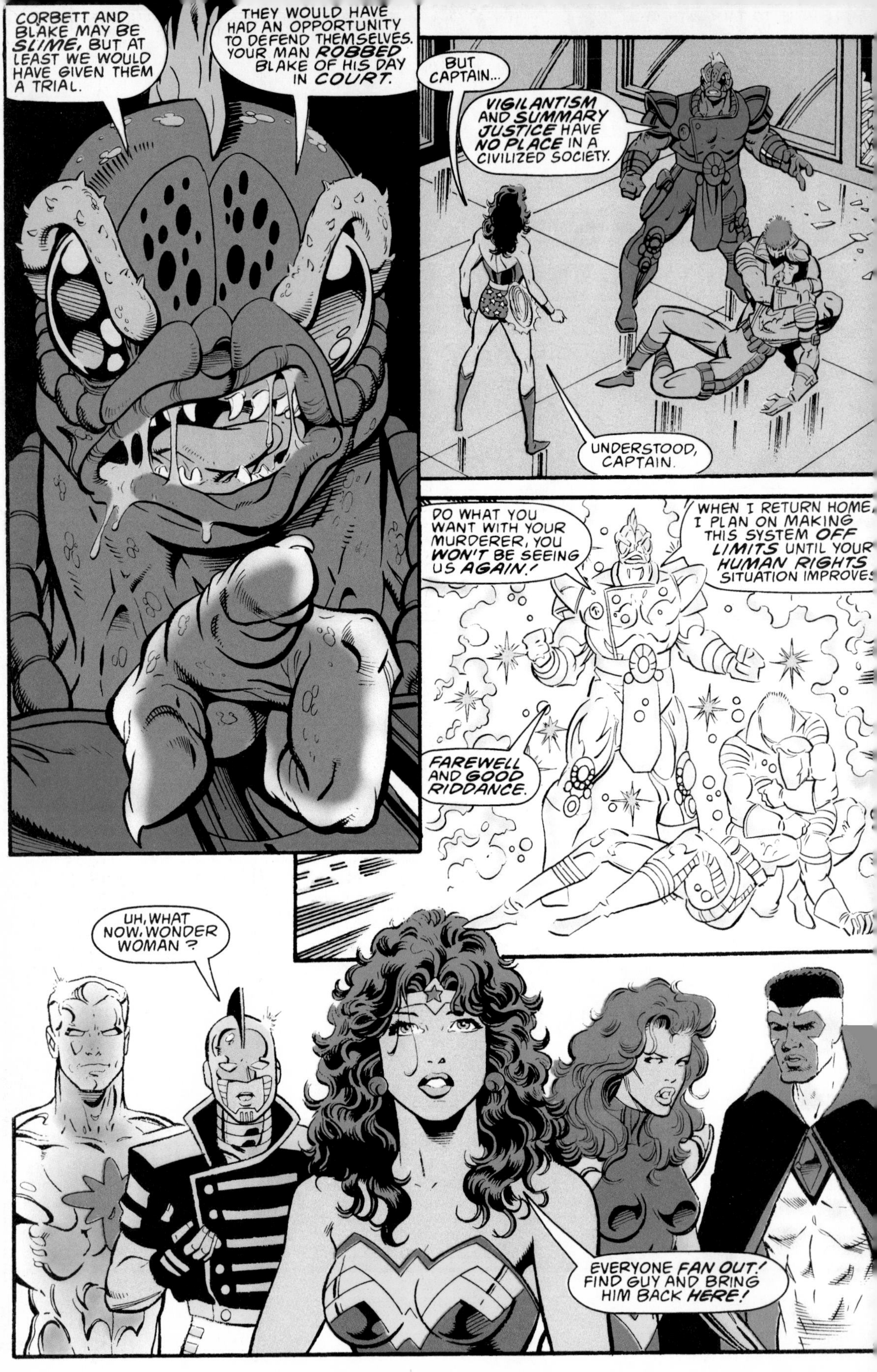
CORBETT AND BLAKE MAY BE SLIME, BUT AT LEAST WE WOULD HAVE GIVEN THEM A TRIAL.
THEY WOULD HAVE HAD AN OPPORTUNITY TO DEFEND THEMSELVES. YOUR MAN ROBBED BLAKE OF HIS DAY IN COURT.
BUT CAPTAIN...
VIGILANTISM AND SUMMARY JUSTICE HAVE NO PLACE IN A CIVILIZED SOCIETY.
UNDERSTOOD, CAPTAIN.
DO WHAT YOU WANT WITH YOUR MURDERER, YOU WON'T BE SEEING US AGAIN!
WHEN I RETURN HOME, I PLAN ON MAKING THIS SYSTEM OFF LIMITS UNTIL YOUR HUMAN RIGHTS SITUATION IMPROVES
FAREWELL AND GOOD RIDDANCE.
UH, WHAT NOW, WONDER WOMAN?
EVERYONE FAN OUT! FIND GUY AND BRING HIM BACK HERE!

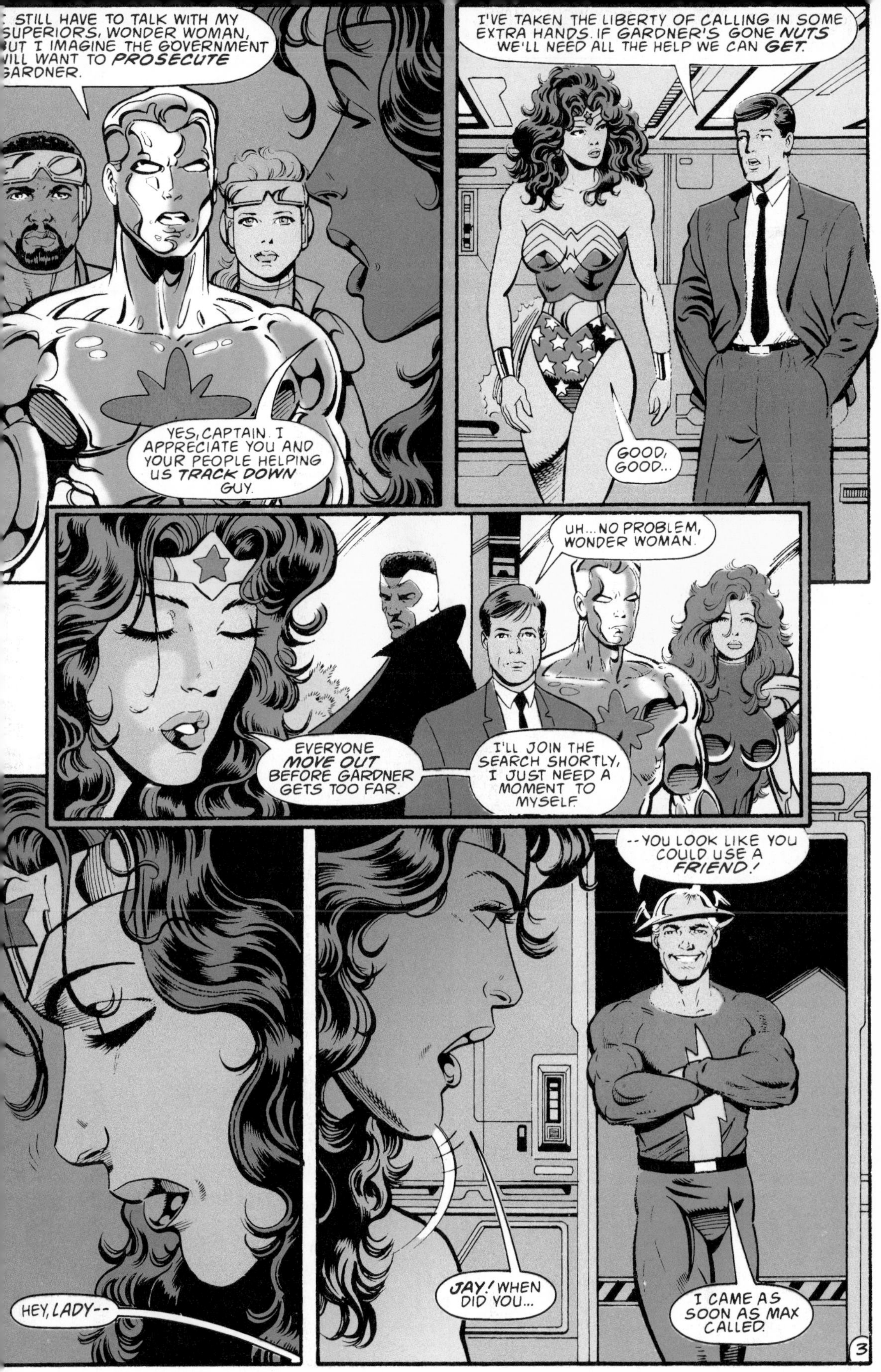
STILL HAVE TO TALK WITH MY SUPERIORS, WONDER WOMAN, UT I IMAGINE THE GOVERNMENT ILL WANT TO PROSECUTE ARDNER.
YES, CAPTAIN. I APPRECIATE YOU AND YOUR PEOPLE HELPING US TRACK DOWN GUY.
I'VE TAKEN THE LIBERTY OF CALLING IN SOME EXTRA HANDS. IF GARDNER'S GONE NUTS WE'LL NEED ALL THE HELP WE CAN GET.
GOOD, GOOD...
EVERYONE MOVE OUT BEFORE GARDNER GETS TOO FAR.
I'LL JOIN THE SEARCH SHORTLY, I JUST NEED A MOMENT TO MYSELF.
UH... NO PROBLEM, WONDER WOMAN.
HEY, LADY--
--YOU LOOK LIKE YOU COULD USE A FRIEND!
JAY! WHEN DID YOU...
I CAME AS SOON AS MAX CALLED.
3

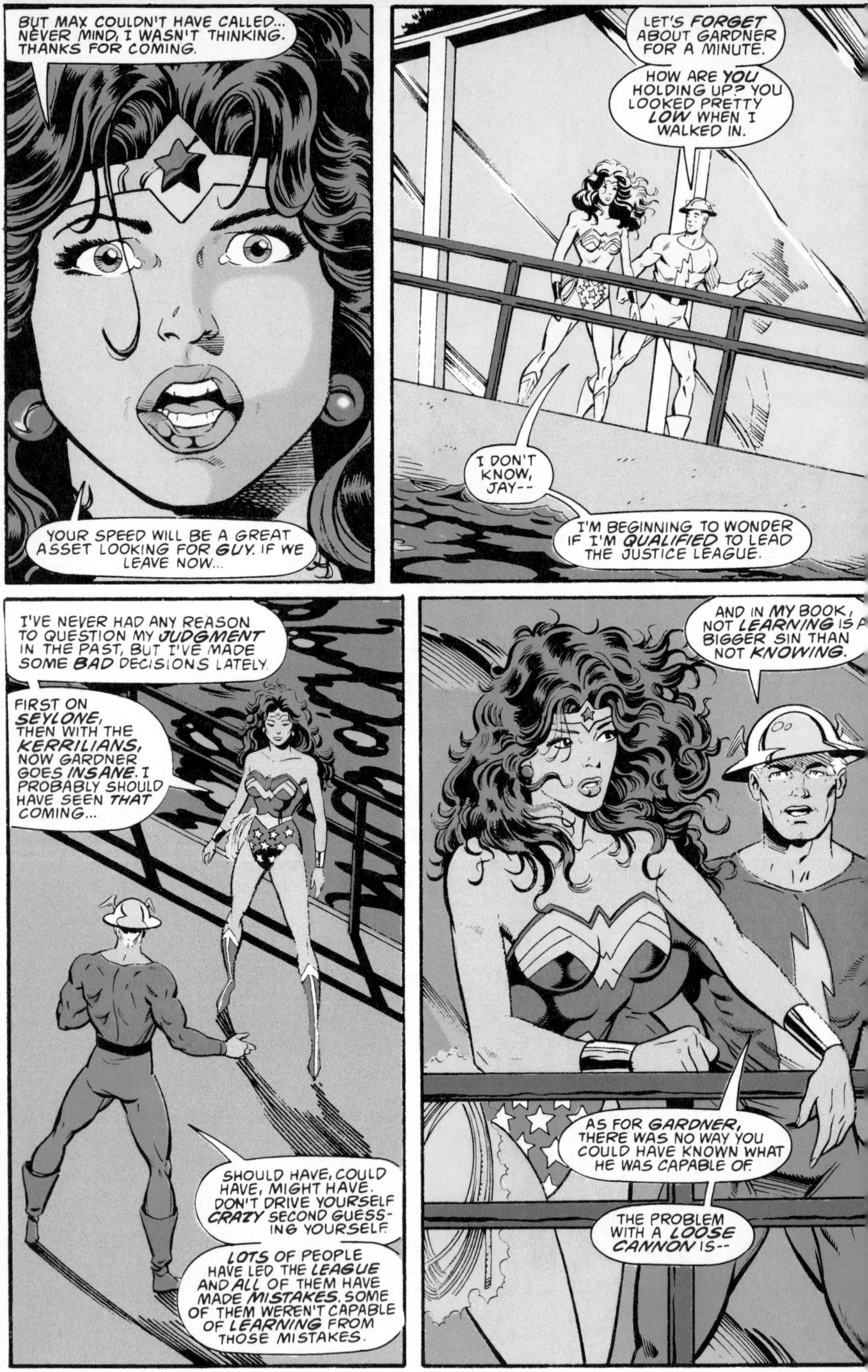

BUT MAX COULDN'T HAVE CALLED... NEVER MIND, I WASN'T THINKING. THANKS FOR COMING.
YOUR SPEED WILL BE A GREAT ASSET LOOKING FOR GUY. IF WE LEAVE NOW...
LET'S FORGET ABOUT GARDNER FOR A MINUTE.
HOW ARE YOU HOLDING UP? YOU LOOKED PRETTY LOW WHEN I WALKED IN.
I DON'T KNOW, JAY--
I'M BEGINNING TO WONDER IF I'M QUALIFIED TO LEAD THE JUSTICE LEAGUE.
I'VE NEVER HAD ANY REASON TO QUESTION MY JUDGMENT IN THE PAST, BUT I'VE MADE SOME BAD DECISIONS LATELY.
FIRST ON SEYLONE, THEN WITH THE KERRILIANS, NOW GARDNER GOES INSANE. I PROBABLY SHOULD HAVE SEEN THAT COMING...
SHOULD HAVE, COULD HAVE, MIGHT HAVE. DON'T DRIVE YOURSELF CRAZY SECOND GUESSING YOURSELF.
LOTS OF PEOPLE HAVE LED THE LEAGUE AND ALL OF THEM HAVE MADE MISTAKES. SOME OF THEM WEREN'T CAPABLE OF LEARNING FROM THOSE MISTAKES.
AND IN MY BOOK, NOT LEARNING IS A BIGGER SIN THAN NOT KNOWING.
AS FOR GARDNER, THERE WAS NO WAY YOU COULD HAVE KNOWN WHAT HE WAS CAPABLE OF.
THE PROBLEM WITH A LOOSE CANNON IS--

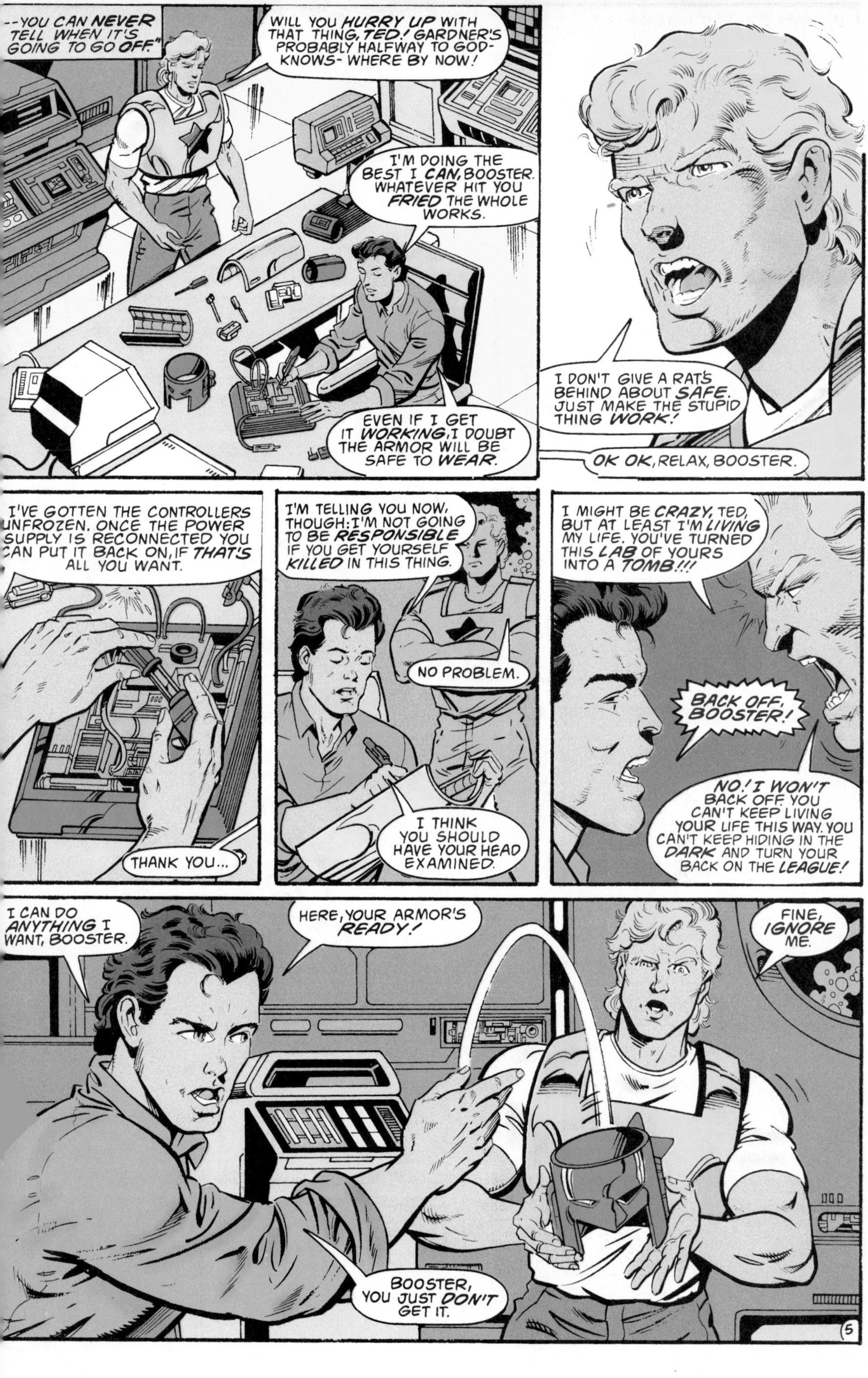
--YOU CAN NEVER TELL WHEN IT'S GOING TO GO OFF."
WILL YOU HURRY UP WITH THAT THING, TED! GARDNER'S PROBABLY HALFWAY TO GOD-KNOWS-WHERE BY NOW!
I'M DOING THE BEST I CAN, BOOSTER. WHATEVER HIT YOU FRIED THE WHOLE WORKS.
EVEN IF I GET IT WORKING, I DOUBT THE ARMOR WILL BE SAFE TO WEAR.
I DON'T GIVE A RAT'S BEHIND ABOUT SAFE. JUST MAKE THE STUPID THING WORK!
OK OK, RELAX, BOOSTER.
I'VE GOTTEN THE CONTROLLERS UNFROZEN. ONCE THE POWER SUPPLY IS RECONNECTED YOU CAN PUT IT BACK ON, IF THAT'S ALL YOU WANT.
THANK YOU...
I'M TELLING YOU NOW, THOUGH: I'M NOT GOING TO BE RESPONSIBLE IF YOU GET YOURSELF KILLED IN THIS THING.
NO PROBLEM.
I THINK YOU SHOULD HAVE YOUR HEAD EXAMINED.
I MIGHT BE CRAZY, TED, BUT AT LEAST I'M LIVING MY LIFE. YOU'VE TURNED THIS LAB OF YOURS INTO A TOMB!!!
BACK OFF, BOOSTER!
NO! I WON'T BACK OFF. YOU CAN'T KEEP LIVING YOUR LIFE THIS WAY. YOU CAN'T KEEP HIDING IN THE DARK AND TURN YOUR BACK ON THE LEAGUE!
I CAN DO ANYTHING I WANT, BOOSTER.
HERE, YOUR ARMOR'S READY!
FINE, IGNORE ME.
BOOSTER, YOU JUST DON'T GET IT.

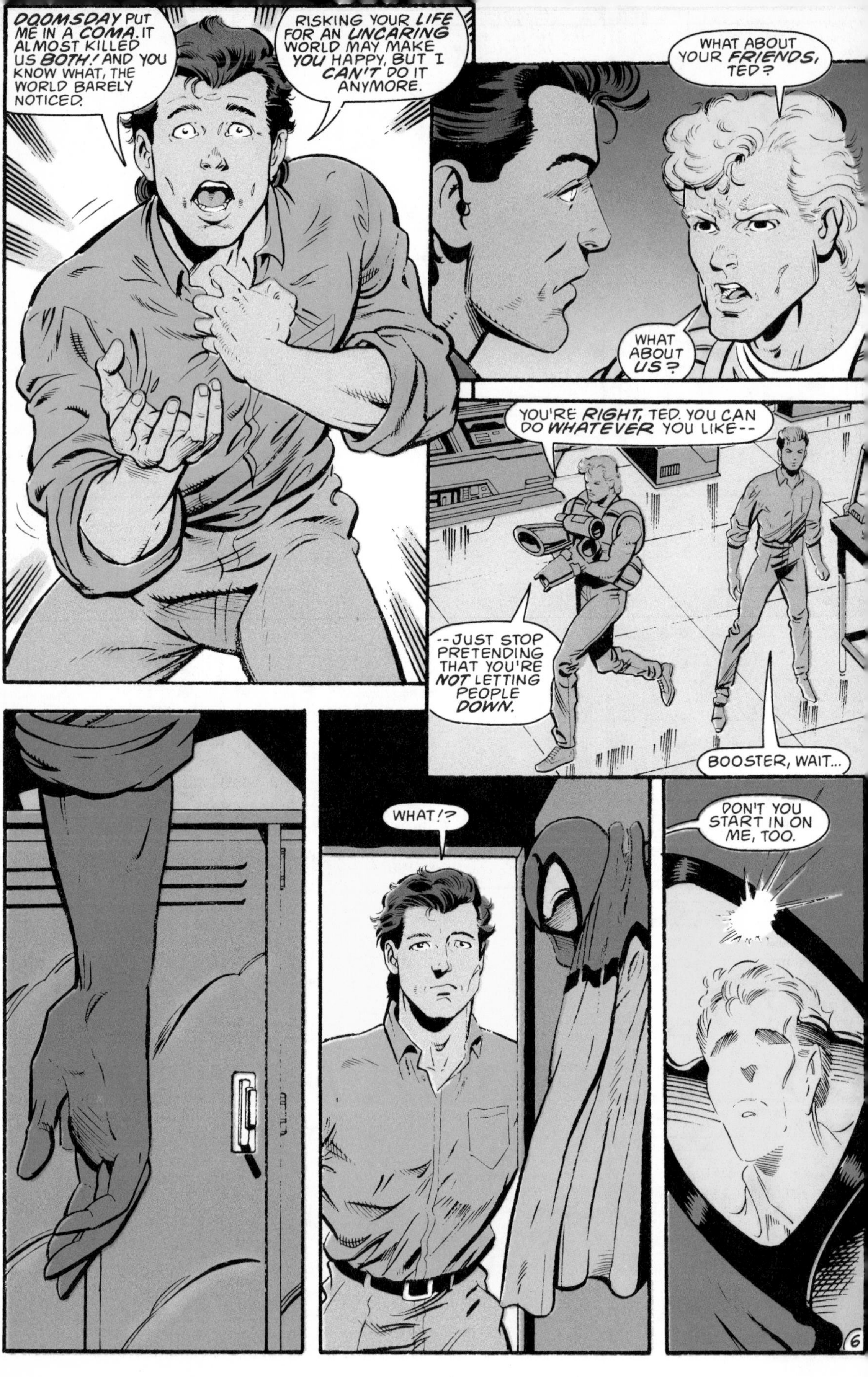
DOOMSDAY PUT ME IN A COMA. IT ALMOST KILLED US BOTH! AND YOU KNOW WHAT, THE WORLD BARELY NOTICED.
RISKING YOUR LIFE FOR AN UNCARING WORLD MAY MAKE YOU HAPPY, BUT I CAN'T DO IT ANYMORE.
WHAT ABOUT YOUR FRIENDS, TED?
WHAT ABOUT US?
YOU'RE RIGHT, TED. YOU CAN DO WHATEVER YOU LIKE--
--JUST STOP PRETENDING THAT YOU'RE NOT LETTING PEOPLE DOWN.
BOOSTER, WAIT...
WHAT!?
DON'T YOU START IN ON ME, TOO.
6

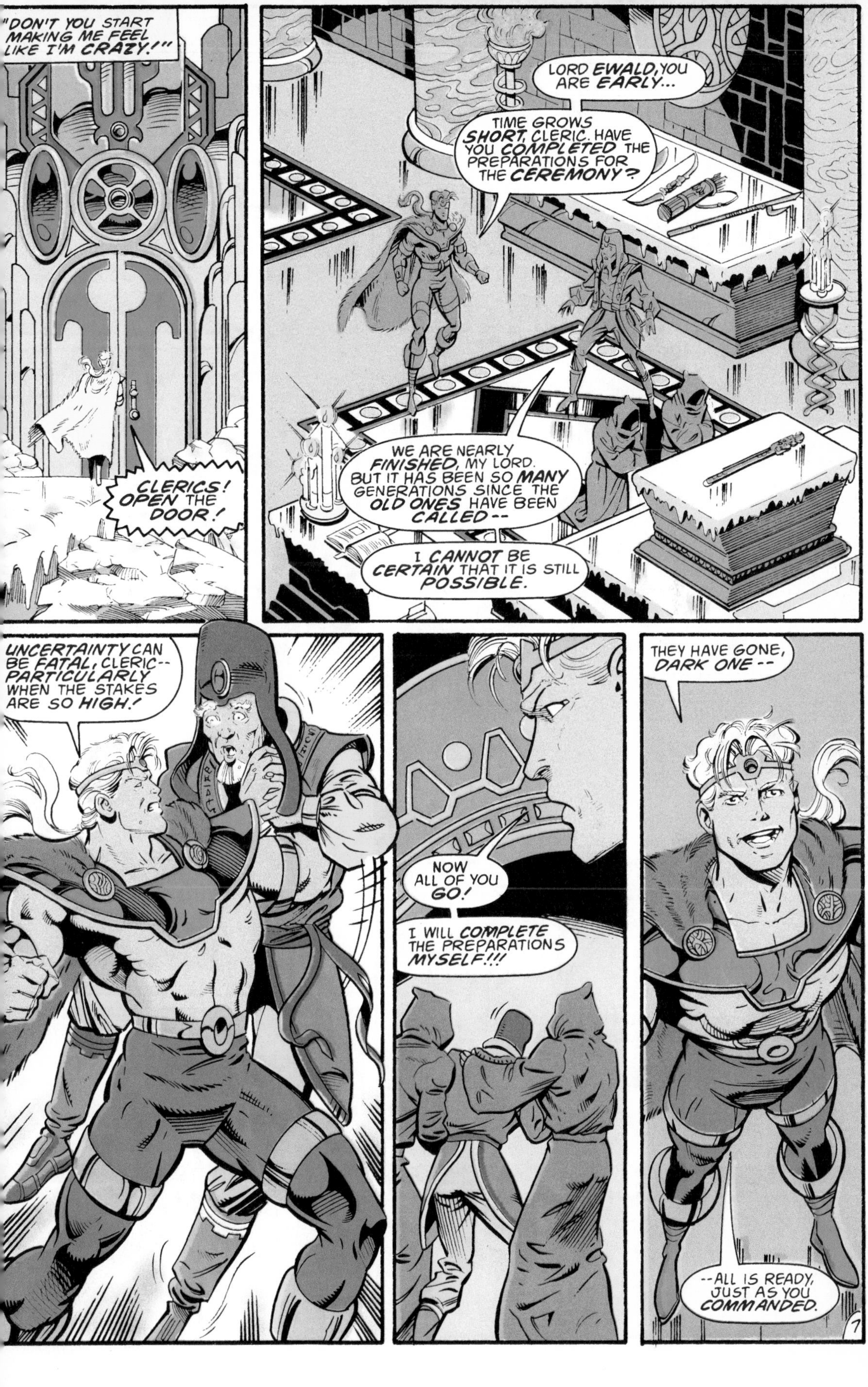
"DON'T YOU START MAKING ME FEEL LIKE I'M CRAZY!"
CLERICS! OPEN THE DOOR!
LORD EWALD, YOU ARE EARLY...
TIME GROWS SHORT, CLERIC. HAVE YOU COMPLETED THE PREPARATIONS FOR THE CEREMONY?
WE ARE NEARLY FINISHED, MY LORD. BUT IT HAS BEEN SO MANY GENERATIONS SINCE THE OLD ONES HAVE BEEN CALLED--
I CANNOT BE CERTAIN THAT IT IS STILL POSSIBLE.
UNCERTAINTY CAN BE FATAL, CLERIC-- PARTICULARLY WHEN THE STAKES ARE SO HIGH!
NOW ALL OF YOU GO!
I WILL COMPLETE THE PREPARATIONS MYSELF!!!
THEY HAVE GONE, DARK ONE--
--ALL IS READY, JUST AS YOU COMMANDED.
7

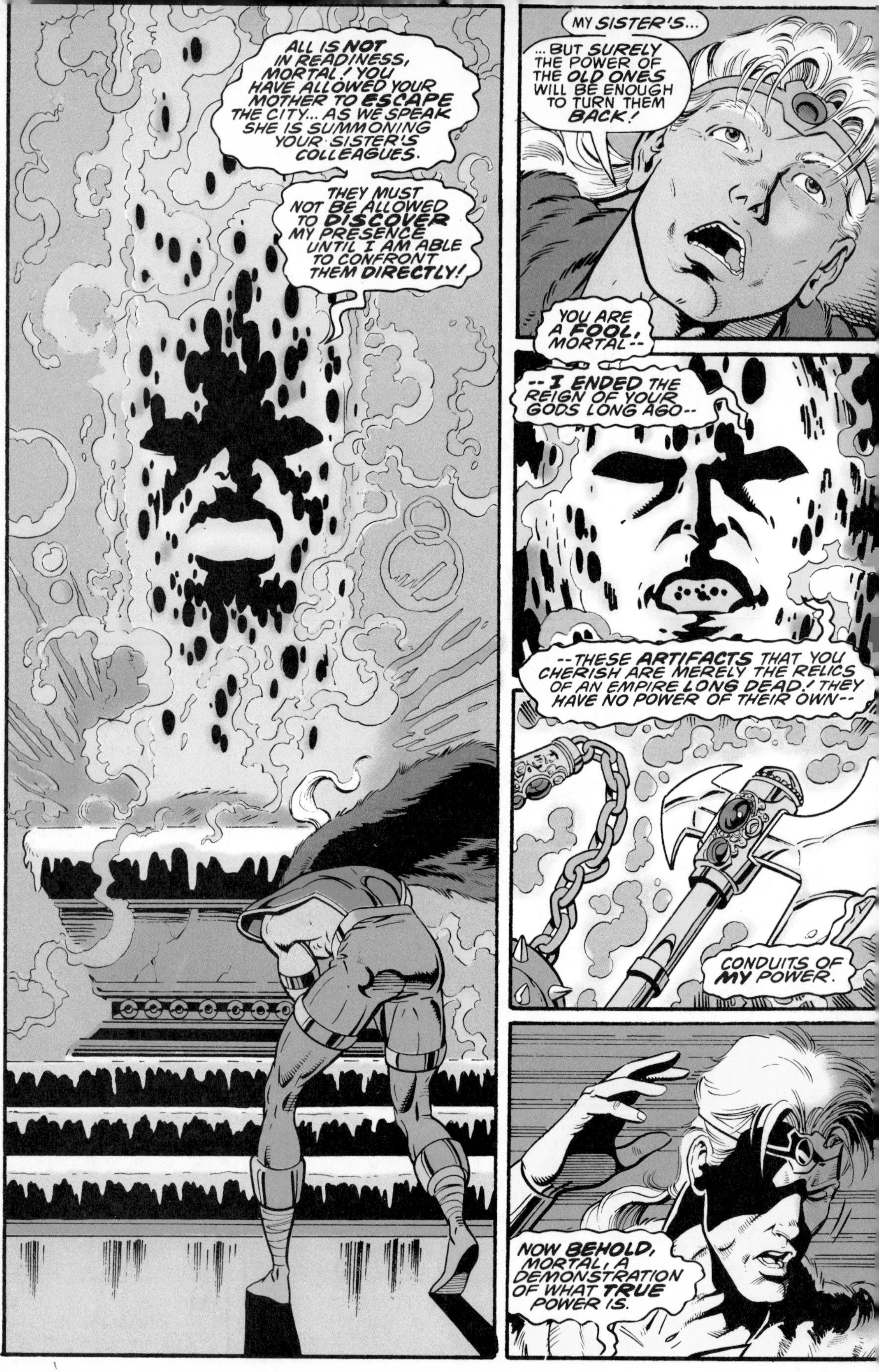

ALL IS NOT IN READINESS, MORTAL! YOU HAVE ALLOWED YOUR MOTHER TO ESCAPE THE CITY... AS WE SPEAK SHE IS SUMMONING YOUR SISTER'S COLLEAGUES.
THEY MUST NOT BE ALLOWED TO DISCOVER MY PRESENCE UNTIL I AM ABLE TO CONFRONT THEM DIRECTLY!
MY SISTER'S...
...BUT SURELY THE POWER OF THE OLD ONES WILL BE ENOUGH TO TURN THEM BACK!
YOU ARE A FOOL, MORTAL--
--I ENDED THE REIGN OF YOUR GODS LONG AGO--
--THESE ARTIFACTS THAT YOU CHERISH ARE MERELY THE RELICS OF AN EMPIRE LONG DEAD! THEY HAVE NO POWER OF THEIR OWN--
CONDUITS OF MY POWER.
NOW BEHOLD, MORTAL, A DEMONSTRATION OF WHAT TRUE POWER IS.

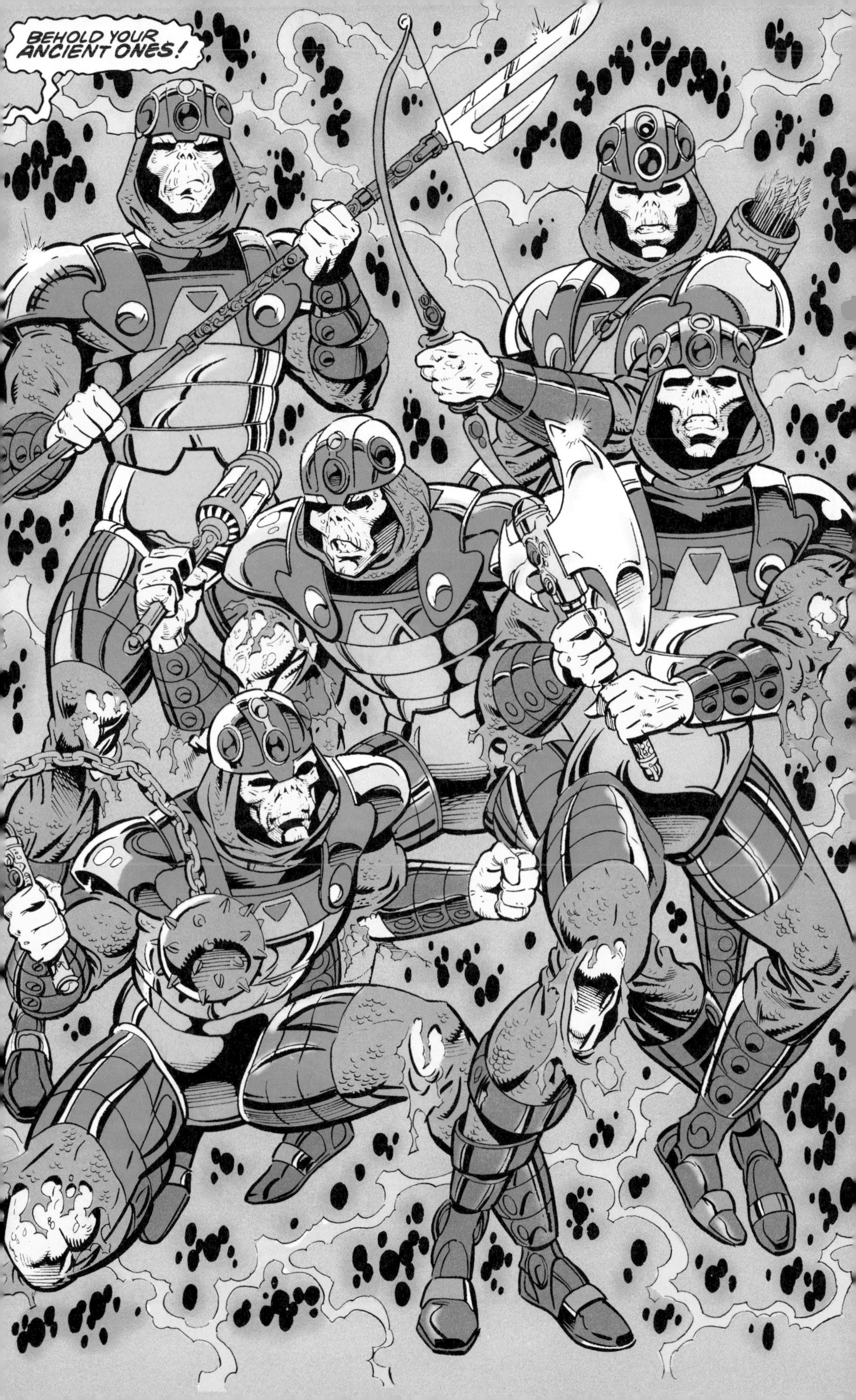
BEHOLD YOUR ANCIENT ONES!

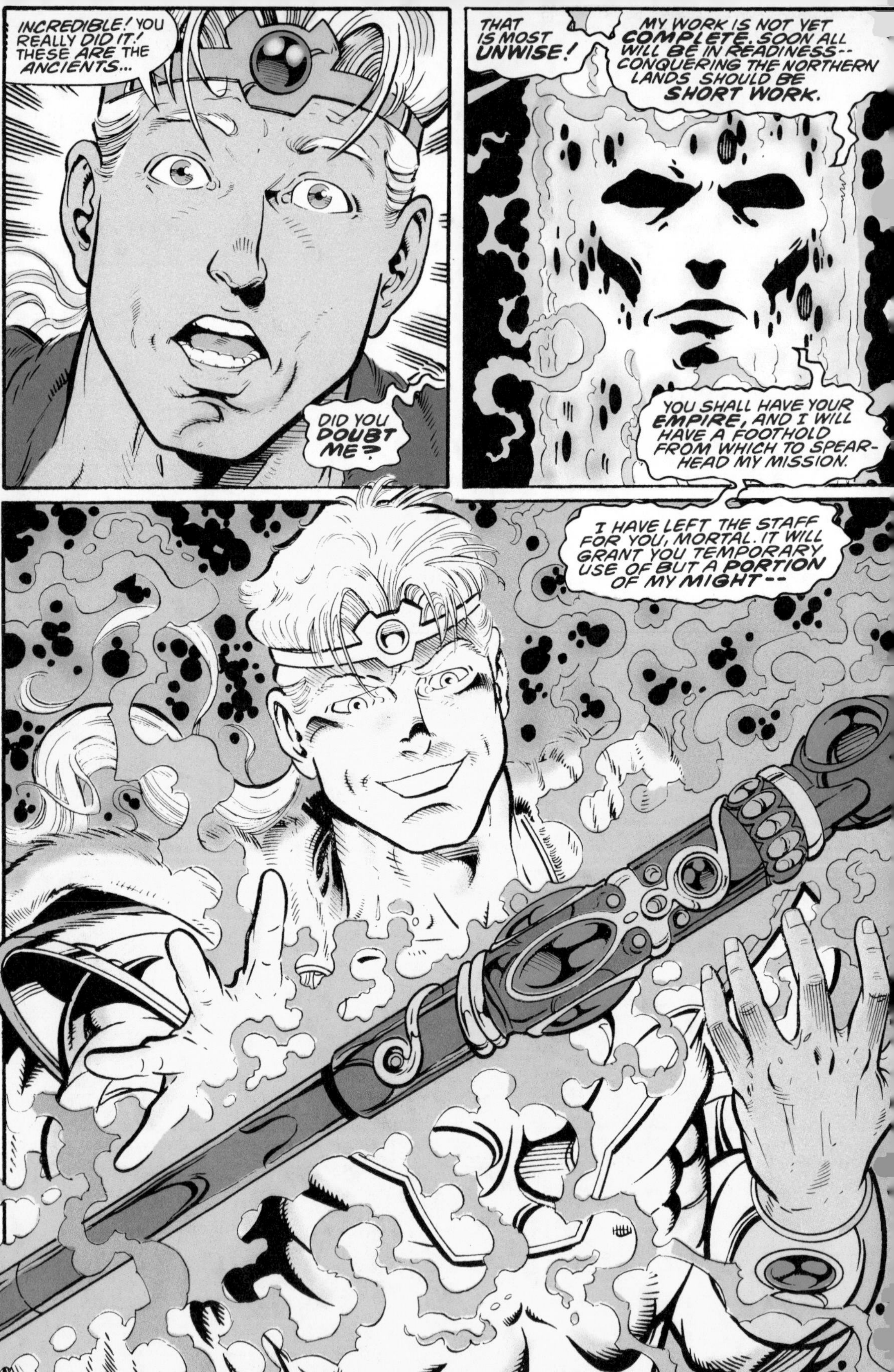
INCREDIBLE! YOU REALLY DID IT! THESE ARE THE ANCIENTS...
DID YOU DOUBT ME?
THAT IS MOST UNWISE!
MY WORK IS NOT YET COMPLETE. SOON ALL WILL BE IN READINESS-- CONQUERING THE NORTHERN LANDS SHOULD BE SHORT WORK.
YOU SHALL HAVE YOUR EMPIRE, AND I WILL HAVE A FOOTHOLD FROM WHICH TO SPEAR-HEAD MY MISSION.
I HAVE LEFT THE STAFF FOR YOU, MORTAL. IT WILL GRANT YOU TEMPORARY USE OF BUT A PORTION OF MY MIGHT--

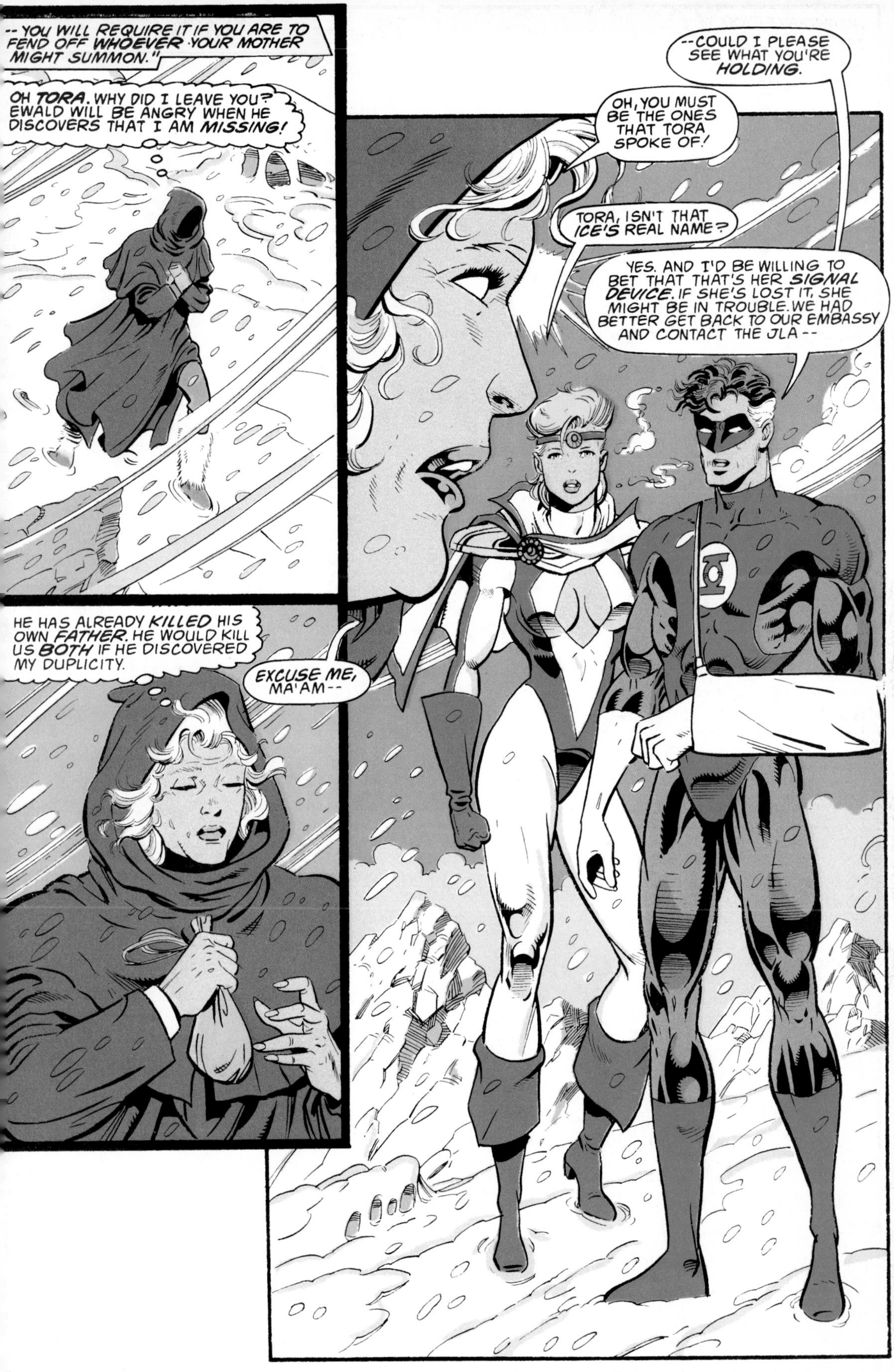
-- YOU WILL REQUIRE IT IF YOU ARE TO FEND OFF WHOEVER YOUR MOTHER MIGHT SUMMON."
OH TORA. WHY DID I LEAVE YOU? EWALD WILL BE ANGRY WHEN HE DISCOVERS THAT I AM MISSING!
HE HAS ALREADY KILLED HIS OWN FATHER. HE WOULD KILL US BOTH IF HE DISCOVERED MY DUPLICITY.
EXCUSE ME, MA'AM--
--COULD I PLEASE SEE WHAT YOU'RE HOLDING.
OH, YOU MUST BE THE ONES THAT TORA SPOKE OF!
TORA, ISN'T THAT ICE'S REAL NAME?
YES. AND I'D BE WILLING TO BET THAT THAT'S HER SIGNAL DEVICE. IF SHE'S LOST IT, SHE MIGHT BE IN TROUBLE. WE HAD BETTER GET BACK TO OUR EMBASSY AND CONTACT THE JLA--

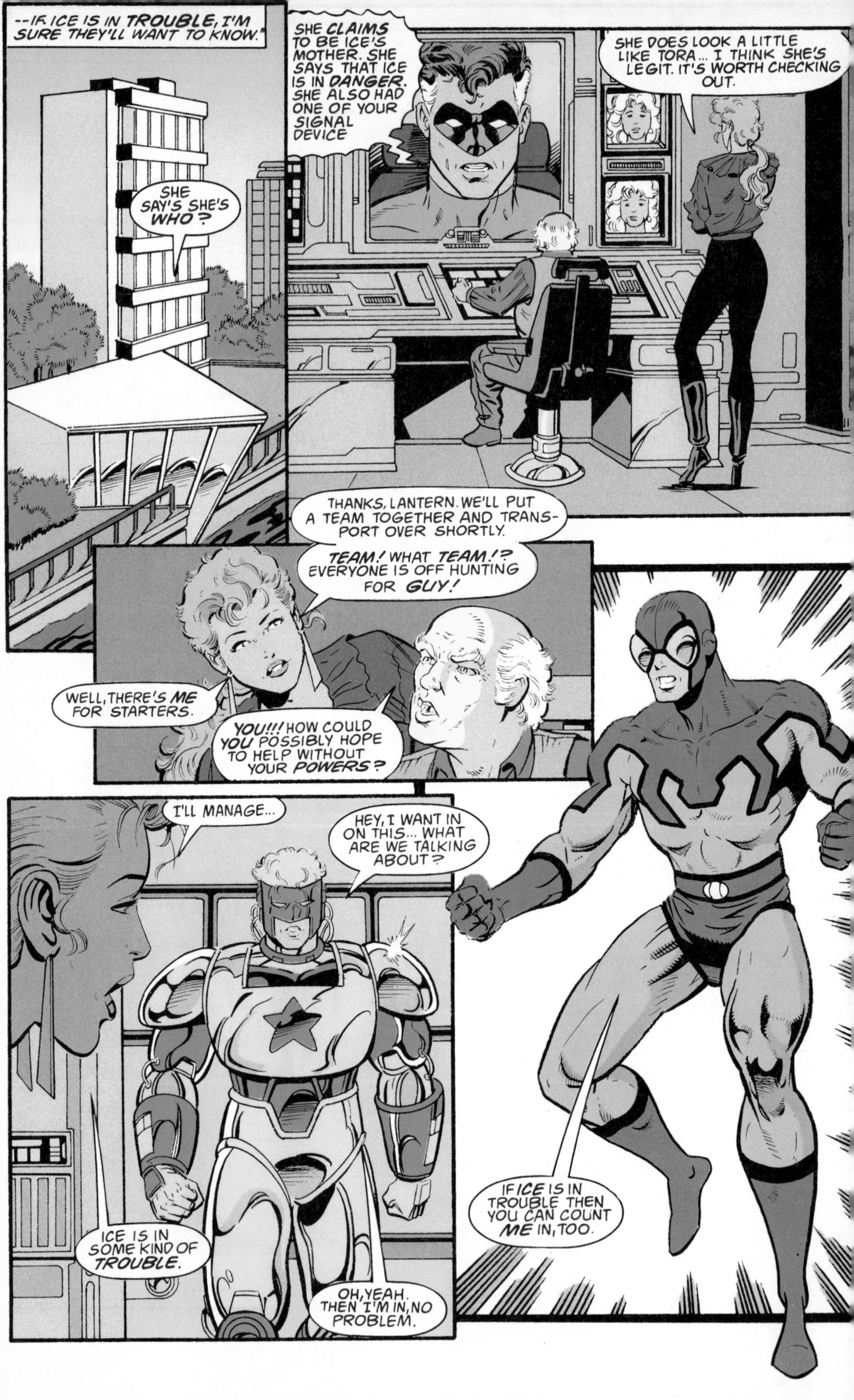
--IF ICE IS IN TROUBLE, I'M SURE THEY'LL WANT TO KNOW."
SHE SAY'S SHE'S WHO?
SHE CLAIMS TO BE ICE'S MOTHER. SHE SAYS THAT ICE IS IN DANGER. SHE ALSO HAD ONE OF YOUR SIGNAL DEVICE
SHE DOES LOOK A LITTLE LIKE TORA... I THINK SHE'S LEGIT. IT'S WORTH CHECKING OUT.
THANKS, LANTERN. WE'LL PUT A TEAM TOGETHER AND TRANSPORT OVER SHORTLY.
TEAM! WHAT TEAM!? EVERYONE IS OFF HUNTING FOR GUY!
WELL, THERE'S ME FOR STARTERS.
YOU!!! HOW COULD YOU POSSIBLY HOPE TO HELP WITHOUT YOUR POWERS?
I'LL MANAGE...
HEY, I WANT IN ON THIS... WHAT ARE WE TALKING ABOUT?
ICE IS IN SOME KIND OF TROUBLE.
OH, YEAH. THEN I'M IN, NO PROBLEM.
IF ICE IS IN TROUBLE THEN YOU CAN COUNT ME IN, TOO.

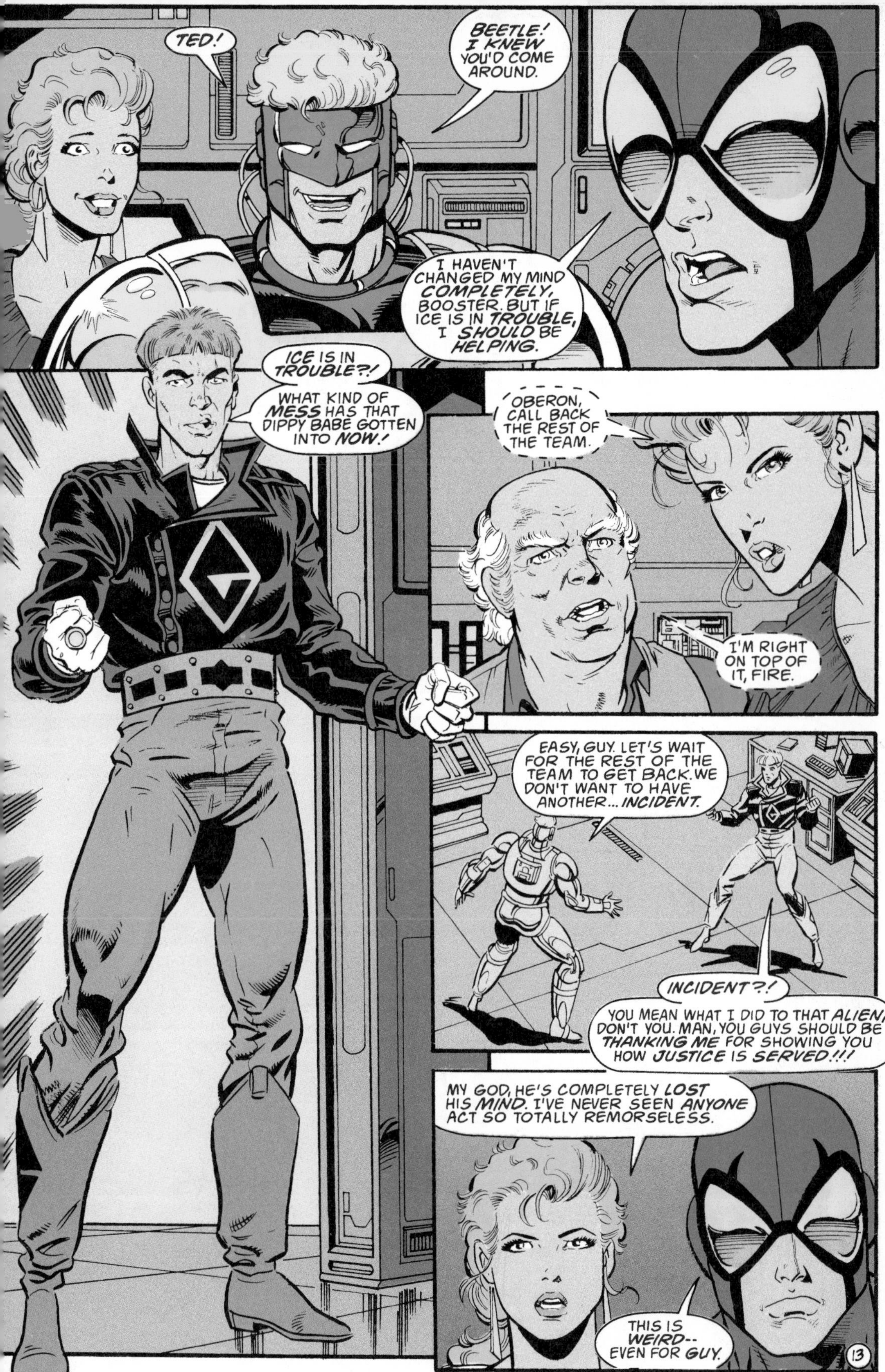
TED!
BEETLE! I KNEW YOU'D COME AROUND.
I HAVEN'T CHANGED MY MIND COMPLETELY, BOOSTER. BUT IF ICE IS IN TROUBLE, I SHOULD BE HELPING.
ICE IS IN TROUBLE?!
WHAT KIND OF MESS HAS THAT DIPPY BABE GOTTEN INTO NOW!
OBERON, CALL BACK THE REST OF THE TEAM.
I'M RIGHT ON TOP OF IT, FIRE.
EASY, GUY. LET'S WAIT FOR THE REST OF THE TEAM TO GET BACK. WE DON'T WANT TO HAVE ANOTHER... INCIDENT.
INCIDENT?!
YOU MEAN WHAT I DID TO THAT ALIEN, DON'T YOU. MAN, YOU GUYS SHOULD BE THANKING ME FOR SHOWING YOU HOW JUSTICE IS SERVED!!!
MY GOD, HE'S COMPLETELY LOST HIS MIND. I'VE NEVER SEEN ANYONE ACT SO TOTALLY REMORSELESS.
THIS IS WEIRD-- EVEN FOR GUY.
13

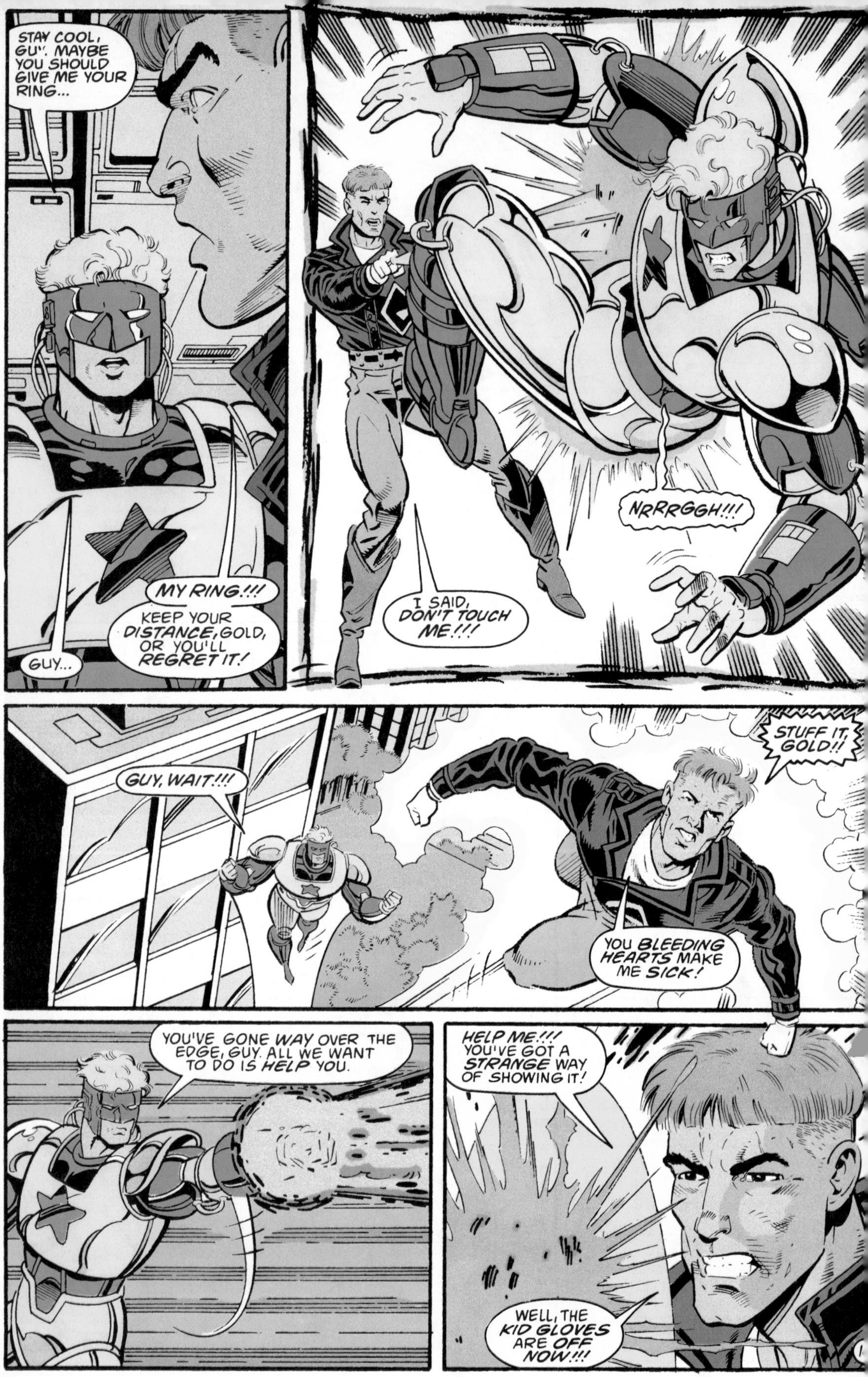
STAY COOL, GU'. MAYBE YOU SHOULD GIVE ME YOUR RING...
MY RING!!!
KEEP YOUR DISTANCE, GOLD, OR YOU'LL REGRET IT!
GUY...
I SAID, DON'T TOUCH ME!!!
NRRRGGH!!!
GUY, WAIT!!!
STUFF IT, GOLD!!
YOU BLEEDING HEARTS MAKE ME SICK!
YOU'VE GONE WAY OVER THE EDGE, GUY. ALL WE WANT TO DO IS HELP YOU.
HELP ME!!! YOU'VE GOT A STRANGE WAY OF SHOWING IT!
WELL, THE KID GLOVES ARE OFF NOW!!!

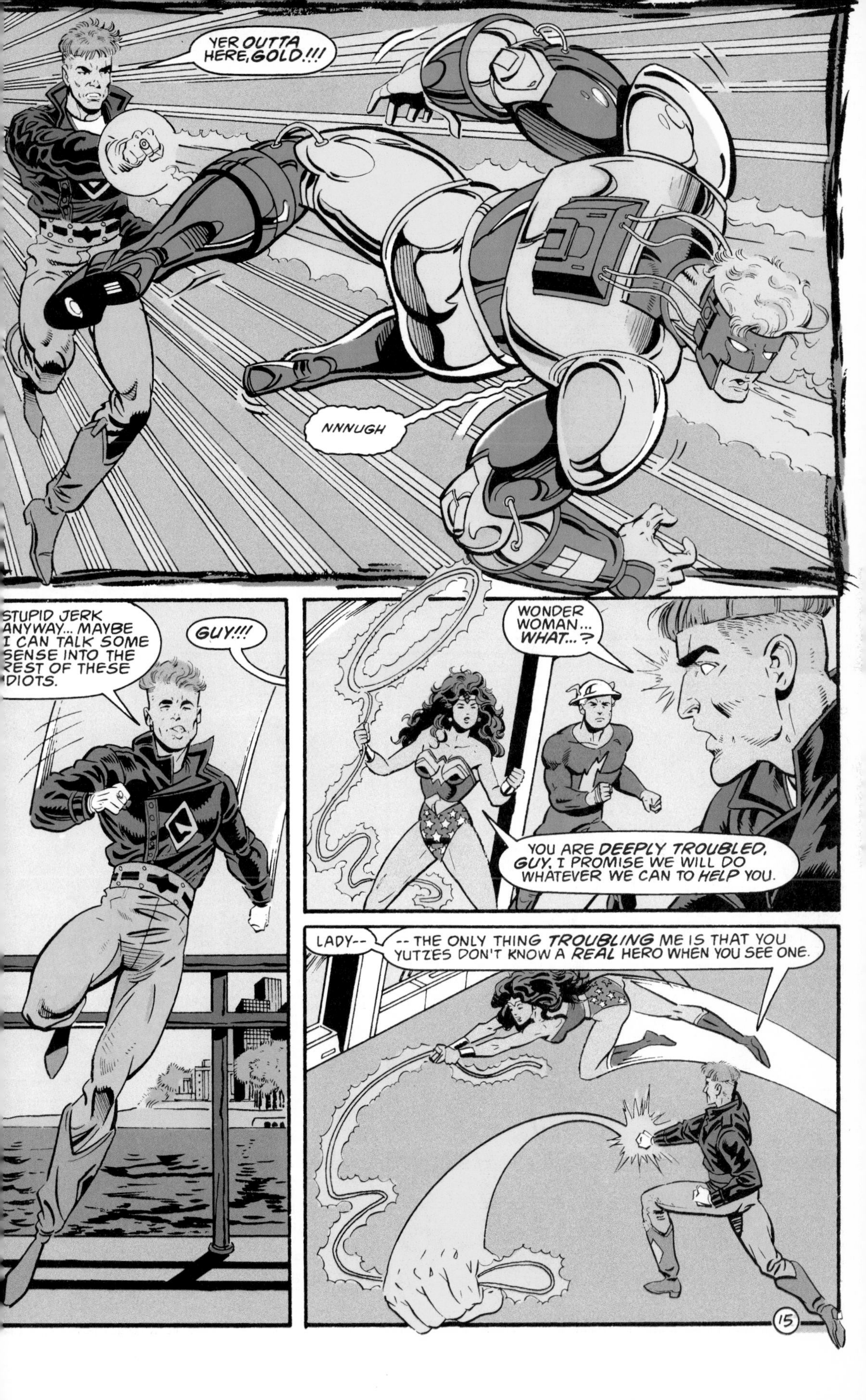
YER OUTTA HERE, GOLD.!!!
NNNUGH
STUPID JERK ANYWAY... MAYBE I CAN TALK SOME SENSE INTO THE REST OF THESE IDIOTS.
GUY!!!
WONDER WOMAN... WHAT...?
YOU ARE DEEPLY TROUBLED, GUY. I PROMISE WE WILL DO WHATEVER WE CAN TO HELP YOU.
LADY--
--THE ONLY THING TROUBLING ME IS THAT YOU YUTZES DON'T KNOW A REAL HERO WHEN YOU SEE ONE.
15

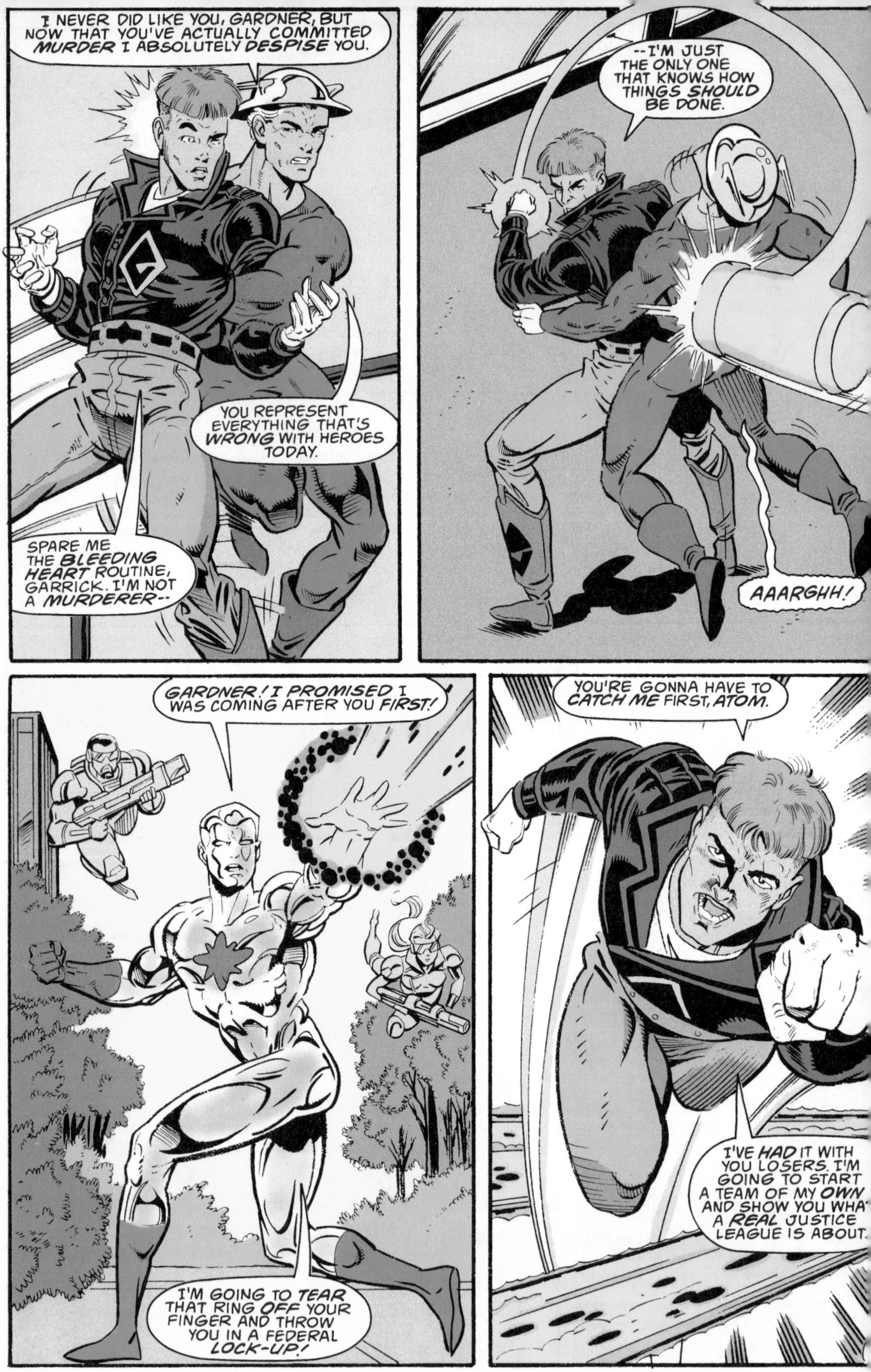
I NEVER DID LIKE YOU, GARDNER, BUT NOW THAT YOU'VE ACTUALLY COMMITTED MURDER I ABSOLUTELY DESPISE YOU.
YOU REPRESENT EVERYTHING THAT'S WRONG WITH HEROES TODAY.
SPARE ME THE BLEEDING HEART ROUTINE, GARRICK. I'M NOT A MURDERER--
--I'M JUST THE ONLY ONE THAT KNOWS HOW THINGS SHOULD BE DONE.
AAARGHH!
GARDNER! I PROMISED I WAS COMING AFTER YOU FIRST!
I'M GOING TO TEAR THAT RING OFF YOUR FINGER AND THROW YOU IN A FEDERAL LOCK-UP!
YOU'RE GONNA HAVE TO CATCH ME FIRST, ATOM.
I'VE HAD IT WITH YOU LOSERS. I'M GOING TO START A TEAM OF MY OWN AND SHOW YOU WHA A REAL JUSTICE LEAGUE IS ABOUT.

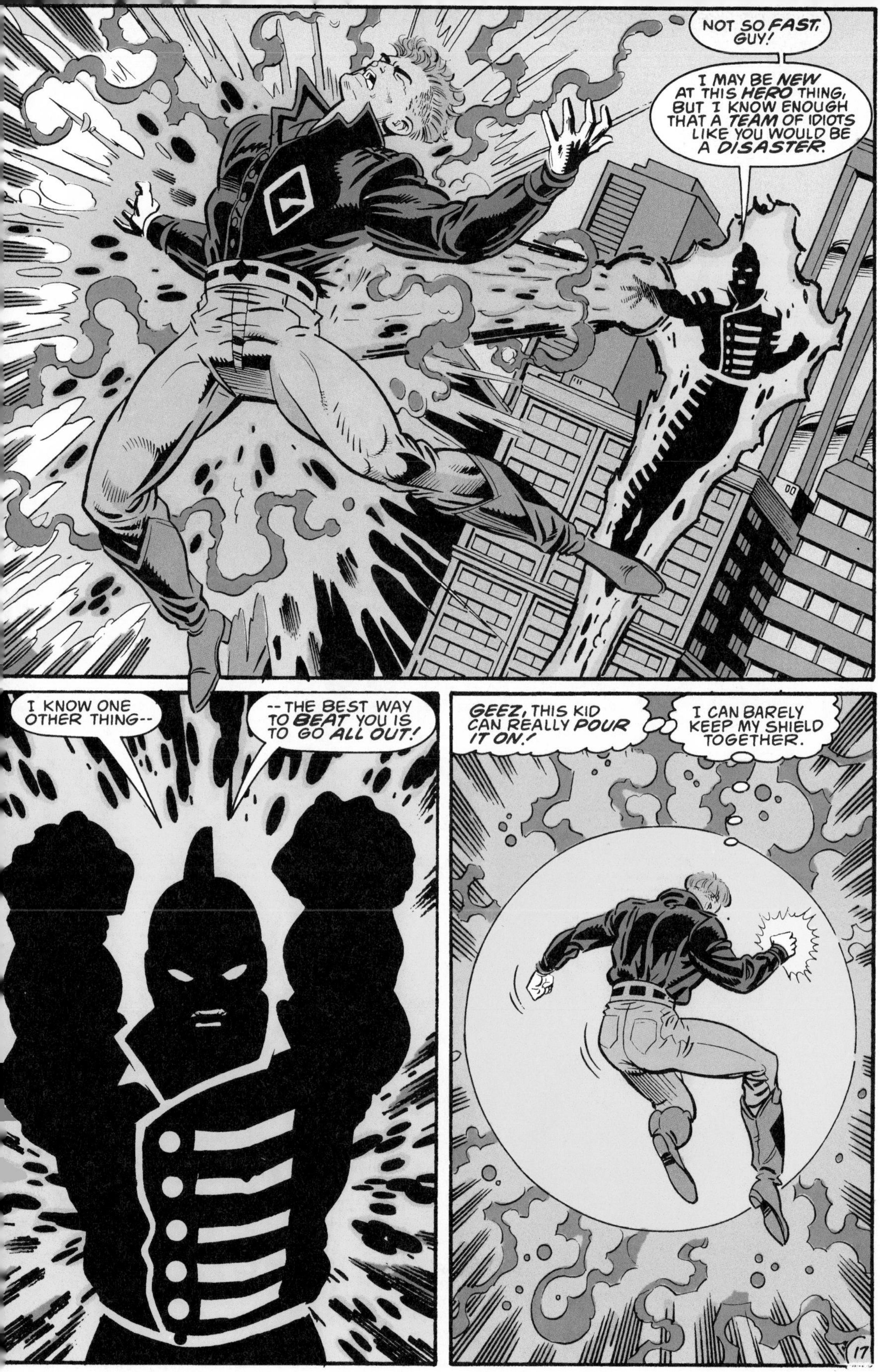
NOT SO FAST, GUY!
I MAY BE NEW AT THIS HERO THING, BUT I KNOW ENOUGH THAT A TEAM OF IDIOTS LIKE YOU WOULD BE A DISASTER.
I KNOW ONE OTHER THING--
--THE BEST WAY TO BEAT YOU IS TO GO ALL OUT!
GEEZ, THIS KID CAN REALLY POUR IT ON!
I CAN BARELY KEEP MY SHIELD TOGETHER.

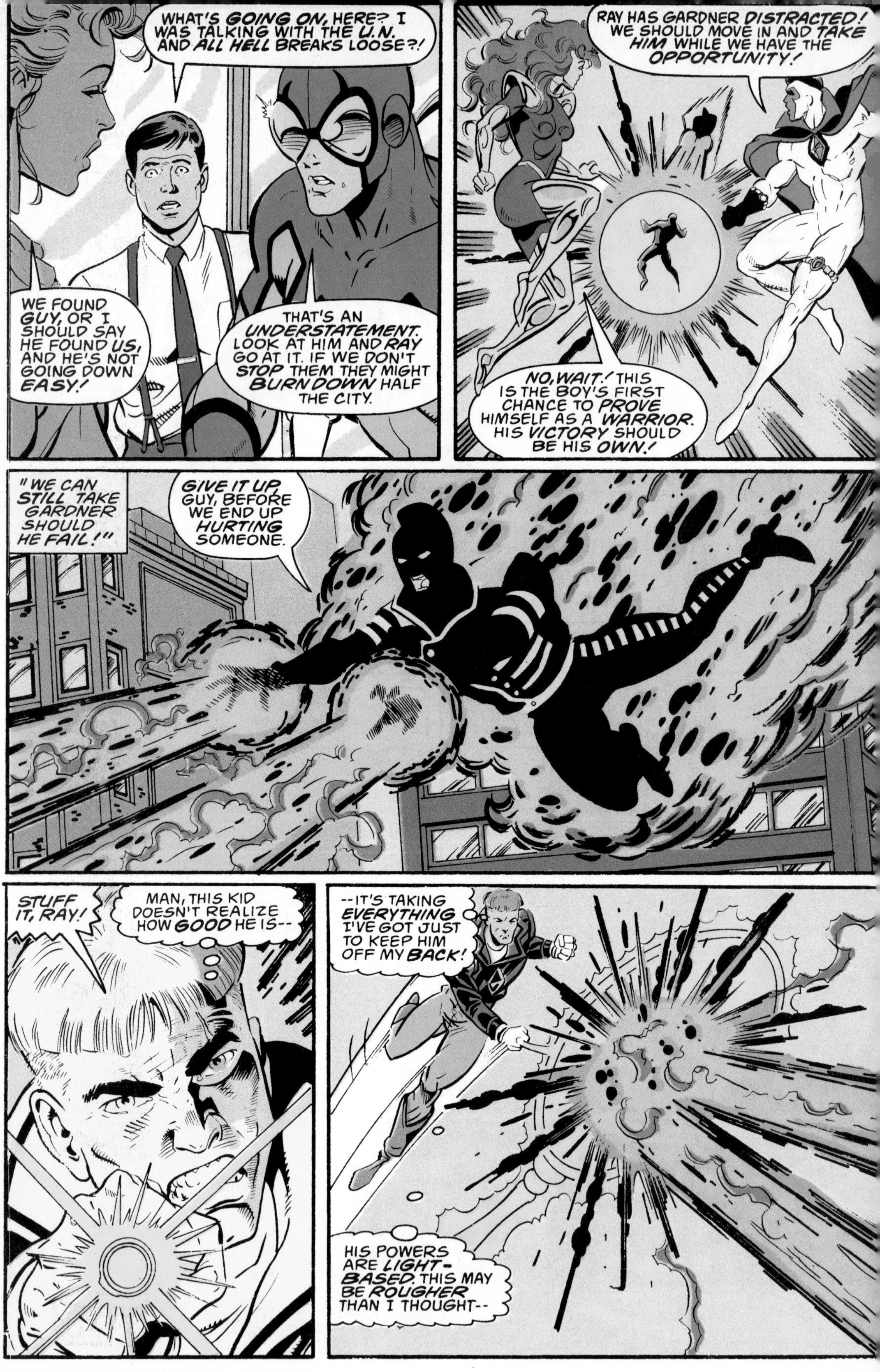
WHAT'S GOING ON, HERE? I WAS TALKING WITH THE U.N. AND ALL HELL BREAKS LOOSE?!
WE FOUND GUY, OR I SHOULD SAY HE FOUND US, AND HE'S NOT GOING DOWN EASY!
THAT'S AN UNDERSTATEMENT. LOOK AT HIM AND RAY GO AT IT. IF WE DON'T STOP THEM THEY MIGHT BURN DOWN HALF THE CITY.
RAY HAS GARDNER DISTRACTED! WE SHOULD MOVE IN AND TAKE HIM WHILE WE HAVE THE OPPORTUNITY!
NO, WAIT! THIS IS THE BOY'S FIRST CHANCE TO PROVE HIMSELF AS A WARRIOR. HIS VICTORY SHOULD BE HIS OWN!
"WE CAN STILL TAKE GARDNER SHOULD HE FAIL!"
GIVE IT UP, GUY, BEFORE WE END UP HURTING SOMEONE.
STUFF IT, RAY!
MAN, THIS KID DOESN'T REALIZE HOW GOOD HE IS--
--IT'S TAKING EVERYTHING I'VE GOT JUST TO KEEP HIM OFF MY BACK!
HIS POWERS ARE LIGHT-BASED. THIS MAY BE ROUGHER THAN I THOUGHT--

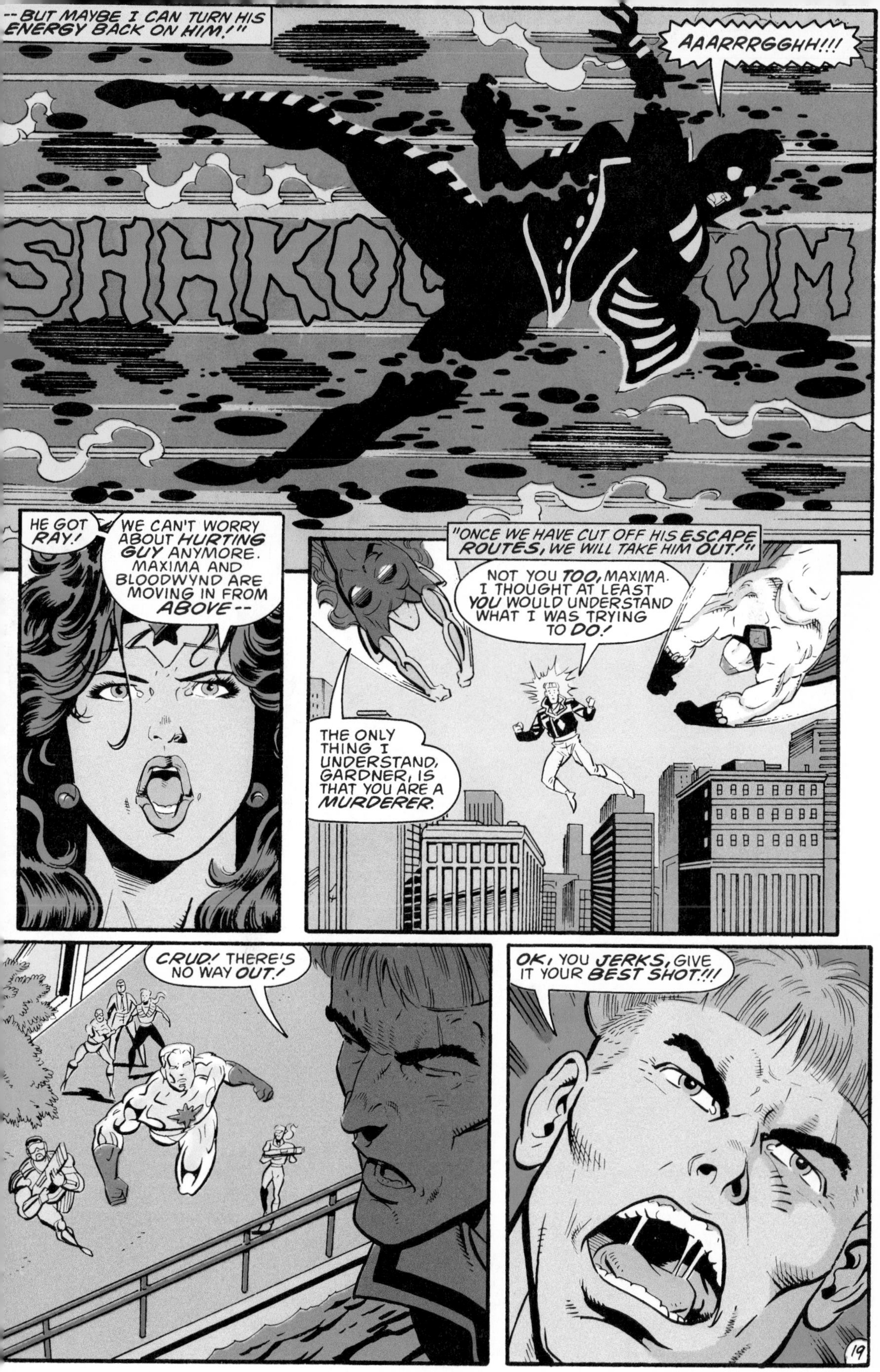
--BUT MAYBE I CAN TURN HIS ENERGY BACK ON HIM!"
AAARRRGGHH!!!
SHHKOOOM
HE GOT RAY!
WE CAN'T WORRY ABOUT HURTING GUY ANYMORE. MAXIMA AND BLOODWYND ARE MOVING IN FROM ABOVE--
"ONCE WE HAVE CUT OFF HIS ESCAPE ROUTES, WE WILL TAKE HIM OUT!"
NOT YOU TOO, MAXIMA. I THOUGHT AT LEAST YOU WOULD UNDERSTAND WHAT I WAS TRYING TO DO!
THE ONLY THING I UNDERSTAND, GARDNER, IS THAT YOU ARE A MURDERER.
CRUD! THERE'S NO WAY OUT!
OK, YOU JERKS, GIVE IT YOUR BEST SHOT!!!
19

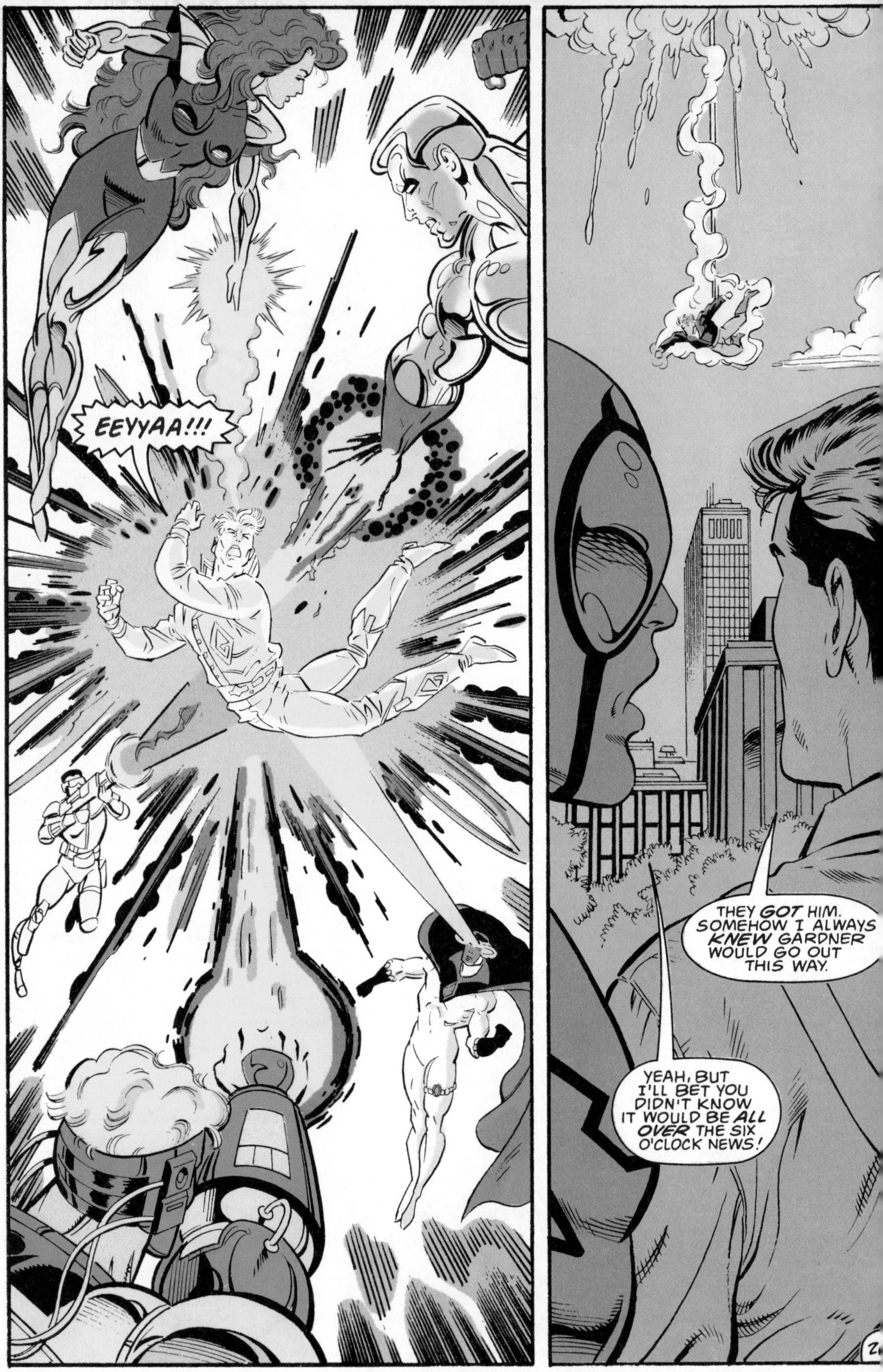
EEYYAA!!!
THEY *GOT* HIM. SOMEHOW I ALWAYS *KNEW* GARDNER WOULD GO OUT THIS WAY.
YEAH, BUT I'LL BET YOU DIDN'T KNOW IT WOULD BE *ALL OVER* THE SIX O'CLOCK NEWS!

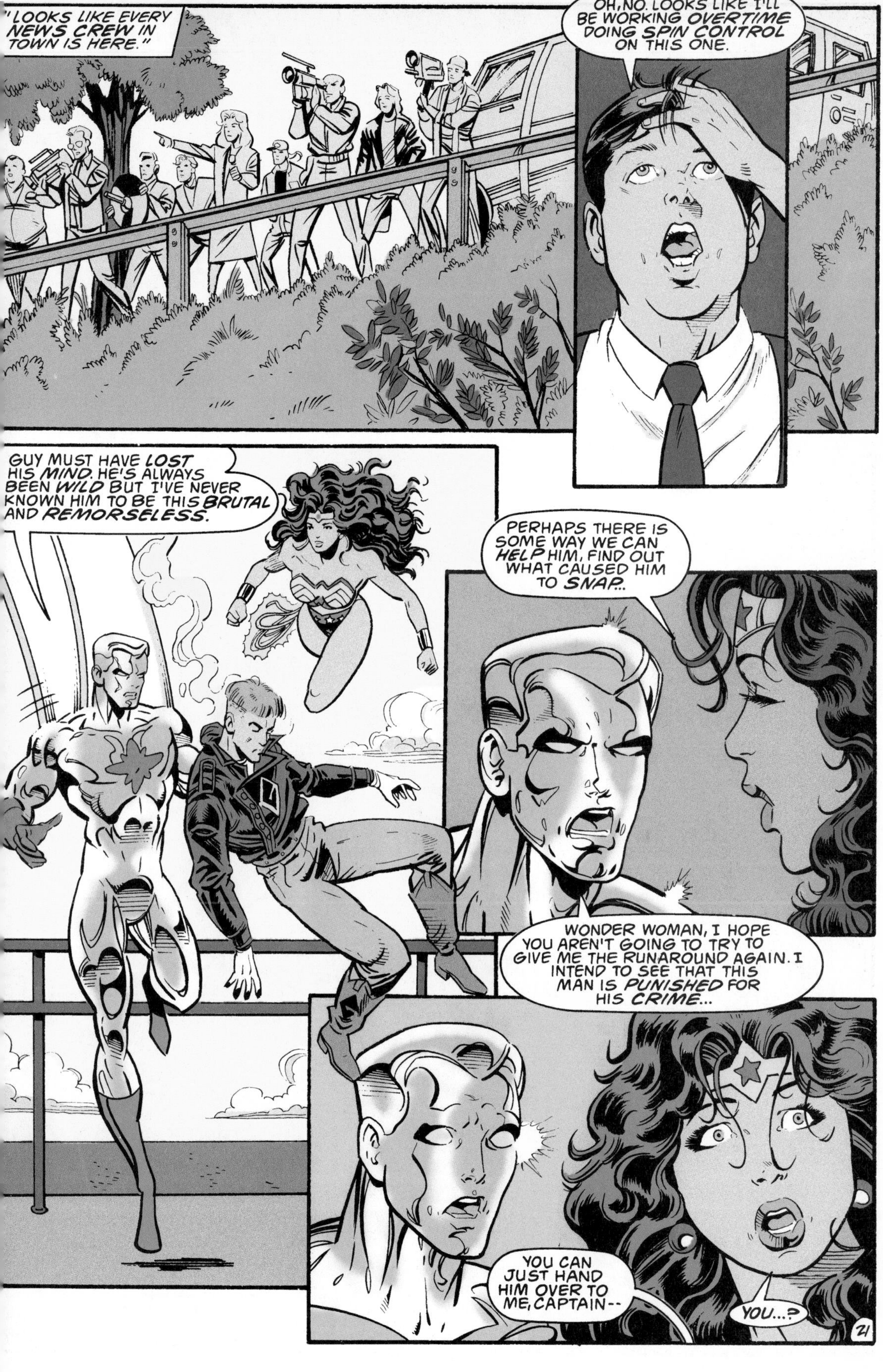
"LOOKS LIKE EVERY NEWS CREW IN TOWN IS HERE."
OH, NO. LOOKS LIKE I'LL BE WORKING OVERTIME DOING SPIN CONTROL ON THIS ONE.
GUY MUST HAVE LOST HIS MIND. HE'S ALWAYS BEEN WILD BUT I'VE NEVER KNOWN HIM TO BE THIS BRUTAL AND REMORSELESS.
PERHAPS THERE IS SOME WAY WE CAN HELP HIM, FIND OUT WHAT CAUSED HIM TO SNAP...
WONDER WOMAN, I HOPE YOU AREN'T GOING TO TRY TO GIVE ME THE RUNAROUND AGAIN. I INTEND TO SEE THAT THIS MAN IS PUNISHED FOR HIS CRIME...
YOU CAN JUST HAND HIM OVER TO ME, CAPTAIN--
YOU...?
21

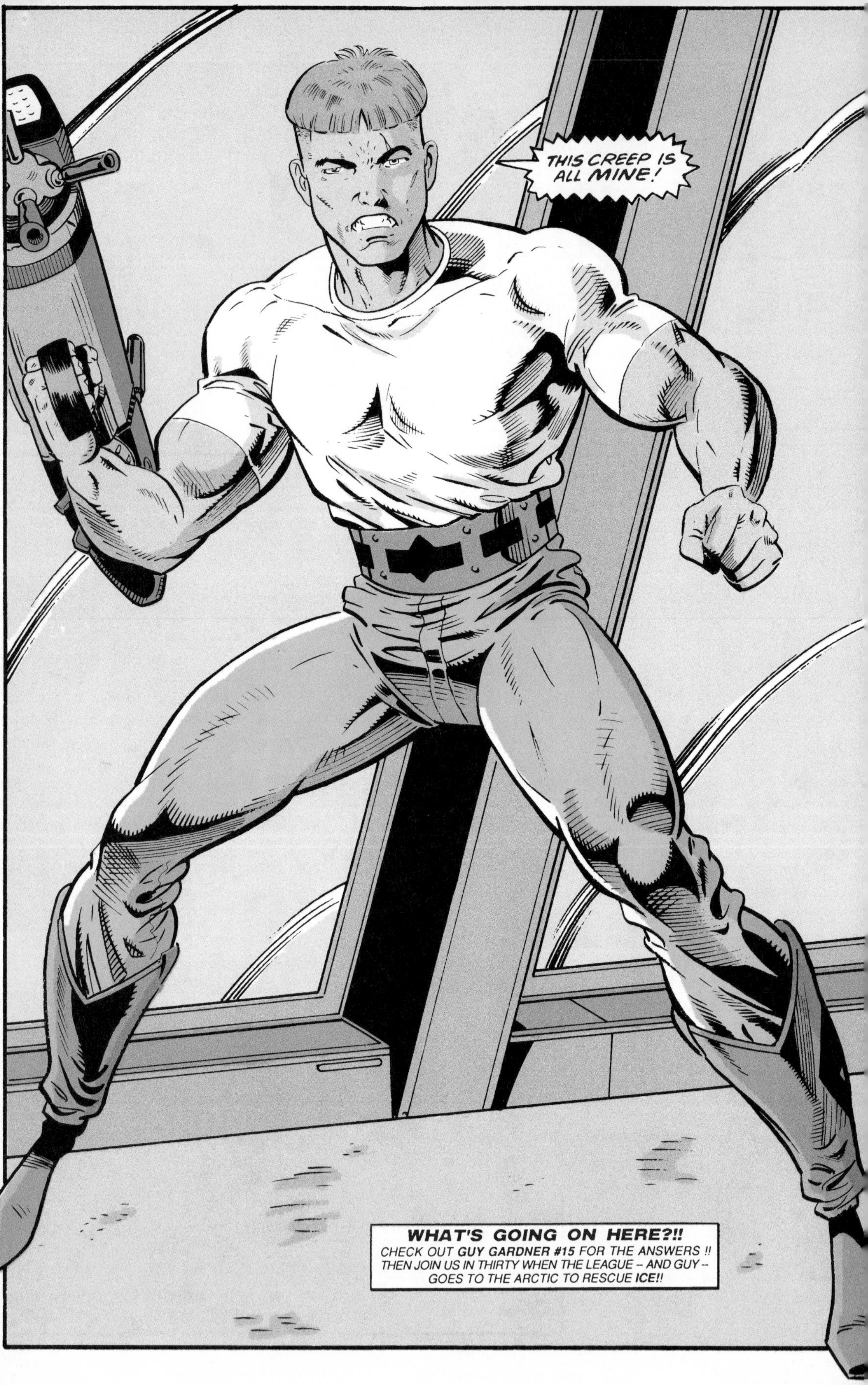
THIS CREEP IS ALL MINE!
WHAT'S GOING ON HERE?!!
CHECK OUT GUY GARDNER #15 FOR THE ANSWERS !!
THEN JOIN US IN THIRTY WHEN THE LEAGUE -- AND GUY --
GOES TO THE ARCTIC TO RESCUE ICE!!

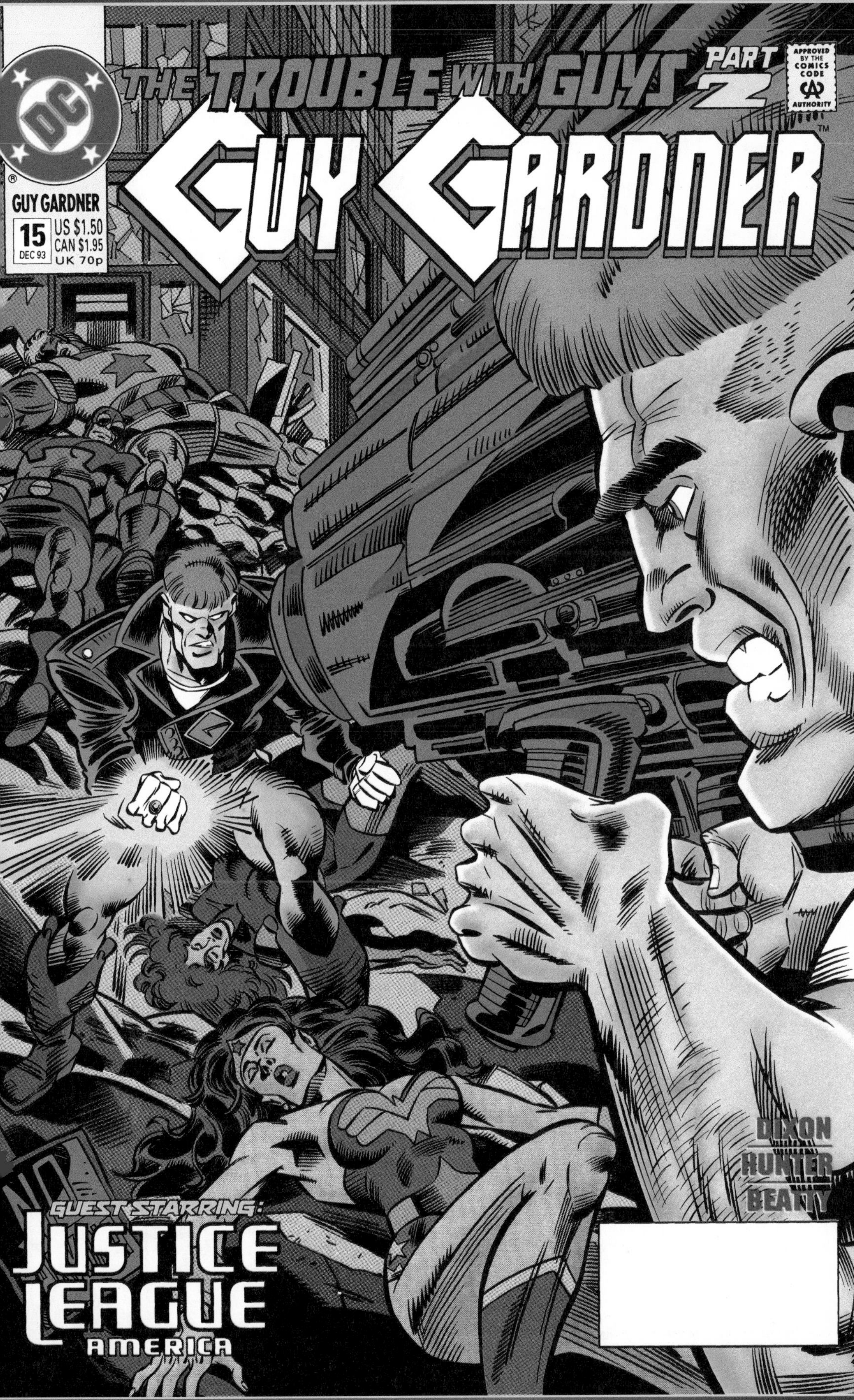

THE TROUBLE WITH GUYS PART 2
APPROVED BY THE COMICS CODE AUTHORITY
GUY GARDNER
GUY GARDNER
15
DEC 93
US $1.50
CAN $1.95
UK 70p
DIXON
HUNTER
BEATTY
GUEST-STARRING:
JUSTICE LEAGUE AMERICA

Cover art by **JOE STATON**

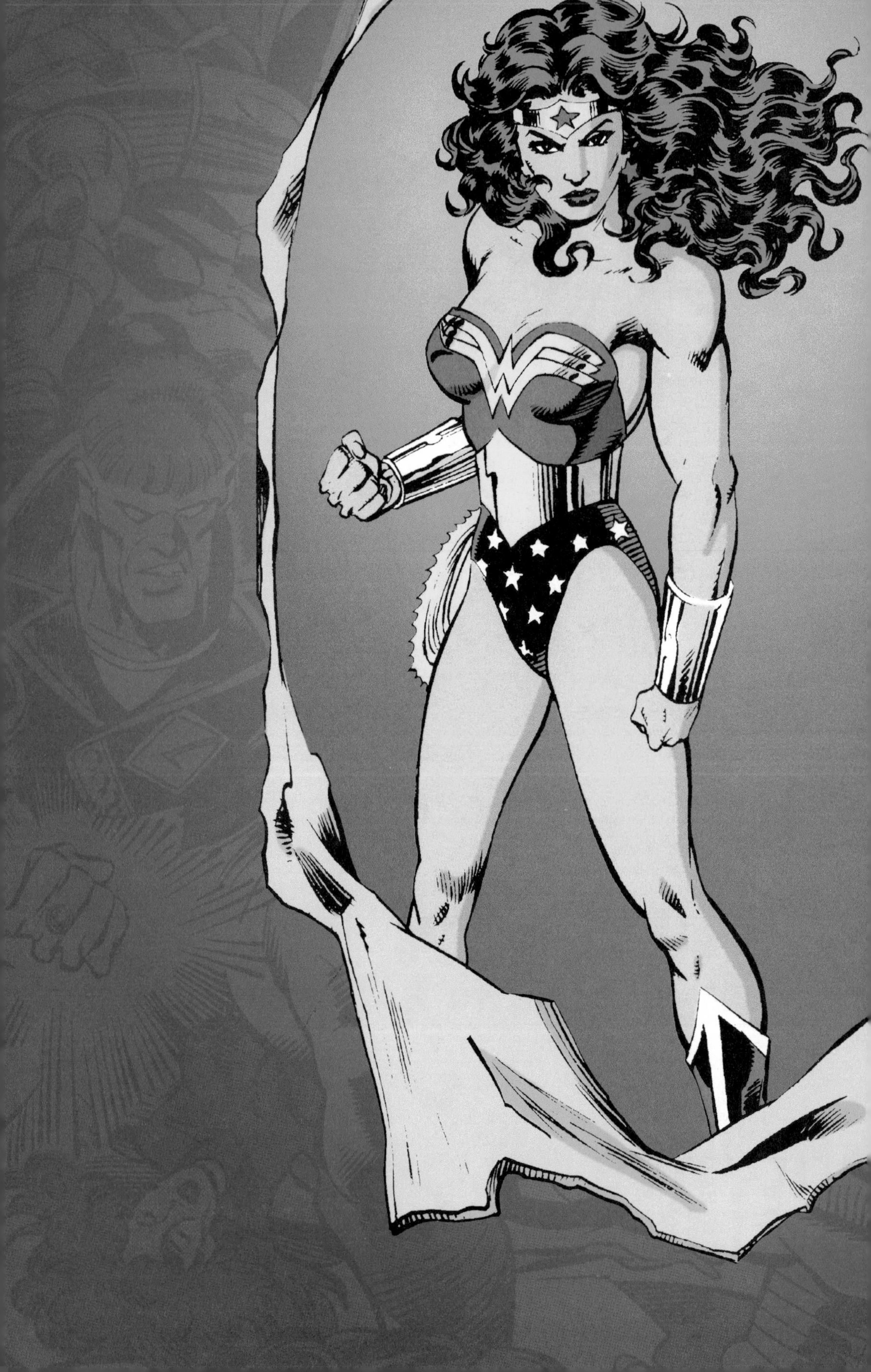

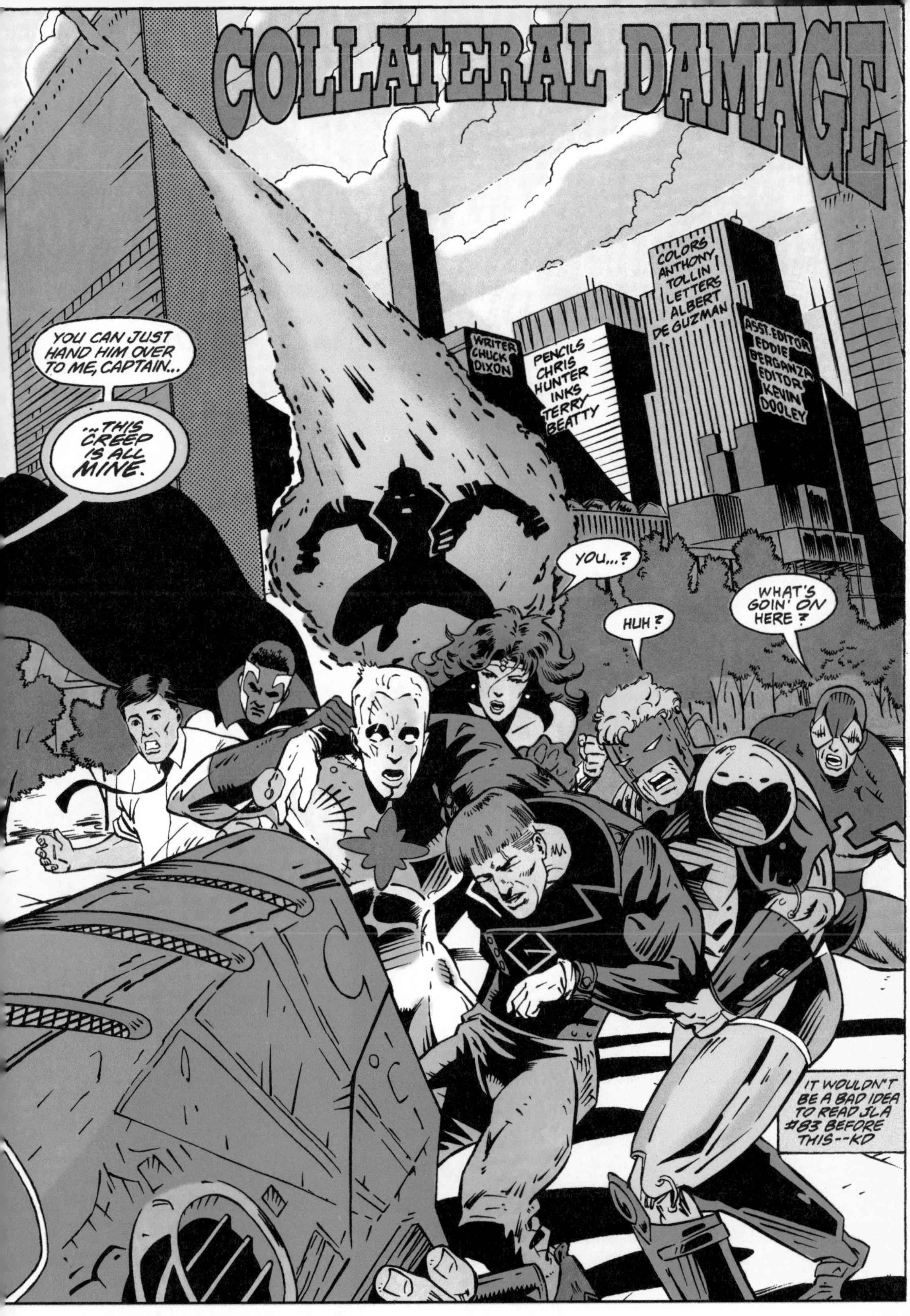
COLLATERAL DAMAGE
WRITER CHUCK DIXON
PENCILS CHRIS HUNTER INKS TERRY BEATTY
COLORS ANTHONY TOLLIN LETTERS ALBERT DE GUZMAN
ASST. EDITOR EDDIE BERGANZA EDITOR KEVIN DOOLEY
YOU CAN JUST HAND HIM OVER TO ME, CAPTAIN...
...THIS CREEP IS ALL MINE.
YOU...?
HUH?
WHAT'S GOIN' ON HERE?
IT WOULDN'T BE A BAD IDEA TO READ JLA #83 BEFORE THIS--KD

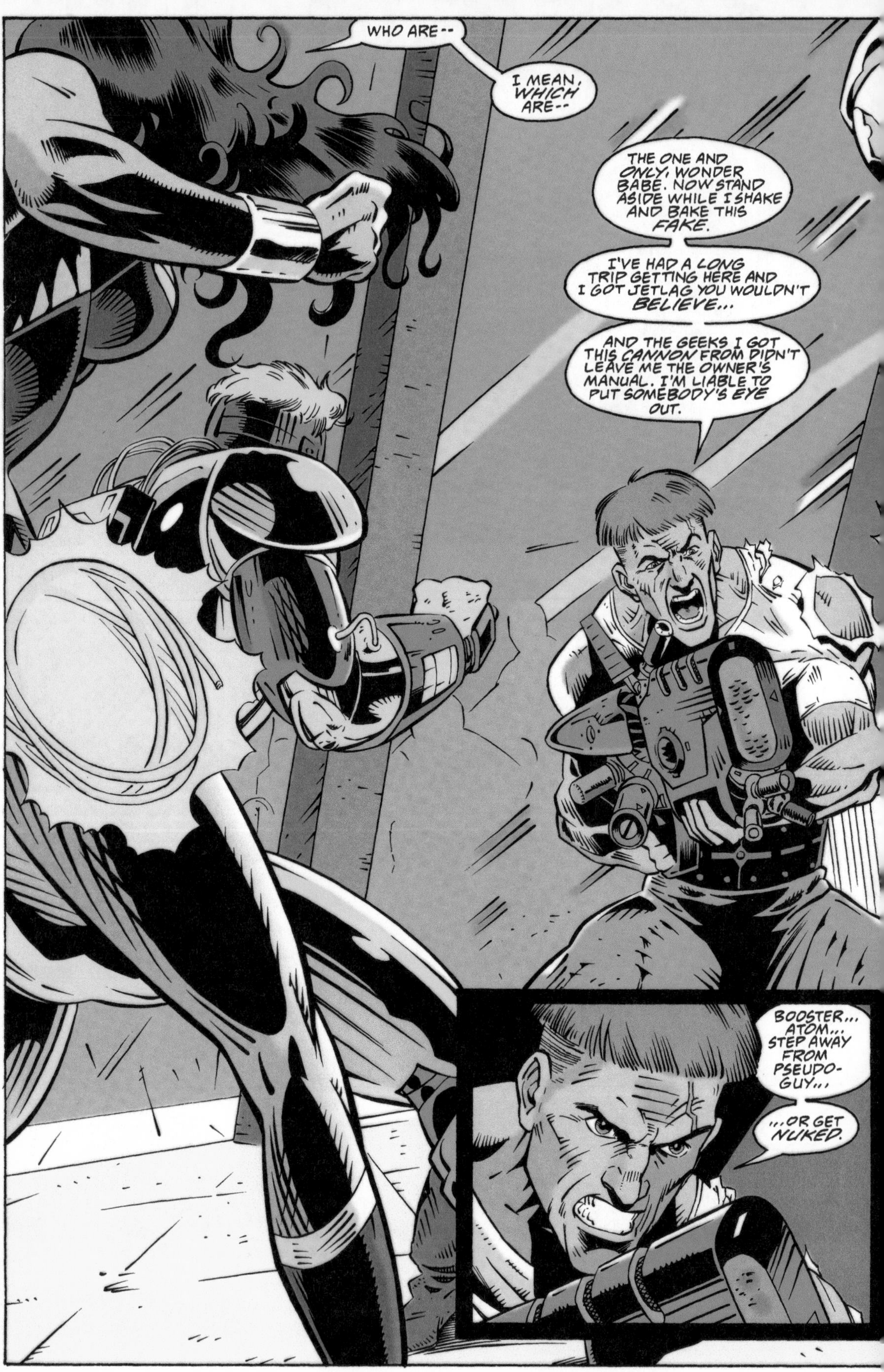
WHO ARE--
I MEAN, WHICH ARE--
THE ONE AND ONLY, WONDER BABE. NOW STAND ASIDE WHILE I SHAKE AND BAKE THIS FAKE.
I'VE HAD A LONG TRIP GETTING HERE AND I GOT JETLAG YOU WOULDN'T BELIEVE...
AND THE GEEKS I GOT THIS CANNON FROM DIDN'T LEAVE ME THE OWNER'S MANUAL. I'M LIABLE TO PUT SOMEBODY'S EYE OUT.
BOOSTER... ATOM... STEP AWAY FROM PSEUDO-GUY...
...OR GET NUKED.

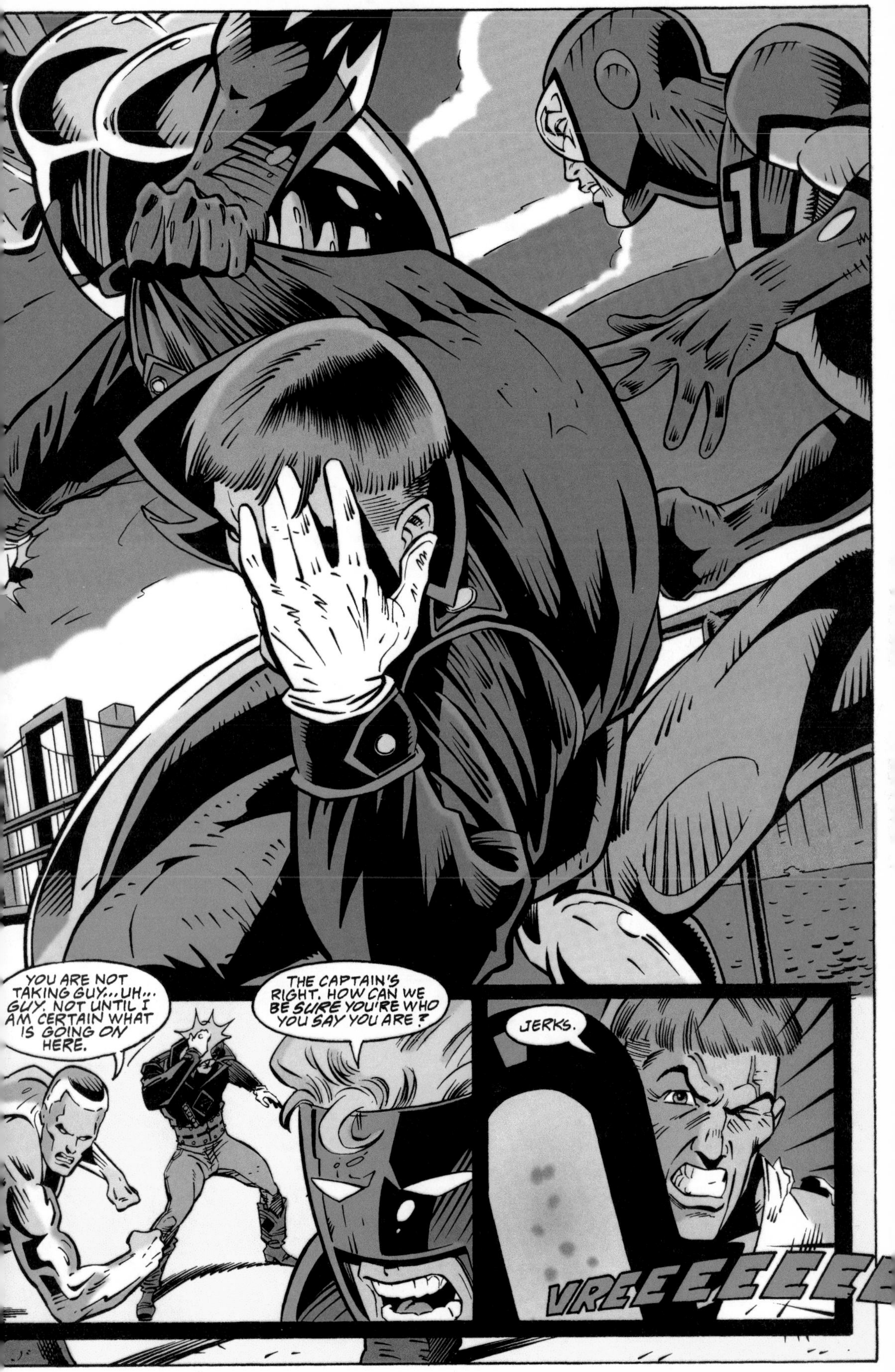
YOU ARE NOT TAKING GUY... UH... GUY. NOT UNTIL I AM CERTAIN WHAT IS GOING ON HERE.
THE CAPTAIN'S RIGHT. HOW CAN WE BE SURE YOU'RE WHO YOU SAY YOU ARE?
JERKS.
VREEEEEEE

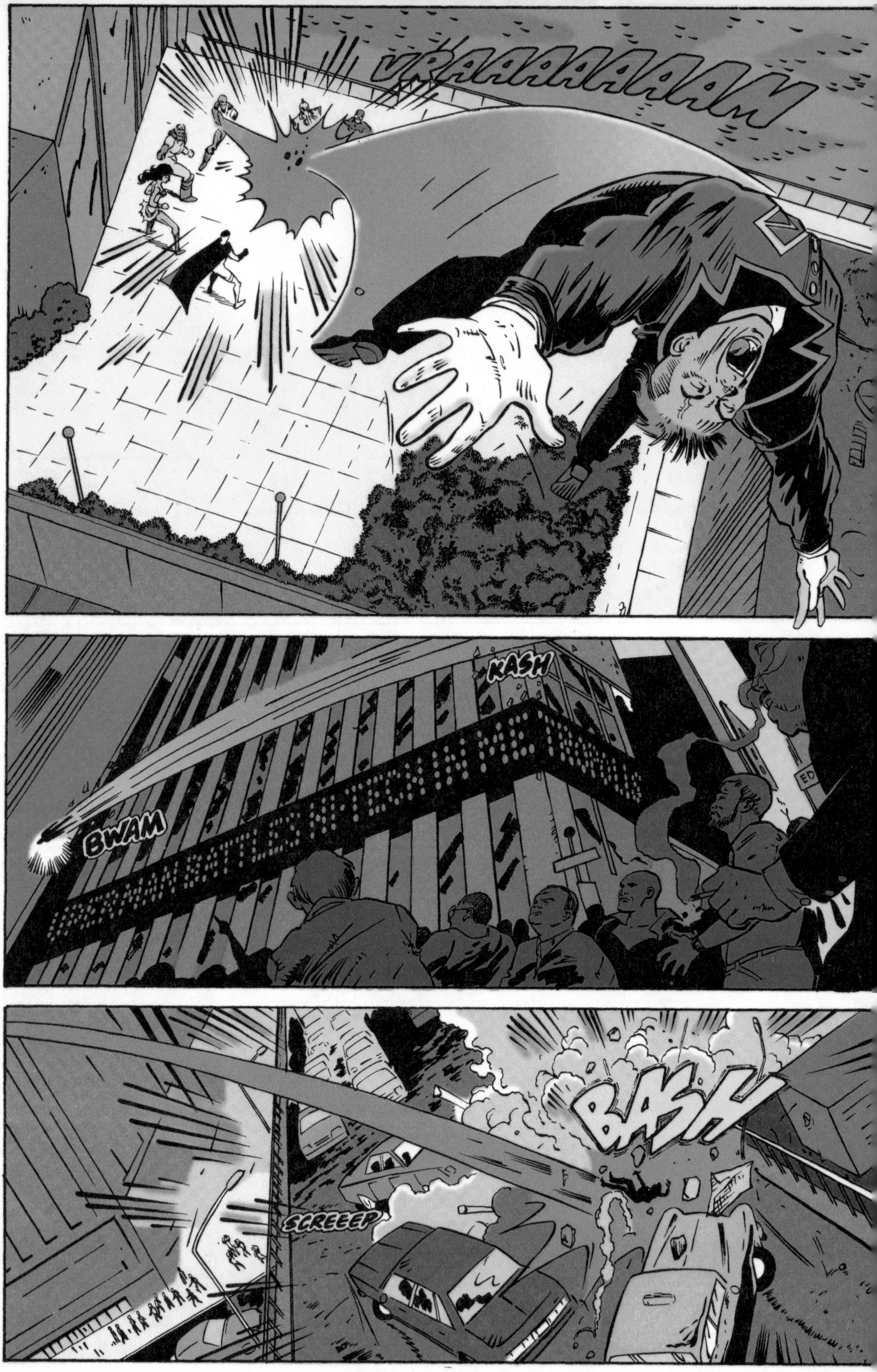
VRAAAAAAAAAM
KASH
BWAM
SCREEEP
BLASH

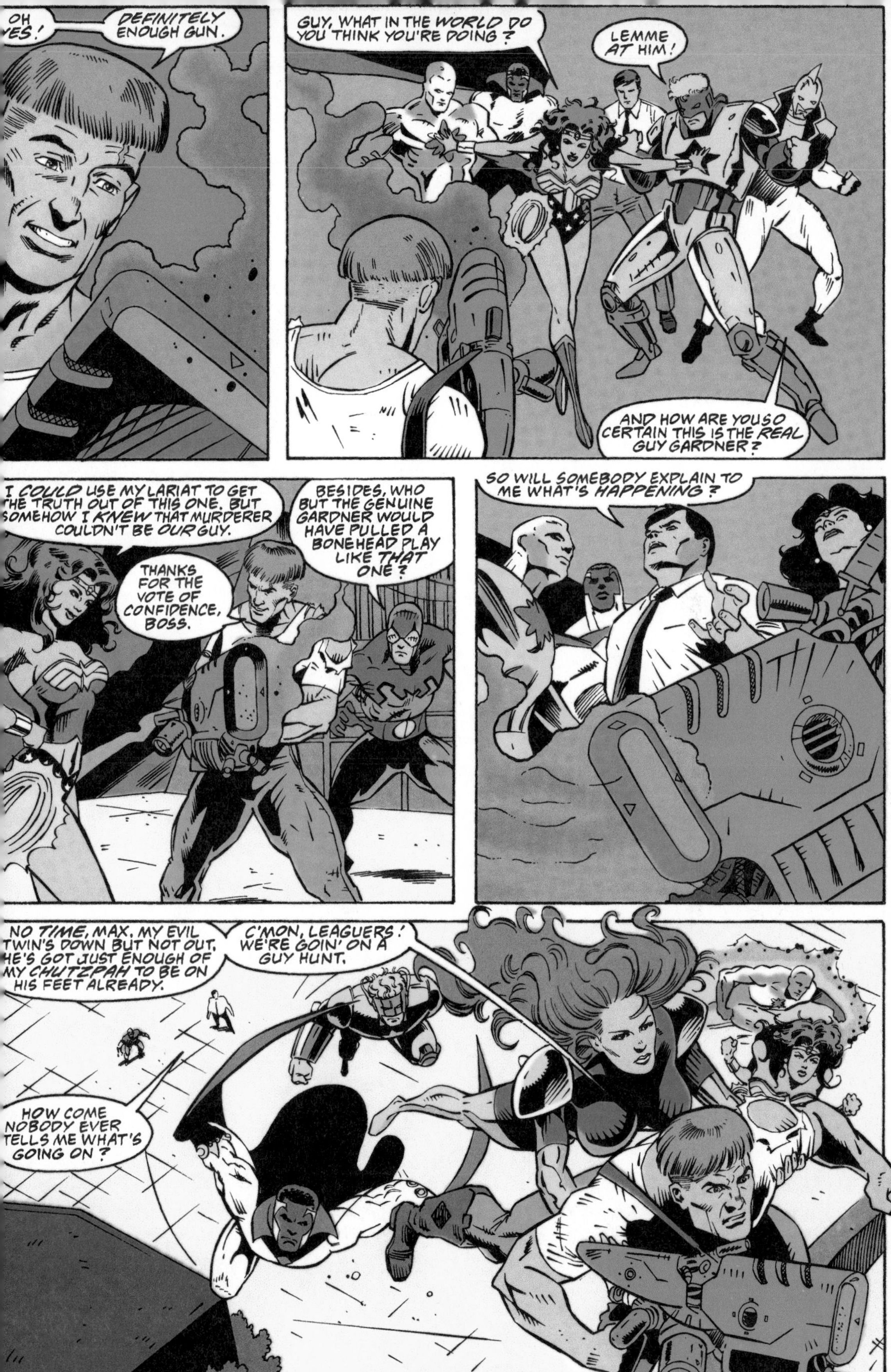
OH YES!
DEFINITELY ENOUGH GUN.
GUY, WHAT IN THE WORLD DO YOU THINK YOU'RE DOING?
LEMME AT HIM!
AND HOW ARE YOU SO CERTAIN THIS IS THE REAL GUY GARDNER?
I COULD USE MY LARIAT TO GET THE TRUTH OUT OF THIS ONE. BUT SOMEHOW I KNEW THAT MURDERER COULDN'T BE OUR GUY.
BESIDES, WHO BUT THE GENUINE GARDNER WOULD HAVE PULLED A BONEHEAD PLAY LIKE THAT ONE?
THANKS FOR THE VOTE OF CONFIDENCE, BOSS.
SO WILL SOMEBODY EXPLAIN TO ME WHAT'S HAPPENING?
NO TIME, MAX. MY EVIL TWIN'S DOWN BUT NOT OUT. HE'S GOT JUST ENOUGH OF MY CHUTZPAH TO BE ON HIS FEET ALREADY.
C'MON, LEAGUERS! WE'RE GOIN' ON A GUY HUNT.
HOW COME NOBODY EVER TELLS ME WHAT'S GOING ON?

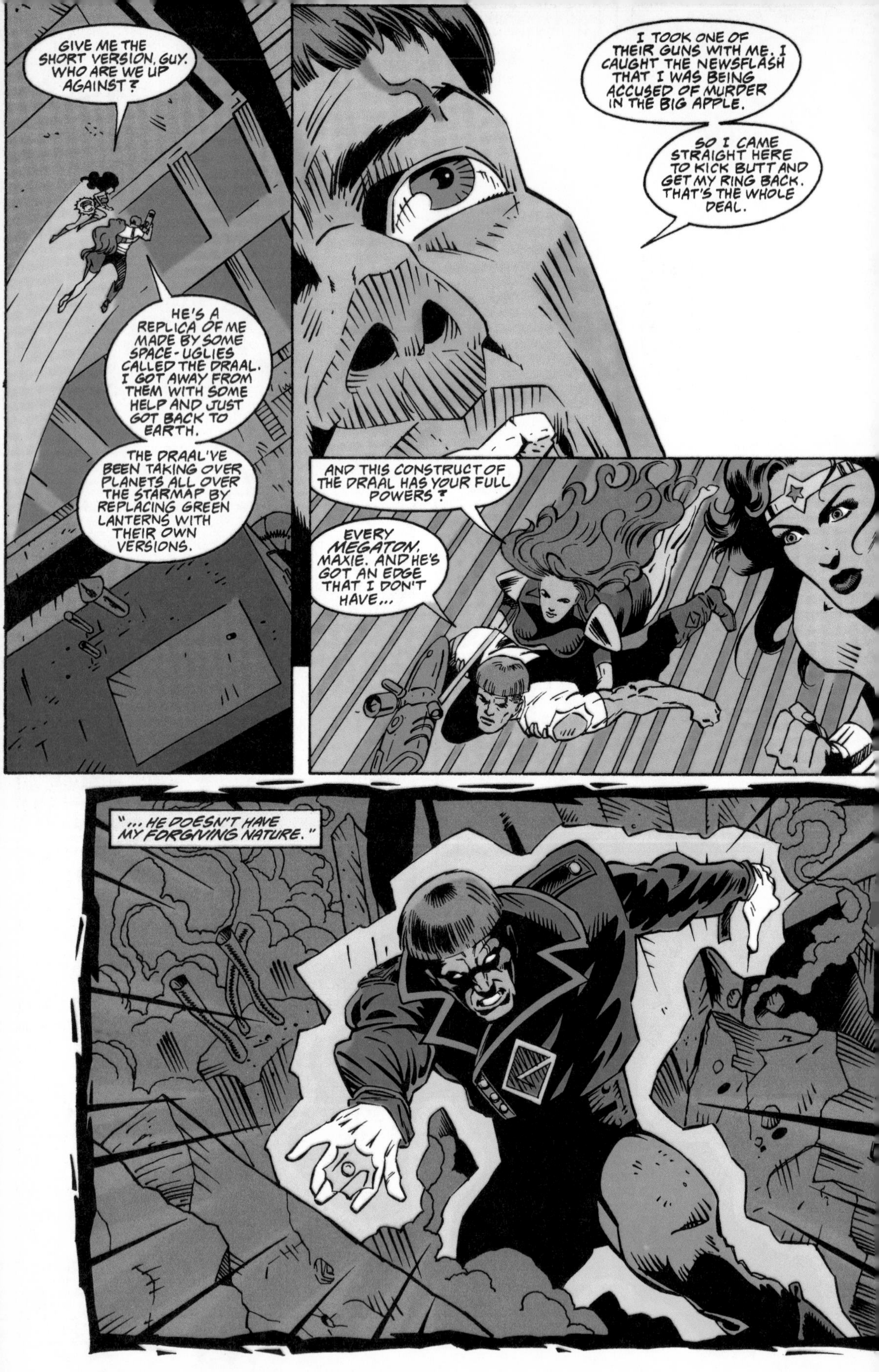
GIVE ME THE SHORT VERSION, GUY. WHO ARE WE UP AGAINST?
HE'S A REPLICA OF ME MADE BY SOME SPACE-UGLIES CALLED THE DRAAL. I GOT AWAY FROM THEM WITH SOME HELP AND JUST GOT BACK TO EARTH.
THE DRAAL'VE BEEN TAKING OVER PLANETS ALL OVER THE STARMAP BY REPLACING GREEN LANTERNS WITH THEIR OWN VERSIONS.
I TOOK ONE OF THEIR GUNS WITH ME. I CAUGHT THE NEWSFLASH THAT I WAS BEING ACCUSED OF MURDER IN THE BIG APPLE.
SO I CAME STRAIGHT HERE TO KICK BUTT AND GET MY RING BACK. THAT'S THE WHOLE DEAL.
AND THIS CONSTRUCT OF THE DRAAL HAS YOUR FULL POWERS?
EVERY MEGATON, MAXIE. AND HE'S GOT AN EDGE THAT I DON'T HAVE...
"...HE DOESN'T HAVE MY FORGIVING NATURE."

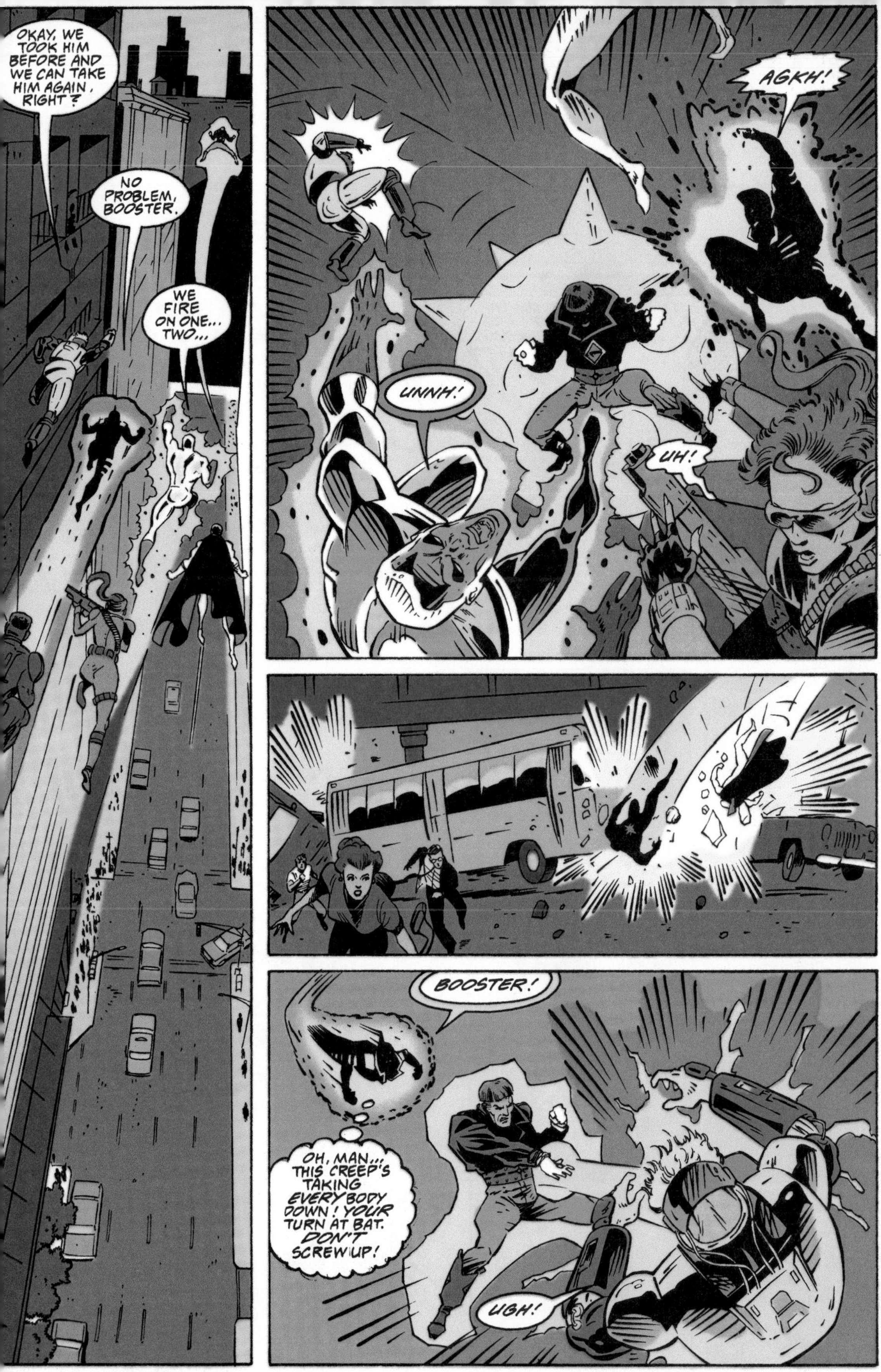
OKAY, WE TOOK HIM BEFORE AND WE CAN TAKE HIM AGAIN, RIGHT?
NO PROBLEM, BOOSTER.
WE FIRE ON ONE... TWO...
AGKH!
UNNH!
UH!
BOOSTER!
OH, MAN... THIS CREEP'S TAKING EVERYBODY DOWN! YOUR TURN AT BAT. DON'T SCREW UP!
UGH!

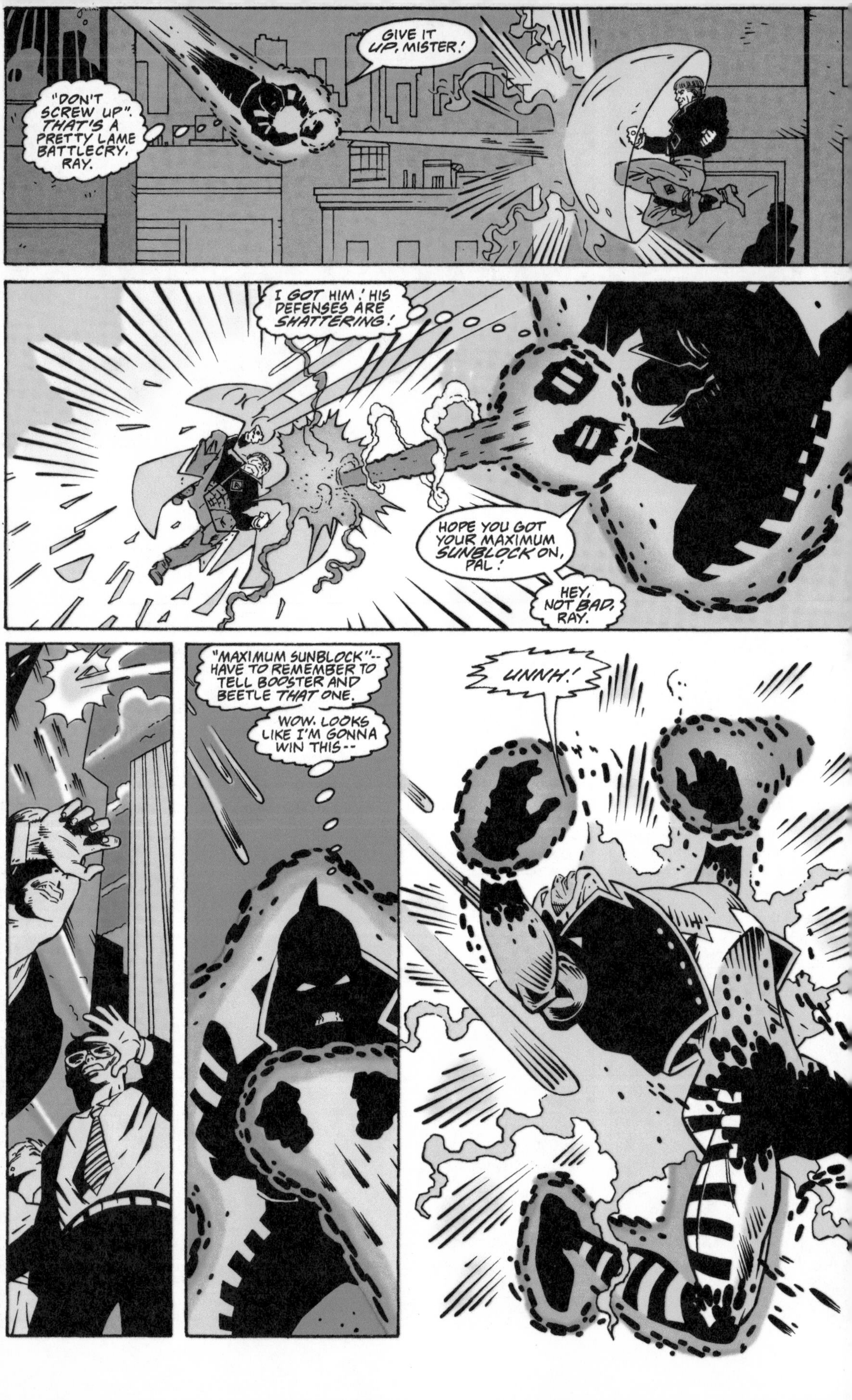
GIVE IT UP, MISTER!
"DON'T SCREW UP". THAT'S A PRETTY LAME BATTLECRY, RAY.
I GOT HIM! HIS DEFENSES ARE SHATTERING!
HOPE YOU GOT YOUR MAXIMUM SUNBLOCK ON, PAL!
HEY, NOT BAD, RAY.
"MAXIMUM SUNBLOCK"-- HAVE TO REMEMBER TO TELL BOOSTER AND BEETLE THAT ONE.
WOW. LOOKS LIKE I'M GONNA WIN THIS--
UNNH!

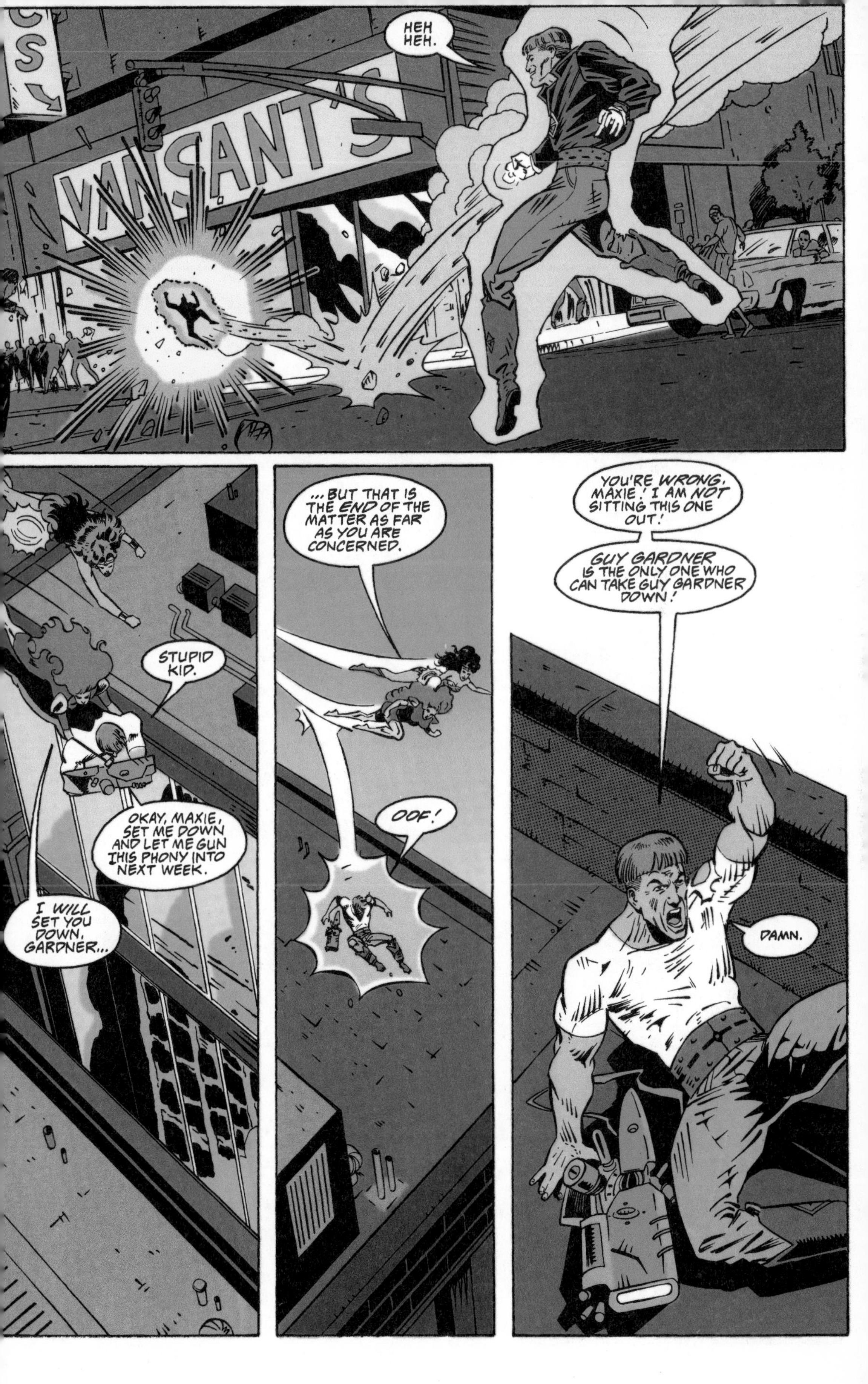
HEH HEH.
VAN SANT'S
STUPID KID.
OKAY, MAXIE, SET ME DOWN AND LET ME GUN THIS PHONY INTO NEXT WEEK.
I WILL SET YOU DOWN, GARDNER...
...BUT THAT IS THE END OF THE MATTER AS FAR AS YOU ARE CONCERNED.
OOF!
YOU'RE WRONG, MAXIE! I AM NOT SITTING THIS ONE OUT!
GUY GARDNER IS THE ONLY ONE WHO CAN TAKE GUY GARDNER DOWN!
DAMN.

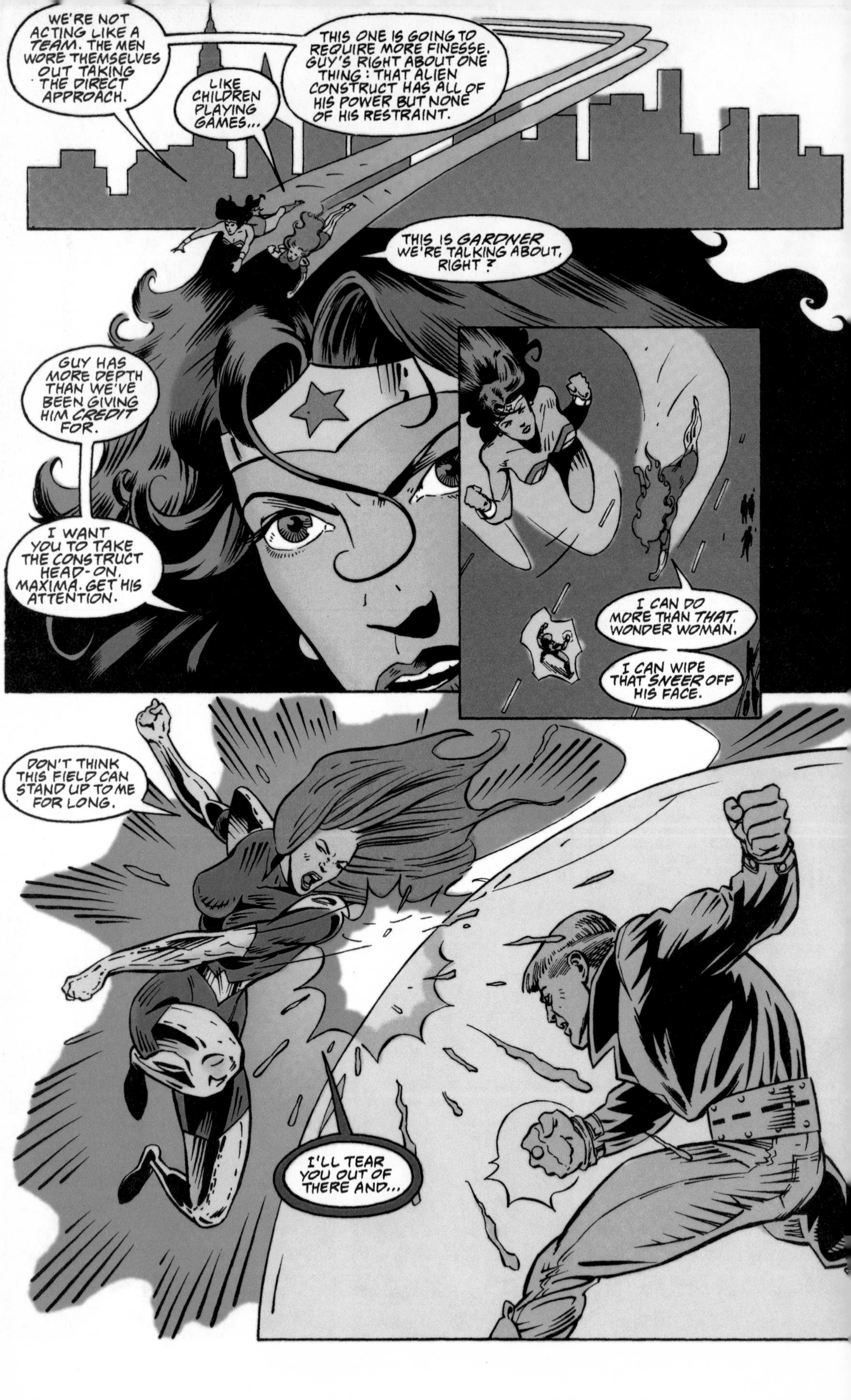
WE'RE NOT ACTING LIKE A TEAM. THE MEN WORE THEMSELVES OUT TAKING THE DIRECT APPROACH.
LIKE CHILDREN PLAYING GAMES...
THIS ONE IS GOING TO REQUIRE MORE FINESSE. GUY'S RIGHT ABOUT ONE THING: THAT ALIEN CONSTRUCT HAS ALL OF HIS POWER BUT NONE OF HIS RESTRAINT.
THIS IS GARDNER WE'RE TALKING ABOUT, RIGHT?
GUY HAS MORE DEPTH THAN WE'VE BEEN GIVING HIM CREDIT FOR.
I WANT YOU TO TAKE THE CONSTRUCT HEAD-ON, MAXIMA. GET HIS ATTENTION.
I CAN DO MORE THAN THAT, WONDER WOMAN.
I CAN WIPE THAT SNEER OFF HIS FACE.
DON'T THINK THIS FIELD CAN STAND UP TO ME FOR LONG.
I'LL TEAR YOU OUT OF THERE AND...

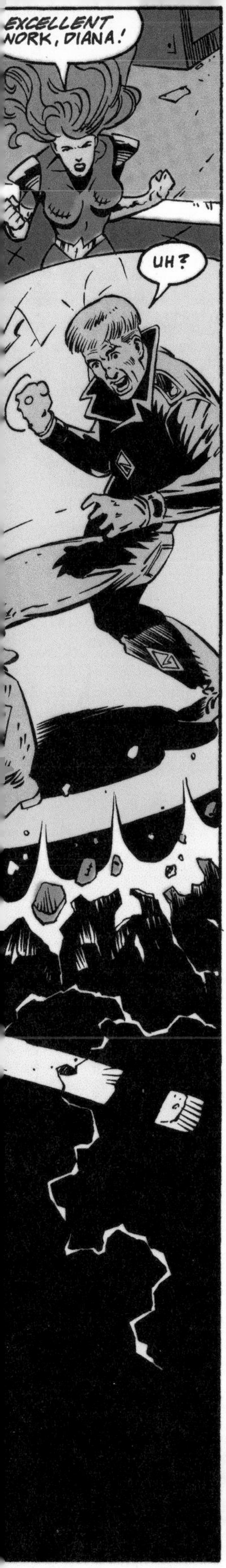
EXCELLENT WORK, DIANA!
UH?

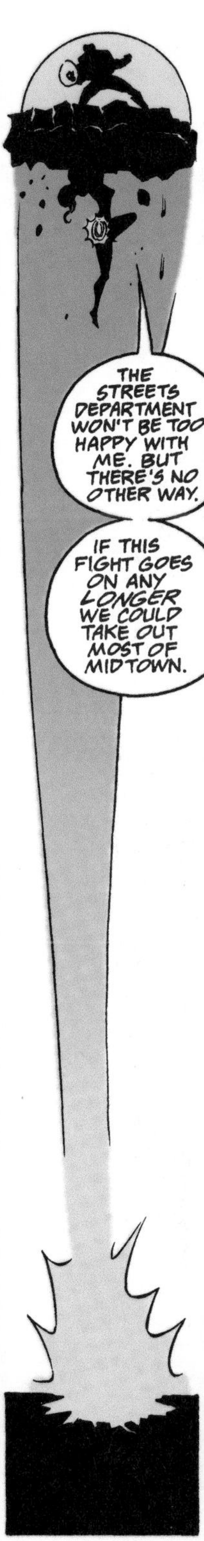
THE STREETS DEPARTMENT WON'T BE TOO HAPPY WITH ME. BUT THERE'S NO OTHER WAY.
IF THIS FIGHT GOES ON ANY LONGER WE COULD TAKE OUT MOST OF MIDTOWN.

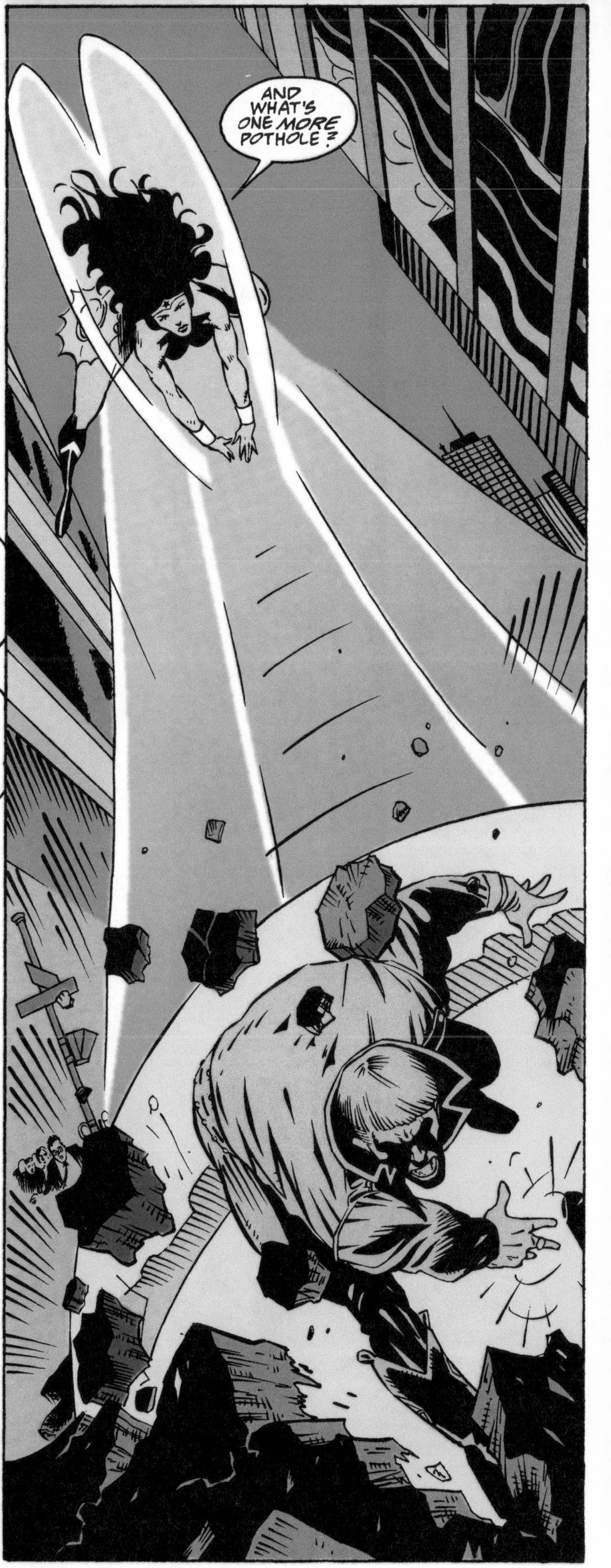
AND WHAT'S ONE MORE POTHOLE?

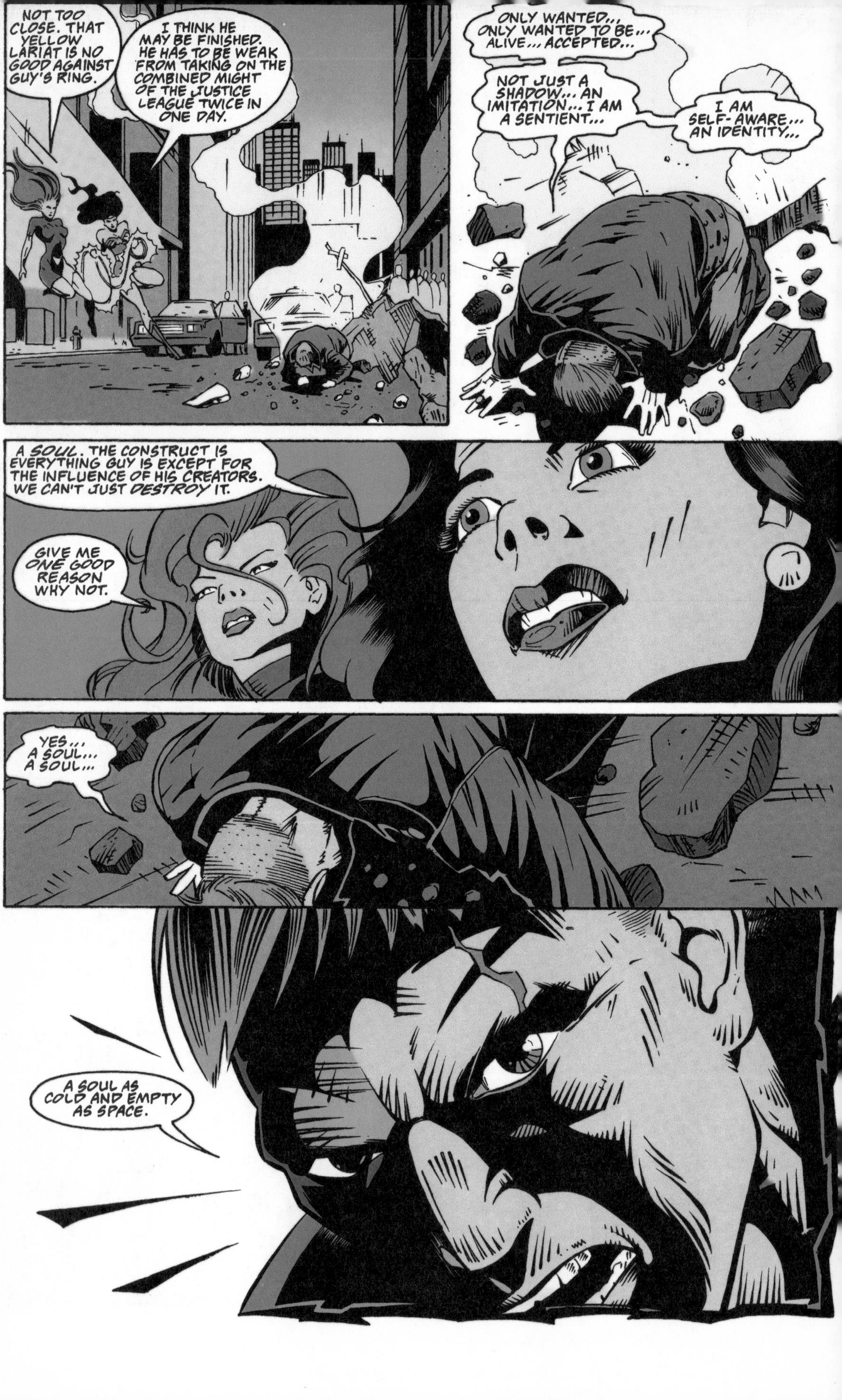
NOT TOO CLOSE. THAT YELLOW LARIAT IS NO GOOD AGAINST GUY'S RING.
I THINK HE MAY BE FINISHED. HE HAS TO BE WEAK FROM TAKING ON THE COMBINED MIGHT OF THE JUSTICE LEAGUE TWICE IN ONE DAY.
ONLY WANTED... ONLY WANTED TO BE... ALIVE... ACCEPTED...
NOT JUST A SHADOW... AN IMITATION... I AM A SENTIENT...
I AM SELF-AWARE... AN IDENTITY...
A SOUL. THE CONSTRUCT IS EVERYTHING GUY IS EXCEPT FOR THE INFLUENCE OF HIS CREATORS. WE CAN'T JUST DESTROY IT.
GIVE ME ONE GOOD REASON WHY NOT.
YES... A SOUL... A SOUL...
A SOUL AS COLD AND EMPTY AS SPACE.

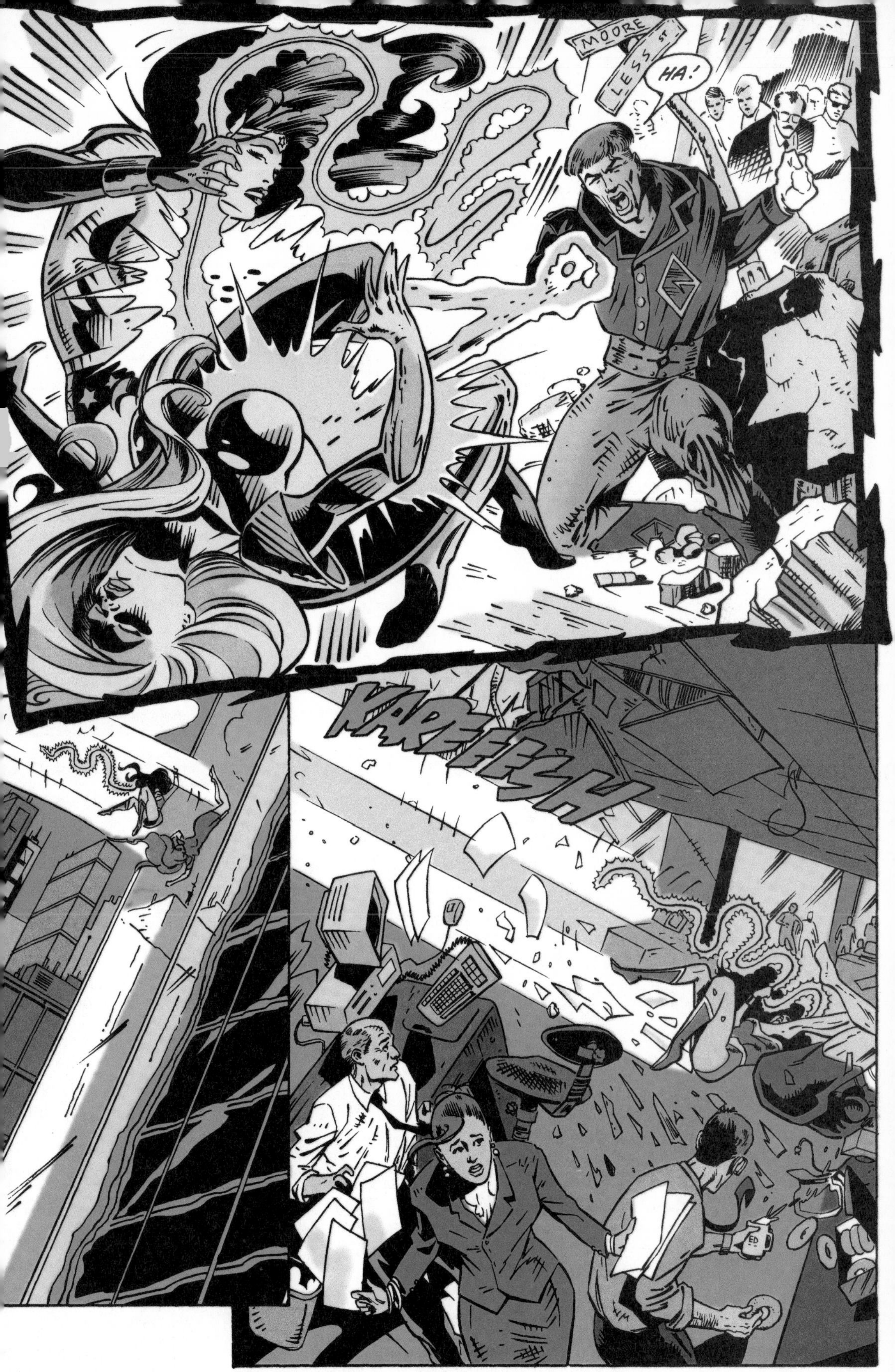
MOORE
LESS ST
HA!
KAREESH
ED

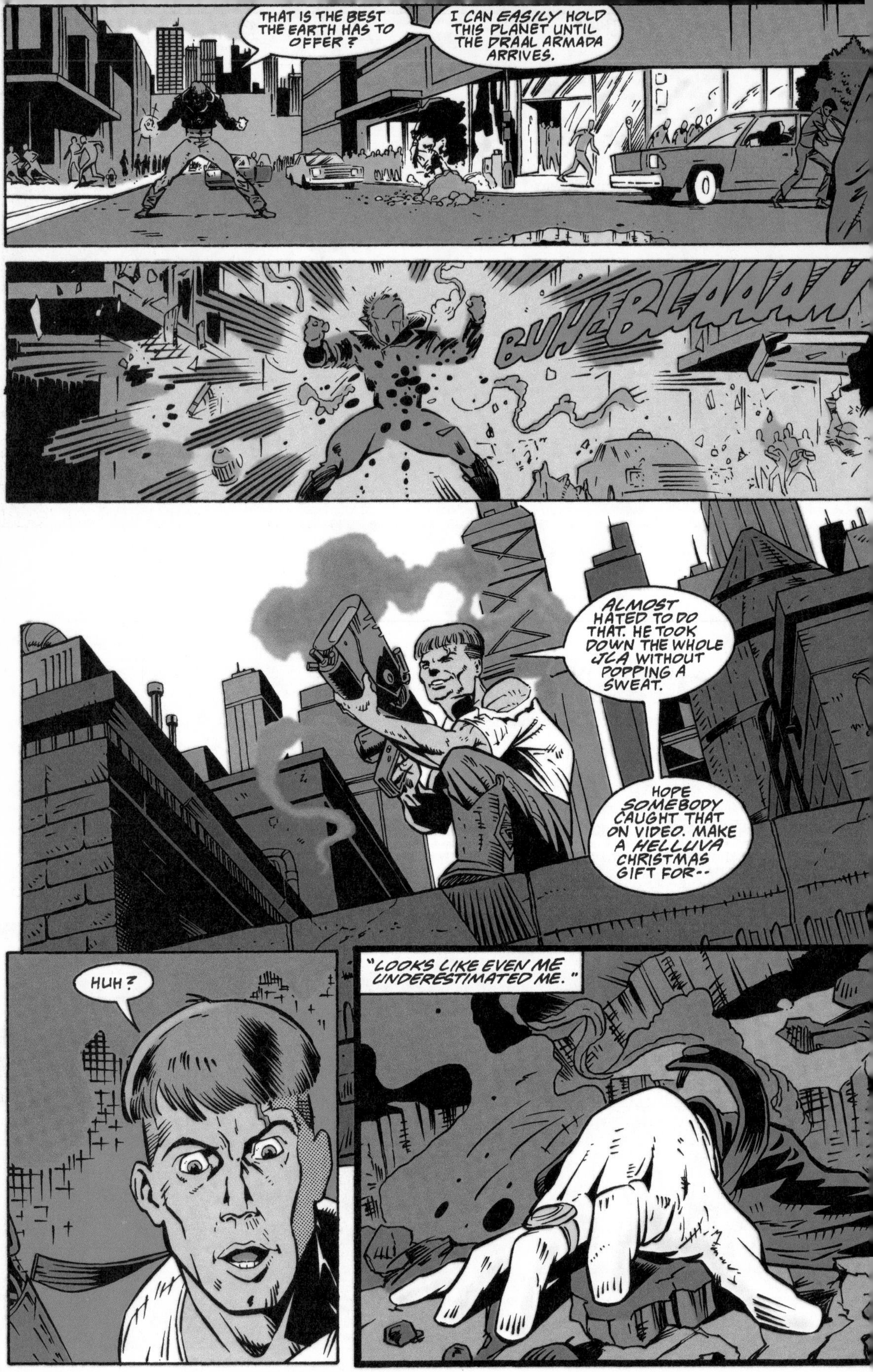
THAT IS THE BEST THE EARTH HAS TO OFFER?
I CAN EASILY HOLD THIS PLANET UNTIL THE DRAAL ARMADA ARRIVES.
BUH-BLAAAM
ALMOST HATED TO DO THAT. HE TOOK DOWN THE WHOLE JLA WITHOUT POPPING A SWEAT.
HOPE SOMEBODY CAUGHT THAT ON VIDEO. MAKE A HELLUVA CHRISTMAS GIFT FOR--
HUH?
"LOOKS LIKE EVEN ME UNDERESTIMATED ME."

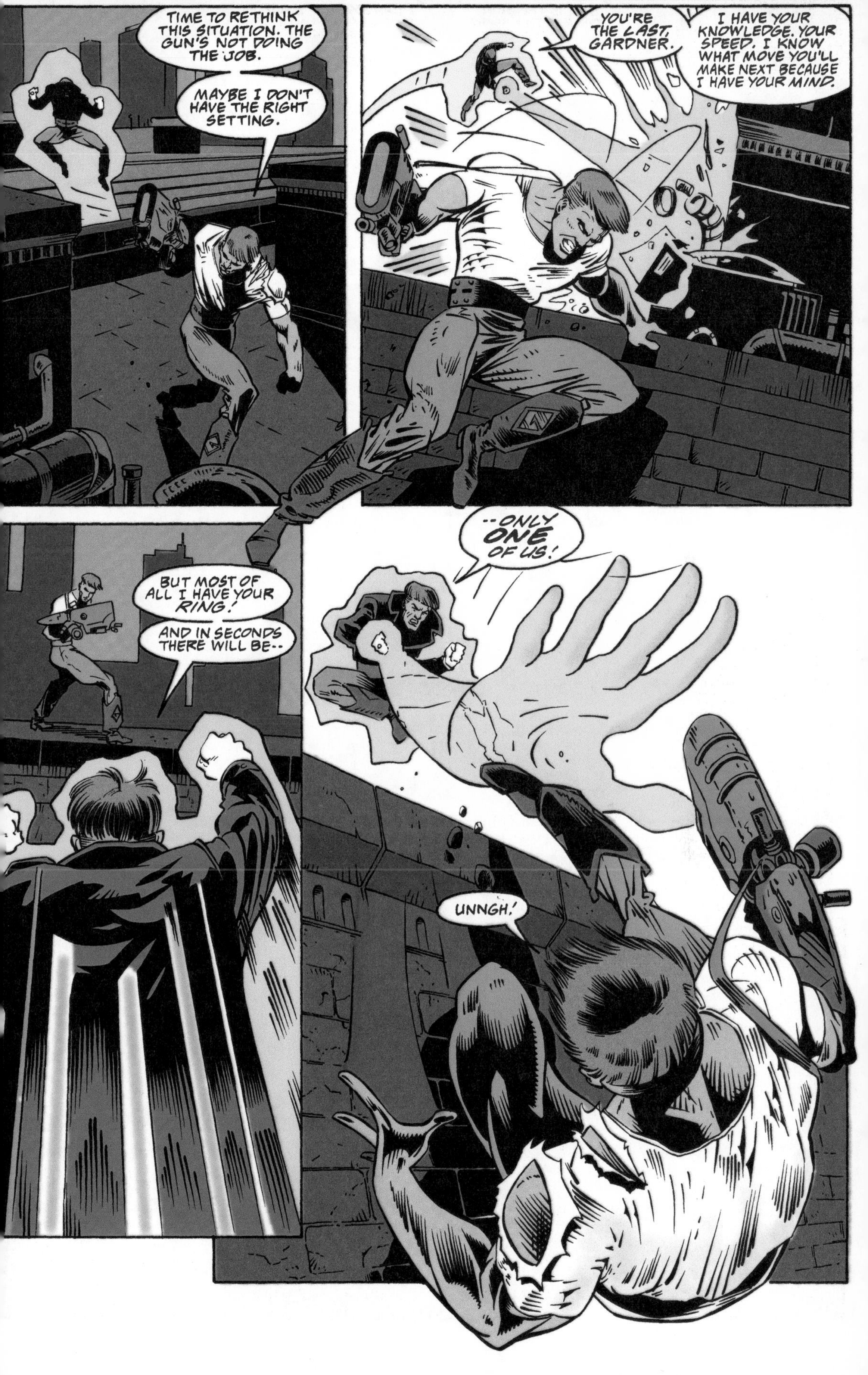
TIME TO RETHINK THIS SITUATION. THE GUN'S NOT DOING THE JOB.
MAYBE I DON'T HAVE THE RIGHT SETTING.
YOU'RE THE LAST, GARDNER.
I HAVE YOUR KNOWLEDGE. YOUR SPEED. I KNOW WHAT MOVE YOU'LL MAKE NEXT BECAUSE I HAVE YOUR MIND.
BUT MOST OF ALL I HAVE YOUR RING!
AND IN SECONDS THERE WILL BE--
--ONLY ONE OF US!
UNNGH!

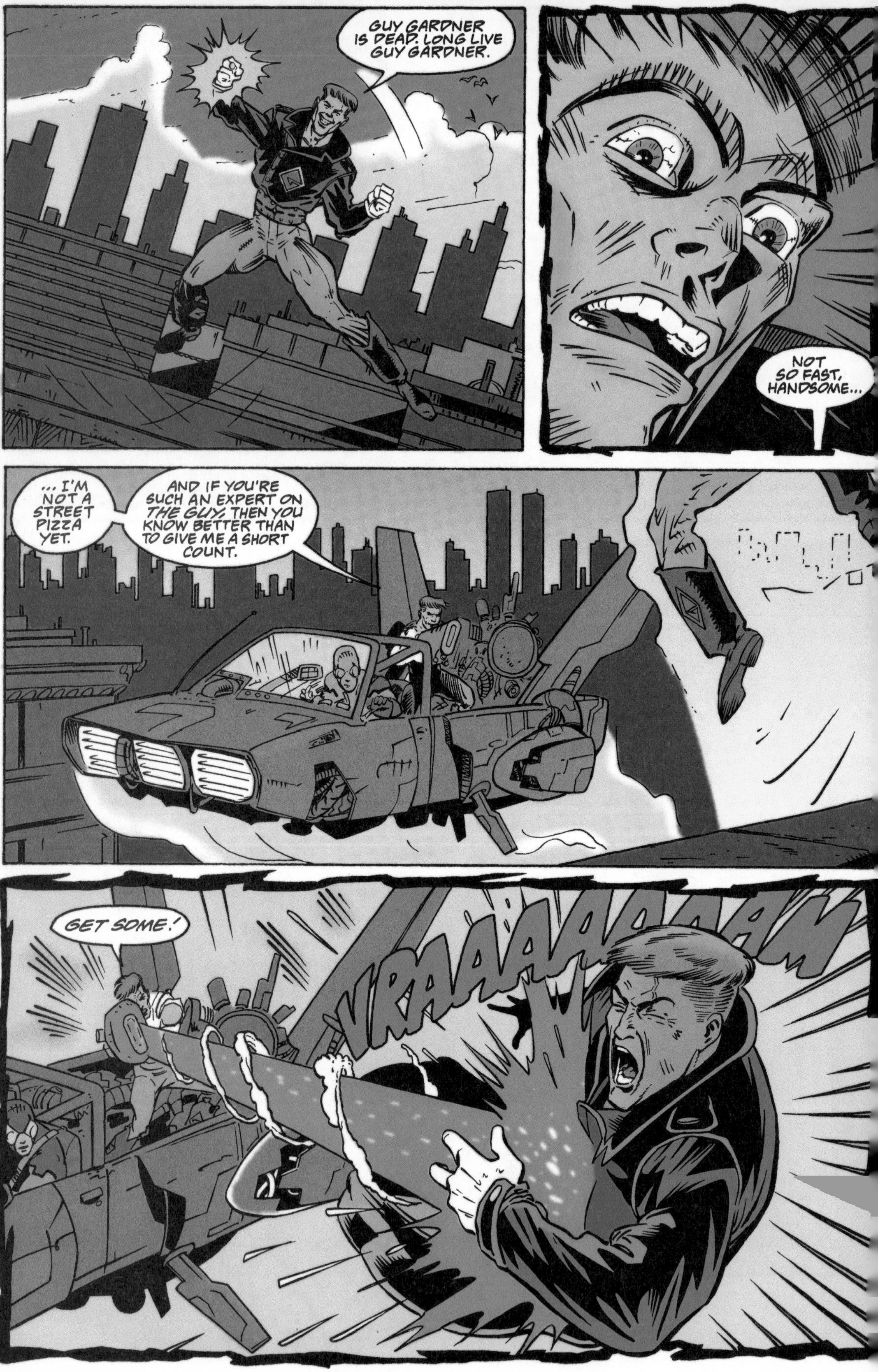

GUY GARDNER IS DEAD. LONG LIVE GUY GARDNER.
NOT SO FAST, HANDSOME...
... I'M NOT A STREET PIZZA YET.
AND IF YOU'RE SUCH AN EXPERT ON THE GUY, THEN YOU KNOW BETTER THAN TO GIVE ME A SHORT COUNT.
GET SOME!
VRAAAAAAAAAN

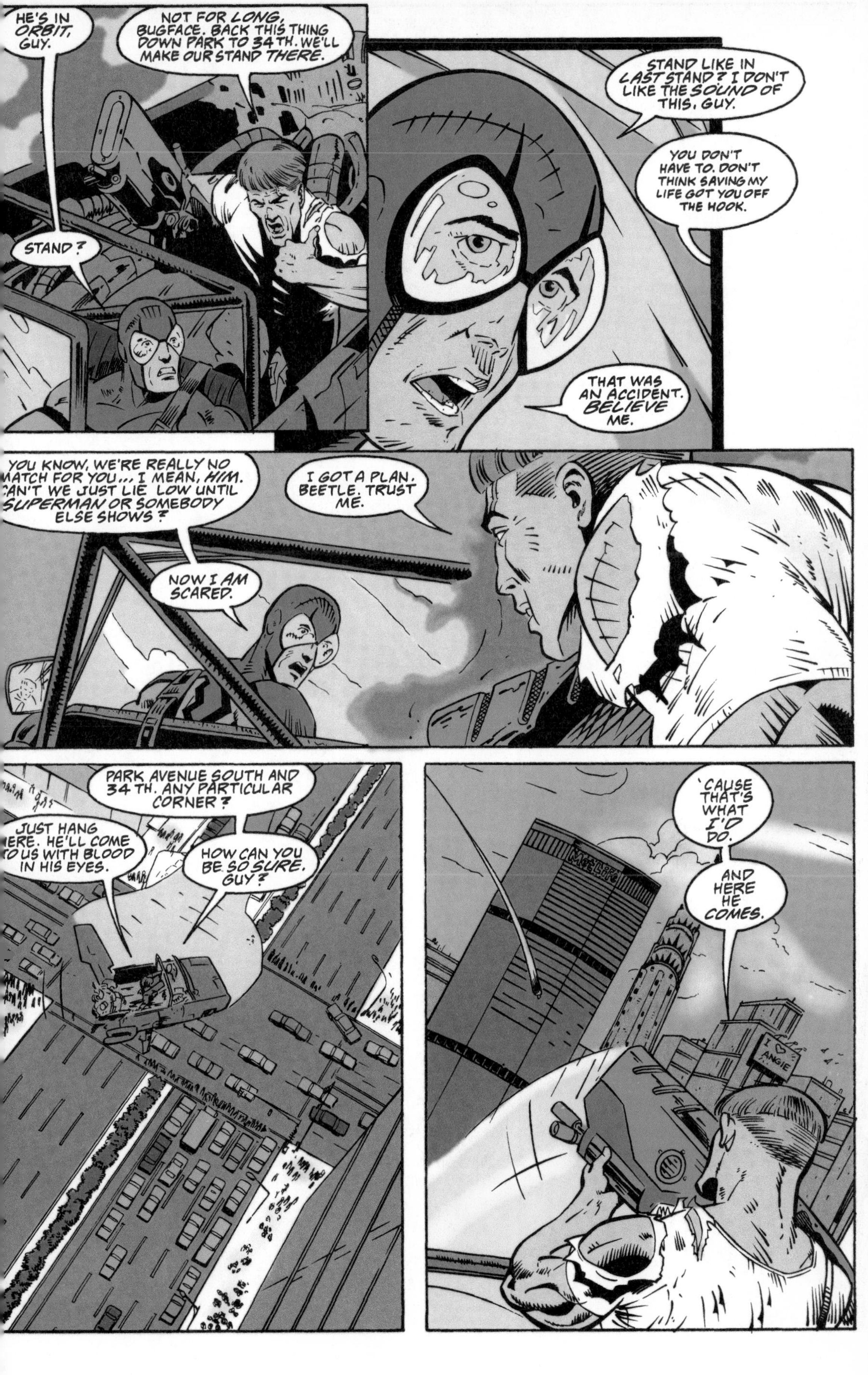
HE'S IN ORBIT, GUY.
NOT FOR LONG, BUGFACE. BACK THIS THING DOWN PARK TO 34 TH. WE'LL MAKE OUR STAND THERE.
STAND?
STAND LIKE IN LAST STAND? I DON'T LIKE THE SOUND OF THIS, GUY.
YOU DON'T HAVE TO. DON'T THINK SAVING MY LIFE GOT YOU OFF THE HOOK.
THAT WAS AN ACCIDENT. BELIEVE ME.
YOU KNOW, WE'RE REALLY NO MATCH FOR YOU... I MEAN, HIM. CAN'T WE JUST LIE LOW UNTIL SUPERMAN OR SOMEBODY ELSE SHOWS?
I GOT A PLAN. BEETLE. TRUST ME.
NOW I AM SCARED.
PARK AVENUE SOUTH AND 34 TH. ANY PARTICULAR CORNER?
JUST HANG HERE. HE'LL COME TO US WITH BLOOD IN HIS EYES.
HOW CAN YOU BE SO SURE, GUY?
'CAUSE THAT'S WHAT I'D DO.
AND HERE HE COMES.
I ♥ ANGIE

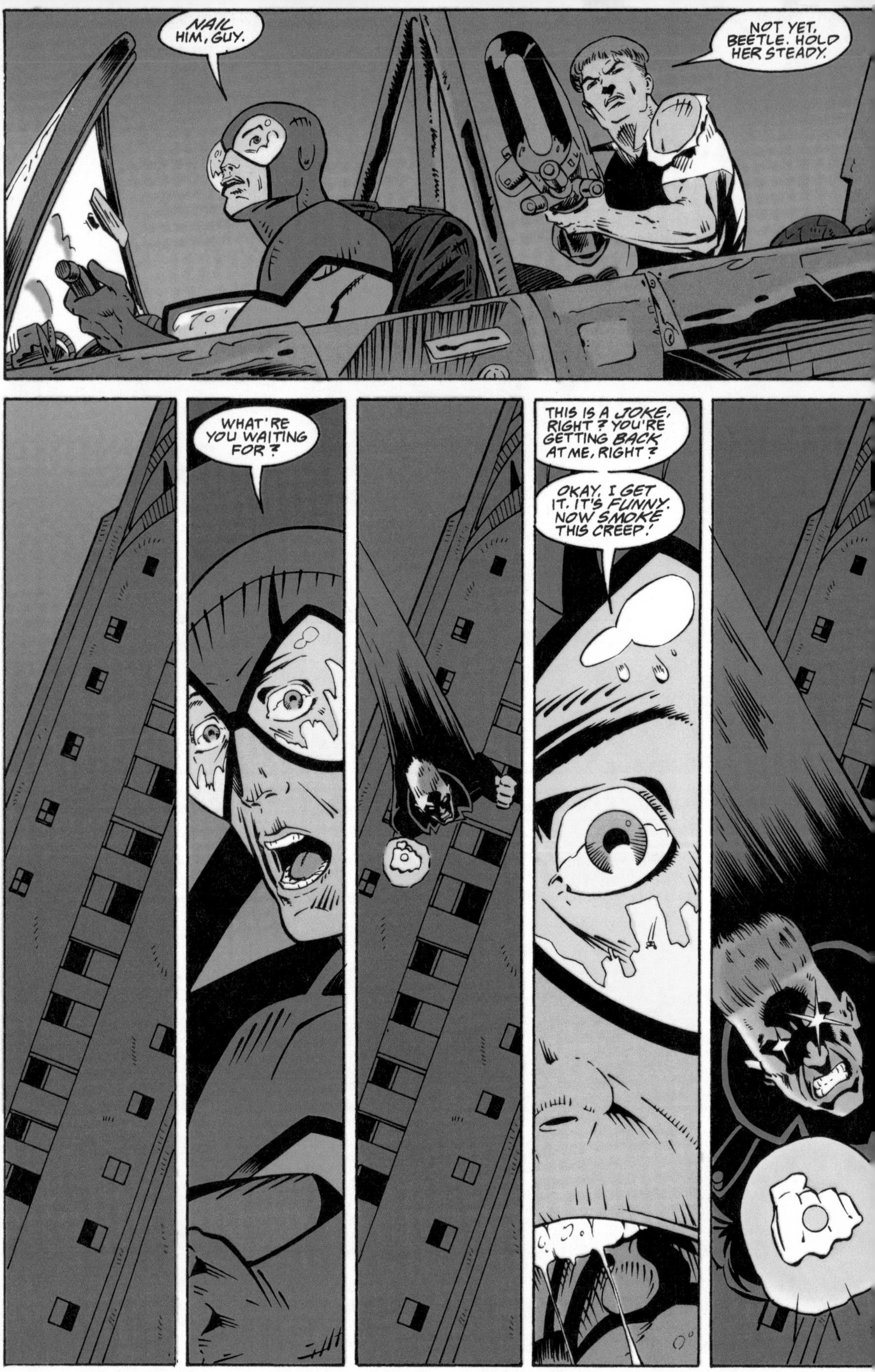
NAIL HIM, GUY.
NOT YET, BEETLE. HOLD HER STEADY.
WHAT'RE YOU WAITING FOR?
THIS IS A JOKE, RIGHT? YOU'RE GETTING BACK AT ME, RIGHT?
OKAY, I GET IT. IT'S FUNNY. NOW SMOKE THIS CREEP!

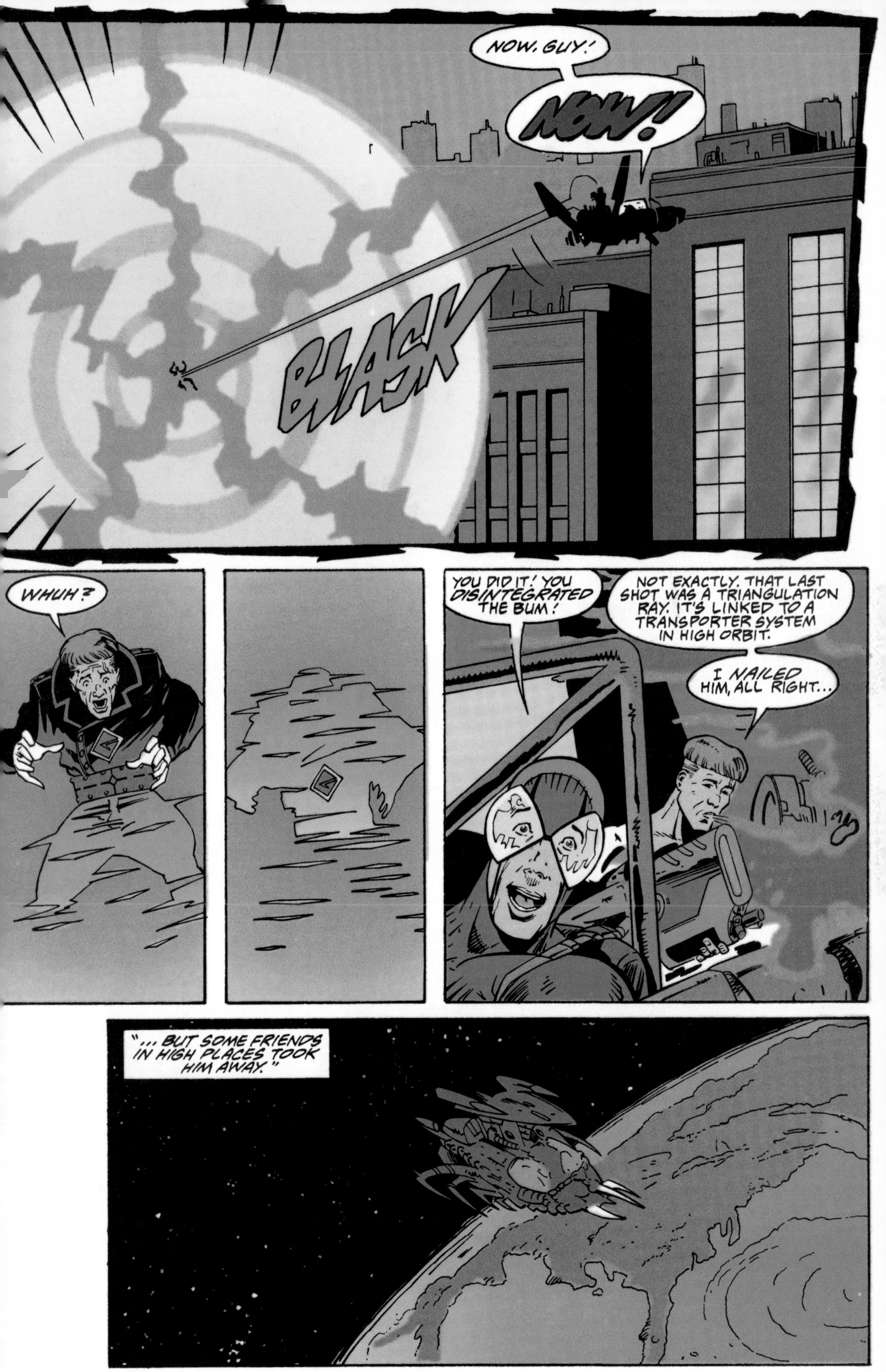
NOW, GUY!
NOW!!
BLASK
WHUH?
YOU DID IT! YOU DISINTEGRATED THE BUM!
NOT EXACTLY. THAT LAST SHOT WAS A TRIANGULATION RAY. IT'S LINKED TO A TRANSPORTER SYSTEM IN HIGH ORBIT.
I NAILED HIM, ALL RIGHT...
"...BUT SOME FRIENDS IN HIGH PLACES TOOK HIM AWAY."

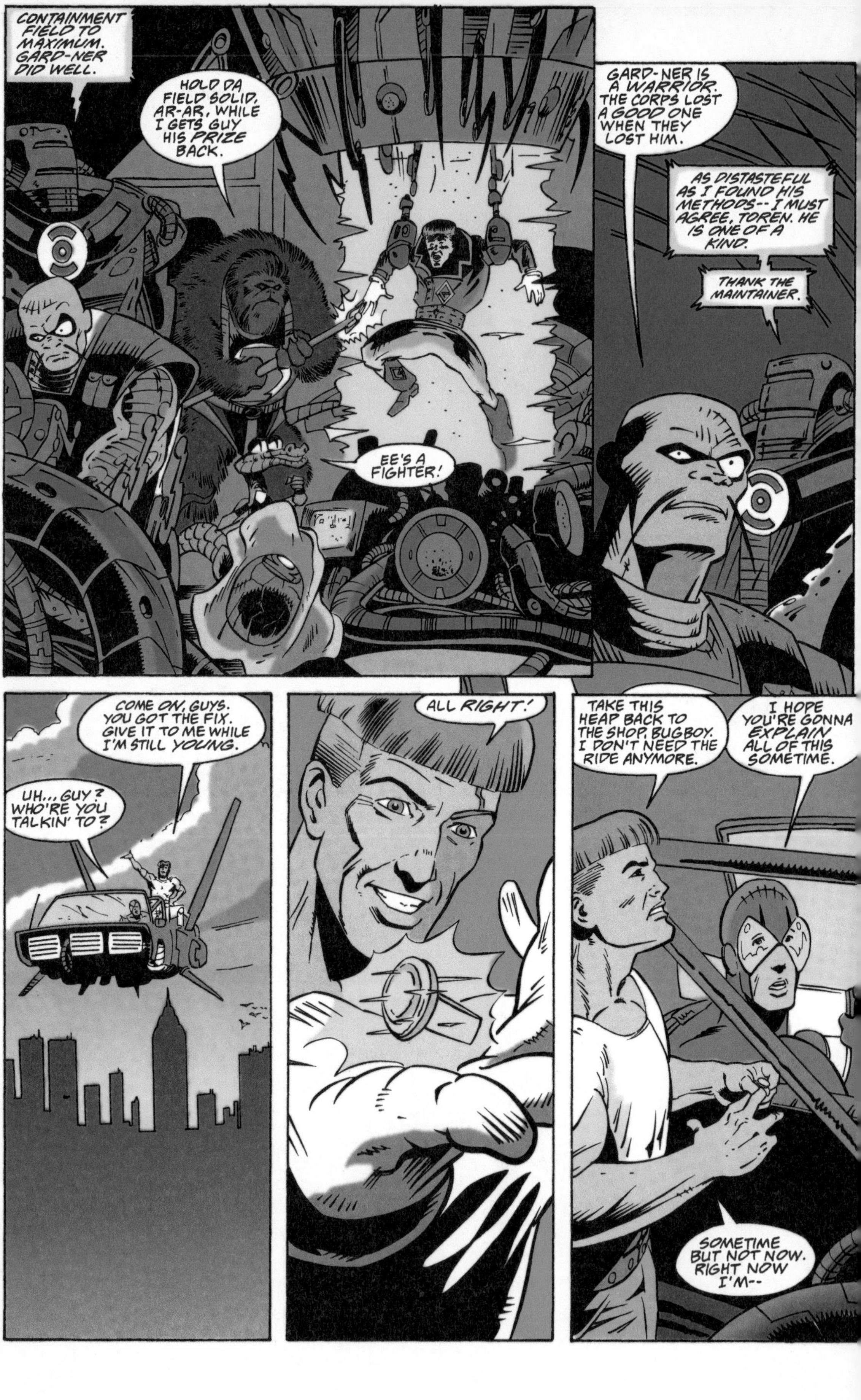
CONTAINMENT FIELD TO MAXIMUM. GARD-NER DID WELL.
HOLD DA FIELD SOLID, AR-AR, WHILE I GETS GUY HIS PRIZE BACK.
EE'S A FIGHTER!
GARD-NER IS A WARRIOR. THE CORPS LOST A GOOD ONE WHEN THEY LOST HIM.
AS DISTASTEFUL AS I FOUND HIS METHODS-- I MUST AGREE, TOREN. HE IS ONE OF A KIND.
THANK THE MAINTAINER.
COME ON, GUYS. YOU GOT THE FIX. GIVE IT TO ME WHILE I'M STILL YOUNG.
UH... GUY? WHO'RE YOU TALKIN' TO?
ALL RIGHT!
TAKE THIS HEAP BACK TO THE SHOP, BUGBOY. I DON'T NEED THE RIDE ANYMORE.
I HOPE YOU'RE GONNA EXPLAIN ALL OF THIS SOMETIME.
SOMETIME BUT NOT NOW. RIGHT NOW I'M--

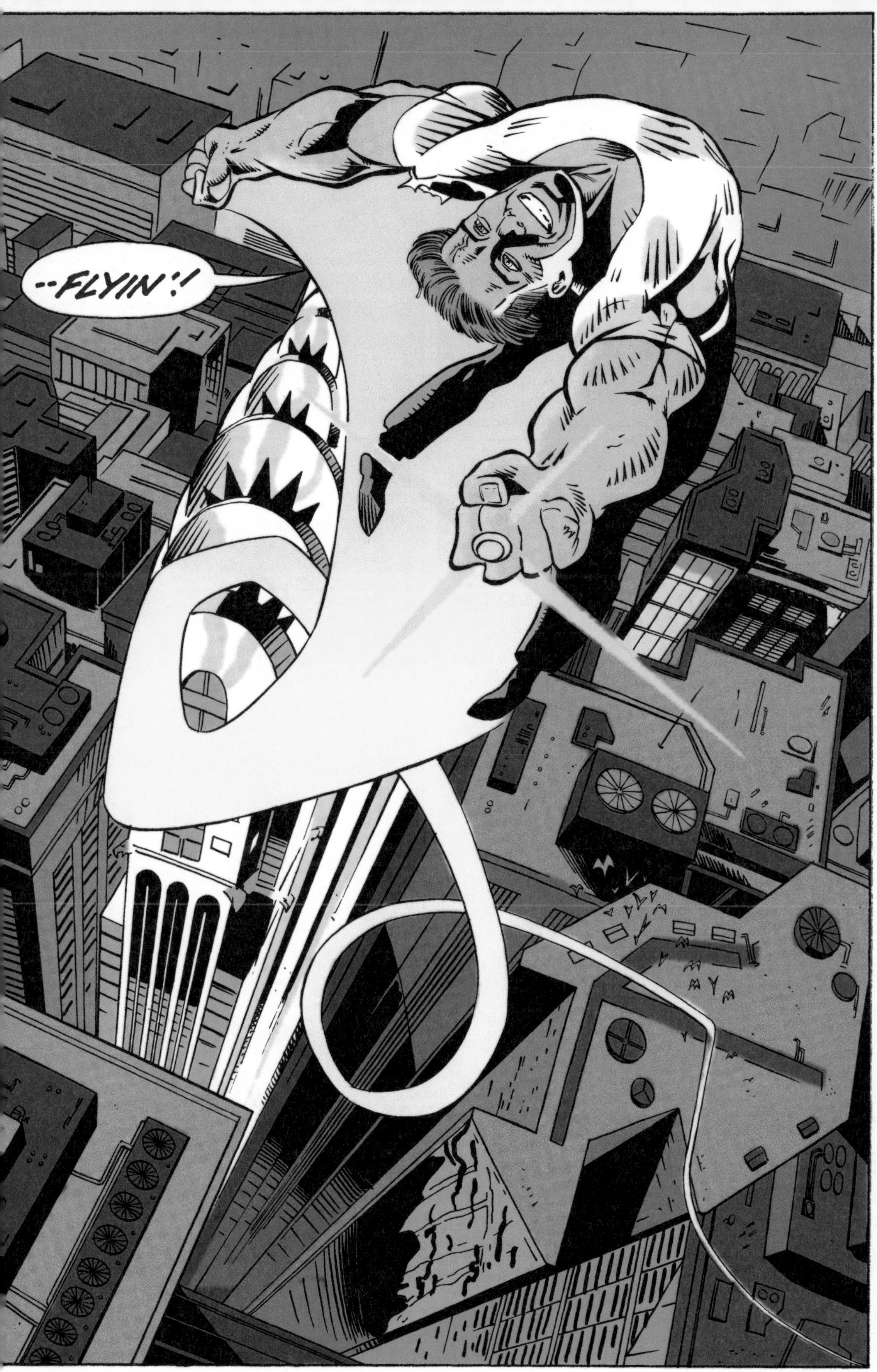
--FLYIN'!

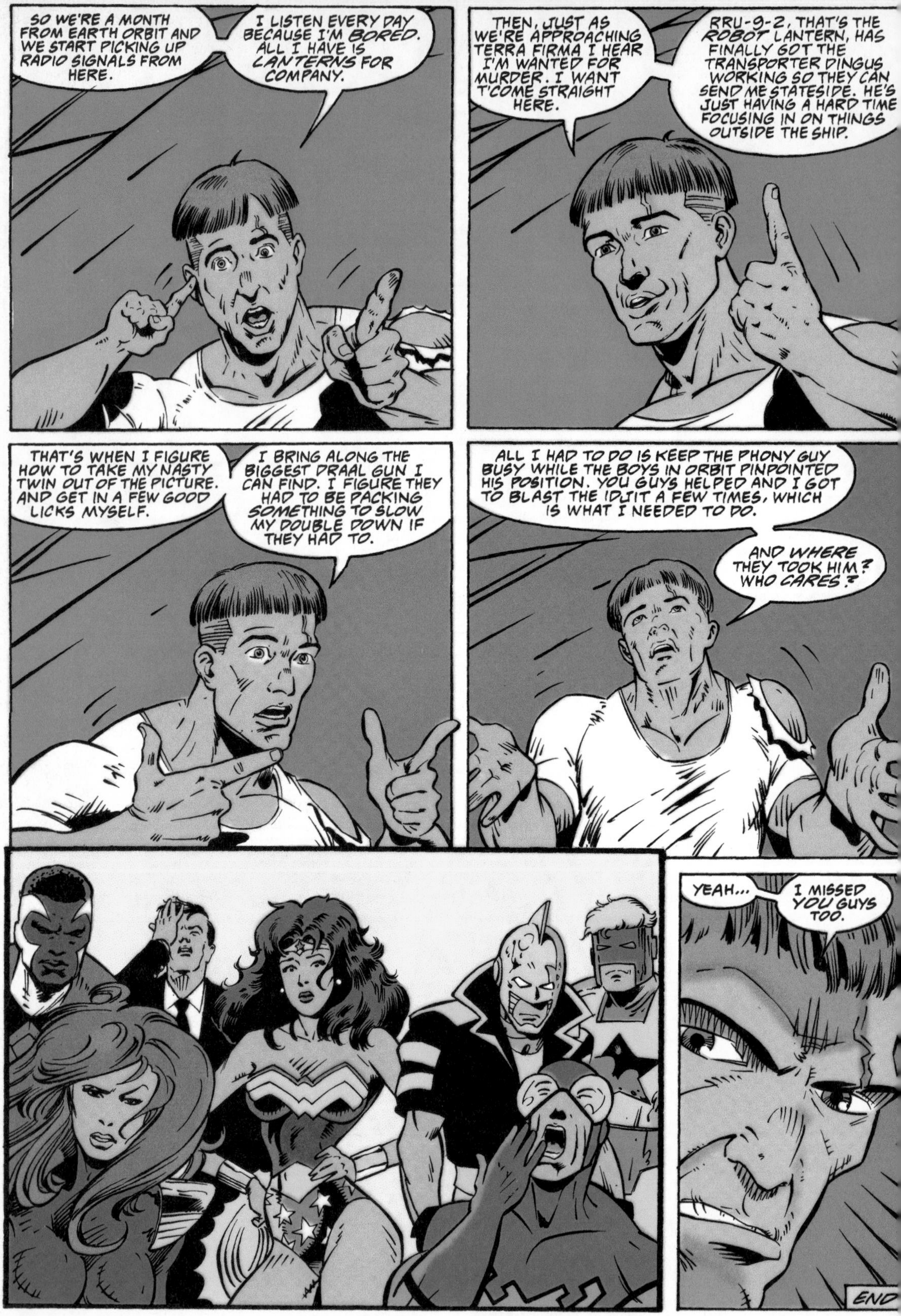

SO WE'RE A MONTH FROM EARTH ORBIT AND WE START PICKING UP RADIO SIGNALS FROM HERE.
I LISTEN EVERY DAY BECAUSE I'M *BORED*. ALL I HAVE IS *LANTERNS* FOR COMPANY.
THEN, JUST AS WE'RE APPROACHING TERRA FIRMA I HEAR I'M WANTED FOR MURDER. I WANT T'COME STRAIGHT HERE.
RRU-9-2, THAT'S THE *ROBOT* LANTERN, HAS FINALLY GOT THE TRANSPORTER DINGUS WORKING SO THEY CAN SEND ME STATESIDE. HE'S JUST HAVING A HARD TIME FOCUSING IN ON THINGS OUTSIDE THE SHIP.
THAT'S WHEN I FIGURE HOW TO TAKE MY NASTY TWIN OUT OF THE PICTURE. AND GET IN A FEW GOOD LICKS MYSELF.
I BRING ALONG THE BIGGEST DRAAL GUN I CAN FIND. I FIGURE THEY HAD TO BE PACKING *SOMETHING* TO SLOW MY DOUBLE *DOWN* IF THEY HAD TO.
ALL I HAD TO DO IS KEEP THE PHONY GUY BUSY WHILE THE BOYS IN ORBIT PINPOINTED HIS POSITION. YOU GUYS HELPED AND I GOT TO BLAST THE ID'JIT A FEW TIMES, WHICH IS WHAT I NEEDED TO DO.
AND *WHERE* THEY TOOK HIM? WHO *CARES*?
YEAH...
I MISSED *YOU* GUYS TOO.
END

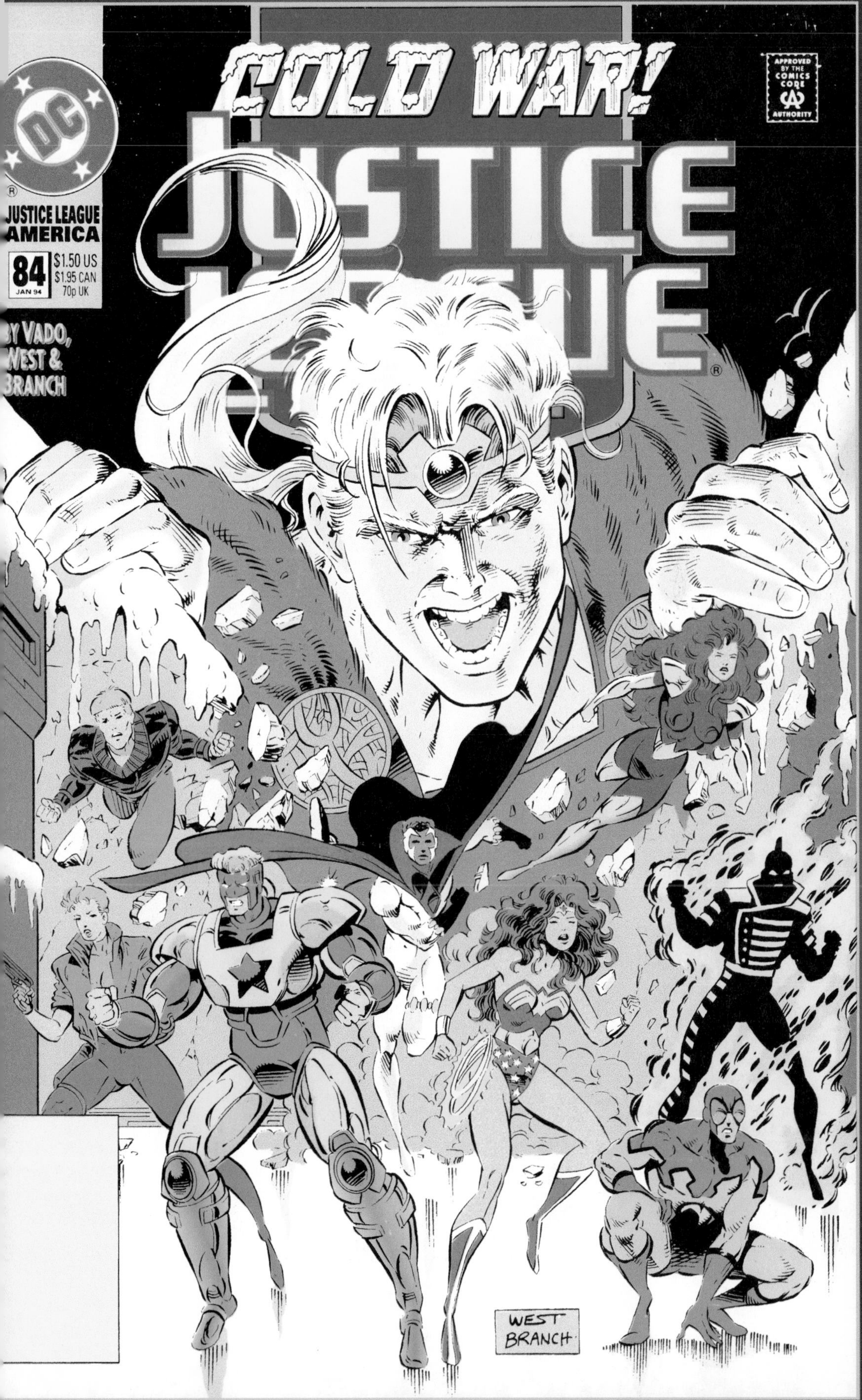

COLD WAR!
JUSTICE
APPROVED BY THE COMICS CODE AUTHORITY
DC
JUSTICE LEAGUE AMERICA
84
JAN 94
$1.50 US
$1.95 CAN
70p UK
Y VADO,
WEST &
BRANCH
WEST
BRANCH

Cover art by **KEVIN WEST**
and **KEN BRANCH**

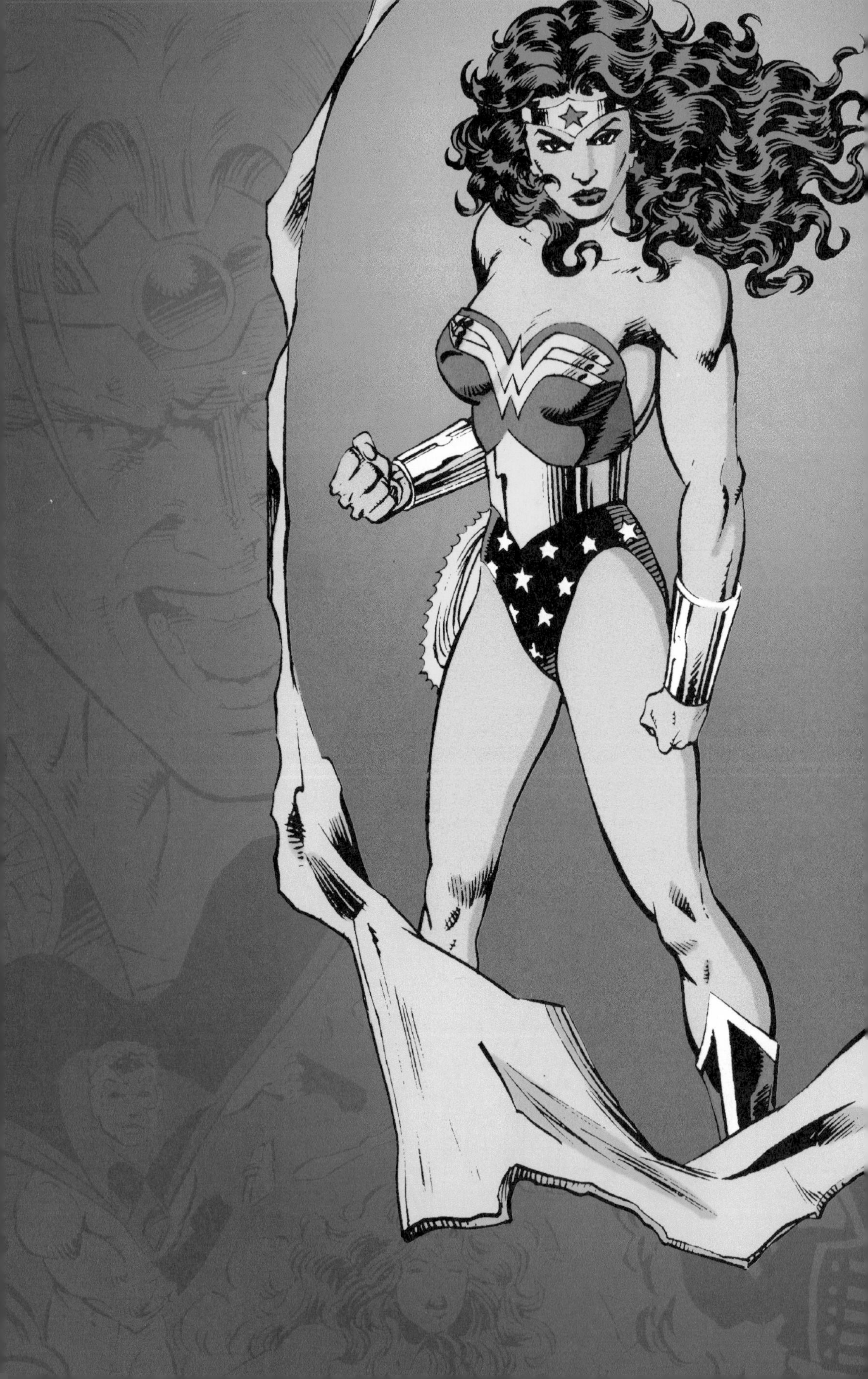

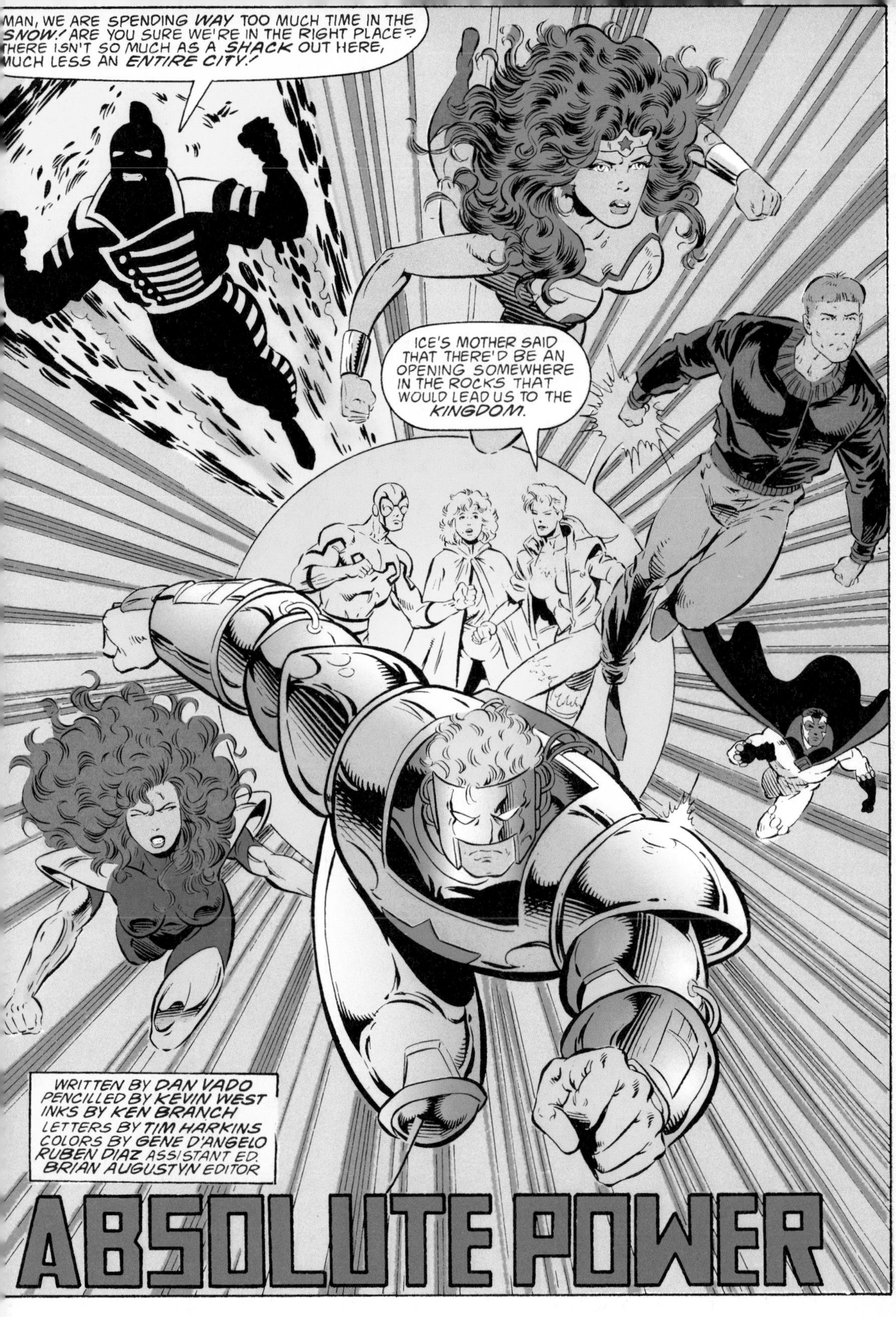
MAN, WE ARE SPENDING WAY TOO MUCH TIME IN THE SNOW! ARE YOU SURE WE'RE IN THE RIGHT PLACE? THERE ISN'T SO MUCH AS A SHACK OUT HERE, MUCH LESS AN ENTIRE CITY!
ICE'S MOTHER SAID THAT THERE'D BE AN OPENING SOMEWHERE IN THE ROCKS THAT WOULD LEAD US TO THE KINGDOM.
WRITTEN BY DAN VADO
PENCILLED BY KEVIN WEST
INKS BY KEN BRANCH
LETTERS BY TIM HARKINS
COLORS BY GENE D'ANGELO
RUBEN DIAZ ASSISTANT ED.
BRIAN AUGUSTYN EDITOR
ABSOLUTE POWER

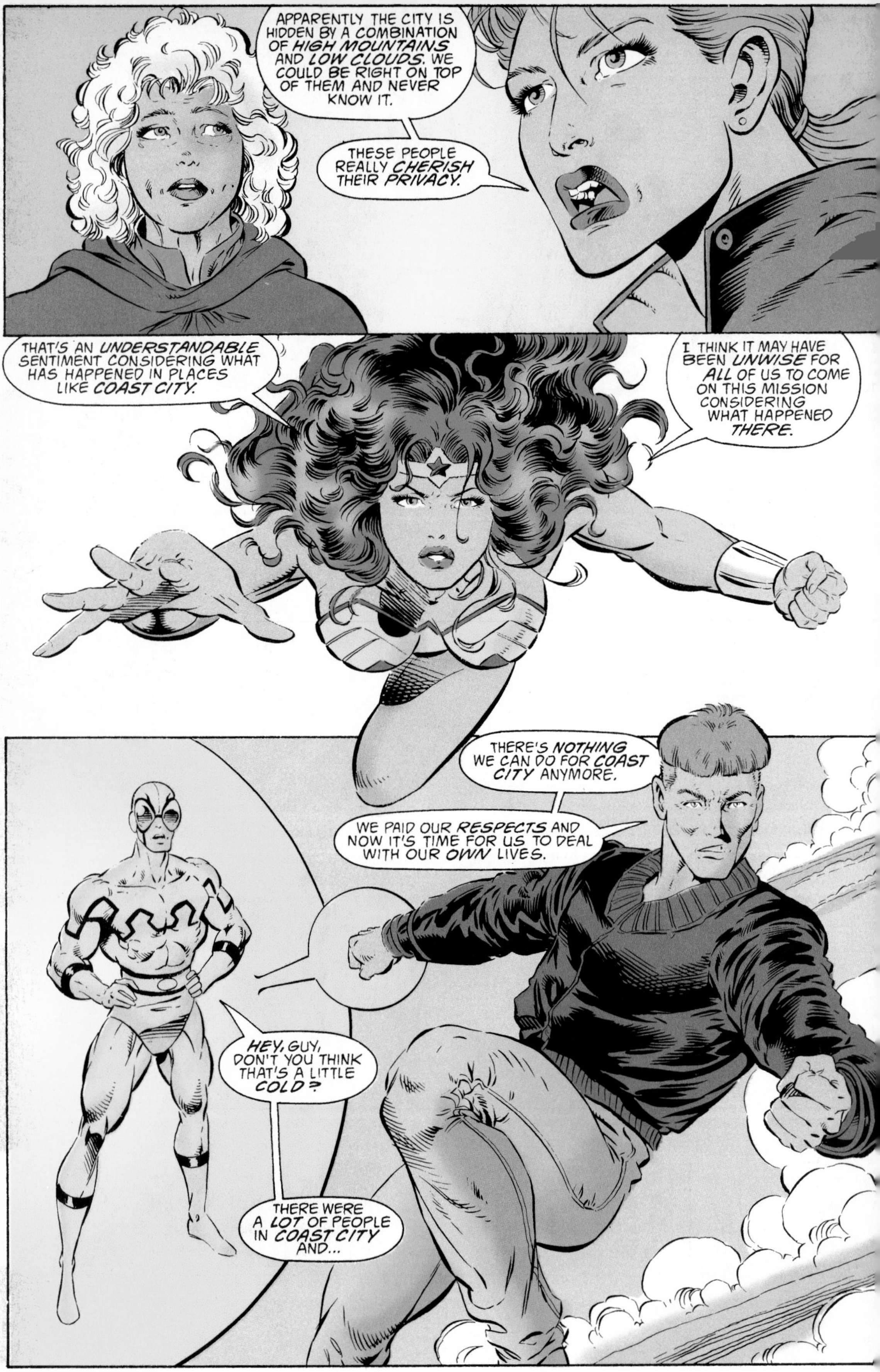
APPARENTLY THE CITY IS HIDDEN BY A COMBINATION OF HIGH MOUNTAINS AND LOW CLOUDS. WE COULD BE RIGHT ON TOP OF THEM AND NEVER KNOW IT.
THESE PEOPLE REALLY CHERISH THEIR PRIVACY.
THAT'S AN UNDERSTANDABLE SENTIMENT CONSIDERING WHAT HAS HAPPENED IN PLACES LIKE COAST CITY.
I THINK IT MAY HAVE BEEN UNWISE FOR ALL OF US TO COME ON THIS MISSION CONSIDERING WHAT HAPPENED THERE.
THERE'S NOTHING WE CAN DO FOR COAST CITY ANYMORE.
WE PAID OUR RESPECTS AND NOW IT'S TIME FOR US TO DEAL WITH OUR OWN LIVES.
HEY, GUY, DON'T YOU THINK THAT'S A LITTLE COLD?
THERE WERE A LOT OF PEOPLE IN COAST CITY AND...

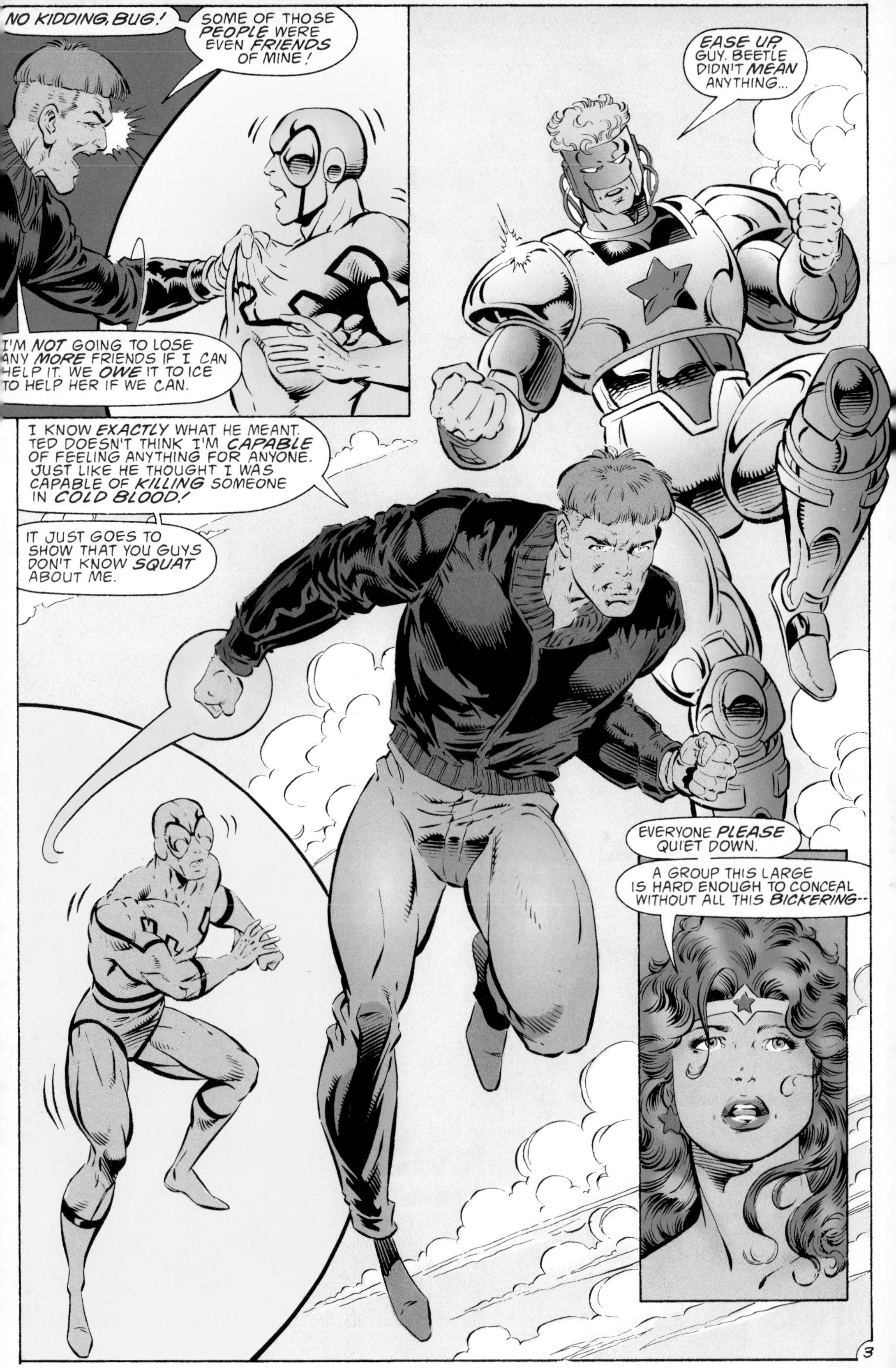
NO KIDDING, BUG!
SOME OF THOSE PEOPLE WERE EVEN FRIENDS OF MINE!
I'M NOT GOING TO LOSE ANY MORE FRIENDS IF I CAN HELP IT. WE OWE IT TO ICE TO HELP HER IF WE CAN.
EASE UP, GUY. BEETLE DIDN'T MEAN ANYTHING...
I KNOW EXACTLY WHAT HE MEANT. TED DOESN'T THINK I'M CAPABLE OF FEELING ANYTHING FOR ANYONE. JUST LIKE HE THOUGHT I WAS CAPABLE OF KILLING SOMEONE IN COLD BLOOD!
IT JUST GOES TO SHOW THAT YOU GUYS DON'T KNOW SQUAT ABOUT ME.
EVERYONE PLEASE QUIET DOWN.
A GROUP THIS LARGE IS HARD ENOUGH TO CONCEAL WITHOUT ALL THIS BICKERING--

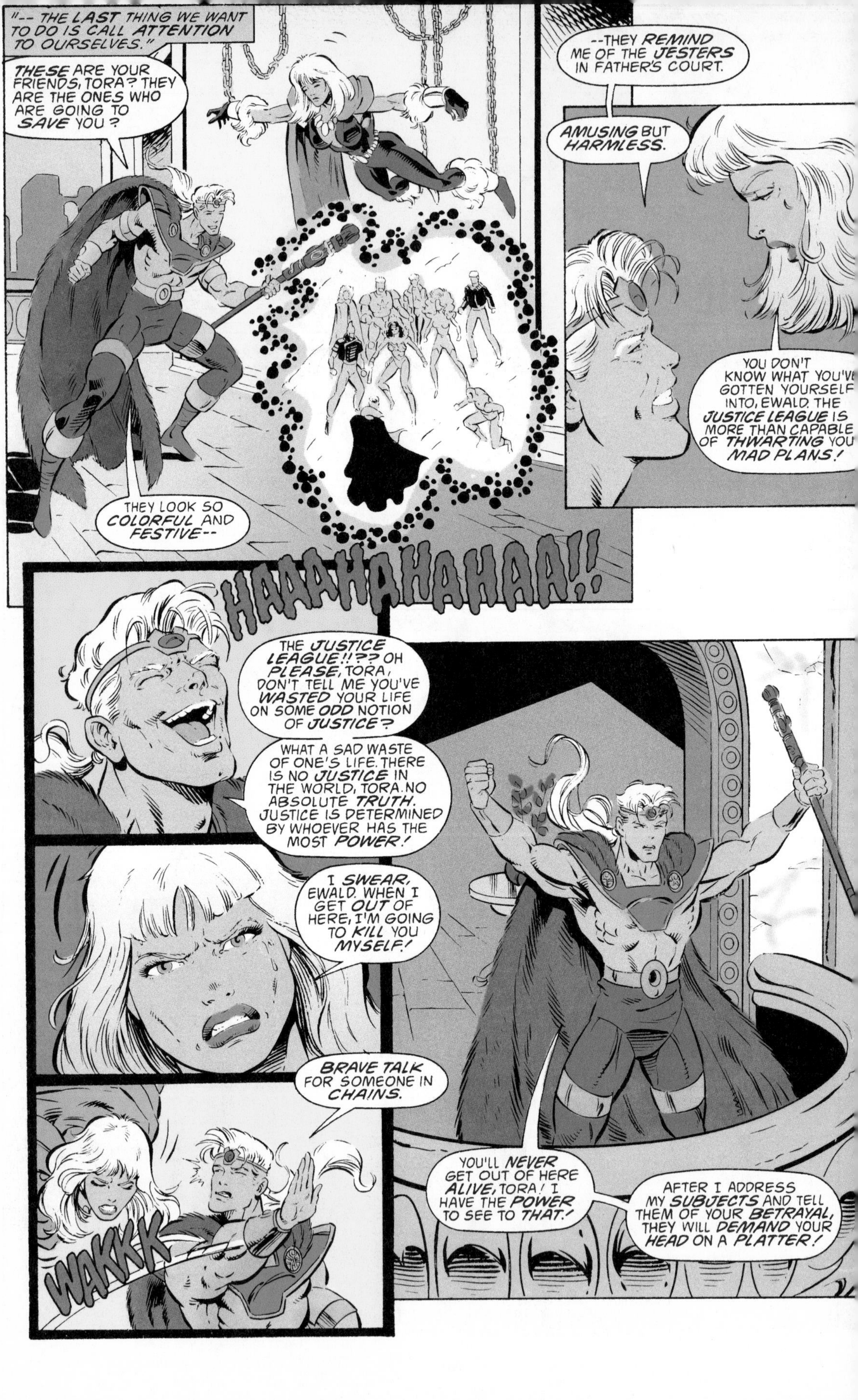
"-- THE LAST THING WE WANT TO DO IS CALL ATTENTION TO OURSELVES."
THESE ARE YOUR FRIENDS, TORA? THEY ARE THE ONES WHO ARE GOING TO SAVE YOU?
THEY LOOK SO COLORFUL AND FESTIVE--
--THEY REMIND ME OF THE JESTERS IN FATHER'S COURT.
AMUSING BUT HARMLESS.
YOU DON'T KNOW WHAT YOU'VE GOTTEN YOURSELF INTO, EWALD. THE JUSTICE LEAGUE IS MORE THAN CAPABLE OF THWARTING YOUR MAD PLANS!
HAAAHAHAHAA!!
THE JUSTICE LEAGUE!!?? OH PLEASE, TORA, DON'T TELL ME YOU'VE WASTED YOUR LIFE ON SOME ODD NOTION OF JUSTICE?
WHAT A SAD WASTE OF ONE'S LIFE. THERE IS NO JUSTICE IN THE WORLD, TORA. NO ABSOLUTE TRUTH. JUSTICE IS DETERMINED BY WHOEVER HAS THE MOST POWER!
I SWEAR, EWALD. WHEN I GET OUT OF HERE, I'M GOING TO KILL YOU MYSELF!
BRAVE TALK FOR SOMEONE IN CHAINS.
WAKKK
YOU'LL NEVER GET OUT OF HERE ALIVE, TORA! I HAVE THE POWER TO SEE TO THAT!
AFTER I ADDRESS MY SUBJECTS AND TELL THEM OF YOUR BETRAYAL, THEY WILL DEMAND YOUR HEAD ON A PLATTER!

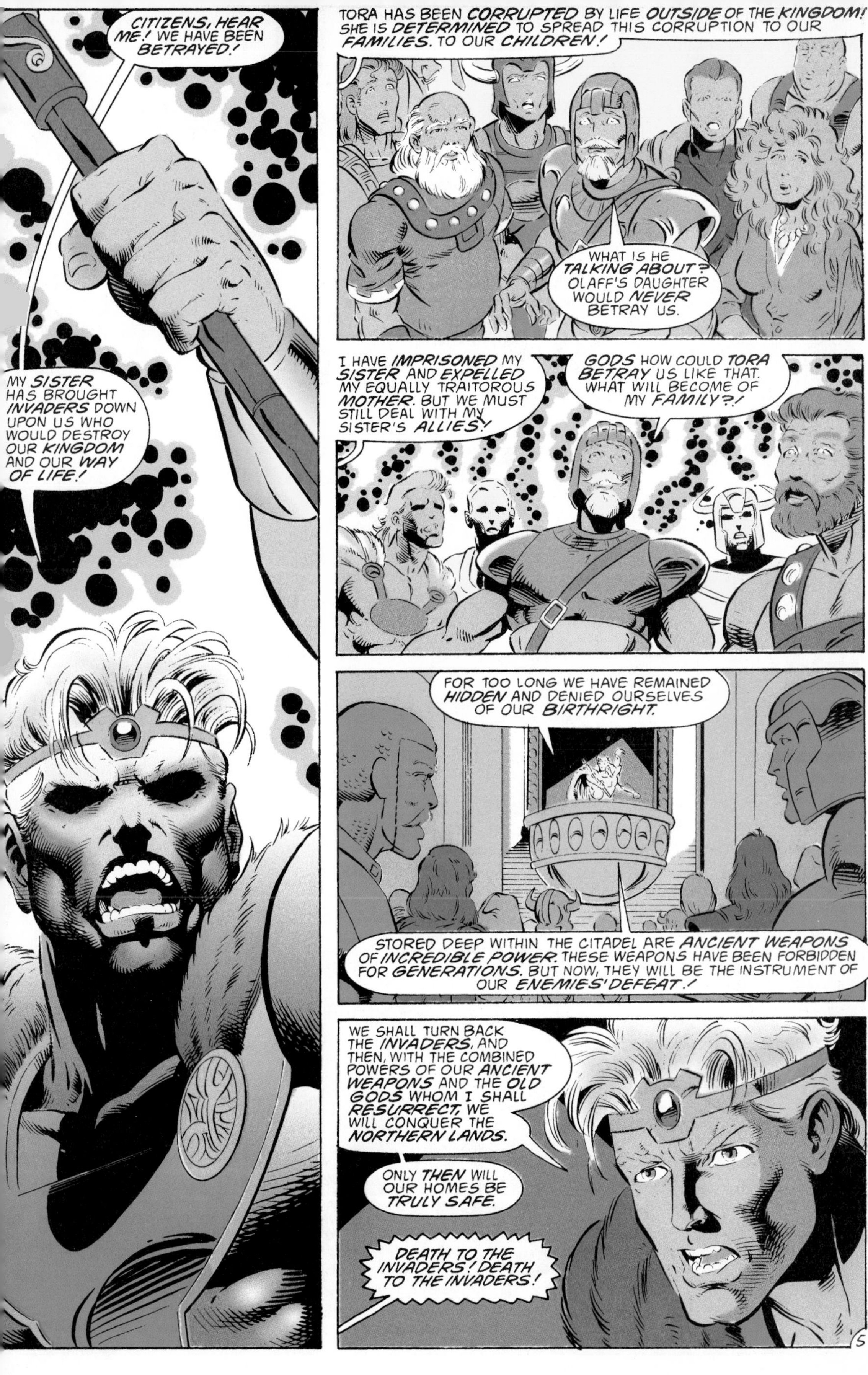

CITIZENS, HEAR ME! WE HAVE BEEN BETRAYED!
MY SISTER HAS BROUGHT INVADERS DOWN UPON US WHO WOULD DESTROY OUR KINGDOM AND OUR WAY OF LIFE!
TORA HAS BEEN CORRUPTED BY LIFE OUTSIDE OF THE KINGDOM! SHE IS DETERMINED TO SPREAD THIS CORRUPTION TO OUR FAMILIES. TO OUR CHILDREN!
WHAT IS HE TALKING ABOUT? OLAFF'S DAUGHTER WOULD NEVER BETRAY US.
I HAVE IMPRISONED MY SISTER AND EXPELLED MY EQUALLY TRAITOROUS MOTHER. BUT WE MUST STILL DEAL WITH MY SISTER'S ALLIES!
GODS HOW COULD TORA BETRAY US LIKE THAT. WHAT WILL BECOME OF MY FAMILY?!
FOR TOO LONG WE HAVE REMAINED HIDDEN AND DENIED OURSELVES OF OUR BIRTHRIGHT.
STORED DEEP WITHIN THE CITADEL ARE ANCIENT WEAPONS OF INCREDIBLE POWER. THESE WEAPONS HAVE BEEN FORBIDDEN FOR GENERATIONS. BUT NOW, THEY WILL BE THE INSTRUMENT OF OUR ENEMIES' DEFEAT!
WE SHALL TURN BACK THE INVADERS, AND THEN, WITH THE COMBINED POWERS OF OUR ANCIENT WEAPONS AND THE OLD GODS WHOM I SHALL RESURRECT, WE WILL CONQUER THE NORTHERN LANDS.
ONLY THEN WILL OUR HOMES BE TRULY SAFE.
DEATH TO THE INVADERS! DEATH TO THE INVADERS!

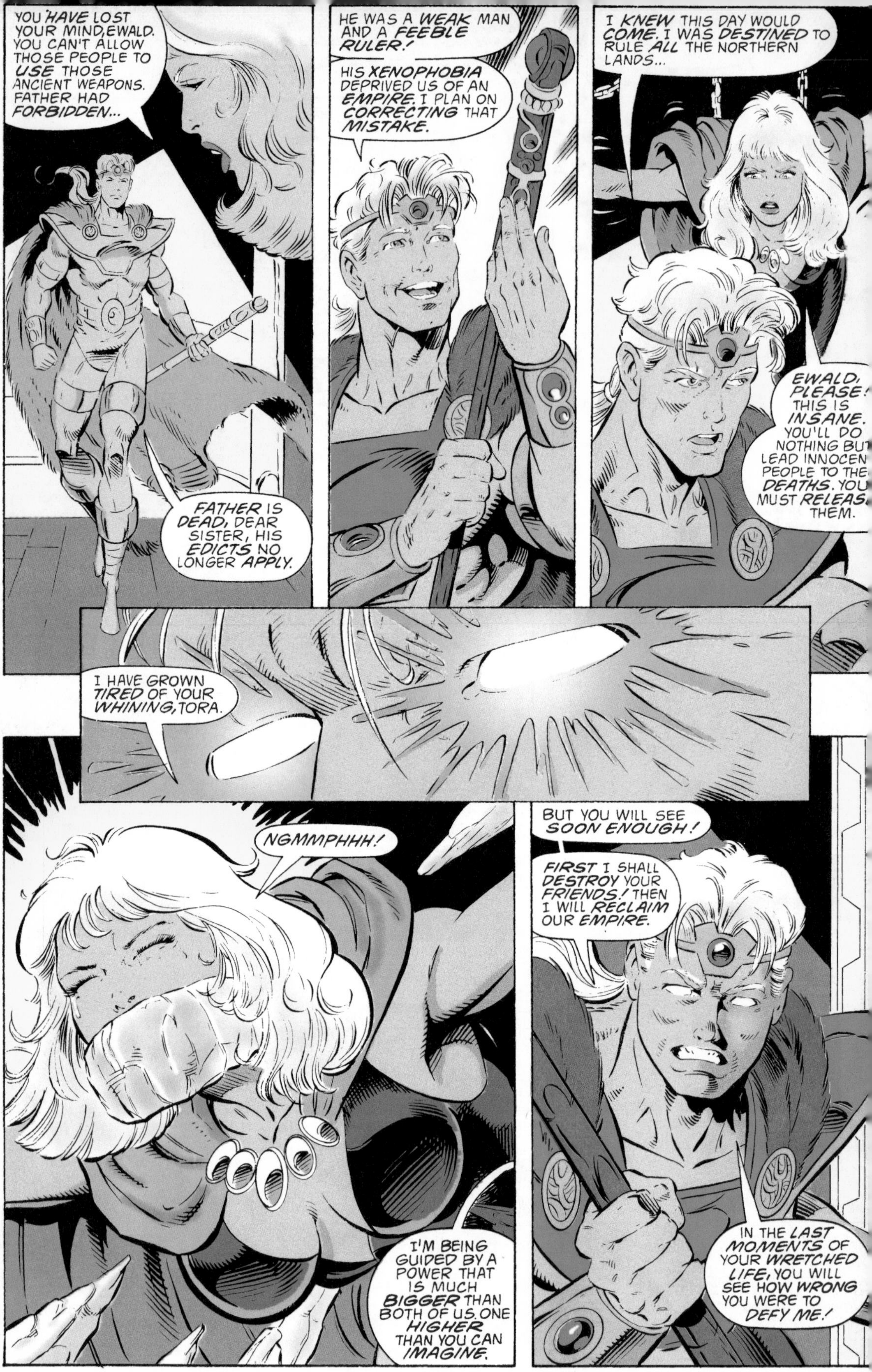

YOU HAVE LOST YOUR MIND, EWALD. YOU CAN'T ALLOW THOSE PEOPLE TO USE THOSE ANCIENT WEAPONS. FATHER HAD FORBIDDEN...
FATHER IS DEAD, DEAR SISTER, HIS EDICTS NO LONGER APPLY.
HE WAS A WEAK MAN AND A FEEBLE RULER!
HIS XENOPHOBIA DEPRIVED US OF AN EMPIRE. I PLAN ON CORRECTING THAT MISTAKE.
I KNEW THIS DAY WOULD COME. I WAS DESTINED TO RULE ALL THE NORTHERN LANDS...
EWALD, PLEASE! THIS IS INSANE. YOU'LL DO NOTHING BUT LEAD INNOCEN PEOPLE TO THE DEATHS. YOU MUST RELEAS THEM.
I HAVE GROWN TIRED OF YOUR WHINING, TORA.
NGMMPHHH!
I'M BEING GUIDED BY A POWER THAT IS MUCH BIGGER THAN BOTH OF US. ONE HIGHER THAN YOU CAN IMAGINE.
BUT YOU WILL SEE SOON ENOUGH!
FIRST I SHALL DESTROY YOUR FRIENDS! THEN I WILL RECLAIM OUR EMPIRE.
IN THE LAST MOMENTS OF YOUR WRETCHED LIFE, YOU WILL SEE HOW WRONG YOU WERE TO DEFY ME!

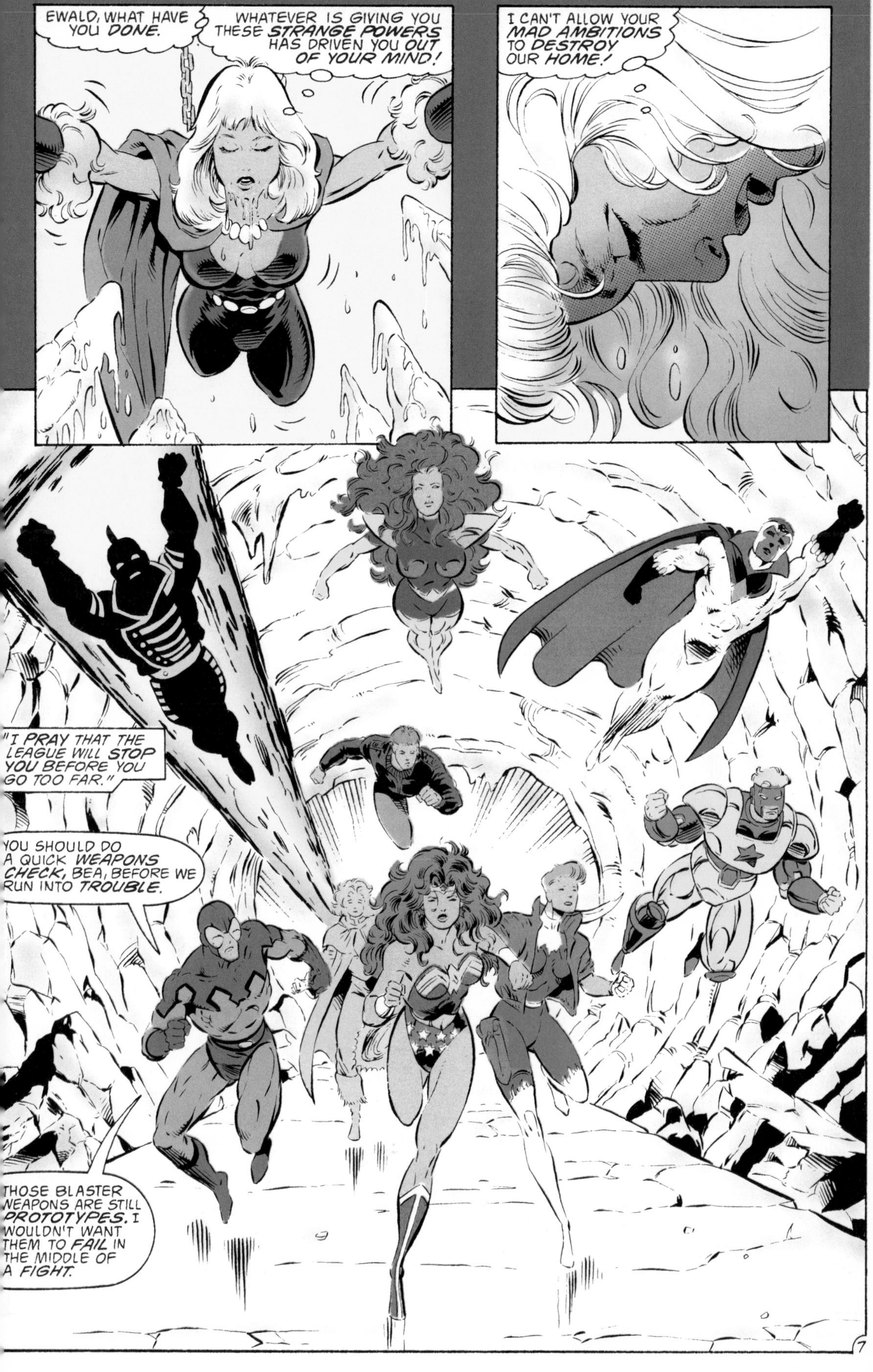
EWALD, WHAT HAVE YOU DONE.
WHATEVER IS GIVING YOU THESE STRANGE POWERS HAS DRIVEN YOU OUT OF YOUR MIND!
I CAN'T ALLOW YOUR MAD AMBITIONS TO DESTROY OUR HOME!
"I PRAY THAT THE LEAGUE WILL STOP YOU BEFORE YOU GO TOO FAR."
YOU SHOULD DO A QUICK WEAPONS CHECK, BEA, BEFORE WE RUN INTO TROUBLE.
THOSE BLASTER WEAPONS ARE STILL PROTOTYPES. I WOULDN'T WANT THEM TO FAIL IN THE MIDDLE OF A FIGHT.

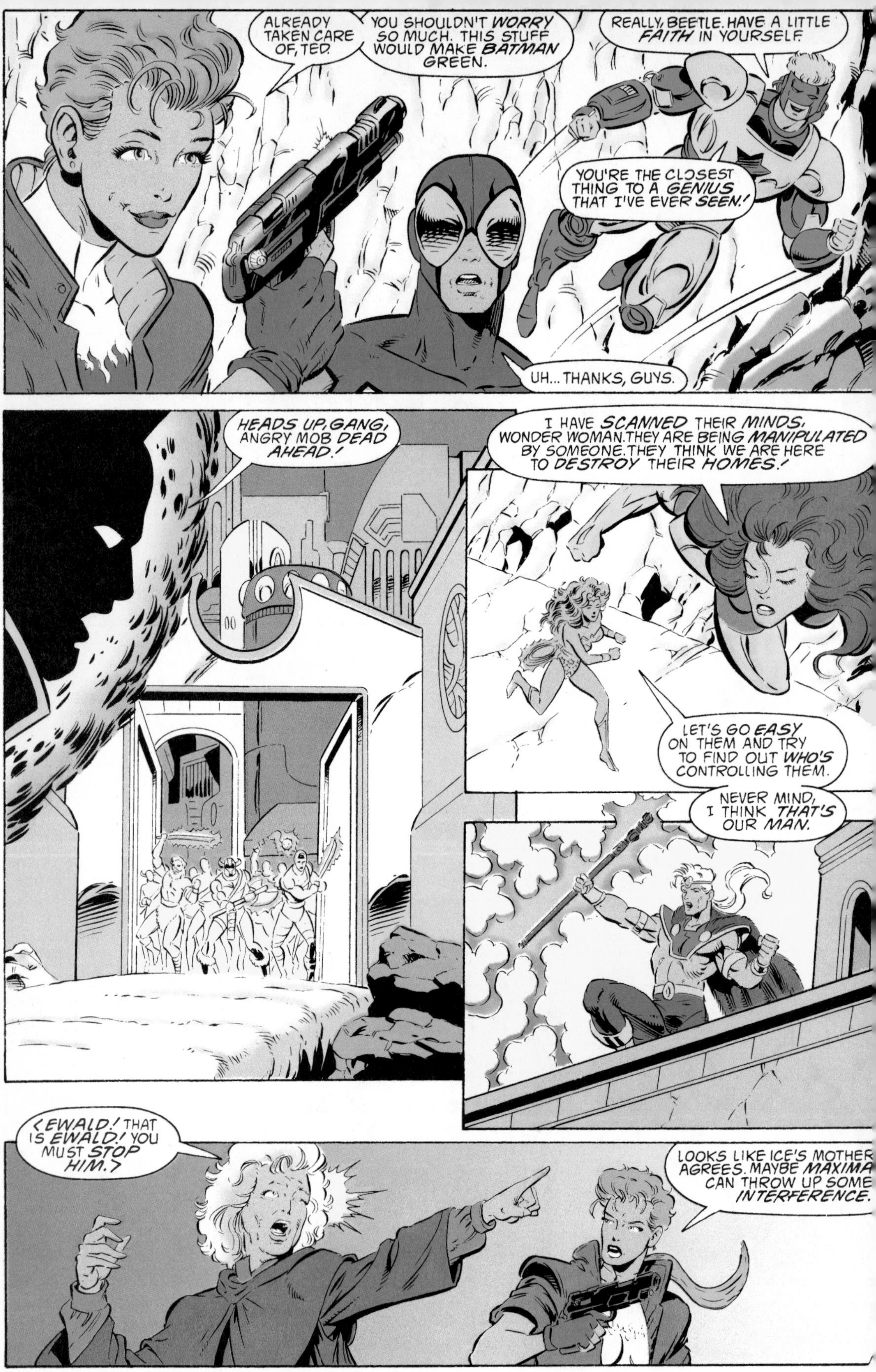
ALREADY TAKEN CARE OF, TED.
YOU SHOULDN'T WORRY SO MUCH. THIS STUFF WOULD MAKE BATMAN GREEN.
REALLY, BEETLE. HAVE A LITTLE FAITH IN YOURSELF.
YOU'RE THE CLOSEST THING TO A GENIUS THAT I'VE EVER SEEN!
UH... THANKS, GUYS.
HEADS UP, GANG, ANGRY MOB DEAD AHEAD!
I HAVE SCANNED THEIR MINDS, WONDER WOMAN. THEY ARE BEING MANIPULATED BY SOMEONE. THEY THINK WE ARE HERE TO DESTROY THEIR HOMES!
LET'S GO EASY ON THEM AND TRY TO FIND OUT WHO'S CONTROLLING THEM.
NEVER MIND, I THINK THAT'S OUR MAN.
<EWALD! THAT IS EWALD! YOU MUST STOP HIM.>
LOOKS LIKE ICE'S MOTHER AGREES. MAYBE MAXIMA CAN THROW UP SOME INTERFERENCE.

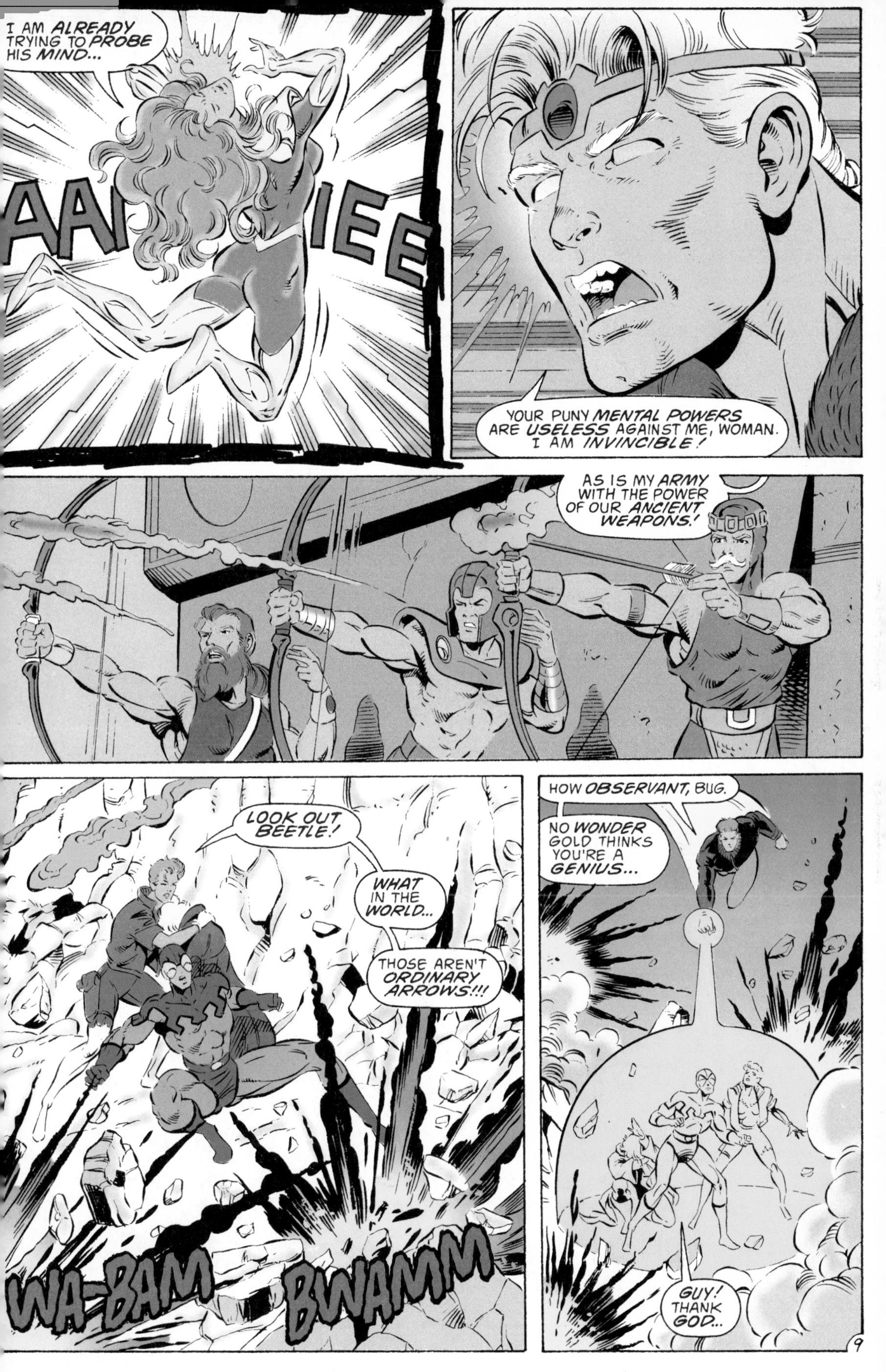
I AM ALREADY TRYING TO PROBE HIS MIND...
AAIEEE
YOUR PUNY MENTAL POWERS ARE USELESS AGAINST ME, WOMAN. I AM INVINCIBLE!
AS IS MY ARMY WITH THE POWER OF OUR ANCIENT WEAPONS!
LOOK OUT BEETLE!
WHAT IN THE WORLD...
THOSE AREN'T ORDINARY ARROWS!!!
WA-BAM
BWAMM
HOW OBSERVANT, BUG.
NO WONDER GOLD THINKS YOU'RE A GENIUS...
GUY! THANK GOD...
9

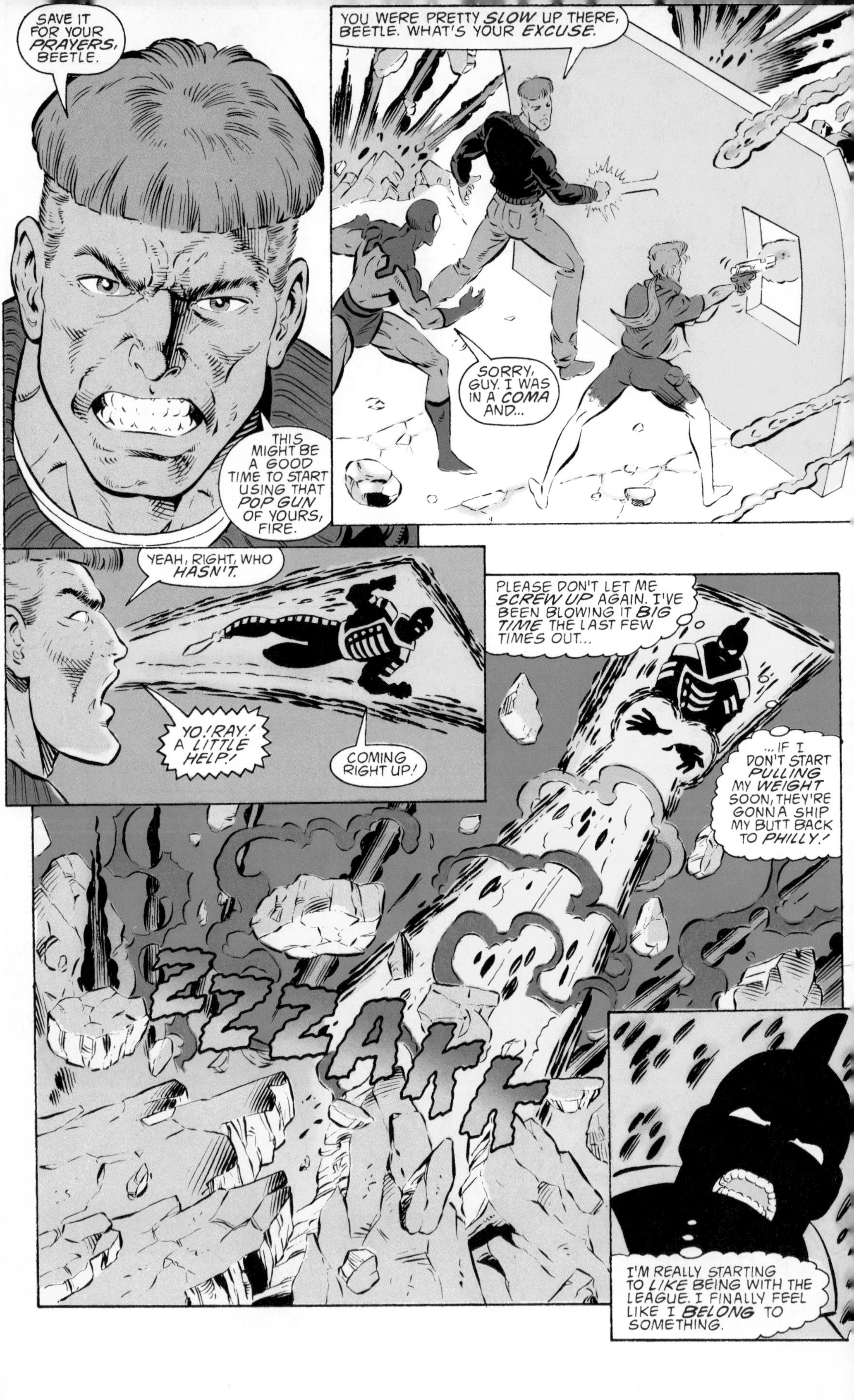
SAVE IT FOR YOUR PRAYERS, BEETLE.
YOU WERE PRETTY SLOW UP THERE, BEETLE. WHAT'S YOUR EXCUSE.
SORRY, GUY. I WAS IN A COMA AND...
THIS MIGHT BE A GOOD TIME TO START USING THAT POP GUN OF YOURS, FIRE.
YEAH, RIGHT, WHO HASN'T.
YO! RAY! A LITTLE HELP!
COMING RIGHT UP!
PLEASE DON'T LET ME SCREW UP AGAIN. I'VE BEEN BLOWING IT BIG TIME THE LAST FEW TIMES OUT...
...IF I DON'T START PULLING MY WEIGHT SOON, THEY'RE GONNA SHIP MY BUTT BACK TO PHILLY!
ZZZAKK
I'M REALLY STARTING TO LIKE BEING WITH THE LEAGUE. I FINALLY FEEL LIKE I BELONG TO SOMETHING.

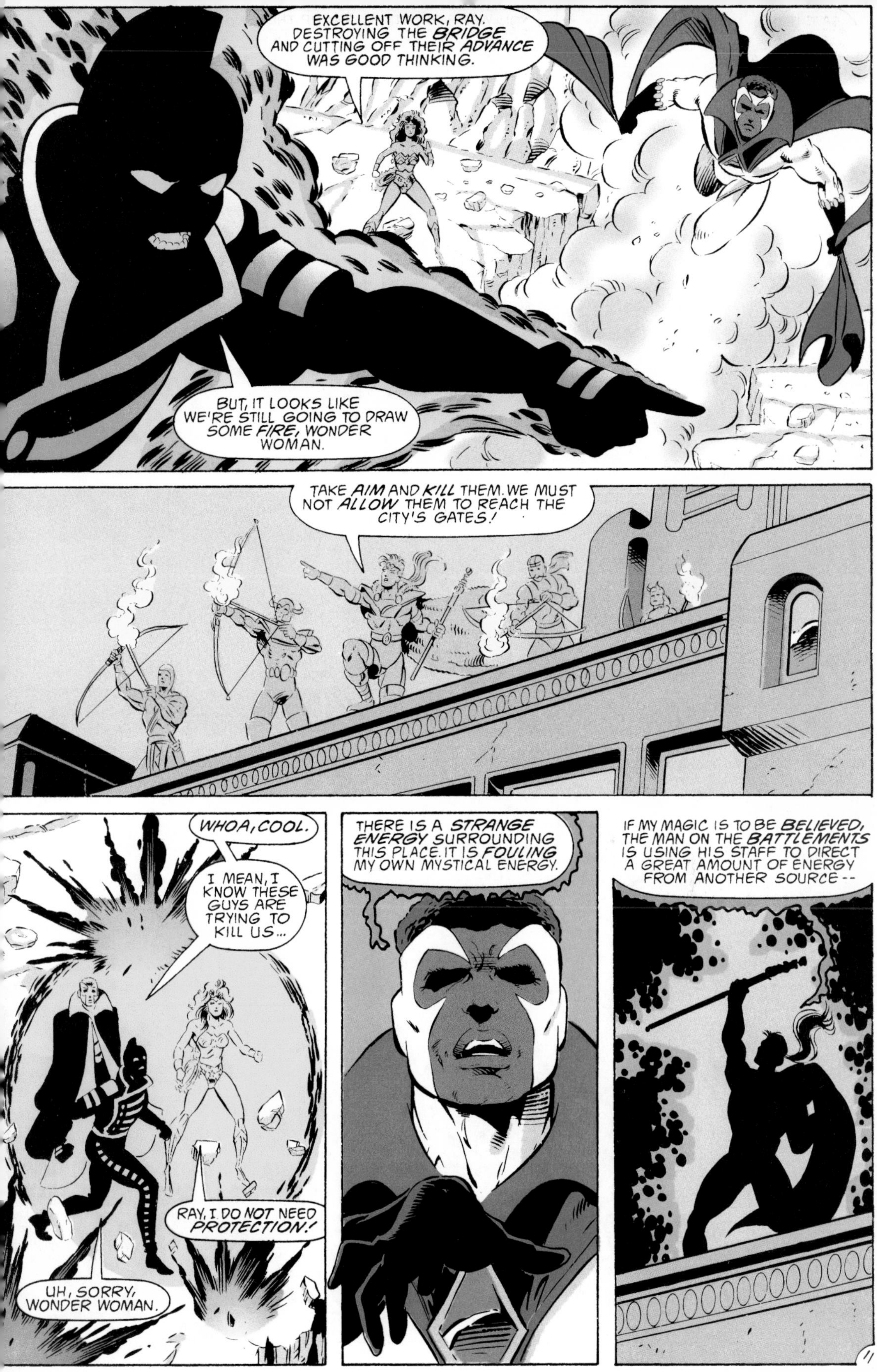

EXCELLENT WORK, RAY. DESTROYING THE *BRIDGE* AND CUTTING OFF THEIR *ADVANCE* WAS GOOD THINKING.
BUT, IT LOOKS LIKE WE'RE STILL GOING TO DRAW SOME *FIRE*, WONDER WOMAN.
TAKE *AIM* AND *KILL* THEM. WE MUST NOT *ALLOW* THEM TO REACH THE CITY'S GATES!
WHOA, COOL.
I MEAN, I KNOW THESE GUYS ARE TRYING TO KILL US...
RAY, I DO *NOT* NEED *PROTECTION!*
UH, SORRY, WONDER WOMAN.
THERE IS A *STRANGE ENERGY* SURROUNDING THIS PLACE. IT IS *FOULING* MY OWN MYSTICAL ENERGY.
IF MY MAGIC IS TO BE *BELIEVED*, THE MAN ON THE *BATTLEMENTS* IS USING HIS STAFF TO DIRECT A GREAT AMOUNT OF ENERGY FROM ANOTHER SOURCE--

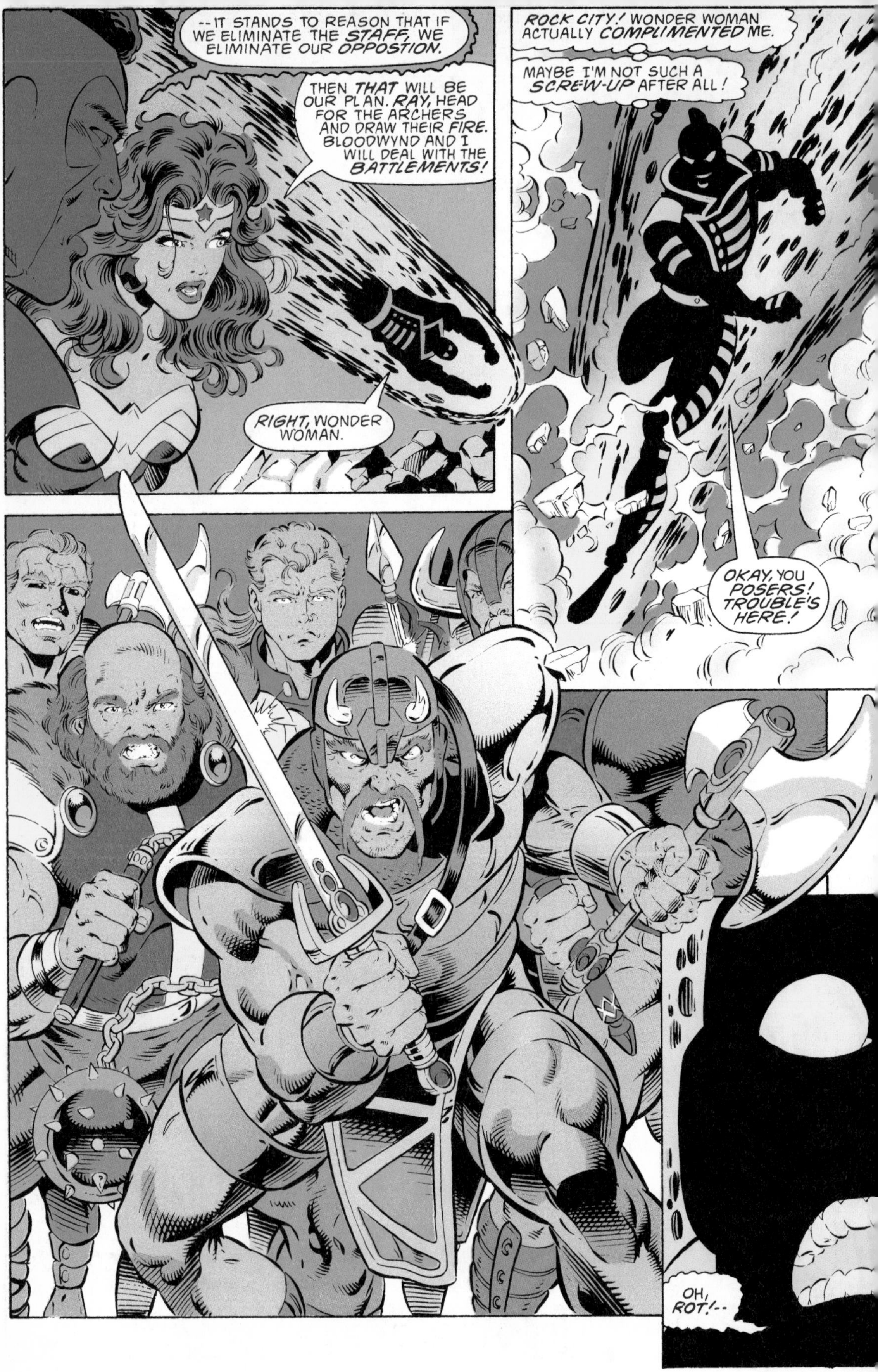
--IT STANDS TO REASON THAT IF WE ELIMINATE THE STAFF, WE ELIMINATE OUR OPPOSTION.
THEN THAT WILL BE OUR PLAN. RAY, HEAD FOR THE ARCHERS AND DRAW THEIR FIRE. BLOODWYND AND I WILL DEAL WITH THE BATTLEMENTS!
RIGHT, WONDER WOMAN.
ROCK CITY! WONDER WOMAN ACTUALLY COMPLIMENTED ME.
MAYBE I'M NOT SUCH A SCREW-UP AFTER ALL!
OKAY, YOU POSERS! TROUBLE'S HERE!
OH, ROT!--

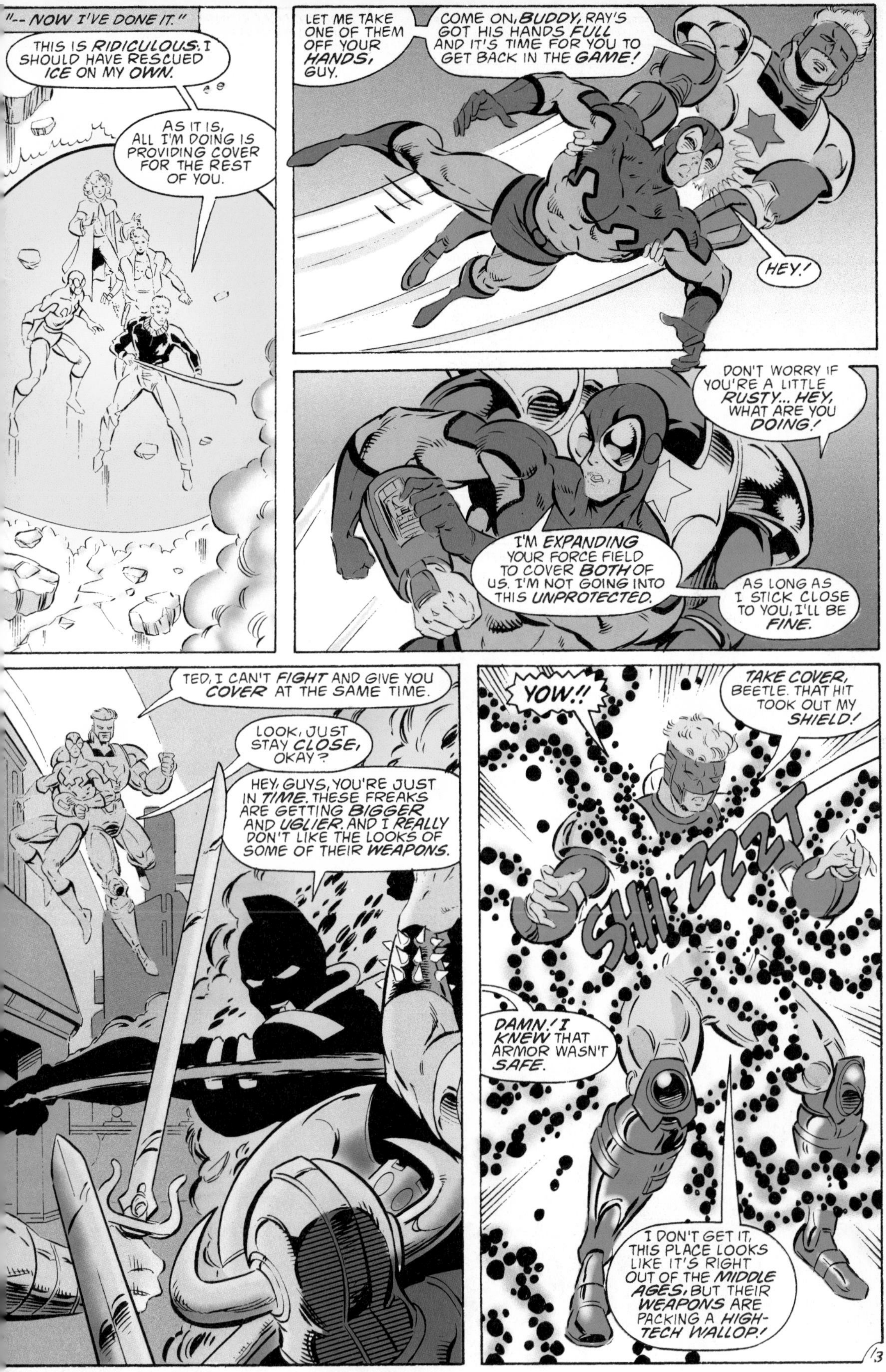

"-- NOW I'VE DONE IT."
THIS IS RIDICULOUS: I SHOULD HAVE RESCUED ICE ON MY OWN.
AS IT IS, ALL I'M DOING IS PROVIDING COVER FOR THE REST OF YOU.
LET ME TAKE ONE OF THEM OFF YOUR HANDS, GUY.
COME ON, BUDDY. RAY'S GOT HIS HANDS FULL AND IT'S TIME FOR YOU TO GET BACK IN THE GAME!
HEY!
DON'T WORRY IF YOU'RE A LITTLE RUSTY... HEY, WHAT ARE YOU DOING!
I'M EXPANDING YOUR FORCE FIELD TO COVER BOTH OF US. I'M NOT GOING INTO THIS UNPROTECTED.
AS LONG AS I STICK CLOSE TO YOU, I'LL BE FINE.
TED, I CAN'T FIGHT AND GIVE YOU COVER AT THE SAME TIME.
LOOK, JUST STAY CLOSE, OKAY?
HEY, GUYS, YOU'RE JUST IN TIME. THESE FREAKS ARE GETTING BIGGER AND UGLIER. AND I REALLY DON'T LIKE THE LOOKS OF SOME OF THEIR WEAPONS.
YOW!!
TAKE COVER, BEETLE. THAT HIT TOOK OUT MY SHIELD!
SHH-ZZZZT
DAMN! I KNEW THAT ARMOR WASN'T SAFE.
I DON'T GET IT, THIS PLACE LOOKS LIKE IT'S RIGHT OUT OF THE MIDDLE AGES, BUT THEIR WEAPONS ARE PACKING A HIGH-TECH WALLOP!

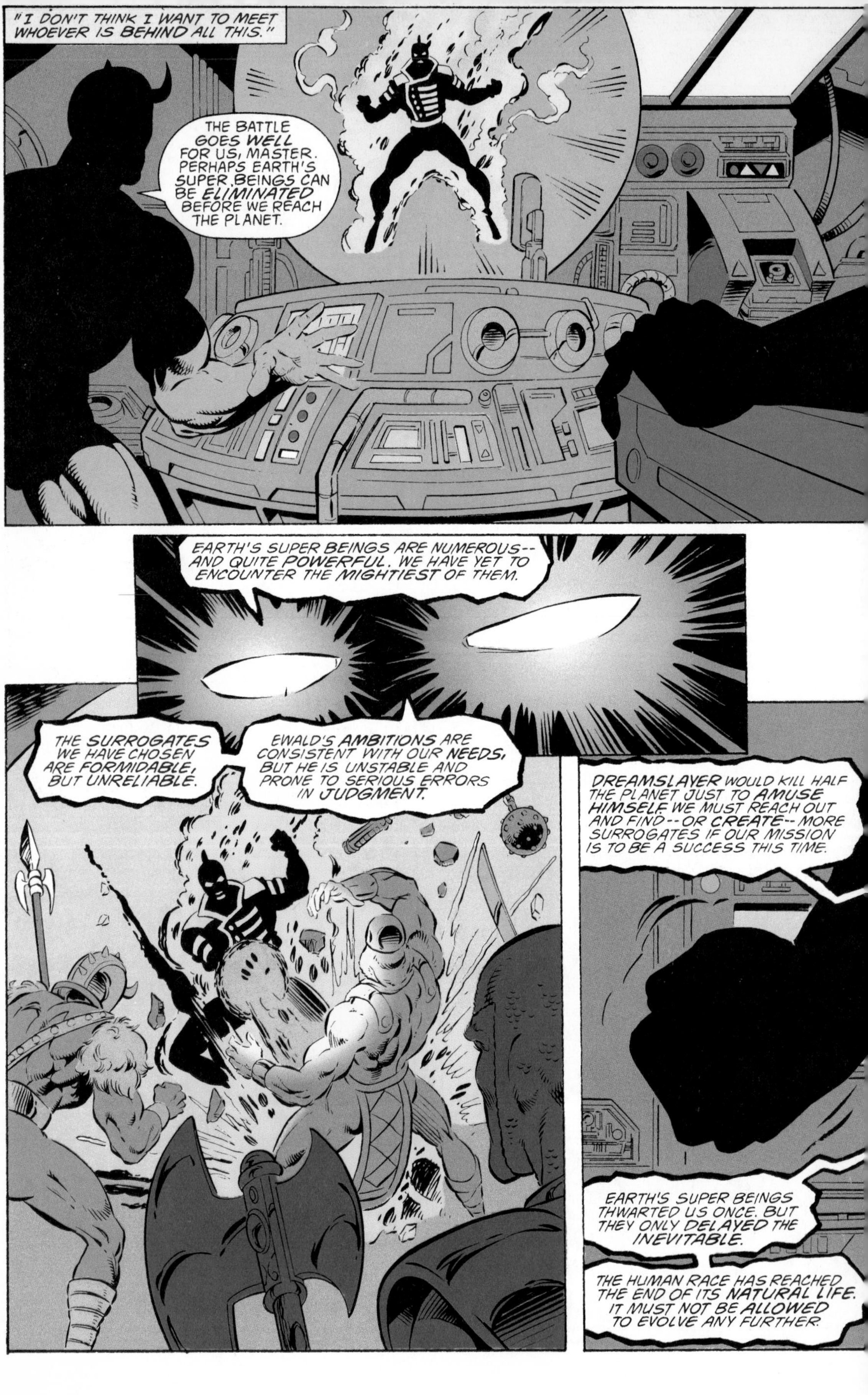
"I DON'T THINK I WANT TO MEET WHOEVER IS BEHIND ALL THIS."
THE BATTLE GOES WELL FOR US, MASTER. PERHAPS EARTH'S SUPER BEINGS CAN BE ELIMINATED BEFORE WE REACH THE PLANET.
EARTH'S SUPER BEINGS ARE NUMEROUS-- AND QUITE POWERFUL. WE HAVE YET TO ENCOUNTER THE MIGHTIEST OF THEM.
THE SURROGATES WE HAVE CHOSEN ARE FORMIDABLE, BUT UNRELIABLE.
EWALD'S AMBITIONS ARE CONSISTENT WITH OUR NEEDS, BUT HE IS UNSTABLE AND PRONE TO SERIOUS ERRORS IN JUDGMENT.
DREAMSLAYER WOULD KILL HALF THE PLANET JUST TO AMUSE HIMSELF. WE MUST REACH OUT AND FIND--OR CREATE--MORE SURROGATES IF OUR MISSION IS TO BE A SUCCESS THIS TIME.
EARTH'S SUPER BEINGS THWARTED US ONCE. BUT THEY ONLY DELAYED THE INEVITABLE.
THE HUMAN RACE HAS REACHED THE END OF ITS NATURAL LIFE. IT MUST NOT BE ALLOWED TO EVOLVE ANY FURTHER.

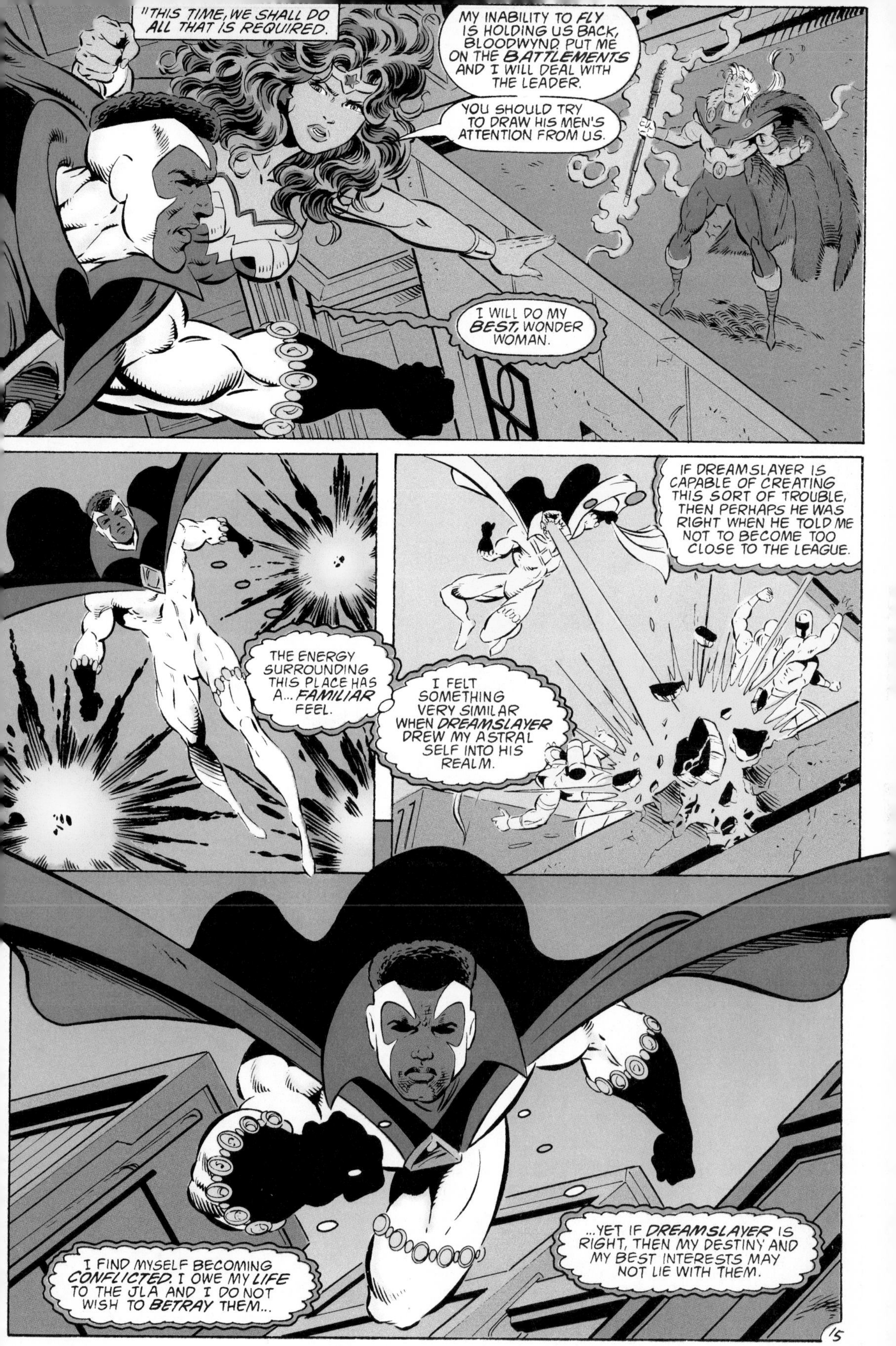
"THIS TIME, WE SHALL DO ALL THAT IS REQUIRED.
MY INABILITY TO FLY IS HOLDING US BACK, BLOODWYND. PUT ME ON THE BATTLEMENTS AND I WILL DEAL WITH THE LEADER.
YOU SHOULD TRY TO DRAW HIS MEN'S ATTENTION FROM US.
I WILL DO MY BEST, WONDER WOMAN.
THE ENERGY SURROUNDING THIS PLACE HAS A... FAMILIAR FEEL.
I FELT SOMETHING VERY SIMILAR WHEN DREAMSLAYER DREW MY ASTRAL SELF INTO HIS REALM.
IF DREAMSLAYER IS CAPABLE OF CREATING THIS SORT OF TROUBLE, THEN PERHAPS HE WAS RIGHT WHEN HE TOLD ME NOT TO BECOME TOO CLOSE TO THE LEAGUE.
I FIND MYSELF BECOMING CONFLICTED. I OWE MY LIFE TO THE JLA AND I DO NOT WISH TO BETRAY THEM...
...YET IF DREAMSLAYER IS RIGHT, THEN MY DESTINY AND MY BEST INTERESTS MAY NOT LIE WITH THEM.
15

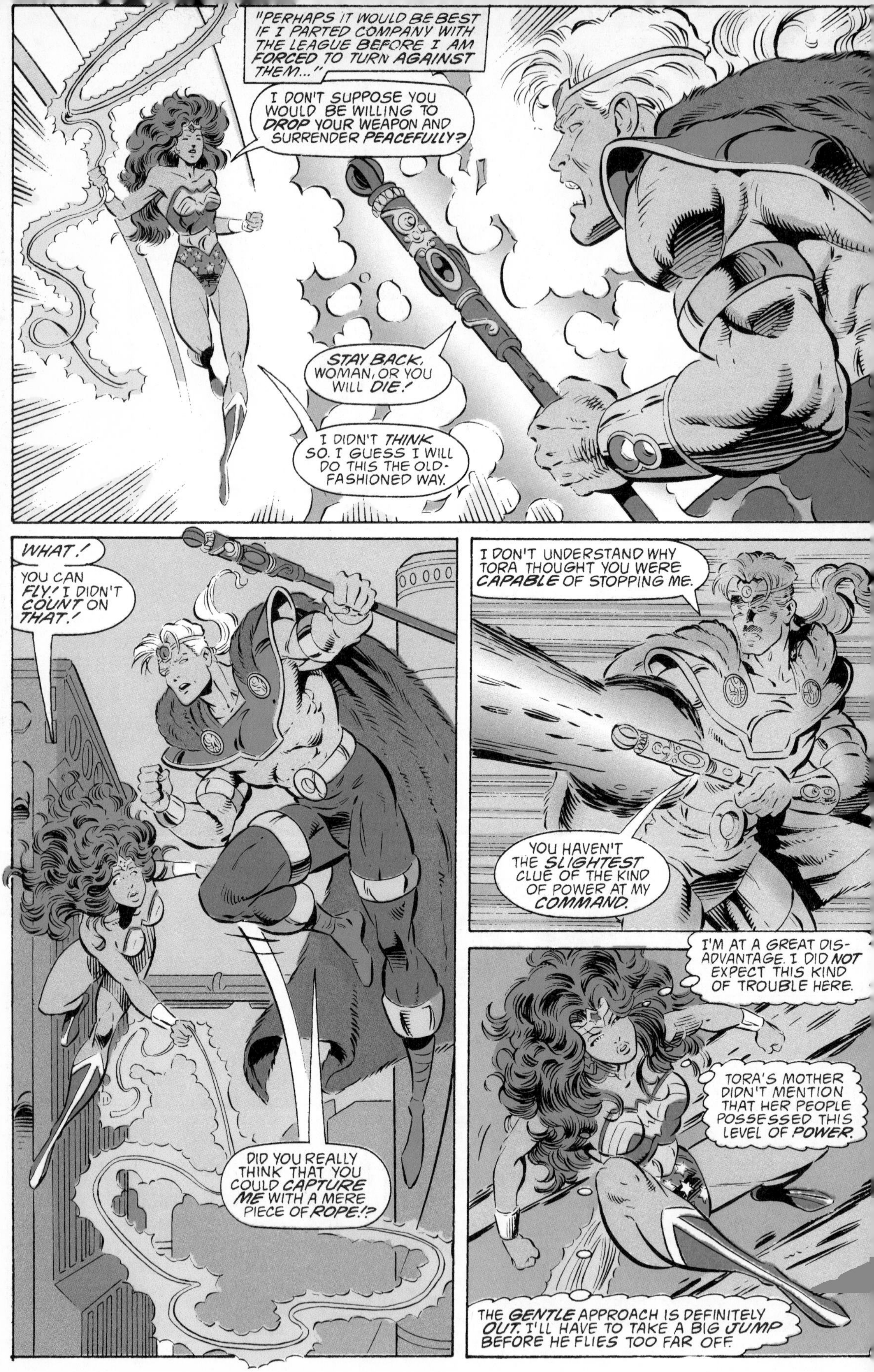
"PERHAPS IT WOULD BE BEST IF I PARTED COMPANY WITH THE LEAGUE BEFORE I AM FORCED TO TURN AGAINST THEM..."
I DON'T SUPPOSE YOU WOULD BE WILLING TO DROP YOUR WEAPON AND SURRENDER PEACEFULLY?
STAY BACK, WOMAN, OR YOU WILL DIE!
I DIDN'T THINK SO. I GUESS I WILL DO THIS THE OLD-FASHIONED WAY.
WHAT.!
YOU CAN FLY.! I DIDN'T COUNT ON THAT.!
DID YOU REALLY THINK THAT YOU COULD CAPTURE ME WITH A MERE PIECE OF ROPE!?
I DON'T UNDERSTAND WHY TORA THOUGHT YOU WERE CAPABLE OF STOPPING ME.
YOU HAVEN'T THE SLIGHTEST CLUE OF THE KIND OF POWER AT MY COMMAND.
I'M AT A GREAT DISADVANTAGE. I DID NOT EXPECT THIS KIND OF TROUBLE HERE.
TORA'S MOTHER DIDN'T MENTION THAT HER PEOPLE POSSESSED THIS LEVEL OF POWER.
THE GENTLE APPROACH IS DEFINITELY OUT. I'LL HAVE TO TAKE A BIG JUMP BEFORE HE FLIES TOO FAR OFF.

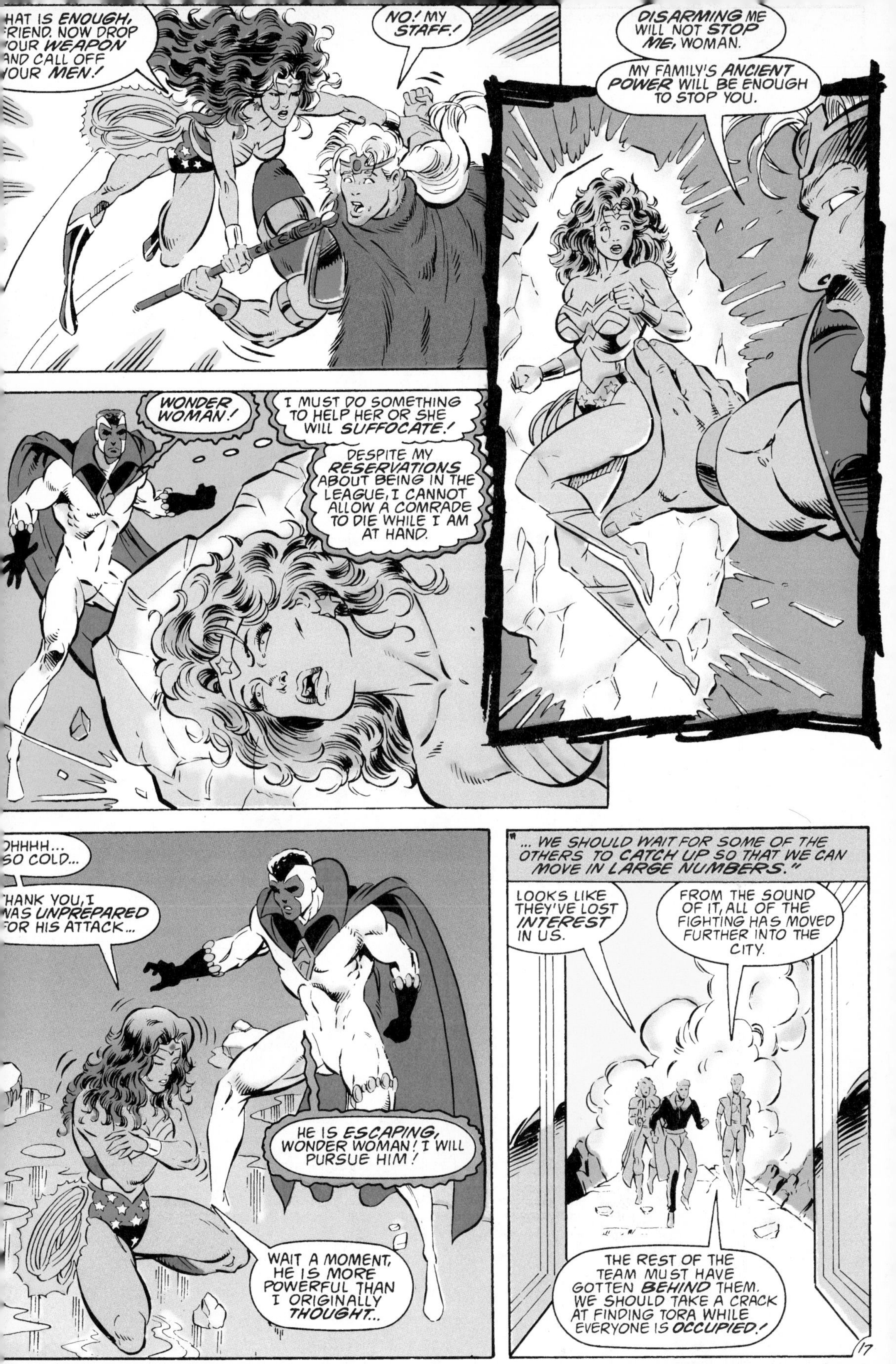
HAT IS ENOUGH, FRIEND. NOW DROP YOUR WEAPON AND CALL OFF YOUR MEN!
NO! MY STAFF!
DISARMING ME WILL NOT STOP ME, WOMAN.
MY FAMILY'S ANCIENT POWER WILL BE ENOUGH TO STOP YOU.
WONDER WOMAN!
I MUST DO SOMETHING TO HELP HER OR SHE WILL SUFFOCATE!
DESPITE MY RESERVATIONS ABOUT BEING IN THE LEAGUE, I CANNOT ALLOW A COMRADE TO DIE WHILE I AM AT HAND.
OHHHH... SO COLD...
THANK YOU, I WAS UNPREPARED FOR HIS ATTACK...
HE IS ESCAPING, WONDER WOMAN! I WILL PURSUE HIM!
WAIT A MOMENT, HE IS MORE POWERFUL THAN I ORIGINALLY THOUGHT...
"... WE SHOULD WAIT FOR SOME OF THE OTHERS TO CATCH UP SO THAT WE CAN MOVE IN LARGE NUMBERS."
LOOKS LIKE THEY'VE LOST INTEREST IN US.
FROM THE SOUND OF IT, ALL OF THE FIGHTING HAS MOVED FURTHER INTO THE CITY.
THE REST OF THE TEAM MUST HAVE GOTTEN BEHIND THEM. WE SHOULD TAKE A CRACK AT FINDING TORA WHILE EVERYONE IS OCCUPIED!
17

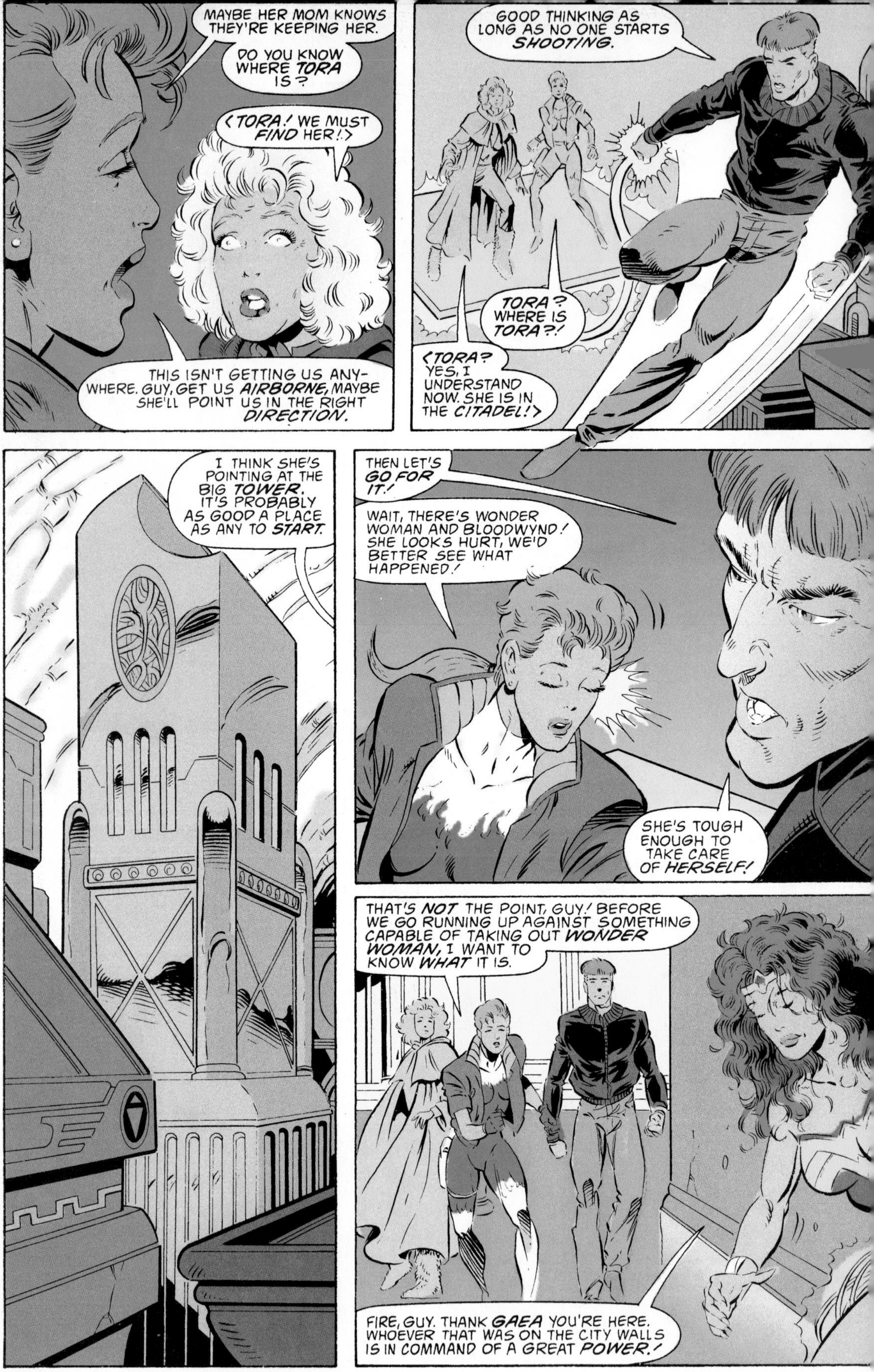
MAYBE HER MOM KNOWS THEY'RE KEEPING HER.
DO YOU KNOW WHERE TORA IS?
<TORA! WE MUST FIND HER!>
THIS ISN'T GETTING US ANY-WHERE. GUY, GET US AIRBORNE, MAYBE SHE'LL POINT US IN THE RIGHT DIRECTION.
GOOD THINKING AS LONG AS NO ONE STARTS SHOOTING.
TORA? WHERE IS TORA?!
<TORA? YES, I UNDERSTAND NOW. SHE IS IN THE CITADEL!>
I THINK SHE'S POINTING AT THE BIG TOWER. IT'S PROBABLY AS GOOD A PLACE AS ANY TO START.
THEN LET'S GO FOR IT!
WAIT, THERE'S WONDER WOMAN AND BLOODWYND! SHE LOOKS HURT, WE'D BETTER SEE WHAT HAPPENED!
SHE'S TOUGH ENOUGH TO TAKE CARE OF HERSELF!
THAT'S NOT THE POINT, GUY! BEFORE WE GO RUNNING UP AGAINST SOMETHING CAPABLE OF TAKING OUT WONDER WOMAN, I WANT TO KNOW WHAT IT IS.
FIRE, GUY. THANK GAEA YOU'RE HERE. WHOEVER THAT WAS ON THE CITY WALLS IS IN COMMAND OF A GREAT POWER!

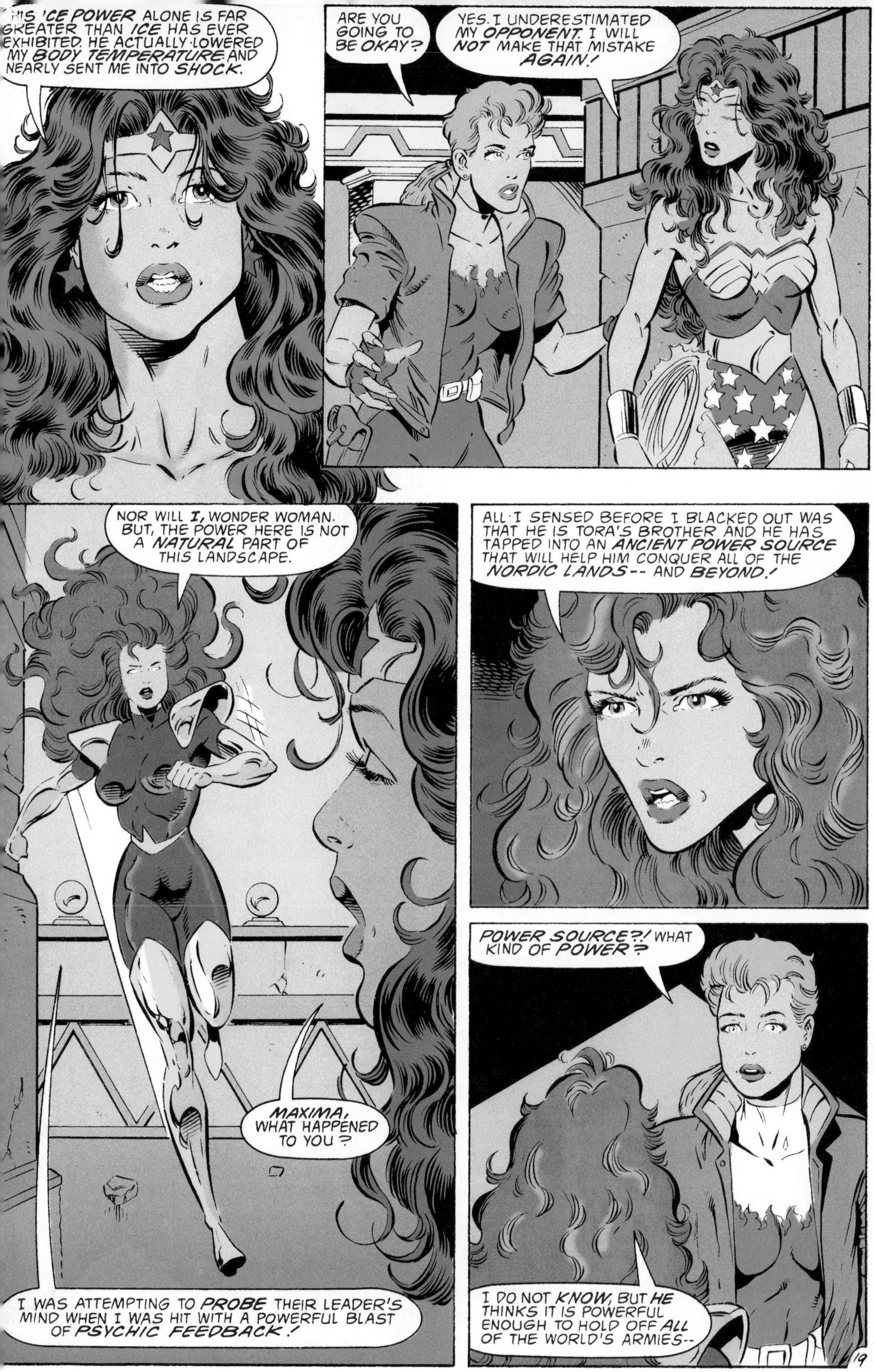
HIS ICE POWER ALONE IS FAR GREATER THAN ICE HAS EVER EXHIBITED. HE ACTUALLY LOWERED MY BODY TEMPERATURE AND NEARLY SENT ME INTO SHOCK.
ARE YOU GOING TO BE OKAY?
YES. I UNDERESTIMATED MY OPPONENT. I WILL NOT MAKE THAT MISTAKE AGAIN!
NOR WILL I, WONDER WOMAN. BUT, THE POWER HERE IS NOT A NATURAL PART OF THIS LANDSCAPE.
MAXIMA, WHAT HAPPENED TO YOU?
I WAS ATTEMPTING TO PROBE THEIR LEADER'S MIND WHEN I WAS HIT WITH A POWERFUL BLAST OF PSYCHIC FEEDBACK!
ALL I SENSED BEFORE I BLACKED OUT WAS THAT HE IS TORA'S BROTHER AND HE HAS TAPPED INTO AN ANCIENT POWER SOURCE THAT WILL HELP HIM CONQUER ALL OF THE NORDIC LANDS-- AND BEYOND!
POWER SOURCE?! WHAT KIND OF POWER?
I DO NOT KNOW, BUT HE THINKS IT IS POWERFUL ENOUGH TO HOLD OFF ALL OF THE WORLD'S ARMIES--
19

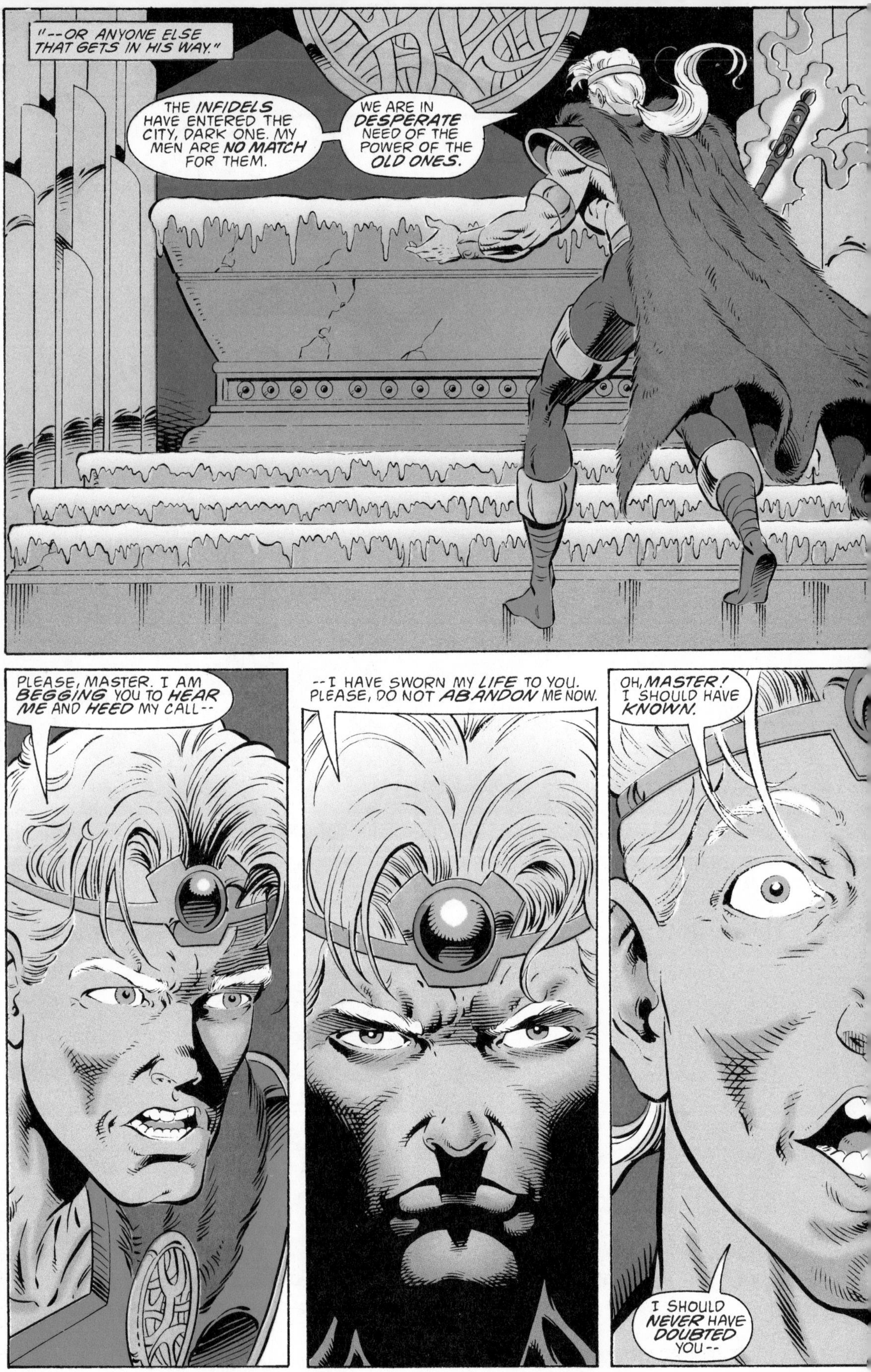
"--OR ANYONE ELSE THAT GETS IN HIS WAY."
THE INFIDELS HAVE ENTERED THE CITY, DARK ONE. MY MEN ARE NO MATCH FOR THEM.
WE ARE IN DESPERATE NEED OF THE POWER OF THE OLD ONES.
PLEASE, MASTER. I AM BEGGING YOU TO HEAR ME AND HEED MY CALL--
--I HAVE SWORN MY LIFE TO YOU. PLEASE, DO NOT ABANDON ME NOW.
OH, MASTER! I SHOULD HAVE KNOWN.
I SHOULD NEVER HAVE DOUBTED YOU--

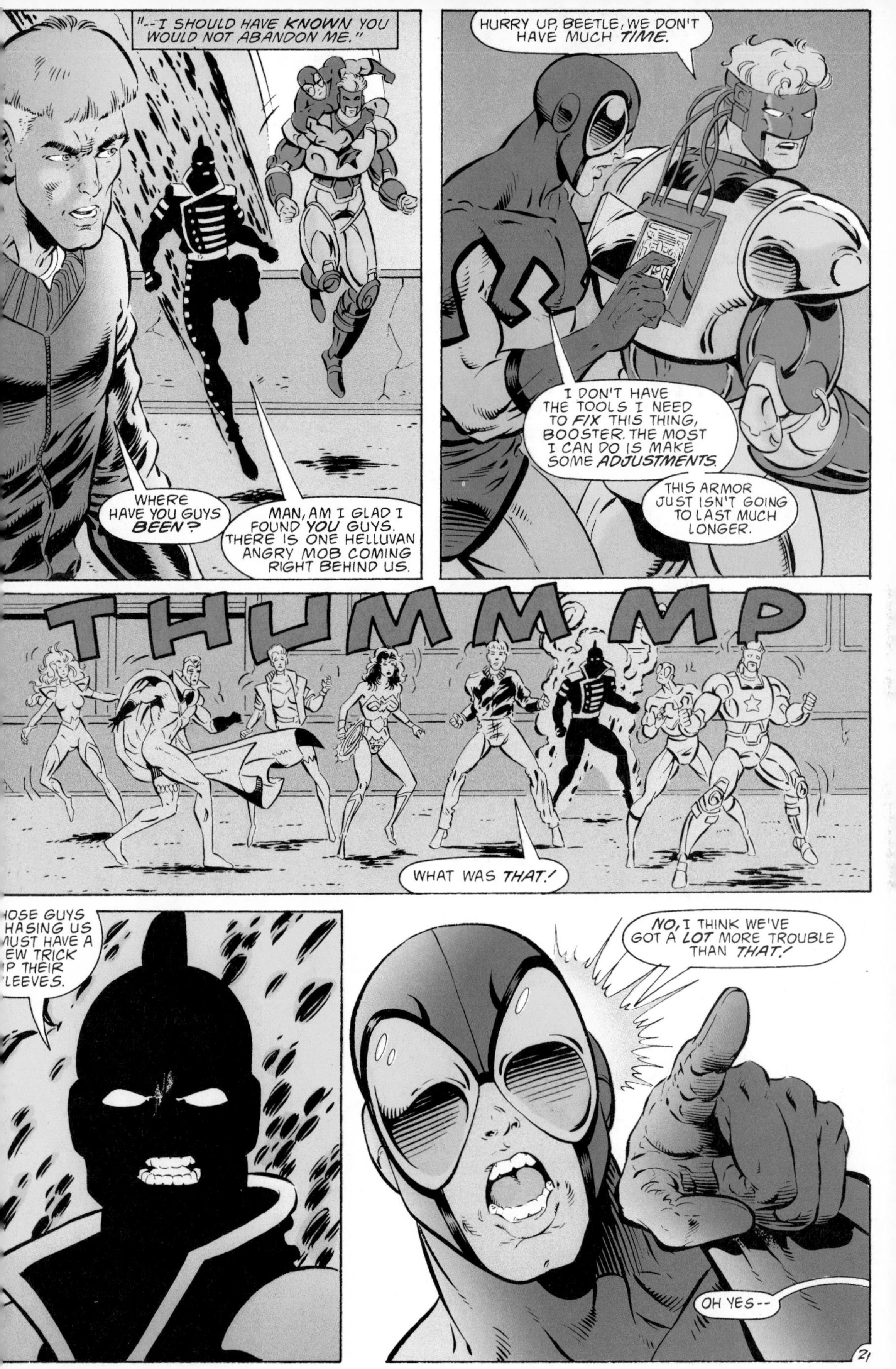
"--I SHOULD HAVE KNOWN YOU WOULD NOT ABANDON ME."
WHERE HAVE YOU GUYS BEEN?
MAN, AM I GLAD I FOUND YOU GUYS. THERE IS ONE HELLUVAN ANGRY MOB COMING RIGHT BEHIND US.
HURRY UP, BEETLE, WE DON'T HAVE MUCH TIME.
I DON'T HAVE THE TOOLS I NEED TO FIX THIS THING, BOOSTER. THE MOST I CAN DO IS MAKE SOME ADJUSTMENTS.
THIS ARMOR JUST ISN'T GOING TO LAST MUCH LONGER.
THUMMMP
WHAT WAS THAT!
HOSE GUYS HASING US MUST HAVE A EW TRICK P THEIR LEEVES.
NO, I THINK WE'VE GOT A LOT MORE TROUBLE THAN THAT!
OH YES--

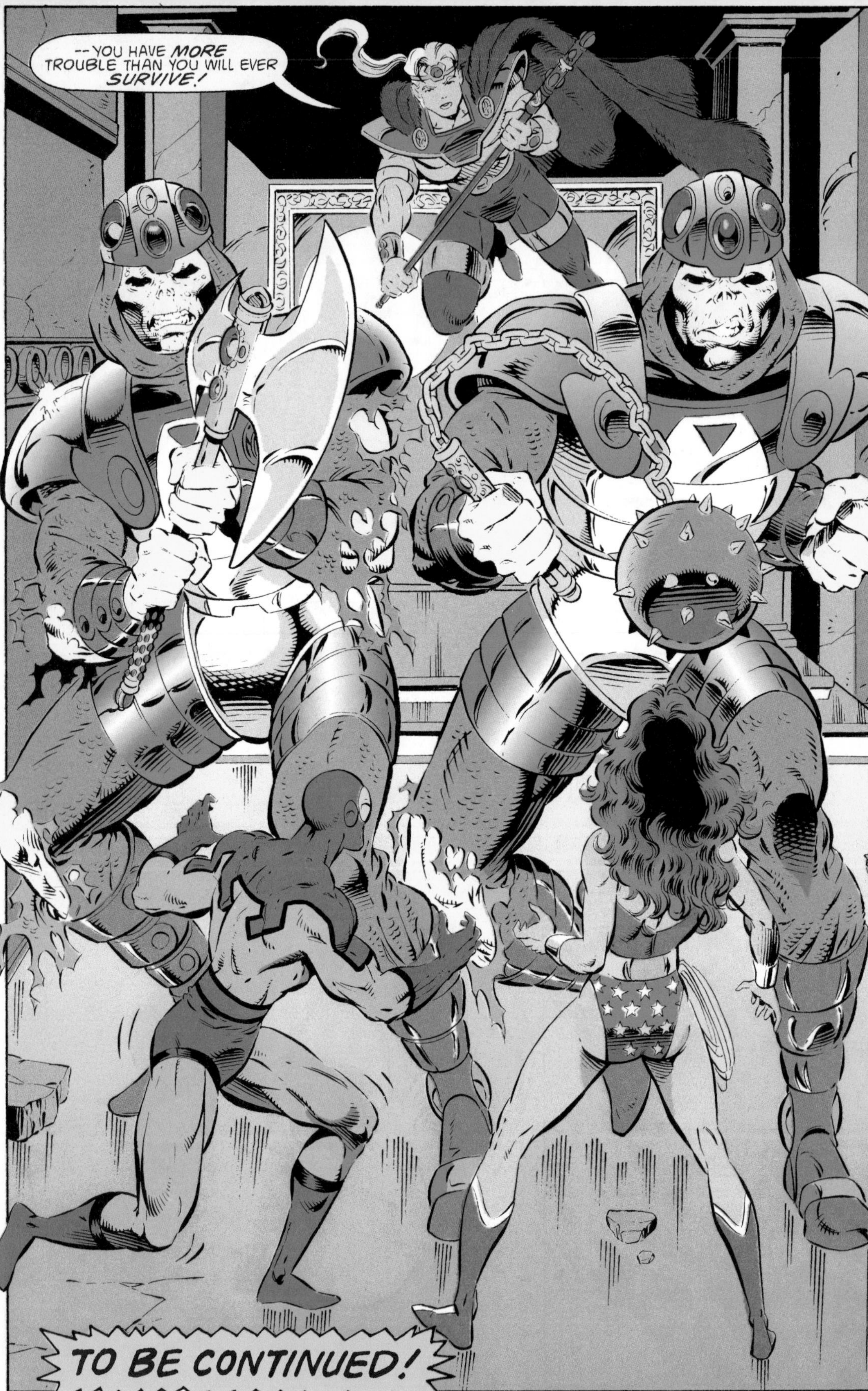
--YOU HAVE MORE TROUBLE THAN YOU WILL EVER SURVIVE!
TO BE CONTINUED!

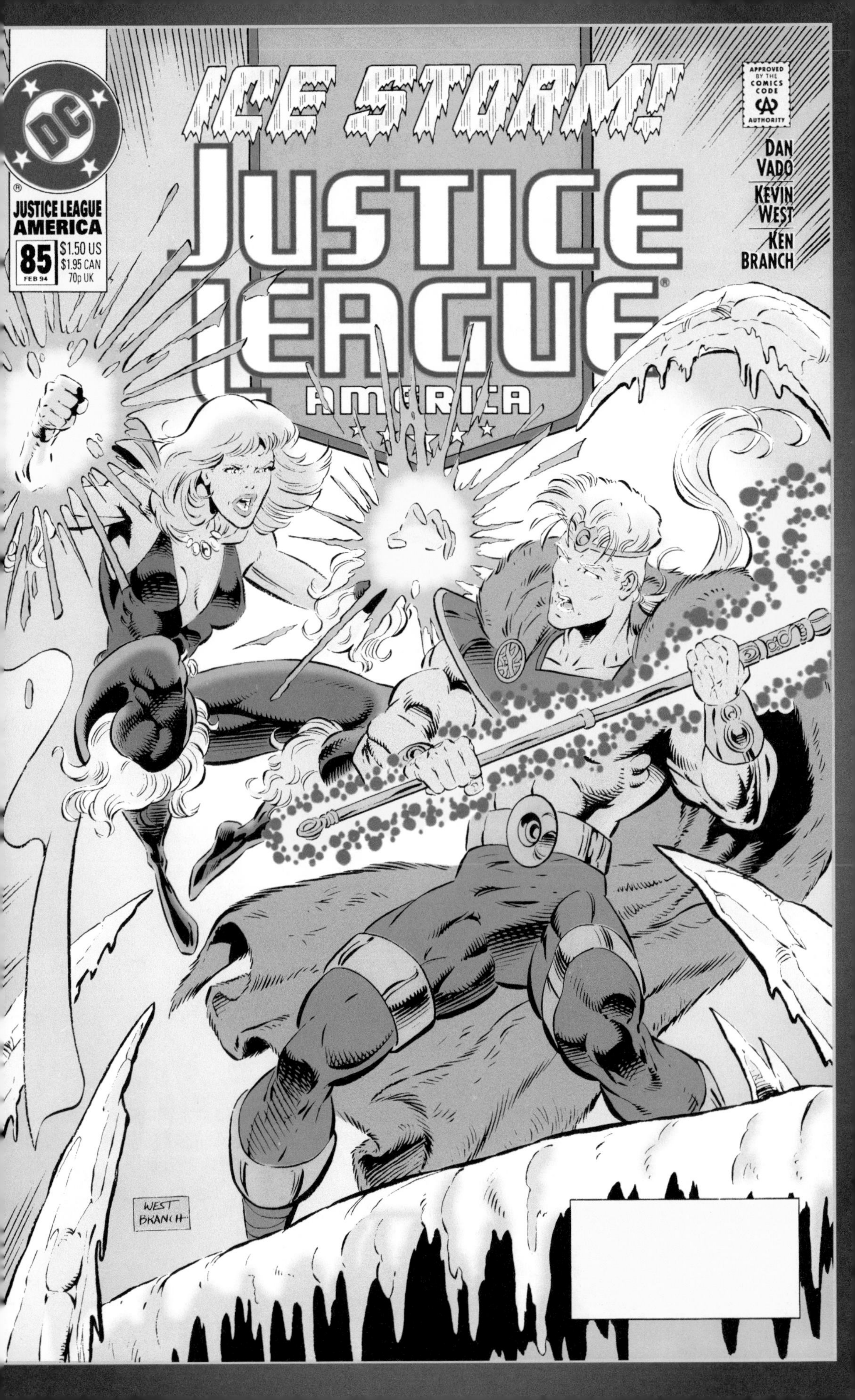

ICE STORM!
JUSTICE LEAGUE AMERICA
JUSTICE LEAGUE AMERICA
85
FEB 94
$1.50 US
$1.95 CAN
70p UK
APPROVED BY THE COMICS CODE AUTHORITY
DAN VADO
KEVIN WEST
KEN BRANCH
WEST BRANCH

Cover art by **KEVIN WEST**
and **KEN BRANCH**

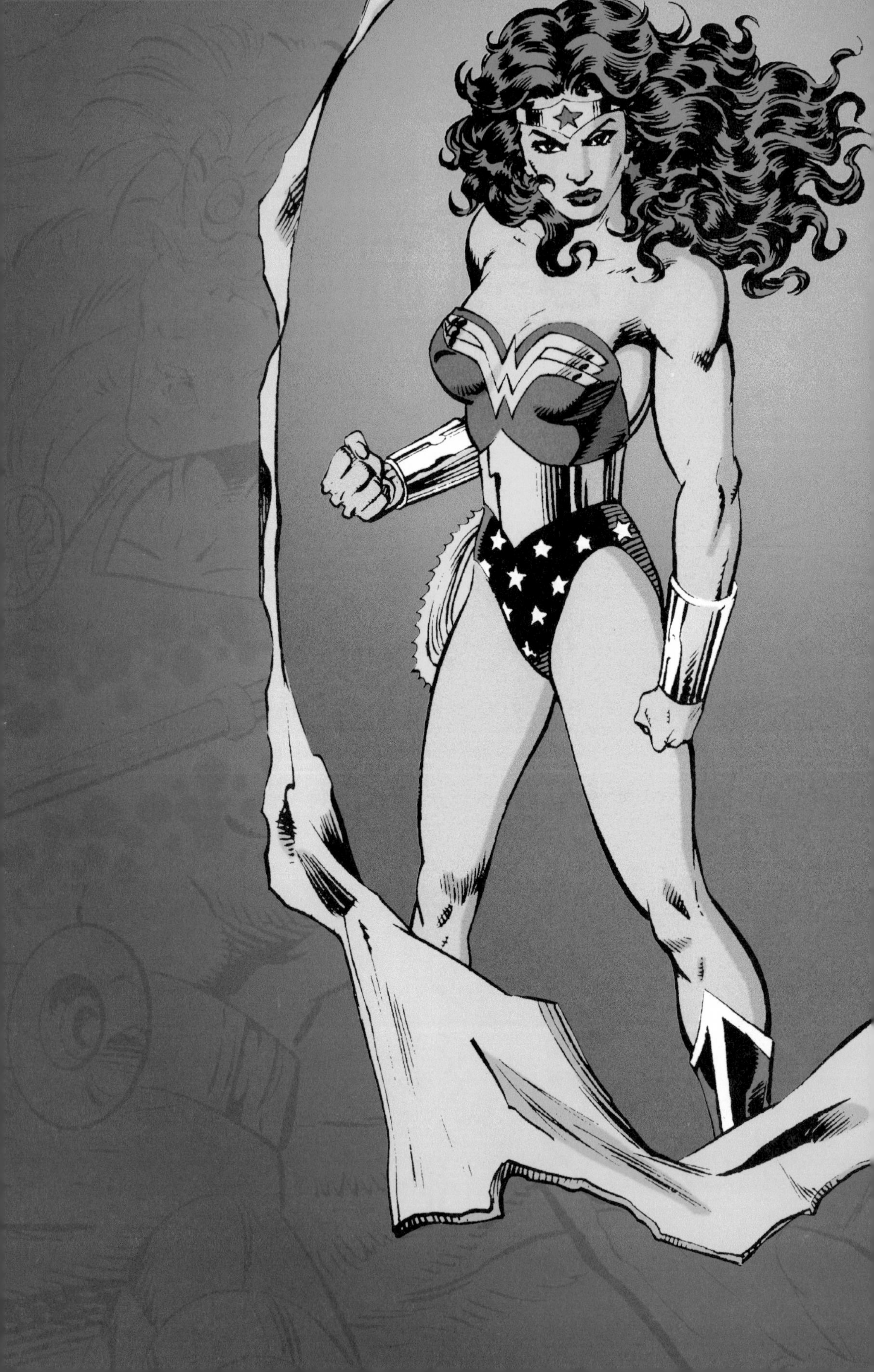

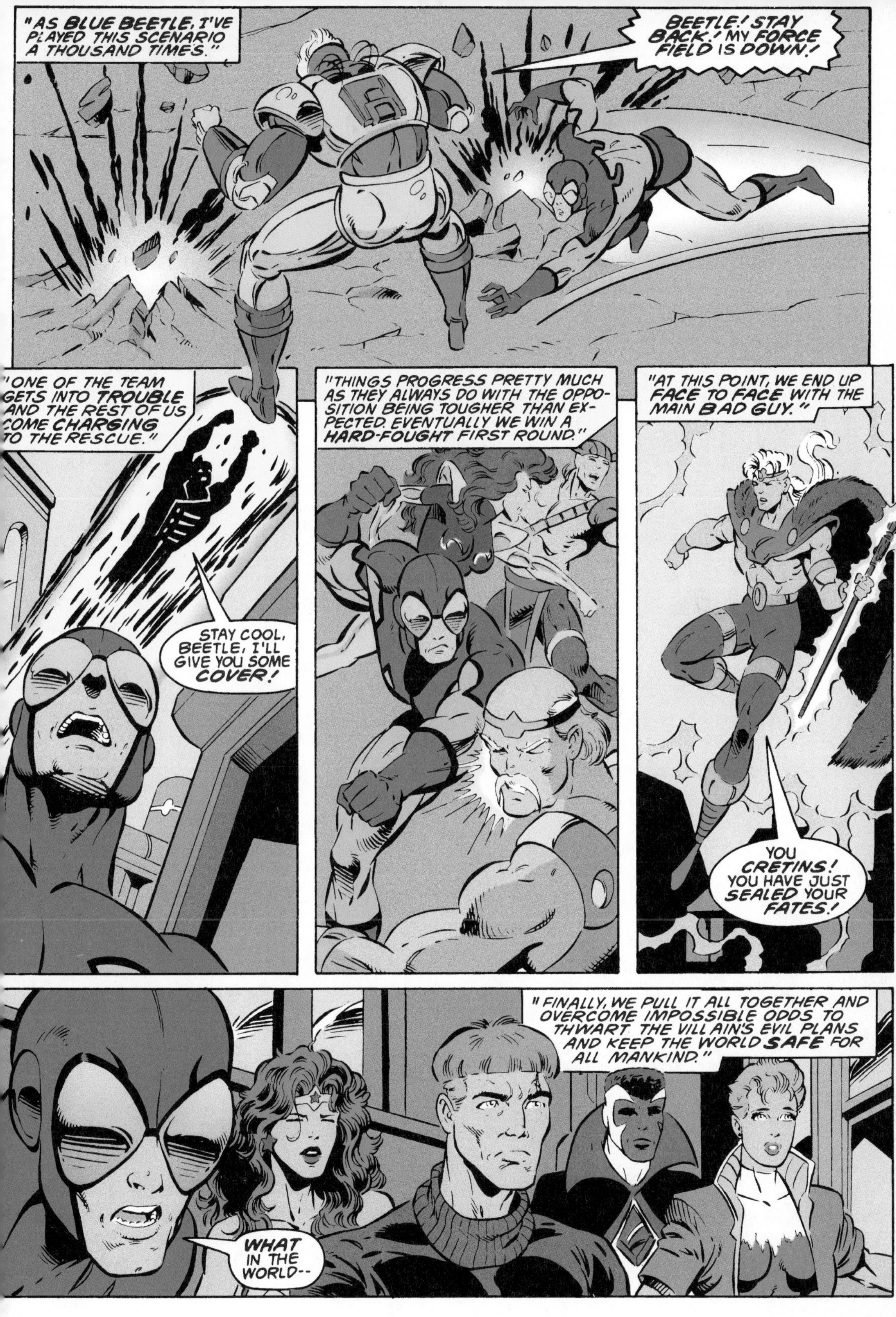
"AS BLUE BEETLE, I'VE PLAYED THIS SCENARIO A THOUSAND TIMES."
BEETLE! STAY BACK! MY FORCE FIELD IS DOWN!
"ONE OF THE TEAM GETS INTO TROUBLE AND THE REST OF US COME CHARGING TO THE RESCUE."
STAY COOL, BEETLE, I'LL GIVE YOU SOME COVER!
"THINGS PROGRESS PRETTY MUCH AS THEY ALWAYS DO WITH THE OPPOSITION BEING TOUGHER THAN EXPECTED. EVENTUALLY WE WIN A HARD-FOUGHT FIRST ROUND."
"AT THIS POINT, WE END UP FACE TO FACE WITH THE MAIN BAD GUY."
YOU CRETINS! YOU HAVE JUST SEALED YOUR FATES!
"FINALLY, WE PULL IT ALL TOGETHER AND OVERCOME IMPOSSIBLE ODDS TO THWART THE VILLAIN'S EVIL PLANS AND KEEP THE WORLD SAFE FOR ALL MANKIND."
WHAT IN THE WORLD--

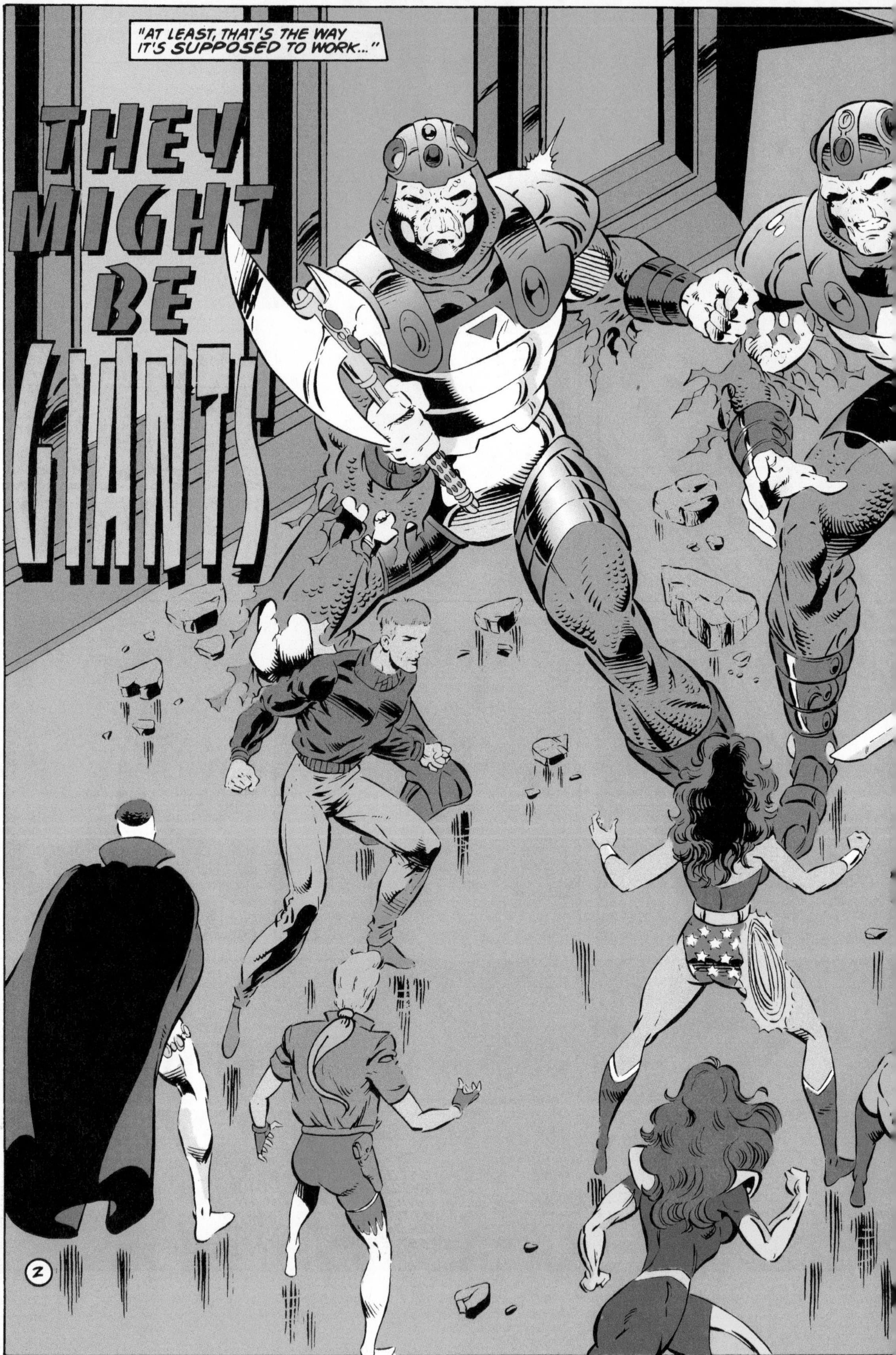
"AT LEAST, THAT'S THE WAY IT'S SUPPOSED TO WORK..."
THEY MIGHT BE GIANTS
2

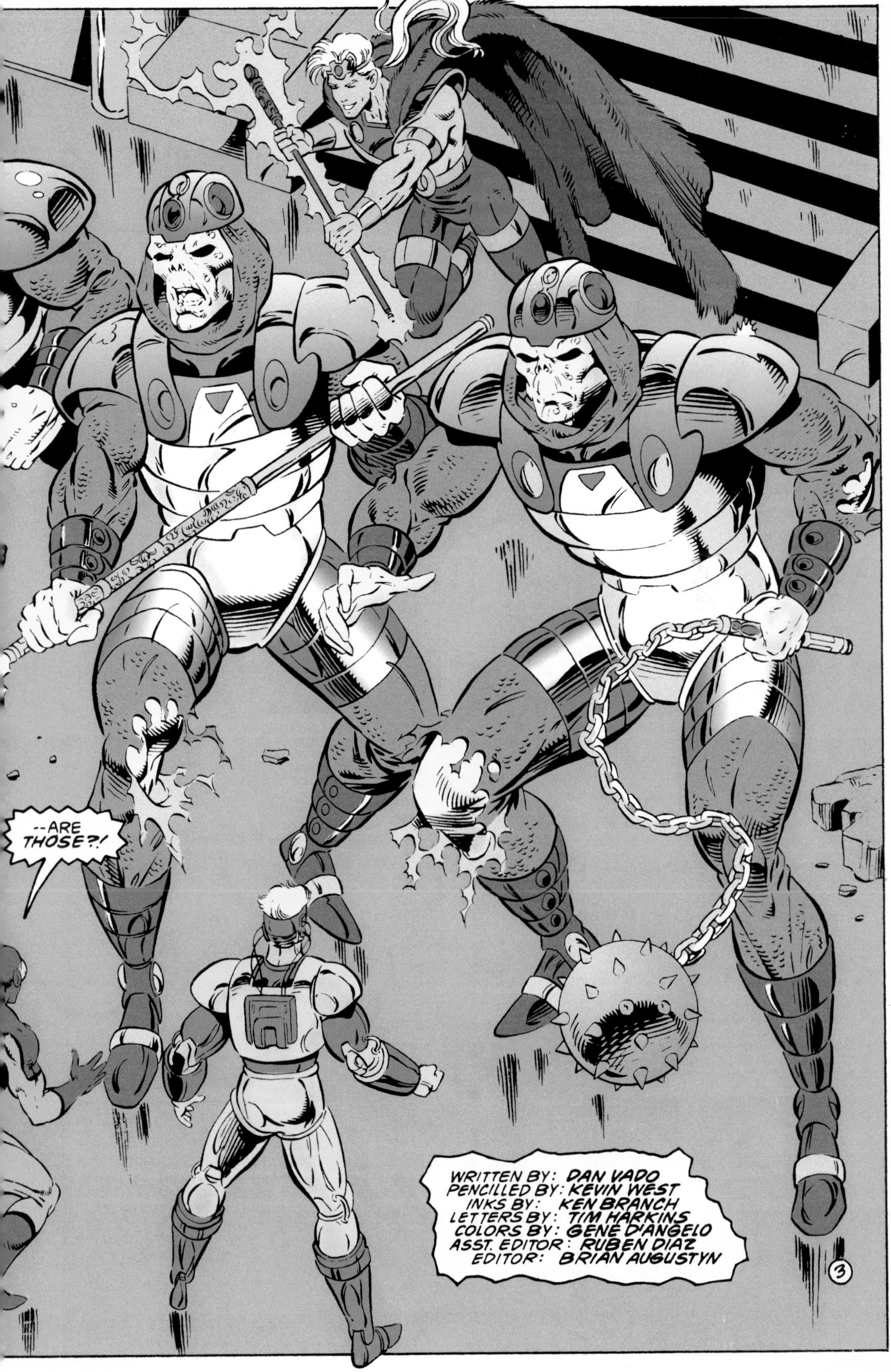
--ARE THOSE?!
WRITTEN BY: DAN VADO
PENCILLED BY: KEVIN WEST
INKS BY: KEN BRANCH
LETTERS BY: TIM HARKINS
COLORS BY: GENE D'ANGELO
ASST. EDITOR: RUBEN DIAZ
EDITOR: BRIAN AUGUSTYN
3

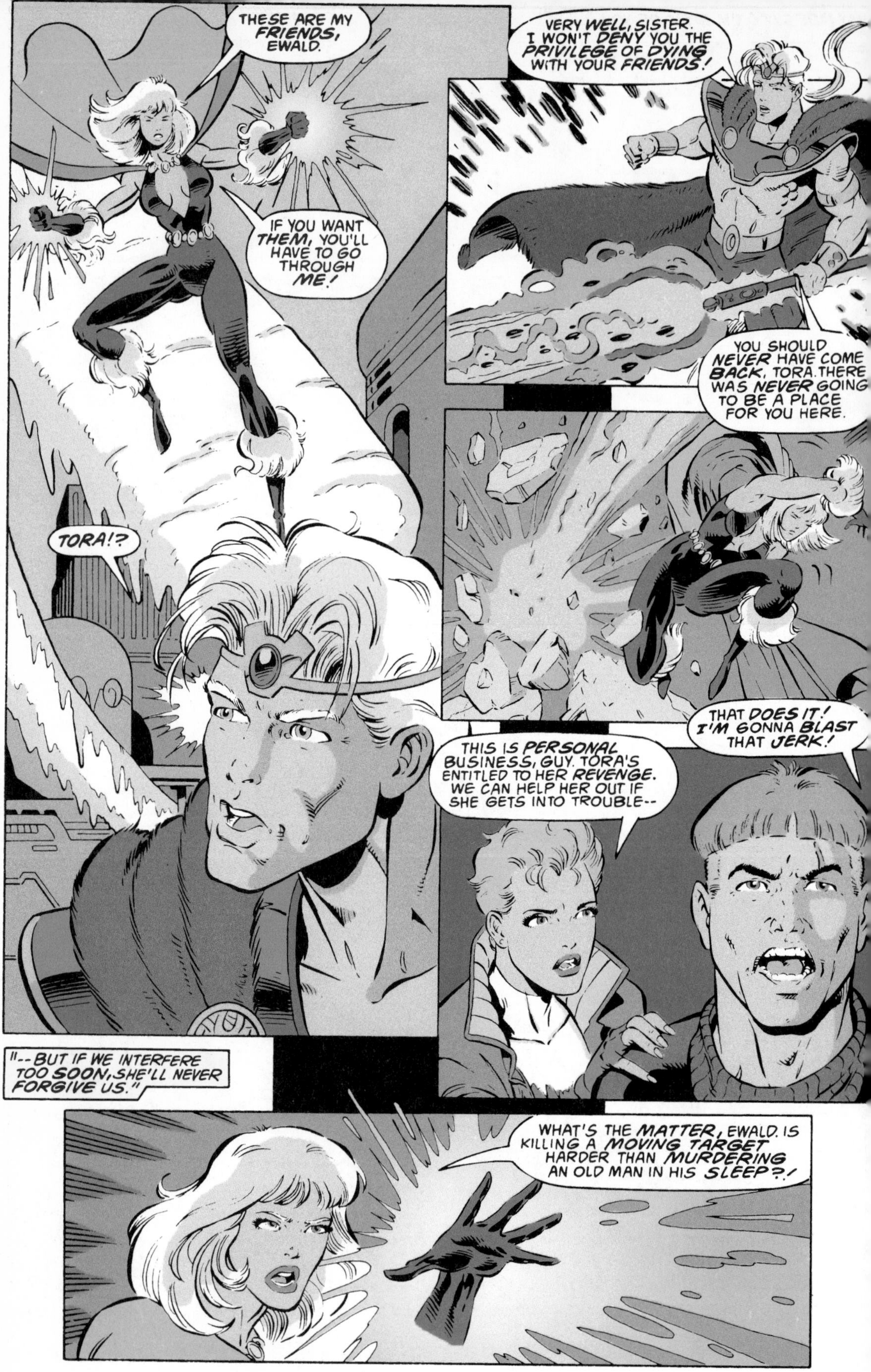
THESE ARE MY FRIENDS, EWALD.
IF YOU WANT THEM, YOU'LL HAVE TO GO THROUGH ME!
VERY WELL, SISTER. I WON'T DENY YOU THE PRIVILEGE OF DYING WITH YOUR FRIENDS!
YOU SHOULD NEVER HAVE COME BACK, TORA. THERE WAS NEVER GOING TO BE A PLACE FOR YOU HERE.
TORA!?
THIS IS PERSONAL BUSINESS, GUY. TORA'S ENTITLED TO HER REVENGE. WE CAN HELP HER OUT IF SHE GETS INTO TROUBLE--
THAT DOES IT! I'M GONNA BLAST THAT JERK!
"--BUT IF WE INTERFERE TOO SOON, SHE'LL NEVER FORGIVE US."
WHAT'S THE MATTER, EWALD. IS KILLING A MOVING TARGET HARDER THAN MURDERING AN OLD MAN IN HIS SLEEP?!

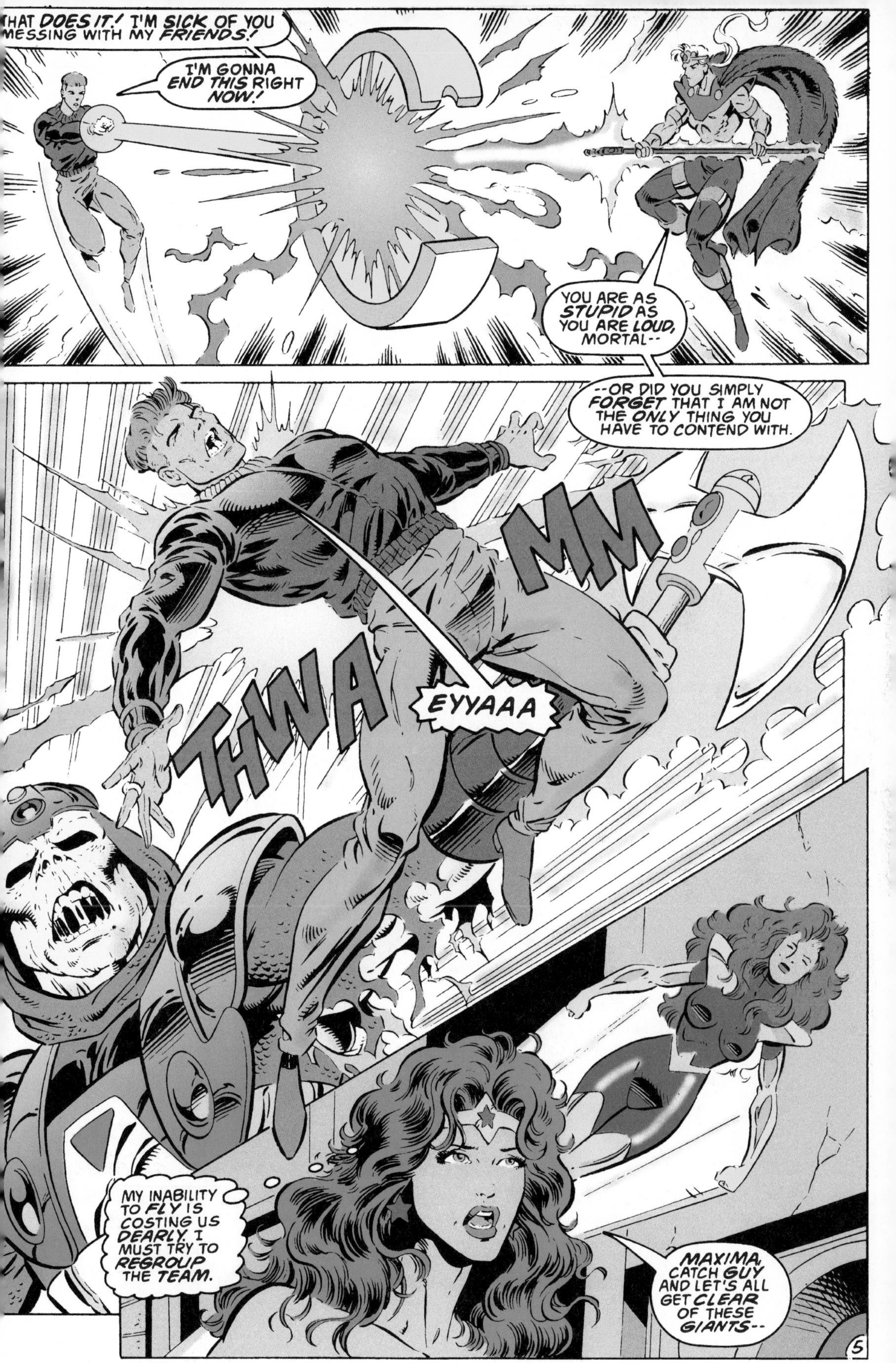

THAT DOES IT! I'M SICK OF YOU MESSING WITH MY FRIENDS!
I'M GONNA END THIS RIGHT NOW!
YOU ARE AS STUPID AS YOU ARE LOUD, MORTAL--
--OR DID YOU SIMPLY FORGET THAT I AM NOT THE ONLY THING YOU HAVE TO CONTEND WITH.
THWAMM
EYYAAA
MY INABILITY TO FLY IS COSTING US DEARLY. I MUST TRY TO REGROUP THE TEAM.
MAXIMA, CATCH GUY AND LET'S ALL GET CLEAR OF THESE GIANTS--

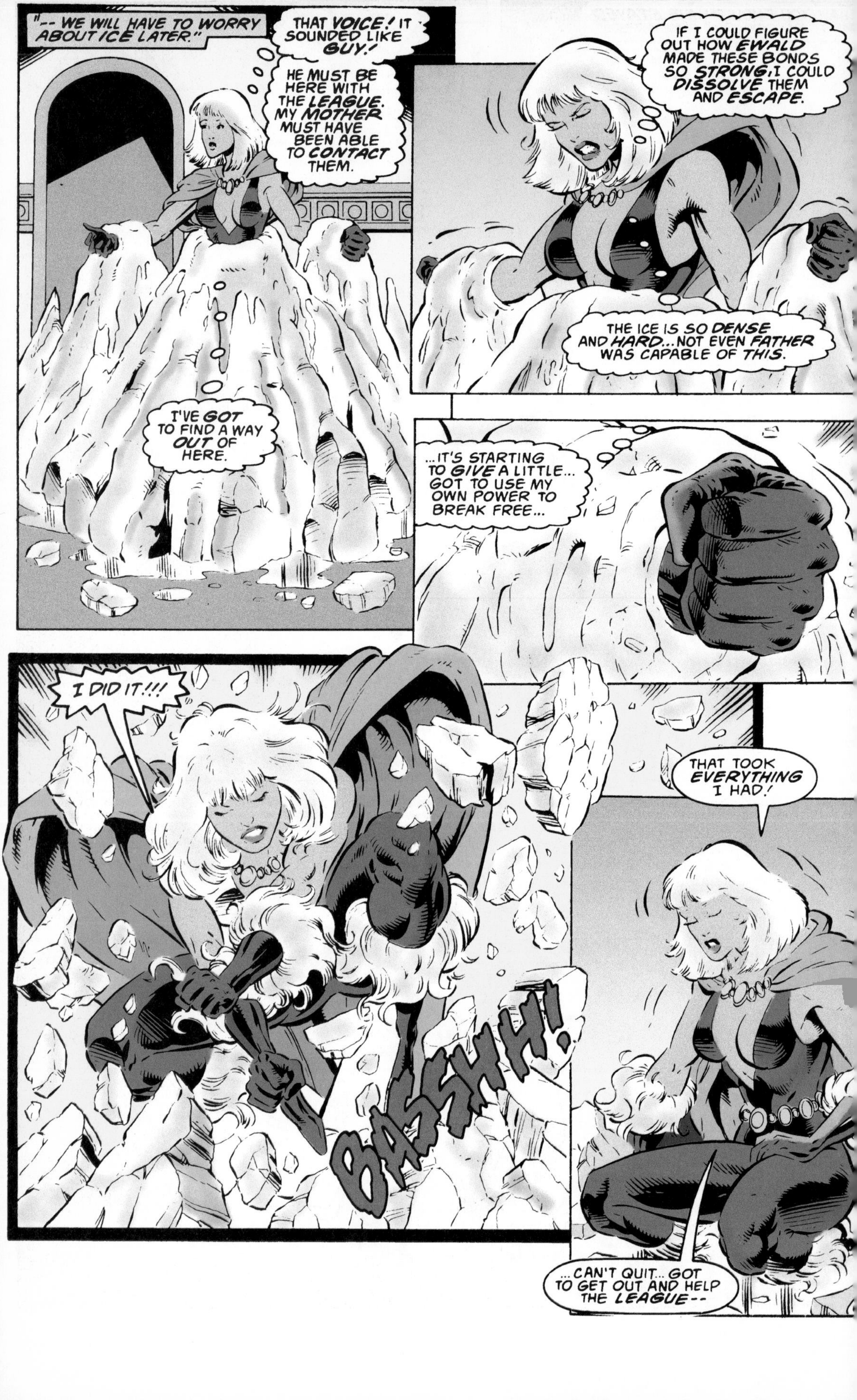
"-- WE WILL HAVE TO WORRY ABOUT ICE LATER."
THAT VOICE! IT SOUNDED LIKE GUY!
HE MUST BE HERE WITH THE LEAGUE. MY MOTHER MUST HAVE BEEN ABLE TO CONTACT THEM.
I'VE GOT TO FIND A WAY OUT OF HERE.
IF I COULD FIGURE OUT HOW EWALD MADE THESE BONDS SO STRONG, I COULD DISSOLVE THEM AND ESCAPE.
THE ICE IS SO DENSE AND HARD... NOT EVEN FATHER WAS CAPABLE OF THIS.
...IT'S STARTING TO GIVE A LITTLE... GOT TO USE MY OWN POWER TO BREAK FREE...
I DID IT!!!
BASHH!
THAT TOOK EVERYTHING I HAD!
...CAN'T QUIT... GOT TO GET OUT AND HELP THE LEAGUE--

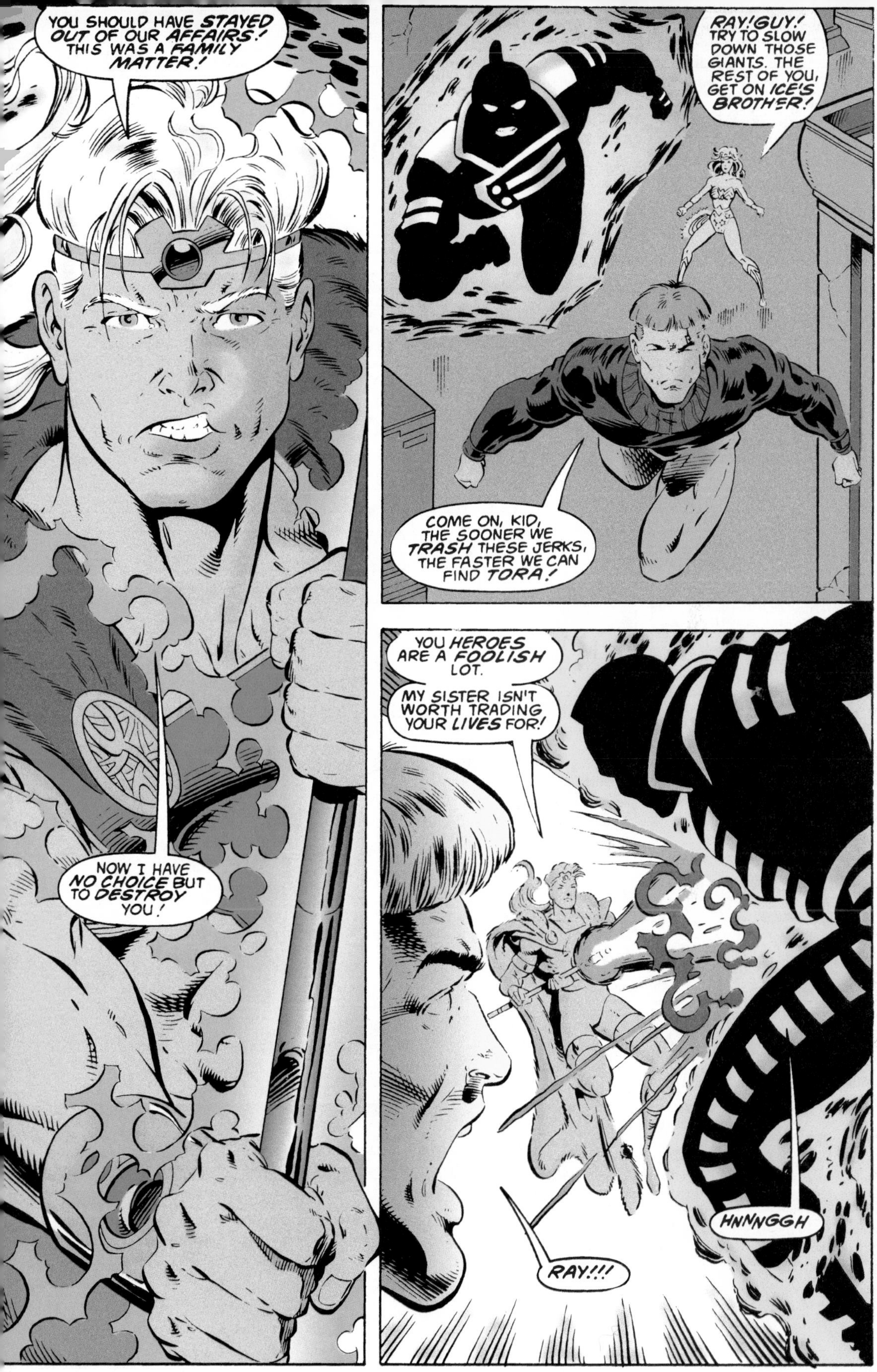
YOU SHOULD HAVE STAYED OUT OF OUR AFFAIRS! THIS WAS A FAMILY MATTER!
NOW I HAVE NO CHOICE BUT TO DESTROY YOU!
RAY! GUY! TRY TO SLOW DOWN THOSE GIANTS. THE REST OF YOU, GET ON ICE'S BROTHER!
COME ON, KID, THE SOONER WE TRASH THESE JERKS, THE FASTER WE CAN FIND TORA!
YOU HEROES ARE A FOOLISH LOT.
MY SISTER ISN'T WORTH TRADING YOUR LIVES FOR!
HNNNGGH
RAY!!!

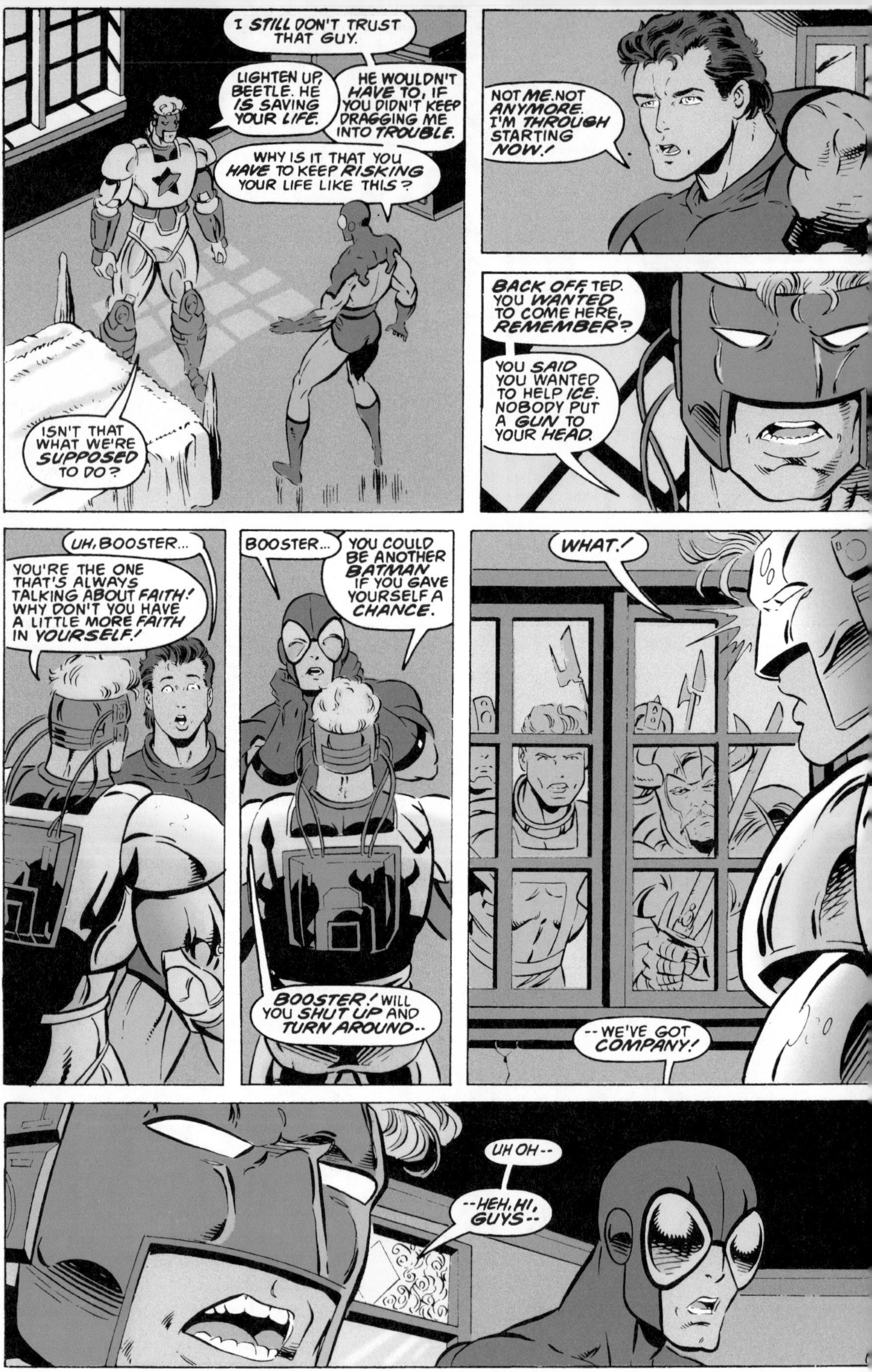

I STILL DON'T TRUST THAT GUY.
LIGHTEN UP, BEETLE. HE IS SAVING YOUR LIFE.
HE WOULDN'T HAVE TO, IF YOU DIDN'T KEEP DRAGGING ME INTO TROUBLE.
WHY IS IT THAT YOU HAVE TO KEEP RISKING YOUR LIFE LIKE THIS?
ISN'T THAT WHAT WE'RE SUPPOSED TO DO?
NOT ME. NOT ANYMORE. I'M THROUGH STARTING NOW!
BACK OFF, TED. YOU WANTED TO COME HERE, REMEMBER?
YOU SAID YOU WANTED TO HELP ICE. NOBODY PUT A GUN TO YOUR HEAD.
UH, BOOSTER...
YOU'RE THE ONE THAT'S ALWAYS TALKING ABOUT FAITH! WHY DON'T YOU HAVE A LITTLE MORE FAITH IN YOURSELF!
BOOSTER...
YOU COULD BE ANOTHER BATMAN IF YOU GAVE YOURSELF A CHANCE.
BOOSTER! WILL YOU SHUT UP AND TURN AROUND--
WHAT!
--WE'VE GOT COMPANY!
UH OH--
--HEH, HI, GUYS--

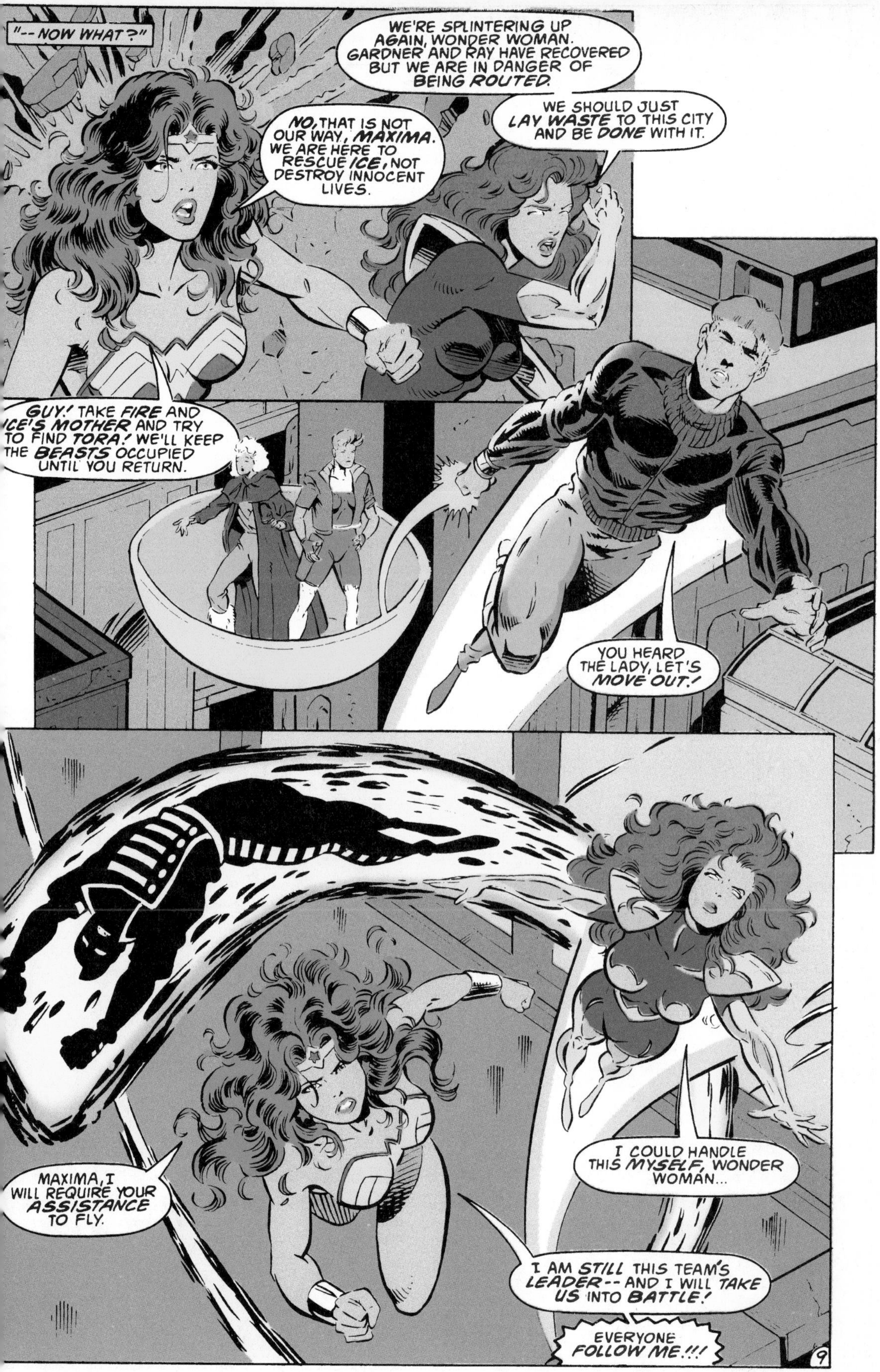
"--NOW WHAT?"
WE'RE SPLINTERING UP AGAIN, WONDER WOMAN. GARDNER AND RAY HAVE RECOVERED BUT WE ARE IN DANGER OF BEING ROUTED.
WE SHOULD JUST LAY WASTE TO THIS CITY AND BE DONE WITH IT.
NO, THAT IS NOT OUR WAY, MAXIMA. WE ARE HERE TO RESCUE ICE, NOT DESTROY INNOCENT LIVES.
GUY! TAKE FIRE AND ICE'S MOTHER AND TRY TO FIND TORA! WE'LL KEEP THE BEASTS OCCUPIED UNTIL YOU RETURN.
YOU HEARD THE LADY, LET'S MOVE OUT!
MAXIMA, I WILL REQUIRE YOUR ASSISTANCE TO FLY.
I COULD HANDLE THIS MYSELF, WONDER WOMAN...
I AM STILL THIS TEAM'S LEADER--AND I WILL TAKE US INTO BATTLE!
EVERYONE FOLLOW ME!!!
9

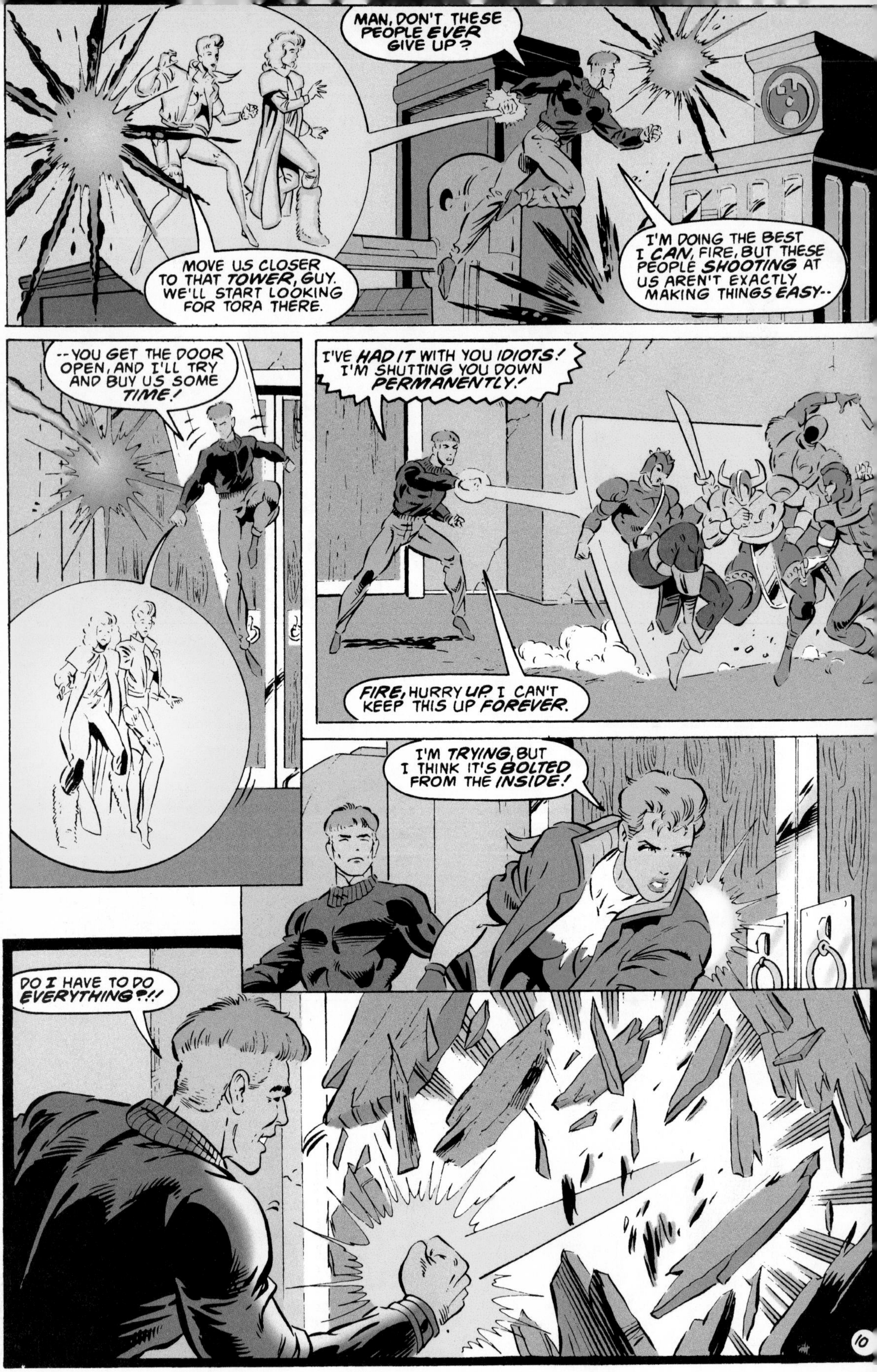

MAN, DON'T THESE PEOPLE EVER GIVE UP?
MOVE US CLOSER TO THAT TOWER, GUY. WE'LL START LOOKING FOR TORA THERE.
I'M DOING THE BEST I CAN, FIRE, BUT THESE PEOPLE SHOOTING AT US AREN'T EXACTLY MAKING THINGS EASY--
--YOU GET THE DOOR OPEN, AND I'LL TRY AND BUY US SOME TIME!
I'VE HAD IT WITH YOU IDIOTS! I'M SHUTTING YOU DOWN PERMANENTLY!
FIRE, HURRY UP. I CAN'T KEEP THIS UP FOREVER.
I'M TRYING, BUT I THINK IT'S BOLTED FROM THE INSIDE!
DO I HAVE TO DO EVERYTHING?!!

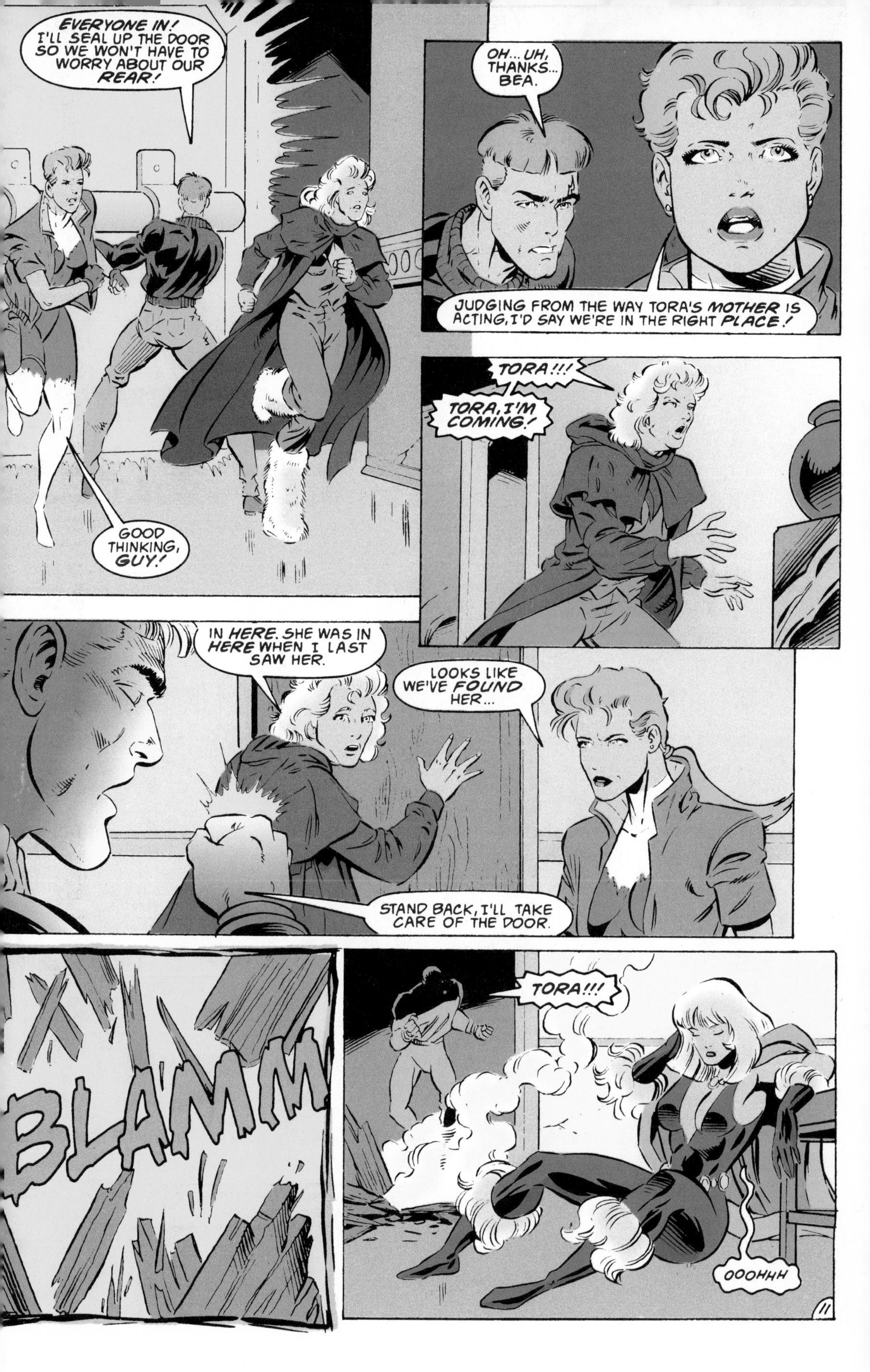
EVERYONE IN! I'LL SEAL UP THE DOOR SO WE WON'T HAVE TO WORRY ABOUT OUR REAR!
GOOD THINKING, GUY!
OH... UH, THANKS... BEA.
JUDGING FROM THE WAY TORA'S MOTHER IS ACTING, I'D SAY WE'RE IN THE RIGHT PLACE!
TORA!!!
TORA, I'M COMING!
IN HERE. SHE WAS IN HERE WHEN I LAST SAW HER.
LOOKS LIKE WE'VE FOUND HER...
STAND BACK, I'LL TAKE CARE OF THE DOOR.
BLAMM
TORA!!!
OOOHHH
11

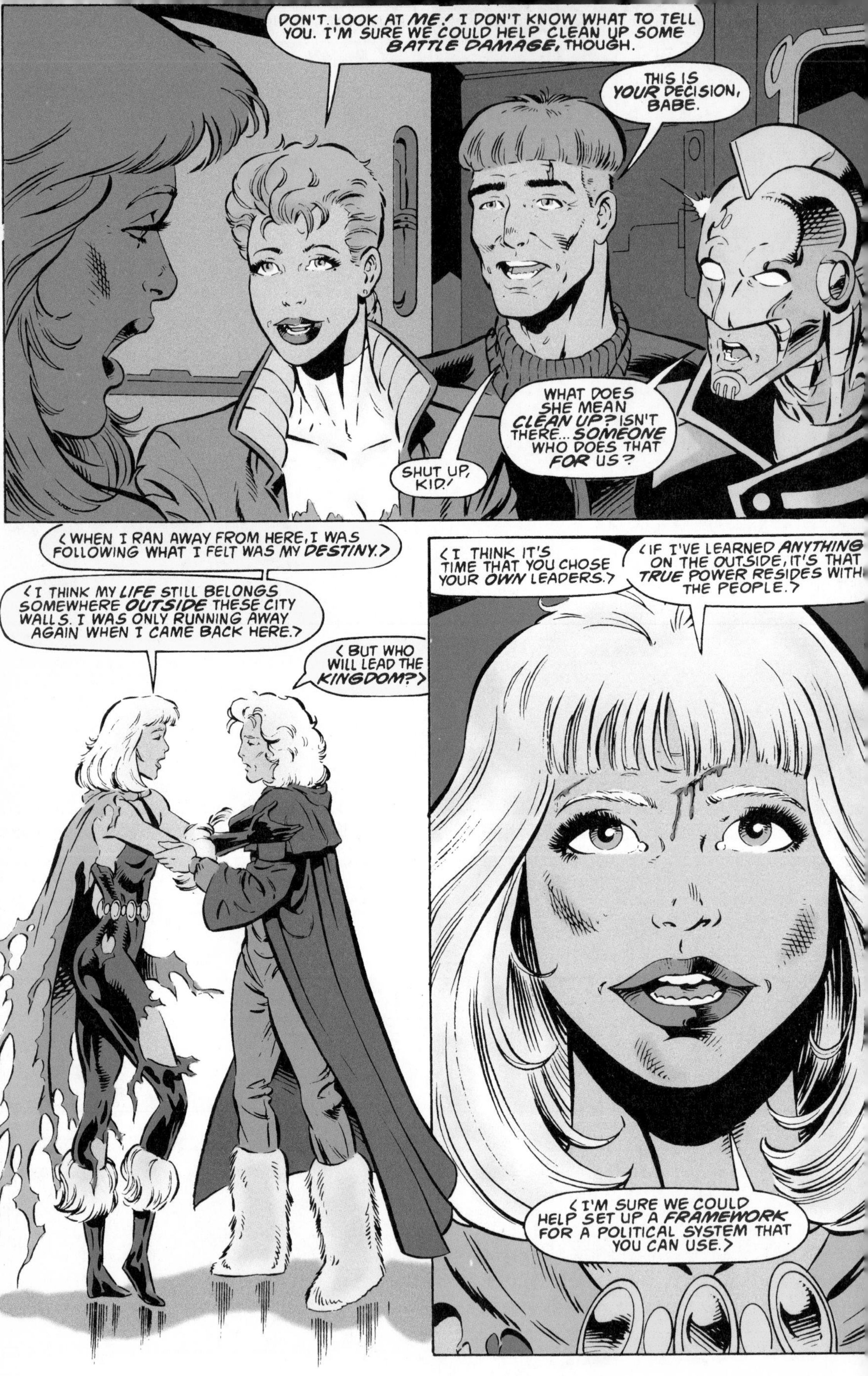
DON'T LOOK AT ME! I DON'T KNOW WHAT TO TELL YOU. I'M SURE WE COULD HELP CLEAN UP SOME BATTLE DAMAGE, THOUGH.
THIS IS YOUR DECISION, BABE.
WHAT DOES SHE MEAN CLEAN UP? ISN'T THERE... SOMEONE WHO DOES THAT FOR US?
SHUT UP, KID!
<WHEN I RAN AWAY FROM HERE, I WAS FOLLOWING WHAT I FELT WAS MY DESTINY.>
<I THINK MY LIFE STILL BELONGS SOMEWHERE OUTSIDE THESE CITY WALLS. I WAS ONLY RUNNING AWAY AGAIN WHEN I CAME BACK HERE.>
<BUT WHO WILL LEAD THE KINGDOM?>
<I THINK IT'S TIME THAT YOU CHOSE YOUR OWN LEADERS.>
<IF I'VE LEARNED ANYTHING ON THE OUTSIDE, IT'S THAT TRUE POWER RESIDES WITH THE PEOPLE.>
<I'M SURE WE COULD HELP SET UP A FRAMEWORK FOR A POLITICAL SYSTEM THAT YOU CAN USE.>

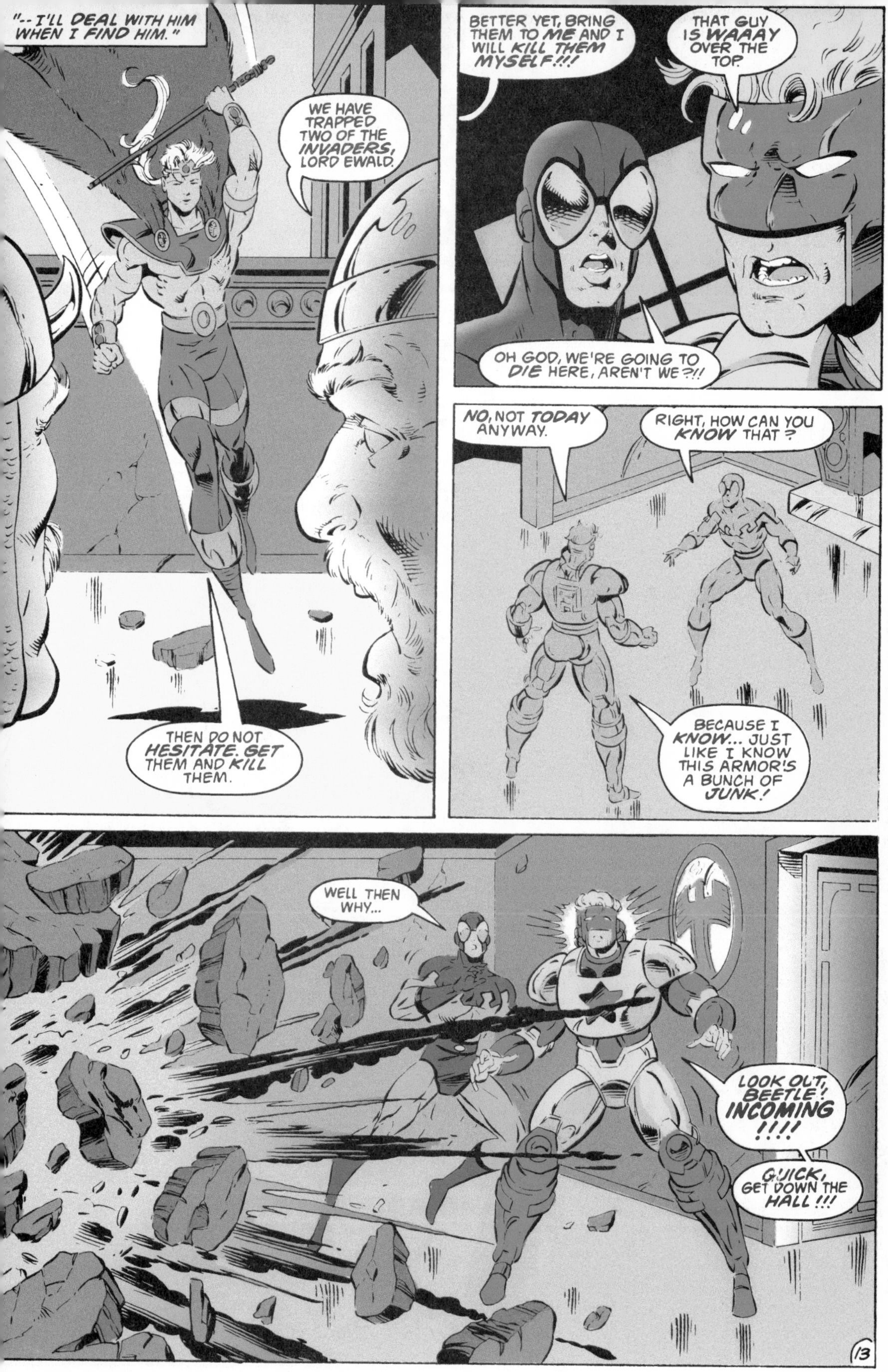
"-- I'LL DEAL WITH HIM WHEN I FIND HIM."
WE HAVE TRAPPED TWO OF THE INVADERS, LORD EWALD.
THEN DO NOT HESITATE. GET THEM AND KILL THEM.
BETTER YET, BRING THEM TO ME AND I WILL KILL THEM MYSELF!!!
THAT GUY IS WAAAY OVER THE TOP.
OH GOD, WE'RE GOING TO DIE HERE, AREN'T WE?!!
NO, NOT TODAY ANYWAY.
RIGHT, HOW CAN YOU KNOW THAT?
BECAUSE I KNOW... JUST LIKE I KNOW THIS ARMOR'S A BUNCH OF JUNK!
WELL THEN WHY...
LOOK OUT, BEETLE! INCOMING!!!!
QUICK, GET DOWN THE HALL!!!
13

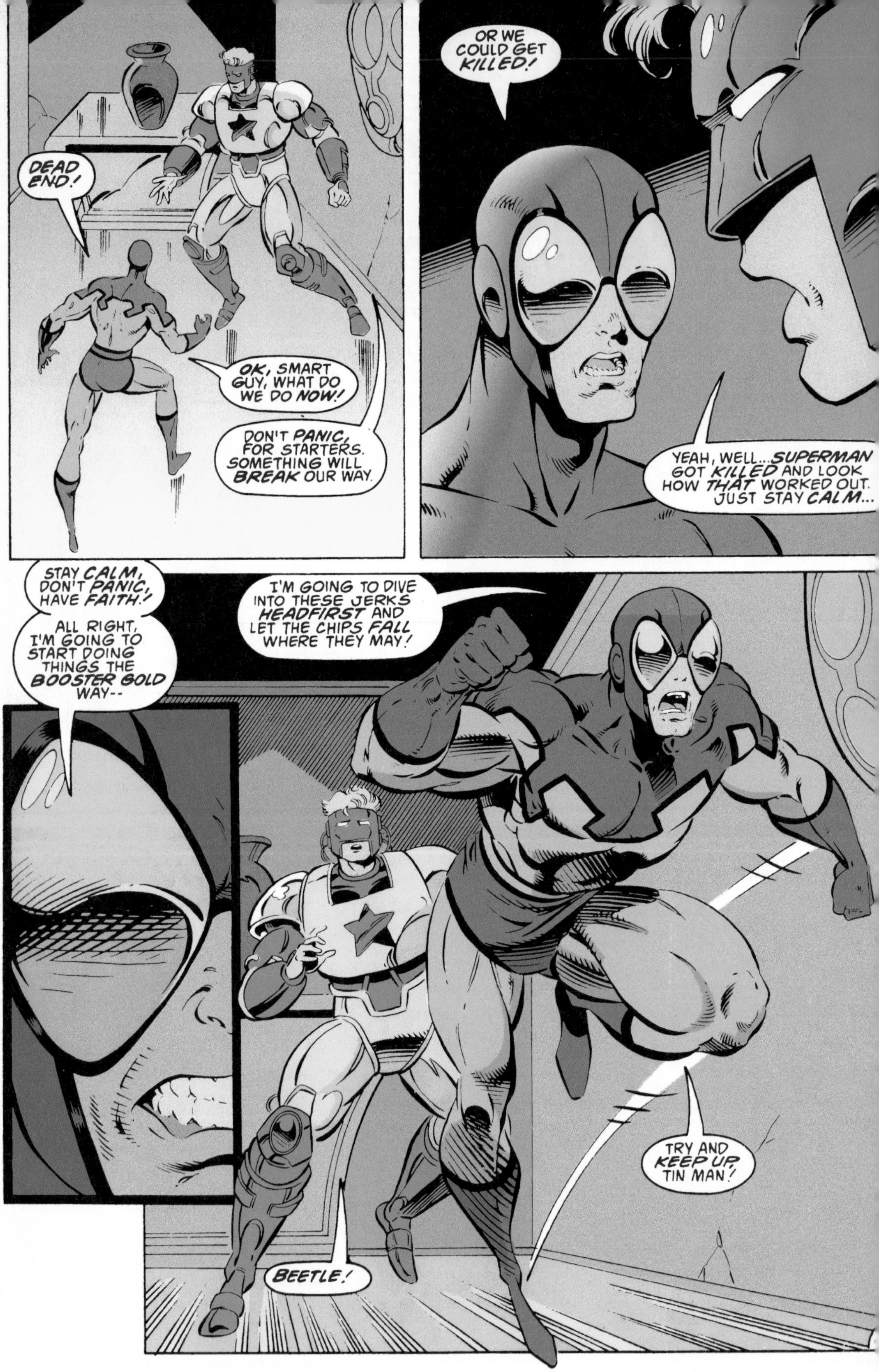
DEAD END!
OK, SMART GUY, WHAT DO WE DO NOW!
DON'T PANIC, FOR STARTERS. SOMETHING WILL BREAK OUR WAY.
OR WE COULD GET KILLED!
YEAH, WELL... SUPERMAN GOT KILLED AND LOOK HOW THAT WORKED OUT. JUST STAY CALM...
STAY CALM, DON'T PANIC, HAVE FAITH!
ALL RIGHT, I'M GOING TO START DOING THINGS THE BOOSTER GOLD WAY--
I'M GOING TO DIVE INTO THESE JERKS HEADFIRST AND LET THE CHIPS FALL WHERE THEY MAY!
TRY AND KEEP UP, TIN MAN!
BEETLE!

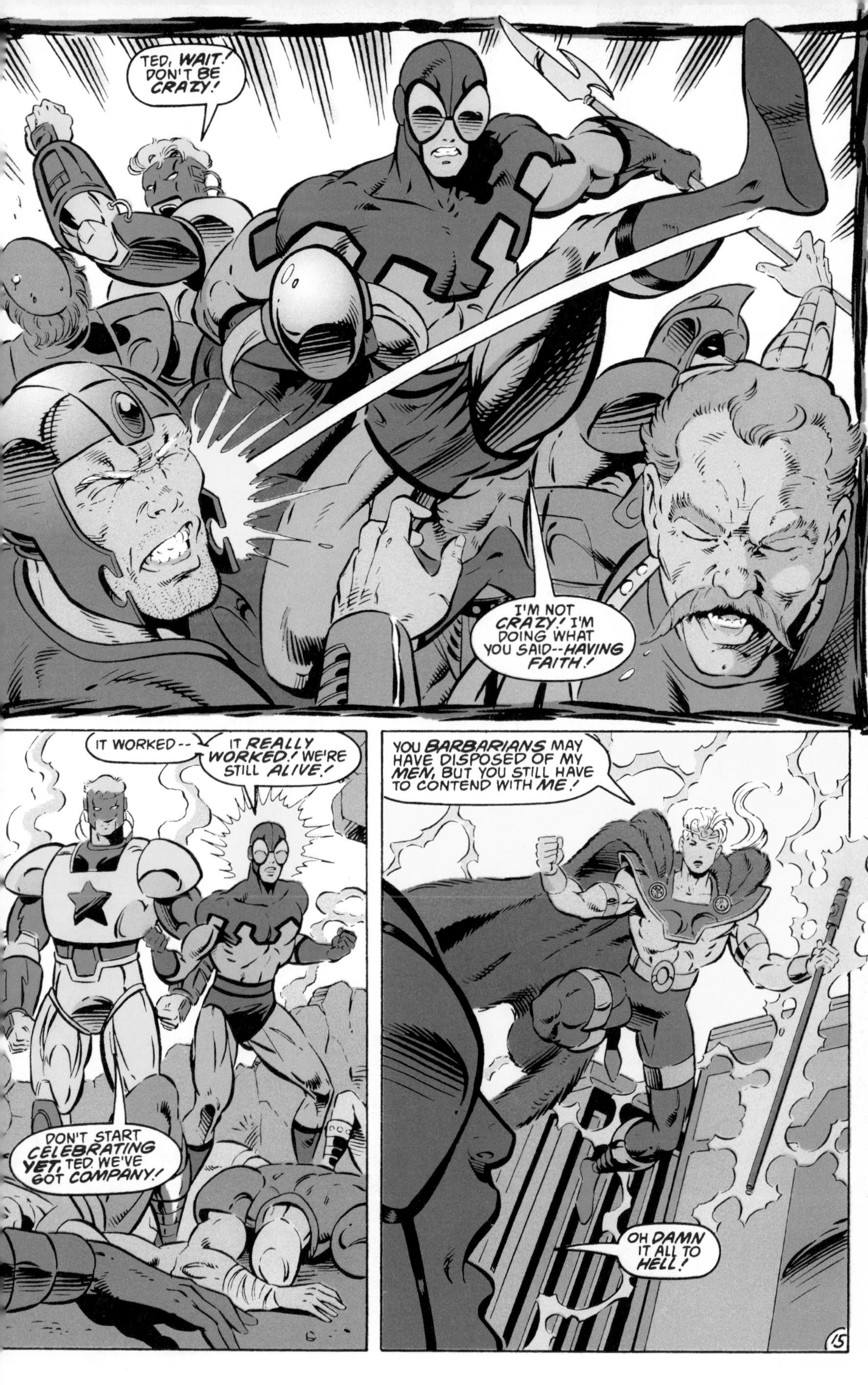
TED, WAIT! DON'T BE CRAZY!
I'M NOT CRAZY! I'M DOING WHAT YOU SAID--HAVING FAITH!
IT WORKED--
IT REALLY WORKED! WE'RE STILL ALIVE!
DON'T START CELEBRATING YET, TED. WE'VE GOT COMPANY!
YOU BARBARIANS MAY HAVE DISPOSED OF MY MEN, BUT YOU STILL HAVE TO CONTEND WITH ME!
OH DAMN IT ALL TO HELL!

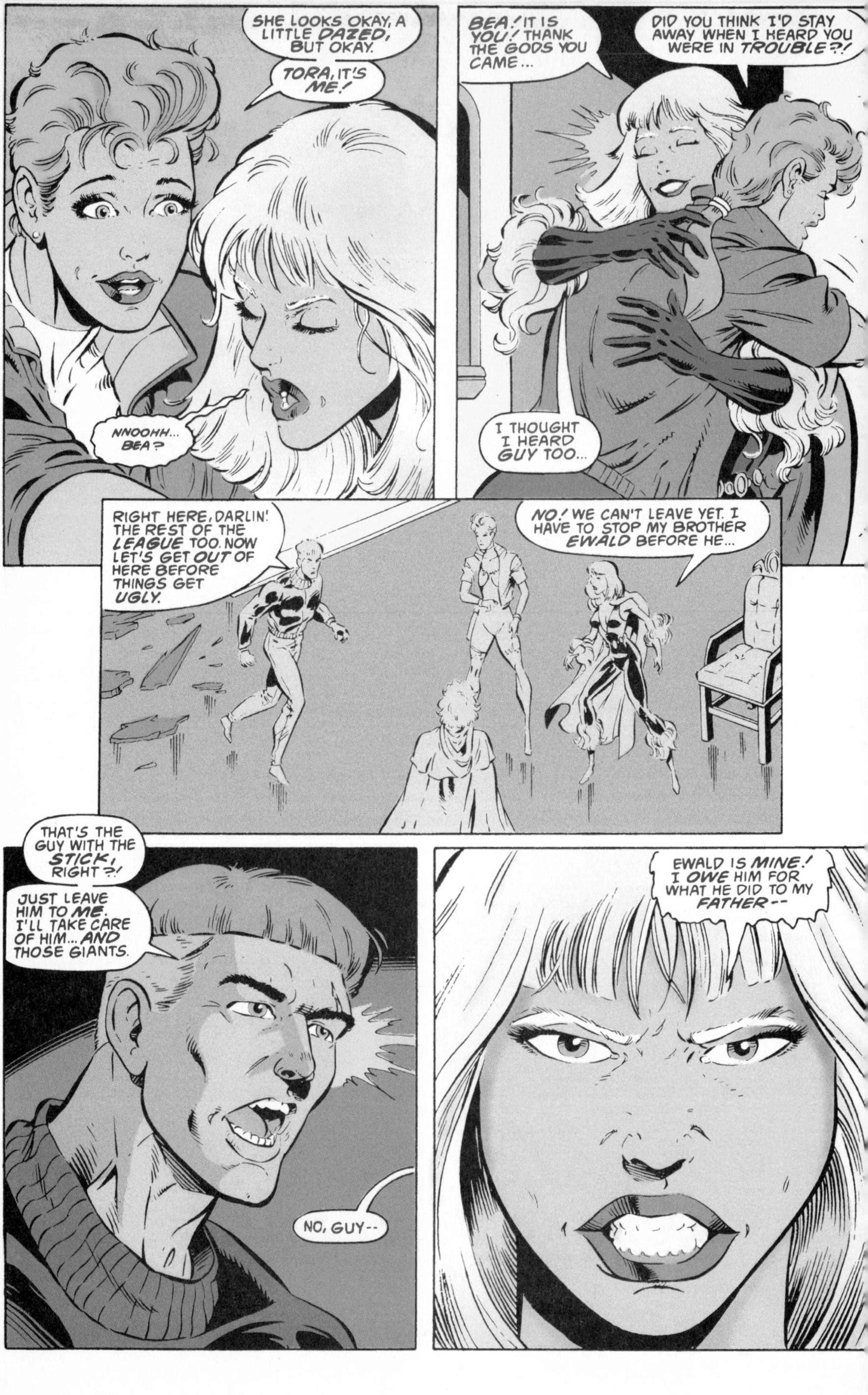
SHE LOOKS OKAY, A LITTLE DAZED, BUT OKAY.
TORA, IT'S ME!
NNOOHH... BEA?
BEA! IT IS YOU! THANK THE GODS YOU CAME...
DID YOU THINK I'D STAY AWAY WHEN I HEARD YOU WERE IN TROUBLE?!
I THOUGHT I HEARD GUY TOO...
RIGHT HERE, DARLIN'. THE REST OF THE LEAGUE TOO. NOW LET'S GET OUT OF HERE BEFORE THINGS GET UGLY.
NO! WE CAN'T LEAVE YET. I HAVE TO STOP MY BROTHER EWALD BEFORE HE...
THAT'S THE GUY WITH THE STICK, RIGHT?!
JUST LEAVE HIM TO ME. I'LL TAKE CARE OF HIM... AND THOSE GIANTS.
NO, GUY--
EWALD IS MINE! I OWE HIM FOR WHAT HE DID TO MY FATHER--

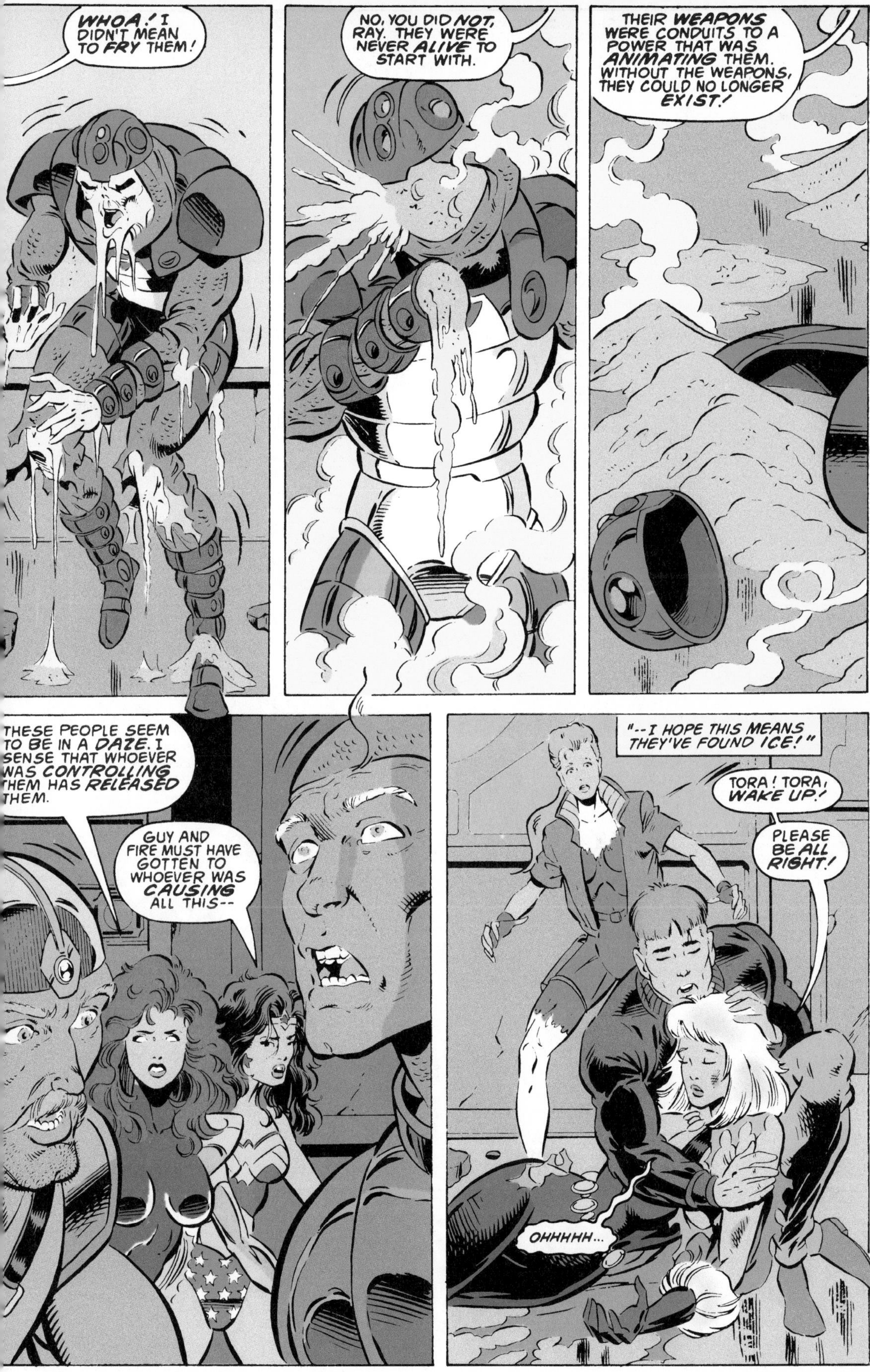
WHOA! I DIDN'T MEAN TO FRY THEM!
NO, YOU DID NOT, RAY. THEY WERE NEVER ALIVE TO START WITH.
THEIR WEAPONS WERE CONDUITS TO A POWER THAT WAS ANIMATING THEM. WITHOUT THE WEAPONS, THEY COULD NO LONGER EXIST!
THESE PEOPLE SEEM TO BE IN A DAZE. I SENSE THAT WHOEVER WAS CONTROLLING THEM HAS RELEASED THEM.
GUY AND FIRE MUST HAVE GOTTEN TO WHOEVER WAS CAUSING ALL THIS--
"--I HOPE THIS MEANS THEY'VE FOUND ICE!"
TORA! TORA, WAKE UP!
PLEASE BE ALL RIGHT!
OHHHHH...

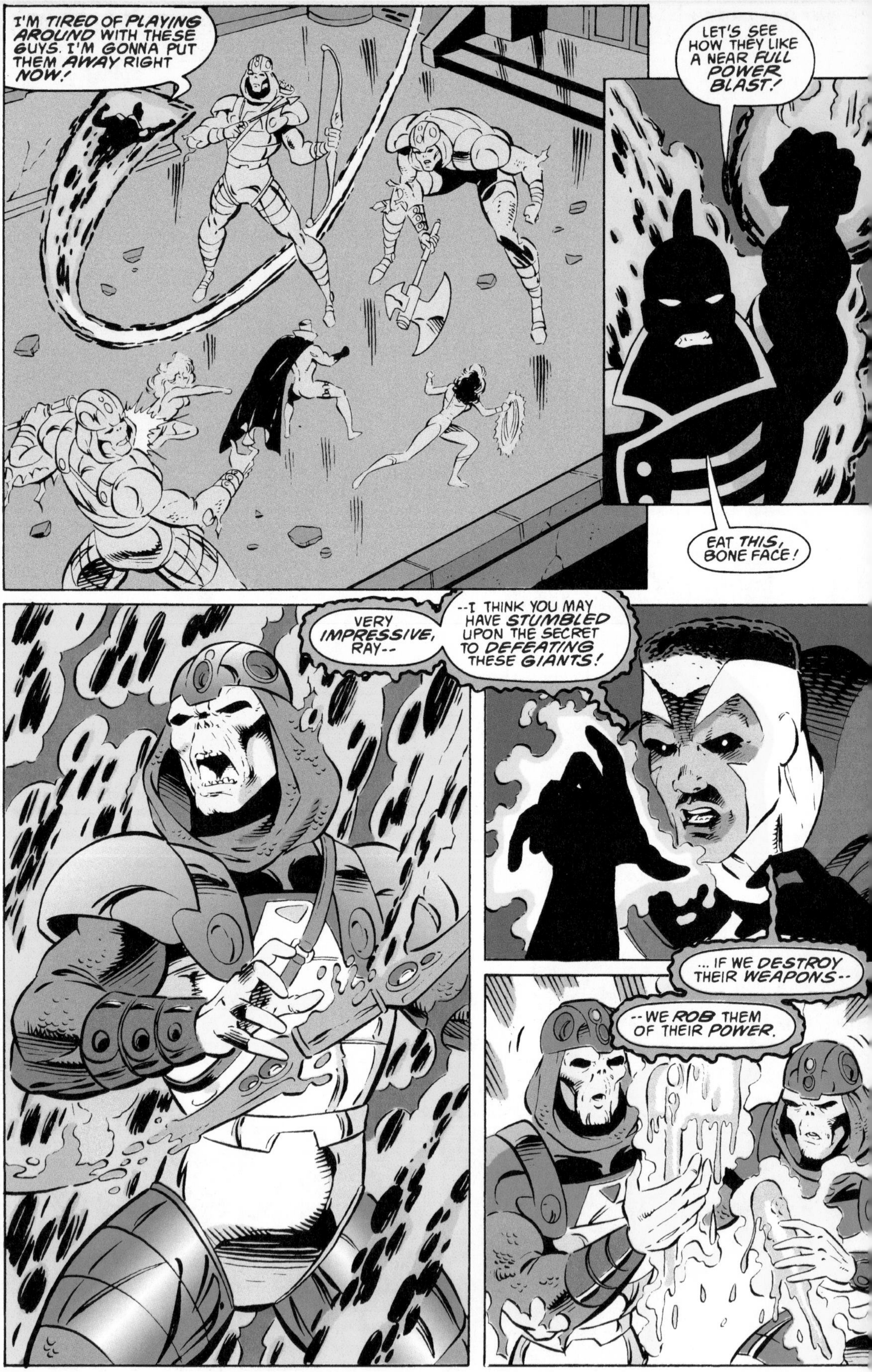
I'M TIRED OF PLAYING AROUND WITH THESE GUYS. I'M GONNA PUT THEM AWAY RIGHT NOW!
LET'S SEE HOW THEY LIKE A NEAR FULL POWER BLAST!
EAT THIS, BONE FACE!
VERY IMPRESSIVE, RAY--
--I THINK YOU MAY HAVE STUMBLED UPON THE SECRET TO DEFEATING THESE GIANTS!
... IF WE DESTROY THEIR WEAPONS--
--WE ROB THEM OF THEIR POWER.

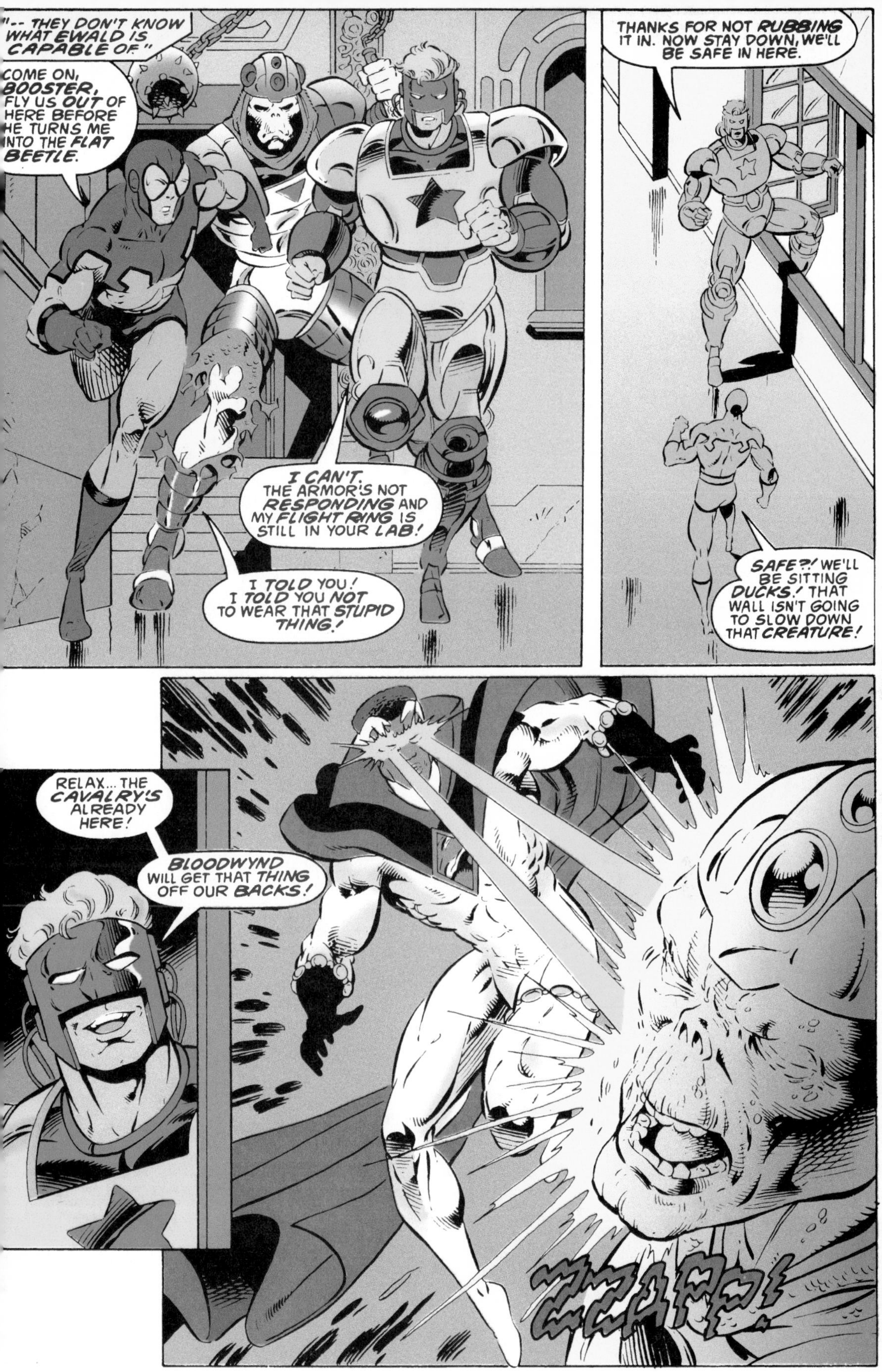
"-- THEY DON'T KNOW WHAT EWALD IS CAPABLE OF."
COME ON, BOOSTER, FLY US OUT OF HERE BEFORE HE TURNS ME INTO THE FLAT BEETLE.
I CAN'T. THE ARMOR'S NOT RESPONDING AND MY FLIGHT RING IS STILL IN YOUR LAB!
I TOLD YOU! I TOLD YOU NOT TO WEAR THAT STUPID THING!
THANKS FOR NOT RUBBING IT IN. NOW STAY DOWN, WE'LL BE SAFE IN HERE.
SAFE?! WE'LL BE SITTING DUCKS! THAT WALL ISN'T GOING TO SLOW DOWN THAT CREATURE!
RELAX... THE CAVALRY'S ALREADY HERE!
BLOODWYND WILL GET THAT THING OFF OUR BACKS!
ZZAPP!

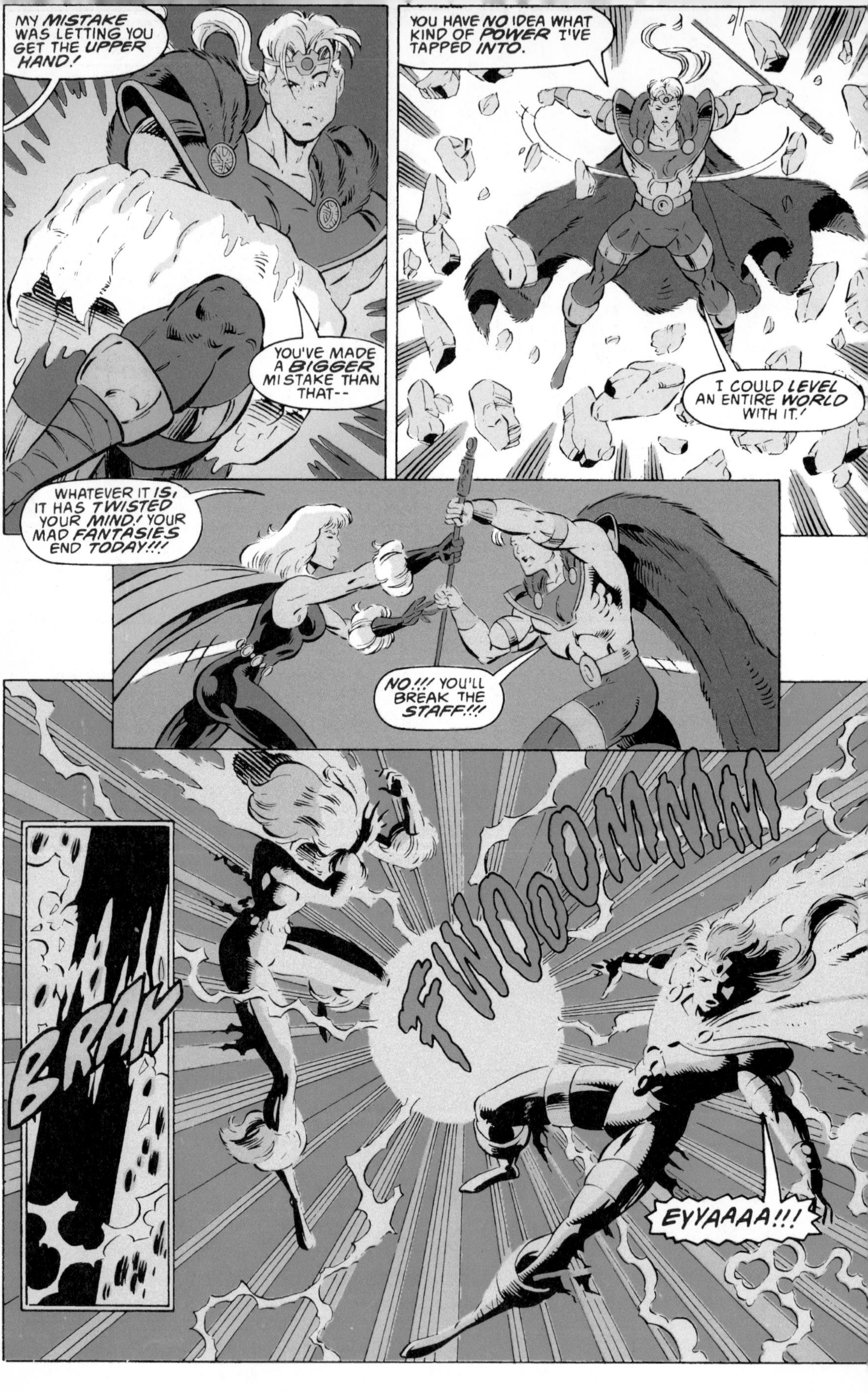
MY MISTAKE WAS LETTING YOU GET THE UPPER HAND!
YOU'VE MADE A BIGGER MISTAKE THAN THAT--
YOU HAVE NO IDEA WHAT KIND OF POWER I'VE TAPPED INTO.
I COULD LEVEL AN ENTIRE WORLD WITH IT!
WHATEVER IT IS, IT HAS TWISTED YOUR MIND! YOUR MAD FANTASIES END TODAY!!!
NO!!! YOU'LL BREAK THE STAFF!!!
BRAK
FWOOOOMMMM
EYYAAAA!!!

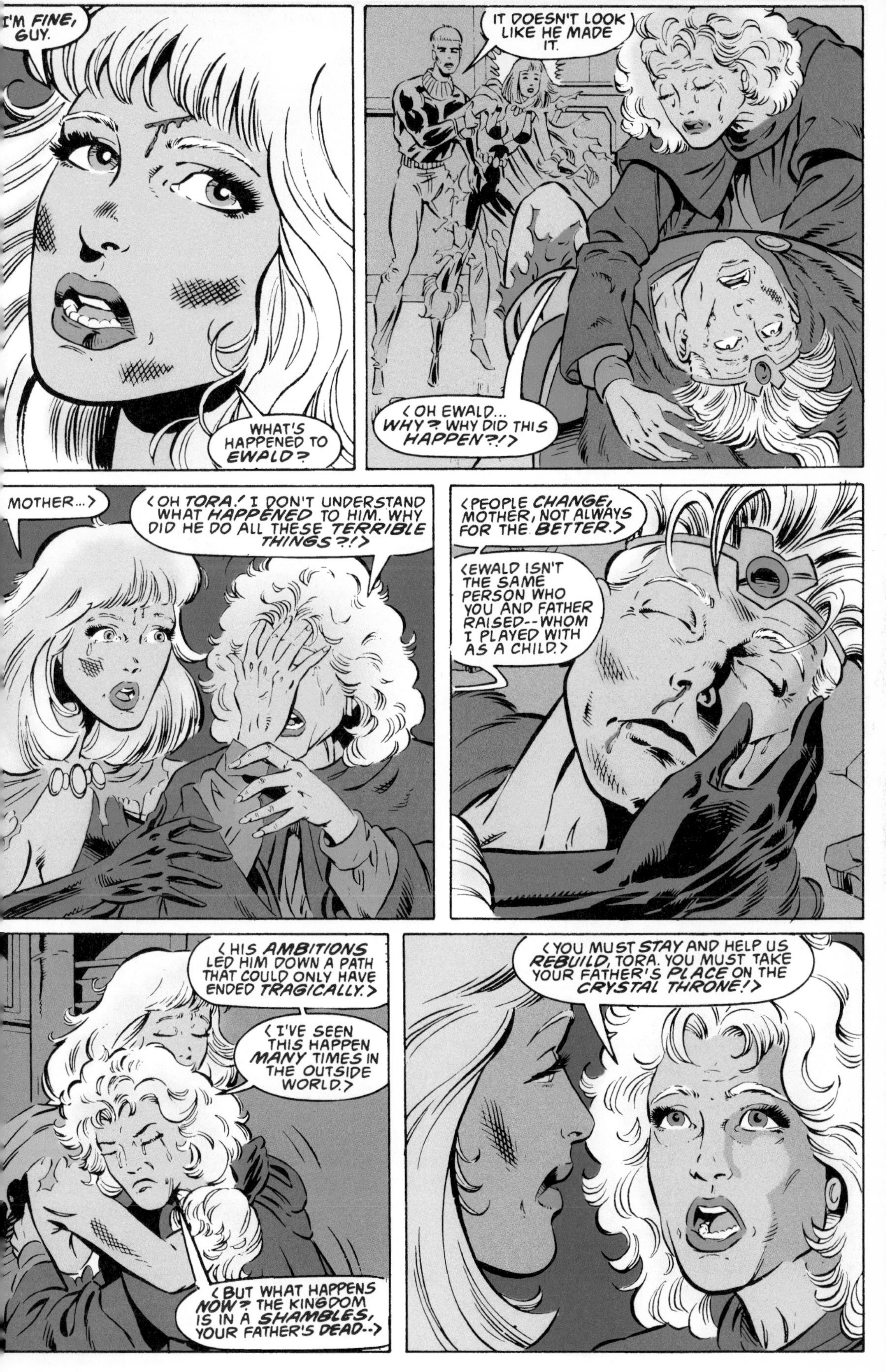

I'M FINE, GUY.
WHAT'S HAPPENED TO EWALD?
IT DOESN'T LOOK LIKE HE MADE IT.
<OH EWALD... WHY? WHY DID THIS HAPPEN?!>
MOTHER...>
<OH TORA! I DON'T UNDERSTAND WHAT HAPPENED TO HIM. WHY DID HE DO ALL THESE TERRIBLE THINGS?!>
<PEOPLE CHANGE, MOTHER, NOT ALWAYS FOR THE BETTER.>
<EWALD ISN'T THE SAME PERSON WHO YOU AND FATHER RAISED--WHOM I PLAYED WITH AS A CHILD.>
<HIS AMBITIONS LED HIM DOWN A PATH THAT COULD ONLY HAVE ENDED TRAGICALLY.>
<I'VE SEEN THIS HAPPEN MANY TIMES IN THE OUTSIDE WORLD.>
<BUT WHAT HAPPENS NOW? THE KINGDOM IS IN A SHAMBLES, YOUR FATHER'S DEAD-->
<YOU MUST STAY AND HELP US REBUILD, TORA. YOU MUST TAKE YOUR FATHER'S PLACE ON THE CRYSTAL THRONE!>

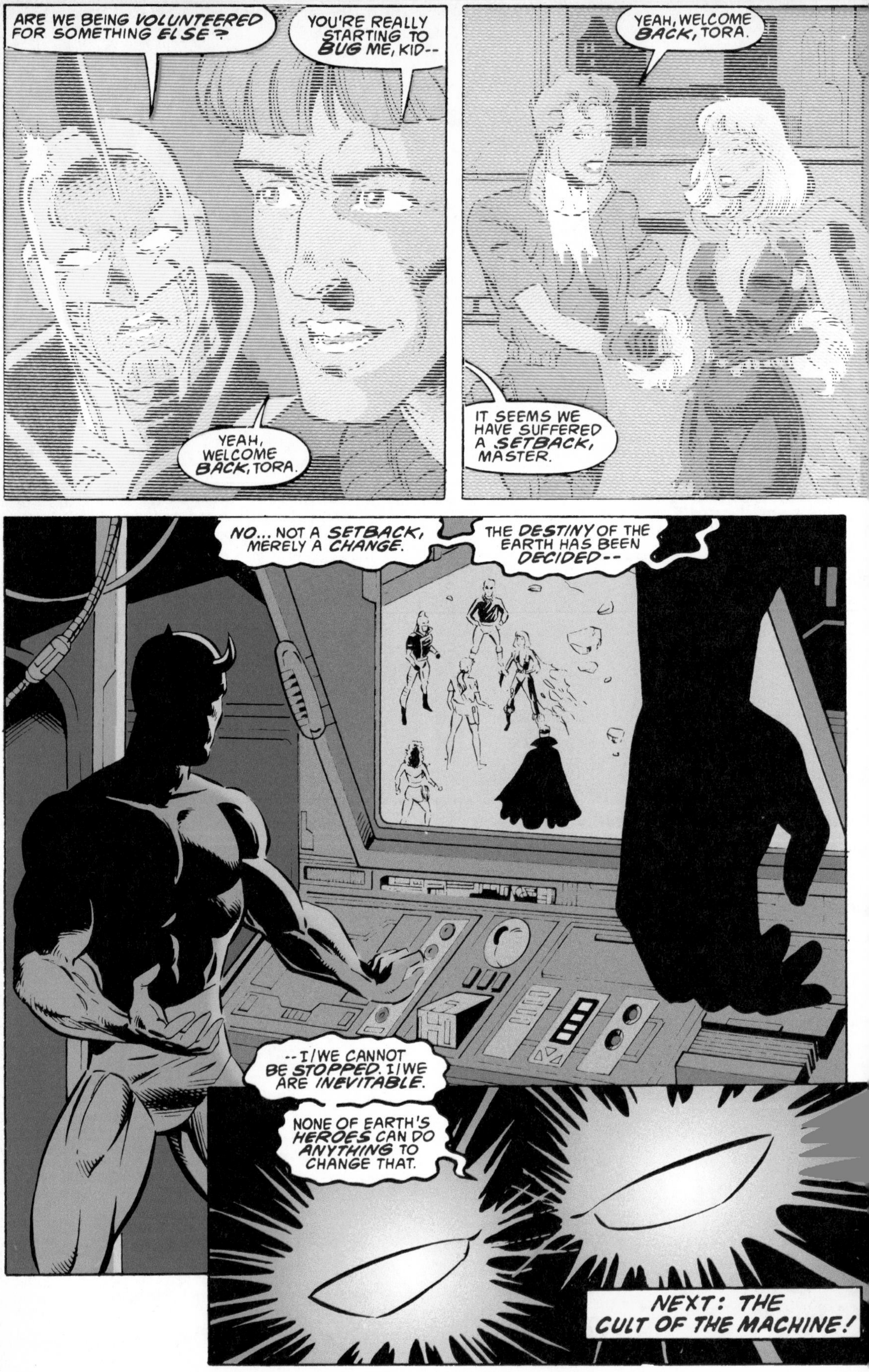
ARE WE BEING VOLUNTEERED FOR SOMETHING ELSE?
YOU'RE REALLY STARTING TO BUG ME, KID--
YEAH, WELCOME BACK, TORA.
YEAH, WELCOME BACK, TORA.
IT SEEMS WE HAVE SUFFERED A SETBACK, MASTER.
NO... NOT A SETBACK, MERELY A CHANGE.
THE DESTINY OF THE EARTH HAS BEEN DECIDED--
--I/WE CANNOT BE STOPPED. I/WE ARE INEVITABLE.
NONE OF EARTH'S HEROES CAN DO ANYTHING TO CHANGE THAT.
NEXT: THE CULT OF THE MACHINE!

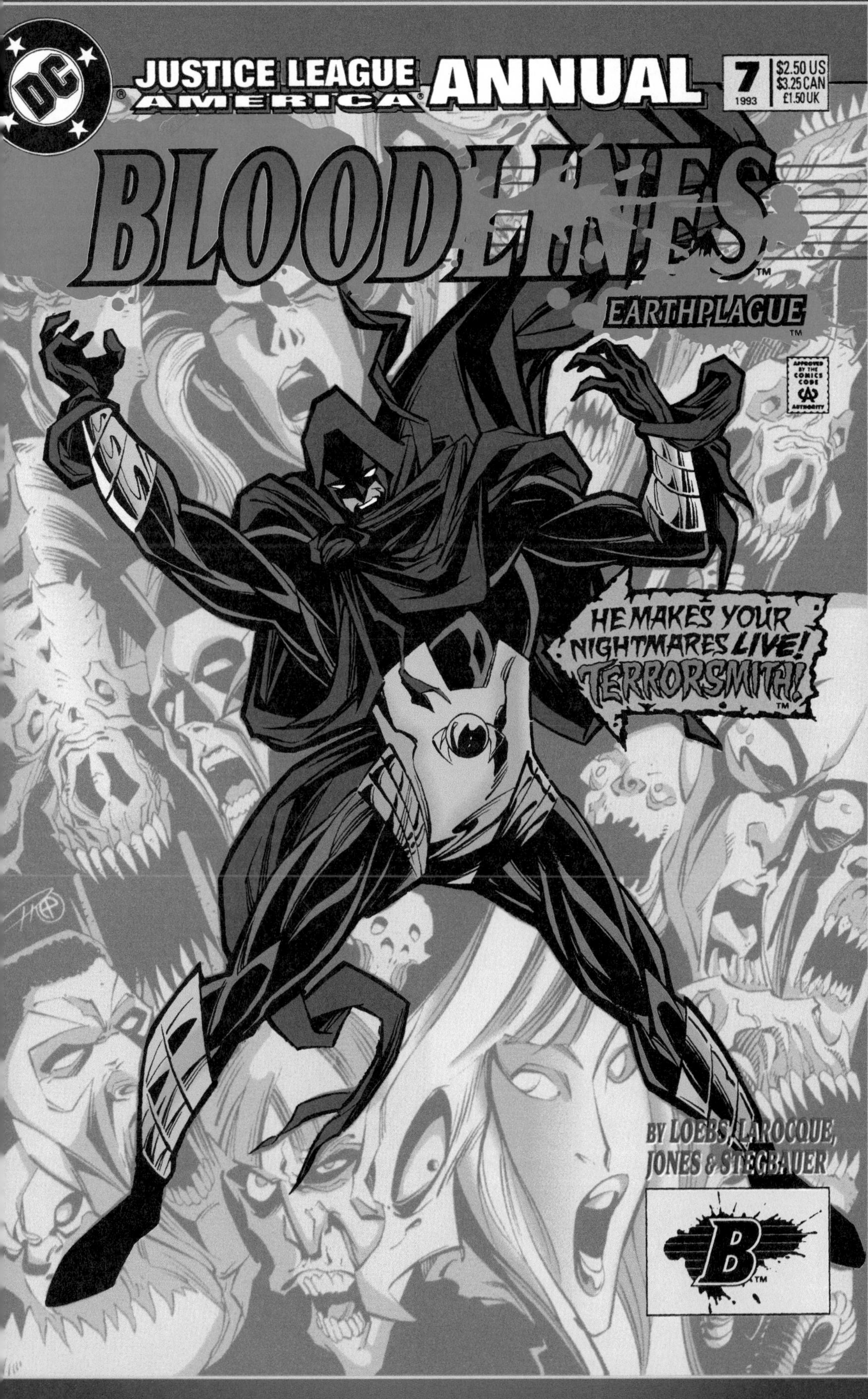
DC
JUSTICE LEAGUE AMERICA ANNUAL
7
1993
$2.50 US
$3.25 CAN
£1.50 UK
BLOODLINES
EARTHPLAGUE
APPROVED BY THE COMICS CODE AUTHORITY
HE MAKES YOUR NIGHTMARES LIVE! TERRORSMITH!
BY LOEBS, LAROCQUE, JONES & STEGBAUER
B

Cover art by **RICK BURCHETT**

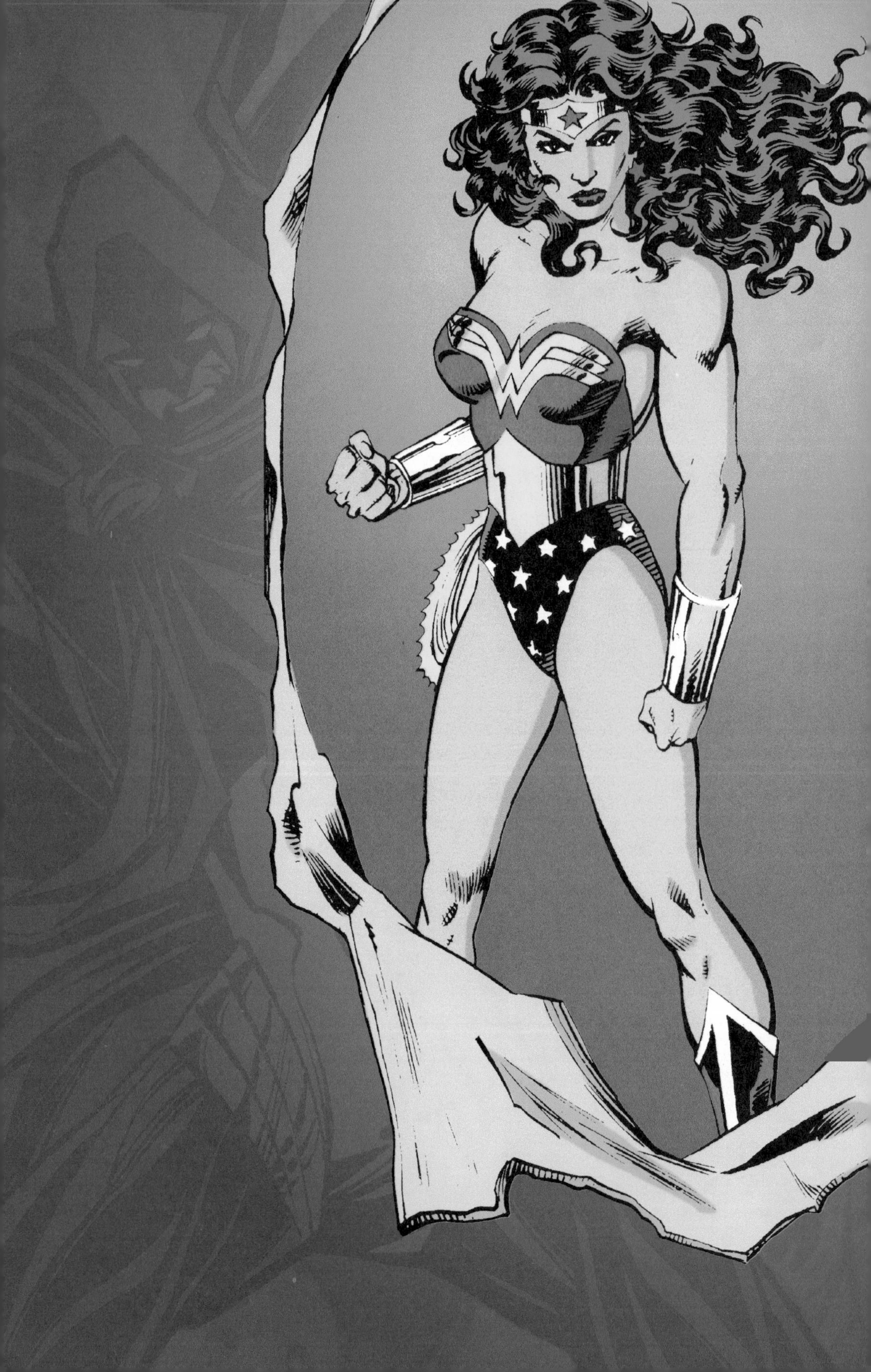

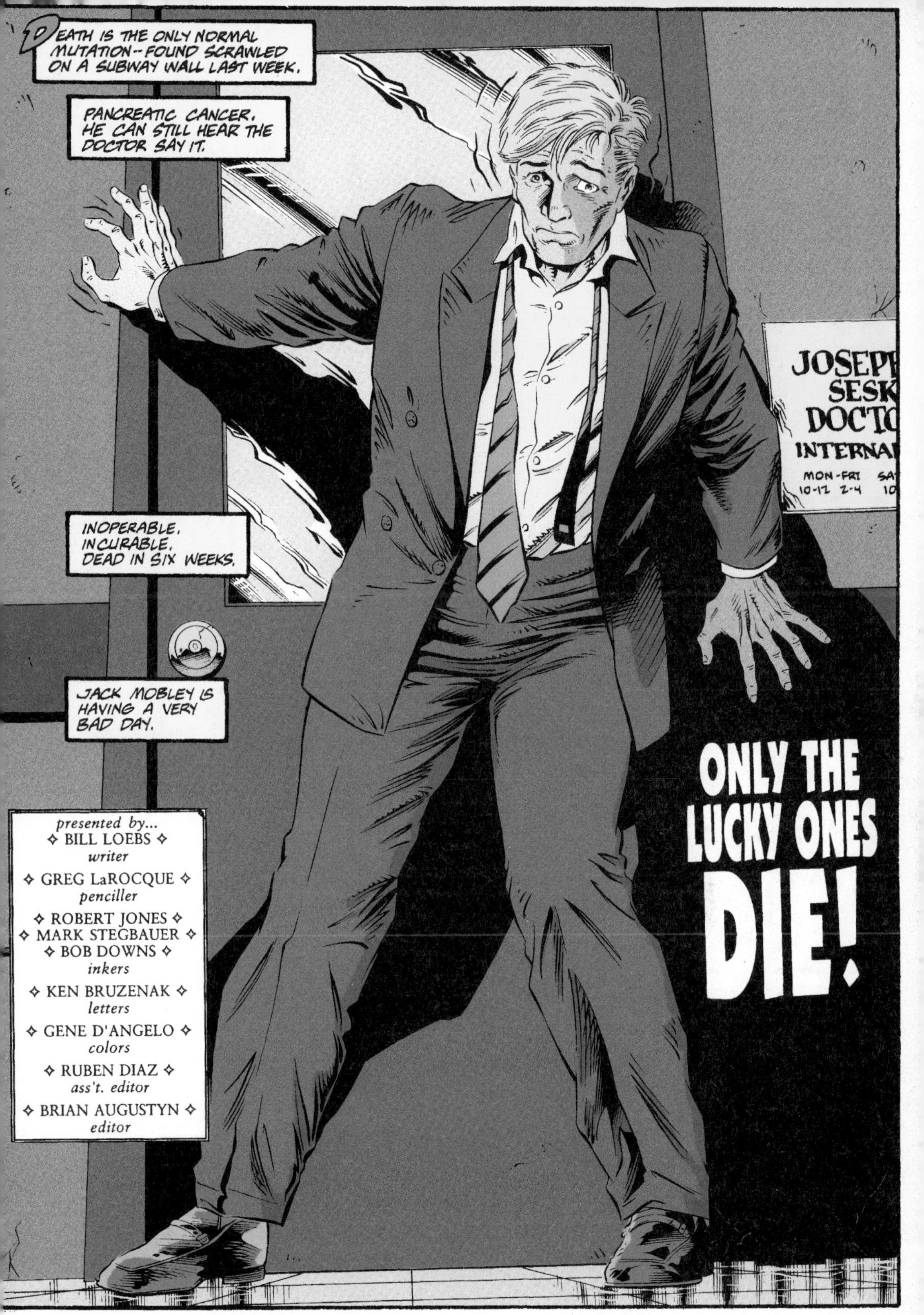
DEATH IS THE ONLY NORMAL MUTATION--FOUND SCRAWLED ON A SUBWAY WALL LAST WEEK.
PANCREATIC CANCER. HE CAN STILL HEAR THE DOCTOR SAY IT.
JOSEPH SESK DOCTO INTERNA
MON-FRI 10-12 2-4
INOPERABLE. INCURABLE. DEAD IN SIX WEEKS.
JACK MOBLEY IS HAVING A VERY BAD DAY.
ONLY THE LUCKY ONES DIE!
presented by...
✧ BILL LOEBS ✧ writer
✧ GREG LaROCQUE ✧ penciller
✧ ROBERT JONES ✧
✧ MARK STEGBAUER ✧
✧ BOB DOWNS ✧ inkers
✧ KEN BRUZENAK ✧ letters
✧ GENE D'ANGELO ✧ colors
✧ RUBEN DIAZ ✧ ass't. editor
✧ BRIAN AUGUSTYN ✧ editor

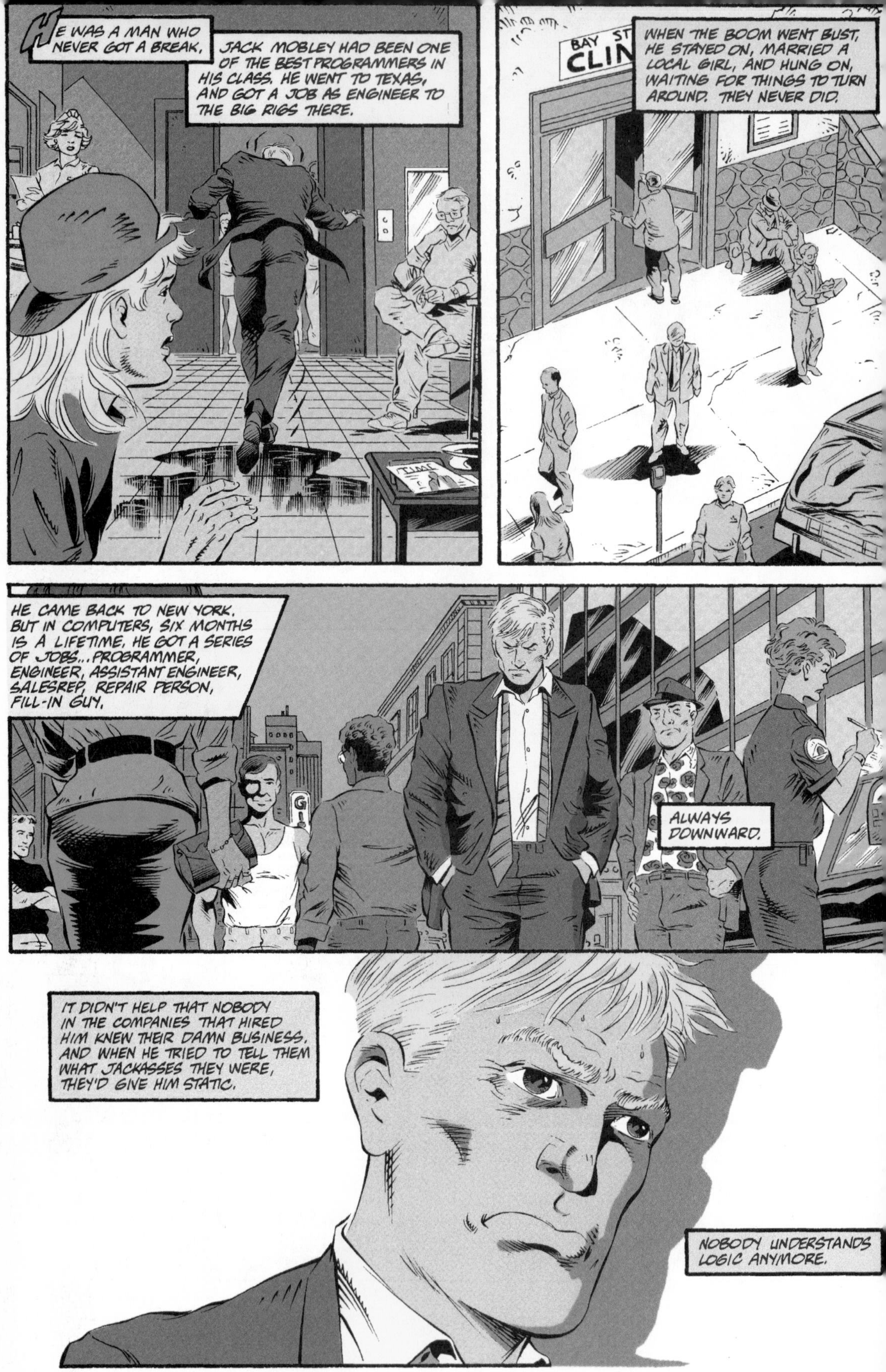
HE WAS A MAN WHO NEVER GOT A BREAK.
JACK MOBLEY HAD BEEN ONE OF THE BEST PROGRAMMERS IN HIS CLASS. HE WENT TO TEXAS, AND GOT A JOB AS ENGINEER TO THE BIG RIGS THERE.
TIME
BAY ST
CLIN
WHEN THE BOOM WENT BUST, HE STAYED ON, MARRIED A LOCAL GIRL, AND HUNG ON, WAITING FOR THINGS TO TURN AROUND. THEY NEVER DID.
HE CAME BACK TO NEW YORK. BUT IN COMPUTERS, SIX MONTHS IS A LIFETIME. HE GOT A SERIES OF JOBS...PROGRAMMER, ENGINEER, ASSISTANT ENGINEER, SALESREP, REPAIR PERSON, FILL-IN GUY.
ALWAYS DOWNWARD.
IT DIDN'T HELP THAT NOBODY IN THE COMPANIES THAT HIRED HIM KNEW THEIR DAMN BUSINESS. AND WHEN HE TRIED TO TELL THEM WHAT JACKASSES THEY WERE, THEY'D GIVE HIM STATIC.
NOBODY UNDERSTANDS LOGIC ANYMORE.

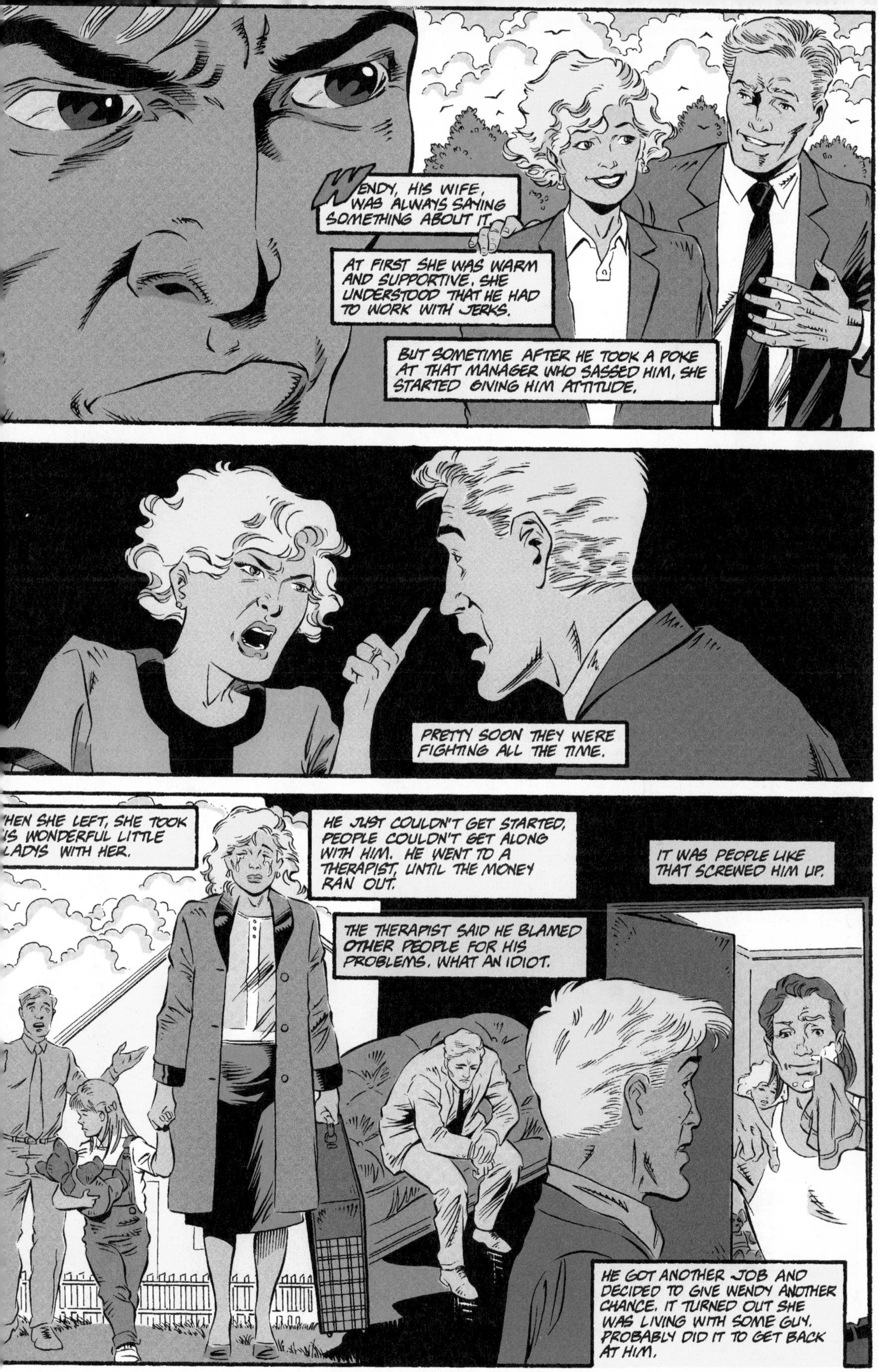
WENDY, HIS WIFE, WAS ALWAYS SAYING SOMETHING ABOUT IT.
AT FIRST SHE WAS WARM AND SUPPORTIVE. SHE UNDERSTOOD THAT HE HAD TO WORK WITH JERKS.
BUT SOMETIME AFTER HE TOOK A POKE AT THAT MANAGER WHO SASSED HIM, SHE STARTED GIVING HIM ATTITUDE.
PRETTY SOON THEY WERE FIGHTING ALL THE TIME.
HEN SHE LEFT, SHE TOOK IS WONDERFUL LITTLE LADYS WITH HER.
HE JUST COULDN'T GET STARTED. PEOPLE COULDN'T GET ALONG WITH HIM. HE WENT TO A THERAPIST, UNTIL THE MONEY RAN OUT.
THE THERAPIST SAID HE BLAMED OTHER PEOPLE FOR HIS PROBLEMS. WHAT AN IDIOT.
IT WAS PEOPLE LIKE THAT SCREWED HIM UP.
HE GOT ANOTHER JOB AND DECIDED TO GIVE WENDY ANOTHER CHANCE. IT TURNED OUT SHE WAS LIVING WITH SOME GUY. PROBABLY DID IT TO GET BACK AT HIM.

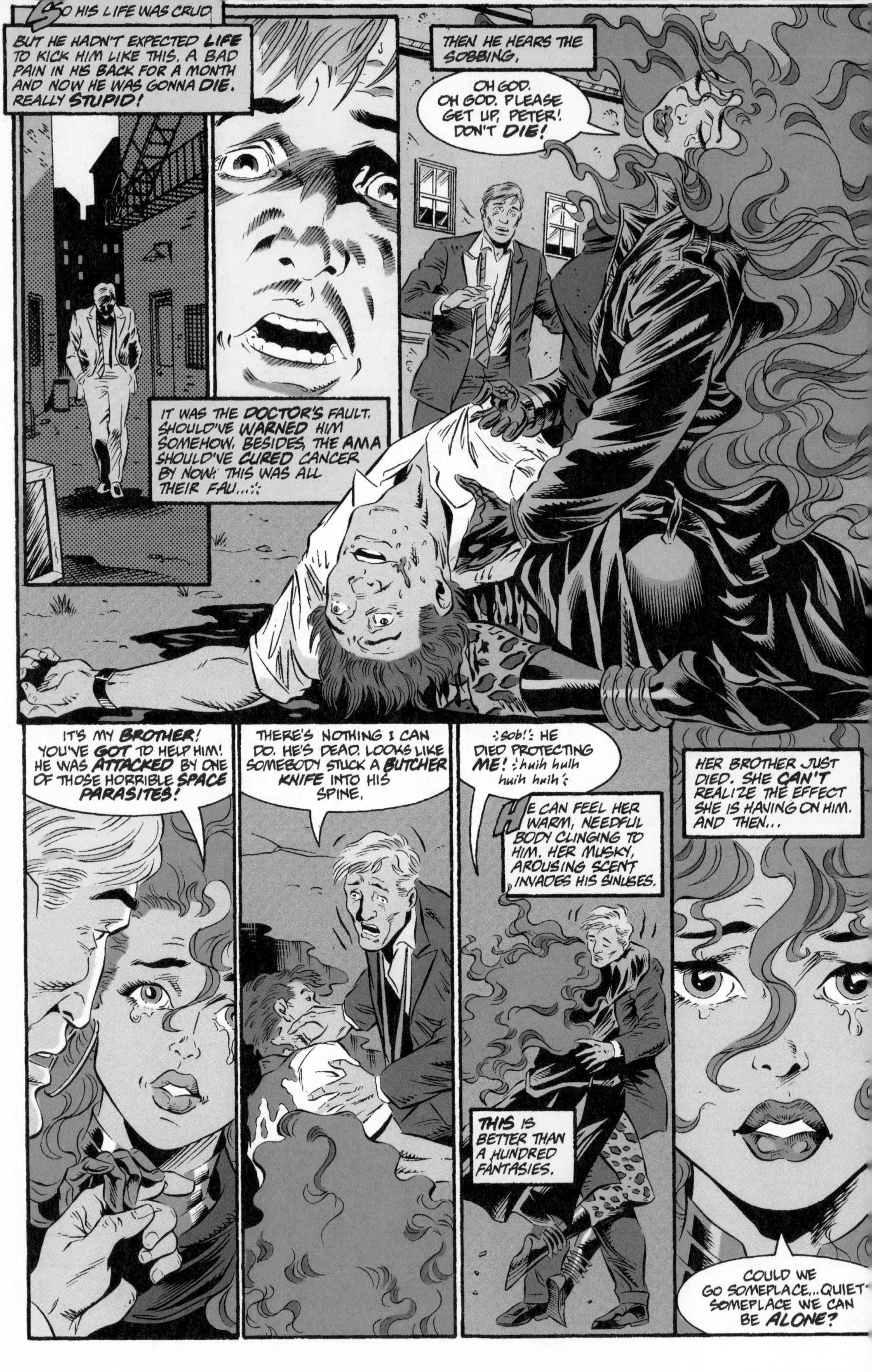
SO HIS LIFE WAS CRUD.
BUT HE HADN'T EXPECTED LIFE TO KICK HIM LIKE THIS. A BAD PAIN IN HIS BACK FOR A MONTH AND NOW HE WAS GONNA DIE. REALLY STUPID!
IT WAS THE DOCTOR'S FAULT. SHOULD'VE WARNED HIM SOMEHOW. BESIDES, THE AMA SHOULD'VE CURED CANCER BY NOW. THIS WAS ALL THEIR FAU...
THEN HE HEARS THE SOBBING.
OH GOD. OH GOD. PLEASE GET UP, PETER! DON'T DIE!
IT'S MY BROTHER! YOU'VE GOT TO HELP HIM! HE WAS ATTACKED BY ONE OF THOSE HORRIBLE SPACE PARASITES!
THERE'S NOTHING I CAN DO. HE'S DEAD. LOOKS LIKE SOMEBODY STUCK A BUTCHER KNIFE INTO HIS SPINE.
:sob!: HE DIED PROTECTING ME! :huih huih huih huih:
HE CAN FEEL HER WARM, NEEDFUL BODY CLINGING TO HIM. HER MUSKY, AROUSING SCENT INVADES HIS SINUSES.
THIS IS BETTER THAN A HUNDRED FANTASIES.
HER BROTHER JUST DIED. SHE CAN'T REALIZE THE EFFECT SHE IS HAVING ON HIM. AND THEN...
COULD WE GO SOMEPLACE... QUIET. SOMEPLACE WE CAN BE ALONE?

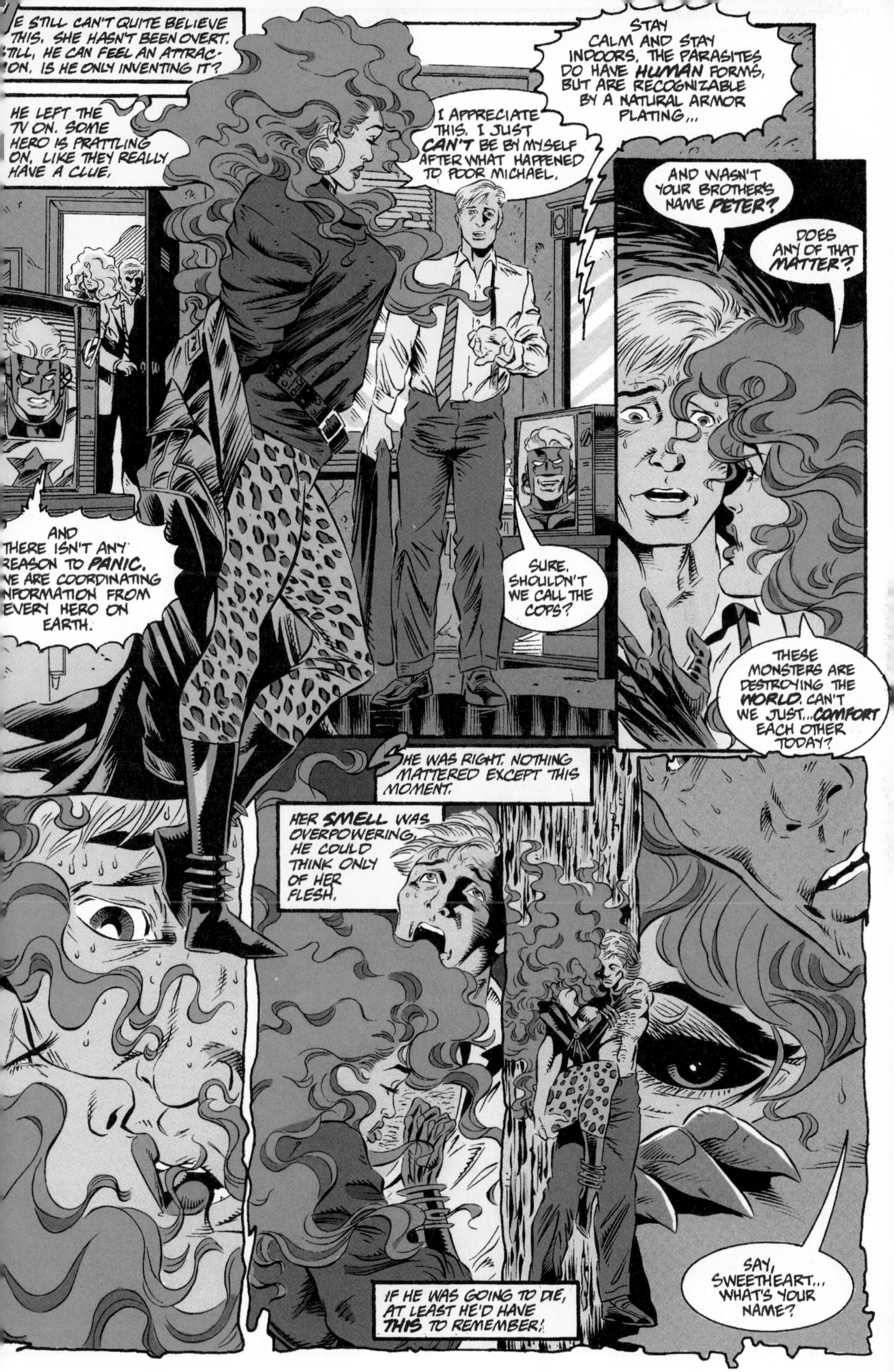

E STILL CAN'T QUITE BELIEVE THIS. SHE HASN'T BEEN OVERT. TILL, HE CAN FEEL AN ATTRAC- ION. IS HE ONLY INVENTING IT?
HE LEFT THE TV ON. SOME HERO IS PRATTLING ON, LIKE THEY REALLY HAVE A CLUE.
STAY CALM AND STAY INDOORS. THE PARASITES DO HAVE HUMAN FORMS, BUT ARE RECOGNIZABLE BY A NATURAL ARMOR PLATING...
I APPRECIATE THIS. I JUST CAN'T BE BY MYSELF AFTER WHAT HAPPENED TO POOR MICHAEL.
AND THERE ISN'T ANY REASON TO PANIC. VE ARE COORDINATING NFORMATION FROM EVERY HERO ON EARTH.
SURE. SHOULDN'T WE CALL THE COPS?
AND WASN'T YOUR BROTHER'S NAME PETER?
DOES ANY OF THAT MATTER?
THESE MONSTERS ARE DESTROYING THE WORLD. CAN'T WE JUST...COMFORT EACH OTHER TODAY?
SHE WAS RIGHT. NOTHING MATTERED EXCEPT THIS MOMENT.
HER SMELL WAS OVERPOWERING. HE COULD THINK ONLY OF HER FLESH.
IF HE WAS GOING TO DIE, AT LEAST HE'D HAVE THIS TO REMEMBER!
SAY, SWEETHEART... WHAT'S YOUR NAME?

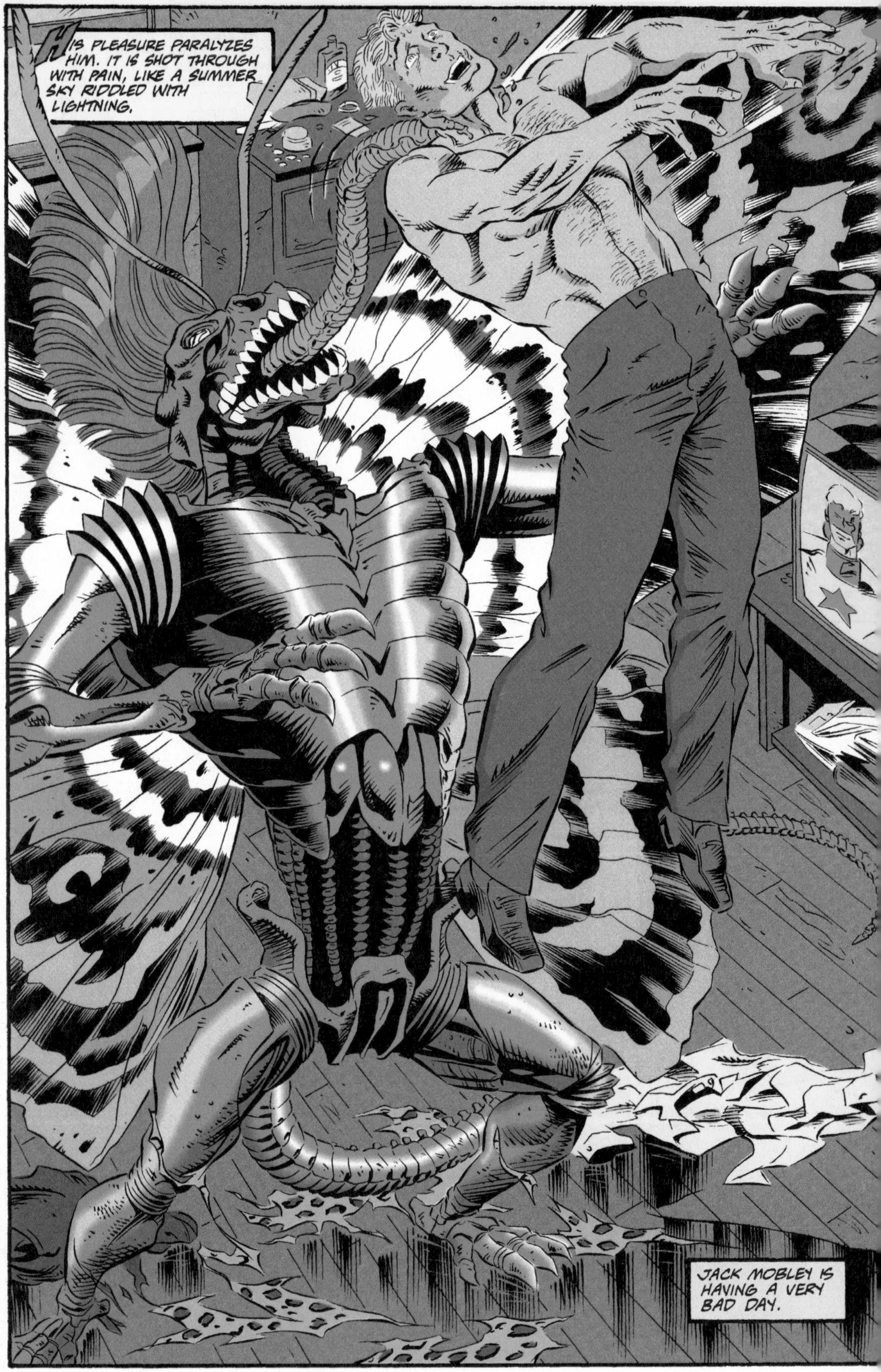
HIS PLEASURE PARALYZES HIM. IT IS SHOT THROUGH WITH PAIN, LIKE A SUMMER SKY RIDDLED WITH LIGHTNING.
JACK MOBLEY IS HAVING A VERY BAD DAY.

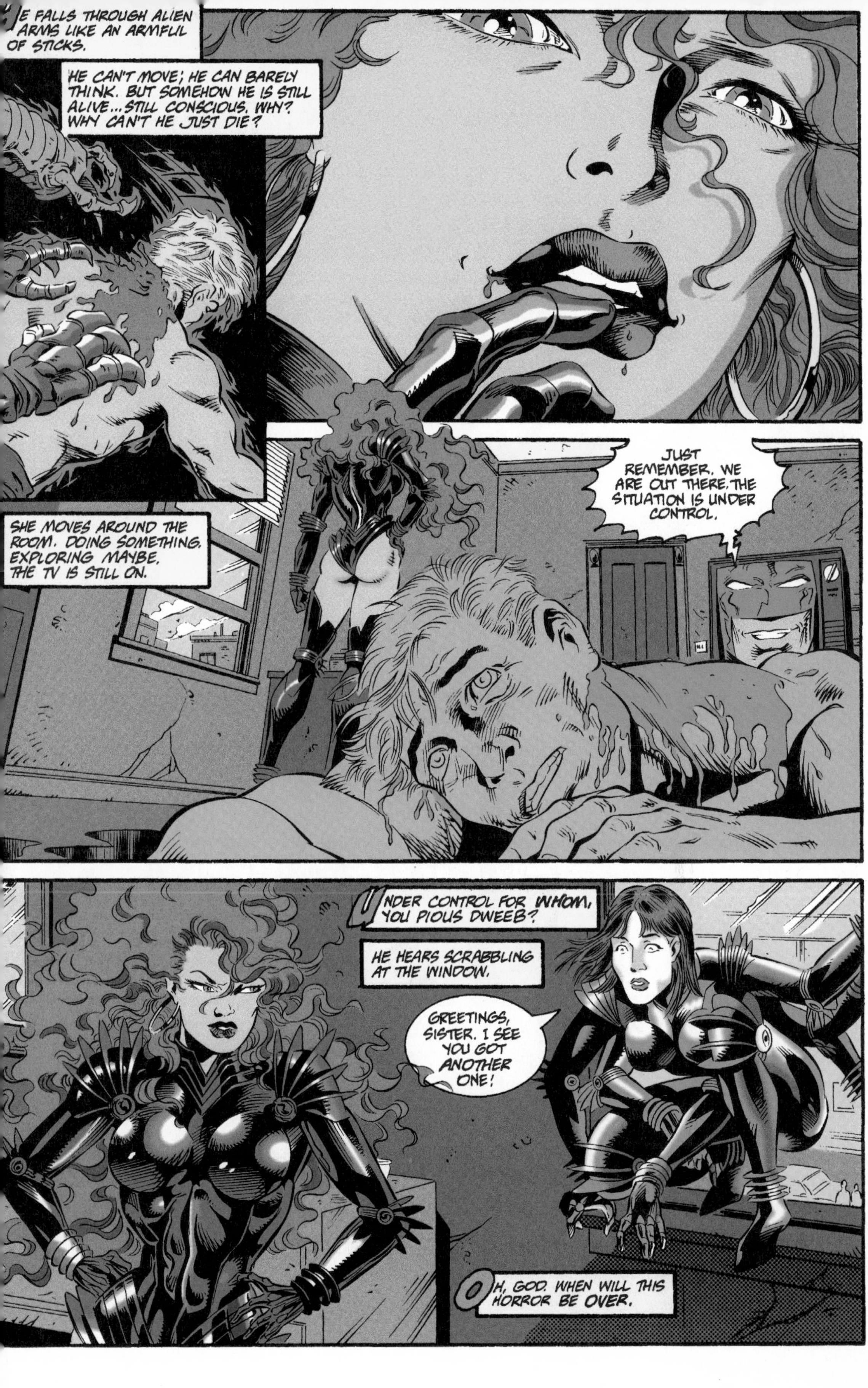
HE FALLS THROUGH ALIEN ARMS LIKE AN ARMFUL OF STICKS.
HE CAN'T MOVE; HE CAN BARELY THINK. BUT SOMEHOW HE IS STILL ALIVE... STILL CONSCIOUS. WHY? WHY CAN'T HE JUST DIE?
SHE MOVES AROUND THE ROOM. DOING SOMETHING. EXPLORING MAYBE. THE TV IS STILL ON.
JUST REMEMBER. WE ARE OUT THERE. THE SITUATION IS UNDER CONTROL.
UNDER CONTROL FOR WHOM, YOU PIOUS DWEEB?
HE HEARS SCRABBLING AT THE WINDOW.
GREETINGS, SISTER. I SEE YOU GOT ANOTHER ONE!
OH, GOD. WHEN WILL THIS HORROR BE OVER.

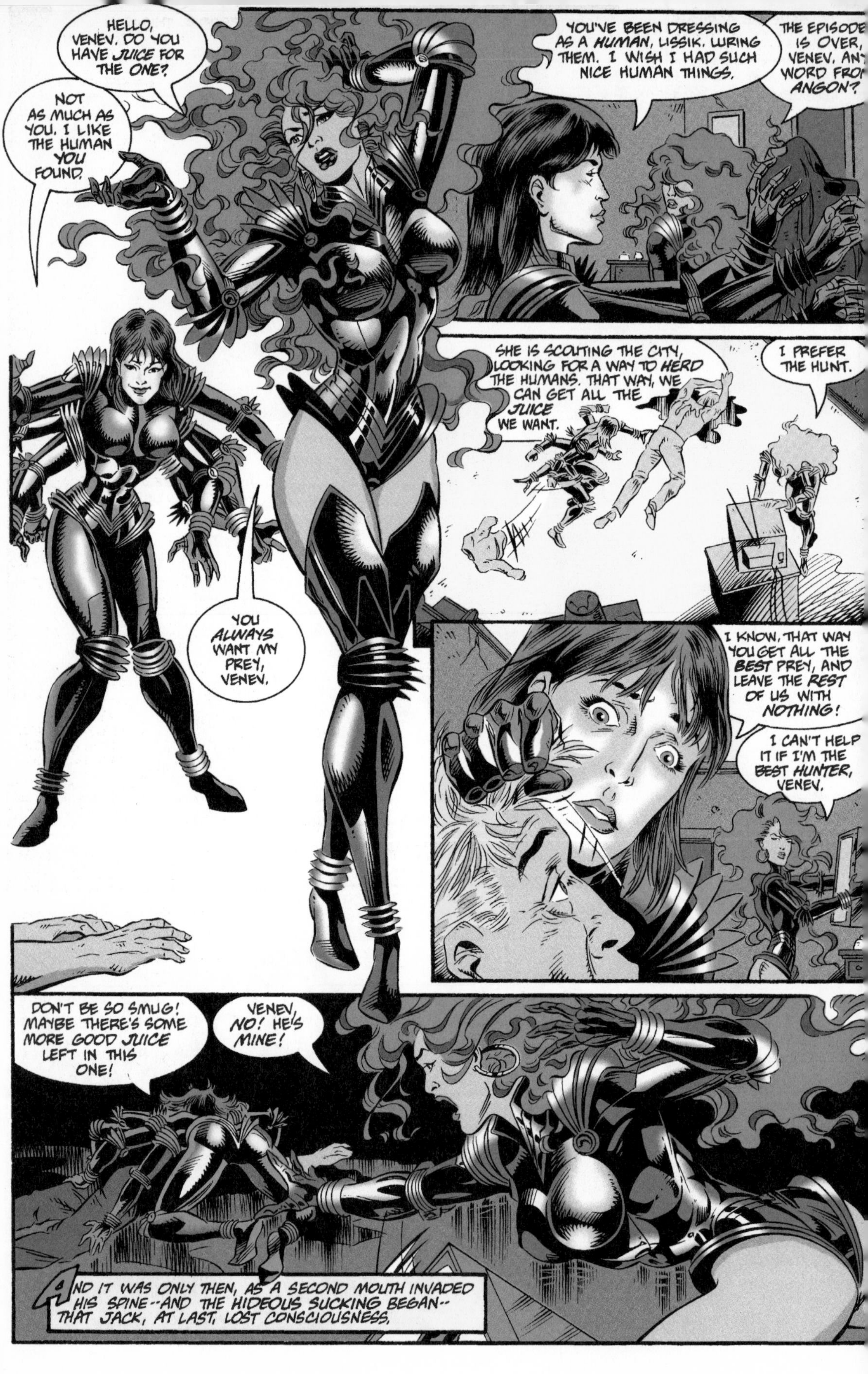
HELLO, VENEV. DO YOU HAVE JUICE FOR THE ONE?
NOT AS MUCH AS YOU. I LIKE THE HUMAN YOU FOUND.
YOU'VE BEEN DRESSING AS A HUMAN, LISSIK. LURING THEM. I WISH I HAD SUCH NICE HUMAN THINGS.
THE EPISODE IS OVER, VENEV. ANY WORD FROM ANGON?
SHE IS SCOUTING THE CITY, LOOKING FOR A WAY TO HERD THE HUMANS. THAT WAY, WE CAN GET ALL THE JUICE WE WANT.
I PREFER THE HUNT.
YOU ALWAYS WANT MY PREY, VENEV.
I KNOW. THAT WAY YOU GET ALL THE BEST PREY, AND LEAVE THE REST OF US WITH NOTHING!
I CAN'T HELP IT IF I'M THE BEST HUNTER, VENEV.
DON'T BE SO SMUG! MAYBE THERE'S SOME MORE GOOD JUICE LEFT IN THIS ONE!
VENEV, NO! HE'S MINE!
AND IT WAS ONLY THEN, AS A SECOND MOUTH INVADED HIS SPINE--AND THE HIDEOUS SUCKING BEGAN--THAT JACK, AT LAST, LOST CONSCIOUSNESS.

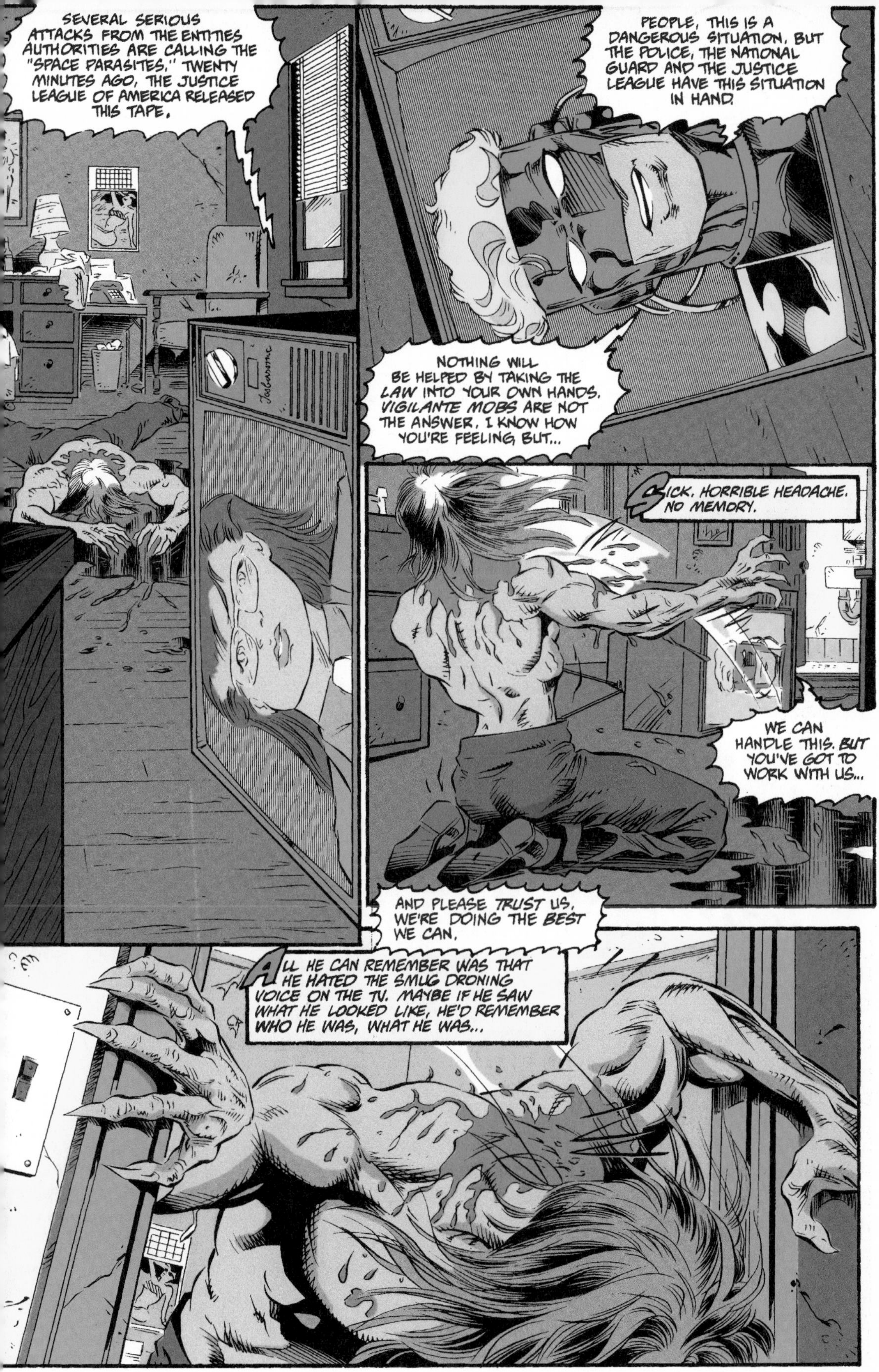
SEVERAL SERIOUS ATTACKS FROM THE ENTITIES AUTHORITIES ARE CALLING THE "SPACE PARASITES." TWENTY MINUTES AGO, THE JUSTICE LEAGUE OF AMERICA RELEASED THIS TAPE.
PEOPLE, THIS IS A DANGEROUS SITUATION, BUT THE POLICE, THE NATIONAL GUARD AND THE JUSTICE LEAGUE HAVE THIS SITUATION IN HAND.
NOTHING WILL BE HELPED BY TAKING THE LAW INTO YOUR OWN HANDS. VIGILANTE MOBS ARE NOT THE ANSWER. I KNOW HOW YOU'RE FEELING, BUT...
SICK. HORRIBLE HEADACHE. NO MEMORY.
WE CAN HANDLE THIS. BUT YOU'VE GOT TO WORK WITH US...
AND PLEASE TRUST US. WE'RE DOING THE BEST WE CAN.
ALL HE CAN REMEMBER WAS THAT HE HATED THE SMUG DRONING VOICE ON THE TV. MAYBE IF HE SAW WHAT HE LOOKED LIKE, HE'D REMEMBER WHO HE WAS, WHAT HE WAS...

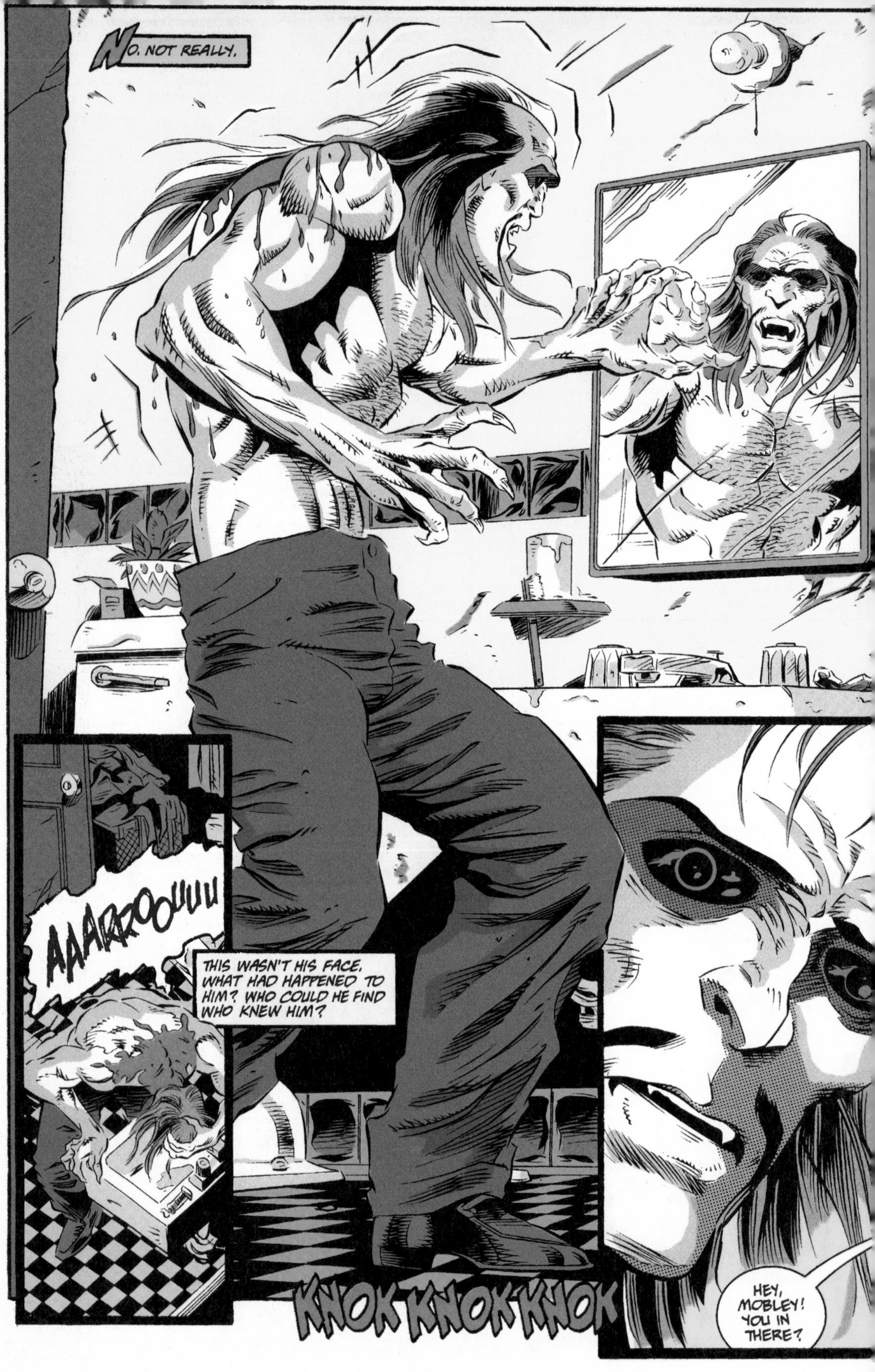
NO. NOT REALLY.
AAARROOUUU
THIS WASN'T HIS FACE. WHAT HAD HAPPENED TO HIM? WHO COULD HE FIND WHO KNEW HIM?
KNOK KNOK KNOK
HEY, MOBLEY! YOU IN THERE?

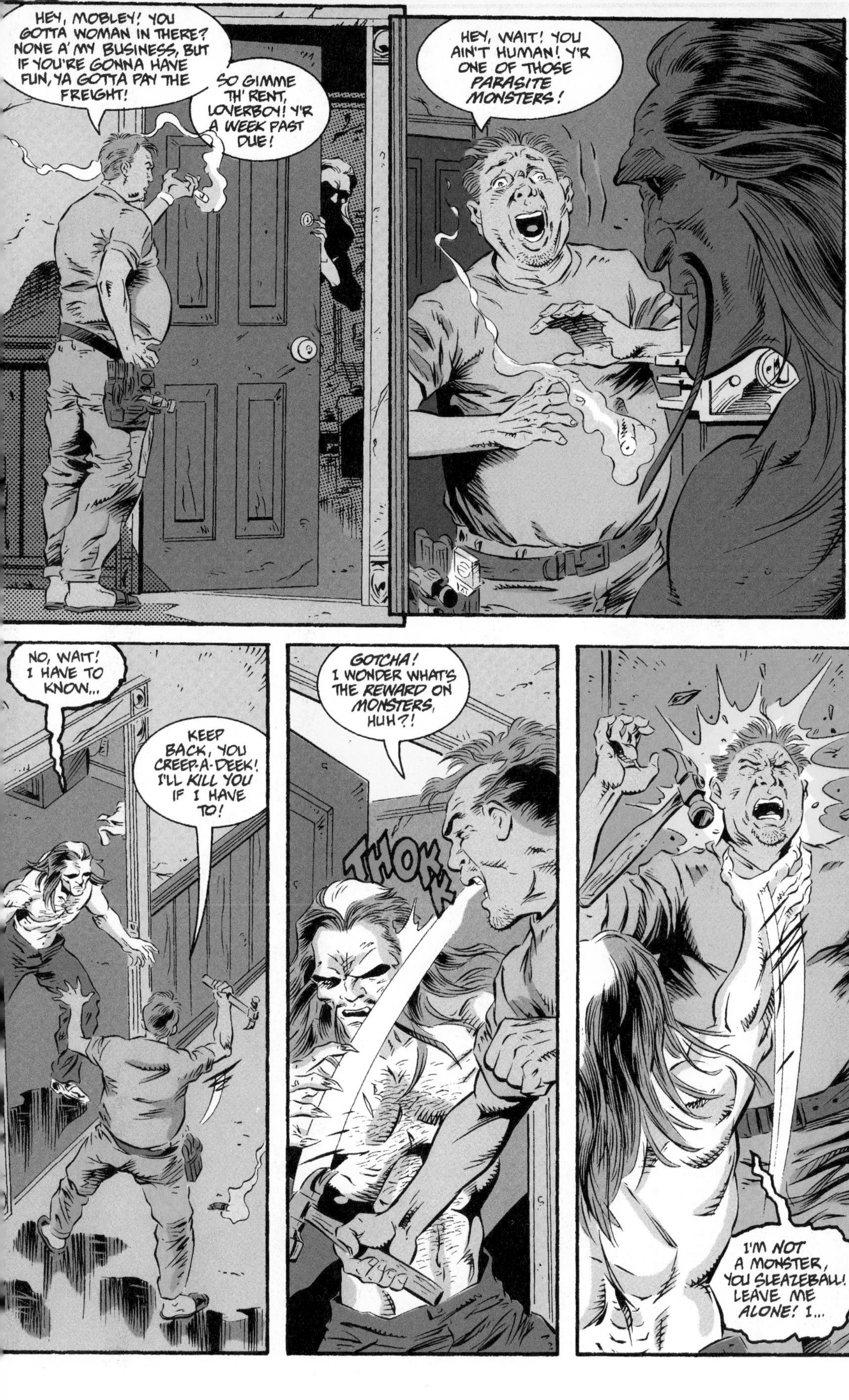
HEY, MOBLEY! YOU GOTTA WOMAN IN THERE? NONE A' MY BUSINESS, BUT IF YOU'RE GONNA HAVE FUN, YA GOTTA PAY THE FREIGHT!
SO GIMME TH' RENT, LOVERBOY! Y'R A WEEK PAST DUE!
HEY, WAIT! YOU AIN'T HUMAN! Y'R ONE OF THOSE PARASITE MONSTERS!
NO, WAIT! I HAVE TO KNOW...
KEEP BACK, YOU CREEP-A-DEEK! I'LL KILL YOU IF I HAVE TO!
GOTCHA! I WONDER WHAT'S THE REWARD ON MONSTERS, HUH?!
THOKK
I'M NOT A MONSTER, YOU SLEAZEBALL! LEAVE ME ALONE! I...

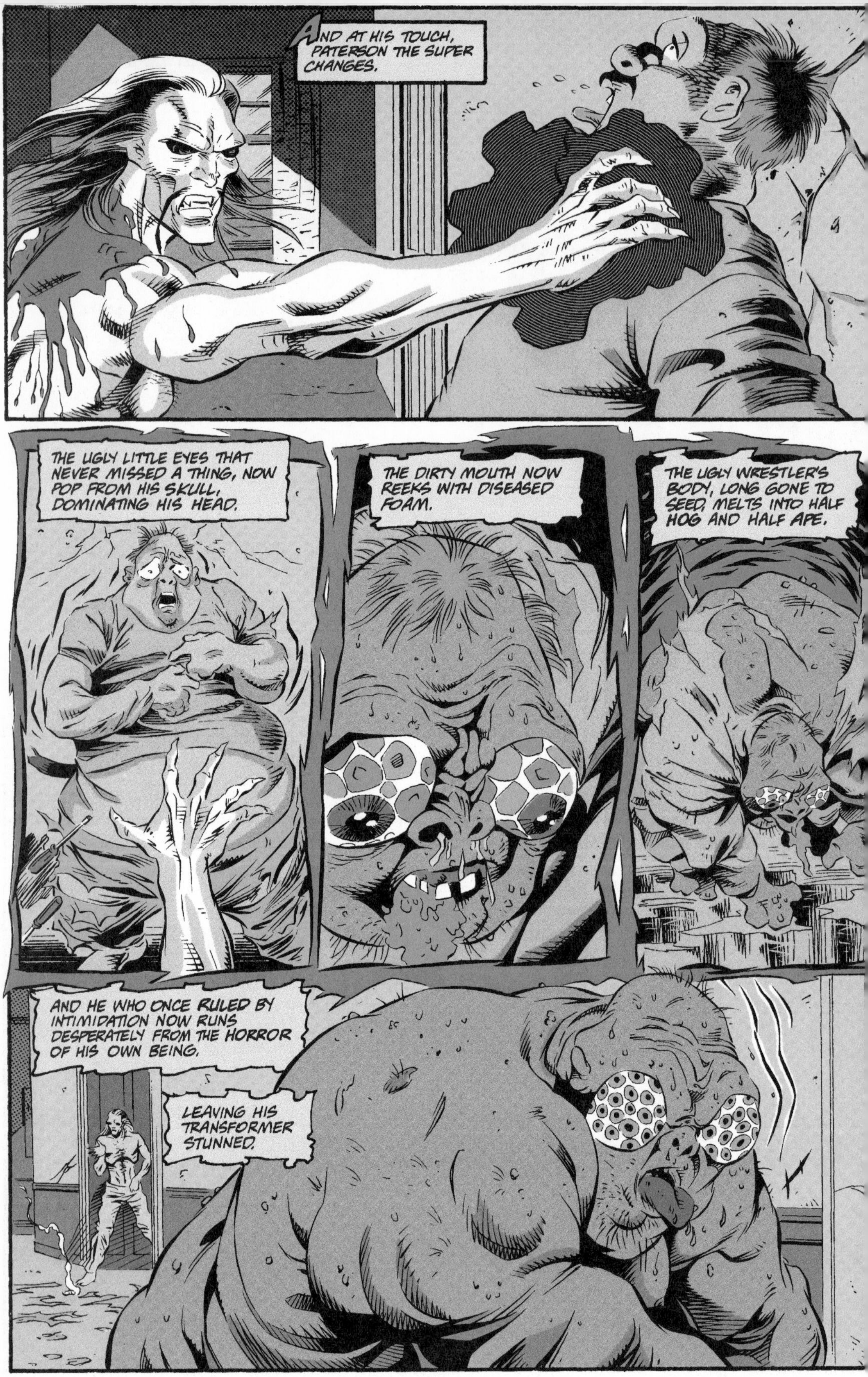
AND AT HIS TOUCH, PATERSON THE SUPER CHANGES.
THE UGLY LITTLE EYES THAT NEVER MISSED A THING, NOW POP FROM HIS SKULL, DOMINATING HIS HEAD.
THE DIRTY MOUTH NOW REEKS WITH DISEASED FOAM.
THE UGLY WRESTLER'S BODY, LONG GONE TO SEED, MELTS INTO HALF HOG AND HALF APE.
AND HE WHO ONCE RULED BY INTIMIDATION NOW RUNS DESPERATELY FROM THE HORROR OF HIS OWN BEING.
LEAVING HIS TRANSFORMER STUNNED.

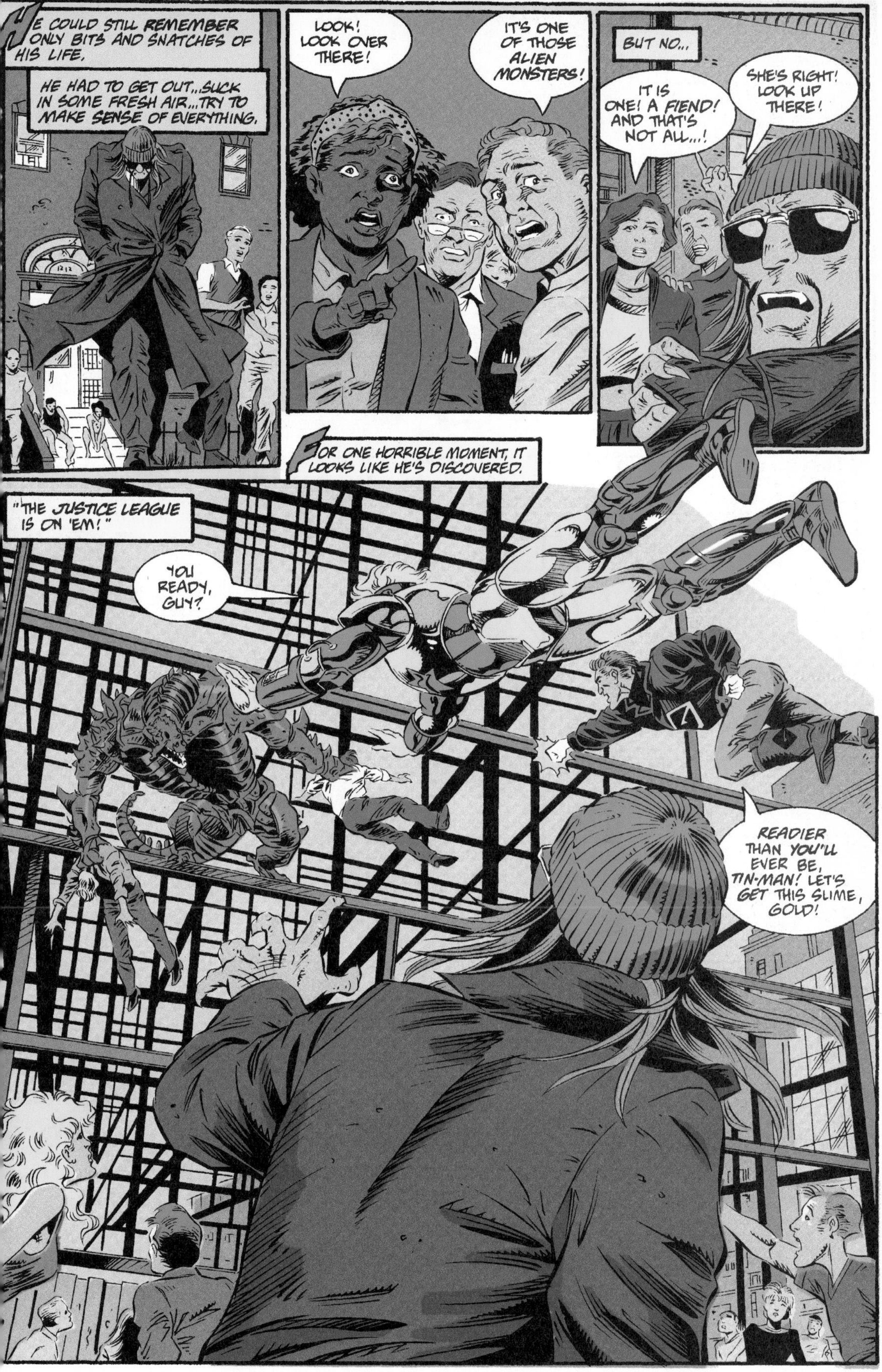
HE COULD STILL REMEMBER ONLY BITS AND SNATCHES OF HIS LIFE.
HE HAD TO GET OUT...SUCK IN SOME FRESH AIR...TRY TO MAKE SENSE OF EVERYTHING.
LOOK! LOOK OVER THERE!
IT'S ONE OF THOSE ALIEN MONSTERS!
BUT NO...
IT IS ONE! A FIEND! AND THAT'S NOT ALL...!
SHE'S RIGHT! LOOK UP THERE!
FOR ONE HORRIBLE MOMENT, IT LOOKS LIKE HE'S DISCOVERED.
"THE JUSTICE LEAGUE IS ON 'EM!"
YOU READY, GUY?
READIER THAN YOU'LL EVER BE, TIN-MAN! LET'S GET THIS SLIME, GOLD!

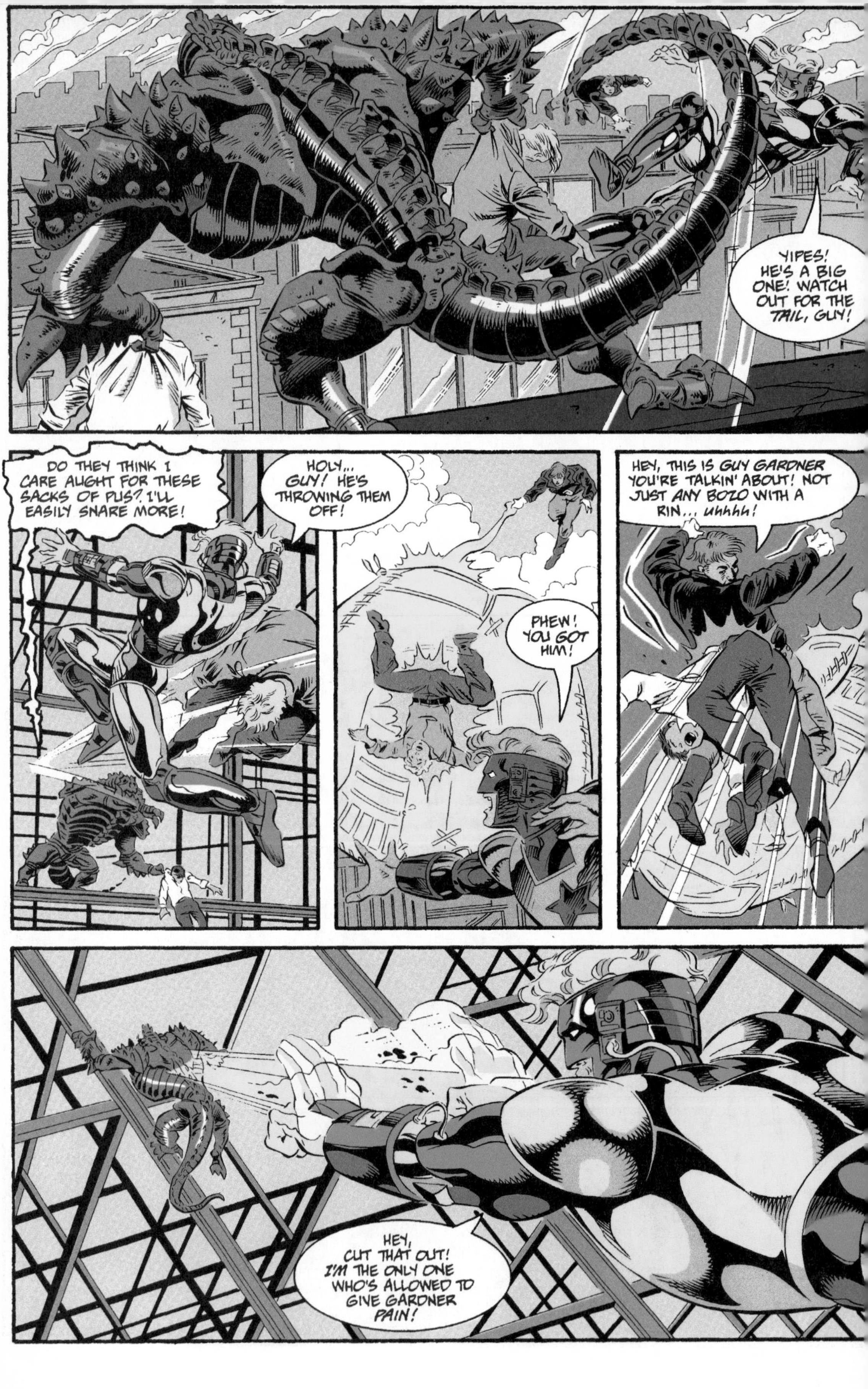
YIPES! HE'S A BIG ONE! WATCH OUT FOR THE TAIL, GUY!
DO THEY THINK I CARE AUGHT FOR THESE SACKS OF PUS? I'LL EASILY SNARE MORE!
HOLY... GUY! HE'S THROWING THEM OFF!
PHEW! YOU GOT HIM!
HEY, THIS IS GUY GARDNER YOU'RE TALKIN' ABOUT! NOT JUST ANY BOZO WITH A RIN... uhhhh!
HEY, CUT THAT OUT! I'M THE ONLY ONE WHO'S ALLOWED TO GIVE GARDNER PAIN!

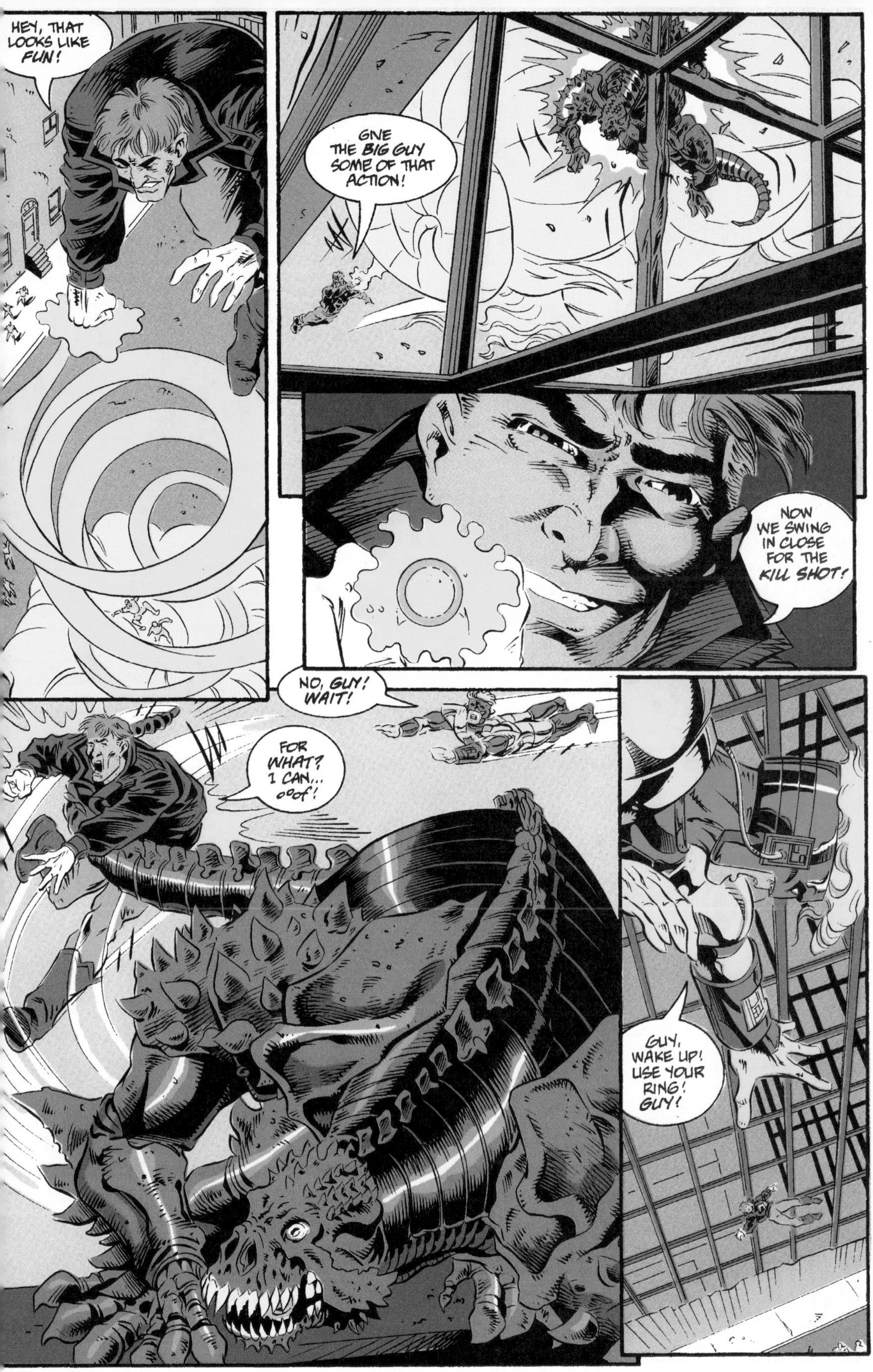
HEY, THAT LOOKS LIKE FUN!
GIVE THE BIG GUY SOME OF THAT ACTION!
NOW WE SWING IN CLOSE FOR THE KILL SHOT!
NO, GUY! WAIT!
FOR WHAT? I CAN... oof!
GUY, WAKE UP! USE YOUR RING! GUY!

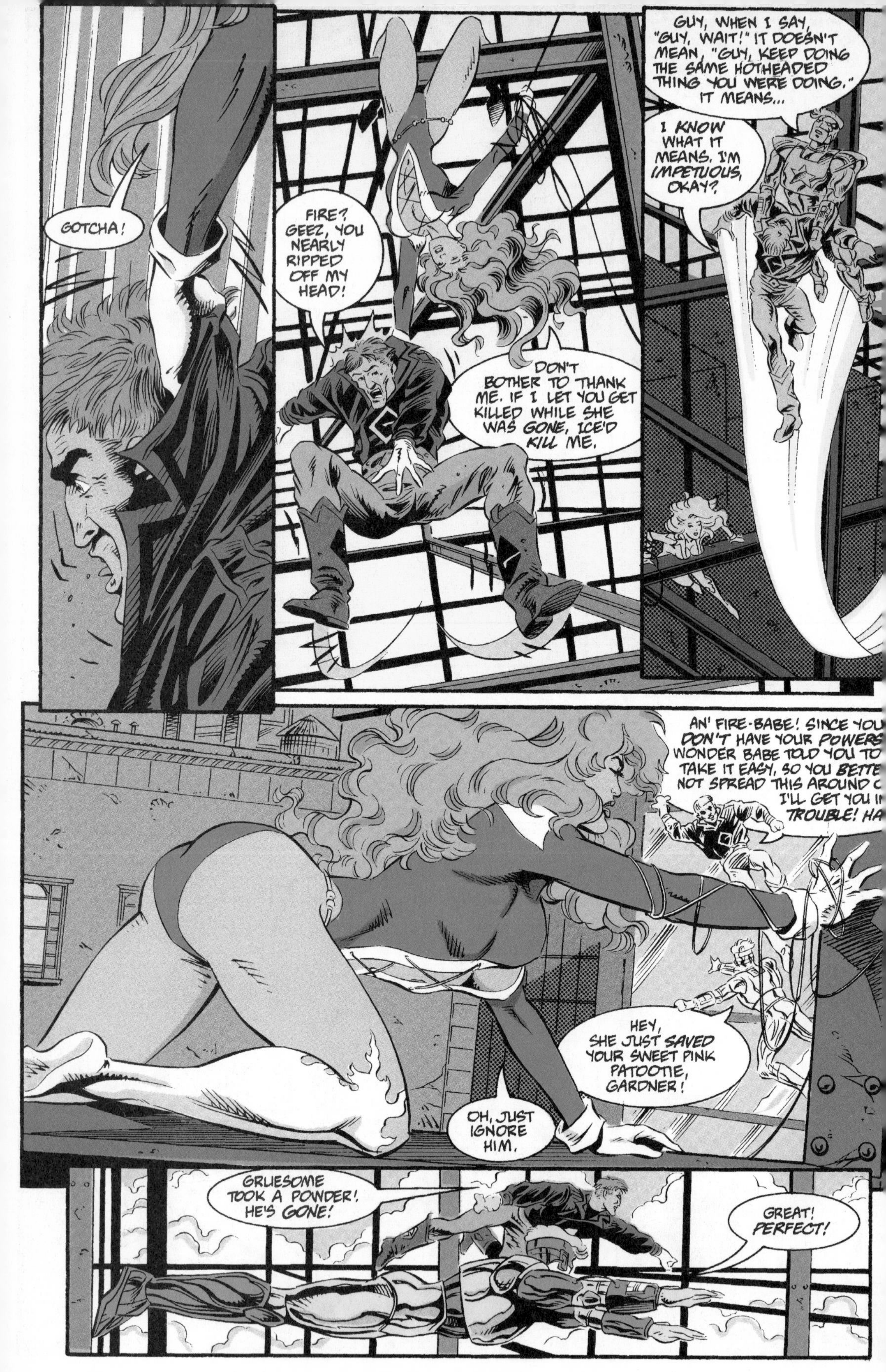
GOTCHA!
FIRE? GEEZ, YOU NEARLY RIPPED OFF MY HEAD!
DON'T BOTHER TO THANK ME. IF I LET YOU GET KILLED WHILE SHE WAS GONE, ICE'D KILL ME.
GUY, WHEN I SAY, "GUY, WAIT!" IT DOESN'T MEAN, "GUY, KEEP DOING THE SAME HOTHEADED THING YOU WERE DOING." IT MEANS...
I KNOW WHAT IT MEANS. I'M IMPETUOUS, OKAY?
AN' FIRE-BABE! SINCE YOU DON'T HAVE YOUR POWERS WONDER BABE TOLD YOU TO TAKE IT EASY, SO YOU BETTE NOT SPREAD THIS AROUND O I'LL GET YOU IN TROUBLE! HA
HEY, SHE JUST SAVED YOUR SWEET PINK PATOOTIE, GARDNER!
OH, JUST IGNORE HIM.
GRUESOME TOOK A POWDER! HE'S GONE!
GREAT! PERFECT!

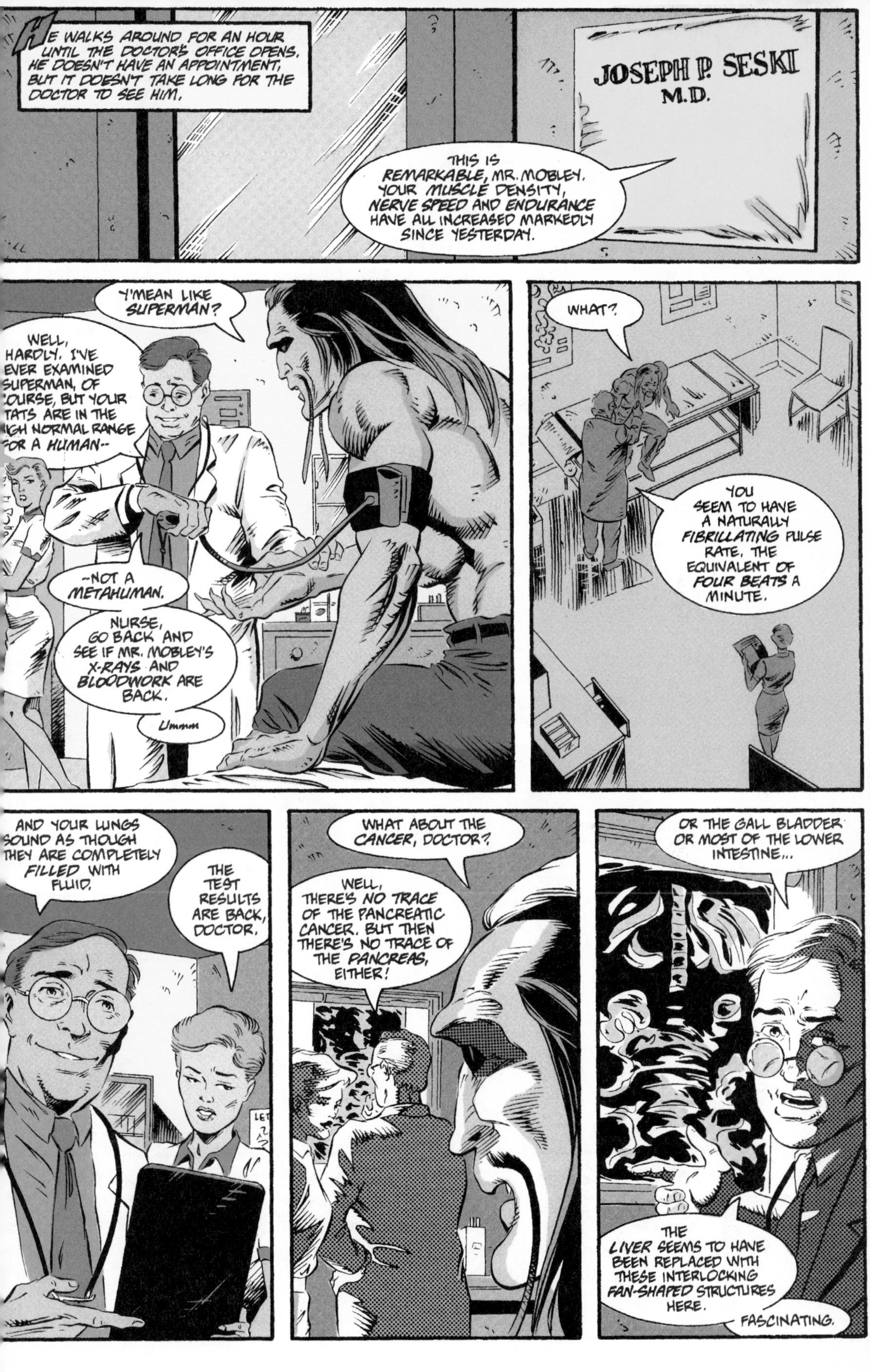
HE WALKS AROUND FOR AN HOUR UNTIL THE DOCTOR'S OFFICE OPENS. HE DOESN'T HAVE AN APPOINTMENT, BUT IT DOESN'T TAKE LONG FOR THE DOCTOR TO SEE HIM.
JOSEPH P. SESKI M.D.
THIS IS REMARKABLE, MR. MOBLEY. YOUR MUSCLE DENSITY, NERVE SPEED AND ENDURANCE HAVE ALL INCREASED MARKEDLY SINCE YESTERDAY.
Y'MEAN LIKE SUPERMAN?
WELL, HARDLY. I'VE EVER EXAMINED SUPERMAN, OF COURSE, BUT YOUR TATS ARE IN THE IGH NORMAL RANGE FOR A HUMAN--
--NOT A METAHUMAN.
NURSE, GO BACK AND SEE IF MR. MOBLEY'S X-RAYS AND BLOODWORK ARE BACK.
Ummm
WHAT?
YOU SEEM TO HAVE A NATURALLY FIBRILLATING PULSE RATE. THE EQUIVALENT OF FOUR BEATS A MINUTE.
AND YOUR LUNGS SOUND AS THOUGH THEY ARE COMPLETELY FILLED WITH FLUID.
THE TEST RESULTS ARE BACK, DOCTOR.
WHAT ABOUT THE CANCER, DOCTOR?
WELL, THERE'S NO TRACE OF THE PANCREATIC CANCER. BUT THEN THERE'S NO TRACE OF THE PANCREAS, EITHER!
OR THE GALL BLADDER OR MOST OF THE LOWER INTESTINE...
THE LIVER SEEMS TO HAVE BEEN REPLACED WITH THESE INTERLOCKING FAN-SHAPED STRUCTURES HERE.
FASCINATING.

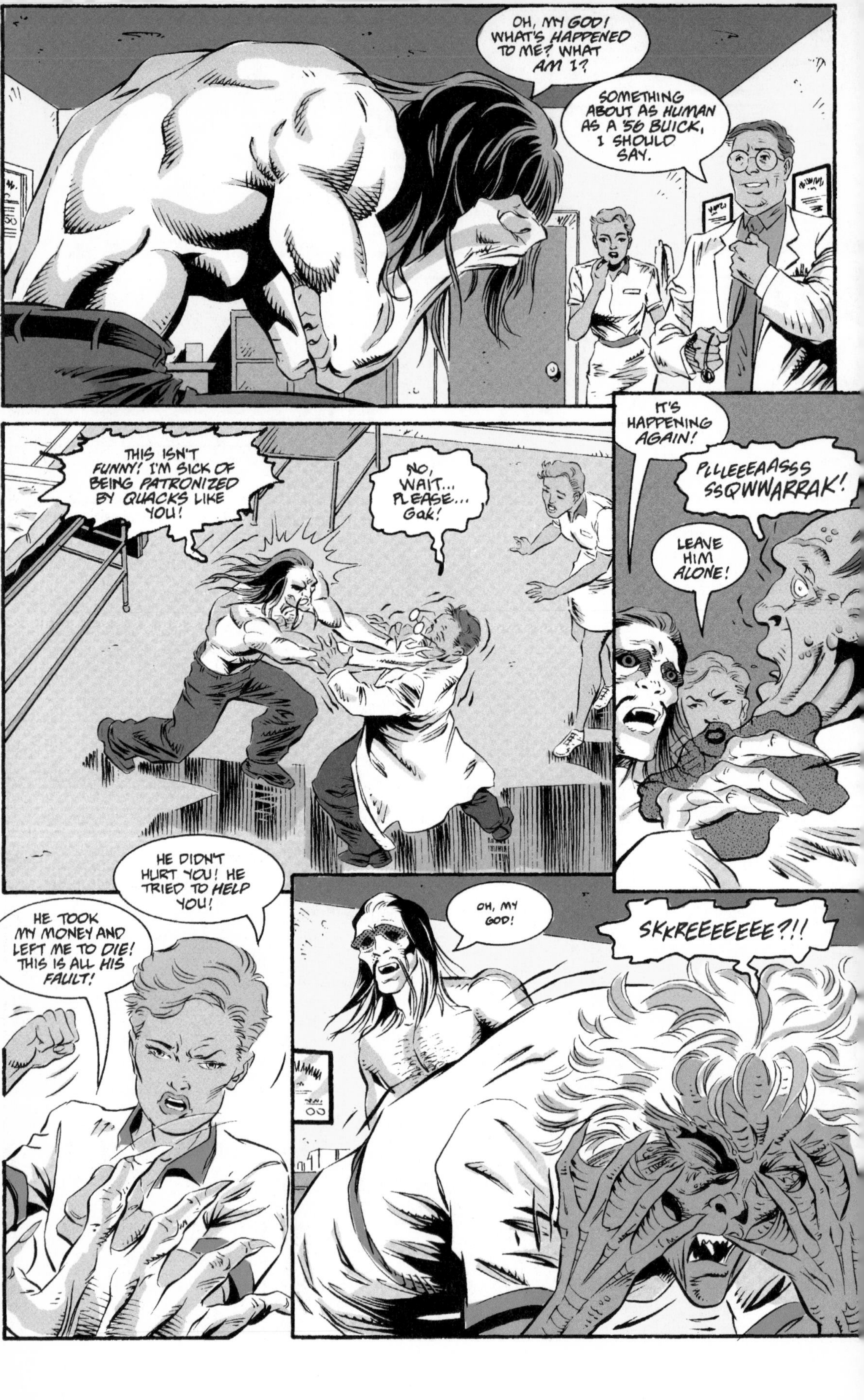
OH, MY GOD! WHAT'S HAPPENED TO ME? WHAT AM I?
SOMETHING ABOUT AS HUMAN AS A '56 BUICK, I SHOULD SAY.
THIS ISN'T FUNNY! I'M SICK OF BEING PATRONIZED BY QUACKS LIKE YOU!
NO, WAIT... PLEASE... Gak!
IT'S HAPPENING AGAIN!
PLLLEEEAASSS SSQWWARRAK!
LEAVE HIM ALONE!
HE DIDN'T HURT YOU! HE TRIED TO HELP YOU!
HE TOOK MY MONEY AND LEFT ME TO DIE! THIS IS ALL HIS FAULT!
OH, MY GOD!
SKKREEEEEEEE?!!

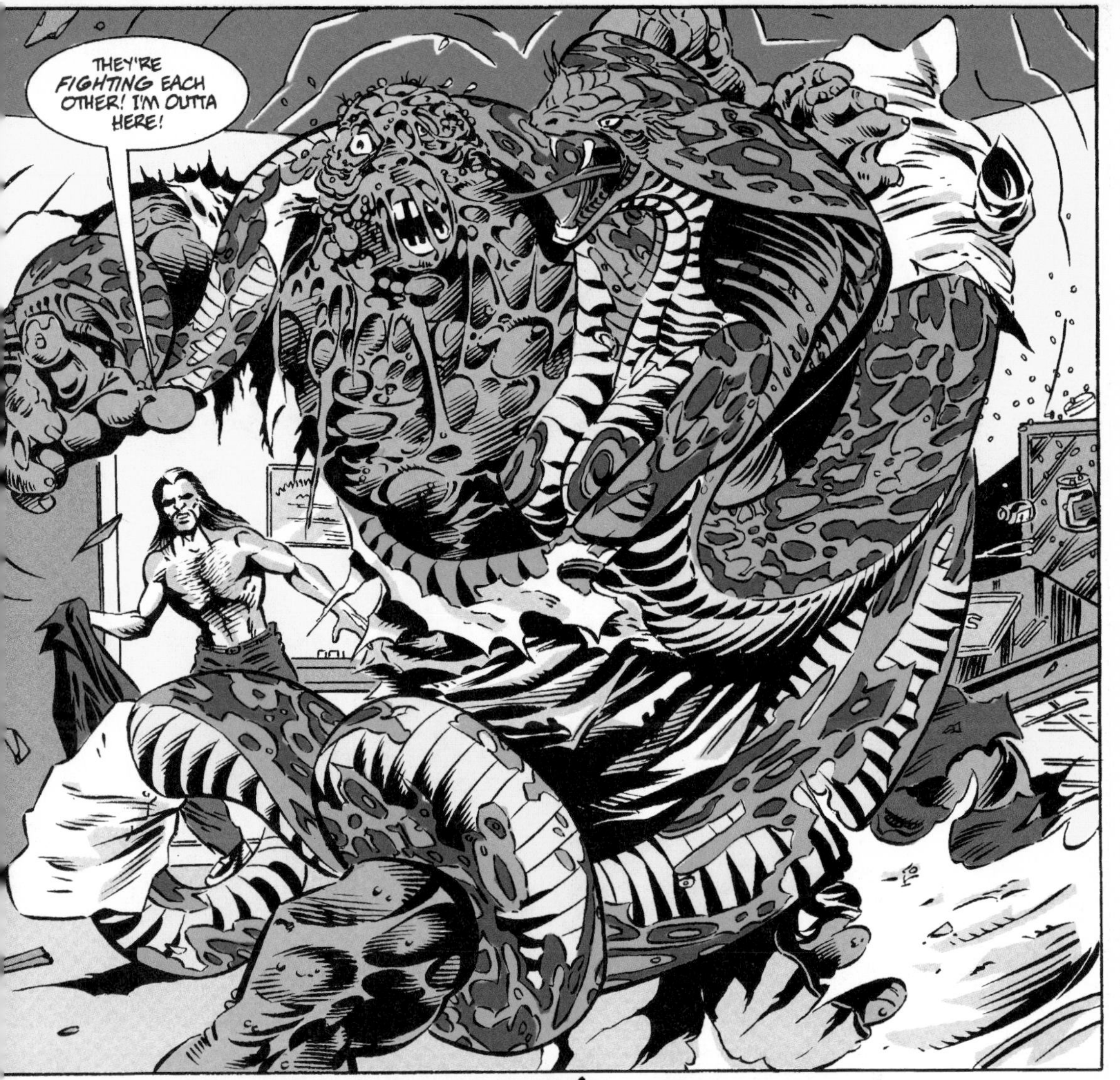
THEY'RE FIGHTING EACH OTHER! I'M OUTTA HERE!

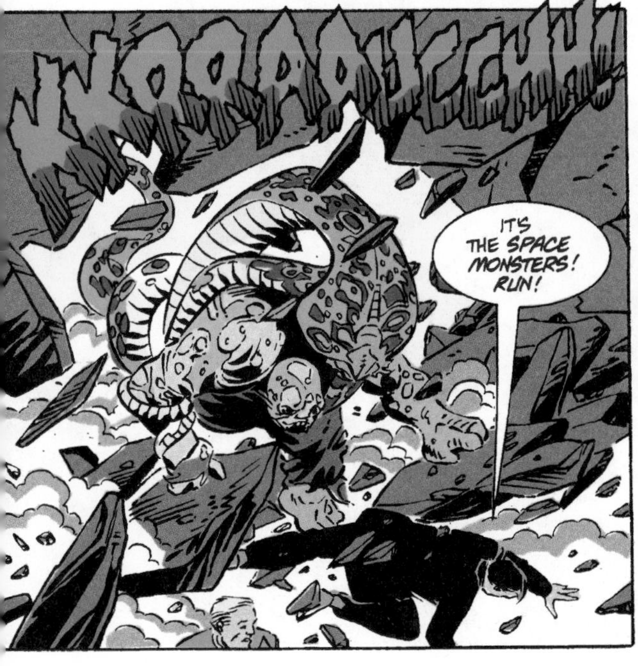
WOOOOUCCHH!
IT'S THE SPACE MONSTERS! RUN!

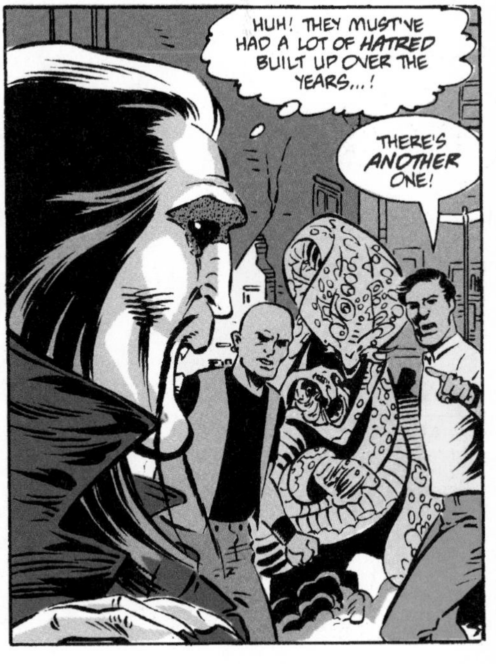
HUH! THEY MUST'VE HAD A LOT OF HATRED BUILT UP OVER THE YEARS...!
THERE'S ANOTHER ONE!

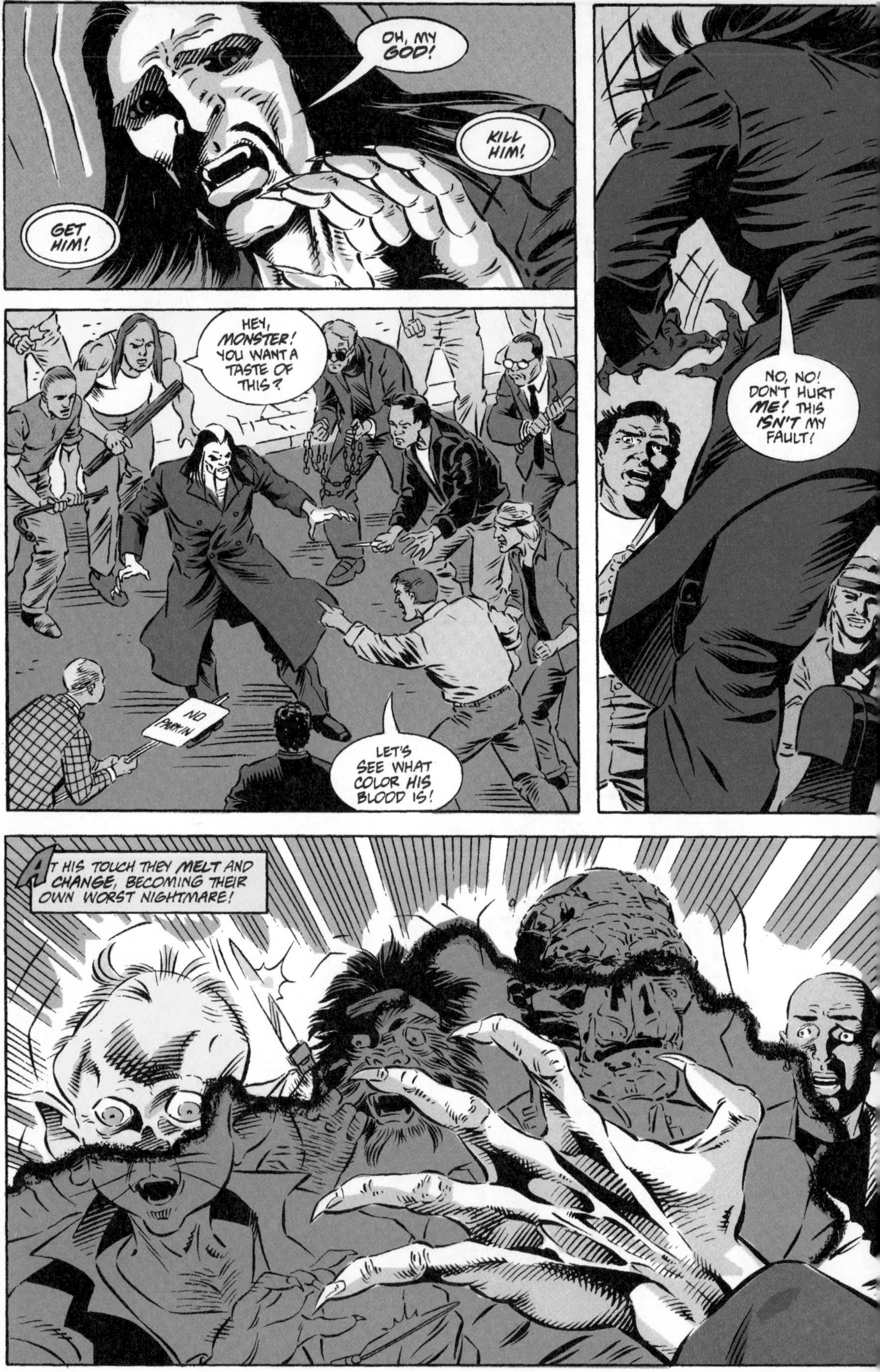
OH, MY GOD!
KILL HIM!
GET HIM!
HEY, MONSTER! YOU WANT A TASTE OF THIS?
NO PARKIN
LET'S SEE WHAT COLOR HIS BLOOD IS!
NO, NO! DON'T HURT ME! THIS ISN'T MY FAULT!
AT HIS TOUCH THEY MELT AND CHANGE, BECOMING THEIR OWN WORST NIGHTMARE!

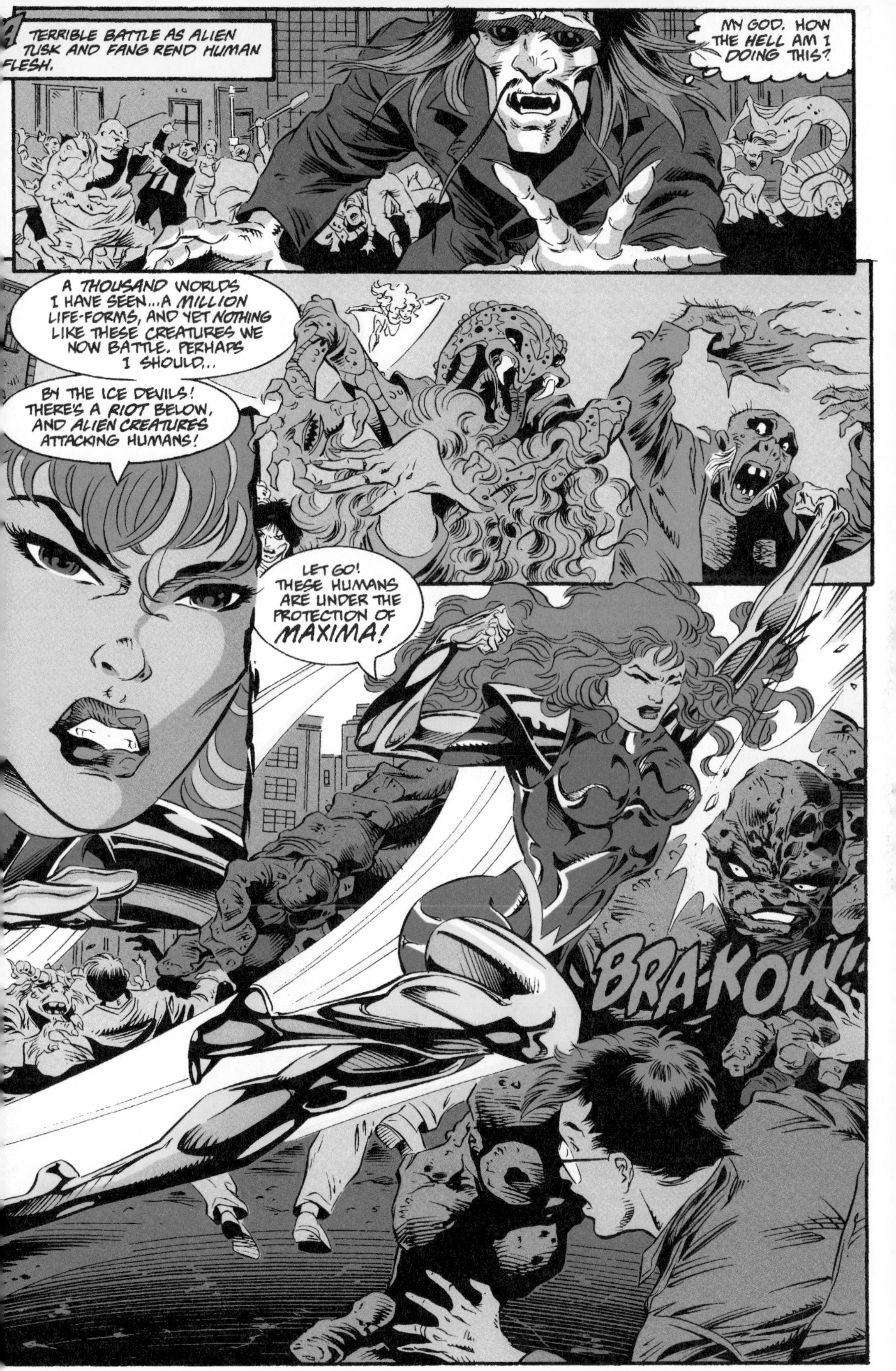
TERRIBLE BATTLE AS ALIEN TUSK AND FANG REND HUMAN FLESH.
MY GOD. HOW THE HELL AM I DOING THIS?
A THOUSAND WORLDS I HAVE SEEN... A MILLION LIFE-FORMS, AND YET NOTHING LIKE THESE CREATURES WE NOW BATTLE. PERHAPS I SHOULD...
BY THE ICE DEVILS! THERE'S A RIOT BELOW, AND ALIEN CREATURES ATTACKING HUMANS!
LET GO! THESE HUMANS ARE UNDER THE PROTECTION OF MAXIMA!
BRA-KOW!!

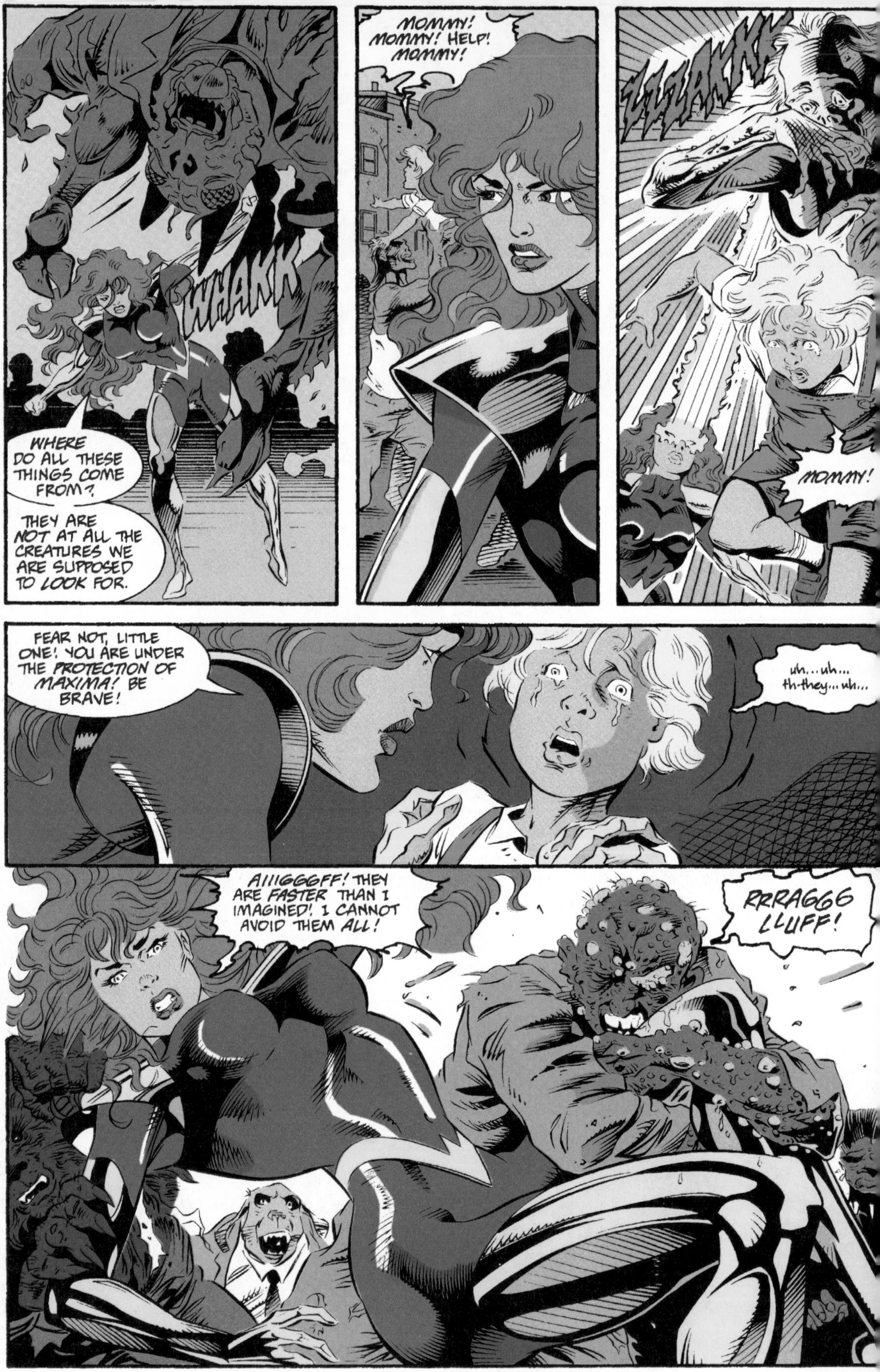
WHAKK
WHERE DO ALL THESE THINGS COME FROM?
THEY ARE NOT AT ALL THE CREATURES WE ARE SUPPOSED TO LOOK FOR.
MOMMY! MOMMY! HELP! MOMMY!
ZZZAKKK
MOMMY!
FEAR NOT, LITTLE ONE! YOU ARE UNDER THE PROTECTION OF MAXIMA! BE BRAVE!
uh... uh... th-they... uh...
AIIIGGGFF! THEY ARE FASTER THAN I IMAGINED! I CANNOT AVOID THEM ALL!
RRRAGGG LLUFF!

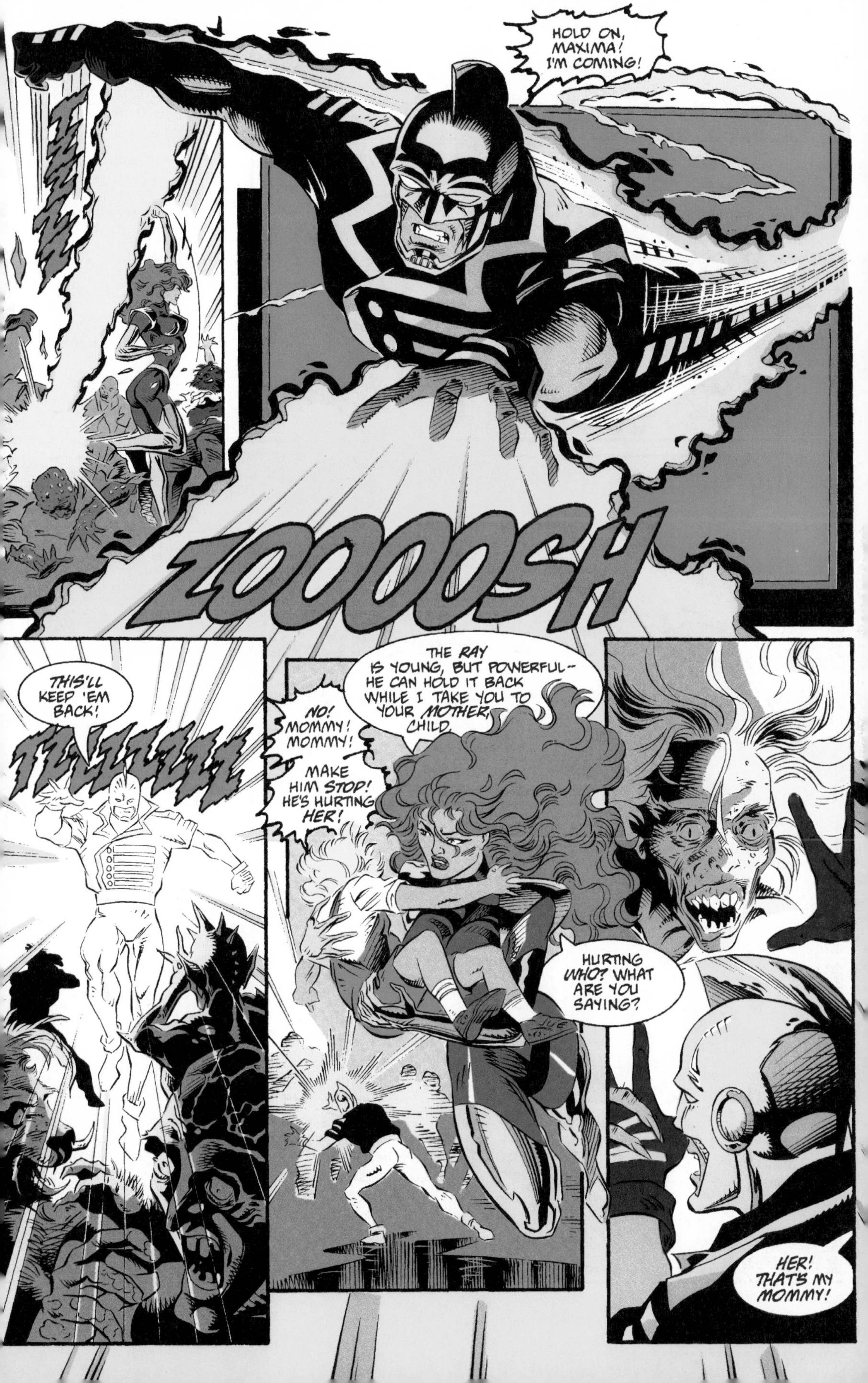
HOLD ON, MAXIMA! I'M COMING!
ZOOOOSH
THIS'LL KEEP 'EM BACK!
TZZZZZZZ
NO! MOMMY! MOMMY!
THE RAY IS YOUNG, BUT POWERFUL-- HE CAN HOLD IT BACK WHILE I TAKE YOU TO YOUR MOTHER, CHILD.
MAKE HIM STOP! HE'S HURTING HER!
HURTING WHO? WHAT ARE YOU SAYING?
HER! THAT'S MY MOMMY!

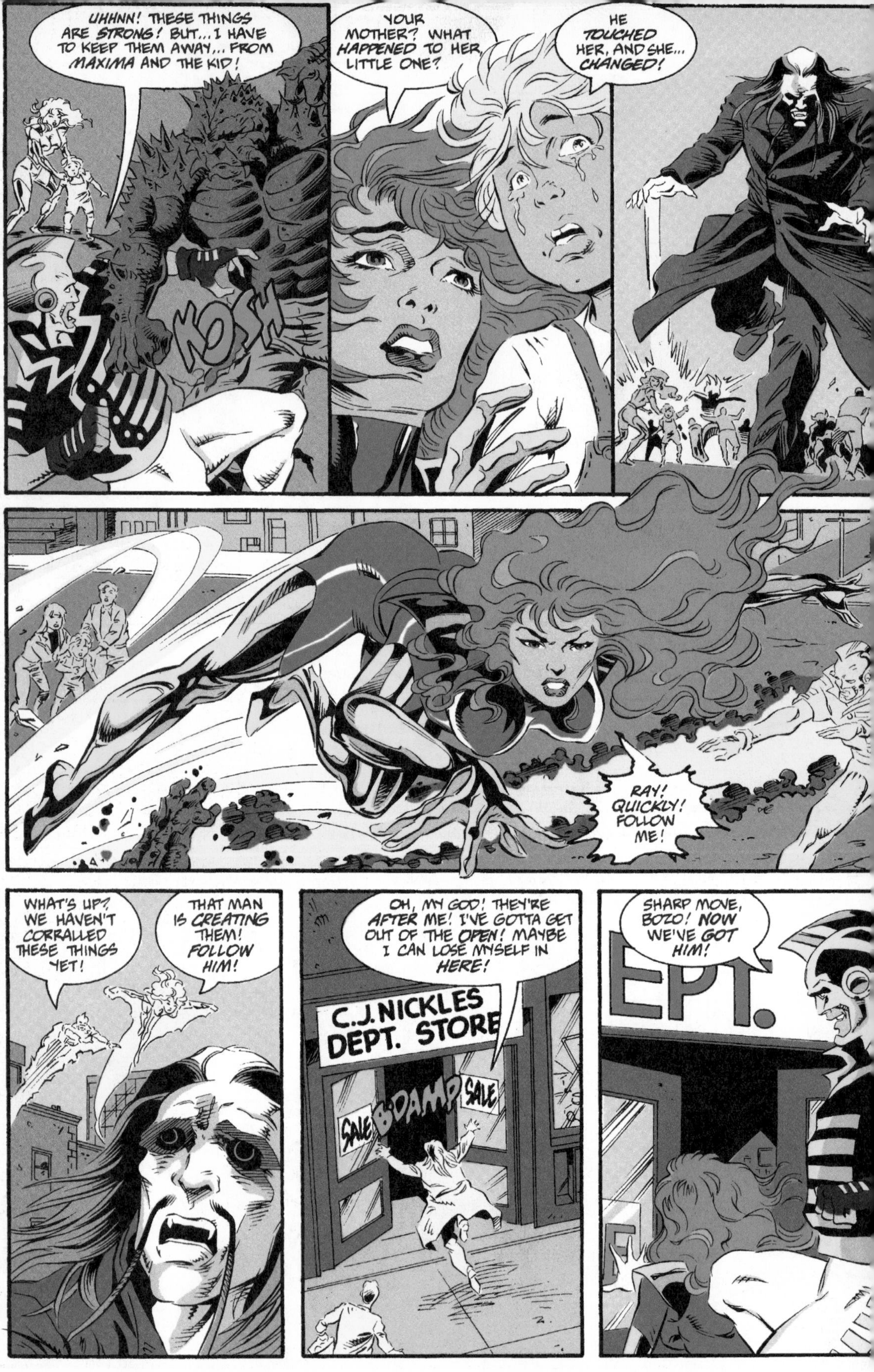

UHHNN! THESE THINGS ARE STRONG! BUT... I HAVE TO KEEP THEM AWAY... FROM MAXIMA AND THE KID!
KOSH
YOUR MOTHER? WHAT HAPPENED TO HER, LITTLE ONE?
HE TOUCHED HER, AND SHE... CHANGED!
RAY! QUICKLY! FOLLOW ME!
WHAT'S UP? WE HAVEN'T CORRALLED THESE THINGS YET!
THAT MAN IS CREATING THEM! FOLLOW HIM!
OH, MY GOD! THEY'RE AFTER ME! I'VE GOTTA GET OUT OF THE OPEN! MAYBE I CAN LOSE MYSELF IN HERE!
C.J. NICKLES DEPT. STORE
SALE
BDAMP
SALE
SHARP MOVE, BOZO! NOW WE'VE GOT HIM!
DEPT.

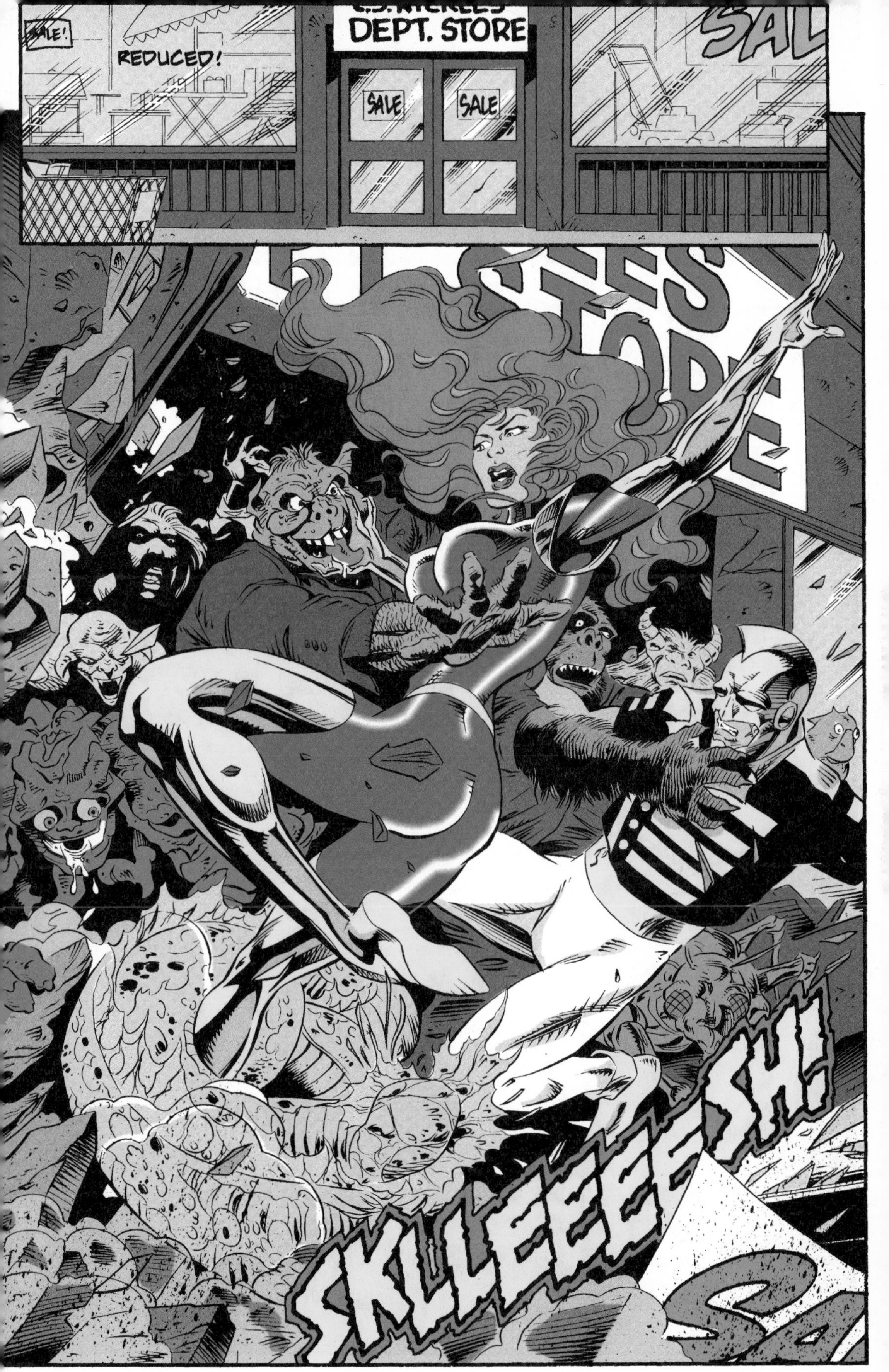
SALE!
REDUCED!
DEPT. STORE
SALE
SALE
SKLEEEEESH!

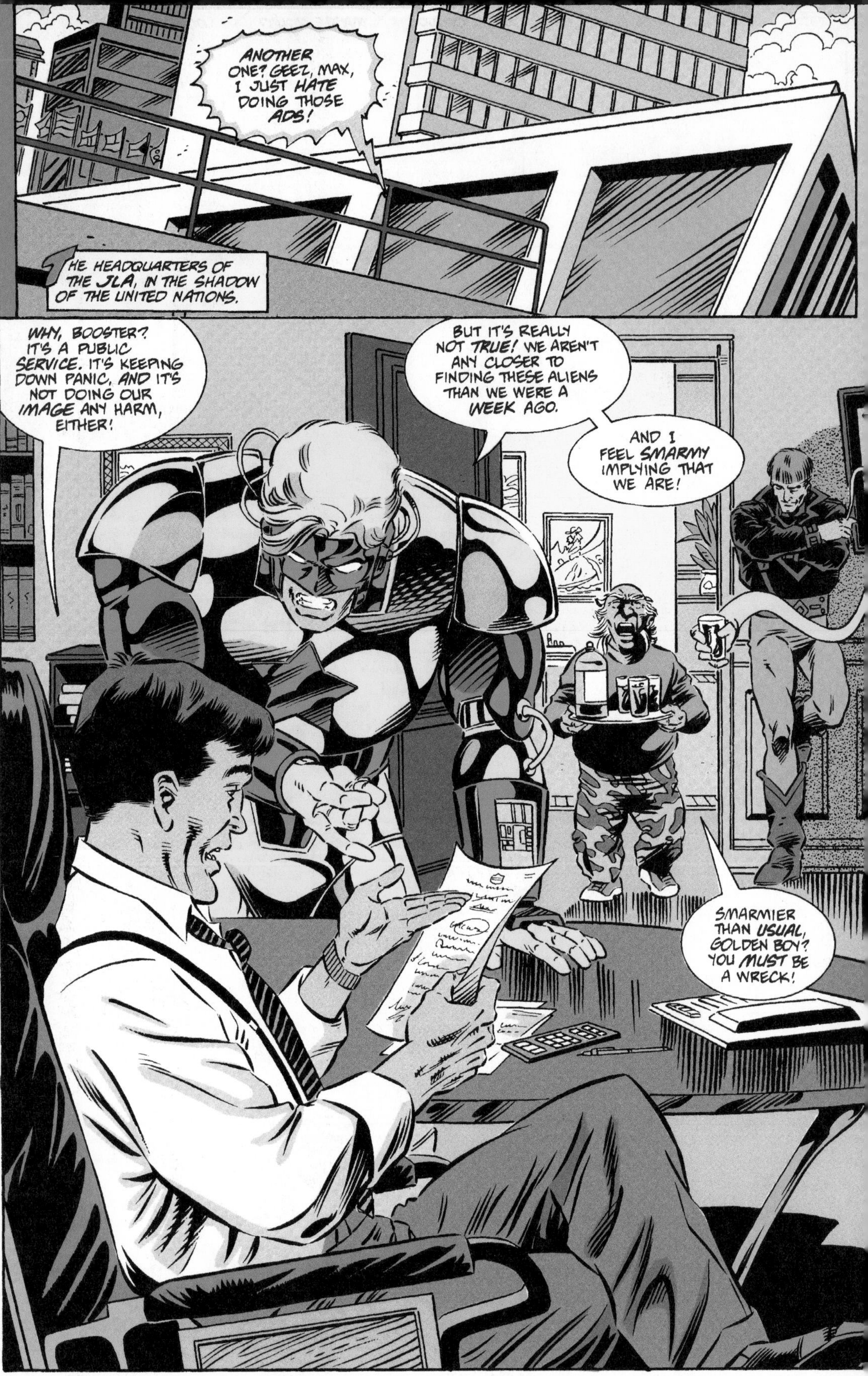
ANOTHER ONE? GEEZ, MAX, I JUST HATE DOING THOSE ADS!
THE HEADQUARTERS OF THE JLA, IN THE SHADOW OF THE UNITED NATIONS.
WHY, BOOSTER? IT'S A PUBLIC SERVICE. IT'S KEEPING DOWN PANIC, AND IT'S NOT DOING OUR IMAGE ANY HARM, EITHER!
BUT IT'S REALLY NOT TRUE! WE AREN'T ANY CLOSER TO FINDING THESE ALIENS THAN WE WERE A WEEK AGO.
AND I FEEL SMARMY IMPLYING THAT WE ARE!
SMARMIER THAN USUAL, GOLDEN BOY? YOU MUST BE A WRECK!

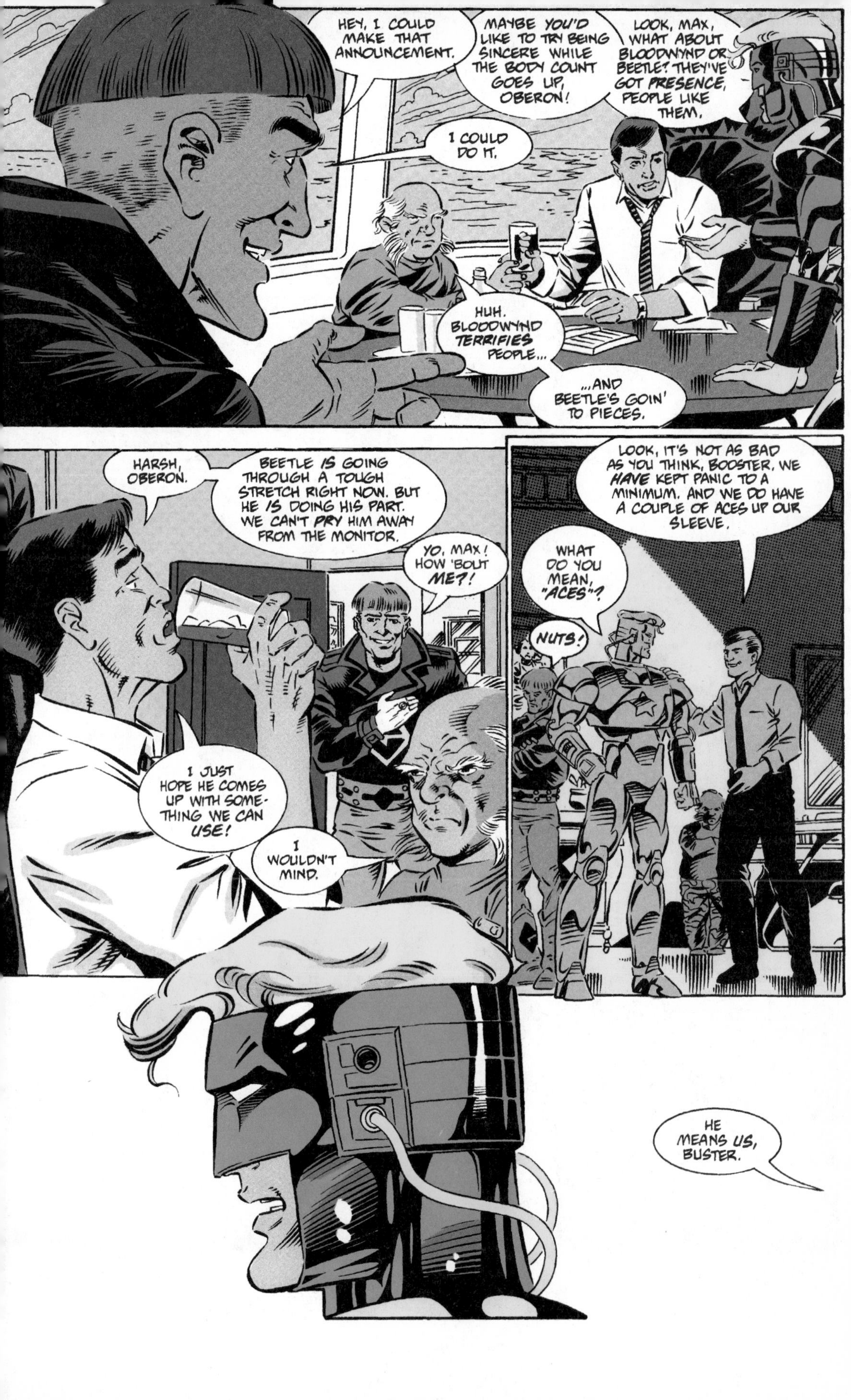
HEY, I COULD MAKE THAT ANNOUNCEMENT.
MAYBE YOU'D LIKE TO TRY BEING SINCERE WHILE THE BODY COUNT GOES UP, OBERON!
LOOK, MAX, WHAT ABOUT BLOODWYND OR BEETLE? THEY'VE GOT PRESENCE, PEOPLE LIKE THEM.
I COULD DO IT.
HUH. BLOODWYND TERRIFIES PEOPLE...
...AND BEETLE'S GOIN' TO PIECES.
HARSH, OBERON.
BEETLE IS GOING THROUGH A TOUGH STRETCH RIGHT NOW. BUT HE IS DOING HIS PART. WE CAN'T PRY HIM AWAY FROM THE MONITOR.
YO, MAX! HOW 'BOUT ME?!
I JUST HOPE HE COMES UP WITH SOME-THING WE CAN USE!
I WOULDN'T MIND.
LOOK, IT'S NOT AS BAD AS YOU THINK, BOOSTER. WE HAVE KEPT PANIC TO A MINIMUM. AND WE DO HAVE A COUPLE OF ACES UP OUR SLEEVE.
WHAT DO YOU MEAN, "ACES"?
NUTS!
HE MEANS US, BUSTER.

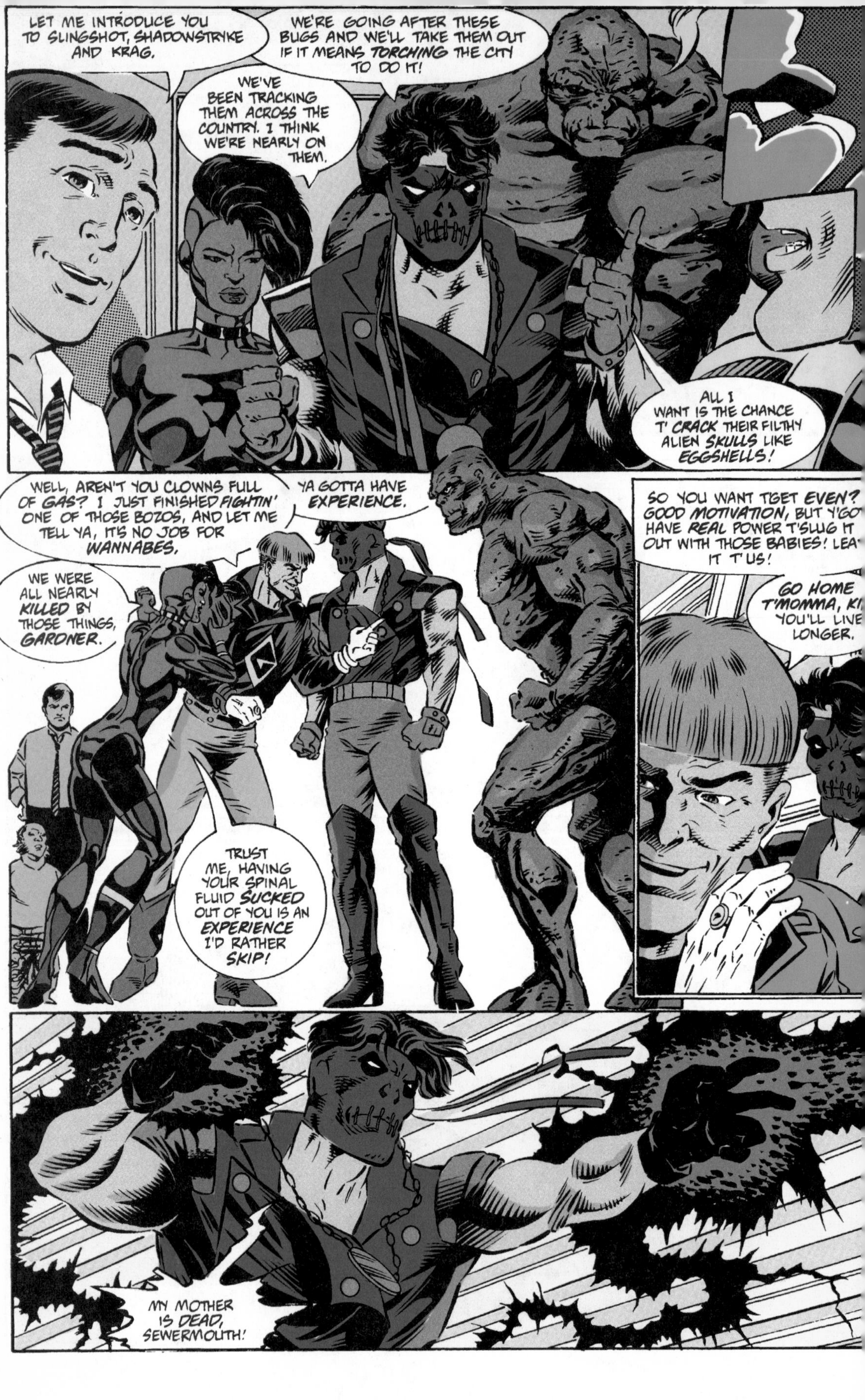
LET ME INTRODUCE YOU TO SLINGSHOT, SHADOWSTRYKE AND KRAG.
WE'RE GOING AFTER THESE BUGS AND WE'LL TAKE THEM OUT IF IT MEANS TORCHING THE CITY TO DO IT!
WE'VE BEEN TRACKING THEM ACROSS THE COUNTRY. I THINK WE'RE NEARLY ON THEM.
ALL I WANT IS THE CHANCE T' CRACK THEIR FILTHY ALIEN SKULLS LIKE EGGSHELLS!
WELL, AREN'T YOU CLOWNS FULL OF GAS? I JUST FINISHED FIGHTIN' ONE OF THOSE BOZOS, AND LET ME TELL YA, IT'S NO JOB FOR WANNABES.
YA GOTTA HAVE EXPERIENCE.
WE WERE ALL NEARLY KILLED BY THOSE THINGS, GARDNER.
TRUST ME, HAVING YOUR SPINAL FLUID SUCKED OUT OF YOU IS AN EXPERIENCE I'D RATHER SKIP!
SO YOU WANT T'GET EVEN? GOOD MOTIVATION, BUT Y'GO HAVE REAL POWER T'SLUG IT OUT WITH THOSE BABIES! LEA IT T'US!
GO HOME T'MOMMA, KI YOU'LL LIVE LONGER.
MY MOTHER IS DEAD, SEWERMOUTH!

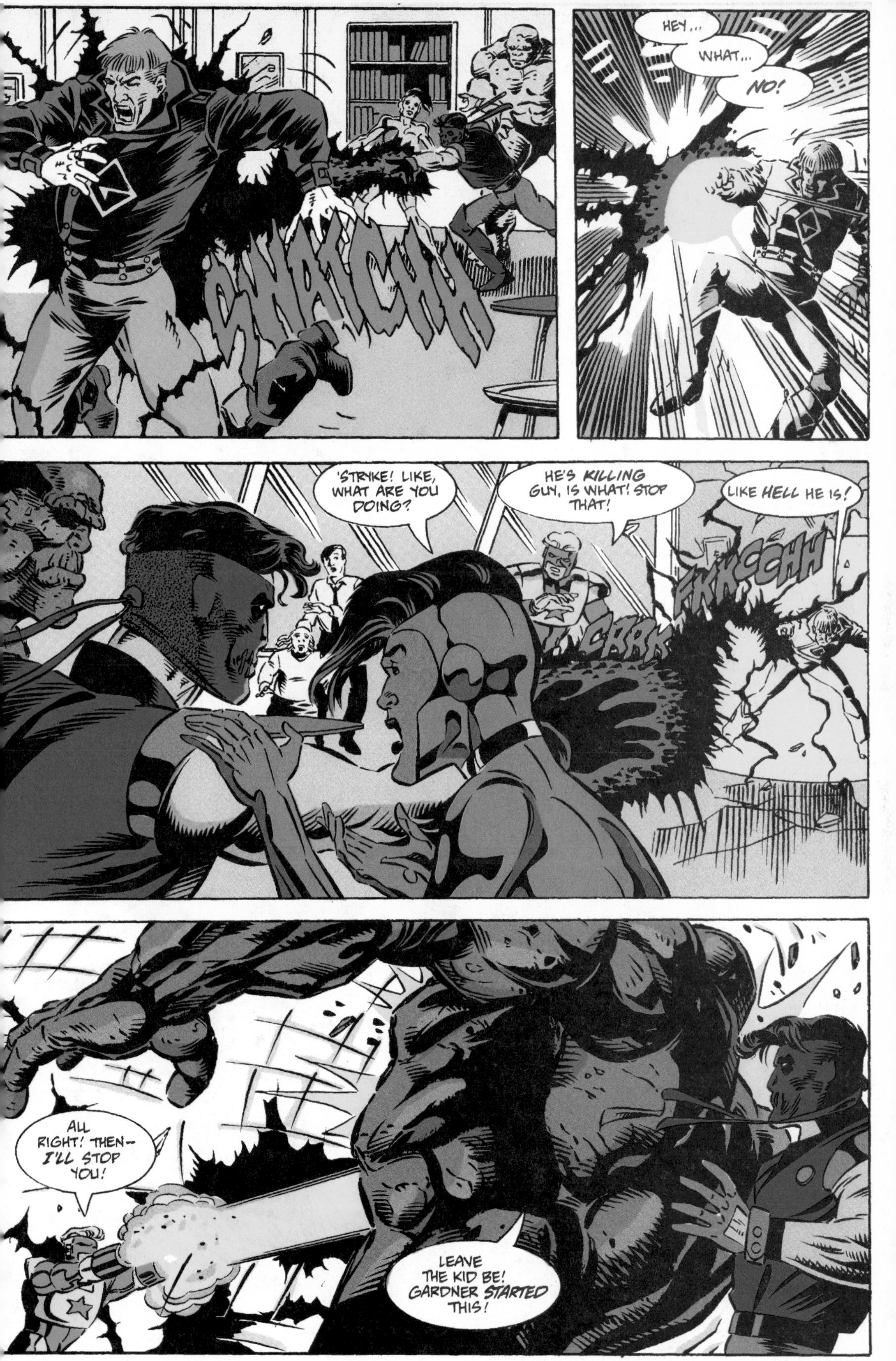
SHATCHH
HEY...
WHAT...
NO!
'STRYKE! LIKE, WHAT ARE YOU DOING?
HE'S KILLING GUY, IS WHAT! STOP THAT!
LIKE HELL HE IS!
FKKCCHH
CRRK
ALL RIGHT! THEN-- I'LL STOP YOU!
LEAVE THE KID BE! GARDNER STARTED THIS!

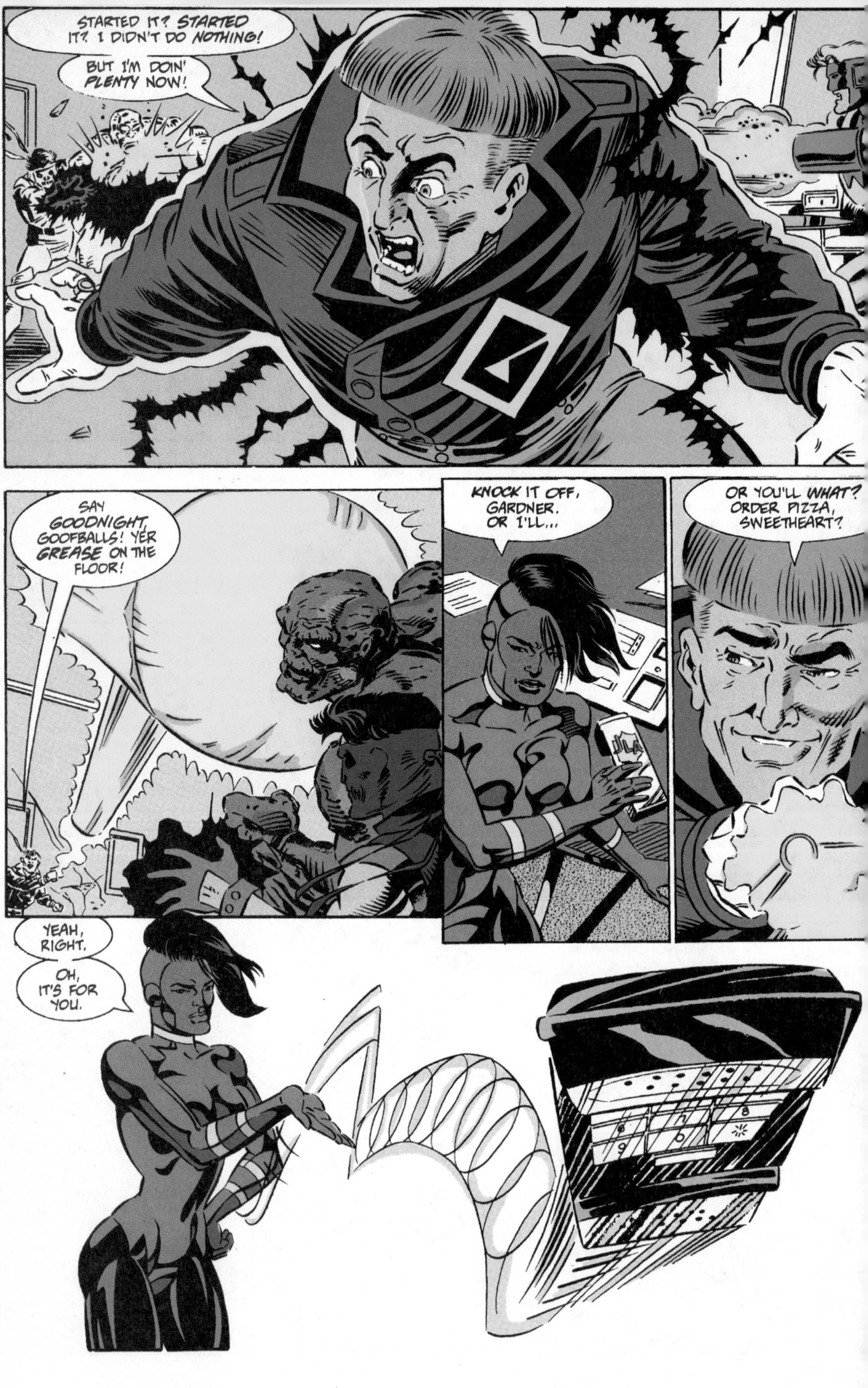
STARTED IT? STARTED IT? I DIDN'T DO NOTHING!
BUT I'M DOIN' PLENTY NOW!
SAY GOODNIGHT, GOOFBALLS! YER GREASE ON THE FLOOR!
KNOCK IT OFF, GARDNER. OR I'LL...
OR YOU'LL WHAT? ORDER PIZZA, SWEETHEART?
YEAH, RIGHT.
OH, IT'S FOR YOU.

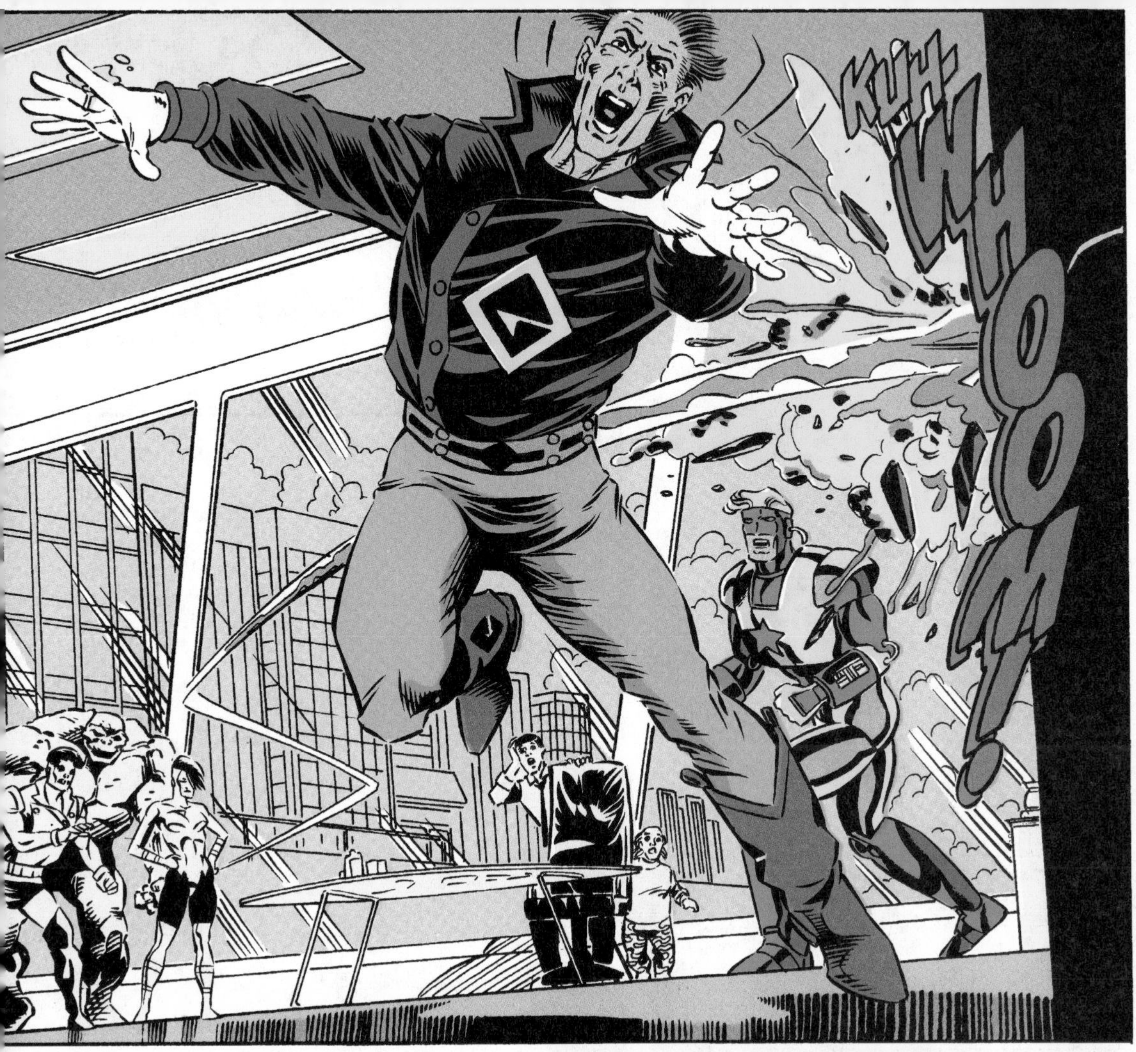
KUH-WHOOOM!

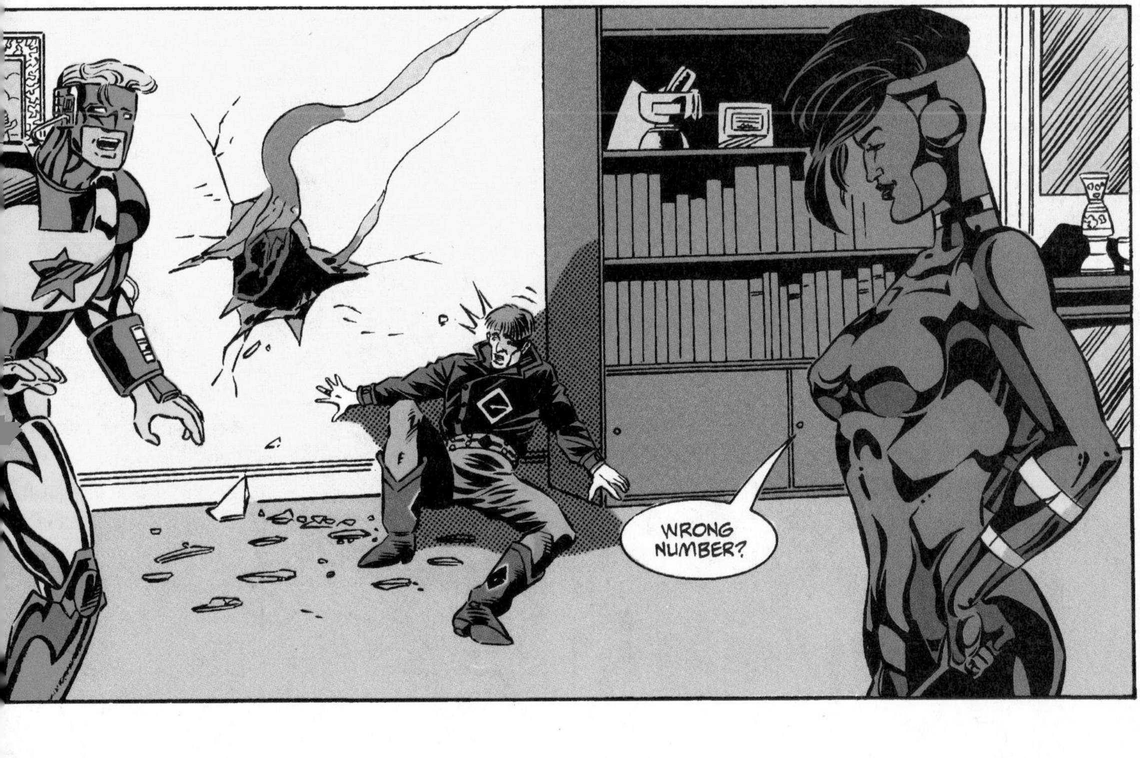
WRONG NUMBER?

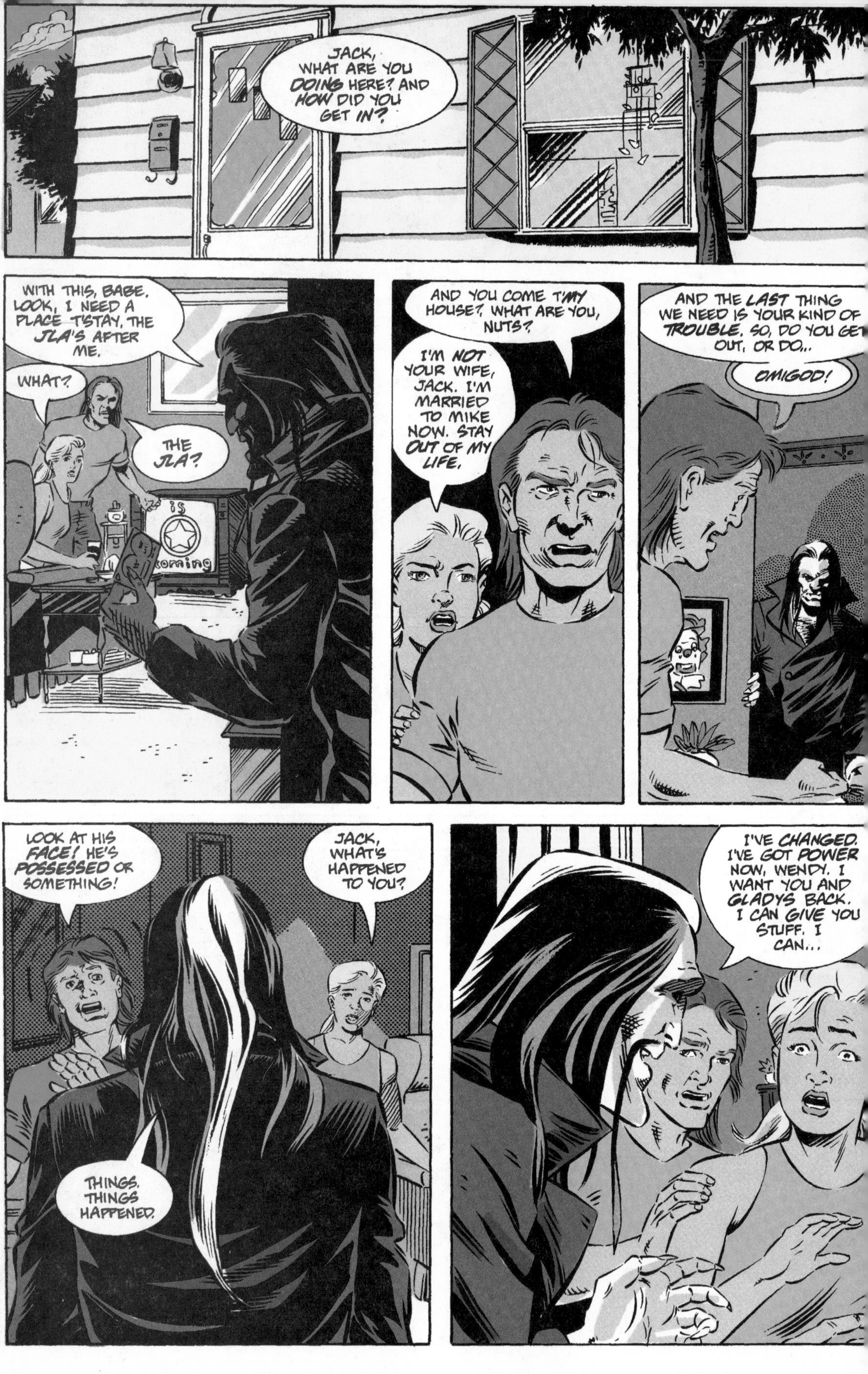
JACK, WHAT ARE YOU DOING HERE? AND HOW DID YOU GET IN?
WITH THIS, BABE. LOOK, I NEED A PLACE T'STAY. THE JLA'S AFTER ME.
WHAT?
THE JLA?
is
coming
AND YOU COME T'MY HOUSE? WHAT ARE YOU, NUTS?
I'M NOT YOUR WIFE, JACK. I'M MARRIED TO MIKE NOW. STAY OUT OF MY LIFE.
AND THE LAST THING WE NEED IS YOUR KIND OF TROUBLE. SO, DO YOU GET OUT, OR DO...
OMIGOD!
LOOK AT HIS FACE! HE'S POSSESSED OR SOMETHING!
JACK, WHAT'S HAPPENED TO YOU?
THINGS. THINGS HAPPENED.
I'VE CHANGED. I'VE GOT POWER NOW, WENDY. I WANT YOU AND GLADYS BACK. I CAN GIVE YOU STUFF. I CAN...

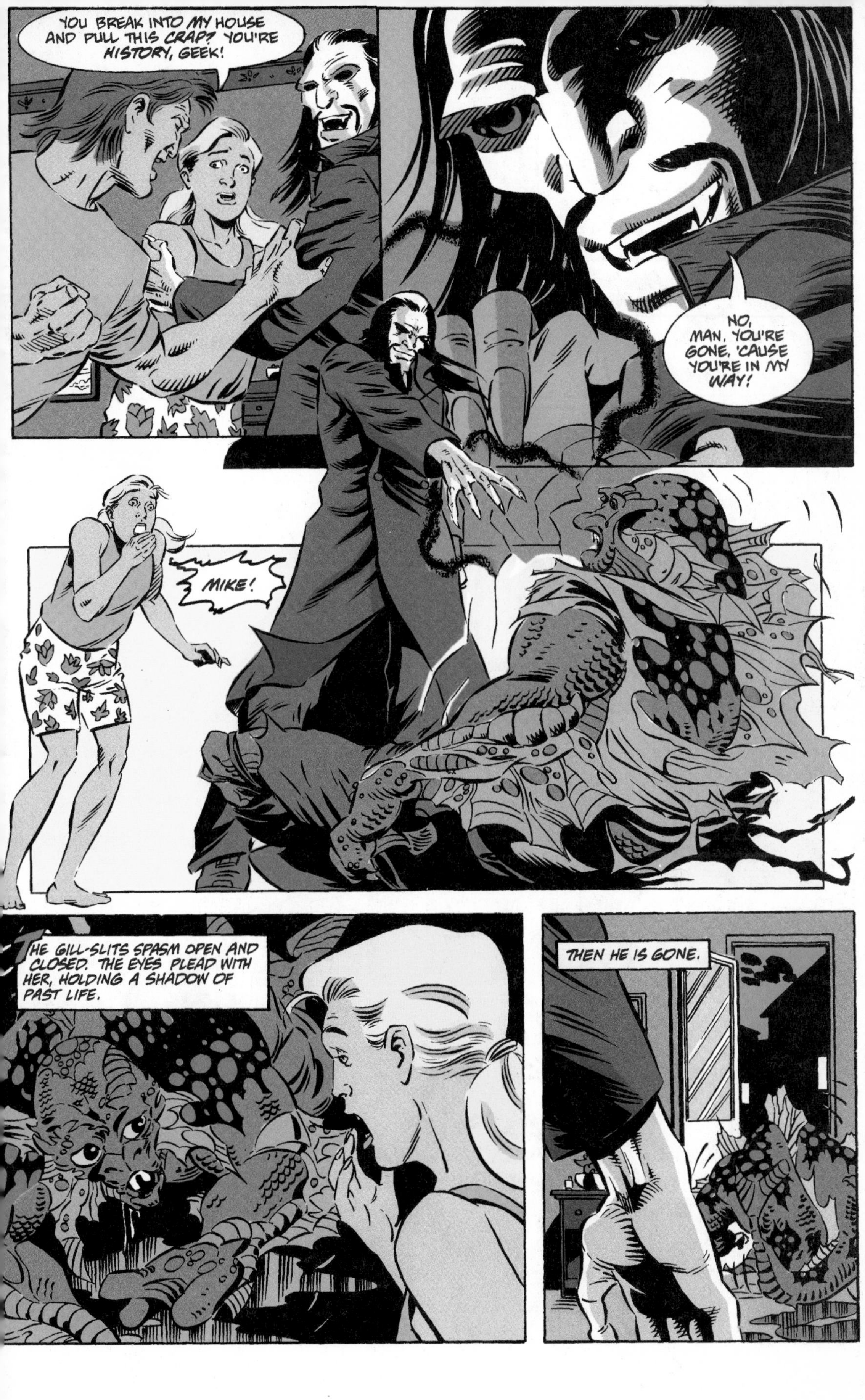
YOU BREAK INTO MY HOUSE AND PULL THIS CRAP? YOU'RE HISTORY, GEEK!
NO, MAN. YOU'RE GONE, 'CAUSE YOU'RE IN MY WAY!
MIKE!
THE GILL-SLITS SPASM OPEN AND CLOSED. THE EYES PLEAD WITH HER, HOLDING A SHADOW OF PAST LIFE.
THEN HE IS GONE.

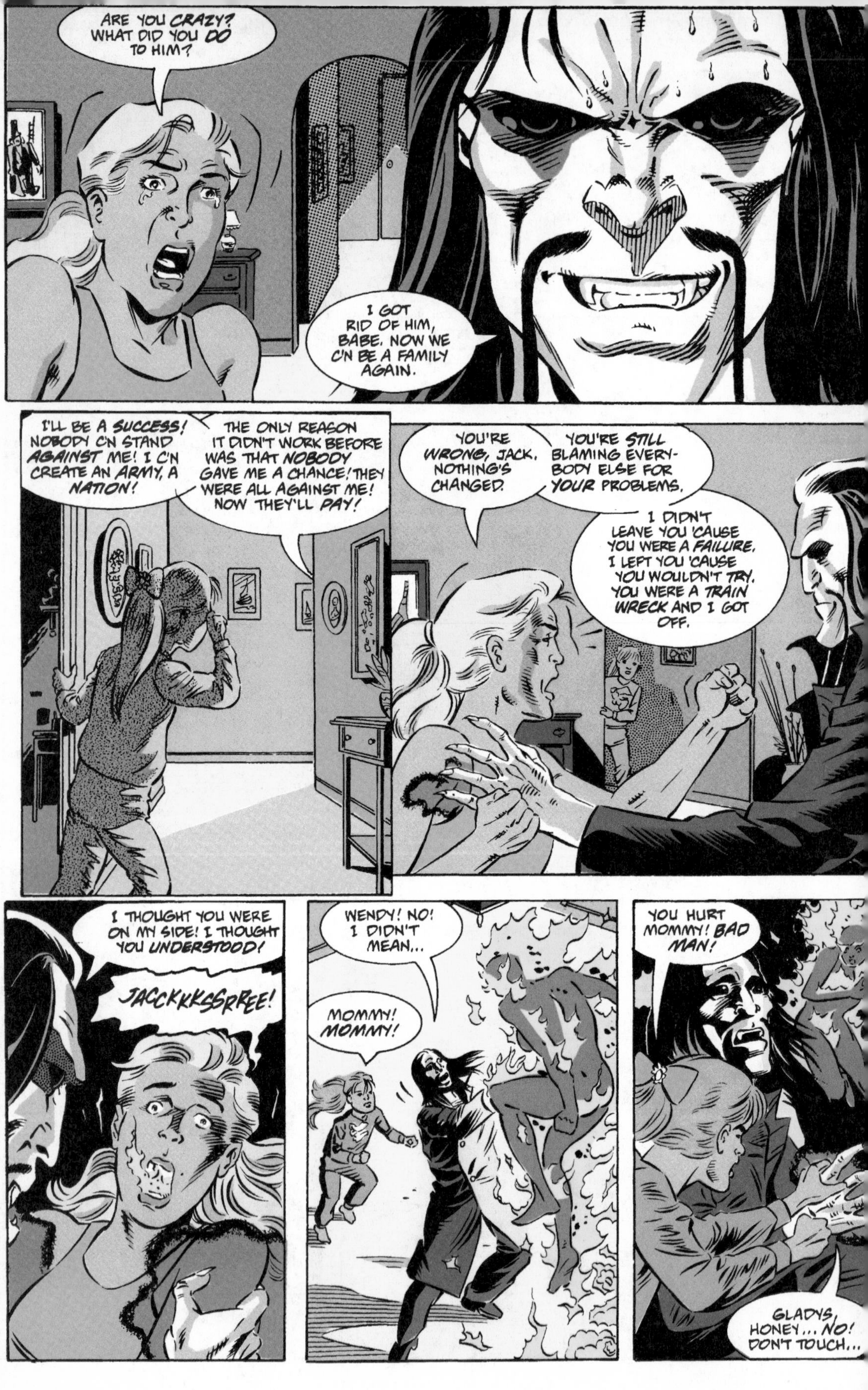

ARE YOU CRAZY? WHAT DID YOU DO TO HIM?
I GOT RID OF HIM, BABE. NOW WE C'N BE A FAMILY AGAIN.
I'LL BE A SUCCESS! NOBODY C'N STAND AGAINST ME! I C'N CREATE AN ARMY, A NATION!
THE ONLY REASON IT DIDN'T WORK BEFORE WAS THAT NOBODY GAVE ME A CHANCE! THEY WERE ALL AGAINST ME! NOW THEY'LL PAY!
YOU'RE WRONG, JACK. NOTHING'S CHANGED.
YOU'RE STILL BLAMING EVERY-BODY ELSE FOR YOUR PROBLEMS.
I DIDN'T LEAVE YOU 'CAUSE YOU WERE A FAILURE. I LEFT YOU 'CAUSE YOU WOULDN'T TRY. YOU WERE A TRAIN WRECK AND I GOT OFF.
I THOUGHT YOU WERE ON MY SIDE! I THOUGHT YOU UNDERSTOOD!
JACCKKKSSRREE!
WENDY! NO! I DIDN'T MEAN...
MOMMY! MOMMY!
YOU HURT MOMMY! BAD MAN!
GLADYS, HONEY... NO! DON'T TOUCH...

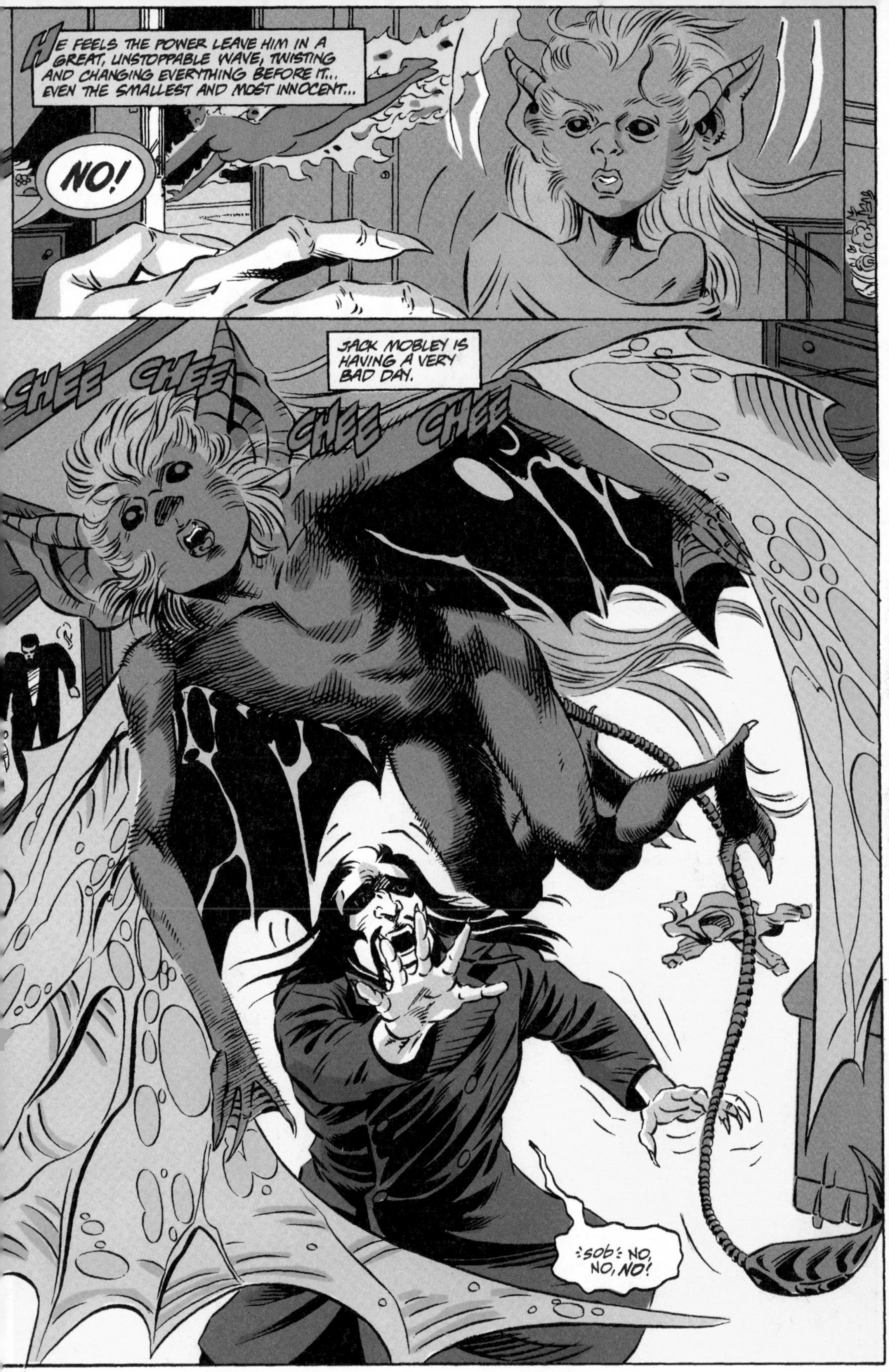
HE FEELS THE POWER LEAVE HIM IN A GREAT, UNSTOPPABLE WAVE, TWISTING AND CHANGING EVERYTHING BEFORE IT... EVEN THE SMALLEST AND MOST INNOCENT...
NO!
JACK MOBLEY IS HAVING A VERY BAD DAY.
CHEE CHEE
CHEE CHEE
:sob: NO, NO, NO!

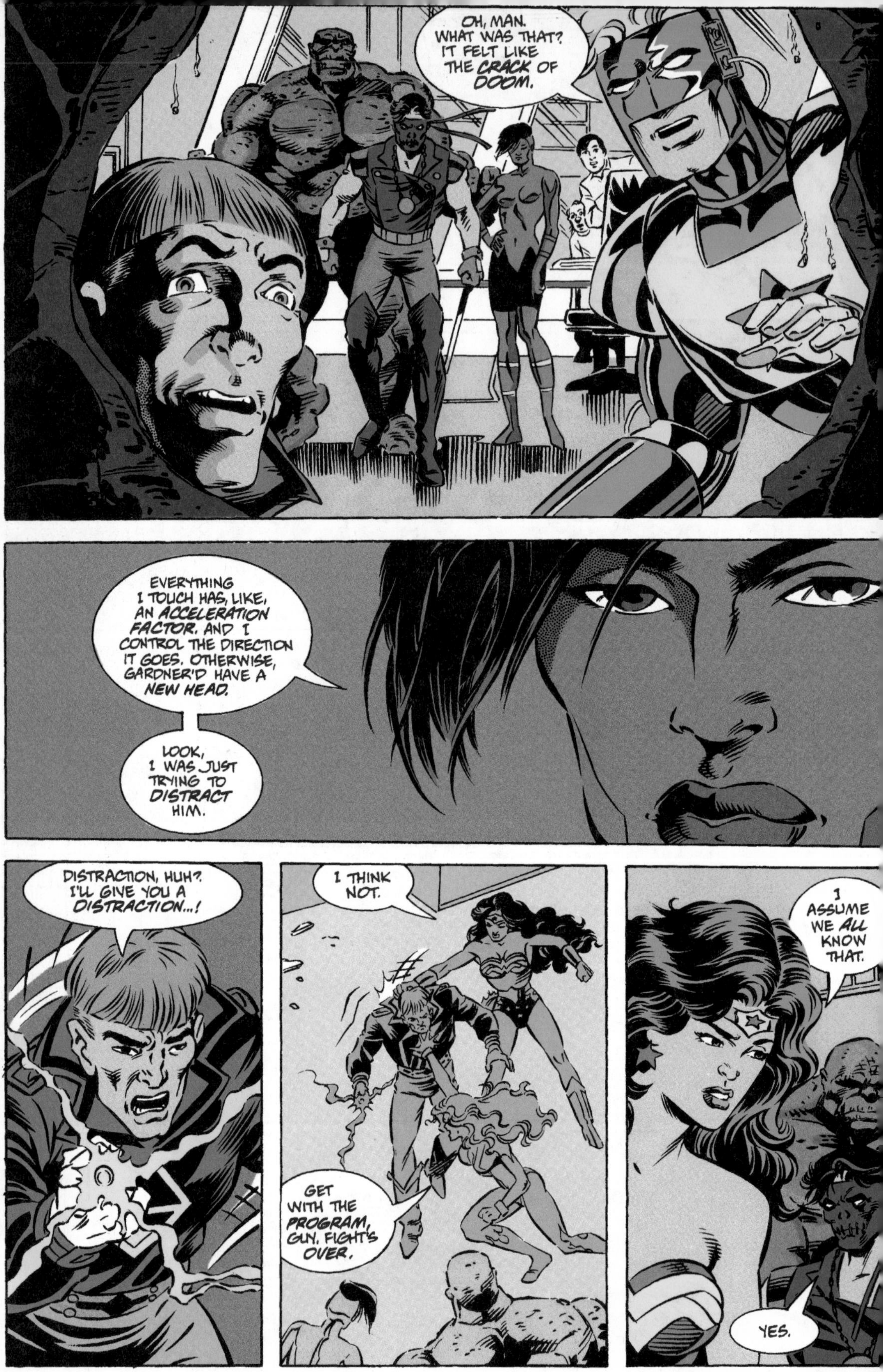
OH, MAN. WHAT WAS THAT? IT FELT LIKE THE CRACK OF DOOM.
EVERYTHING I TOUCH HAS, LIKE, AN ACCELERATION FACTOR. AND I CONTROL THE DIRECTION IT GOES. OTHERWISE, GARDNER'D HAVE A NEW HEAD.
LOOK, I WAS JUST TRYING TO DISTRACT HIM.
DISTRACTION, HUH? I'LL GIVE YOU A DISTRACTION...!
I THINK NOT.
GET WITH THE PROGRAM, GUY. FIGHT'S OVER.
I ASSUME WE ALL KNOW THAT.
YES.

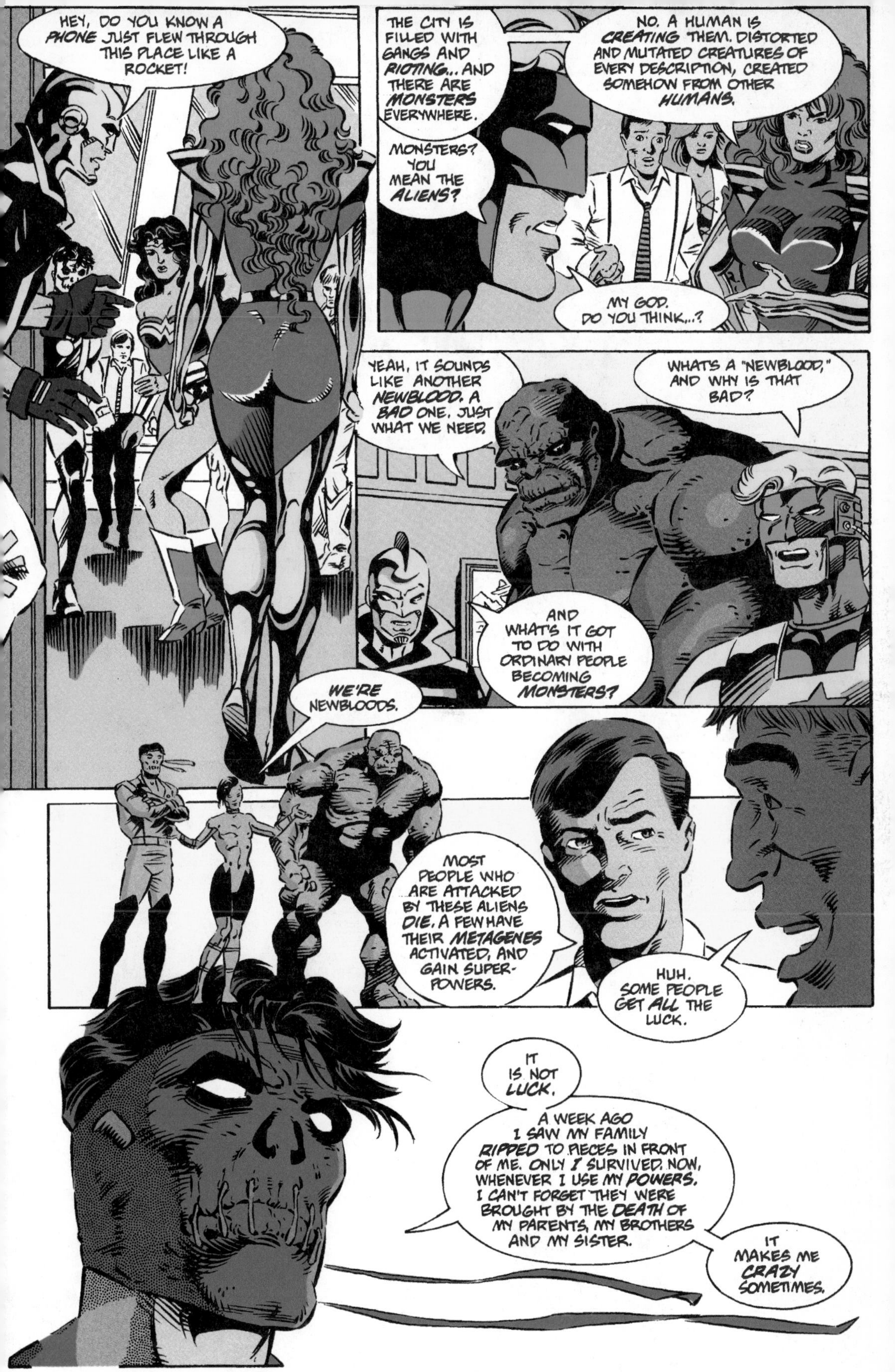
HEY, DO YOU KNOW A PHONE JUST FLEW THROUGH THIS PLACE LIKE A ROCKET!
THE CITY IS FILLED WITH GANGS AND RIOTING... AND THERE ARE MONSTERS EVERYWHERE.
MONSTERS? YOU MEAN THE ALIENS?
NO. A HUMAN IS CREATING THEM. DISTORTED AND MUTATED CREATURES OF EVERY DESCRIPTION, CREATED SOMEHOW FROM OTHER HUMANS.
MY GOD. DO YOU THINK...?
YEAH, IT SOUNDS LIKE ANOTHER NEWBLOOD. A BAD ONE. JUST WHAT WE NEED.
WHAT'S A "NEWBLOOD," AND WHY IS THAT BAD?
AND WHAT'S IT GOT TO DO WITH ORDINARY PEOPLE BECOMING MONSTERS?
WE'RE NEWBLOODS.
MOST PEOPLE WHO ARE ATTACKED BY THESE ALIENS DIE. A FEW HAVE THEIR METAGENES ACTIVATED, AND GAIN SUPER-POWERS.
HUH. SOME PEOPLE GET ALL THE LUCK.
IT IS NOT LUCK.
A WEEK AGO I SAW MY FAMILY RIPPED TO PIECES IN FRONT OF ME. ONLY I SURVIVED. NOW, WHENEVER I USE MY POWERS, I CAN'T FORGET THEY WERE BROUGHT BY THE DEATH OF MY PARENTS, MY BROTHERS AND MY SISTER.
IT MAKES ME CRAZY SOMETIMES.

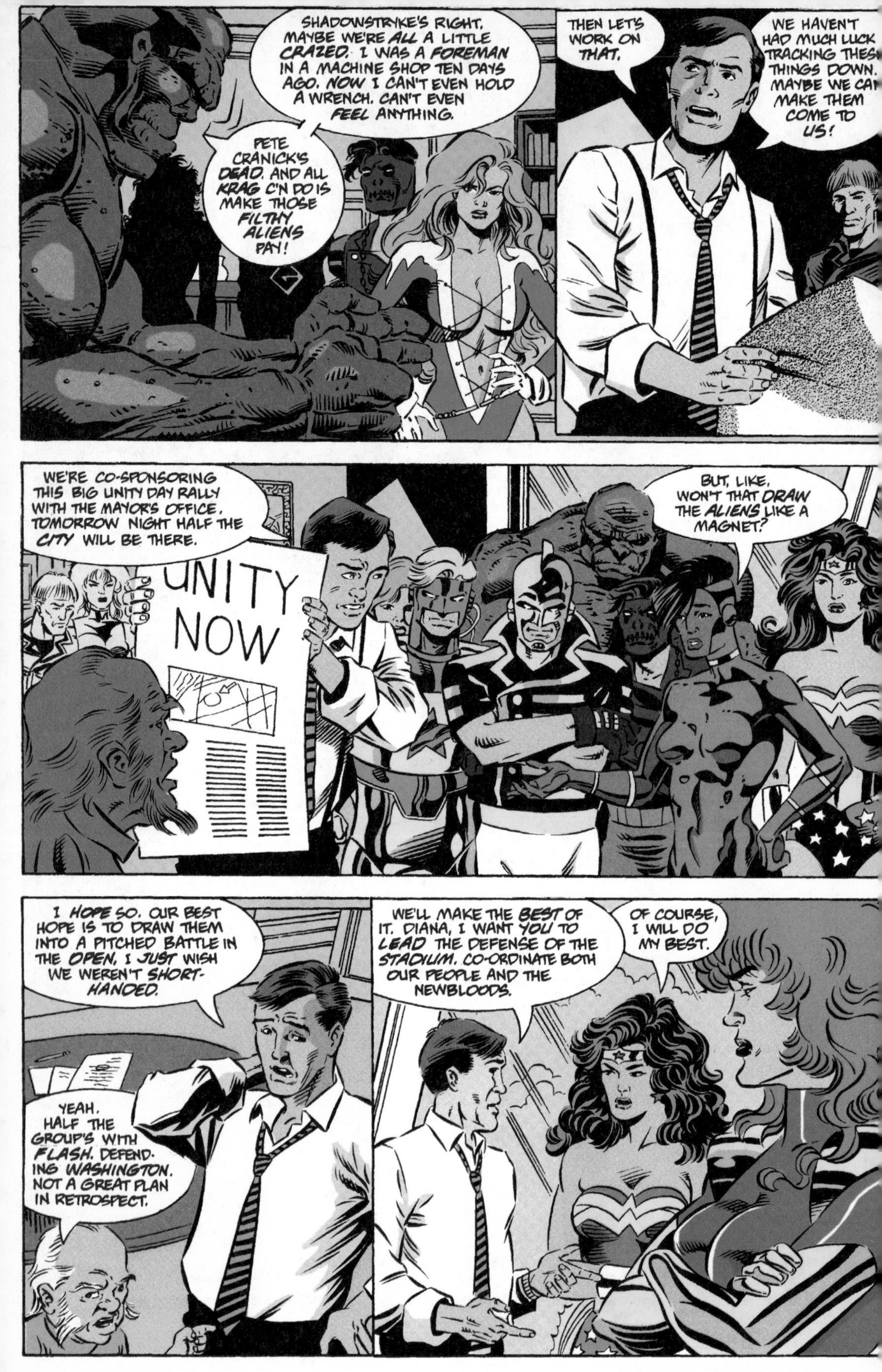

SHADOWSTRYKE'S RIGHT. MAYBE WE'RE ALL A LITTLE CRAZED. I WAS A FOREMAN IN A MACHINE SHOP TEN DAYS AGO. NOW I CAN'T EVEN HOLD A WRENCH. CAN'T EVEN FEEL ANYTHING.
PETE CRANICK'S DEAD. AND ALL KRAG C'N DO IS MAKE THOSE FILTHY ALIENS PAY!
THEN LET'S WORK ON THAT.
WE HAVEN'T HAD MUCH LUCK TRACKING THES THINGS DOWN. MAYBE WE CA MAKE THEM COME TO US!
WE'RE CO-SPONSORING THIS BIG UNITY DAY RALLY WITH THE MAYOR'S OFFICE. TOMORROW NIGHT HALF THE CITY WILL BE THERE.
UNITY NOW
BUT, LIKE, WON'T THAT DRAW THE ALIENS LIKE A MAGNET?
I HOPE SO. OUR BEST HOPE IS TO DRAW THEM INTO A PITCHED BATTLE IN THE OPEN. I JUST WISH WE WEREN'T SHORT-HANDED.
YEAH. HALF THE GROUP'S WITH FLASH. DEFEND-ING WASHINGTON. NOT A GREAT PLAN IN RETROSPECT.
WE'LL MAKE THE BEST OF IT. DIANA, I WANT YOU TO LEAD THE DEFENSE OF THE STADIUM. CO-ORDINATE BOTH OUR PEOPLE AND THE NEWBLOODS.
OF COURSE, I WILL DO MY BEST.

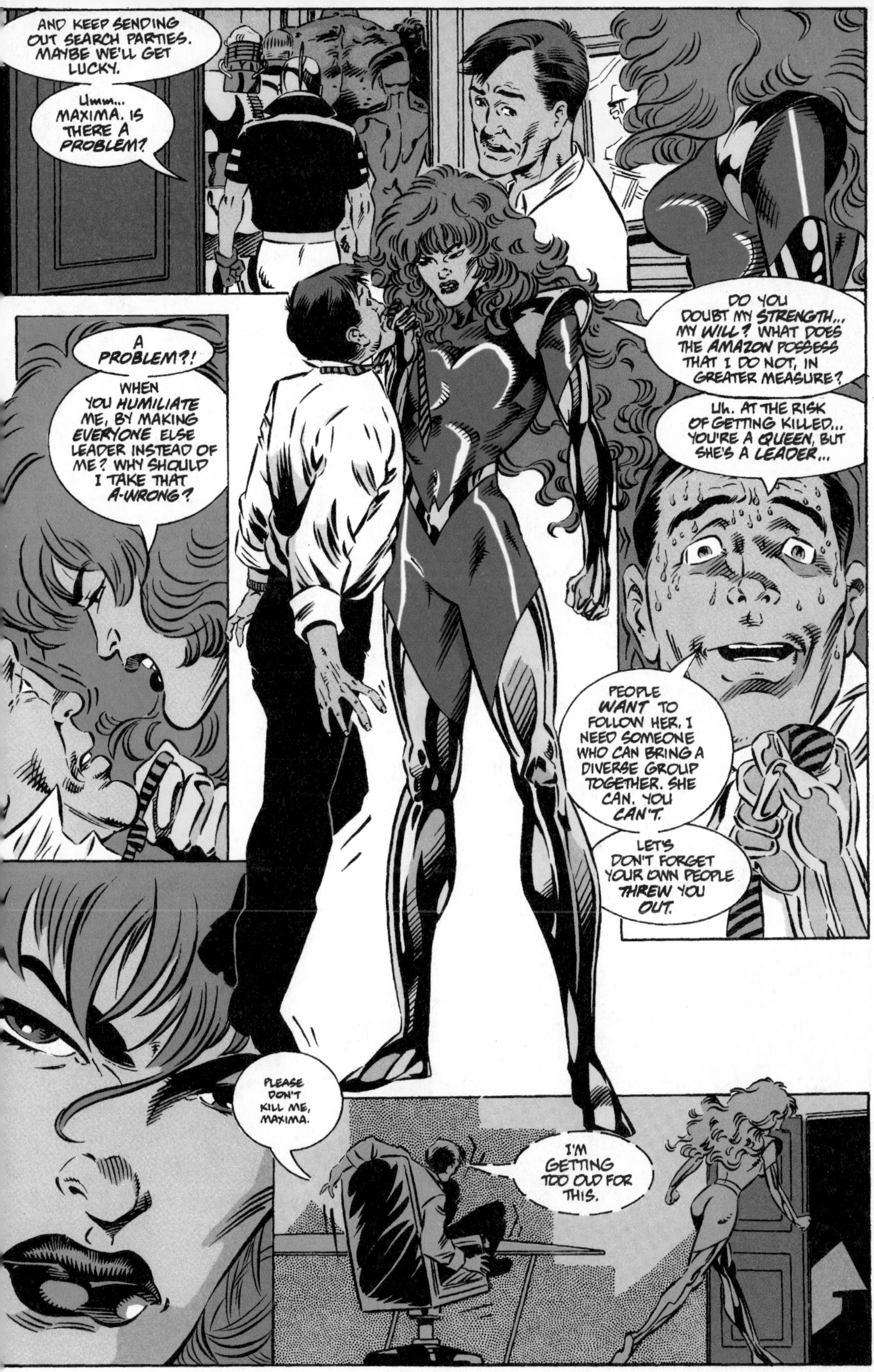
AND KEEP SENDING OUT SEARCH PARTIES. MAYBE WE'LL GET LUCKY.
Umm... MAXIMA. IS THERE A PROBLEM?
A PROBLEM?!
WHEN YOU HUMILIATE ME, BY MAKING EVERYONE ELSE LEADER INSTEAD OF ME? WHY SHOULD I TAKE THAT A-WRONG?
DO YOU DOUBT MY STRENGTH... MY WILL? WHAT DOES THE AMAZON POSSESS THAT I DO NOT, IN GREATER MEASURE?
Uh. AT THE RISK OF GETTING KILLED... YOU'RE A QUEEN, BUT SHE'S A LEADER...
PEOPLE WANT TO FOLLOW HER. I NEED SOMEONE WHO CAN BRING A DIVERSE GROUP TOGETHER. SHE CAN. YOU CAN'T.
LET'S DON'T FORGET YOUR OWN PEOPLE THREW YOU OUT.
PLEASE DON'T KILL ME, MAXIMA.
I'M GETTING TOO OLD FOR THIS.

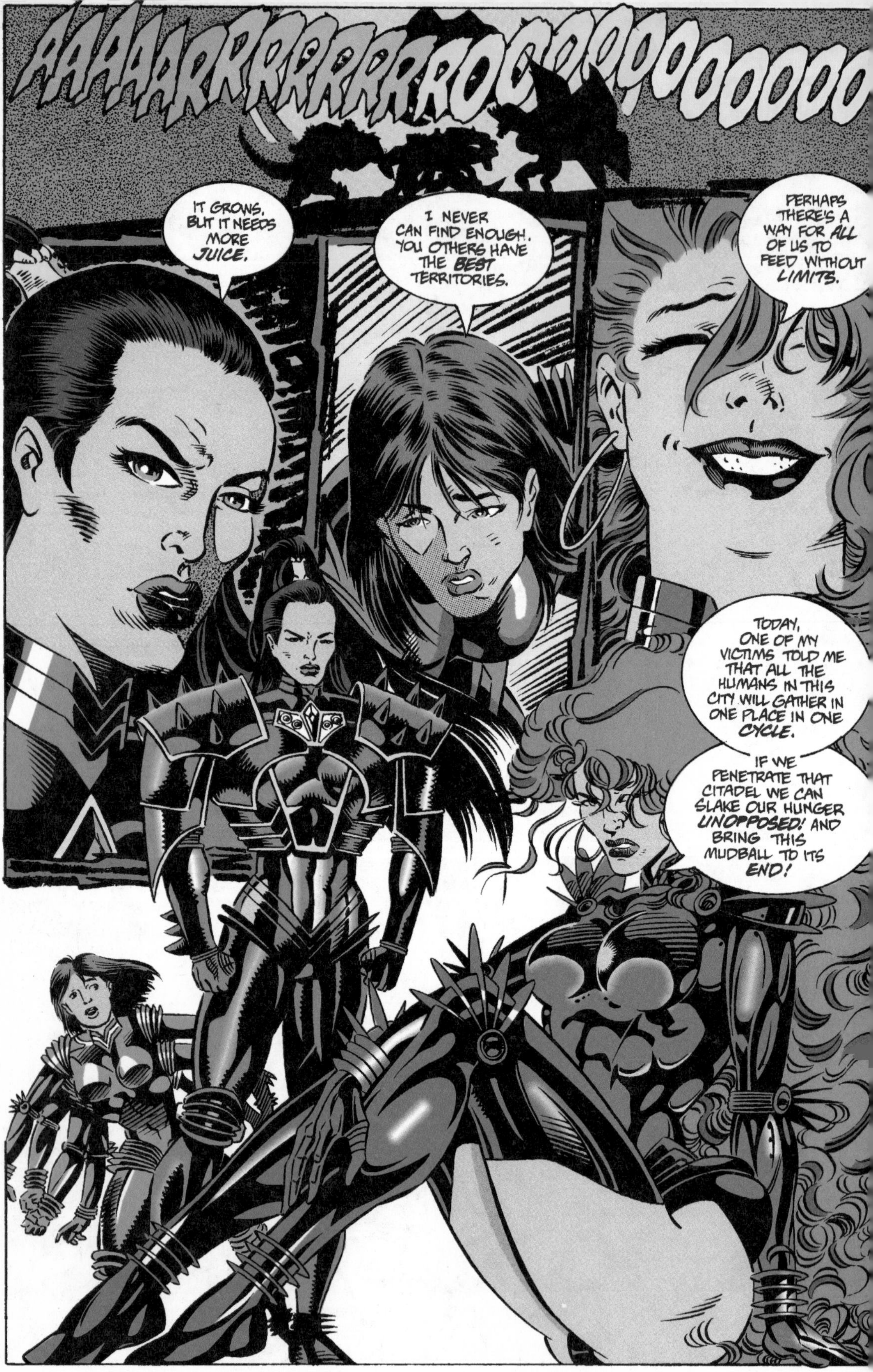
AAAAARRRRRRRRROOOOOOOOOOO
IT GROWS, BUT IT NEEDS MORE JUICE.
I NEVER CAN FIND ENOUGH. YOU OTHERS HAVE THE BEST TERRITORIES.
PERHAPS THERE'S A WAY FOR ALL OF US TO FEED WITHOUT LIMITS.
TODAY, ONE OF MY VICTIMS TOLD ME THAT ALL THE HUMANS IN THIS CITY WILL GATHER IN ONE PLACE IN ONE CYCLE.
IF WE PENETRATE THAT CITADEL WE CAN SLAKE OUR HUNGER UNOPPOSED! AND BRING THIS MUDBALL TO ITS END!

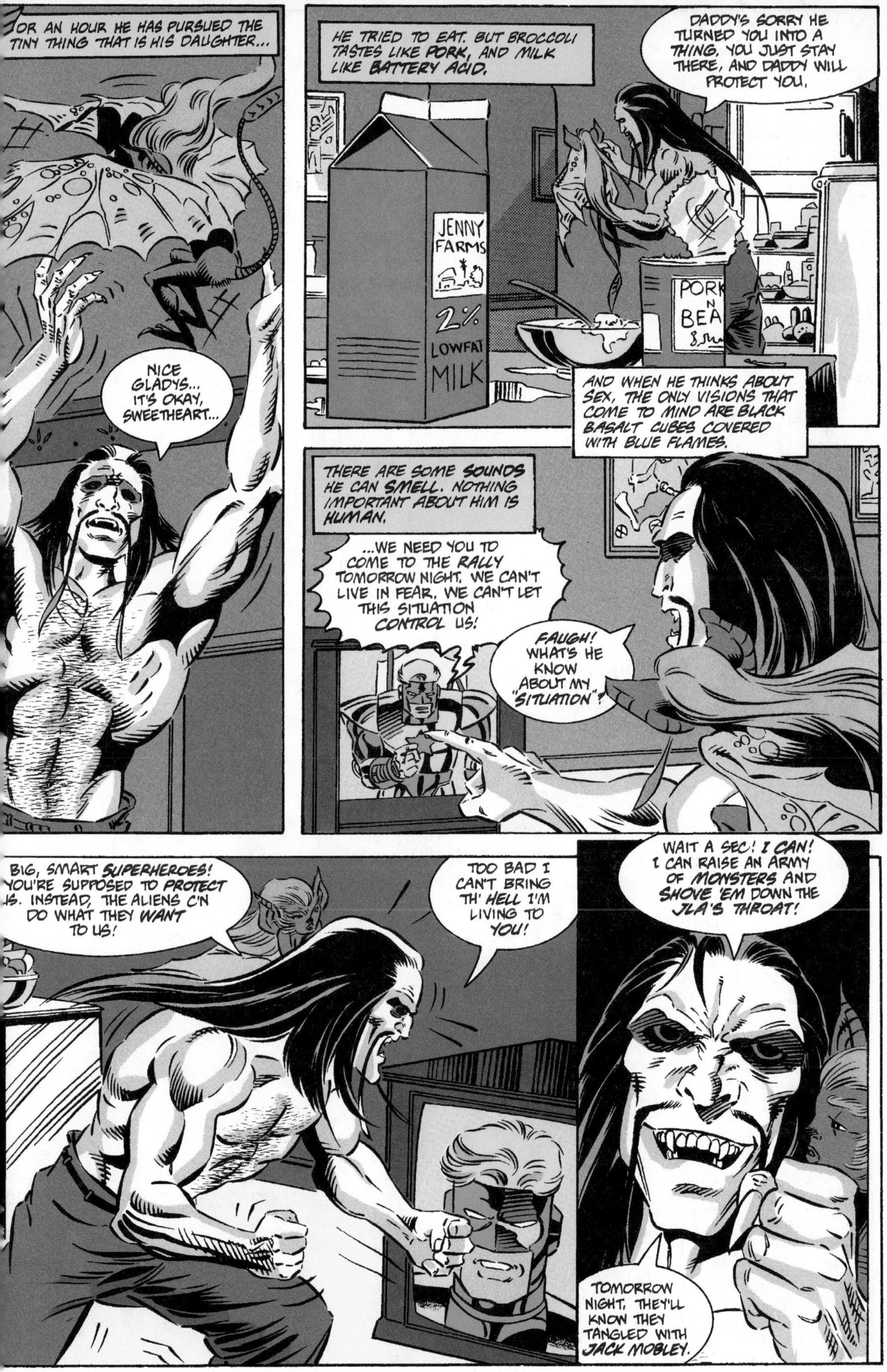

FOR AN HOUR HE HAS PURSUED THE TINY THING THAT IS HIS DAUGHTER...
NICE GLADYS... IT'S OKAY, SWEETHEART...
HE TRIED TO EAT. BUT BROCCOLI TASTES LIKE PORK, AND MILK LIKE BATTERY ACID.
DADDY'S SORRY HE TURNED YOU INTO A THING. YOU JUST STAY THERE, AND DADDY WILL PROTECT YOU.
JENNY FARMS
2%
LOWFAT
MILK
PORK N BEA
AND WHEN HE THINKS ABOUT SEX, THE ONLY VISIONS THAT COME TO MIND ARE BLACK BASALT CUBES COVERED WITH BLUE FLAMES.
THERE ARE SOME SOUNDS HE CAN SMELL. NOTHING IMPORTANT ABOUT HIM IS HUMAN.
...WE NEED YOU TO COME TO THE RALLY TOMORROW NIGHT. WE CAN'T LIVE IN FEAR. WE CAN'T LET THIS SITUATION CONTROL US!
FAUGH! WHAT'S HE KNOW ABOUT MY "SITUATION"?
BIG, SMART SUPERHEROES! YOU'RE SUPPOSED TO PROTECT US. INSTEAD, THE ALIENS C'N DO WHAT THEY WANT TO US!
TOO BAD I CAN'T BRING TH' HELL I'M LIVING TO YOU!
WAIT A SEC! I CAN! I CAN RAISE AN ARMY OF MONSTERS AND SHOVE 'EM DOWN THE JLA'S THROAT!
TOMORROW NIGHT, THEY'LL KNOW THEY TANGLED WITH JACK MOBLEY.

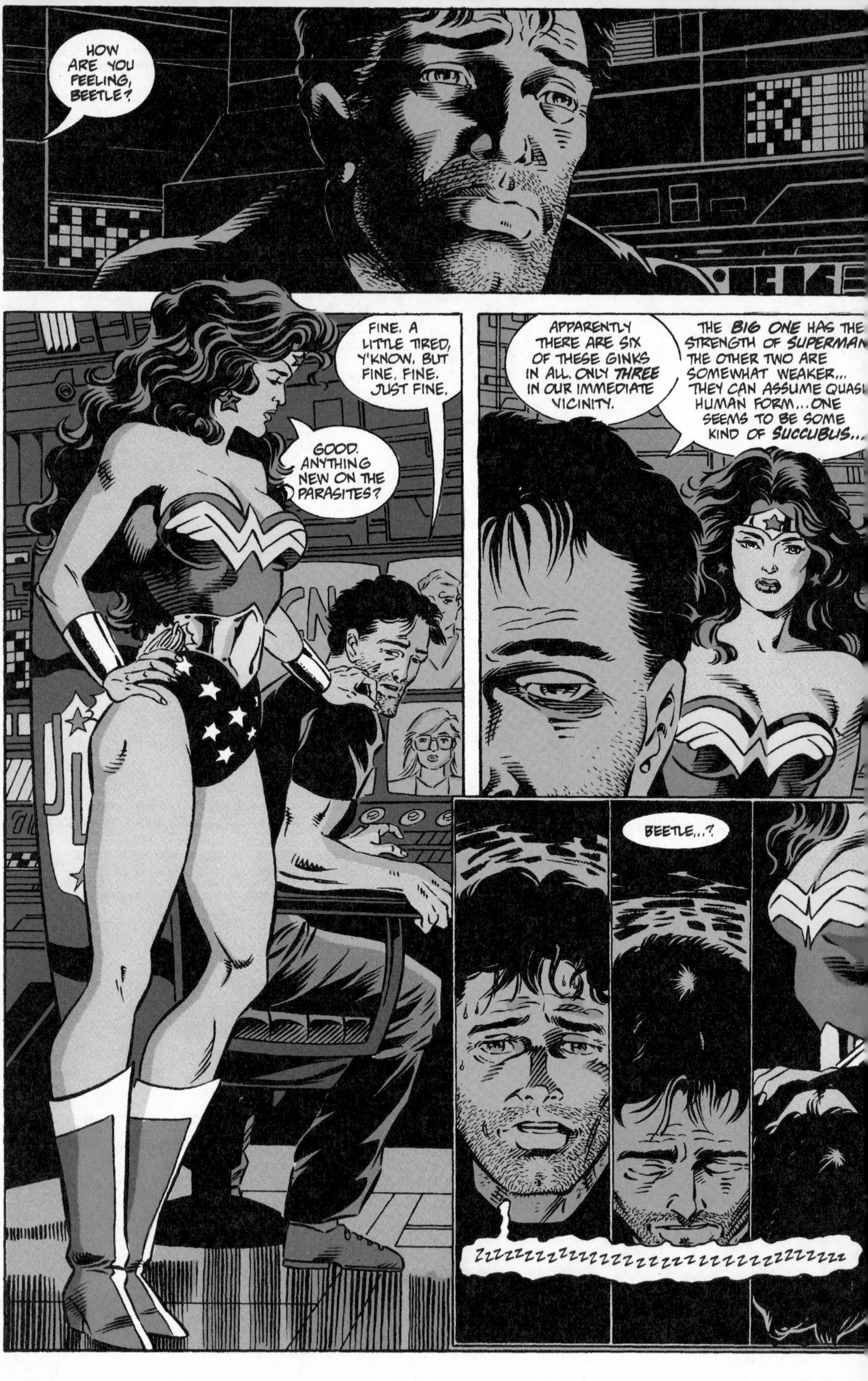
HOW ARE YOU FEELING, BEETLE?
GOOD. ANYTHING NEW ON THE PARASITES?
FINE. A LITTLE TIRED, Y'KNOW. BUT FINE. FINE. JUST FINE.
APPARENTLY THERE ARE SIX OF THESE GINKS IN ALL. ONLY THREE IN OUR IMMEDIATE VICINITY.
THE BIG ONE HAS THE STRENGTH OF SUPERMAN THE OTHER TWO ARE SOMEWHAT WEAKER... THEY CAN ASSUME QUASI HUMAN FORM...ONE SEEMS TO BE SOME KIND OF SUCCUBUS...
BEETLE...?
ZZZZZZZZZZZZZZZZZZZZZZZZZZZZZZZZZZ

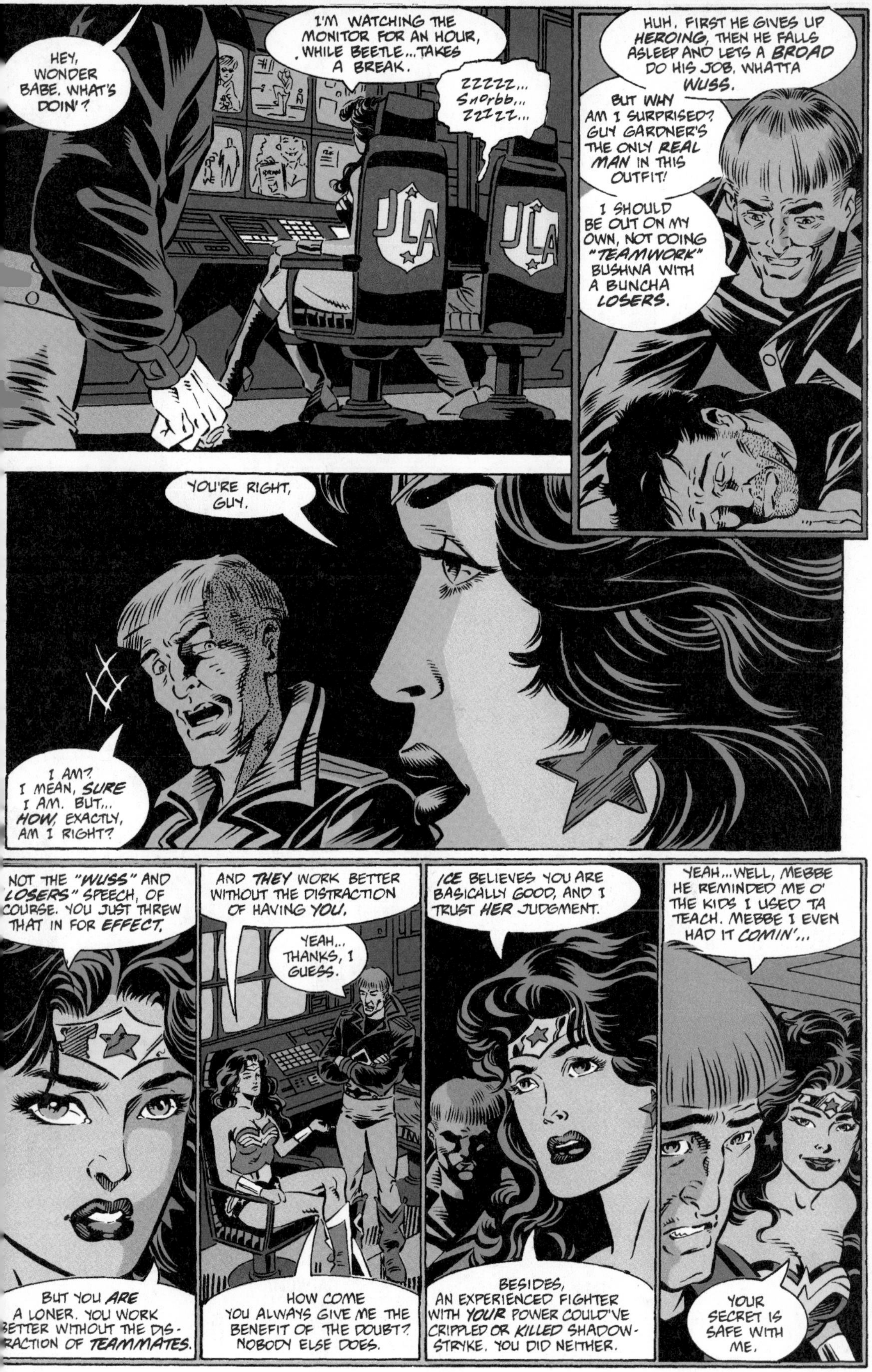
HEY, WONDER BABE. WHAT'S DOIN'?
I'M WATCHING THE MONITOR FOR AN HOUR, WHILE BEETLE... TAKES A BREAK.
ZZZZZ... SNORBB... ZZZZZ...
HUH. FIRST HE GIVES UP HEROING, THEN HE FALLS ASLEEP AND LETS A BROAD DO HIS JOB. WHATTA WUSS.
BUT WHY AM I SURPRISED? GUY GARDNER'S THE ONLY REAL MAN IN THIS OUTFIT!
I SHOULD BE OUT ON MY OWN, NOT DOING "TEAMWORK" BUSHWA WITH A BUNCHA LOSERS.
YOU'RE RIGHT, GUY.
I AM? I MEAN, SURE I AM. BUT... HOW, EXACTLY, AM I RIGHT?
NOT THE "WUSS" AND "LOSERS" SPEECH, OF COURSE. YOU JUST THREW THAT IN FOR EFFECT.
BUT YOU ARE A LONER. YOU WORK BETTER WITHOUT THE DISTRACTION OF TEAMMATES.
AND THEY WORK BETTER WITHOUT THE DISTRACTION OF HAVING YOU.
YEAH... THANKS, I GUESS.
HOW COME YOU ALWAYS GIVE ME THE BENEFIT OF THE DOUBT? NOBODY ELSE DOES.
ICE BELIEVES YOU ARE BASICALLY GOOD, AND I TRUST HER JUDGMENT.
BESIDES, AN EXPERIENCED FIGHTER WITH YOUR POWER COULD'VE CRIPPLED OR KILLED SHADOW-STRYKE. YOU DID NEITHER.
YEAH... WELL, MEBBE HE REMINDED ME O' THE KIDS I USED TA TEACH. MEBBE I EVEN HAD IT COMIN'...
YOUR SECRET IS SAFE WITH ME.

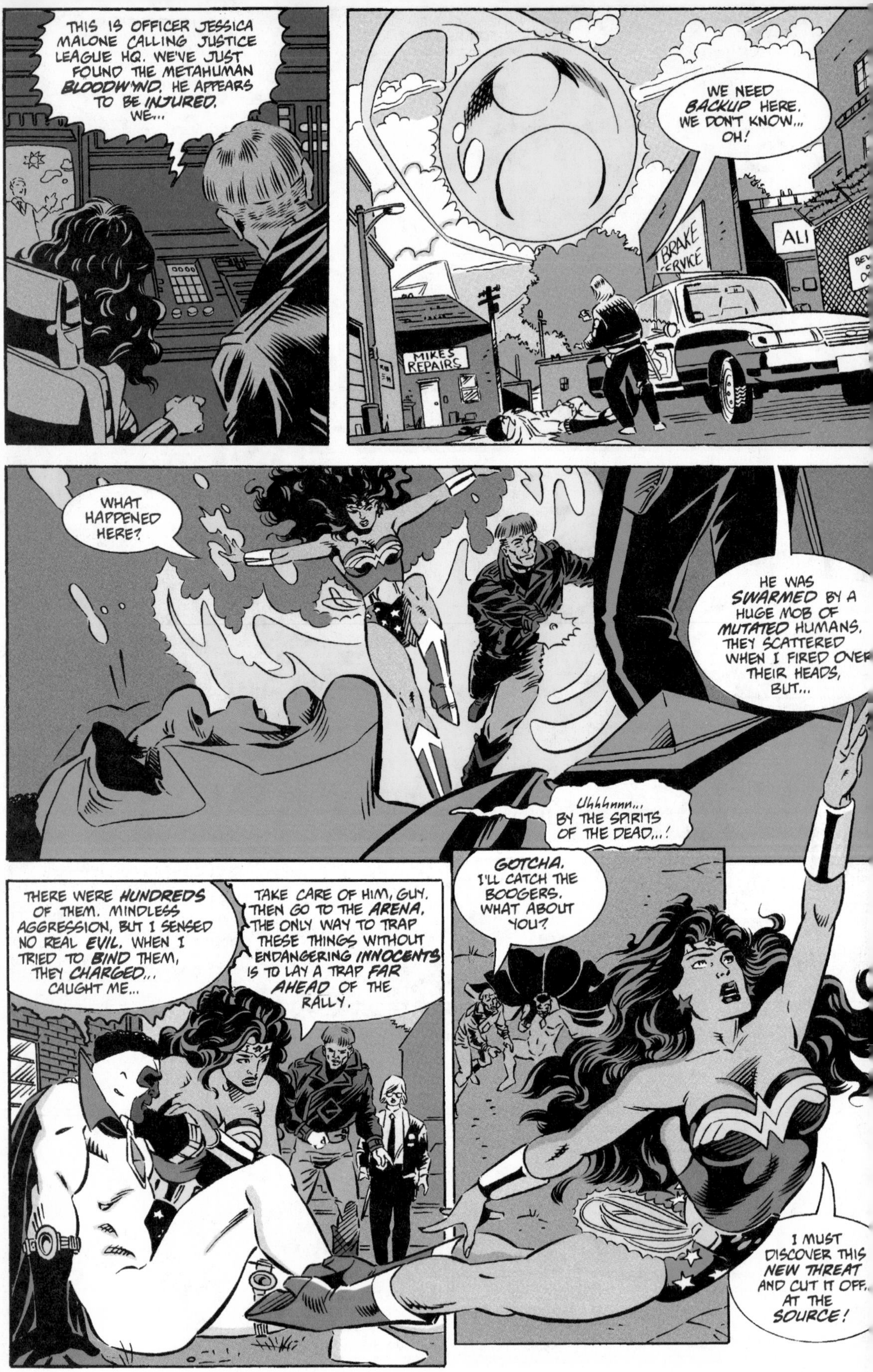
THIS IS OFFICER JESSICA MALONE CALLING JUSTICE LEAGUE HQ. WE'VE JUST FOUND THE METAHUMAN BLOODWYND. HE APPEARS TO BE INJURED. WE...
WE NEED BACKUP HERE. WE DON'T KNOW... OH!
BRAKE SERVICE
ALI
MIKE'S REPAIRS
WHAT HAPPENED HERE?
HE WAS SWARMED BY A HUGE MOB OF MUTATED HUMANS. THEY SCATTERED WHEN I FIRED OVER THEIR HEADS, BUT...
Uhhhnnn... BY THE SPIRITS OF THE DEAD...!
THERE WERE HUNDREDS OF THEM. MINDLESS AGGRESSION, BUT I SENSED NO REAL EVIL. WHEN I TRIED TO BIND THEM, THEY CHARGED... CAUGHT ME...
TAKE CARE OF HIM, GUY. THEN GO TO THE ARENA. THE ONLY WAY TO TRAP THESE THINGS WITHOUT ENDANGERING INNOCENTS IS TO LAY A TRAP FAR AHEAD OF THE RALLY.
GOTCHA. I'LL CATCH THE BOOGERS. WHAT ABOUT YOU?
I MUST DISCOVER THIS NEW THREAT AND CUT IT OFF... AT THE SOURCE!

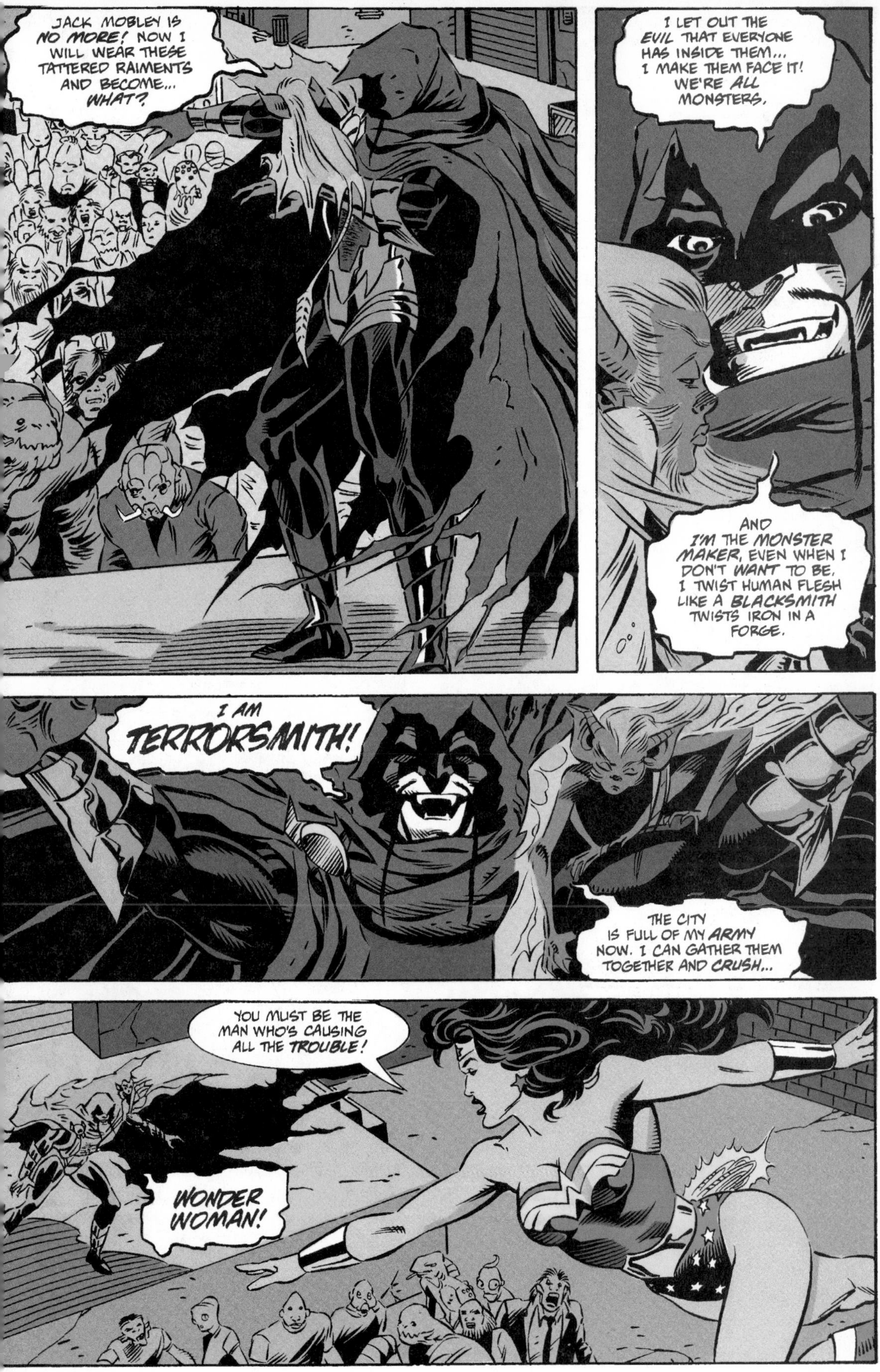
JACK MOBLEY IS NO MORE! NOW I WILL WEAR THESE TATTERED RAIMENTS AND BECOME... WHAT?
I LET OUT THE EVIL THAT EVERYONE HAS INSIDE THEM... I MAKE THEM FACE IT! WE'RE ALL MONSTERS.
AND I'M THE MONSTER MAKER, EVEN WHEN I DON'T WANT TO BE. I TWIST HUMAN FLESH LIKE A BLACKSMITH TWISTS IRON IN A FORGE.
I AM TERRORSMITH!
THE CITY IS FULL OF MY ARMY NOW. I CAN GATHER THEM TOGETHER AND CRUSH...
YOU MUST BE THE MAN WHO'S CAUSING ALL THE TROUBLE!
WONDER WOMAN!

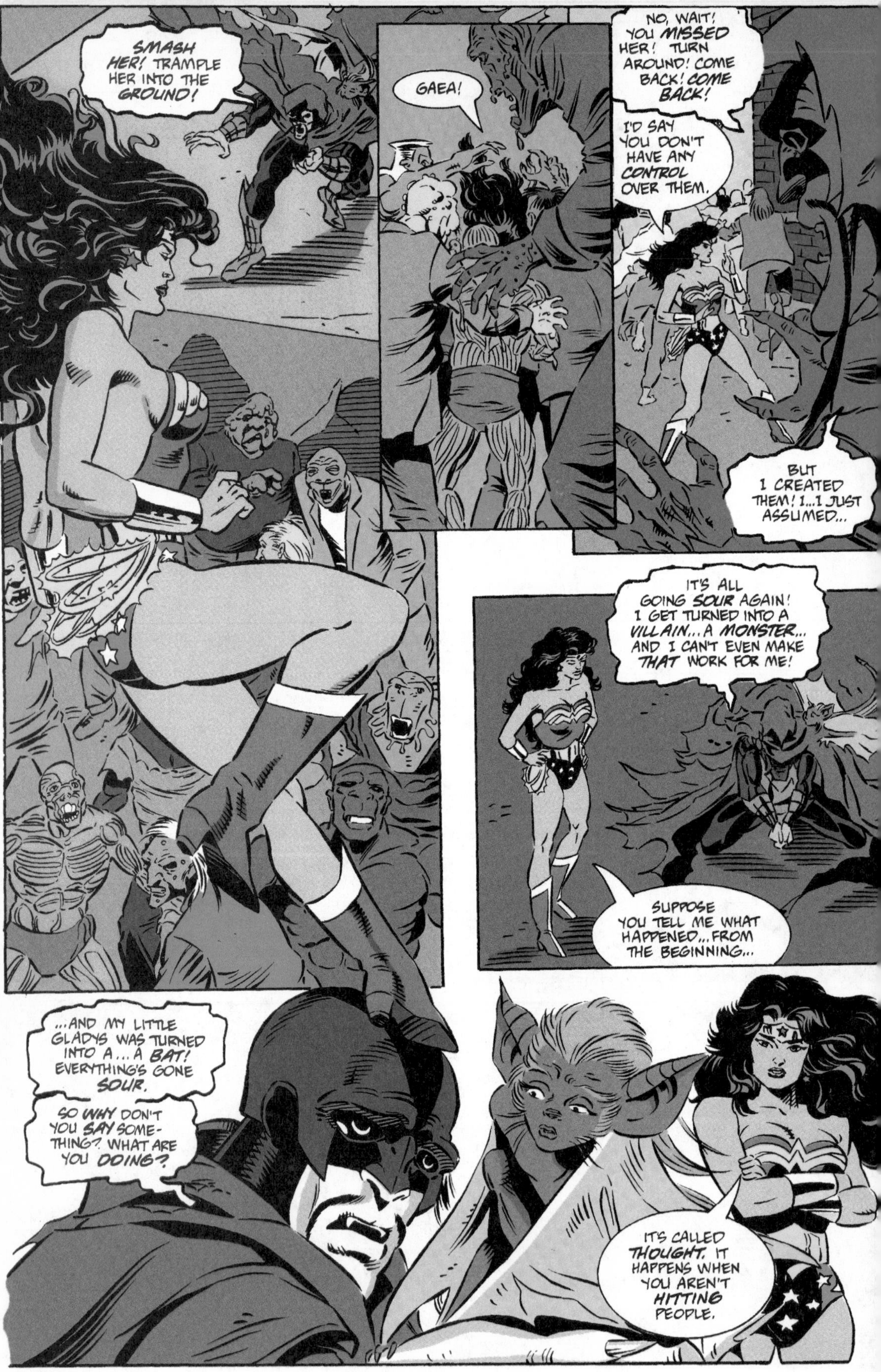
SMASH HER! TRAMPLE HER INTO THE GROUND!
GAEA!
NO, WAIT! YOU MISSED HER! TURN AROUND! COME BACK! COME BACK!
I'D SAY YOU DON'T HAVE ANY CONTROL OVER THEM.
BUT I CREATED THEM! I...I JUST ASSUMED...
IT'S ALL GOING SOUR AGAIN! I GET TURNED INTO A VILLAIN... A MONSTER... AND I CAN'T EVEN MAKE THAT WORK FOR ME!
SUPPOSE YOU TELL ME WHAT HAPPENED... FROM THE BEGINNING...
...AND MY LITTLE GLADYS WAS TURNED INTO A... A BAT! EVERYTHING'S GONE SOUR.
SO WHY DON'T YOU SAY SOME-THING? WHAT ARE YOU DOING?
IT'S CALLED THOUGHT. IT HAPPENS WHEN YOU AREN'T HITTING PEOPLE.

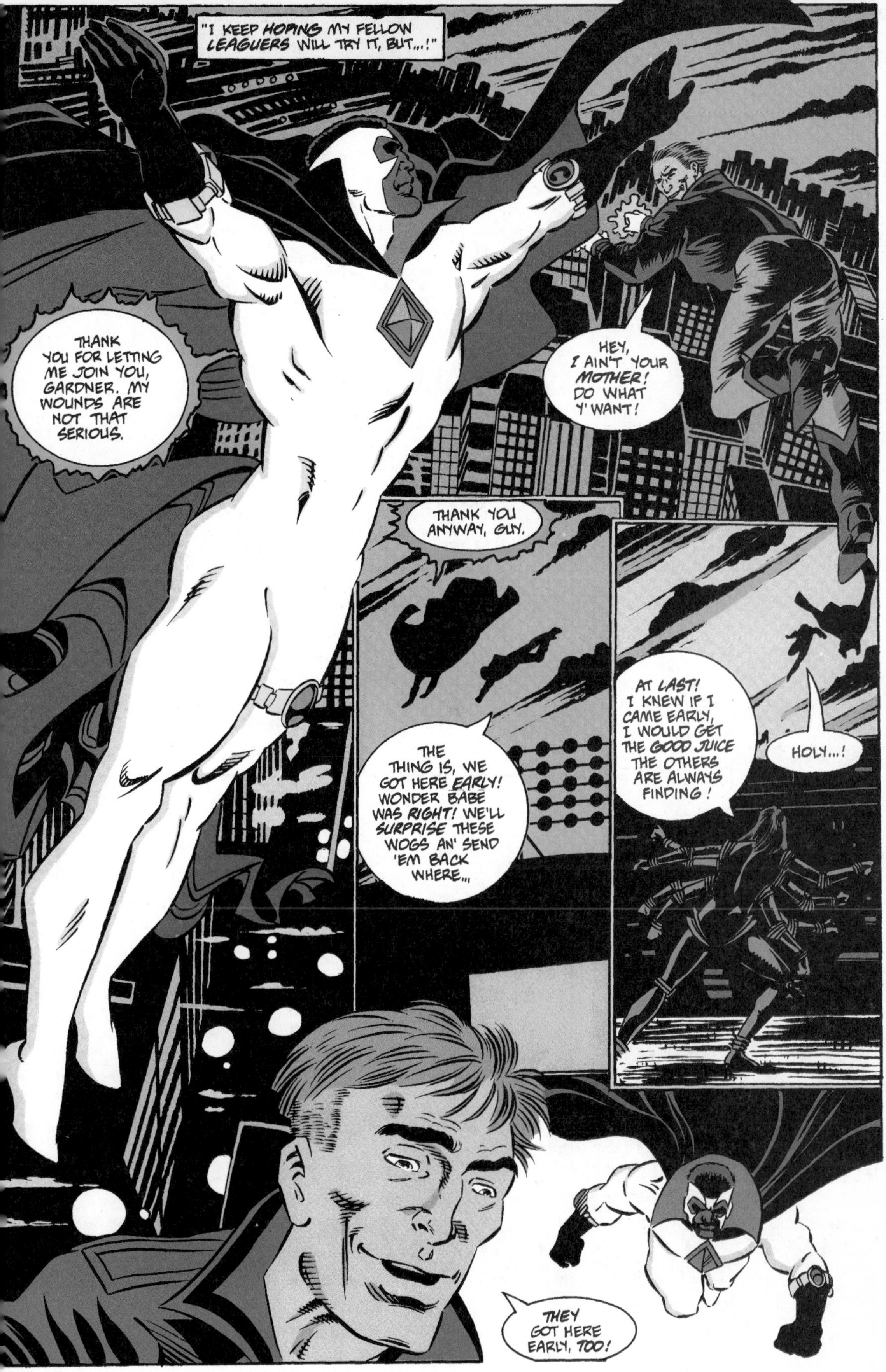
"I KEEP HOPING MY FELLOW LEAGUERS WILL TRY IT, BUT...!"
THANK YOU FOR LETTING ME JOIN YOU, GARDNER. MY WOUNDS ARE NOT THAT SERIOUS.
HEY, I AIN'T YOUR MOTHER! DO WHAT Y' WANT!
THANK YOU ANYWAY, GUY.
THE THING IS, WE GOT HERE EARLY! WONDER BABE WAS RIGHT! WE'LL SURPRISE THESE WOGS AN' SEND 'EM BACK WHERE...
AT LAST! I KNEW IF I CAME EARLY, I WOULD GET THE GOOD JUICE THE OTHERS ARE ALWAYS FINDING!
HOLY...!
THEY GOT HERE EARLY, TOO!

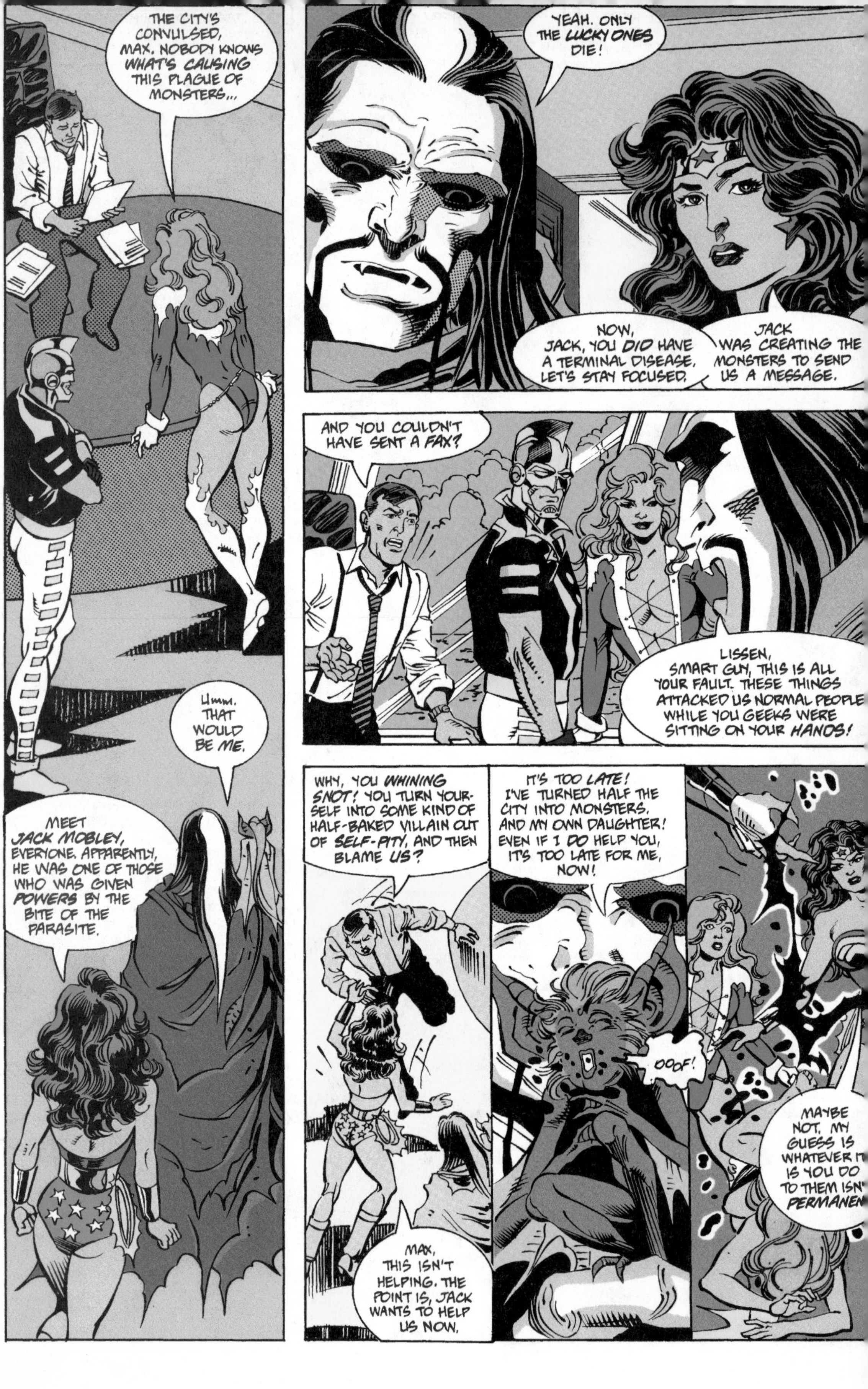
THE CITY'S CONVULSED, MAX. NOBODY KNOWS WHAT'S CAUSING THIS PLAGUE OF MONSTERS...
UMM. THAT WOULD BE ME.
MEET JACK MOBLEY, EVERYONE. APPARENTLY, HE WAS ONE OF THOSE WHO WAS GIVEN POWERS BY THE BITE OF THE PARASITE.
YEAH. ONLY THE LUCKY ONES DIE!
NOW, JACK, YOU DID HAVE A TERMINAL DISEASE. LET'S STAY FOCUSED.
JACK WAS CREATING THE MONSTERS TO SEND US A MESSAGE.
AND YOU COULDN'T HAVE SENT A FAX?
LISSEN, SMART GUY, THIS IS ALL YOUR FAULT. THESE THINGS ATTACKED US NORMAL PEOPLE WHILE YOU GEEKS WERE SITTING ON YOUR HANDS!
WHY, YOU WHINING SNOT! YOU TURN YOURSELF INTO SOME KIND OF HALF-BAKED VILLAIN OUT OF SELF-PITY, AND THEN BLAME US?
MAX, THIS ISN'T HELPING. THE POINT IS, JACK WANTS TO HELP US NOW.
IT'S TOO LATE! I'VE TURNED HALF THE CITY INTO MONSTERS, AND MY OWN DAUGHTER! EVEN IF I DO HELP YOU, IT'S TOO LATE FOR ME, NOW!
OOOF!
MAYBE NOT. MY GUESS IS WHATEVER IT IS YOU DO TO THEM ISN'T PERMANENT

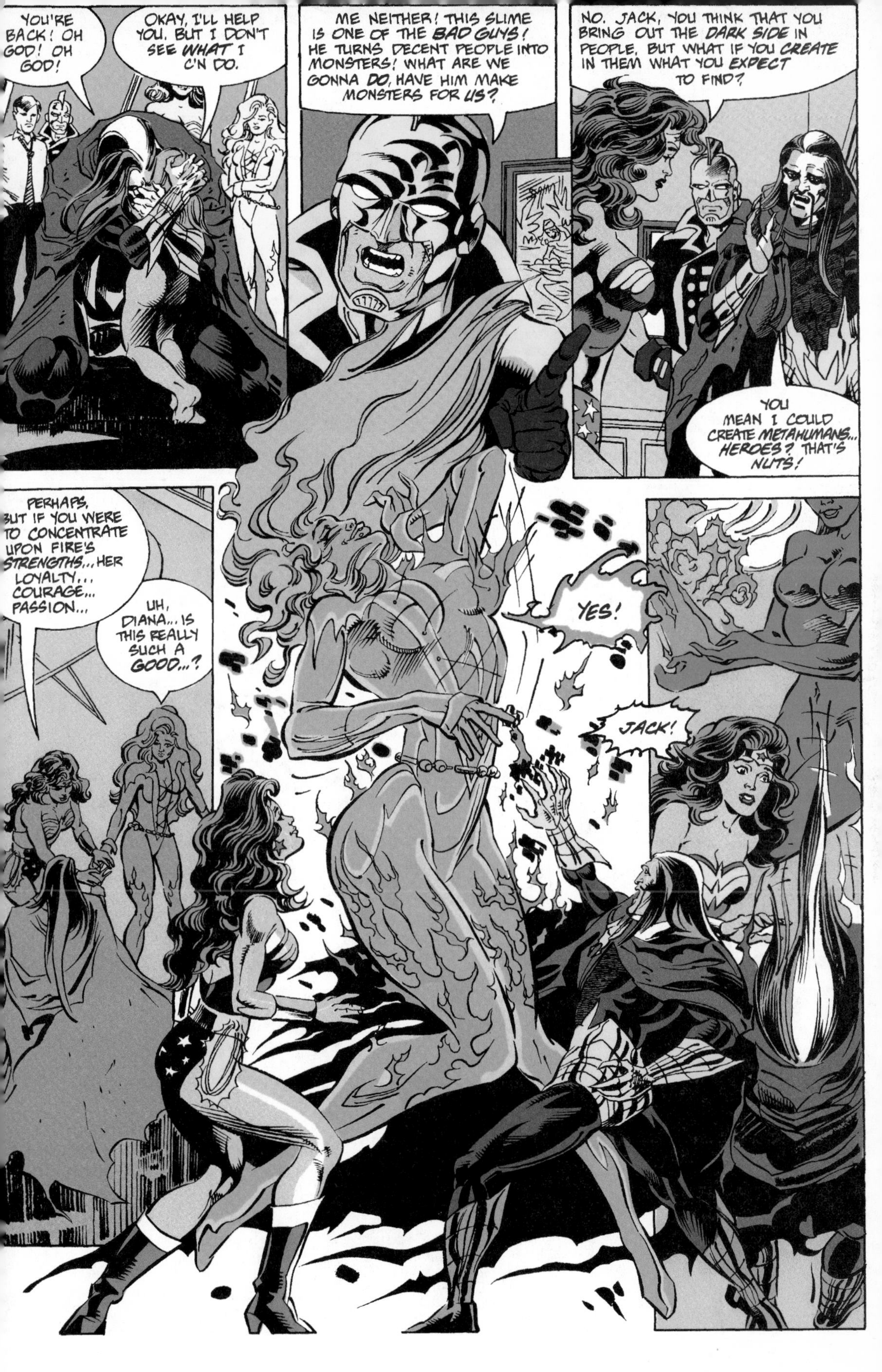
YOU'RE BACK! OH GOD! OH GOD!
OKAY, I'LL HELP YOU. BUT I DON'T SEE WHAT I C'N DO.
ME NEITHER! THIS SLIME IS ONE OF THE BAD GUYS! HE TURNS DECENT PEOPLE INTO MONSTERS! WHAT ARE WE GONNA DO, HAVE HIM MAKE MONSTERS FOR US?
NO. JACK, YOU THINK THAT YOU BRING OUT THE DARK SIDE IN PEOPLE, BUT WHAT IF YOU CREATE IN THEM WHAT YOU EXPECT TO FIND?
YOU MEAN I COULD CREATE METAHUMANS... HEROES? THAT'S NUTS!
PERHAPS, BUT IF YOU WERE TO CONCENTRATE UPON FIRE'S STRENGTHS... HER LOYALTY... COURAGE... PASSION...
UH, DIANA... IS THIS REALLY SUCH A GOOD...?
YES!
JACK!

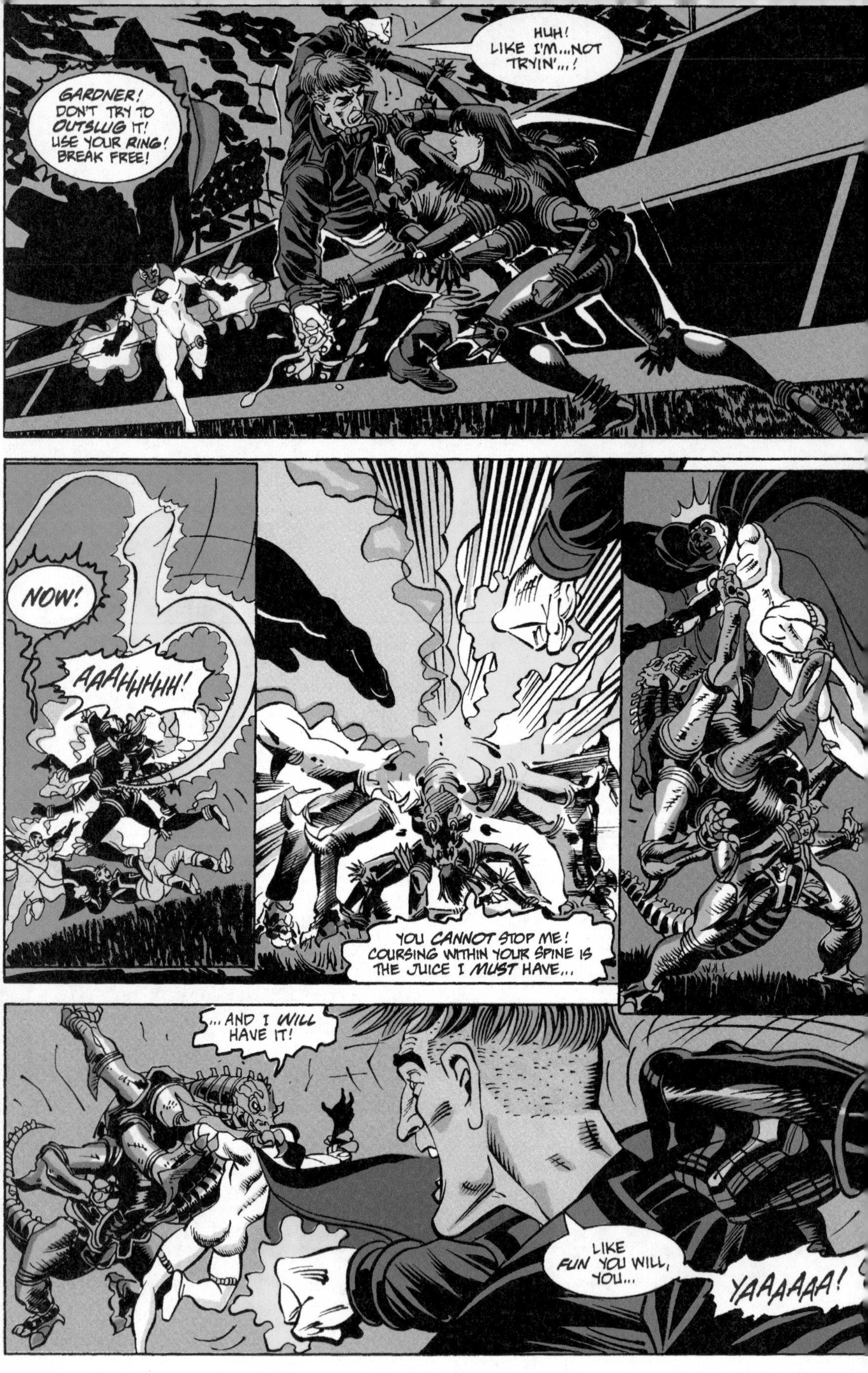
HUH! LIKE I'M...NOT TRYIN'...!
GARDNER! DON'T TRY TO OUTSLUG IT! USE YOUR RING! BREAK FREE!
NOW!
AAAHHHHH!
YOU CANNOT STOP ME! COURSING WITHIN YOUR SPINE IS THE JUICE I MUST HAVE...
...AND I WILL HAVE IT!
LIKE FUN YOU WILL, YOU...
YAAAAAA!

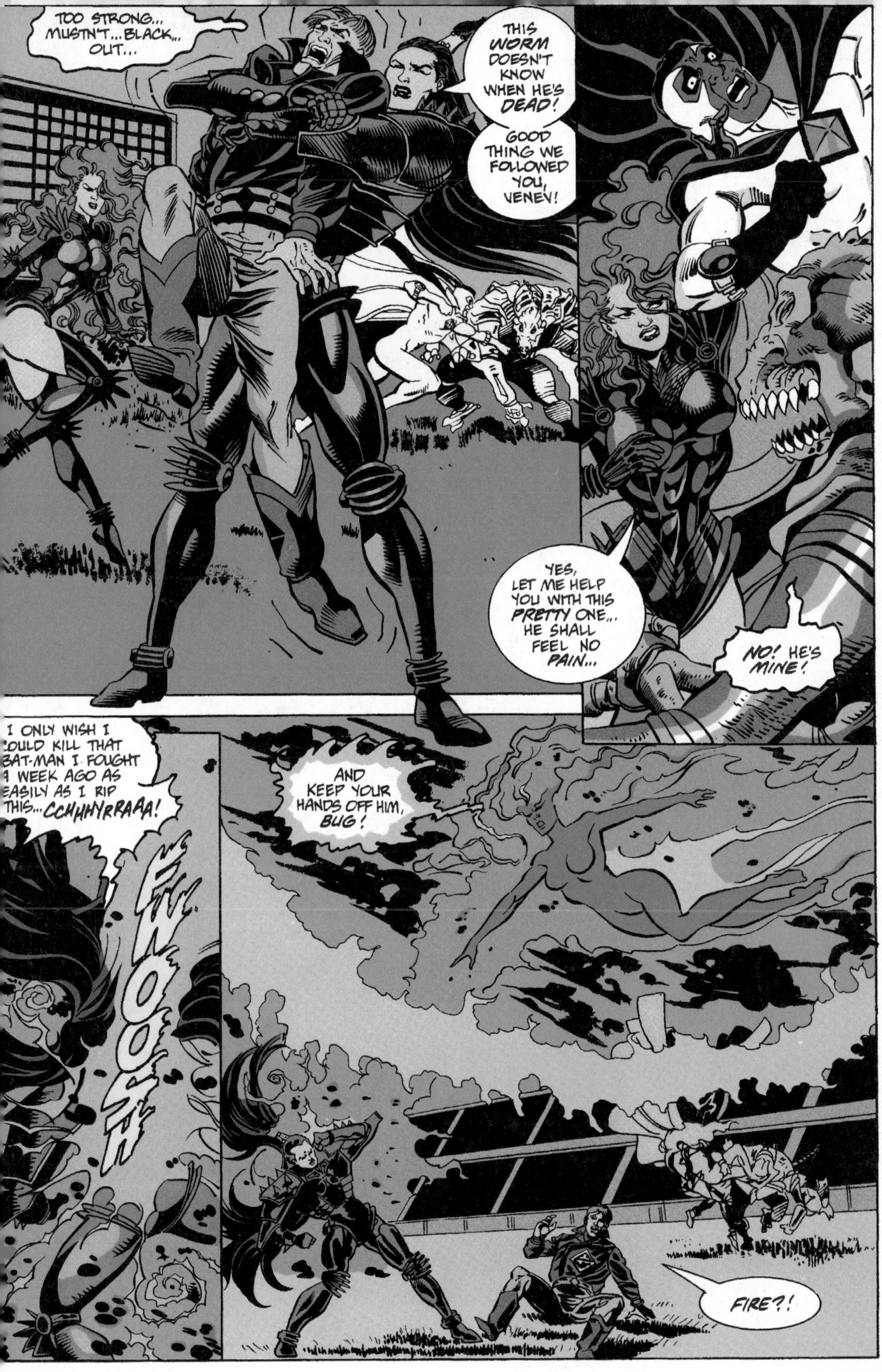
TOO STRONG... MUSTN'T... BLACK... OUT...
THIS WORM DOESN'T KNOW WHEN HE'S DEAD!
GOOD THING WE FOLLOWED YOU, VENEV!
YES, LET ME HELP YOU WITH THIS PRETTY ONE... HE SHALL FEEL NO PAIN...
NO! HE'S MINE!
I ONLY WISH I COULD KILL THAT BAT-MAN I FOUGHT A WEEK AGO AS EASILY AS I RIP THIS... CCHHHYRRAAA!
FWOOOOM
AND KEEP YOUR HANDS OFF HIM, BUG!
FIRE?!

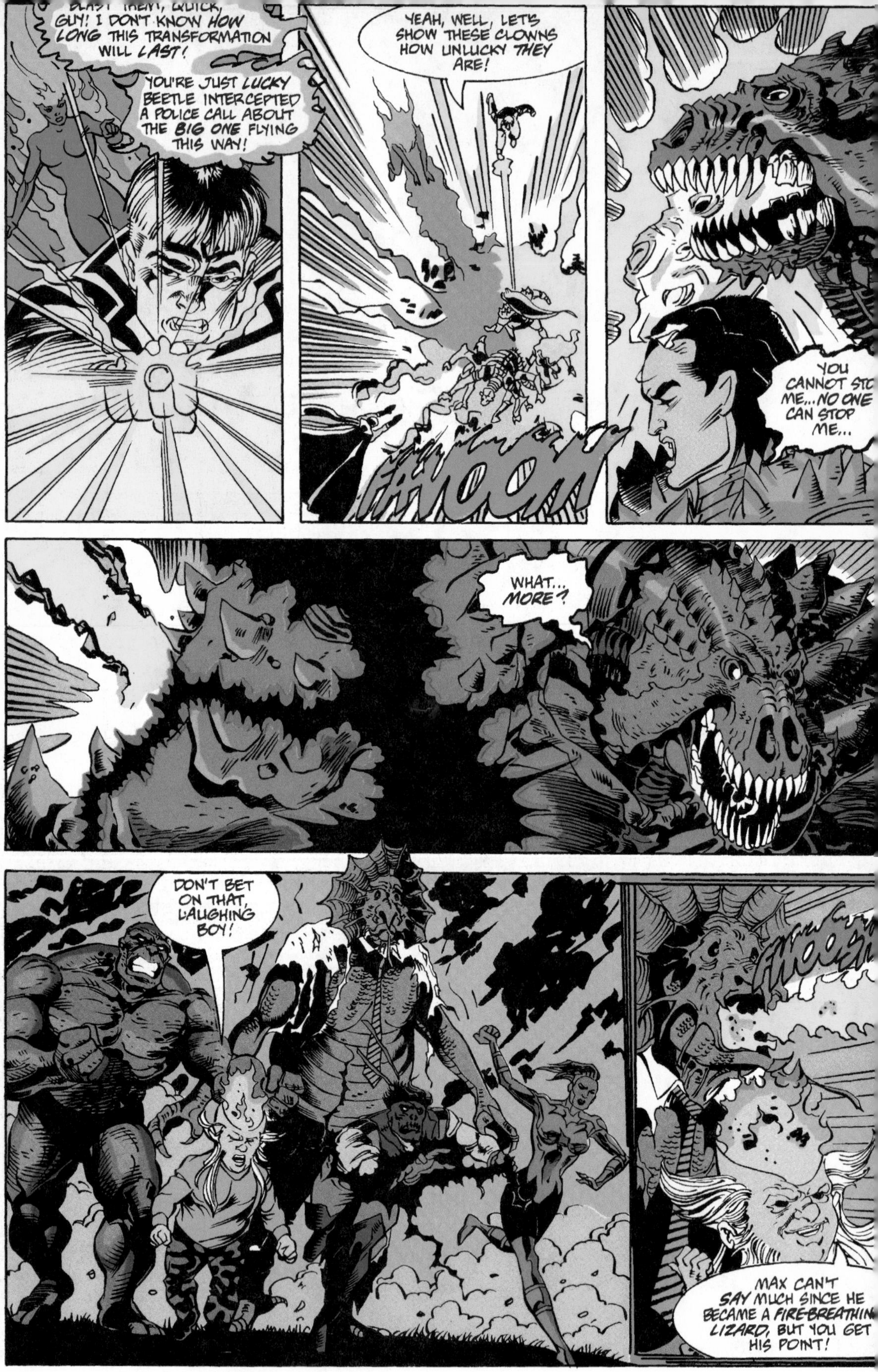
BLAST THEM, QUICK, GUY! I DON'T KNOW HOW LONG THIS TRANSFORMATION WILL LAST!
YOU'RE JUST LUCKY BEETLE INTERCEPTED A POLICE CALL ABOUT THE BIG ONE FLYING THIS WAY!
YEAH, WELL, LET'S SHOW THESE CLOWNS HOW UNLUCKY THEY ARE!
FWOOM
YOU CANNOT STO ME... NO ONE CAN STOP ME...
WHAT... MORE?
DON'T BET ON THAT, LAUGHING BOY!
MAX CAN'T SAY MUCH SINCE HE BECAME A FIRE-BREATHIN LIZARD, BUT YOU GET HIS POINT!

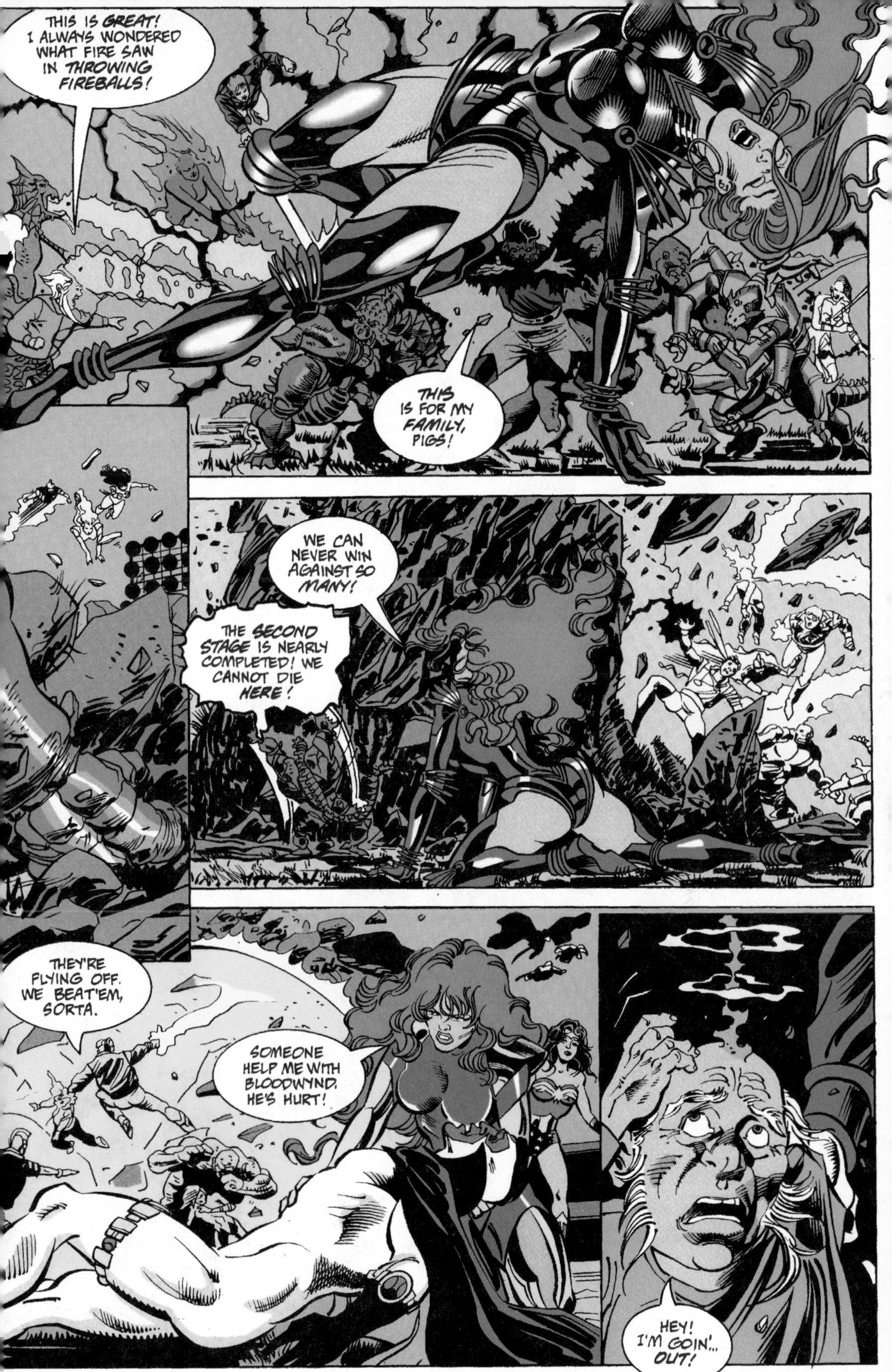
THIS IS GREAT! I ALWAYS WONDERED WHAT FIRE SAW IN THROWING FIREBALLS!
THIS IS FOR MY FAMILY, PIGS!
WE CAN NEVER WIN AGAINST SO MANY!
THE SECOND STAGE IS NEARLY COMPLETED! WE CANNOT DIE HERE!
THEY'RE FLYING OFF. WE BEAT'EM, SORTA.
SOMEONE HELP ME WITH BLOODWYND. HE'S HURT!
HEY! I'M GOIN'... OUT!

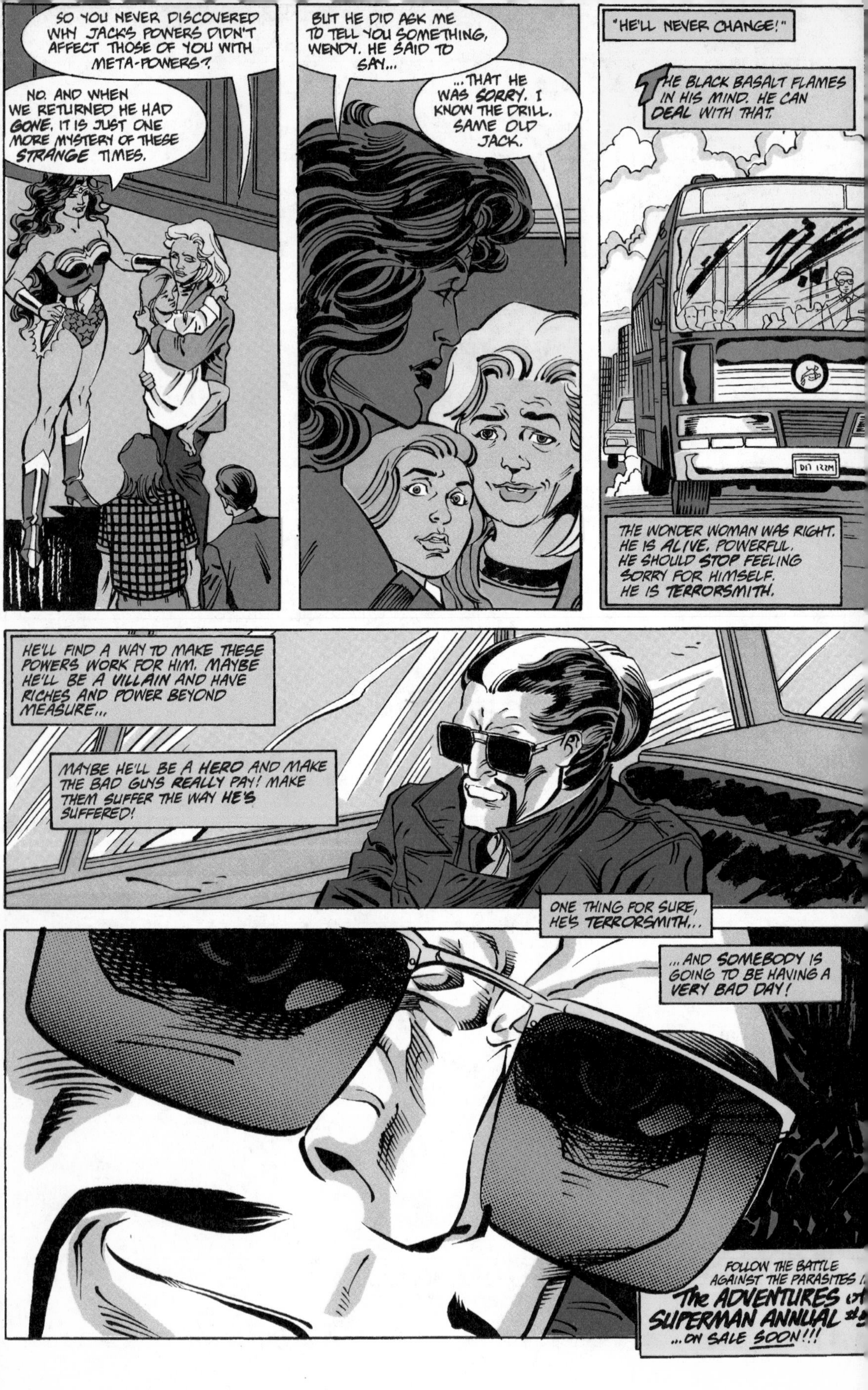
SO YOU NEVER DISCOVERED WHY JACKS POWERS DIDN'T AFFECT THOSE OF YOU WITH META-POWERS?
NO. AND WHEN WE RETURNED HE HAD GONE. IT IS JUST ONE MORE MYSTERY OF THESE STRANGE TIMES.
BUT HE DID ASK ME TO TELL YOU SOMETHING, WENDY. HE SAID TO SAY...
...THAT HE WAS SORRY. I KNOW THE DRILL. SAME OLD JACK.
"HE'LL NEVER CHANGE!"
THE BLACK BASALT FLAMES IN HIS MIND. HE CAN DEAL WITH THAT.
THE WONDER WOMAN WAS RIGHT. HE IS ALIVE. POWERFUL. HE SHOULD STOP FEELING SORRY FOR HIMSELF. HE IS TERRORSMITH.
HE'LL FIND A WAY TO MAKE THESE POWERS WORK FOR HIM. MAYBE HE'LL BE A VILLAIN AND HAVE RICHES AND POWER BEYOND MEASURE...
MAYBE HE'LL BE A HERO AND MAKE THE BAD GUYS REALLY PAY! MAKE THEM SUFFER THE WAY HE'S SUFFERED!
ONE THING FOR SURE, HE'S TERRORSMITH...
...AND SOMEBODY IS GOING TO BE HAVING A VERY BAD DAY!
FOLLOW THE BATTLE AGAINST THE PARASITES
The ADVENTURES
SUPERMAN ANNUAL
...ON SALE SOON!!!

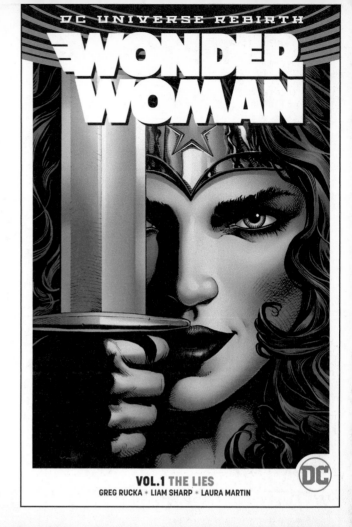

"Some really thrilling artwork that establishes incredible scope and danger."

–IGN

DC UNIVERSE REBIRTH

JUSTICE LEAGUE

VOL. 1: The Extinction Machines

BRYAN HITCH
with TONY S. DANIEL

VOL.1 THE EXTINCTION MACHINES

BRYAN HITCH • TONY S. DANIEL • SANDU FLOREA • TOMEU MOREY

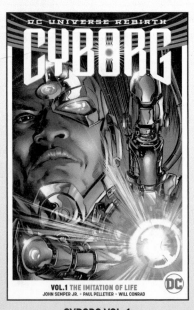

VOL.1 THE IMITATION OF LIFE
JOHN SEMPER JR. • PAUL PELLETIER • WILL CONRAD

**CYBORG VOL. 1:
THE IMITATION OF LIFE**

VOL.1 RAGE PLANET
SAM HUMPHRIES • ROBSON ROCHA • ETHAN VAN SCIVER • ED BENES

**GREEN LANTERNS VOL. 1:
RAGE PLANET**

VOL.1 THE DROWNING
DAN ABNETT • PHILIPPE BRIONES • SCOT EATON • BRAD WALKER

**AQUAMAN VOL. 1:
THE DROWNING**

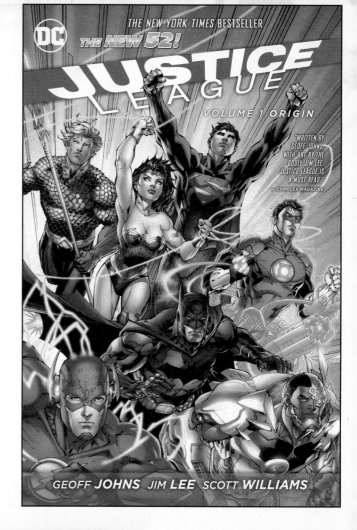

"The cartoonist Darwyn Cooke is an extraordinary talent...[THE NEW FRONTIER] is an audacious revisionist look at the formation of the Justice League."
– THE NEW YORK TIMES

"Using a classic style, Cooke creates a classic of his own."
– A.V. CLUB/THE ONION

FROM EISNER AWARD WINNER DARWYN COOKE

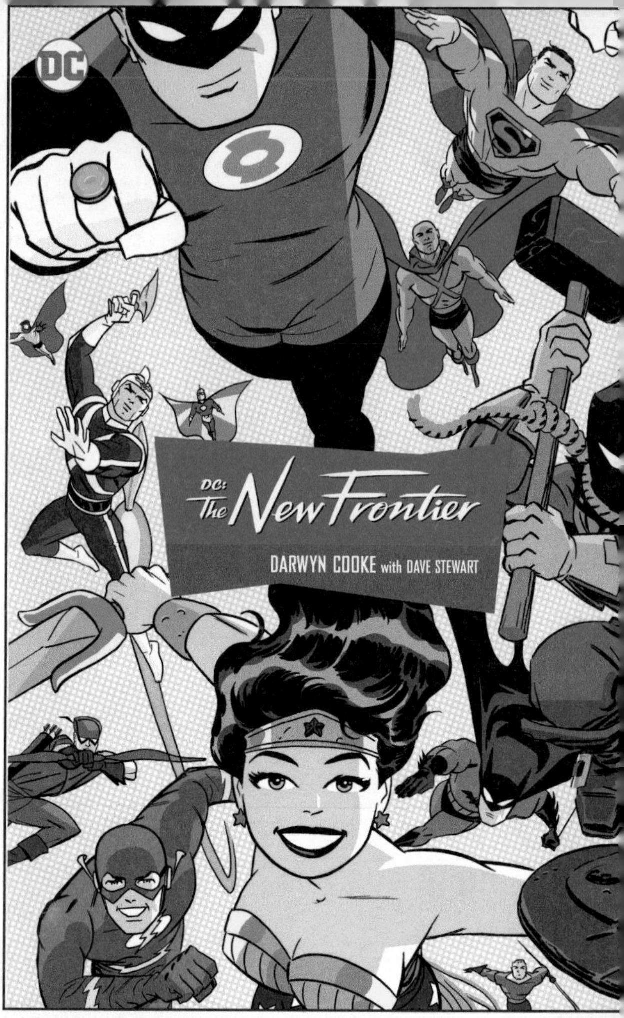
DC
DC: The New Frontier
DARWYN COOKE with DAVE STEWART

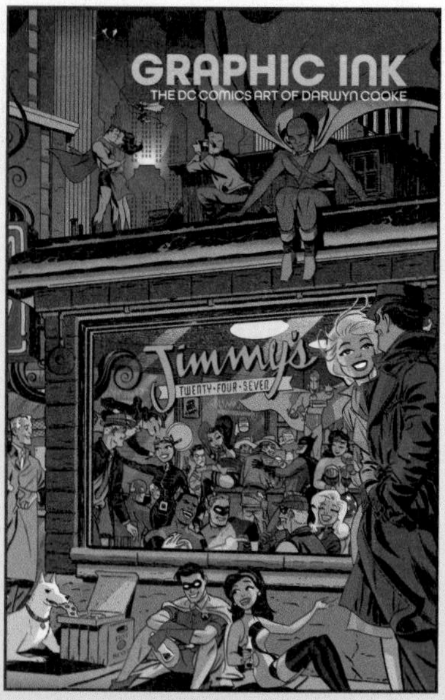
GRAPHIC INK
THE DC COMICS ART OF DARWYN COOKE
Jimmy's
TWENTY-FOUR-SEVEN

GRAPHIC INK:
THE DC COMICS ART OF
DARWYN COOKE

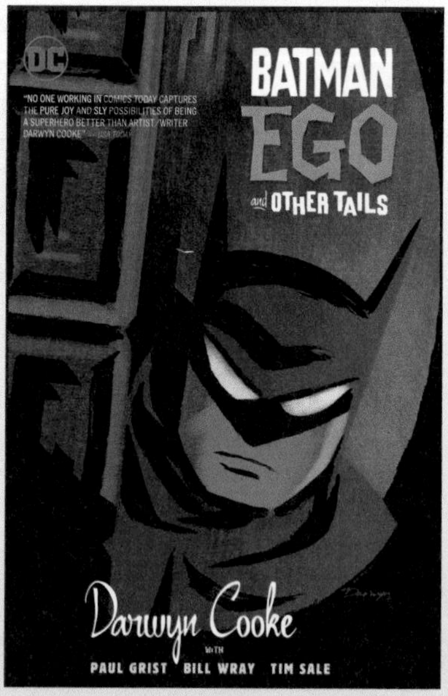
DC
BATMAN
EGO
and OTHER TAILS
Darwyn Cooke
WITH
PAUL GRIST BILL WRAY TIM SALE

BATMAN:
EGO AND OTHER TAILS

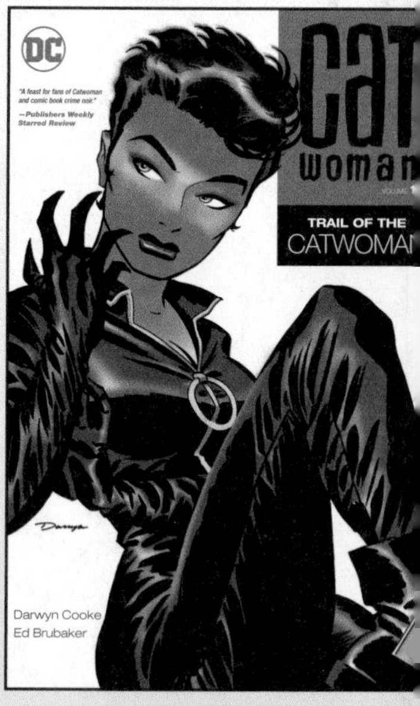
DC
Cat
woman
TRAIL OF THE
CATWOMAN
Darwyn Cooke
Ed Brubaker

CATWOMAN:
TRAIL OF THE CATWOMAN

Get more DC graphic novels wherever comics and books are sold!